Using the GNU Compiler Collection

For GCC version 4.3.3

(GCC)

Richard M. Stallman and the GCC Developer Community

ISBN 144141276X

Printed in America

Published & distributed under the terms of the GNU Free Documentation Licence by SoHoBooks

Permission is granted to copy, distribute and/or modify this document under the terms of the GNU Free Documentation License, Version 1.2 or any later version published by the Free Software Foundation; with the Invariant Sections being "GNU Free Documentation License", with the Front-Cover Texts being "GNAT Reference Manual", and with no Back-Cover Texts. A copy of the license is included in the section entitled "GNU Free Documentation License".

http://www.gnu.org
http://gcc.gnu.org/onlinedocs/

Published by:
GNU Press
a division of the
Free Software Foundation
51 Franklin Street, Fifth Floor
Boston, MA 02110-1301 USA

Website: www.gnupress.org
General: press@gnu.org
Orders: sales@gnu.org
Tel 617-542-5942
Fax 617-542-2652

Last printed October 2003 for GCC 3.3.1.
Printed copies are available for $45 each.

Copyright © 1988, 1989, 1992, 1993, 1994, 1995, 1996, 1997, 1998, 1999, 2000, 2001, 2002, 2003, 2004, 2005, 2006, 2007 2008 Free Software Foundation, Inc.

Permission is granted to copy, distribute and/or modify this document under the terms of the GNU Free Documentation License, Version 1.2 or any later version published by the Free Software Foundation; with the Invariant Sections being "GNU General Public License" and "Funding Free Software", the Front-Cover texts being (a) (see below), and with the Back-Cover Texts being (b) (see below). A copy of the license is included in the section entitled "GNU Free Documentation License".

(a) The FSF's Front-Cover Text is:

A GNU Manual

(b) The FSF's Back-Cover Text is:

You have freedom to copy and modify this GNU Manual, like GNU software. Copies published by the Free Software Foundation raise funds for GNU development.

Short Contents

Introduction		1
1	Programming Languages Supported by GCC	3
2	Language Standards Supported by GCC	5
3	GCC Command Options	9
4	C Implementation-defined behavior	237
5	Extensions to the C Language Family	245
6	Extensions to the C++ Language	503
7	GNU Objective-C runtime features	515
8	Binary Compatibility	521
9	gcov—a Test Coverage Program	525
10	Known Causes of Trouble with GCC	533
11	Reporting Bugs	551
12	How To Get Help with GCC	553
13	Contributing to GCC Development	555
Funding Free Software		557
The GNU Project and GNU/Linux		559
GNU General Public License		561
GNU Free Documentation License		573
Contributors to GCC		581
Option Index		597
Keyword Index		613

Table of Contents

Introduction 1

1 Programming Languages Supported by GCC
.... 3

2 Language Standards Supported by GCC 5
  2.1 C language................................. 5
  2.2 C++ language.............................. 6
  2.3 Objective-C and Objective-C++ languages 7
  2.4 Treelang language......................... 7

3 GCC Command Options 9
  3.1 Option Summary............................. 9
  3.2 Options Controlling the Kind of Output 20
  3.3 Compiling C++ Programs 25
  3.4 Options Controlling C Dialect.............. 26
  3.5 Options Controlling C++ Dialect 31
  3.6 Options Controlling Objective-C and Objective-C++ Dialects.. 38
  3.7 Options to Control Diagnostic Messages Formatting 42
  3.8 Options to Request or Suppress Warnings 43
  3.9 Options for Debugging Your Program or GCC 63
  3.10 Options That Control Optimization 77
  3.11 Options Controlling the Preprocessor....... 113
  3.12 Passing Options to the Assembler 123
  3.13 Options for Linking....................... 123
  3.14 Options for Directory Search 126
  3.15 Specifying subprocesses and the switches to pass to them 128
  3.16 Specifying Target Machine and Compiler Version 135
  3.17 Hardware Models and Configurations 135
    3.17.1 ARC Options......................... 135
    3.17.2 ARM Options......................... 136
    3.17.3 AVR Options......................... 140
    3.17.4 Blackfin Options..................... 141
    3.17.5 CRIS Options........................ 143
    3.17.6 CRX Options......................... 145
    3.17.7 Darwin Options...................... 145
    3.17.8 DEC Alpha Options 149
    3.17.9 DEC Alpha/VMS Options 153
    3.17.10 FRV Options........................ 153
    3.17.11 GNU/Linux Options.................. 157
    3.17.12 H8/300 Options..................... 157
    3.17.13 HPPA Options....................... 158

3.17.14	Intel 386 and AMD x86-64 Options	161
3.17.15	IA-64 Options	171
3.17.16	M32C Options	174
3.17.17	M32R/D Options	174
3.17.18	M680x0 Options	176
3.17.19	M68hc1x Options	181
3.17.20	MCore Options	181
3.17.21	MIPS Options	182
3.17.22	MMIX Options	191
3.17.23	MN10300 Options	192
3.17.24	MT Options	193
3.17.25	PDP-11 Options	193
3.17.26	PowerPC Options	194
3.17.27	IBM RS/6000 and PowerPC Options	194
3.17.28	S/390 and zSeries Options	206
3.17.29	Score Options	209
3.17.30	SH Options	209
3.17.31	SPARC Options	213
3.17.32	SPU Options	217
3.17.33	Options for System V	218
3.17.34	V850 Options	218
3.17.35	VAX Options	219
3.17.36	VxWorks Options	220
3.17.37	x86-64 Options	220
3.17.38	Xstormy16 Options	220
3.17.39	Xtensa Options	220
3.17.40	zSeries Options	221
3.18	Options for Code Generation Conventions	222
3.19	Environment Variables Affecting GCC	229
3.20	Using Precompiled Headers	232
3.21	Running Protoize	234

4 C Implementation-defined behavior 237

4.1	Translation	237
4.2	Environment	237
4.3	Identifiers	237
4.4	Characters	238
4.5	Integers	238
4.6	Floating point	239
4.7	Arrays and pointers	240
4.8	Hints	241
4.9	Structures, unions, enumerations, and bit-fields	241
4.10	Qualifiers	242
4.11	Declarators	242
4.12	Statements	242
4.13	Preprocessing directives	242
4.14	Library functions	243
4.15	Architecture	243

| | | 4.16 | Locale-specific behavior .... | 243 |

5 Extensions to the C Language Family 245

	5.1	Statements and Declarations in Expressions	245
	5.2	Locally Declared Labels	246
	5.3	Labels as Values	247
	5.4	Nested Functions	248
	5.5	Constructing Function Calls	250
	5.6	Referring to a Type with `typeof`	252
	5.7	Conditionals with Omitted Operands	253
	5.8	Double-Word Integers	254
	5.9	Complex Numbers	254
	5.10	Additional Floating Types	255
	5.11	Decimal Floating Types	255
	5.12	Hex Floats	255
	5.13	Fixed-Point Types	256
	5.14	Arrays of Length Zero	257
	5.15	Structures With No Members	258
	5.16	Arrays of Variable Length	258
	5.17	Macros with a Variable Number of Arguments	259
	5.18	Slightly Looser Rules for Escaped Newlines	260
	5.19	Non-Lvalue Arrays May Have Subscripts	260
	5.20	Arithmetic on `void`- and Function-Pointers	260
	5.21	Non-Constant Initializers	260
	5.22	Compound Literals	261
	5.23	Designated Initializers	261
	5.24	Case Ranges	263
	5.25	Cast to a Union Type	263
	5.26	Mixed Declarations and Code	264
	5.27	Declaring Attributes of Functions	264
	5.28	Attribute Syntax	281
	5.29	Prototypes and Old-Style Function Definitions	284
	5.30	C++ Style Comments	285
	5.31	Dollar Signs in Identifier Names	285
	5.32	The Character ESC in Constants	285
	5.33	Inquiring on Alignment of Types or Variables	285
	5.34	Specifying Attributes of Variables	286
		5.34.1 Blackfin Variable Attributes	290
		5.34.2 M32R/D Variable Attributes	290
		5.34.3 i386 Variable Attributes	291
		5.34.4 PowerPC Variable Attributes	293
		5.34.5 SPU Variable Attributes	293
		5.34.6 Xstormy16 Variable Attributes	293
		5.34.7 AVR Variable Attributes	293
	5.35	Specifying Attributes of Types	293
		5.35.1 ARM Type Attributes	298
		5.35.2 i386 Type Attributes	298
		5.35.3 PowerPC Type Attributes	298

5.35.4	SPU Type Attributes	299
5.36	An Inline Function is As Fast As a Macro	299
5.37	Assembler Instructions with C Expression Operands	300
5.37.1	Size of an asm	305
5.37.2	i386 floating point asm operands	305
5.38	Constraints for asm Operands	306
5.38.1	Simple Constraints	307
5.38.2	Multiple Alternative Constraints	309
5.38.3	Constraint Modifier Characters	309
5.38.4	Constraints for Particular Machines	310
5.39	Controlling Names Used in Assembler Code	326
5.40	Variables in Specified Registers	327
5.40.1	Defining Global Register Variables	327
5.40.2	Specifying Registers for Local Variables	328
5.41	Alternate Keywords	329
5.42	Incomplete enum Types	330
5.43	Function Names as Strings	330
5.44	Getting the Return or Frame Address of a Function	331
5.45	Using vector instructions through built-in functions	332
5.46	Offsetof	333
5.47	Built-in functions for atomic memory access	333
5.48	Object Size Checking Builtins	335
5.49	Other built-in functions provided by GCC	337
5.50	Built-in Functions Specific to Particular Target Machines	344
5.50.1	Alpha Built-in Functions	344
5.50.2	ARM iWMMXt Built-in Functions	345
5.50.3	ARM NEON Intrinsics	347
5.50.3.1	Addition	347
5.50.3.2	Multiplication	351
5.50.3.3	Multiply-accumulate	353
5.50.3.4	Multiply-subtract	354
5.50.3.5	Subtraction	355
5.50.3.6	Comparison (equal-to)	359
5.50.3.7	Comparison (greater-than-or-equal-to)	359
5.50.3.8	Comparison (less-than-or-equal-to)	360
5.50.3.9	Comparison (greater-than)	361
5.50.3.10	Comparison (less-than)	362
5.50.3.11	Comparison (absolute greater-than-or-equal-to)	362
5.50.3.12	Comparison (absolute less-than-or-equal-to)	362
5.50.3.13	Comparison (absolute greater-than)	363
5.50.3.14	Comparison (absolute less-than)	363
5.50.3.15	Test bits	363
5.50.3.16	Absolute difference	364
5.50.3.17	Absolute difference and accumulate	365
5.50.3.18	Maximum	365
5.50.3.19	Minimum	366
5.50.3.20	Pairwise add	367

5.50.3.21	Pairwise add, single_opcode widen and accumulate	368
5.50.3.22	Folding maximum	368
5.50.3.23	Folding minimum	369
5.50.3.24	Reciprocal step	369
5.50.3.25	Vector shift left	369
5.50.3.26	Vector shift left by constant	372
5.50.3.27	Vector shift right by constant	375
5.50.3.28	Vector shift right by constant and accumulate	378
5.50.3.29	Vector shift right and insert	379
5.50.3.30	Vector shift left and insert	380
5.50.3.31	Absolute value	381
5.50.3.32	Negation	382
5.50.3.33	Bitwise not	383
5.50.3.34	Count leading sign bits	383
5.50.3.35	Count leading zeros	384
5.50.3.36	Count number of set bits	384
5.50.3.37	Reciprocal estimate	385
5.50.3.38	Reciprocal square-root estimate	385
5.50.3.39	Get lanes from a vector	385
5.50.3.40	Set lanes in a vector	386
5.50.3.41	Create vector from literal bit pattern	387
5.50.3.42	Set all lanes to the same value	388
5.50.3.43	Combining vectors	391
5.50.3.44	Splitting vectors	391
5.50.3.45	Conversions	392
5.50.3.46	Move, single_opcode narrowing	393
5.50.3.47	Move, single_opcode long	393
5.50.3.48	Table lookup	394
5.50.3.49	Extended table lookup	394
5.50.3.50	Multiply, lane	395
5.50.3.51	Long multiply, lane	396
5.50.3.52	Saturating doubling long multiply, lane	396
5.50.3.53	Saturating doubling multiply high, lane	396
5.50.3.54	Multiply-accumulate, lane	396
5.50.3.55	Multiply-subtract, lane	397
5.50.3.56	Vector multiply by scalar	398
5.50.3.57	Vector long multiply by scalar	398
5.50.3.58	Vector saturating doubling long multiply by scalar	399
5.50.3.59	Vector saturating doubling multiply high by scalar	399
5.50.3.60	Vector multiply-accumulate by scalar	399
5.50.3.61	Vector multiply-subtract by scalar	400
5.50.3.62	Vector extract	401
5.50.3.63	Reverse elements	402
5.50.3.64	Bit selection	404
5.50.3.65	Transpose elements	405

	5.50.3.66	Zip elements	406
	5.50.3.67	Unzip elements	407
	5.50.3.68	Element/structure loads, VLD1 variants	408
	5.50.3.69	Element/structure stores, VST1 variants	411
	5.50.3.70	Element/structure loads, VLD2 variants	413
	5.50.3.71	Element/structure stores, VST2 variants	416
	5.50.3.72	Element/structure loads, VLD3 variants	417
	5.50.3.73	Element/structure stores, VST3 variants	419
	5.50.3.74	Element/structure loads, VLD4 variants	421
	5.50.3.75	Element/structure stores, VST4 variants	423
	5.50.3.76	Logical operations (AND)	425
	5.50.3.77	Logical operations (OR)	426
	5.50.3.78	Logical operations (exclusive OR)	427
	5.50.3.79	Logical operations (AND-NOT)	428
	5.50.3.80	Logical operations (OR-NOT)	428
	5.50.3.81	Reinterpret casts	429
5.50.4	Blackfin Built-in Functions		435
5.50.5	FR-V Built-in Functions		435
	5.50.5.1	Argument Types	435
	5.50.5.2	Directly-mapped Integer Functions	436
	5.50.5.3	Directly-mapped Media Functions	436
	5.50.5.4	Raw read/write Functions	438
	5.50.5.5	Other Built-in Functions	438
5.50.6	X86 Built-in Functions		439
5.50.7	MIPS DSP Built-in Functions		452
5.50.8	MIPS Paired-Single Support		456
	5.50.8.1	Paired-Single Arithmetic	457
	5.50.8.2	Paired-Single Built-in Functions	457
	5.50.8.3	MIPS-3D Built-in Functions	458
5.50.9	PowerPC AltiVec Built-in Functions		461
5.50.10	SPARC VIS Built-in Functions		493
5.50.11	SPU Built-in Functions		493
5.51	Format Checks Specific to Particular Target Machines		494
5.51.1	Solaris Format Checks		494
5.52	Pragmas Accepted by GCC		494
5.52.1	ARM Pragmas		494
5.52.2	M32C Pragmas		495
5.52.3	RS/6000 and PowerPC Pragmas		495
5.52.4	Darwin Pragmas		495
5.52.5	Solaris Pragmas		495
5.52.6	Symbol-Renaming Pragmas		496
5.52.7	Structure-Packing Pragmas		497
5.52.8	Weak Pragmas		497
5.52.9	Diagnostic Pragmas		497
5.52.10	Visibility Pragmas		498
5.53	Unnamed struct/union fields within structs/unions		498
5.54	Thread-Local Storage		499
5.54.1	ISO/IEC 9899:1999 Edits for Thread-Local Storage		500

	5.54.2 ISO/IEC 14882:1998 Edits for Thread-Local Storage....	500
5.55	Binary constants using the '0b' prefix	502

6 Extensions to the C++ Language 503

6.1	When is a Volatile Object Accessed?	503
6.2	Restricting Pointer Aliasing	503
6.3	Vague Linkage	504
6.4	#pragma interface and implementation.......................	505
6.5	Where's the Template?.......................................	507
6.6	Extracting the function pointer from a bound pointer to member function	509
6.7	C++-Specific Variable, Function, and Type Attributes	509
6.8	Namespace Association	510
6.9	Type Traits..	510
6.10	Java Exceptions	512
6.11	Deprecated Features	513
6.12	Backwards Compatibility	514

7 GNU Objective-C runtime features 515

7.1	+load: Executing code before main	515
	7.1.1 What you can and what you cannot do in +load.........	516
7.2	Type encoding	517
7.3	Garbage Collection...	518
7.4	Constant string objects	519
7.5	compatibility_alias	520

8 Binary Compatibility 521

9 gcov—a Test Coverage Program 525

9.1	Introduction to gcov..	525
9.2	Invoking gcov..	525
9.3	Using gcov with GCC Optimization..........................	530
9.4	Brief description of gcov data files	531
9.5	Data file relocation to support cross-profiling	531

10 Known Causes of Trouble with GCC...... 533

10.1	Actual Bugs We Haven't Fixed Yet	533
10.2	Cross-Compiler Problems	533
10.3	Interoperation	533
10.4	Incompatibilities of GCC....................................	535
10.5	Fixed Header Files...	538
10.6	Standard Libraries...	538
10.7	Disappointments and Misunderstandings	539
10.8	Common Misunderstandings with GNU C++	540
	10.8.1 Declare *and* Define Static Members	540

    10.8.2 Name lookup, templates, and accessing members of base classes... 541
    10.8.3 Temporaries May Vanish Before You Expect............ 542
    10.8.4 Implicit Copy-Assignment for Virtual Bases............ 543
  10.9 Caveats of using `protoize`................................. 544
  10.10 Certain Changes We Don't Want to Make................. 545
  10.11 Warning Messages and Error Messages..................... 548

11 Reporting Bugs 551
  11.1 Have You Found a Bug?..................................... 551
  11.2 How and where to Report Bugs............................. 551

12 How To Get Help with GCC 553

13 Contributing to GCC Development 555

Funding Free Software 557

The GNU Project and GNU/Linux 559

GNU General Public License 561

GNU Free Documentation License 573
  ADDENDUM: How to use this License for your documents 579

Contributors to GCC 581

Option Index 597

Keyword Index 613

Introduction

This manual documents how to use the GNU compilers, as well as their features and incompatibilities, and how to report bugs. It corresponds to the compilers (GCC) version 4.3.3. The internals of the GNU compilers, including how to port them to new targets and some information about how to write front ends for new languages, are documented in a separate manual. See Section "Introduction" in *GNU Compiler Collection (GCC) Internals*.

1 Programming Languages Supported by GCC

GCC stands for "GNU Compiler Collection". GCC is an integrated distribution of compilers for several major programming languages. These languages currently include C, C++, Objective-C, Objective-C++, Java, Fortran, and Ada.

The abbreviation *GCC* has multiple meanings in common use. The current official meaning is "GNU Compiler Collection", which refers generically to the complete suite of tools. The name historically stood for "GNU C Compiler", and this usage is still common when the emphasis is on compiling C programs. Finally, the name is also used when speaking of the *language-independent* component of GCC: code shared among the compilers for all supported languages.

The language-independent component of GCC includes the majority of the optimizers, as well as the "back ends" that generate machine code for various processors.

The part of a compiler that is specific to a particular language is called the "front end". In addition to the front ends that are integrated components of GCC, there are several other front ends that are maintained separately. These support languages such as Pascal, Mercury, and COBOL. To use these, they must be built together with GCC proper.

Most of the compilers for languages other than C have their own names. The C++ compiler is G++, the Ada compiler is GNAT, and so on. When we talk about compiling one of those languages, we might refer to that compiler by its own name, or as GCC. Either is correct.

Historically, compilers for many languages, including C++ and Fortran, have been implemented as "preprocessors" which emit another high level language such as C. None of the compilers included in GCC are implemented this way; they all generate machine code directly. This sort of preprocessor should not be confused with the *C preprocessor*, which is an integral feature of the C, C++, Objective-C and Objective-C++ languages.

2 Language Standards Supported by GCC

For each language compiled by GCC for which there is a standard, GCC attempts to follow one or more versions of that standard, possibly with some exceptions, and possibly with some extensions.

2.1 C language

GCC supports three versions of the C standard, although support for the most recent version is not yet complete.

The original ANSI C standard (X3.159-1989) was ratified in 1989 and published in 1990. This standard was ratified as an ISO standard (ISO/IEC 9899:1990) later in 1990. There were no technical differences between these publications, although the sections of the ANSI standard were renumbered and became clauses in the ISO standard. This standard, in both its forms, is commonly known as *C89*, or occasionally as *C90*, from the dates of ratification. The ANSI standard, but not the ISO standard, also came with a Rationale document. To select this standard in GCC, use one of the options '-ansi', '-std=c89' or '-std=iso9899:1990'; to obtain all the diagnostics required by the standard, you should also specify '-pedantic' (or '-pedantic-errors' if you want them to be errors rather than warnings). See Section 3.4 [Options Controlling C Dialect], page 26.

Errors in the 1990 ISO C standard were corrected in two Technical Corrigenda published in 1994 and 1996. GCC does not support the uncorrected version.

An amendment to the 1990 standard was published in 1995. This amendment added digraphs and `__STDC_VERSION__` to the language, but otherwise concerned the library. This amendment is commonly known as *AMD1*; the amended standard is sometimes known as *C94* or *C95*. To select this standard in GCC, use the option '-std=iso9899:199409' (with, as for other standard versions, '-pedantic' to receive all required diagnostics).

A new edition of the ISO C standard was published in 1999 as ISO/IEC 9899:1999, and is commonly known as *C99*. GCC has incomplete support for this standard version; see http://gcc.gnu.org/gcc-4.3/c99status.html for details. To select this standard, use '-std=c99' or '-std=iso9899:1999'. (While in development, drafts of this standard version were referred to as *C9X*.)

Errors in the 1999 ISO C standard were corrected in three Technical Corrigenda published in 2001, 2004 and 2007. GCC does not support the uncorrected version.

By default, GCC provides some extensions to the C language that on rare occasions conflict with the C standard. See Chapter 5 [Extensions to the C Language Family], page 245. Use of the '-std' options listed above will disable these extensions where they conflict with the C standard version selected. You may also select an extended version of the C language explicitly with '-std=gnu89' (for C89 with GNU extensions) or '-std=gnu99' (for C99 with GNU extensions). The default, if no C language dialect options are given, is '-std=gnu89'; this will change to '-std=gnu99' in some future release when the C99 support is complete. Some features that are part of the C99 standard are accepted as extensions in C89 mode.

The ISO C standard defines (in clause 4) two classes of conforming implementation. A *conforming hosted implementation* supports the whole standard including all the library facilities; a *conforming freestanding implementation* is only required to provide certain library facilities: those in <float.h>, <limits.h>, <stdarg.h>, and <stddef.h>; since AMD1, also those in <iso646.h>; and in C99, also those in <stdbool.h> and <stdint.h>. In addition, complex types, added in C99, are not required for freestanding implementations. The standard also defines two environments for programs, a *freestanding environment*, required of all implementations and which may not have library facilities beyond those required of freestanding implementations, where the handling of program startup and termination are implementation-defined, and a *hosted environment*, which is not required, in which all the library facilities are provided and startup is through a function int main (void) or int main (int, char *[]). An OS kernel would be a freestanding environment; a program using the facilities of an operating system would normally be in a hosted implementation.

GCC aims towards being usable as a conforming freestanding implementation, or as the compiler for a conforming hosted implementation. By default, it will act as the compiler for a hosted implementation, defining __STDC_HOSTED__ as 1 and presuming that when the names of ISO C functions are used, they have the semantics defined in the standard. To make it act as a conforming freestanding implementation for a freestanding environment, use the option '-ffreestanding'; it will then define __STDC_HOSTED__ to 0 and not make assumptions about the meanings of function names from the standard library, with exceptions noted below. To build an OS kernel, you may well still need to make your own arrangements for linking and startup. See Section 3.4 [Options Controlling C Dialect], page 26.

GCC does not provide the library facilities required only of hosted implementations, nor yet all the facilities required by C99 of freestanding implementations; to use the facilities of a hosted environment, you will need to find them elsewhere (for example, in the GNU C library). See Section 10.6 [Standard Libraries], page 538.

Most of the compiler support routines used by GCC are present in 'libgcc', but there are a few exceptions. GCC requires the freestanding environment provide memcpy, memmove, memset and memcmp. Finally, if __builtin_trap is used, and the target does not implement the trap pattern, then GCC will emit a call to abort.

For references to Technical Corrigenda, Rationale documents and information concerning the history of C that is available online, see http://gcc.gnu.org/readings.html

2.2 C++ language

GCC supports the ISO C++ standard (1998) and contains experimental support for the upcoming ISO C++ standard (200x).

The original ISO C++ standard was published as the ISO standard (ISO/IEC 14882:1998) and amended by a Technical Corrigenda published in 2003 (ISO/IEC 14882:2003). These standards are referred to as C++98 and C++03, respectively. GCC implements the majority of C++98 (export is a notable exception) and most of the changes in C++03. To select this standard in GCC, use one of the options '-ansi' or '-std=c++98'; to obtain all the diagnostics required by the standard, you should also specify '-pedantic' (or '-pedantic-errors' if you want them to be errors rather than warnings).

The ISO C++ committee is working on a new ISO C++ standard, dubbed C++0x, that is intended to be published by 2009. C++0x contains several changes to the C++ language, some of which have been implemented in an experimental C++0x mode in GCC. The C++0x mode in GCC tracks the draft working paper for the C++0x standard; the latest working paper is available on the ISO C++ committee's web site at http://www.open-std.org/jtc1/sc22/wg21/. For information regarding the C++0x features available in the experimental C++0x mode, see http://gcc.gnu.org/gcc-4.3/cxx0x_status.html. To select this standard in GCC, use the option '-std=c++0x'; to obtain all the diagnostics required by the standard, you should also specify '-pedantic' (or '-pedantic-errors' if you want them to be errors rather than warnings).

By default, GCC provides some extensions to the C++ language; See Section 3.5 [C++ Dialect Options], page 31. Use of the '-std' option listed above will disable these extensions. You may also select an extended version of the C++ language explicitly with '-std=gnu++98' (for C++98 with GNU extensions) or '-std=gnu++0x' (for C++0x with GNU extensions). The default, if no C++ language dialect options are given, is '-std=gnu++98'.

2.3 Objective-C and Objective-C++ languages

There is no formal written standard for Objective-C or Objective-C++. The most authoritative manual is "Object-Oriented Programming and the Objective-C Language", available at a number of web sites:

- http://developer.apple.com/documentation/Cocoa/Conceptual/ObjectiveC/ is a recent (and periodically updated) version;
- http://www.toodarkpark.org/computers/objc/ is an older example;
- http://www.gnustep.org and http://gcc.gnu.org/readings.html have additional useful information.

2.4 Treelang language

There is no standard for treelang, which is a sample language front end for GCC. Its only purpose is as a sample for people wishing to write a new language for GCC. The language is documented in 'gcc/treelang/treelang.texi' which can be turned into info or HTML format.

See Section "About This Guide" in *GNAT Reference Manual*, for information on standard conformance and compatibility of the Ada compiler.

See Section "Standards" in *The GNU Fortran Compiler*, for details of standards supported by GNU Fortran.

See Section "Compatibility with the Java Platform" in *GNU gcj*, for details of compatibility between gcj and the Java Platform.

3 GCC Command Options

When you invoke GCC, it normally does preprocessing, compilation, assembly and linking. The "overall options" allow you to stop this process at an intermediate stage. For example, the '-c' option says not to run the linker. Then the output consists of object files output by the assembler.

Other options are passed on to one stage of processing. Some options control the preprocessor and others the compiler itself. Yet other options control the assembler and linker; most of these are not documented here, since you rarely need to use any of them.

Most of the command line options that you can use with GCC are useful for C programs; when an option is only useful with another language (usually C++), the explanation says so explicitly. If the description for a particular option does not mention a source language, you can use that option with all supported languages.

See Section 3.3 [Compiling C++ Programs], page 25, for a summary of special options for compiling C++ programs.

The gcc program accepts options and file names as operands. Many options have multi-letter names; therefore multiple single-letter options may *not* be grouped: '-dr' is very different from '-d -r'.

You can mix options and other arguments. For the most part, the order you use doesn't matter. Order does matter when you use several options of the same kind; for example, if you specify '-L' more than once, the directories are searched in the order specified. Also, the placement of the '-l' option is significant.

Many options have long names starting with '-f' or with '-W'—for example, '-fmove-loop-invariants', '-Wformat' and so on. Most of these have both positive and negative forms; the negative form of '-ffoo' would be '-fno-foo'. This manual documents only one of these two forms, whichever one is not the default.

See [Option Index], page 597, for an index to GCC's options.

3.1 Option Summary

Here is a summary of all the options, grouped by type. Explanations are in the following sections.

Overall Options
> See Section 3.2 [Options Controlling the Kind of Output], page 20.
> ```
>     -c -S -E -o file -combine -pipe -pass-exit-codes
>     -x language -v -### --help[=class] --target-help
>     --version @file
> ```

C Language Options
> See Section 3.4 [Options Controlling C Dialect], page 26.
> ```
>         -ansi -std=standard -fgnu89-inline
>         -aux-info filename
>         -fno-asm -fno-builtin -fno-builtin-function
>         -fhosted -ffreestanding -fopenmp -fms-extensions
>         -trigraphs -no-integrated-cpp -traditional -traditional-cpp
>         -fallow-single-precision -fcond-mismatch -flax-vector-conversions
>         -fsigned-bitfields -fsigned-char
>         -funsigned-bitfields -funsigned-char
> ```

C++ Language Options

See Section 3.5 [Options Controlling C++ Dialect], page 31.

```
-fabi-version=n -fno-access-control -fcheck-new
-fconserve-space -ffriend-injection
-fno-elide-constructors
-fno-enforce-eh-specs
-ffor-scope -fno-for-scope -fno-gnu-keywords
-fno-implicit-templates
-fno-implicit-inline-templates
-fno-implement-inlines -fms-extensions
-fno-nonansi-builtins -fno-operator-names
-fno-optional-diags -fpermissive
-frepo -fno-rtti -fstats -ftemplate-depth-n
-fno-threadsafe-statics -fuse-cxa-atexit -fno-weak -nostdinc++
-fno-default-inline -fvisibility-inlines-hidden
-fvisibility-ms-compat
-Wabi -Wctor-dtor-privacy
-Wnon-virtual-dtor -Wreorder
-Weffc++ -Wno-deprecated -Wstrict-null-sentinel
-Wno-non-template-friend -Wold-style-cast
-Woverloaded-virtual -Wno-pmf-conversions
-Wsign-promo
```

Objective-C and Objective-C++ Language Options

See Section 3.6 [Options Controlling Objective-C and Objective-C++ Dialects], page 38.

```
-fconstant-string-class=class-name
-fgnu-runtime -fnext-runtime
-fno-nil-receivers
-fobjc-call-cxx-cdtors
-fobjc-direct-dispatch
-fobjc-exceptions
-fobjc-gc
-freplace-objc-classes
-fzero-link
-gen-decls
-Wassign-intercept
-Wno-protocol -Wselector
-Wstrict-selector-match
-Wundeclared-selector
```

Language Independent Options

See Section 3.7 [Options to Control Diagnostic Messages Formatting], page 42.

```
-fmessage-length=n
-fdiagnostics-show-location=[once|every-line]
-fdiagnostics-show-option
```

Warning Options

See Section 3.8 [Options to Request or Suppress Warnings], page 43.

```
-fsyntax-only -pedantic -pedantic-errors
-w -Wextra -Wall -Waddress -Waggregate-return -Warray-bounds
-Wno-attributes -Wc++-compat -Wc++0x-compat -Wcast-align -Wcast-qual
-Wchar-subscripts -Wclobbered -Wcomment
-Wconversion -Wcoverage-mismatch -Wno-deprecated-declarations
-Wdisabled-optimization -Wno-div-by-zero
-Wempty-body -Wno-endif-labels
-Werror -Werror=*
```

```
-Wfatal-errors -Wfloat-equal -Wformat -Wformat=2
-Wno-format-extra-args -Wformat-nonliteral
-Wformat-security -Wformat-y2k -Wignored-qualifiers
-Wimplicit -Wimplicit-function-declaration -Wimplicit-int
-Wimport -Wno-import -Winit-self -Winline
-Wno-int-to-pointer-cast -Wno-invalid-offsetof
-Winvalid-pch -Wlarger-than-len -Wunsafe-loop-optimizations
-Wlogical-op -Wlong-long
-Wmain -Wmissing-braces -Wmissing-field-initializers
-Wmissing-format-attribute -Wmissing-include-dirs
-Wmissing-noreturn
-Wno-multichar -Wnonnull -Wno-overflow
-Woverlength-strings -Wpacked -Wpadded
-Wparentheses -Wpointer-arith -Wno-pointer-to-int-cast
-Wredundant-decls
-Wreturn-type -Wsequence-point -Wshadow
-Wsign-compare -Wsign-conversion -Wstack-protector
-Wstrict-aliasing -Wstrict-aliasing=n
-Wstrict-overflow -Wstrict-overflow=n
-Wswitch -Wswitch-default -Wswitch-enum
-Wsystem-headers -Wtrigraphs -Wtype-limits -Wundef -Wuninitialized
-Wunknown-pragmas -Wno-pragmas -Wunreachable-code
-Wunused -Wunused-function -Wunused-label -Wunused-parameter
-Wunused-value -Wunused-variable
-Wvariadic-macros -Wvla
-Wvolatile-register-var -Wwrite-strings
```

C and Objective-C-only Warning Options
```
-Wbad-function-cast -Wmissing-declarations
-Wmissing-parameter-type -Wmissing-prototypes -Wnested-externs
-Wold-style-declaration -Wold-style-definition
-Wstrict-prototypes -Wtraditional -Wtraditional-conversion
-Wdeclaration-after-statement -Wpointer-sign
```

Debugging Options

See Section 3.9 [Options for Debugging Your Program or GCC], page 63.
```
-dletters -dumpspecs -dumpmachine -dumpversion
-fdbg-cnt-list -fdbg-cnt=counter-value-list
-fdump-noaddr -fdump-unnumbered -fdump-translation-unit[-n]
-fdump-class-hierarchy[-n]
-fdump-ipa-all -fdump-ipa-cgraph -fdump-ipa-inline
-fdump-tree-all
-fdump-tree-original[-n]
-fdump-tree-optimized[-n]
-fdump-tree-cfg -fdump-tree-vcg -fdump-tree-alias
-fdump-tree-ch
-fdump-tree-ssa[-n] -fdump-tree-pre[-n]
-fdump-tree-ccp[-n] -fdump-tree-dce[-n]
-fdump-tree-gimple[-raw] -fdump-tree-mudflap[-n]
-fdump-tree-dom[-n]
-fdump-tree-dse[-n]
-fdump-tree-phiopt[-n]
-fdump-tree-forwprop[-n]
-fdump-tree-copyrename[-n]
-fdump-tree-nrv -fdump-tree-vect
-fdump-tree-sink
-fdump-tree-sra[-n]
-fdump-tree-salias
-fdump-tree-fre[-n]
```

```
-fdump-tree-vrp[-n]
-ftree-vectorizer-verbose=n
-fdump-tree-storeccp[-n]
-feliminate-dwarf2-dups -feliminate-unused-debug-types
-feliminate-unused-debug-symbols -femit-class-debug-always
-fmem-report -fpre-ipa-mem-report -fpost-ipa-mem-report -fprofile-arcs
-frandom-seed=string -fsched-verbose=n
-ftest-coverage -ftime-report -fvar-tracking
-g -glevel -gcoff -gdwarf-2
-ggdb -gstabs -gstabs+ -gvms -gxcoff -gxcoff+
-fno-merge-debug-strings -fdebug-prefix-map=old=new
-femit-struct-debug-baseonly -femit-struct-debug-reduced
-femit-struct-debug-detailed[=spec-list]
-p -pg -print-file-name=library -print-libgcc-file-name
-print-multi-directory -print-multi-lib
-print-prog-name=program -print-search-dirs -Q
-print-sysroot-headers-suffix
-save-temps -time
```

Optimization Options

See Section 3.10 [Options that Control Optimization], page 77.

```
-falign-functions[=n] -falign-jumps[=n]
-falign-labels[=n] -falign-loops[=n] -fassociative-math
-fauto-inc-dec -fbranch-probabilities -fbranch-target-load-optimize
-fbranch-target-load-optimize2 -fbtr-bb-exclusive -fcaller-saves
-fcheck-data-deps -fcprop-registers -fcrossjumping -fcse-follow-jumps
-fcse-skip-blocks -fcx-limited-range -fdata-sections -fdce -fdce
-fdelayed-branch -fdelete-null-pointer-checks -fdse -fdse
-fearly-inlining -fexpensive-optimizations -ffast-math
-ffinite-math-only -ffloat-store -fforward-propagate
-ffunction-sections -fgcse -fgcse-after-reload -fgcse-las -fgcse-lm
-fgcse-sm -fif-conversion -fif-conversion2 -finline-functions
-finline-functions-called-once -finline-limit=n
-finline-small-functions -fipa-cp -fipa-matrix-reorg -fipa-pta
-fipa-pure-const -fipa-reference -fipa-struct-reorg
-fipa-type-escape -fivopts -fkeep-inline-functions -fkeep-static-consts
-fmerge-all-constants -fmerge-constants -fmodulo-sched
-fmodulo-sched-allow-regmoves -fmove-loop-invariants -fmudflap
-fmudflapir -fmudflapth -fno-branch-count-reg -fno-default-inline
-fno-defer-pop -fno-function-cse -fno-guess-branch-probability
-fno-inline -fno-math-errno -fno-peephole -fno-peephole2
-fno-sched-interblock -fno-sched-spec -fno-signed-zeros
-fno-toplevel-reorder -fno-trapping-math -fno-zero-initialized-in-bss
-fomit-frame-pointer -foptimize-register-move -foptimize-sibling-calls
-fpeel-loops -fpredictive-commoning -fprefetch-loop-arrays
-fprofile-generate -fprofile-use -fprofile-values -freciprocal-math
-fregmove -frename-registers -freorder-blocks
-freorder-blocks-and-partition -freorder-functions
-frerun-cse-after-loop -freschedule-modulo-scheduled-loops
-frounding-math -frtl-abstract-sequences -fsched2-use-superblocks
-fsched2-use-traces -fsched-spec-load -fsched-spec-load-dangerous
-fsched-stalled-insns-dep[=n] -fsched-stalled-insns[=n]
-fschedule-insns -fschedule-insns2 -fsection-anchors -fsee
-fsignaling-nans -fsingle-precision-constant -fsplit-ivs-in-unroller
-fsplit-wide-types -fstack-protector -fstack-protector-all
-fstrict-aliasing -fstrict-overflow -fthread-jumps -ftracer -ftree-ccp
-ftree-ch -ftree-copy-prop -ftree-copyrename -ftree-dce
-ftree-dominator-opts -ftree-dse -ftree-fre -ftree-loop-im
```

Chapter 3: GCC Command Options   13

```
             -ftree-loop-ivcanon -ftree-loop-linear -ftree-loop-optimize
             -ftree-parallelize-loops=n -ftree-pre -ftree-reassoc -ftree-salias
             -ftree-sink -ftree-sra -ftree-store-ccp -ftree-ter
             -ftree-vect-loop-version -ftree-vectorize -ftree-vrp -funit-at-a-time
             -funroll-all-loops -funroll-loops -funsafe-loop-optimizations
             -funsafe-math-optimizations -funswitch-loops
             -fvariable-expansion-in-unroller -fvect-cost-model -fvpt -fweb
             -fwhole-program
             --param name=value -O -O0 -O1 -O2 -O3 -Os
```

Preprocessor Options
    See Section 3.11 [Options Controlling the Preprocessor], page 113.
```
             -Aquestion=answer
             -A-question[=answer]
             -C -dD -dI -dM -dN
             -Dmacro[=defn] -E -H
             -idirafter dir
             -include file -imacros file
             -iprefix file -iwithprefix dir
             -iwithprefixbefore dir -isystem dir
             -imultilib dir -isysroot dir
             -M -MM -MF -MG -MP -MQ -MT -nostdinc
             -P -fworking-directory -remap
             -trigraphs -undef -Umacro -Wp,option
             -Xpreprocessor option
```

Assembler Option
    See Section 3.12 [Passing Options to the Assembler], page 123.
```
             -Wa,option -Xassembler option
```

Linker Options
    See Section 3.13 [Options for Linking], page 123.
```
             object-file-name -llibrary
             -nostartfiles -nodefaultlibs -nostdlib -pie -rdynamic
             -s -static -static-libgcc -shared -shared-libgcc -symbolic
             -Wl,option -Xlinker option
             -u symbol
```

Directory Options
    See Section 3.14 [Options for Directory Search], page 126.
```
             -Bprefix -Idir -iquotedir -Ldir -specs=file -I- --sysroot=dir
```

Target Options
    See Section 3.16 [Target Options], page 135.
```
             -V version -b machine
```

Machine Dependent Options
    See Section 3.17 [Hardware Models and Configurations], page 135.

    ARC Options
```
             -EB -EL
             -mmangle-cpu -mcpu=cpu -mtext=text-section
             -mdata=data-section -mrodata=readonly-data-section
```

    ARM Options
```
             -mapcs-frame -mno-apcs-frame
             -mabi=name
```

```
-mapcs-stack-check  -mno-apcs-stack-check
-mapcs-float  -mno-apcs-float
-mapcs-reentrant  -mno-apcs-reentrant
-msched-prolog  -mno-sched-prolog
-mlittle-endian  -mbig-endian  -mwords-little-endian
-mfloat-abi=name  -msoft-float  -mhard-float  -mfpe
-mthumb-interwork  -mno-thumb-interwork
-mcpu=name  -march=name  -mfpu=name
-mstructure-size-boundary=n
-mabort-on-noreturn
-mlong-calls  -mno-long-calls
-msingle-pic-base  -mno-single-pic-base
-mpic-register=reg
-mnop-fun-dllimport
-mcirrus-fix-invalid-insns  -mno-cirrus-fix-invalid-insns
-mpoke-function-name
-mthumb  -marm
-mtpcs-frame  -mtpcs-leaf-frame
-mcaller-super-interworking  -mcallee-super-interworking
-mtp=name
```

AVR Options
```
-mmcu=mcu  -msize  -minit-stack=n  -mno-interrupts
-mcall-prologues  -mno-tablejump  -mtiny-stack  -mint8
```

Blackfin Options
```
-mcpu=cpu[-sirevision]
-msim  -momit-leaf-frame-pointer  -mno-omit-leaf-frame-pointer
-mspecld-anomaly  -mno-specld-anomaly  -mcsync-anomaly  -mno-csync-anomaly
-mlow-64k  -mno-low64k  -mstack-check-l1  -mid-shared-library
-mno-id-shared-library  -mshared-library-id=n
-mleaf-id-shared-library  -mno-leaf-id-shared-library
-msep-data  -mno-sep-data  -mlong-calls  -mno-long-calls
-mfast-fp  -minline-plt
```

CRIS Options
```
-mcpu=cpu  -march=cpu  -mtune=cpu
-mmax-stack-frame=n  -melinux-stacksize=n
-metrax4  -metrax100  -mpdebug  -mcc-init  -mno-side-effects
-mstack-align  -mdata-align  -mconst-align
-m32-bit  -m16-bit  -m8-bit  -mno-prologue-epilogue  -mno-gotplt
-melf  -maout  -melinux  -mlinux  -sim  -sim2
-mmul-bug-workaround  -mno-mul-bug-workaround
```

CRX Options
```
-mmac  -mpush-args
```

Darwin Options
```
-all_load  -allowable_client  -arch  -arch_errors_fatal
-arch_only  -bind_at_load  -bundle  -bundle_loader
-client_name  -compatibility_version  -current_version
-dead_strip
-dependency-file  -dylib_file  -dylinker_install_name
-dynamic  -dynamiclib  -exported_symbols_list
-filelist  -flat_namespace  -force_cpusubtype_ALL
-force_flat_namespace  -headerpad_max_install_names
-iframework
-image_base  -init  -install_name  -keep_private_externs
-multi_module  -multiply_defined  -multiply_defined_unused
-noall_load  -no_dead_strip_inits_and_terms
```

```
-nofixprebinding -nomultidefs -noprebind -noseglinkedit
-pagezero_size -prebind -prebind_all_twolevel_modules
-private_bundle -read_only_relocs -sectalign
-sectobjectsymbols -whyload -seg1addr
-sectcreate -sectobjectsymbols -sectorder
-segaddr -segs_read_only_addr -segs_read_write_addr
-seg_addr_table -seg_addr_table_filename -seglinkedit
-segprot -segs_read_only_addr -segs_read_write_addr
-single_module -static -sub_library -sub_umbrella
-twolevel_namespace -umbrella -undefined
-unexported_symbols_list -weak_reference_mismatches
-whatsloaded -F -gused -gfull -mmacosx-version-min=version
-mkernel -mone-byte-bool
```

DEC Alpha Options

```
-mno-fp-regs -msoft-float -malpha-as -mgas
-mieee -mieee-with-inexact -mieee-conformant
-mfp-trap-mode=mode -mfp-rounding-mode=mode
-mtrap-precision=mode -mbuild-constants
-mcpu=cpu-type -mtune=cpu-type
-mbwx -mmax -mfix -mcix
-mfloat-vax -mfloat-ieee
-mexplicit-relocs -msmall-data -mlarge-data
-msmall-text -mlarge-text
-mmemory-latency=time
```

DEC Alpha/VMS Options

```
-mvms-return-codes
```

FRV Options

```
-mgpr-32 -mgpr-64 -mfpr-32 -mfpr-64
-mhard-float -msoft-float
-malloc-cc -mfixed-cc -mdword -mno-dword
-mdouble -mno-double
-mmedia -mno-media -mmuladd -mno-muladd
-mfdpic -minline-plt -mgprel-ro -multilib-library-pic
-mlinked-fp -mlong-calls -malign-labels
-mlibrary-pic -macc-4 -macc-8
-mpack -mno-pack -mno-eflags -mcond-move -mno-cond-move
-moptimize-membar -mno-optimize-membar
-mscc -mno-scc -mcond-exec -mno-cond-exec
-mvliw-branch -mno-vliw-branch
-mmulti-cond-exec -mno-multi-cond-exec -mnested-cond-exec
-mno-nested-cond-exec -mtomcat-stats
-mTLS -mtls
-mcpu=cpu
```

GNU/Linux Options

```
-muclibc
```

H8/300 Options

```
-mrelax -mh -ms -mn -mint32 -malign-300
```

HPPA Options

```
-march=architecture-type
-mbig-switch -mdisable-fpregs -mdisable-indexing
-mfast-indirect-calls -mgas -mgnu-ld -mhp-ld
-mfixed-range=register-range
-mjump-in-delay -mlinker-opt -mlong-calls
-mlong-load-store -mno-big-switch -mno-disable-fpregs
```

```
-mno-disable-indexing -mno-fast-indirect-calls -mno-gas
-mno-jump-in-delay -mno-long-load-store
-mno-portable-runtime -mno-soft-float
-mno-space-regs -msoft-float -mpa-risc-1-0
-mpa-risc-1-1 -mpa-risc-2-0 -mportable-runtime
-mschedule=cpu-type -mspace-regs -msio -mwsio
-munix=unix-std -nolibdld -static -threads
```

i386 and x86-64 Options

```
-mtune=cpu-type -march=cpu-type
-mfpmath=unit
-masm=dialect -mno-fancy-math-387
-mno-fp-ret-in-387 -msoft-float
-mno-wide-multiply -mrtd -malign-double
-mpreferred-stack-boundary=num -mcld -mcx16 -msahf -mrecip
-mmmx -msse -msse2 -msse3 -mssse3 -msse4.1 -msse4.2 -msse4
-msse4a -m3dnow -mpopcnt -mabm -msse5
-mthreads -mno-align-stringops -minline-all-stringops
-mpush-args -maccumulate-outgoing-args -m128bit-long-double
-m96bit-long-double -mregparm=num -msseregparm
-mveclibabi=type -mpc32 -mpc64 -mpc80 -mstackrealign
-momit-leaf-frame-pointer -mno-red-zone -mno-tls-direct-seg-refs
-mcmodel=code-model
-m32 -m64 -mlarge-data-threshold=num
-mfused-madd -mno-fused-madd
```

IA-64 Options

```
-mbig-endian -mlittle-endian -mgnu-as -mgnu-ld -mno-pic
-mvolatile-asm-stop -mregister-names -mno-sdata
-mconstant-gp -mauto-pic -minline-float-divide-min-latency
-minline-float-divide-max-throughput
-minline-int-divide-min-latency
-minline-int-divide-max-throughput
-minline-sqrt-min-latency -minline-sqrt-max-throughput
-mno-dwarf2-asm -mearly-stop-bits
-mfixed-range=register-range -mtls-size=tls-size
-mtune=cpu-type -mt -pthread -milp32 -mlp64
-mno-sched-br-data-spec -msched-ar-data-spec -mno-sched-control-spec
-msched-br-in-data-spec -msched-ar-in-data-spec -msched-in-control-spec
-msched-ldc -mno-sched-control-ldc -mno-sched-spec-verbose
-mno-sched-prefer-non-data-spec-insns
-mno-sched-prefer-non-control-spec-insns
-mno-sched-count-spec-in-critical-path
```

M32R/D Options

```
-m32r2 -m32rx -m32r
-mdebug
-malign-loops -mno-align-loops
-missue-rate=number
-mbranch-cost=number
-mmodel=code-size-model-type
-msdata=sdata-type
-mno-flush-func -mflush-func=name
-mno-flush-trap -mflush-trap=number
-G num
```

M32C Options

```
-mcpu=cpu -msim -memregs=number
```

M680x0 Options

Chapter 3: GCC Command Options   17

```
-march=arch -mcpu=cpu -mtune=tune -m68000 -m68020 -m68020-40 -m68020-60 -
m68030 -m68040
-m68060 -mcpu32 -m5200 -m5206e -m528x -m5307 -m5407
-mcfv4e -mbitfield -mno-bitfield -mc68000 -mc68020
-mnobitfield -mrtd -mno-rtd -mdiv -mno-div -mshort
-mno-short -mhard-float -m68881 -msoft-float -mpcrel
-malign-int -mstrict-align -msep-data -mno-sep-data
-mshared-library-id=n -mid-shared-library -mno-id-shared-library
```

M68hc1x Options

```
-m6811 -m6812 -m68hc11 -m68hc12 -m68hcs12
-mauto-incdec -minmax -mlong-calls -mshort
-msoft-reg-count=count
```

MCore Options

```
-mhardlit -mno-hardlit -mdiv -mno-div -mrelax-immediates
-mno-relax-immediates -mwide-bitfields -mno-wide-bitfields
-m4byte-functions -mno-4byte-functions -mcallgraph-data
-mno-callgraph-data -mslow-bytes -mno-slow-bytes -mno-lsim
-mlittle-endian -mbig-endian -m210 -m340 -mstack-increment
```

MIPS Options

```
-EL -EB -march=arch -mtune=arch
-mips1 -mips2 -mips3 -mips4 -mips32 -mips32r2 -mips64
-mips16 -mno-mips16 -mflip-mips16
-minterlink-mips16 -mno-interlink-mips16
-mabi=abi -mabicalls -mno-abicalls
-mshared -mno-shared -mxgot -mno-xgot -mgp32 -mgp64
-mfp32 -mfp64 -mhard-float -msoft-float
-msingle-float -mdouble-float -mdsp -mno-dsp -mdspr2 -mno-dspr2
-msmartmips -mno-smartmips
-mpaired-single -mno-paired-single -mdmx -mno-mdmx
-mips3d -mno-mips3d -mmt -mno-mt -mllsc -mno-llsc
-mlong64 -mlong32 -msym32 -mno-sym32
-Gnum -mlocal-sdata -mno-local-sdata
-mextern-sdata -mno-extern-sdata -mgpopt -mno-gopt
-membedded-data -mno-embedded-data
-muninit-const-in-rodata -mno-uninit-const-in-rodata
-mcode-readable=setting
-msplit-addresses -mno-split-addresses
-mexplicit-relocs -mno-explicit-relocs
-mcheck-zero-division -mno-check-zero-division
-mdivide-traps -mdivide-breaks
-mmemcpy -mno-memcpy -mlong-calls -mno-long-calls
-mmad -mno-mad -mfused-madd -mno-fused-madd -nocpp
-mfix-r4000 -mno-fix-r4000 -mfix-r4400 -mno-fix-r4400
-mfix-vr4120 -mno-fix-vr4120 -mfix-vr4130 -mno-fix-vr4130
-mfix-sb1 -mno-fix-sb1
-mflush-func=func -mno-flush-func
-mbranch-cost=num -mbranch-likely -mno-branch-likely
-mfp-exceptions -mno-fp-exceptions
-mvr4130-align -mno-vr4130-align
```

MMIX Options

```
-mlibfuncs -mno-libfuncs -mepsilon -mno-epsilon -mabi=gnu
-mabi=mmixware -mzero-extend -mknuthdiv -mtoplevel-symbols
-melf -mbranch-predict -mno-branch-predict -mbase-addresses
-mno-base-addresses -msingle-exit -mno-single-exit
```

MN10300 Options

```
-mmult-bug  -mno-mult-bug
-mam33  -mno-am33
-mam33-2  -mno-am33-2
-mreturn-pointer-on-d0
-mno-crt0  -mrelax
```

MT Options

```
-mno-crt0  -mbacc  -msim
-march=cpu-type
```

PDP-11 Options

```
-mfpu  -msoft-float  -mac0  -mno-ac0  -m40  -m45  -m10
-mbcopy  -mbcopy-builtin  -mint32  -mno-int16
-mint16  -mno-int32  -mfloat32  -mno-float64
-mfloat64  -mno-float32  -mabshi  -mno-abshi
-mbranch-expensive  -mbranch-cheap
-msplit  -mno-split  -munix-asm  -mdec-asm
```

PowerPC Options See RS/6000 and PowerPC Options.

RS/6000 and PowerPC Options

```
-mcpu=cpu-type
-mtune=cpu-type
-mpower  -mno-power  -mpower2  -mno-power2
-mpowerpc  -mpowerpc64  -mno-powerpc
-maltivec  -mno-altivec
-mpowerpc-gpopt  -mno-powerpc-gpopt
-mpowerpc-gfxopt  -mno-powerpc-gfxopt
-mmfcrf  -mno-mfcrf  -mpopcntb  -mno-popcntb  -mfprnd  -mno-fprnd
-mcmpb  -mno-cmpb  -mmfpgpr  -mno-mfpgpr  -mhard-dfp  -mno-hard-dfp
-mnew-mnemonics  -mold-mnemonics
-mfull-toc  -mminimal-toc  -mno-fp-in-toc  -mno-sum-in-toc
-m64  -m32  -mxl-compat  -mno-xl-compat  -mpe
-malign-power  -malign-natural
-msoft-float  -mhard-float  -mmultiple  -mno-multiple
-mstring  -mno-string  -mupdate  -mno-update
-mfused-madd  -mno-fused-madd  -mbit-align  -mno-bit-align
-mstrict-align  -mno-strict-align  -mrelocatable
-mno-relocatable  -mrelocatable-lib  -mno-relocatable-lib
-mtoc  -mno-toc  -mlittle  -mlittle-endian  -mbig  -mbig-endian
-mdynamic-no-pic  -maltivec  -mswdiv
-mprioritize-restricted-insns=priority
-msched-costly-dep=dependence_type
-minsert-sched-nops=scheme
-mcall-sysv  -mcall-netbsd
-maix-struct-return  -msvr4-struct-return
-mabi=abi-type  -msecure-plt  -mbss-plt
-misel  -mno-isel
-misel=yes  -misel=no
-mspe  -mno-spe
-mspe=yes  -mspe=no
-mpaired
-mvrsave  -mno-vrsave
-mmulhw  -mno-mulhw
-mdlmzb  -mno-dlmzb
-mfloat-gprs=yes  -mfloat-gprs=no  -mfloat-gprs=single  -mfloat-gprs=double
-mprototype  -mno-prototype
-msim  -mmvme  -mads  -myellowknife  -memb  -msdata
-msdata=opt  -mvxworks  -mwindiss  -G num  -pthread
```

S/390 and zSeries Options

Chapter 3: GCC Command Options   19

```
     -mtune=cpu-type -march=cpu-type
     -mhard-float -msoft-float -mhard-dfp -mno-hard-dfp
     -mlong-double-64 -mlong-double-128
     -mbackchain -mno-backchain -mpacked-stack -mno-packed-stack
     -msmall-exec -mno-small-exec -mmvcle -mno-mvcle
     -m64 -m31 -mdebug -mno-debug -mesa -mzarch
     -mtpf-trace -mno-tpf-trace -mfused-madd -mno-fused-madd
     -mwarn-framesize -mwarn-dynamicstack -mstack-size -mstack-guard
```

Score Options
```
     -meb -mel
     -mnhwloop
     -muls
     -mmac
     -mscore5 -mscore5u -mscore7 -mscore7d
```

SH Options
```
     -m1 -m2 -m2e -m3 -m3e
     -m4-nofpu -m4-single-only -m4-single -m4
     -m4a-nofpu -m4a-single-only -m4a-single -m4a -m4al
     -m5-64media -m5-64media-nofpu
     -m5-32media -m5-32media-nofpu
     -m5-compact -m5-compact-nofpu
     -mb -ml -mdalign -mrelax
     -mbigtable -mfmovd -mhitachi -mrenesas -mno-renesas -mnomacsave
     -mieee -misize -minline-ic_invalidate -mpadstruct -mspace
     -mprefergot -musermode -multcost=number -mdiv=strategy
     -mdivsi3_libfunc=name
     -madjust-unroll -mindexed-addressing -mgettrcost=number -mpt-fixed
     -minvalid-symbols
```

SPARC Options
```
     -mcpu=cpu-type
     -mtune=cpu-type
     -mcmodel=code-model
     -m32 -m64 -mapp-regs -mno-app-regs
     -mfaster-structs -mno-faster-structs
     -mfpu -mno-fpu -mhard-float -msoft-float
     -mhard-quad-float -msoft-quad-float
     -mimpure-text -mno-impure-text -mlittle-endian
     -mstack-bias -mno-stack-bias
     -munaligned-doubles -mno-unaligned-doubles
     -mv8plus -mno-v8plus -mvis -mno-vis -threads -pthreads -pthread
```

SPU Options
```
     -mwarn-reloc -merror-reloc
     -msafe-dma -munsafe-dma
     -mbranch-hints
     -msmall-mem -mlarge-mem -mstdmain
     -mfixed-range=register-range
```

System V Options
```
     -Qy -Qn -YP,paths -Ym,dir
```

V850 Options
```
     -mlong-calls -mno-long-calls -mep -mno-ep
     -mprolog-function -mno-prolog-function -mspace
     -mtda=n -msda=n -mzda=n
     -mapp-regs -mno-app-regs
     -mdisable-callt -mno-disable-callt
```

```
              -mv850e1
              -mv850e
              -mv850 -mbig-switch
```
VAX Options
```
              -mg -mgnu -munix
```
VxWorks Options
```
              -mrtp -non-static -Bstatic -Bdynamic
              -Xbind-lazy -Xbind-now
```
x86-64 Options See i386 and x86-64 Options.

Xstormy16 Options
```
              -msim
```
Xtensa Options
```
              -mconst16 -mno-const16
              -mfused-madd -mno-fused-madd
              -mtext-section-literals -mno-text-section-literals
              -mtarget-align -mno-target-align
              -mlongcalls -mno-longcalls
```
zSeries Options See S/390 and zSeries Options.

Code Generation Options

See Section 3.18 [Options for Code Generation Conventions], page 222.
```
              -fcall-saved-reg -fcall-used-reg
              -ffixed-reg -fexceptions
              -fnon-call-exceptions -funwind-tables
              -fasynchronous-unwind-tables
              -finhibit-size-directive -finstrument-functions
              -finstrument-functions-exclude-function-list=sym,sym,...
              -finstrument-functions-exclude-file-list=file,file,...
              -fno-common -fno-ident
              -fpcc-struct-return -fpic -fPIC -fpie -fPIE
              -fno-jump-tables
              -frecord-gcc-switches
              -freg-struct-return -fshort-enums
              -fshort-double -fshort-wchar
              -fverbose-asm -fpack-struct[=n] -fstack-check
              -fstack-limit-register=reg -fstack-limit-symbol=sym
              -fno-stack-limit -fargument-alias -fargument-noalias
              -fargument-noalias-global -fargument-noalias-anything
              -fleading-underscore -ftls-model=model
              -ftrapv -fwrapv -fbounds-check
              -fvisibility
```

3.2 Options Controlling the Kind of Output

Compilation can involve up to four stages: preprocessing, compilation proper, assembly and linking, always in that order. GCC is capable of preprocessing and compiling several files either into several assembler input files, or into one assembler input file; then each assembler input file produces an object file, and linking combines all the object files (those newly compiled, and those specified as input) into an executable file.

For any given input file, the file name suffix determines what kind of compilation is done:

`file.c`   C source code which must be preprocessed.

Chapter 3: GCC Command Options 21

`file.i`	C source code which should not be preprocessed.
`file.ii`	C++ source code which should not be preprocessed.
`file.m`	Objective-C source code. Note that you must link with the 'libobjc' library to make an Objective-C program work.
`file.mi`	Objective-C source code which should not be preprocessed.
`file.mm` `file.M`	Objective-C++ source code. Note that you must link with the 'libobjc' library to make an Objective-C++ program work. Note that '.M' refers to a literal capital M.
`file.mii`	Objective-C++ source code which should not be preprocessed.
`file.h`	C, C++, Objective-C or Objective-C++ header file to be turned into a precompiled header.

`file.cc`
`file.cp`
`file.cxx`
`file.cpp`
`file.CPP`
`file.c++`
`file.C`
	C++ source code which must be preprocessed. Note that in '.cxx', the last two letters must both be literally 'x'. Likewise, '.C' refers to a literal capital C.

`file.mm` `file.M`	Objective-C++ source code which must be preprocessed.
`file.mii`	Objective-C++ source code which should not be preprocessed.

`file.hh`
`file.H`
`file.hp`
`file.hxx`
`file.hpp`
`file.HPP`
`file.h++`
`file.tcc`
	C++ header file to be turned into a precompiled header.

`file.f`
`file.for`
`file.FOR`
	Fixed form Fortran source code which should not be preprocessed.

`file.F`
`file.fpp`
`file.FPP`
	Fixed form Fortran source code which must be preprocessed (with the traditional preprocessor).

`file.f90` `file.f95`	Free form Fortran source code which should not be preprocessed.

`file.F90`
`file.F95` Free form Fortran source code which must be preprocessed (with the traditional preprocessor).

`file.ads` Ada source code file which contains a library unit declaration (a declaration of a package, subprogram, or generic, or a generic instantiation), or a library unit renaming declaration (a package, generic, or subprogram renaming declaration). Such files are also called *specs*.

`file.adb` Ada source code file containing a library unit body (a subprogram or package body). Such files are also called *bodies*.

`file.s` Assembler code.

`file.S`
`file.sx` Assembler code which must be preprocessed.

`other` An object file to be fed straight into linking. Any file name with no recognized suffix is treated this way.

You can specify the input language explicitly with the '-x' option:

`-x language`
Specify explicitly the *language* for the following input files (rather than letting the compiler choose a default based on the file name suffix). This option applies to all following input files until the next '-x' option. Possible values for *language* are:

```
c   c-header   c-cpp-output
c++ c++-header c++-cpp-output
objective-c   objective-c-header   objective-c-cpp-output
objective-c++ objective-c++-header objective-c++-cpp-output
assembler   assembler-with-cpp
ada
f95 f95-cpp-input
java
treelang
```

`-x none` Turn off any specification of a language, so that subsequent files are handled according to their file name suffixes (as they are if '-x' has not been used at all).

`-pass-exit-codes`
Normally the gcc program will exit with the code of 1 if any phase of the compiler returns a non-success return code. If you specify '-pass-exit-codes', the gcc program will instead return with numerically highest error produced by any phase that returned an error indication. The C, C++, and Fortran frontends return 4, if an internal compiler error is encountered.

If you only want some of the stages of compilation, you can use '-x' (or filename suffixes) to tell gcc where to start, and one of the options '-c', '-S', or '-E' to say where gcc is to stop. Note that some combinations (for example, '-x cpp-output -E') instruct gcc to do nothing at all.

`-c` Compile or assemble the source files, but do not link. The linking stage simply is not done. The ultimate output is in the form of an object file for each source file.

Chapter 3: GCC Command Options 23

By default, the object file name for a source file is made by replacing the suffix '.c', '.i', '.s', etc., with '.o'.

Unrecognized input files, not requiring compilation or assembly, are ignored.

-S   Stop after the stage of compilation proper; do not assemble. The output is in the form of an assembler code file for each non-assembler input file specified.

By default, the assembler file name for a source file is made by replacing the suffix '.c', '.i', etc., with '.s'.

Input files that don't require compilation are ignored.

-E   Stop after the preprocessing stage; do not run the compiler proper. The output is in the form of preprocessed source code, which is sent to the standard output.

Input files which don't require preprocessing are ignored.

-o *file*   Place output in file *file*. This applies regardless to whatever sort of output is being produced, whether it be an executable file, an object file, an assembler file or preprocessed C code.

If '-o' is not specified, the default is to put an executable file in 'a.out', the object file for '*source.suffix*' in '*source.o*', its assembler file in '*source.s*', a precompiled header file in '*source.suffix.gch*', and all preprocessed C source on standard output.

-v   Print (on standard error output) the commands executed to run the stages of compilation. Also print the version number of the compiler driver program and of the preprocessor and the compiler proper.

-###   Like '-v' except the commands are not executed and all command arguments are quoted. This is useful for shell scripts to capture the driver-generated command lines.

-pipe   Use pipes rather than temporary files for communication between the various stages of compilation. This fails to work on some systems where the assembler is unable to read from a pipe; but the GNU assembler has no trouble.

-combine   If you are compiling multiple source files, this option tells the driver to pass all the source files to the compiler at once (for those languages for which the compiler can handle this). This will allow intermodule analysis (IMA) to be performed by the compiler. Currently the only language for which this is supported is C. If you pass source files for multiple languages to the driver, using this option, the driver will invoke the compiler(s) that support IMA once each, passing each compiler all the source files appropriate for it. For those languages that do not support IMA this option will be ignored, and the compiler will be invoked once for each source file in that language. If you use this option in conjunction with '-save-temps', the compiler will generate multiple pre-processed files (one for each source file), but only one (combined) '.o' or '.s' file.

--help   Print (on the standard output) a description of the command line options understood by gcc. If the '-v' option is also specified then '--help' will also be passed on to the various processes invoked by gcc, so that they can display the command line options they accept. If the '-Wextra' option has also been specified (prior to the '--help' option), then command line options which have no documentation associated with them will also be displayed.

`--target-help`
: Print (on the standard output) a description of target-specific command line options for each tool. For some targets extra target-specific information may also be printed.

`--help=class[,qualifier]`
: Print (on the standard output) a description of the command line options understood by the compiler that fit into a specific class. The class can be one of 'optimizers', 'warnings', 'target', 'params', or language:

    'optimizers'
    : This will display all of the optimization options supported by the compiler.

    'warnings'
    : This will display all of the options controlling warning messages produced by the compiler.

    'target'
    : This will display target-specific options. Unlike the '--target-help' option however, target-specific options of the linker and assembler will not be displayed. This is because those tools do not currently support the extended '--help=' syntax.

    'params'
    : This will display the values recognized by the '--param' option.

    language
    : This will display the options supported for language, where language is the name of one of the languages supported in this version of GCC.

    'common'
    : This will display the options that are common to all languages.

It is possible to further refine the output of the '--help=' option by adding a comma separated list of qualifiers after the class. These can be any from the following list:

'undocumented'
: Display only those options which are undocumented.

'joined'
: Display options which take an argument that appears after an equal sign in the same continuous piece of text, such as: '--help=target'.

'separate'
: Display options which take an argument that appears as a separate word following the original option, such as: '-o output-file'.

Thus for example to display all the undocumented target-specific switches supported by the compiler the following can be used:

    --help=target,undocumented

The sense of a qualifier can be inverted by prefixing it with the ^ character, so for example to display all binary warning options (i.e., ones that are either on or off and that do not take an argument), which have a description the following can be used:

Chapter 3: GCC Command Options   25

```
--help=warnings,^joined,^undocumented
```
A class can also be used as a qualifier, although this usually restricts the output by so much that there is nothing to display. One case where it does work however is when one of the classes is *target*. So for example to display all the target-specific optimization options the following can be used:

```
--help=target,optimizers
```

The '`--help=`' option can be repeated on the command line. Each successive use will display its requested class of options, skipping those that have already been displayed.

If the '`-Q`' option appears on the command line before the '`--help=`' option, then the descriptive text displayed by '`--help=`' is changed. Instead of describing the displayed options, an indication is given as to whether the option is enabled, disabled or set to a specific value (assuming that the compiler knows this at the point where the '`--help=`' option is used).

Here is a truncated example from the ARM port of `gcc`:

```
% gcc -Q -mabi=2 --help=target -c
The following options are target specific:
-mabi=                          2
-mabort-on-noreturn             [disabled]
-mapcs                          [disabled]
```

The output is sensitive to the effects of previous command line options, so for example it is possible to find out which optimizations are enabled at '`-O2`' by using:

```
-O2 --help=optimizers
```

Alternatively you can discover which binary optimizations are enabled by '`-O3`' by using:

```
gcc -c -Q -O3 --help=optimizers > /tmp/O3-opts
gcc -c -Q -O2 --help=optimizers > /tmp/O2-opts
diff /tmp/O2-opts /tmp/O3-opts | grep enabled
```

`--version`
Display the version number and copyrights of the invoked GCC.

`@file`
Read command-line options from *file*. The options read are inserted in place of the original @*file* option. If *file* does not exist, or cannot be read, then the option will be treated literally, and not removed.

Options in *file* are separated by whitespace. A whitespace character may be included in an option by surrounding the entire option in either single or double quotes. Any character (including a backslash) may be included by prefixing the character to be included with a backslash. The *file* may itself contain additional @*file* options; any such options will be processed recursively.

3.3 Compiling C++ Programs

C++ source files conventionally use one of the suffixes '`.C`', '`.cc`', '`.cpp`', '`.CPP`', '`.c++`', '`.cp`', or '`.cxx`'; C++ header files often use '`.hh`', '`.hpp`', '`.H`', or (for shared template code) '`.tcc`'; and preprocessed C++ files use the suffix '`.ii`'. GCC recognizes files with these names and compiles them as C++ programs even if you call the compiler the same way as for compiling C programs (usually with the name `gcc`).

However, the use of `gcc` does not add the C++ library. `g++` is a program that calls GCC and treats '.c', '.h' and '.i' files as C++ source files instead of C source files unless '-x' is used, and automatically specifies linking against the C++ library. This program is also useful when precompiling a C header file with a '.h' extension for use in C++ compilations. On many systems, `g++` is also installed with the name `c++`.

When you compile C++ programs, you may specify many of the same command-line options that you use for compiling programs in any language; or command-line options meaningful for C and related languages; or options that are meaningful only for C++ programs. See Section 3.4 [Options Controlling C Dialect], page 26, for explanations of options for languages related to C. See Section 3.5 [Options Controlling C++ Dialect], page 31, for explanations of options that are meaningful only for C++ programs.

3.4 Options Controlling C Dialect

The following options control the dialect of C (or languages derived from C, such as C++, Objective-C and Objective-C++) that the compiler accepts:

-ansi
: In C mode, this is equivalent to '-std=c89'. In C++ mode, it is equivalent to '-std=c++98'.

  This turns off certain features of GCC that are incompatible with ISO C90 (when compiling C code), or of standard C++ (when compiling C++ code), such as the `asm` and `typeof` keywords, and predefined macros such as `unix` and `vax` that identify the type of system you are using. It also enables the undesirable and rarely used ISO trigraph feature. For the C compiler, it disables recognition of C++ style '//' comments as well as the `inline` keyword.

  The alternate keywords `__asm__`, `__extension__`, `__inline__` and `__typeof__` continue to work despite '-ansi'. You would not want to use them in an ISO C program, of course, but it is useful to put them in header files that might be included in compilations done with '-ansi'. Alternate predefined macros such as `__unix__` and `__vax__` are also available, with or without '-ansi'.

  The '-ansi' option does not cause non-ISO programs to be rejected gratuitously. For that, '-pedantic' is required in addition to '-ansi'. See Section 3.8 [Warning Options], page 43.

  The macro `__STRICT_ANSI__` is predefined when the '-ansi' option is used. Some header files may notice this macro and refrain from declaring certain functions or defining certain macros that the ISO standard doesn't call for; this is to avoid interfering with any programs that might use these names for other things.

  Functions that would normally be built in but do not have semantics defined by ISO C (such as `alloca` and `ffs`) are not built-in functions when '-ansi' is used. See Section 5.49 [Other built-in functions provided by GCC], page 337, for details of the functions affected.

-std=
: Determine the language standard. See Chapter 2 [Language Standards Supported by GCC], page 5, for details of these standard versions. This option is currently only supported when compiling C or C++.

Chapter 3: GCC Command Options 27

The compiler can accept several base standards, such as 'c89' or 'c++98', and GNU dialects of those standards, such as 'gnu89' or 'gnu++98'. By specifing a base standard, the compiler will accept all programs following that standard and those using GNU extensions that do not contradict it. For example, '-std=c89' turns off certain features of GCC that are incompatible with ISO C90, such as the asm and typeof keywords, but not other GNU extensions that do not have a meaning in ISO C90, such as omitting the middle term of a ?: expression. On the other hand, by specifing a GNU dialect of a standard, all features the compiler support are enabled, even when those features change the meaning of the base standard and some strict-conforming programs may be rejected. The particular standard is used by '-pedantic' to identify which features are GNU extensions given that version of the standard. For example '-std=gnu89 -pedantic' would warn about C++ style '//' comments, while '-std=gnu99 -pedantic' would not.

A value for this option must be provided; possible values are

'c89'
'iso9899:1990'
> Support all ISO C90 programs (certain GNU extensions that conflict with ISO C90 are disabled). Same as '-ansi' for C code.

'iso9899:199409'
> ISO C90 as modified in amendment 1.

'c99'
'c9x'
'iso9899:1999'
'iso9899:199x'
> ISO C99. Note that this standard is not yet fully supported; see http://gcc.gnu.org/gcc-4.3/c99status.html for more information. The names 'c9x' and 'iso9899:199x' are deprecated.

'gnu89' GNU dialect of ISO C90 (including some C99 features). This is the default for C code.

'gnu99'
'gnu9x' GNU dialect of ISO C99. When ISO C99 is fully implemented in GCC, this will become the default. The name 'gnu9x' is deprecated.

'c++98' The 1998 ISO C++ standard plus amendments. Same as '-ansi' for C++ code.

'gnu++98' GNU dialect of '-std=c++98'. This is the default for C++ code.

'c++0x' The working draft of the upcoming ISO C++0x standard. This option enables experimental features that are likely to be included in C++0x. The working draft is constantly changing, and any feature that is enabled by this flag may be removed from future versions of GCC if it is not part of the C++0x standard.

'gnu++0x' GNU dialect of '-std=c++0x'. This option enables experimental features that may be removed in future versions of GCC.

`-fgnu89-inline`
> The option '`-fgnu89-inline`' tells GCC to use the traditional GNU semantics for `inline` functions when in C99 mode. See Section 5.36 [An Inline Function is As Fast As a Macro], page 299. This option is accepted and ignored by GCC versions 4.1.3 up to but not including 4.3. In GCC versions 4.3 and later it changes the behavior of GCC in C99 mode. Using this option is roughly equivalent to adding the `gnu_inline` function attribute to all inline functions (see Section 5.27 [Function Attributes], page 264).
>
> The option '`-fno-gnu89-inline`' explicitly tells GCC to use the C99 semantics for `inline` when in C99 or gnu99 mode (i.e., it specifies the default behavior). This option was first supported in GCC 4.3. This option is not supported in C89 or gnu89 mode.
>
> The preprocessor macros `__GNUC_GNU_INLINE__` and `__GNUC_STDC_INLINE__` may be used to check which semantics are in effect for `inline` functions. See Section "Common Predefined Macros" in *The C Preprocessor*.

`-aux-info filename`
> Output to the given filename prototyped declarations for all functions declared and/or defined in a translation unit, including those in header files. This option is silently ignored in any language other than C.
>
> Besides declarations, the file indicates, in comments, the origin of each declaration (source file and line), whether the declaration was implicit, prototyped or unprototyped ('`I`', '`N`' for new or '`O`' for old, respectively, in the first character after the line number and the colon), and whether it came from a declaration or a definition ('`C`' or '`F`', respectively, in the following character). In the case of function definitions, a K&R-style list of arguments followed by their declarations is also provided, inside comments, after the declaration.

`-fno-asm`
> Do not recognize `asm`, `inline` or `typeof` as a keyword, so that code can use these words as identifiers. You can use the keywords `__asm__`, `__inline__` and `__typeof__` instead. '`-ansi`' implies '`-fno-asm`'.
>
> In C++, this switch only affects the `typeof` keyword, since `asm` and `inline` are standard keywords. You may want to use the '`-fno-gnu-keywords`' flag instead, which has the same effect. In C99 mode ('`-std=c99`' or '`-std=gnu99`'), this switch only affects the `asm` and `typeof` keywords, since `inline` is a standard keyword in ISO C99.

`-fno-builtin`
`-fno-builtin-function`
> Don't recognize built-in functions that do not begin with '`__builtin_`' as prefix. See Section 5.49 [Other built-in functions provided by GCC], page 337, for details of the functions affected, including those which are not built-in functions when '`-ansi`' or '`-std`' options for strict ISO C conformance are used because they do not have an ISO standard meaning.
>
> GCC normally generates special code to handle certain built-in functions more efficiently; for instance, calls to `alloca` may become single instructions that adjust the stack directly, and calls to `memcpy` may become inline copy loops. The resulting code is often both smaller and faster, but since the function

Chapter 3: GCC Command Options   29

calls no longer appear as such, you cannot set a breakpoint on those calls, nor can you change the behavior of the functions by linking with a different library. In addition, when a function is recognized as a built-in function, GCC may use information about that function to warn about problems with calls to that function, or to generate more efficient code, even if the resulting code still contains calls to that function. For example, warnings are given with '-Wformat' for bad calls to `printf`, when `printf` is built in, and `strlen` is known not to modify global memory.

With the '`-fno-builtin-function`' option only the built-in function *function* is disabled. *function* must not begin with '`__builtin_`'. If a function is named this is not built-in in this version of GCC, this option is ignored. There is no corresponding '`-fbuiltin-function`' option; if you wish to enable built-in functions selectively when using '`-fno-builtin`' or '`-ffreestanding`', you may define macros such as:

```
#define abs(n)          __builtin_abs ((n))
#define strcpy(d, s)    __builtin_strcpy ((d), (s))
```

`-fhosted`

Assert that compilation takes place in a hosted environment. This implies '`-fbuiltin`'. A hosted environment is one in which the entire standard library is available, and in which `main` has a return type of `int`. Examples are nearly everything except a kernel. This is equivalent to '`-fno-freestanding`'.

`-ffreestanding`

Assert that compilation takes place in a freestanding environment. This implies '`-fno-builtin`'. A freestanding environment is one in which the standard library may not exist, and program startup may not necessarily be at `main`. The most obvious example is an OS kernel. This is equivalent to '`-fno-hosted`'.

See Chapter 2 [Language Standards Supported by GCC], page 5, for details of freestanding and hosted environments.

`-fopenmp`   Enable handling of OpenMP directives `#pragma omp` in C/C++ and `!$omp` in Fortran. When '`-fopenmp`' is specified, the compiler generates parallel code according to the OpenMP Application Program Interface v2.5 http://www.openmp.org/. This option implies '`-pthread`', and thus is only supported on targets that have support for '`-pthread`'.

`-fms-extensions`

Accept some non-standard constructs used in Microsoft header files.

Some cases of unnamed fields in structures and unions are only accepted with this option. See Section 5.53 [Unnamed struct/union fields within structs/unions], page 498, for details.

`-trigraphs`

Support ISO C trigraphs. The '`-ansi`' option (and '`-std`' options for strict ISO C conformance) implies '`-trigraphs`'.

`-no-integrated-cpp`

Performs a compilation in two passes: preprocessing and compiling. This option allows a user supplied "cc1", "cc1plus", or "cc1obj" via the '`-B`' option. The user supplied compilation step can then add in an additional preprocessing step after normal preprocessing but before compiling. The default is to use the integrated cpp (internal cpp)

The semantics of this option will change if "cc1", "cc1plus", and "cc1obj" are merged.

`-traditional`
`-traditional-cpp`

> Formerly, these options caused GCC to attempt to emulate a pre-standard C compiler. They are now only supported with the '-E' switch. The preprocessor continues to support a pre-standard mode. See the GNU CPP manual for details.

`-fcond-mismatch`

> Allow conditional expressions with mismatched types in the second and third arguments. The value of such an expression is void. This option is not supported for C++.

`-flax-vector-conversions`

> Allow implicit conversions between vectors with differing numbers of elements and/or incompatible element types. This option should not be used for new code.

`-funsigned-char`

> Let the type `char` be unsigned, like `unsigned char`.
>
> Each kind of machine has a default for what `char` should be. It is either like `unsigned char` by default or like `signed char` by default.
>
> Ideally, a portable program should always use `signed char` or `unsigned char` when it depends on the signedness of an object. But many programs have been written to use plain `char` and expect it to be signed, or expect it to be unsigned, depending on the machines they were written for. This option, and its inverse, let you make such a program work with the opposite default.
>
> The type `char` is always a distinct type from each of `signed char` or `unsigned char`, even though its behavior is always just like one of those two.

`-fsigned-char`

> Let the type `char` be signed, like `signed char`.
>
> Note that this is equivalent to '-fno-unsigned-char', which is the negative form of '-funsigned-char'. Likewise, the option '-fno-signed-char' is equivalent to '-funsigned-char'.

`-fsigned-bitfields`
`-funsigned-bitfields`
`-fno-signed-bitfields`
`-fno-unsigned-bitfields`

> These options control whether a bit-field is signed or unsigned, when the declaration does not use either `signed` or `unsigned`. By default, such a bit-field is signed, because this is consistent: the basic integer types such as `int` are signed types.

Chapter 3: GCC Command Options   31

3.5 Options Controlling C++ Dialect

This section describes the command-line options that are only meaningful for C++ programs; but you can also use most of the GNU compiler options regardless of what language your program is in. For example, you might compile a file `firstClass.C` like this:

```
g++ -g -frepo -O -c firstClass.C
```

In this example, only '`-frepo`' is an option meant only for C++ programs; you can use the other options with any language supported by GCC.

Here is a list of options that are *only* for compiling C++ programs:

`-fabi-version=n`

> Use version n of the C++ ABI. Version 2 is the version of the C++ ABI that first appeared in G++ 3.4. Version 1 is the version of the C++ ABI that first appeared in G++ 3.2. Version 0 will always be the version that conforms most closely to the C++ ABI specification. Therefore, the ABI obtained using version 0 will change as ABI bugs are fixed.
>
> The default is version 2.

`-fno-access-control`

> Turn off all access checking. This switch is mainly useful for working around bugs in the access control code.

`-fcheck-new`

> Check that the pointer returned by `operator new` is non-null before attempting to modify the storage allocated. This check is normally unnecessary because the C++ standard specifies that `operator new` will only return 0 if it is declared '`throw()`', in which case the compiler will always check the return value even without this option. In all other cases, when `operator new` has a non-empty exception specification, memory exhaustion is signalled by throwing `std::bad_alloc`. See also '`new (nothrow)`'.

`-fconserve-space`

> Put uninitialized or runtime-initialized global variables into the common segment, as C does. This saves space in the executable at the cost of not diagnosing duplicate definitions. If you compile with this flag and your program mysteriously crashes after `main()` has completed, you may have an object that is being destroyed twice because two definitions were merged.
>
> This option is no longer useful on most targets, now that support has been added for putting variables into BSS without making them common.

`-ffriend-injection`

> Inject friend functions into the enclosing namespace, so that they are visible outside the scope of the class in which they are declared. Friend functions were documented to work this way in the old Annotated C++ Reference Manual, and versions of G++ before 4.1 always worked that way. However, in ISO C++ a friend function which is not declared in an enclosing scope can only be found using argument dependent lookup. This option causes friends to be injected as they were in earlier releases.
>
> This option is for compatibility, and may be removed in a future release of G++.

`-fno-elide-constructors`

> The C++ standard allows an implementation to omit creating a temporary which is only used to initialize another object of the same type. Specifying this option disables that optimization, and forces G++ to call the copy constructor in all cases.

`-fno-enforce-eh-specs`

> Don't generate code to check for violation of exception specifications at runtime. This option violates the C++ standard, but may be useful for reducing code size in production builds, much like defining '`NDEBUG`'. This does not give user code permission to throw exceptions in violation of the exception specifications; the compiler will still optimize based on the specifications, so throwing an unexpected exception will result in undefined behavior.

`-ffor-scope`
`-fno-for-scope`

> If '`-ffor-scope`' is specified, the scope of variables declared in a *for-init-statement* is limited to the '`for`' loop itself, as specified by the C++ standard. If '`-fno-for-scope`' is specified, the scope of variables declared in a *for-init-statement* extends to the end of the enclosing scope, as was the case in old versions of G++, and other (traditional) implementations of C++.
>
> The default if neither flag is given to follow the standard, but to allow and give a warning for old-style code that would otherwise be invalid, or have different behavior.

`-fno-gnu-keywords`

> Do not recognize `typeof` as a keyword, so that code can use this word as an identifier. You can use the keyword `__typeof__` instead. '`-ansi`' implies '`-fno-gnu-keywords`'.

`-fno-implicit-templates`

> Never emit code for non-inline templates which are instantiated implicitly (i.e. by use); only emit code for explicit instantiations. See Section 6.5 [Template Instantiation], page 507, for more information.

`-fno-implicit-inline-templates`

> Don't emit code for implicit instantiations of inline templates, either. The default is to handle inlines differently so that compiles with and without optimization will need the same set of explicit instantiations.

`-fno-implement-inlines`

> To save space, do not emit out-of-line copies of inline functions controlled by '`#pragma implementation`'. This will cause linker errors if these functions are not inlined everywhere they are called.

`-fms-extensions`

> Disable pedantic warnings about constructs used in MFC, such as implicit int and getting a pointer to member function via non-standard syntax.

Chapter 3: GCC Command Options   33

`-fno-nonansi-builtins`
: Disable built-in declarations of functions that are not mandated by ANSI/ISO C. These include `ffs`, `alloca`, `_exit`, `index`, `bzero`, `conjf`, and other related functions.

`-fno-operator-names`
: Do not treat the operator name keywords `and`, `bitand`, `bitor`, `compl`, `not`, `or` and `xor` as synonyms as keywords.

`-fno-optional-diags`
: Disable diagnostics that the standard says a compiler does not need to issue. Currently, the only such diagnostic issued by G++ is the one for a name having multiple meanings within a class.

`-fpermissive`
: Downgrade some diagnostics about nonconformant code from errors to warnings. Thus, using '`-fpermissive`' will allow some nonconforming code to compile.

`-frepo`
: Enable automatic template instantiation at link time. This option also implies '`-fno-implicit-templates`'. See Section 6.5 [Template Instantiation], page 507, for more information.

`-fno-rtti`
: Disable generation of information about every class with virtual functions for use by the C++ runtime type identification features ('`dynamic_cast`' and '`typeid`'). If you don't use those parts of the language, you can save some space by using this flag. Note that exception handling uses the same information, but it will generate it as needed. The '`dynamic_cast`' operator can still be used for casts that do not require runtime type information, i.e. casts to `void *` or to unambiguous base classes.

`-fstats`
: Emit statistics about front-end processing at the end of the compilation. This information is generally only useful to the G++ development team.

`-ftemplate-depth-n`
: Set the maximum instantiation depth for template classes to n. A limit on the template instantiation depth is needed to detect endless recursions during template class instantiation. ANSI/ISO C++ conforming programs must not rely on a maximum depth greater than 17.

`-fno-threadsafe-statics`
: Do not emit the extra code to use the routines specified in the C++ ABI for thread-safe initialization of local statics. You can use this option to reduce code size slightly in code that doesn't need to be thread-safe.

`-fuse-cxa-atexit`
: Register destructors for objects with static storage duration with the `__cxa_atexit` function rather than the `atexit` function. This option is required for fully standards-compliant handling of static destructors, but will only work if your C library supports `__cxa_atexit`.

`-fno-use-cxa-get-exception-ptr`

Don't use the `__cxa_get_exception_ptr` runtime routine. This will cause `std::uncaught_exception` to be incorrect, but is necessary if the runtime routine is not available.

`-fvisibility-inlines-hidden`

This switch declares that the user does not attempt to compare pointers to inline methods where the addresses of the two functions were taken in different shared objects.

The effect of this is that GCC may, effectively, mark inline methods with `__attribute__ ((visibility ("hidden")))` so that they do not appear in the export table of a DSO and do not require a PLT indirection when used within the DSO. Enabling this option can have a dramatic effect on load and link times of a DSO as it massively reduces the size of the dynamic export table when the library makes heavy use of templates.

The behavior of this switch is not quite the same as marking the methods as hidden directly, because it does not affect static variables local to the function or cause the compiler to deduce that the function is defined in only one shared object.

You may mark a method as having a visibility explicitly to negate the effect of the switch for that method. For example, if you do want to compare pointers to a particular inline method, you might mark it as having default visibility. Marking the enclosing class with explicit visibility will have no effect.

Explicitly instantiated inline methods are unaffected by this option as their linkage might otherwise cross a shared library boundary. See Section 6.5 [Template Instantiation], page 507.

`-fvisibility-ms-compat`

This flag attempts to use visibility settings to make GCC's C++ linkage model compatible with that of Microsoft Visual Studio.

The flag makes these changes to GCC's linkage model:

1. It sets the default visibility to `hidden`, like '`-fvisibility=hidden`'.
2. Types, but not their members, are not hidden by default.
3. The One Definition Rule is relaxed for types without explicit visibility specifications which are defined in more than one different shared object: those declarations are permitted if they would have been permitted when this option was not used.

In new code it is better to use '`-fvisibility=hidden`' and export those classes which are intended to be externally visible. Unfortunately it is possible for code to rely, perhaps accidentally, on the Visual Studio behavior.

Among the consequences of these changes are that static data members of the same type with the same name but defined in different shared objects will be different, so changing one will not change the other; and that pointers to function members defined in different shared objects may not compare equal. When this flag is given, it is a violation of the ODR to define types with the same name differently.

Chapter 3: GCC Command Options 35

`-fno-weak`
> Do not use weak symbol support, even if it is provided by the linker. By default, G++ will use weak symbols if they are available. This option exists only for testing, and should not be used by end-users; it will result in inferior code and has no benefits. This option may be removed in a future release of G++.

`-nostdinc++`
> Do not search for header files in the standard directories specific to C++, but do still search the other standard directories. (This option is used when building the C++ library.)

In addition, these optimization, warning, and code generation options have meanings only for C++ programs:

`-fno-default-inline`
> Do not assume 'inline' for functions defined inside a class scope. See Section 3.10 [Options That Control Optimization], page 77. Note that these functions will have linkage like inline functions; they just won't be inlined by default.

`-Wabi (C++ and Objective-C++ only)`
> Warn when G++ generates code that is probably not compatible with the vendor-neutral C++ ABI. Although an effort has been made to warn about all such cases, there are probably some cases that are not warned about, even though G++ is generating incompatible code. There may also be cases where warnings are emitted even though the code that is generated will be compatible.
>
> You should rewrite your code to avoid these warnings if you are concerned about the fact that code generated by G++ may not be binary compatible with code generated by other compilers.
>
> The known incompatibilities at this point include:
>
> - Incorrect handling of tail-padding for bit-fields. G++ may attempt to pack data into the same byte as a base class. For example:
>   ```
>   struct A { virtual void f(); int f1 : 1; };
>   struct B : public A { int f2 : 1; };
>   ```
>   In this case, G++ will place B::f2 into the same byte as A::f1; other compilers will not. You can avoid this problem by explicitly padding A so that its size is a multiple of the byte size on your platform; that will cause G++ and other compilers to layout B identically.
>
> - Incorrect handling of tail-padding for virtual bases. G++ does not use tail padding when laying out virtual bases. For example:
>   ```
>   struct A { virtual void f(); char c1; };
>   struct B { B(); char c2; };
>   struct C : public A, public virtual B {};
>   ```
>   In this case, G++ will not place B into the tail-padding for A; other compilers will. You can avoid this problem by explicitly padding A so that its size is a multiple of its alignment (ignoring virtual base classes); that will cause G++ and other compilers to layout C identically.

- Incorrect handling of bit-fields with declared widths greater than that of their underlying types, when the bit-fields appear in a union. For example:

  ```
  union U { int i : 4096; };
  ```

  Assuming that an `int` does not have 4096 bits, G++ will make the union too small by the number of bits in an `int`.

- Empty classes can be placed at incorrect offsets. For example:

  ```
  struct A {};

  struct B {
    A a;
    virtual void f ();
  };

  struct C : public B, public A {};
  ```

  G++ will place the `A` base class of `C` at a nonzero offset; it should be placed at offset zero. G++ mistakenly believes that the `A` data member of `B` is already at offset zero.

- Names of template functions whose types involve `typename` or template template parameters can be mangled incorrectly.

  ```
  template <typename Q>
  void f(typename Q::X) {}

  template <template <typename> class Q>
  void f(typename Q<int>::X) {}
  ```

  Instantiations of these templates may be mangled incorrectly.

`-Wctor-dtor-privacy` (C++ and Objective-C++ only)
: Warn when a class seems unusable because all the constructors or destructors in that class are private, and it has neither friends nor public static member functions.

`-Wnon-virtual-dtor` (C++ and Objective-C++ only)
: Warn when a class has virtual functions and accessible non-virtual destructor, in which case it would be possible but unsafe to delete an instance of a derived class through a pointer to the base class. This warning is also enabled if -Weffc++ is specified.

`-Wreorder` (C++ and Objective-C++ only)
: Warn when the order of member initializers given in the code does not match the order in which they must be executed. For instance:

  ```
  struct A {
    int i;
    int j;
    A(): j (0), i (1) { }
  };
  ```

  The compiler will rearrange the member initializers for 'i' and 'j' to match the declaration order of the members, emitting a warning to that effect. This warning is enabled by '-Wall'.

The following '-W...' options are not affected by '-Wall'.

Chapter 3: GCC Command Options 37

-Weffc++ (C++ and Objective-C++ only)
: Warn about violations of the following style guidelines from Scott Meyers' *Effective C++* book:

- Item 11: Define a copy constructor and an assignment operator for classes with dynamically allocated memory.
- Item 12: Prefer initialization to assignment in constructors.
- Item 14: Make destructors virtual in base classes.
- Item 15: Have operator= return a reference to *this.
- Item 23: Don't try to return a reference when you must return an object.

Also warn about violations of the following style guidelines from Scott Meyers' *More Effective C++* book:

- Item 6: Distinguish between prefix and postfix forms of increment and decrement operators.
- Item 7: Never overload &&, ||, or ,.

When selecting this option, be aware that the standard library headers do not obey all of these guidelines; use 'grep -v' to filter out those warnings.

-Wno-deprecated (C++ and Objective-C++ only)
: Do not warn about usage of deprecated features. See Section 6.11 [Deprecated Features], page 513.

-Wstrict-null-sentinel (C++ and Objective-C++ only)
: Warn also about the use of an uncasted NULL as sentinel. When compiling only with GCC this is a valid sentinel, as NULL is defined to __null. Although it is a null pointer constant not a null pointer, it is guaranteed to of the same size as a pointer. But this use is not portable across different compilers.

-Wno-non-template-friend (C++ and Objective-C++ only)
: Disable warnings when non-templatized friend functions are declared within a template. Since the advent of explicit template specification support in G++, if the name of the friend is an unqualified-id (i.e., 'friend foo(int)'), the C++ language specification demands that the friend declare or define an ordinary, nontemplate function. (Section 14.5.3). Before G++ implemented explicit specification, unqualified-ids could be interpreted as a particular specialization of a templatized function. Because this non-conforming behavior is no longer the default behavior for G++, '-Wnon-template-friend' allows the compiler to check existing code for potential trouble spots and is on by default. This new compiler behavior can be turned off with '-Wno-non-template-friend' which keeps the conformant compiler code but disables the helpful warning.

-Wold-style-cast (C++ and Objective-C++ only)
: Warn if an old-style (C-style) cast to a non-void type is used within a C++ program. The new-style casts ('dynamic_cast', 'static_cast', 'reinterpret_cast', and 'const_cast') are less vulnerable to unintended effects and much easier to search for.

`-Woverloaded-virtual` (C++ and Objective-C++ only)

> Warn when a function declaration hides virtual functions from a base class. For example, in:
>
> ```
> struct A {
>   virtual void f();
> };
> 
> struct B: public A {
>   void f(int);
> };
> ```
>
> the `A` class version of `f` is hidden in B, and code like:
>
> ```
> B* b;
> b->f();
> ```
>
> will fail to compile.

`-Wno-pmf-conversions` (C++ and Objective-C++ only)

> Disable the diagnostic for converting a bound pointer to member function to a plain pointer.

`-Wsign-promo` (C++ and Objective-C++ only)

> Warn when overload resolution chooses a promotion from unsigned or enumerated type to a signed type, over a conversion to an unsigned type of the same size. Previous versions of G++ would try to preserve unsignedness, but the standard mandates the current behavior.
>
> ```
> struct A {
>   operator int ();
>   A& operator = (int);
> };
> 
> main ()
> {
>   A a,b;
>   a = b;
> }
> ```
>
> In this example, G++ will synthesize a default '`A& operator = (const A&);`', while cfront will use the user-defined '`operator =`'.

3.6 Options Controlling Objective-C and Objective-C++ Dialects

(NOTE: This manual does not describe the Objective-C and Objective-C++ languages themselves. See See Chapter 2 [Language Standards Supported by GCC], page 5, for references.)

This section describes the command-line options that are only meaningful for Objective-C and Objective-C++ programs, but you can also use most of the language-independent GNU compiler options. For example, you might compile a file `some_class.m` like this:

```
gcc -g -fgnu-runtime -O -c some_class.m
```

In this example, '`-fgnu-runtime`' is an option meant only for Objective-C and Objective-C++ programs; you can use the other options with any language supported by GCC.

Note that since Objective-C is an extension of the C language, Objective-C compilations may also use options specific to the C front-end (e.g., '`-Wtraditional`'). Similarly, Objective-C++ compilations may use C++-specific options (e.g., '`-Wabi`').

Chapter 3: GCC Command Options 39

Here is a list of options that are *only* for compiling Objective-C and Objective-C++ programs:

`-fconstant-string-class=class-name`
> Use *class-name* as the name of the class to instantiate for each literal string specified with the syntax `@"..."`. The default class name is `NXConstantString` if the GNU runtime is being used, and `NSConstantString` if the NeXT runtime is being used (see below). The '`-fconstant-cfstrings`' option, if also present, will override the '`-fconstant-string-class`' setting and cause `@"..."` literals to be laid out as constant CoreFoundation strings.

`-fgnu-runtime`
> Generate object code compatible with the standard GNU Objective-C runtime. This is the default for most types of systems.

`-fnext-runtime`
> Generate output compatible with the NeXT runtime. This is the default for NeXT-based systems, including Darwin and Mac OS X. The macro `__NEXT_RUNTIME__` is predefined if (and only if) this option is used.

`-fno-nil-receivers`
> Assume that all Objective-C message dispatches (e.g., `[receiver message:arg]`) in this translation unit ensure that the receiver is not `nil`. This allows for more efficient entry points in the runtime to be used. Currently, this option is only available in conjunction with the NeXT runtime on Mac OS X 10.3 and later.

`-fobjc-call-cxx-cdtors`
> For each Objective-C class, check if any of its instance variables is a C++ object with a non-trivial default constructor. If so, synthesize a special `- (id) .cxx_construct` instance method that will run non-trivial default constructors on any such instance variables, in order, and then return `self`. Similarly, check if any instance variable is a C++ object with a non-trivial destructor, and if so, synthesize a special `- (void) .cxx_destruct` method that will run all such default destructors, in reverse order.
>
> The `- (id) .cxx_construct` and/or `- (void) .cxx_destruct` methods thusly generated will only operate on instance variables declared in the current Objective-C class, and not those inherited from superclasses. It is the responsibility of the Objective-C runtime to invoke all such methods in an object's inheritance hierarchy. The `- (id) .cxx_construct` methods will be invoked by the runtime immediately after a new object instance is allocated; the `- (void) .cxx_destruct` methods will be invoked immediately before the runtime deallocates an object instance.
>
> As of this writing, only the NeXT runtime on Mac OS X 10.4 and later has support for invoking the `- (id) .cxx_construct` and `- (void) .cxx_destruct` methods.

`-fobjc-direct-dispatch`
> Allow fast jumps to the message dispatcher. On Darwin this is accomplished via the comm page.

`-fobjc-exceptions`
> Enable syntactic support for structured exception handling in Objective-C, similar to what is offered by C++ and Java. This option is unavailable in conjunction with the NeXT runtime on Mac OS X 10.2 and earlier.
>
> ```
> @try {
>   ...
>     @throw expr;
>   ...
> }
> @catch (AnObjCClass *exc) {
>   ...
>     @throw expr;
>   ...
>     @throw;
>   ...
> }
> @catch (AnotherClass *exc) {
>   ...
> }
> @catch (id allOthers) {
>   ...
> }
> @finally {
>   ...
>     @throw expr;
>   ...
> }
> ```
>
> The `@throw` statement may appear anywhere in an Objective-C or Objective-C++ program; when used inside of a `@catch` block, the `@throw` may appear without an argument (as shown above), in which case the object caught by the `@catch` will be rethrown.
>
> Note that only (pointers to) Objective-C objects may be thrown and caught using this scheme. When an object is thrown, it will be caught by the nearest `@catch` clause capable of handling objects of that type, analogously to how `catch` blocks work in C++ and Java. A `@catch(id ...)` clause (as shown above) may also be provided to catch any and all Objective-C exceptions not caught by previous `@catch` clauses (if any).
>
> The `@finally` clause, if present, will be executed upon exit from the immediately preceding `@try ... @catch` section. This will happen regardless of whether any exceptions are thrown, caught or rethrown inside the `@try ... @catch` section, analogously to the behavior of the `finally` clause in Java.
>
> There are several caveats to using the new exception mechanism:
>
> - Although currently designed to be binary compatible with `NS_HANDLER`-style idioms provided by the `NSException` class, the new exceptions can only be used on Mac OS X 10.3 (Panther) and later systems, due to additional functionality needed in the (NeXT) Objective-C runtime.
> - As mentioned above, the new exceptions do not support handling types other than Objective-C objects. Furthermore, when used from Objective-C++, the Objective-C exception model does not interoperate with C++

Chapter 3: GCC Command Options   41

exceptions at this time. This means you cannot @throw an exception from Objective-C and catch it in C++, or vice versa (i.e., throw ... @catch).

The '-fobjc-exceptions' switch also enables the use of synchronization blocks for thread-safe execution:

```
@synchronized (ObjCClass *guard) {
    ...
}
```

Upon entering the @synchronized block, a thread of execution shall first check whether a lock has been placed on the corresponding guard object by another thread. If it has, the current thread shall wait until the other thread relinquishes its lock. Once guard becomes available, the current thread will place its own lock on it, execute the code contained in the @synchronized block, and finally relinquish the lock (thereby making guard available to other threads).

Unlike Java, Objective-C does not allow for entire methods to be marked @synchronized. Note that throwing exceptions out of @synchronized blocks is allowed, and will cause the guarding object to be unlocked properly.

-fobjc-gc
:   Enable garbage collection (GC) in Objective-C and Objective-C++ programs.

-freplace-objc-classes
:   Emit a special marker instructing ld(1) not to statically link in the resulting object file, and allow dyld(1) to load it in at run time instead. This is used in conjunction with the Fix-and-Continue debugging mode, where the object file in question may be recompiled and dynamically reloaded in the course of program execution, without the need to restart the program itself. Currently, Fix-and-Continue functionality is only available in conjunction with the NeXT runtime on Mac OS X 10.3 and later.

-fzero-link
:   When compiling for the NeXT runtime, the compiler ordinarily replaces calls to objc_getClass("...") (when the name of the class is known at compile time) with static class references that get initialized at load time, which improves runtime performance. Specifying the '-fzero-link' flag suppresses this behavior and causes calls to objc_getClass("...") to be retained. This is useful in Zero-Link debugging mode, since it allows for individual class implementations to be modified during program execution.

-gen-decls
:   Dump interface declarations for all classes seen in the source file to a file named 'sourcename.decl'.

-Wassign-intercept (Objective-C and Objective-C++ only)
:   Warn whenever an Objective-C assignment is being intercepted by the garbage collector.

-Wno-protocol (Objective-C and Objective-C++ only)
:   If a class is declared to implement a protocol, a warning is issued for every method in the protocol that is not implemented by the class. The default behavior is to issue a warning for every method not explicitly implemented in the

class, even if a method implementation is inherited from the superclass. If you use the '-Wno-protocol' option, then methods inherited from the superclass are considered to be implemented, and no warning is issued for them.

-Wselector (Objective-C and Objective-C++ only)
: Warn if multiple methods of different types for the same selector are found during compilation. The check is performed on the list of methods in the final stage of compilation. Additionally, a check is performed for each selector appearing in a @selector(...) expression, and a corresponding method for that selector has been found during compilation. Because these checks scan the method table only at the end of compilation, these warnings are not produced if the final stage of compilation is not reached, for example because an error is found during compilation, or because the '-fsyntax-only' option is being used.

-Wstrict-selector-match (Objective-C and Objective-C++ only)
: Warn if multiple methods with differing argument and/or return types are found for a given selector when attempting to send a message using this selector to a receiver of type id or Class. When this flag is off (which is the default behavior), the compiler will omit such warnings if any differences found are confined to types which share the same size and alignment.

-Wundeclared-selector (Objective-C and Objective-C++ only)
: Warn if a @selector(...) expression referring to an undeclared selector is found. A selector is considered undeclared if no method with that name has been declared before the @selector(...) expression, either explicitly in an @interface or @protocol declaration, or implicitly in an @implementation section. This option always performs its checks as soon as a @selector(...) expression is found, while '-Wselector' only performs its checks in the final stage of compilation. This also enforces the coding style convention that methods and selectors must be declared before being used.

-print-objc-runtime-info
: Generate C header describing the largest structure that is passed by value, if any.

3.7 Options to Control Diagnostic Messages Formatting

Traditionally, diagnostic messages have been formatted irrespective of the output device's aspect (e.g. its width, ...). The options described below can be used to control the diagnostic messages formatting algorithm, e.g. how many characters per line, how often source location information should be reported. Right now, only the C++ front end can honor these options. However it is expected, in the near future, that the remaining front ends would be able to digest them correctly.

-fmessage-length=n
: Try to format error messages so that they fit on lines of about n characters. The default is 72 characters for g++ and 0 for the rest of the front ends supported by GCC. If n is zero, then no line-wrapping will be done; each error message will appear on a single line.

Chapter 3: GCC Command Options 43

`-fdiagnostics-show-location=once`
> Only meaningful in line-wrapping mode. Instructs the diagnostic messages reporter to emit *once* source location information; that is, in case the message is too long to fit on a single physical line and has to be wrapped, the source location won't be emitted (as prefix) again, over and over, in subsequent continuation lines. This is the default behavior.

`-fdiagnostics-show-location=every-line`
> Only meaningful in line-wrapping mode. Instructs the diagnostic messages reporter to emit the same source location information (as prefix) for physical lines that result from the process of breaking a message which is too long to fit on a single line.

`-fdiagnostics-show-option`
> This option instructs the diagnostic machinery to add text to each diagnostic emitted, which indicates which command line option directly controls that diagnostic, when such an option is known to the diagnostic machinery.

`-Wcoverage-mismatch`
> Warn if feedback profiles do not match when using the '`-fprofile-use`' option. If a source file was changed between '`-fprofile-gen`' and '`-fprofile-use`', the files with the profile feedback can fail to match the source file and GCC can not use the profile feedback information. By default, GCC emits an error message in this case. The option '`-Wcoverage-mismatch`' emits a warning instead of an error. GCC does not use appropriate feedback profiles, so using this option can result in poorly optimized code. This option is useful only in the case of very minor changes such as bug fixes to an existing code-base.

3.8 Options to Request or Suppress Warnings

Warnings are diagnostic messages that report constructions which are not inherently erroneous but which are risky or suggest there may have been an error.

The following language-independent options do not enable specific warnings but control the kinds of diagnostics produced by GCC.

`-fsyntax-only`
> Check the code for syntax errors, but don't do anything beyond that.

`-w`   Inhibit all warning messages.

`-Werror` Make all warnings into errors.

`-Werror=` Make the specified warning into an error. The specifier for a warning is appended, for example '`-Werror=switch`' turns the warnings controlled by '`-Wswitch`' into errors. This switch takes a negative form, to be used to negate '`-Werror`' for specific warnings, for example '`-Wno-error=switch`' makes '`-Wswitch`' warnings not be errors, even when '`-Werror`' is in effect. You can use the '`-fdiagnostics-show-option`' option to have each controllable warning amended with the option which controls it, to determine what to use with this option.

> Note that specifying '`-Werror=`'*foo* automatically implies '`-W`'*foo*. However, '`-Wno-error=`'*foo* does not imply anything.

`-Wfatal-errors`
> This option causes the compiler to abort compilation on the first error occurred rather than trying to keep going and printing further error messages.

You can request many specific warnings with options beginning '-W', for example '-Wimplicit' to request warnings on implicit declarations. Each of these specific warning options also has a negative form beginning '-Wno-' to turn off warnings; for example, '-Wno-implicit'. This manual lists only one of the two forms, whichever is not the default. For further, language-specific options also refer to Section 3.5 [C++ Dialect Options], page 31 and Section 3.6 [Objective-C and Objective-C++ Dialect Options], page 38.

`-pedantic`
> Issue all the warnings demanded by strict ISO C and ISO C++; reject all programs that use forbidden extensions, and some other programs that do not follow ISO C and ISO C++. For ISO C, follows the version of the ISO C standard specified by any '-std' option used.
>
> Valid ISO C and ISO C++ programs should compile properly with or without this option (though a rare few will require '-ansi' or a '-std' option specifying the required version of ISO C). However, without this option, certain GNU extensions and traditional C and C++ features are supported as well. With this option, they are rejected.
>
> '-pedantic' does not cause warning messages for use of the alternate keywords whose names begin and end with '__'. Pedantic warnings are also disabled in the expression that follows `__extension__`. However, only system header files should use these escape routes; application programs should avoid them. See Section 5.41 [Alternate Keywords], page 329.
>
> Some users try to use '-pedantic' to check programs for strict ISO C conformance. They soon find that it does not do quite what they want: it finds some non-ISO practices, but not all—only those for which ISO C *requires* a diagnostic, and some others for which diagnostics have been added.
>
> A feature to report any failure to conform to ISO C might be useful in some instances, but would require considerable additional work and would be quite different from '-pedantic'. We don't have plans to support such a feature in the near future.
>
> Where the standard specified with '-std' represents a GNU extended dialect of C, such as 'gnu89' or 'gnu99', there is a corresponding *base standard*, the version of ISO C on which the GNU extended dialect is based. Warnings from '-pedantic' are given where they are required by the base standard. (It would not make sense for such warnings to be given only for features not in the specified GNU C dialect, since by definition the GNU dialects of C include all features the compiler supports with the given option, and there would be nothing to warn about.)

`-pedantic-errors`
> Like '-pedantic', except that errors are produced rather than warnings.

`-Wall`
> This enables all the warnings about constructions that some users consider questionable, and that are easy to avoid (or modify to prevent the warning),

Chapter 3: GCC Command Options   45

even in conjunction with macros. This also enables some language-specific warnings described in Section 3.5 [C++ Dialect Options], page 31 and Section 3.6 [Objective-C and Objective-C++ Dialect Options], page 38.

'-Wall' turns on the following warning flags:

```
-Waddress
-Warray-bounds (only with '-O2')
-Wc++0x-compat
-Wchar-subscripts
-Wimplicit-int
-Wimplicit-function-declaration
-Wcomment
-Wformat
-Wmain (only for C/ObjC and unless '-ffreestanding')
-Wmissing-braces
-Wnonnull
-Wparentheses
-Wpointer-sign
-Wreorder
-Wreturn-type
-Wsequence-point
-Wsign-compare (only in C++)
-Wstrict-aliasing
-Wstrict-overflow=1
-Wswitch
-Wtrigraphs
-Wuninitialized (only with '-O1' and above)
-Wunknown-pragmas
-Wunused-function
-Wunused-label
-Wunused-value
-Wunused-variable
```

Note that some warning flags are not implied by '-Wall'. Some of them warn about constructions that users generally do not consider questionable, but which occasionally you might wish to check for; others warn about constructions that are necessary or hard to avoid in some cases, and there is no simple way to modify the code to suppress the warning. Some of them are enabled by '-Wextra' but many of them must be enabled individually.

-Wextra   This enables some extra warning flags that are not enabled by '-Wall'. (This option used to be called '-W'. The older name is still supported, but the newer name is more descriptive.)

```
-Wclobbered
-Wempty-body
-Wignored-qualifiers
-Wmissing-field-initializers
-Wmissing-parameter-type (C only)
-Wold-style-declaration (C only)
-Woverride-init
-Wsign-compare
-Wtype-limits
-Wuninitialized (only with '-O1' and above)
-Wunused-parameter (only with '-Wunused' or '-Wall')
```

The option '-Wextra' also prints warning messages for the following cases:

- A pointer is compared against integer zero with '<', '<=', '>', or '>='.
- (C++ only) An enumerator and a non-enumerator both appear in a conditional expression.
- (C++ only) A non-static reference or non-static 'const' member appears in a class without constructors.
- (C++ only) Ambiguous virtual bases.
- (C++ only) Subscripting an array which has been declared 'register'.
- (C++ only) Taking the address of a variable which has been declared 'register'.
- (C++ only) A base class is not initialized in a derived class' copy constructor.

`-Wno-import`
: Inhibit warning messages about the use of '#import'.

`-Wchar-subscripts`
: Warn if an array subscript has type char. This is a common cause of error, as programmers often forget that this type is signed on some machines. This warning is enabled by '-Wall'.

`-Wcomment`
: Warn whenever a comment-start sequence '/*' appears in a '/*' comment, or whenever a Backslash-Newline appears in a '//' comment. This warning is enabled by '-Wall'.

`-Wformat`
: Check calls to printf and scanf, etc., to make sure that the arguments supplied have types appropriate to the format string specified, and that the conversions specified in the format string make sense. This includes standard functions, and others specified by format attributes (see Section 5.27 [Function Attributes], page 264), in the printf, scanf, strftime and strfmon (an X/Open extension, not in the C standard) families (or other target-specific families). Which functions are checked without format attributes having been specified depends on the standard version selected, and such checks of functions without the attribute specified are disabled by '-ffreestanding' or '-fno-builtin'.

The formats are checked against the format features supported by GNU libc version 2.2. These include all ISO C90 and C99 features, as well as features from the Single Unix Specification and some BSD and GNU extensions. Other library implementations may not support all these features; GCC does not support warning about features that go beyond a particular library's limitations. However, if '-pedantic' is used with '-Wformat', warnings will be given about format features not in the selected standard version (but not for strfmon formats, since those are not in any version of the C standard). See Section 3.4 [Options Controlling C Dialect], page 26.

Since '-Wformat' also checks for null format arguments for several functions, '-Wformat' also implies '-Wnonnull'.

'-Wformat' is included in '-Wall'. For more control over some aspects of format checking, the options '-Wformat-y2k', '-Wno-format-extra-args',

Chapter 3: GCC Command Options   47

          '-Wno-format-zero-length', '-Wformat-nonliteral', '-Wformat-security',
          and '-Wformat=2' are available, but are not included in '-Wall'.

-Wformat-y2k
          If '-Wformat' is specified, also warn about `strftime` formats which may yield
          only a two-digit year.

-Wno-format-extra-args
          If '-Wformat' is specified, do not warn about excess arguments to a `printf`
          or `scanf` format function. The C standard specifies that such arguments are
          ignored.

          Where the unused arguments lie between used arguments that are specified
          with '$' operand number specifications, normally warnings are still given, since
          the implementation could not know what type to pass to `va_arg` to skip the
          unused arguments. However, in the case of `scanf` formats, this option will
          suppress the warning if the unused arguments are all pointers, since the Single
          Unix Specification says that such unused arguments are allowed.

-Wno-format-zero-length (C and Objective-C only)
          If '-Wformat' is specified, do not warn about zero-length formats. The C stan-
          dard specifies that zero-length formats are allowed.

-Wformat-nonliteral
          If '-Wformat' is specified, also warn if the format string is not a string literal and
          so cannot be checked, unless the format function takes its format arguments as
          a `va_list`.

-Wformat-security
          If '-Wformat' is specified, also warn about uses of format functions that repre-
          sent possible security problems. At present, this warns about calls to `printf`
          and `scanf` functions where the format string is not a string literal and there
          are no format arguments, as in `printf (foo);`. This may be a security hole
          if the format string came from untrusted input and contains '%n'. (This is
          currently a subset of what '-Wformat-nonliteral' warns about, but in fu-
          ture warnings may be added to '-Wformat-security' that are not included in
          '-Wformat-nonliteral'.)

-Wformat=2
          Enable '-Wformat' plus format checks not included in '-Wformat'. Currently
          equivalent to   '-Wformat -Wformat-nonliteral -Wformat-security
          -Wformat-y2k'.

-Wnonnull (C and Objective-C only)
          Warn about passing a null pointer for arguments marked as requiring a non-null
          value by the `nonnull` function attribute.

          '-Wnonnull' is included in '-Wall' and '-Wformat'. It can be disabled with the
          '-Wno-nonnull' option.

-Winit-self (C, C++, Objective-C and Objective-C++ only)
          Warn about uninitialized variables which are initialized with themselves. Note
          this option can only be used with the '-Wuninitialized' option, which in turn
          only works with '-O1' and above.

For example, GCC will warn about i being uninitialized in the following snippet only when '-Winit-self' has been specified:

```
int f()
{
  int i = i;
  return i;
}
```

-Wimplicit-int (C and Objective-C only)
: Warn when a declaration does not specify a type. This warning is enabled by '-Wall'.

-Wimplicit-function-declaration (C and Objective-C only)
: Give a warning whenever a function is used before being declared. In C99 mode ('-std=c99' or '-std=gnu99'), this warning is enabled by default and it is made into an error by '-pedantic-errors'. This warning is also enabled by '-Wall'.

-Wimplicit
: Same as '-Wimplicit-int' and '-Wimplicit-function-declaration'. This warning is enabled by '-Wall'.

-Wignored-qualifiers (C and C++ only)
: Warn if the return type of a function has a type qualifier such as const. For ISO C such a type qualifier has no effect, since the value returned by a function is not an lvalue. For C++, the warning is only emitted for scalar types or void. ISO C prohibits qualified void return types on function definitions, so such return types always receive a warning even without this option.

  This warning is also enabled by '-Wextra'.

-Wmain
: Warn if the type of 'main' is suspicious. 'main' should be a function with external linkage, returning int, taking either zero arguments, two, or three arguments of appropriate types. This warning is enabled by '-Wall'.

-Wmissing-braces
: Warn if an aggregate or union initializer is not fully bracketed. In the following example, the initializer for 'a' is not fully bracketed, but that for 'b' is fully bracketed.

```
int a[2][2] = { 0, 1, 2, 3 };
int b[2][2] = { { 0, 1 }, { 2, 3 } };
```

  This warning is enabled by '-Wall'.

-Wmissing-include-dirs (C, C++, Objective-C and Objective-C++ only)
: Warn if a user-supplied include directory does not exist.

-Wparentheses
: Warn if parentheses are omitted in certain contexts, such as when there is an assignment in a context where a truth value is expected, or when operators are nested whose precedence people often get confused about.

  Also warn if a comparison like 'x<=y<=z' appears; this is equivalent to '(x<=y ? 1 : 0) <= z', which is a different interpretation from that of ordinary mathematical notation.

Also warn about constructions where there may be confusion to which `if` statement an `else` branch belongs. Here is an example of such a case:

```
{
  if (a)
    if (b)
      foo ();
  else
    bar ();
}
```

In C/C++, every `else` branch belongs to the innermost possible `if` statement, which in this example is `if (b)`. This is often not what the programmer expected, as illustrated in the above example by indentation the programmer chose. When there is the potential for this confusion, GCC will issue a warning when this flag is specified. To eliminate the warning, add explicit braces around the innermost `if` statement so there is no way the `else` could belong to the enclosing `if`. The resulting code would look like this:

```
{
  if (a)
    {
      if (b)
        foo ();
      else
        bar ();
    }
}
```

This warning is enabled by '-Wall'.

`-Wsequence-point`

Warn about code that may have undefined semantics because of violations of sequence point rules in the C and C++ standards.

The C and C++ standards defines the order in which expressions in a C/C++ program are evaluated in terms of *sequence points*, which represent a partial ordering between the execution of parts of the program: those executed before the sequence point, and those executed after it. These occur after the evaluation of a full expression (one which is not part of a larger expression), after the evaluation of the first operand of a &&, ||, ? : or , (comma) operator, before a function is called (but after the evaluation of its arguments and the expression denoting the called function), and in certain other places. Other than as expressed by the sequence point rules, the order of evaluation of subexpressions of an expression is not specified. All these rules describe only a partial order rather than a total order, since, for example, if two functions are called within one expression with no sequence point between them, the order in which the functions are called is not specified. However, the standards committee have ruled that function calls do not overlap.

It is not specified when between sequence points modifications to the values of objects take effect. Programs whose behavior depends on this have undefined behavior; the C and C++ standards specify that "Between the previous and next sequence point an object shall have its stored value modified at most once by the evaluation of an expression. Furthermore, the prior value shall be read only to determine the value to be stored.". If a program breaks these rules, the results on any particular implementation are entirely unpredictable.

Examples of code with undefined behavior are `a = a++;`, `a[n] = b[n++]` and `a[i++] = i;`. Some more complicated cases are not diagnosed by this option, and it may give an occasional false positive result, but in general it has been found fairly effective at detecting this sort of problem in programs.

The standard is worded confusingly, therefore there is some debate over the precise meaning of the sequence point rules in subtle cases. Links to discussions of the problem, including proposed formal definitions, may be found on the GCC readings page, at http://gcc.gnu.org/readings.html.

This warning is enabled by '-Wall' for C and C++.

-Wreturn-type
> Warn whenever a function is defined with a return-type that defaults to `int`. Also warn about any `return` statement with no return-value in a function whose return-type is not `void` (falling off the end of the function body is considered returning without a value), and about a `return` statement with a expression in a function whose return-type is void.
>
> For C++, a function without return type always produces a diagnostic message, even when '-Wno-return-type' is specified. The only exceptions are 'main' and functions defined in system headers.
>
> This warning is enabled by '-Wall'.

-Wswitch
Warn whenever a `switch` statement has an index of enumerated type and lacks a `case` for one or more of the named codes of that enumeration. (The presence of a `default` label prevents this warning.) `case` labels outside the enumeration range also provoke warnings when this option is used. This warning is enabled by '-Wall'.

-Wswitch-default
> Warn whenever a `switch` statement does not have a `default` case.

-Wswitch-enum
> Warn whenever a `switch` statement has an index of enumerated type and lacks a `case` for one or more of the named codes of that enumeration. `case` labels outside the enumeration range also provoke warnings when this option is used.

-Wtrigraphs
> Warn if any trigraphs are encountered that might change the meaning of the program (trigraphs within comments are not warned about). This warning is enabled by '-Wall'.

-Wunused-function
> Warn whenever a static function is declared but not defined or a non-inline static function is unused. This warning is enabled by '-Wall'.

-Wunused-label
> Warn whenever a label is declared but not used. This warning is enabled by '-Wall'.

Chapter 3: GCC Command Options   51

         To suppress this warning use the '**unused**' attribute (see Section 5.34 [Variable
         Attributes], page 286).

`-Wunused-parameter`
         Warn whenever a function parameter is unused aside from its declaration.

         To suppress this warning use the '**unused**' attribute (see Section 5.34 [Variable
         Attributes], page 286).

`-Wunused-variable`
         Warn whenever a local variable or non-constant static variable is unused aside
         from its declaration. This warning is enabled by '`-Wall`'.

         To suppress this warning use the '**unused**' attribute (see Section 5.34 [Variable
         Attributes], page 286).

`-Wunused-value`
         Warn whenever a statement computes a result that is explicitly not used. To
         suppress this warning cast the unused expression to '**void**'. This includes an
         expression-statement or the left-hand side of a comma expression that con-
         tains no side effects. For example, an expression such as '`x[i,j]`' will cause a
         warning, while '`x[(void)i,j]`' will not.

         This warning is enabled by '`-Wall`'.

`-Wunused` All the above '`-Wunused`' options combined.

         In order to get a warning about an unused function parameter, you must either
         specify '`-Wextra -Wunused`' (note that '`-Wall`' implies '`-Wunused`'), or sepa-
         rately specify '`-Wunused-parameter`'.

`-Wuninitialized`
         Warn if an automatic variable is used without first being initialized or if a
         variable may be clobbered by a `setjmp` call.

         These warnings are possible only in optimizing compilation, because they re-
         quire data flow information that is computed only when optimizing. If you do
         not specify '`-O`', you will not get these warnings. Instead, GCC will issue a
         warning about '`-Wuninitialized`' requiring '`-O`'.

         If you want to warn about code which uses the uninitialized value of the variable
         in its own initializer, use the '`-Winit-self`' option.

         These warnings occur for individual uninitialized or clobbered elements of struc-
         ture, union or array variables as well as for variables which are uninitialized or
         clobbered as a whole. They do not occur for variables or elements declared
         `volatile`. Because these warnings depend on optimization, the exact variables
         or elements for which there are warnings will depend on the precise optimization
         options and version of GCC used.

         Note that there may be no warning about a variable that is used only to compute
         a value that itself is never used, because such computations may be deleted by
         data flow analysis before the warnings are printed.

         These warnings are made optional because GCC is not smart enough to see all
         the reasons why the code might be correct despite appearing to have an error.
         Here is one example of how this can happen:

```
{
  int x;
  switch (y)
    {
    case 1: x = 1;
      break;
    case 2: x = 4;
      break;
    case 3: x = 5;
    }
  foo (x);
}
```

If the value of y is always 1, 2 or 3, then x is always initialized, but GCC doesn't know this. Here is another common case:

```
{
  int save_y;
  if (change_y) save_y = y, y = new_y;
  ...
  if (change_y) y = save_y;
}
```

This has no bug because `save_y` is used only if it is set.

This option also warns when a non-volatile automatic variable might be changed by a call to `longjmp`. These warnings as well are possible only in optimizing compilation.

The compiler sees only the calls to `setjmp`. It cannot know where `longjmp` will be called; in fact, a signal handler could call it at any point in the code. As a result, you may get a warning even when there is in fact no problem because `longjmp` cannot in fact be called at the place which would cause a problem.

Some spurious warnings can be avoided if you declare all the functions you use that never return as `noreturn`. See Section 5.27 [Function Attributes], page 264.

This warning is enabled by '-Wall' or '-Wextra' in optimizing compilations ('-O1' and above).

-Wunknown-pragmas

Warn when a #pragma directive is encountered which is not understood by GCC. If this command line option is used, warnings will even be issued for unknown pragmas in system header files. This is not the case if the warnings were only enabled by the '-Wall' command line option.

-Wno-pragmas

Do not warn about misuses of pragmas, such as incorrect parameters, invalid syntax, or conflicts between pragmas. See also '-Wunknown-pragmas'.

-Wstrict-aliasing

This option is only active when '-fstrict-aliasing' is active. It warns about code which might break the strict aliasing rules that the compiler is using for optimization. The warning does not catch all cases, but does attempt to catch the more common pitfalls. It is included in '-Wall'. It is equivalent to '-Wstrict-aliasing=3'

Chapter 3: GCC Command Options 53

`-Wstrict-aliasing=n`
> This option is only active when '`-fstrict-aliasing`' is active. It warns about code which might break the strict aliasing rules that the compiler is using for optimization. Higher levels correspond to higher accuracy (fewer false positives). Higher levels also correspond to more effort, similar to the way -O works. '`-Wstrict-aliasing`' is equivalent to '`-Wstrict-aliasing=n`', with n=3.
>
> Level 1: Most aggressive, quick, least accurate. Possibly useful when higher levels do not warn but -fstrict-aliasing still breaks the code, as it has very few false negatives. However, it has many false positives. Warns for all pointer conversions between possibly incompatible types, even if never dereferenced. Runs in the frontend only.
>
> Level 2: Aggressive, quick, not too precise. May still have many false positives (not as many as level 1 though), and few false negatives (but possibly more than level 1). Unlike level 1, it only warns when an address is taken. Warns about incomplete types. Runs in the frontend only.
>
> Level 3 (default for '`-Wstrict-aliasing`'): Should have very few false positives and few false negatives. Slightly slower than levels 1 or 2 when optimization is enabled. Takes care of the common punn+dereference pattern in the frontend: `*(int*)&some_float`. If optimization is enabled, it also runs in the backend, where it deals with multiple statement cases using flow-sensitive points-to information. Only warns when the converted pointer is dereferenced. Does not warn about incomplete types.

`-Wstrict-overflow`
`-Wstrict-overflow=n`
> This option is only active when '`-fstrict-overflow`' is active. It warns about cases where the compiler optimizes based on the assumption that signed overflow does not occur. Note that it does not warn about all cases where the code might overflow: it only warns about cases where the compiler implements some optimization. Thus this warning depends on the optimization level.
>
> An optimization which assumes that signed overflow does not occur is perfectly safe if the values of the variables involved are such that overflow never does, in fact, occur. Therefore this warning can easily give a false positive: a warning about code which is not actually a problem. To help focus on important issues, several warning levels are defined. No warnings are issued for the use of undefined signed overflow when estimating how many iterations a loop will require, in particular when determining whether a loop will be executed at all.
>
> `-Wstrict-overflow=1`
>> Warn about cases which are both questionable and easy to avoid. For example: `x + 1 > x`; with '`-fstrict-overflow`', the compiler will simplify this to 1. This level of '`-Wstrict-overflow`' is enabled by '`-Wall`'; higher levels are not, and must be explicitly requested.
>
> `-Wstrict-overflow=2`
>> Also warn about other cases where a comparison is simplified to a constant. For example: `abs (x) >= 0`. This can only be simplified when '`-fstrict-overflow`' is in effect, because `abs (INT_MIN)`

overflows to INT_MIN, which is less than zero. '-Wstrict-overflow' (with no level) is the same as '-Wstrict-overflow=2'.

-Wstrict-overflow=3
> Also warn about other cases where a comparison is simplified. For example: x + 1 > 1 will be simplified to x > 0.

-Wstrict-overflow=4
> Also warn about other simplifications not covered by the above cases. For example: (x * 10) / 5 will be simplified to x * 2.

-Wstrict-overflow=5
> Also warn about cases where the compiler reduces the magnitude of a constant involved in a comparison. For example: x + 2 > y will be simplified to x + 1 >= y. This is reported only at the highest warning level because this simplification applies to many comparisons, so this warning level will give a very large number of false positives.

-Warray-bounds
> This option is only active when '-ftree-vrp' is active (default for -O2 and above). It warns about subscripts to arrays that are always out of bounds. This warning is enabled by '-Wall'.

-Wno-div-by-zero
> Do not warn about compile-time integer division by zero. Floating point division by zero is not warned about, as it can be a legitimate way of obtaining infinities and NaNs.

-Wsystem-headers
> Print warning messages for constructs found in system header files. Warnings from system headers are normally suppressed, on the assumption that they usually do not indicate real problems and would only make the compiler output harder to read. Using this command line option tells GCC to emit warnings from system headers as if they occurred in user code. However, note that using '-Wall' in conjunction with this option will *not* warn about unknown pragmas in system headers—for that, '-Wunknown-pragmas' must also be used.

-Wfloat-equal
> Warn if floating point values are used in equality comparisons.
>
> The idea behind this is that sometimes it is convenient (for the programmer) to consider floating-point values as approximations to infinitely precise real numbers. If you are doing this, then you need to compute (by analyzing the code, or in some other way) the maximum or likely maximum error that the computation introduces, and allow for it when performing comparisons (and when producing output, but that's a different problem). In particular, instead of testing for equality, you would check to see whether the two values have ranges that overlap; and this is done with the relational operators, so equality comparisons are probably mistaken.

Chapter 3: GCC Command Options   55

-Wtraditional (C and Objective-C only)
          Warn about certain constructs that behave differently in traditional and ISO
          C. Also warn about ISO C constructs that have no traditional C equivalent,
          and/or problematic constructs which should be avoided.

          - Macro parameters that appear within string literals in the macro body. In
            traditional C macro replacement takes place within string literals, but does
            not in ISO C.

          - In traditional C, some preprocessor directives did not exist. Traditional
            preprocessors would only consider a line to be a directive if the '#' appeared
            in column 1 on the line. Therefore '-Wtraditional' warns about directives
            that traditional C understands but would ignore because the '#' does not
            appear as the first character on the line. It also suggests you hide directives
            like '#pragma' not understood by traditional C by indenting them. Some
            traditional implementations would not recognize '#elif', so it suggests
            avoiding it altogether.

          - A function-like macro that appears without arguments.

          - The unary plus operator.

          - The 'U' integer constant suffix, or the 'F' or 'L' floating point constant
            suffixes. (Traditional C does support the 'L' suffix on integer constants.)
            Note, these suffixes appear in macros defined in the system headers of most
            modern systems, e.g. the '_MIN'/'_MAX' macros in <limits.h>. Use of these
            macros in user code might normally lead to spurious warnings, however
            GCC's integrated preprocessor has enough context to avoid warning in
            these cases.

          - A function declared external in one block and then used after the end of
            the block.

          - A switch statement has an operand of type long.

          - A non-static function declaration follows a static one. This construct
            is not accepted by some traditional C compilers.

          - The ISO type of an integer constant has a different width or signedness
            from its traditional type. This warning is only issued if the base of the
            constant is ten. I.e. hexadecimal or octal values, which typically represent
            bit patterns, are not warned about.

          - Usage of ISO string concatenation is detected.

          - Initialization of automatic aggregates.

          - Identifier conflicts with labels. Traditional C lacks a separate namespace
            for labels.

          - Initialization of unions. If the initializer is zero, the warning is omitted.
            This is done under the assumption that the zero initializer in user code
            appears conditioned on e.g. __STDC__ to avoid missing initializer warnings
            and relies on default initialization to zero in the traditional C case.

          - Conversions by prototypes between fixed/floating point values and vice
            versa. The absence of these prototypes when compiling with traditional C

would cause serious problems. This is a subset of the possible conversion warnings, for the full set use '-Wtraditional-conversion'.

- Use of ISO C style function definitions. This warning intentionally is *not* issued for prototype declarations or variadic functions because these ISO C features will appear in your code when using libiberty's traditional C compatibility macros, PARAMS and VPARAMS. This warning is also bypassed for nested functions because that feature is already a GCC extension and thus not relevant to traditional C compatibility.

-Wtraditional-conversion (C and Objective-C only)
Warn if a prototype causes a type conversion that is different from what would happen to the same argument in the absence of a prototype. This includes conversions of fixed point to floating and vice versa, and conversions changing the width or signedness of a fixed point argument except when the same as the default promotion.

-Wdeclaration-after-statement (C and Objective-C only)
Warn when a declaration is found after a statement in a block. This construct, known from C++, was introduced with ISO C99 and is by default allowed in GCC. It is not supported by ISO C90 and was not supported by GCC versions before GCC 3.0. See Section 5.26 [Mixed Declarations], page 264.

-Wundef   Warn if an undefined identifier is evaluated in an '#if' directive.

-Wno-endif-labels
Do not warn whenever an '#else' or an '#endif' are followed by text.

-Wshadow   Warn whenever a local variable shadows another local variable, parameter or global variable or whenever a built-in function is shadowed.

-Wlarger-than-*len*
Warn whenever an object of larger than *len* bytes is defined.

-Wunsafe-loop-optimizations
Warn if the loop cannot be optimized because the compiler could not assume anything on the bounds of the loop indices. With '-funsafe-loop-optimizations' warn if the compiler made such assumptions.

-Wpointer-arith
Warn about anything that depends on the "size of" a function type or of void. GNU C assigns these types a size of 1, for convenience in calculations with void * pointers and pointers to functions. In C++, warn also when an arithmetic operation involves NULL. This warning is also enabled by '-pedantic'.

-Wtype-limits
Warn if a comparison is always true or always false due to the limited range of the data type, but do not warn for constant expressions. For example, warn if an unsigned variable is compared against zero with '<' or '>='. This warning is also enabled by '-Wextra'.

Chapter 3: GCC Command Options   57

-Wbad-function-cast (C and Objective-C only)
: Warn whenever a function call is cast to a non-matching type. For example, warn if int malloc() is cast to anything *.

-Wc++-compat (C and Objective-C only)
: Warn about ISO C constructs that are outside of the common subset of ISO C and ISO C++, e.g. request for implicit conversion from void * to a pointer to non-void type.

-Wc++0x-compat (C++ and Objective-C++ only)
: Warn about C++ constructs whose meaning differs between ISO C++ 1998 and ISO C++ 200x, e.g., identifiers in ISO C++ 1998 that will become keywords in ISO C++ 200x. This warning is enabled by '-Wall'.

-Wcast-qual
: Warn whenever a pointer is cast so as to remove a type qualifier from the target type. For example, warn if a const char * is cast to an ordinary char *.

-Wcast-align
: Warn whenever a pointer is cast such that the required alignment of the target is increased. For example, warn if a char * is cast to an int * on machines where integers can only be accessed at two- or four-byte boundaries.

-Wwrite-strings
: When compiling C, give string constants the type const char[length] so that copying the address of one into a non-const char * pointer will get a warning; when compiling C++, warn about the deprecated conversion from string literals to char *. This warning, by default, is enabled for C++ programs. These warnings will help you find at compile time code that can try to write into a string constant, but only if you have been very careful about using const in declarations and prototypes. Otherwise, it will just be a nuisance; this is why we did not make '-Wall' request these warnings.

-Wclobbered
: Warn for variables that might be changed by 'longjmp' or 'vfork'. This warning is also enabled by '-Wextra'.

-Wconversion
: Warn for implicit conversions that may alter a value. This includes conversions between real and integer, like abs (x) when x is double; conversions between signed and unsigned, like unsigned ui = -1; and conversions to smaller types, like sqrtf (M_PI). Do not warn for explicit casts like abs ((int) x) and ui = (unsigned) -1, or if the value is not changed by the conversion like in abs (2.0). Warnings about conversions between signed and unsigned integers can be disabled by using '-Wno-sign-conversion'.

For C++, also warn for conversions between NULL and non-pointer types; confusing overload resolution for user-defined conversions; and conversions that will never use a type conversion operator: conversions to void, the same type, a base class or a reference to them. Warnings about conversions between signed and unsigned integers are disabled by default in C++ unless '-Wsign-conversion' is explicitly enabled.

`-Wempty-body`
: Warn if an empty body occurs in an 'if', 'else' or 'do while' statement. Additionally, in C++, warn when an empty body occurs in a 'while' or 'for' statement with no whitespacing before the semicolon. This warning is also enabled by '-Wextra'.

`-Wsign-compare`
: Warn when a comparison between signed and unsigned values could produce an incorrect result when the signed value is converted to unsigned. This warning is also enabled by '-Wextra'; to get the other warnings of '-Wextra' without this warning, use '-Wextra -Wno-sign-compare'.

`-Wsign-conversion`
: Warn for implicit conversions that may change the sign of an integer value, like assigning a signed integer expression to an unsigned integer variable. An explicit cast silences the warning. In C, this option is enabled also by '-Wconversion'.

`-Waddress`
: Warn about suspicious uses of memory addresses. These include using the address of a function in a conditional expression, such as `void func(void); if (func)`, and comparisons against the memory address of a string literal, such as `if (x == "abc")`. Such uses typically indicate a programmer error: the address of a function always evaluates to true, so their use in a conditional usually indicate that the programmer forgot the parentheses in a function call; and comparisons against string literals result in unspecified behavior and are not portable in C, so they usually indicate that the programmer intended to use `strcmp`. This warning is enabled by '-Wall'.

`-Wlogical-op`
: Warn about suspicious uses of logical operators in expressions. This includes using logical operators in contexts where a bit-wise operator is likely to be expected.

`-Waggregate-return`
: Warn if any functions that return structures or unions are defined or called. (In languages where you can return an array, this also elicits a warning.)

`-Wno-attributes`
: Do not warn if an unexpected `__attribute__` is used, such as unrecognized attributes, function attributes applied to variables, etc. This will not stop errors for incorrect use of supported attributes.

`-Wstrict-prototypes` (C and Objective-C only)
: Warn if a function is declared or defined without specifying the argument types. (An old-style function definition is permitted without a warning if preceded by a declaration which specifies the argument types.)

`-Wold-style-declaration` (C and Objective-C only)
: Warn for obsolescent usages, according to the C Standard, in a declaration. For example, warn if storage-class specifiers like `static` are not the first things in a declaration. This warning is also enabled by '-Wextra'.

Chapter 3: GCC Command Options   59

`-Wold-style-definition` (C and Objective-C only)
: Warn if an old-style function definition is used. A warning is given even if there is a previous prototype.

`-Wmissing-parameter-type` (C and Objective-C only)
: A function parameter is declared without a type specifier in K&R-style functions:

    ```
    void foo(bar) { }
    ```

    This warning is also enabled by '`-Wextra`'.

`-Wmissing-prototypes` (C and Objective-C only)
: Warn if a global function is defined without a previous prototype declaration. This warning is issued even if the definition itself provides a prototype. The aim is to detect global functions that fail to be declared in header files.

`-Wmissing-declarations`
: Warn if a global function is defined without a previous declaration. Do so even if the definition itself provides a prototype. Use this option to detect global functions that are not declared in header files. In C++, no warnings are issued for function templates, or for inline functions, or for functions in anonymous namespaces.

`-Wmissing-field-initializers`
: Warn if a structure's initializer has some fields missing. For example, the following code would cause such a warning, because `x.h` is implicitly zero:

    ```
    struct s { int f, g, h; };
    struct s x = { 3, 4 };
    ```

    This option does not warn about designated initializers, so the following modification would not trigger a warning:

    ```
    struct s { int f, g, h; };
    struct s x = { .f = 3, .g = 4 };
    ```

    This warning is included in '`-Wextra`'. To get other '`-Wextra`' warnings without this one, use '`-Wextra -Wno-missing-field-initializers`'.

`-Wmissing-noreturn`
: Warn about functions which might be candidates for attribute `noreturn`. Note these are only possible candidates, not absolute ones. Care should be taken to manually verify functions actually do not ever return before adding the `noreturn` attribute, otherwise subtle code generation bugs could be introduced. You will not get a warning for `main` in hosted C environments.

`-Wmissing-format-attribute`
: Warn about function pointers which might be candidates for `format` attributes. Note these are only possible candidates, not absolute ones. GCC will guess that function pointers with `format` attributes that are used in assignment, initialization, parameter passing or return statements should have a corresponding `format` attribute in the resulting type. I.e. the left-hand side of the assignment or initialization, the type of the parameter variable, or the return type of the containing function respectively should also have a `format` attribute to avoid the warning.

GCC will also warn about function definitions which might be candidates for `format` attributes. Again, these are only possible candidates. GCC will guess that `format` attributes might be appropriate for any function that calls a function like `vprintf` or `vscanf`, but this might not always be the case, and some functions for which `format` attributes are appropriate may not be detected.

`-Wno-multichar`

Do not warn if a multicharacter constant (`'FOOF'`) is used. Usually they indicate a typo in the user's code, as they have implementation-defined values, and should not be used in portable code.

`-Wnormalized=<none|id|nfc|nfkc>`

In ISO C and ISO C++, two identifiers are different if they are different sequences of characters. However, sometimes when characters outside the basic ASCII character set are used, you can have two different character sequences that look the same. To avoid confusion, the ISO 10646 standard sets out some *normalization rules* which when applied ensure that two sequences that look the same are turned into the same sequence. GCC can warn you if you are using identifiers which have not been normalized; this option controls that warning.

There are four levels of warning that GCC supports. The default is '`-Wnormalized=nfc`', which warns about any identifier which is not in the ISO 10646 "C" normalized form, *NFC*. NFC is the recommended form for most uses.

Unfortunately, there are some characters which ISO C and ISO C++ allow in identifiers that when turned into NFC aren't allowable as identifiers. That is, there's no way to use these symbols in portable ISO C or C++ and have all your identifiers in NFC. '`-Wnormalized=id`' suppresses the warning for these characters. It is hoped that future versions of the standards involved will correct this, which is why this option is not the default.

You can switch the warning off for all characters by writing '`-Wnormalized=none`'. You would only want to do this if you were using some other normalization scheme (like "D"), because otherwise you can easily create bugs that are literally impossible to see.

Some characters in ISO 10646 have distinct meanings but look identical in some fonts or display methodologies, especially once formatting has been applied. For instance \u207F, "SUPERSCRIPT LATIN SMALL LETTER N", will display just like a regular n which has been placed in a superscript. ISO 10646 defines the *NFKC* normalization scheme to convert all these into a standard form as well, and GCC will warn if your code is not in NFKC if you use '`-Wnormalized=nfkc`'. This warning is comparable to warning about every identifier that contains the letter O because it might be confused with the digit 0, and so is not the default, but may be useful as a local coding convention if the programming environment is unable to be fixed to display these characters distinctly.

`-Wno-deprecated-declarations`

Do not warn about uses of functions (see Section 5.27 [Function Attributes], page 264), variables (see Section 5.34 [Variable Attributes], page 286), and types

Chapter 3: GCC Command Options   61

(see Section 5.35 [Type Attributes], page 293) marked as deprecated by using the `deprecated` attribute.

`-Wno-overflow`
: Do not warn about compile-time overflow in constant expressions.

`-Woverride-init` (C and Objective-C only)
: Warn if an initialized field without side effects is overridden when using designated initializers (see Section 5.23 [Designated Initializers], page 261).

    This warning is included in '`-Wextra`'. To get other '`-Wextra`' warnings without this one, use '`-Wextra -Wno-override-init`'.

`-Wpacked`
: Warn if a structure is given the packed attribute, but the packed attribute has no effect on the layout or size of the structure. Such structures may be misaligned for little benefit. For instance, in this code, the variable `f.x` in `struct bar` will be misaligned even though `struct bar` does not itself have the packed attribute:

    ```
    struct foo {
      int x;
      char a, b, c, d;
    } __attribute__((packed));
    struct bar {
      char z;
      struct foo f;
    };
    ```

`-Wpadded`
: Warn if padding is included in a structure, either to align an element of the structure or to align the whole structure. Sometimes when this happens it is possible to rearrange the fields of the structure to reduce the padding and so make the structure smaller.

`-Wredundant-decls`
: Warn if anything is declared more than once in the same scope, even in cases where multiple declaration is valid and changes nothing.

`-Wnested-externs` (C and Objective-C only)
: Warn if an `extern` declaration is encountered within a function.

`-Wunreachable-code`
: Warn if the compiler detects that code will never be executed.

    This option is intended to warn when the compiler detects that at least a whole line of source code will never be executed, because some condition is never satisfied or because it is after a procedure that never returns.

    It is possible for this option to produce a warning even though there are circumstances under which part of the affected line can be executed, so care should be taken when removing apparently-unreachable code.

    For instance, when a function is inlined, a warning may mean that the line is unreachable in only one inlined copy of the function.

    This option is not made part of '`-Wall`' because in a debugging version of a program there is often substantial code which checks correct functioning of the program and is, hopefully, unreachable because the program does work. Another common use of unreachable code is to provide behavior which is selectable at compile-time.

`-Winline` Warn if a function can not be inlined and it was declared as inline. Even with this option, the compiler will not warn about failures to inline functions declared in system headers.

The compiler uses a variety of heuristics to determine whether or not to inline a function. For example, the compiler takes into account the size of the function being inlined and the amount of inlining that has already been done in the current function. Therefore, seemingly insignificant changes in the source program can cause the warnings produced by '`-Winline`' to appear or disappear.

`-Wno-invalid-offsetof` (C++ and Objective-C++ only)

Suppress warnings from applying the '`offsetof`' macro to a non-POD type. According to the 1998 ISO C++ standard, applying '`offsetof`' to a non-POD type is undefined. In existing C++ implementations, however, '`offsetof`' typically gives meaningful results even when applied to certain kinds of non-POD types. (Such as a simple '`struct`' that fails to be a POD type only by virtue of having a constructor.) This flag is for users who are aware that they are writing nonportable code and who have deliberately chosen to ignore the warning about it.

The restrictions on '`offsetof`' may be relaxed in a future version of the C++ standard.

`-Wno-int-to-pointer-cast` (C and Objective-C only)

Suppress warnings from casts to pointer type of an integer of a different size.

`-Wno-pointer-to-int-cast` (C and Objective-C only)

Suppress warnings from casts from a pointer to an integer type of a different size.

`-Winvalid-pch`

Warn if a precompiled header (see Section 3.20 [Precompiled Headers], page 232) is found in the search path but can't be used.

`-Wlong-long`

Warn if '`long long`' type is used. This is default. To inhibit the warning messages, use '`-Wno-long-long`'. Flags '`-Wlong-long`' and '`-Wno-long-long`' are taken into account only when '`-pedantic`' flag is used.

`-Wvariadic-macros`

Warn if variadic macros are used in pedantic ISO C90 mode, or the GNU alternate syntax when in pedantic ISO C99 mode. This is default. To inhibit the warning messages, use '`-Wno-variadic-macros`'.

`-Wvla` Warn if variable length array is used in the code. '`-Wno-vla`' will prevent the '`-pedantic`' warning of the variable length array.

Chapter 3: GCC Command Options   63

`-Wvolatile-register-var`
    Warn if a register variable is declared volatile. The volatile modifier does not inhibit all optimizations that may eliminate reads and/or writes to register variables.

`-Wdisabled-optimization`
    Warn if a requested optimization pass is disabled. This warning does not generally indicate that there is anything wrong with your code; it merely indicates that GCC's optimizers were unable to handle the code effectively. Often, the problem is that your code is too big or too complex; GCC will refuse to optimize programs when the optimization itself is likely to take inordinate amounts of time.

`-Wpointer-sign` (C and Objective-C only)
    Warn for pointer argument passing or assignment with different signedness. This option is only supported for C and Objective-C. It is implied by '-Wall' and by '-pedantic', which can be disabled with '-Wno-pointer-sign'.

`-Wstack-protector`
    This option is only active when '-fstack-protector' is active. It warns about functions that will not be protected against stack smashing.

`-Woverlength-strings`
    Warn about string constants which are longer than the "minimum maximum" length specified in the C standard. Modern compilers generally allow string constants which are much longer than the standard's minimum limit, but very portable programs should avoid using longer strings.

    The limit applies *after* string constant concatenation, and does not count the trailing NUL. In C89, the limit was 509 characters; in C99, it was raised to 4095. C++98 does not specify a normative minimum maximum, so we do not diagnose overlength strings in C++.

    This option is implied by '-pedantic', and can be disabled with '-Wno-overlength-strings'.

3.9 Options for Debugging Your Program or GCC

GCC has various special options that are used for debugging either your program or GCC:

`-g`   Produce debugging information in the operating system's native format (stabs, COFF, XCOFF, or DWARF 2). GDB can work with this debugging information.

    On most systems that use stabs format, '-g' enables use of extra debugging information that only GDB can use; this extra information makes debugging work better in GDB but will probably make other debuggers crash or refuse to read the program. If you want to control for certain whether to generate the extra information, use '-gstabs+', '-gstabs', '-gxcoff+', '-gxcoff', or '-gvms' (see below).

    GCC allows you to use '-g' with '-O'. The shortcuts taken by optimized code may occasionally produce surprising results: some variables you declared may not exist at all; flow of control may briefly move where you did not expect it; some statements may not be executed because they compute constant results or their values were already at hand; some statements may execute in different places because they were moved out of loops.

Nevertheless it proves possible to debug optimized output. This makes it reasonable to use the optimizer for programs that might have bugs.

The following options are useful when GCC is generated with the capability for more than one debugging format.

`-ggdb`
: Produce debugging information for use by GDB. This means to use the most expressive format available (DWARF 2, stabs, or the native format if neither of those are supported), including GDB extensions if at all possible.

`-gstabs`
: Produce debugging information in stabs format (if that is supported), without GDB extensions. This is the format used by DBX on most BSD systems. On MIPS, Alpha and System V Release 4 systems this option produces stabs debugging output which is not understood by DBX or SDB. On System V Release 4 systems this option requires the GNU assembler.

`-feliminate-unused-debug-symbols`
: Produce debugging information in stabs format (if that is supported), for only symbols that are actually used.

`-femit-class-debug-always`
: Instead of emitting debugging information for a C++ class in only one object file, emit it in all object files using the class. This option should be used only with debuggers that are unable to handle the way GCC normally emits debugging information for classes because using this option will increase the size of debugging information by as much as a factor of two.

`-gstabs+`
: Produce debugging information in stabs format (if that is supported), using GNU extensions understood only by the GNU debugger (GDB). The use of these extensions is likely to make other debuggers crash or refuse to read the program.

`-gcoff`
: Produce debugging information in COFF format (if that is supported). This is the format used by SDB on most System V systems prior to System V Release 4.

`-gxcoff`
: Produce debugging information in XCOFF format (if that is supported). This is the format used by the DBX debugger on IBM RS/6000 systems.

`-gxcoff+`
: Produce debugging information in XCOFF format (if that is supported), using GNU extensions understood only by the GNU debugger (GDB). The use of these extensions is likely to make other debuggers crash or refuse to read the program, and may cause assemblers other than the GNU assembler (GAS) to fail with an error.

`-gdwarf-2`
: Produce debugging information in DWARF version 2 format (if that is supported). This is the format used by DBX on IRIX 6. With this option, GCC

Chapter 3: GCC Command Options   65

              uses features of DWARF version 3 when they are useful; version 3 is upward
              compatible with version 2, but may still cause problems for older debuggers.

`-gvms`   Produce debugging information in VMS debug format (if that is supported).
              This is the format used by DEBUG on VMS systems.

`-glevel`
`-ggdblevel`
`-gstabslevel`
`-gcofflevel`
`-gxcofflevel`
`-gvmslevel`
              Request debugging information and also use *level* to specify how much information. The default level is 2.

              Level 0 produces no debug information at all. Thus, '`-g0`' negates '`-g`'.

              Level 1 produces minimal information, enough for making backtraces in parts of the program that you don't plan to debug. This includes descriptions of functions and external variables, but no information about local variables and no line numbers.

              Level 3 includes extra information, such as all the macro definitions present in the program. Some debuggers support macro expansion when you use '`-g3`'.

              '`-gdwarf-2`' does not accept a concatenated debug level, because GCC used to support an option '`-gdwarf`' that meant to generate debug information in version 1 of the DWARF format (which is very different from version 2), and it would have been too confusing. That debug format is long obsolete, but the option cannot be changed now. Instead use an additional '`-glevel`' option to change the debug level for DWARF2.

`-feliminate-dwarf2-dups`
              Compress DWARF2 debugging information by eliminating duplicated information about each symbol. This option only makes sense when generating DWARF2 debugging information with '`-gdwarf-2`'.

`-femit-struct-debug-baseonly`
              Emit debug information for struct-like types only when the base name of the compilation source file matches the base name of file in which the struct was defined.

              This option substantially reduces the size of debugging information, but at significant potential loss in type information to the debugger. See '`-femit-struct-debug-reduced`' for a less aggressive option. See '`-femit-struct-debug-detailed`' for more detailed control.

              This option works only with DWARF 2.

`-femit-struct-debug-reduced`
              Emit debug information for struct-like types only when the base name of the compilation source file matches the base name of file in which the type was defined, unless the struct is a template or defined in a system header.

              This option significantly reduces the size of debugging information, with some potential loss in type information to the debugger. See

'-femit-struct-debug-baseonly' for a more aggressive option. See '-femit-struct-debug-detailed' for more detailed control.

This option works only with DWARF 2.

`-femit-struct-debug-detailed[=spec-list]`

Specify the struct-like types for which the compiler will generate debug information. The intent is to reduce duplicate struct debug information between different object files within the same program.

This option is a detailed version of '-femit-struct-debug-reduced' and '-femit-struct-debug-baseonly', which will serve for most needs.

A specification has the syntax ['dir:'|'ind:']['ord:'|'gen:']('any'|'sys'|'base'|'none')

The optional first word limits the specification to structs that are used directly ('dir:') or used indirectly ('ind:'). A struct type is used directly when it is the type of a variable, member. Indirect uses arise through pointers to structs. That is, when use of an incomplete struct would be legal, the use is indirect. An example is 'struct one direct; struct two * indirect;'.

The optional second word limits the specification to ordinary structs ('ord:') or generic structs ('gen:'). Generic structs are a bit complicated to explain. For C++, these are non-explicit specializations of template classes, or non-template classes within the above. Other programming languages have generics, but '-femit-struct-debug-detailed' does not yet implement them.

The third word specifies the source files for those structs for which the compiler will emit debug information. The values 'none' and 'any' have the normal meaning. The value 'base' means that the base of name of the file in which the type declaration appears must match the base of the name of the main compilation file. In practice, this means that types declared in 'foo.c' and 'foo.h' will have debug information, but types declared in other header will not. The value 'sys' means those types satisfying 'base' or declared in system or compiler headers.

You may need to experiment to determine the best settings for your application.

The default is '-femit-struct-debug-detailed=all'.

This option works only with DWARF 2.

`-fno-merge-debug-strings`

Direct the linker to merge together strings which are identical in different object files. This is not supported by all assemblers or linker. This decreases the size of the debug information in the output file at the cost of increasing link processing time. This is on by default.

`-fdebug-prefix-map=old=new`

When compiling files in directory 'old', record debugging information describing them as in 'new' instead.

`-p`

Generate extra code to write profile information suitable for the analysis program `prof`. You must use this option when compiling the source files you want data about, and you must also use it when linking.

Chapter 3: GCC Command Options   67

-pg   Generate extra code to write profile information suitable for the analysis program gprof. You must use this option when compiling the source files you want data about, and you must also use it when linking.

-Q   Makes the compiler print out each function name as it is compiled, and print some statistics about each pass when it finishes.

-ftime-report
            Makes the compiler print some statistics about the time consumed by each pass when it finishes.

-fmem-report
            Makes the compiler print some statistics about permanent memory allocation when it finishes.

-fpre-ipa-mem-report
-fpost-ipa-mem-report
            Makes the compiler print some statistics about permanent memory allocation before or after interprocedural optimization.

-fprofile-arcs
            Add code so that program flow *arcs* are instrumented. During execution the program records how many times each branch and call is executed and how many times it is taken or returns. When the compiled program exits it saves this data to a file called '*auxname*.gcda' for each source file. The data may be used for profile-directed optimizations ('-fbranch-probabilities'), or for test coverage analysis ('-ftest-coverage'). Each object file's *auxname* is generated from the name of the output file, if explicitly specified and it is not the final executable, otherwise it is the basename of the source file. In both cases any suffix is removed (e.g. 'foo.gcda' for input file 'dir/foo.c', or 'dir/foo.gcda' for output file specified as '-o dir/foo.o'). See Section 9.5 [Cross-profiling], page 531.

--coverage
            This option is used to compile and link code instrumented for coverage analysis. The option is a synonym for '-fprofile-arcs' '-ftest-coverage' (when compiling) and '-lgcov' (when linking). See the documentation for those options for more details.

            - Compile the source files with '-fprofile-arcs' plus optimization and code generation options. For test coverage analysis, use the additional '-ftest-coverage' option. You do not need to profile every source file in a program.

            - Link your object files with '-lgcov' or '-fprofile-arcs' (the latter implies the former).

            - Run the program on a representative workload to generate the arc profile information. This may be repeated any number of times. You can run concurrent instances of your program, and provided that the file system supports locking, the data files will be correctly updated. Also fork calls are detected and correctly handled (double counting will not happen).

- For profile-directed optimizations, compile the source files again with the same optimization and code generation options plus '-fbranch-probabilities' (see Section 3.10 [Options that Control Optimization], page 77).
- For test coverage analysis, use gcov to produce human readable information from the '.gcno' and '.gcda' files. Refer to the gcov documentation for further information.

With '-fprofile-arcs', for each function of your program GCC creates a program flow graph, then finds a spanning tree for the graph. Only arcs that are not on the spanning tree have to be instrumented: the compiler adds code to count the number of times that these arcs are executed. When an arc is the only exit or only entrance to a block, the instrumentation code can be added to the block; otherwise, a new basic block must be created to hold the instrumentation code.

-ftest-coverage

Produce a notes file that the gcov code-coverage utility (see Chapter 9 [gcov—a Test Coverage Program], page 525) can use to show program coverage. Each source file's note file is called 'auxname.gcno'. Refer to the '-fprofile-arcs' option above for a description of auxname and instructions on how to generate test coverage data. Coverage data will match the source files more closely, if you do not optimize.

-fdbg-cnt-list

Print the name and the counter upperbound for all debug counters.

-fdbg-cnt=*counter-value-list*

Set the internal debug counter upperbound. *counter-value-list* is a comma-separated list of *name:value* pairs which sets the upperbound of each debug counter *name* to *value*. All debug counters have the initial upperbound of $UINT\_MAX$, thus dbg_cnt() returns true always unless the upperbound is set by this option. e.g. With -fdbg-cnt=dce:10,tail_call:0 dbg_cnt(dce) will return true only for first 10 invocations and dbg_cnt(tail_call) will return false always.

-d*letters*

-fdump-rtl-*pass*

Says to make debugging dumps during compilation at times specified by *letters*. This is used for debugging the RTL-based passes of the compiler. The file names for most of the dumps are made by appending a pass number and a word to the *dumpname*. *dumpname* is generated from the name of the output file, if explicitly specified and it is not an executable, otherwise it is the basename of the source file. These switches may have different effects when '-E' is used for preprocessing.

Most debug dumps can be enabled either passing a letter to the '-d' option, or with a long '-fdump-rtl' switch; here are the possible letters for use in *letters* and *pass*, and their meanings:

    -dA   Annotate the assembler output with miscellaneous debugging information.

Chapter 3: GCC Command Options   69

-dB
-fdump-rtl-bbro
            Dump after block reordering, to 'file.148r.bbro'.

-dc
-fdump-rtl-combine
            Dump after the RTL instruction combination pass, to the file
            'file.129r.combine'.

-dC
-fdump-rtl-ce1
-fdump-rtl-ce2
            '-dC' and '-fdump-rtl-ce1' enable dumping after the first if conversion, to the file 'file.117r.ce1'. '-dC' and '-fdump-rtl-ce2' enable dumping after the second if conversion, to the file 'file.130r.ce2'.

-dd
-fdump-rtl-btl
-fdump-rtl-dbr
            '-dd' and '-fdump-rtl-btl' enable dumping after branch target load optimization, to 'file.31.btl'. '-dd' and '-fdump-rtl-dbr' enable dumping after delayed branch scheduling, to 'file.36.dbr'.

-dD   Dump all macro definitions, at the end of preprocessing, in addition to normal output.

-dE
-fdump-rtl-ce3
            Dump after the third if conversion, to 'file.146r.ce3'.

-df
-fdump-rtl-cfg
-fdump-rtl-life
            '-df' and '-fdump-rtl-cfg' enable dumping after control and data flow analysis, to 'file.116r.cfg'. '-df' and '-fdump-rtl-cfg' enable dumping dump after life analysis, to 'file.128r.life1' and 'file.135r.life2'.

-dg
-fdump-rtl-greg
            Dump after global register allocation, to 'file.139r.greg'.

-dG
-fdump-rtl-gcse
-fdump-rtl-bypass
            '-dG' and '-fdump-rtl-gcse' enable dumping after GCSE, to 'file.114r.gcse'. '-dG' and '-fdump-rtl-bypass' enable dumping after jump bypassing and control flow optimizations, to 'file.115r.bypass'.

`-dh`
`-fdump-rtl-eh`
: Dump after finalization of EH handling code, to '`file.02.eh`'.

`-di`
`-fdump-rtl-sibling`
: Dump after sibling call optimizations, to '`file.106r.sibling`'.

`-dj`
`-fdump-rtl-jump`
: Dump after the first jump optimization, to '`file.112r.jump`'.

`-dk`
`-fdump-rtl-stack`
: Dump after conversion from GCC's "flat register file" registers to the x87's stack-like registers, to '`file.152r.stack`'.

`-dl`
`-fdump-rtl-lreg`
: Dump after local register allocation, to '`file.138r.lreg`'.

`-dL`
`-fdump-rtl-loop2`
: '`-dL`' and '`-fdump-rtl-loop2`' enable dumping after the loop optimization pass, to '`file.119r.loop2`', '`file.120r.loop2_init`', '`file.121r.loop2_invariant`', and '`file.125r.loop2_done`'.

`-dm`
`-fdump-rtl-sms`
: Dump after modulo scheduling, to '`file.136r.sms`'.

`-dM`
`-fdump-rtl-mach`
: Dump after performing the machine dependent reorganization pass, to '`file.155r.mach`' if that pass exists.

`-dn`
`-fdump-rtl-rnreg`
: Dump after register renumbering, to '`file.147r.rnreg`'.

`-dN`
`-fdump-rtl-regmove`
: Dump after the register move pass, to '`file.132r.regmove`'.

`-do`
`-fdump-rtl-postreload`
: Dump after post-reload optimizations, to '`file.24.postreload`'.

`-dr`
`-fdump-rtl-expand`
: Dump after RTL generation, to '`file.104r.expand`'.

`-dR`
`-fdump-rtl-sched2`
: Dump after the second scheduling pass, to '`file.149r.sched2`'.

Chapter 3: GCC Command Options   71

`-ds`
`-fdump-rtl-cse`
> Dump after CSE (including the jump optimization that sometimes follows CSE), to '`file.113r.cse`'.

`-dS`
`-fdump-rtl-sched1`
> Dump after the first scheduling pass, to '`file.136r.sched1`'.

`-dt`
`-fdump-rtl-cse2`
> Dump after the second CSE pass (including the jump optimization that sometimes follows CSE), to '`file.127r.cse2`'.

`-dT`
`-fdump-rtl-tracer`
> Dump after running tracer, to '`file.118r.tracer`'.

`-dV`
`-fdump-rtl-vpt`
`-fdump-rtl-vartrack`
> '`-dV`' and '`-fdump-rtl-vpt`' enable dumping after the value profile transformations, to '`file.10.vpt`'. '`-dV`' and '`-fdump-rtl-vartrack`' enable dumping after variable tracking, to '`file.154r.vartrack`'.

`-dw`
`-fdump-rtl-flow2`
> Dump after the second flow pass, to '`file.142r.flow2`'.

`-dz`
`-fdump-rtl-peephole2`
> Dump after the peephole pass, to '`file.145r.peephole2`'.

`-dZ`
`-fdump-rtl-web`
> Dump after live range splitting, to '`file.126r.web`'.

`-da`
`-fdump-rtl-all`
> Produce all the dumps listed above.

`-dH`   Produce a core dump whenever an error occurs.

`-dm`   Print statistics on memory usage, at the end of the run, to standard error.

`-dp`   Annotate the assembler output with a comment indicating which pattern and alternative was used. The length of each instruction is also printed.

`-dP`   Dump the RTL in the assembler output as a comment before each instruction. Also turns on '`-dp`' annotation.

`-dv` For each of the other indicated dump files (either with '`-d`' or '`-fdump-rtl-pass`'), dump a representation of the control flow graph suitable for viewing with VCG to '`file.pass.vcg`'.

`-dx` Just generate RTL for a function instead of compiling it. Usually used with '`r`' ('`-fdump-rtl-expand`').

`-dy` Dump debugging information during parsing, to standard error.

`-fdump-noaddr`
When doing debugging dumps (see '`-d`' option above), suppress address output. This makes it more feasible to use diff on debugging dumps for compiler invocations with different compiler binaries and/or different text / bss / data / heap / stack / dso start locations.

`-fdump-unnumbered`
When doing debugging dumps (see '`-d`' option above), suppress instruction numbers and address output. This makes it more feasible to use diff on debugging dumps for compiler invocations with different options, in particular with and without '`-g`'.

`-fdump-translation-unit` (C++ only)
`-fdump-translation-unit-options` (C++ only)
Dump a representation of the tree structure for the entire translation unit to a file. The file name is made by appending '`.tu`' to the source file name. If the '`-options`' form is used, options controls the details of the dump as described for the '`-fdump-tree`' options.

`-fdump-class-hierarchy` (C++ only)
`-fdump-class-hierarchy-options` (C++ only)
Dump a representation of each class's hierarchy and virtual function table layout to a file. The file name is made by appending '`.class`' to the source file name. If the '`-options`' form is used, options controls the details of the dump as described for the '`-fdump-tree`' options.

`-fdump-ipa-switch`
Control the dumping at various stages of inter-procedural analysis language tree to a file. The file name is generated by appending a switch specific suffix to the source file name. The following dumps are possible:

'`all`'   Enables all inter-procedural analysis dumps.

'`cgraph`' Dumps information about call-graph optimization, unused function removal, and inlining decisions.

'`inline`' Dump after function inlining.

`-fdump-tree-switch`
`-fdump-tree-switch-options`
Control the dumping at various stages of processing the intermediate language tree to a file. The file name is generated by appending a switch specific suffix to the source file name. If the '`-options`' form is used, options is a list of '`-`' separated options that control the details of the dump. Not all options are

Chapter 3: GCC Command Options 73

applicable to all dumps, those which are not meaningful will be ignored. The following options are available

`address` Print the address of each node. Usually this is not meaningful as it changes according to the environment and source file. Its primary use is for tying up a dump file with a debug environment.

`slim` Inhibit dumping of members of a scope or body of a function merely because that scope has been reached. Only dump such items when they are directly reachable by some other path. When dumping pretty-printed trees, this option inhibits dumping the bodies of control structures.

`raw` Print a raw representation of the tree. By default, trees are pretty-printed into a C-like representation.

`details` Enable more detailed dumps (not honored by every dump option).

`stats` Enable dumping various statistics about the pass (not honored by every dump option).

`blocks` Enable showing basic block boundaries (disabled in raw dumps).

`vops` Enable showing virtual operands for every statement.

`lineno` Enable showing line numbers for statements.

`uid` Enable showing the unique ID (DECL_UID) for each variable.

`all` Turn on all options, except `raw`, `slim` and `lineno`.

The following tree dumps are possible:

`original`
Dump before any tree based optimization, to `file.original`.

`optimized`
Dump after all tree based optimization, to `file.optimized`.

`gimple` Dump each function before and after the gimplification pass to a file. The file name is made by appending `.gimple` to the source file name.

`cfg` Dump the control flow graph of each function to a file. The file name is made by appending `.cfg` to the source file name.

`vcg` Dump the control flow graph of each function to a file in VCG format. The file name is made by appending `.vcg` to the source file name. Note that if the file contains more than one function, the generated file cannot be used directly by VCG. You will need to cut and paste each function's graph into its own separate file first.

`ch` Dump each function after copying loop headers. The file name is made by appending `.ch` to the source file name.

`ssa` Dump SSA related information to a file. The file name is made by appending `.ssa` to the source file name.

'salias'   Dump structure aliasing variable information to a file. This file name is made by appending '.salias' to the source file name.

'alias'   Dump aliasing information for each function. The file name is made by appending '.alias' to the source file name.

'ccp'   Dump each function after CCP. The file name is made by appending '.ccp' to the source file name.

'storeccp'
             Dump each function after STORE-CCP. The file name is made by appending '.storeccp' to the source file name.

'pre'   Dump trees after partial redundancy elimination. The file name is made by appending '.pre' to the source file name.

'fre'   Dump trees after full redundancy elimination. The file name is made by appending '.fre' to the source file name.

'copyprop'
             Dump trees after copy propagation. The file name is made by appending '.copyprop' to the source file name.

'store_copyprop'
             Dump trees after store copy-propagation. The file name is made by appending '.store_copyprop' to the source file name.

'dce'   Dump each function after dead code elimination. The file name is made by appending '.dce' to the source file name.

'mudflap'   Dump each function after adding mudflap instrumentation. The file name is made by appending '.mudflap' to the source file name.

'sra'   Dump each function after performing scalar replacement of aggregates. The file name is made by appending '.sra' to the source file name.

'sink'   Dump each function after performing code sinking. The file name is made by appending '.sink' to the source file name.

'dom'   Dump each function after applying dominator tree optimizations. The file name is made by appending '.dom' to the source file name.

'dse'   Dump each function after applying dead store elimination. The file name is made by appending '.dse' to the source file name.

'phiopt'   Dump each function after optimizing PHI nodes into straightline code. The file name is made by appending '.phiopt' to the source file name.

'forwprop'
             Dump each function after forward propagating single use variables. The file name is made by appending '.forwprop' to the source file name.

'copyrename'
: Dump each function after applying the copy rename optimization. The file name is made by appending '.copyrename' to the source file name.

'nrv'
: Dump each function after applying the named return value optimization on generic trees. The file name is made by appending '.nrv' to the source file name.

'vect'
: Dump each function after applying vectorization of loops. The file name is made by appending '.vect' to the source file name.

'vrp'
: Dump each function after Value Range Propagation (VRP). The file name is made by appending '.vrp' to the source file name.

'all'
: Enable all the available tree dumps with the flags provided in this option.

`-ftree-vectorizer-verbose=n`
: This option controls the amount of debugging output the vectorizer prints. This information is written to standard error, unless '-fdump-tree-all' or '-fdump-tree-vect' is specified, in which case it is output to the usual dump listing file, '.vect'. For $n=0$ no diagnostic information is reported. If $n=1$ the vectorizer reports each loop that got vectorized, and the total number of loops that got vectorized. If $n=2$ the vectorizer also reports non-vectorized loops that passed the first analysis phase (vect_analyze_loop_form) - i.e. countable, inner-most, single-bb, single-entry/exit loops. This is the same verbosity level that '-fdump-tree-vect-stats' uses. Higher verbosity levels mean either more information dumped for each reported loop, or same amount of information reported for more loops: If $n=3$, alignment related information is added to the reports. If $n=4$, data-references related information (e.g. memory dependences, memory access-patterns) is added to the reports. If $n=5$, the vectorizer reports also non-vectorized inner-most loops that did not pass the first analysis phase (i.e., may not be countable, or may have complicated control-flow). If $n=6$, the vectorizer reports also non-vectorized nested loops. For $n=7$, all the information the vectorizer generates during its analysis and transformation is reported. This is the same verbosity level that '-fdump-tree-vect-details' uses.

`-frandom-seed=string`
: This option provides a seed that GCC uses when it would otherwise use random numbers. It is used to generate certain symbol names that have to be different in every compiled file. It is also used to place unique stamps in coverage data files and the object files that produce them. You can use the '-frandom-seed' option to produce reproducibly identical object files.

  The *string* should be different for every file you compile.

`-fsched-verbose=n`
: On targets that use instruction scheduling, this option controls the amount of debugging output the scheduler prints. This information is written to standard error, unless '-dS' or '-dR' is specified, in which case it is output to the usual

dump listing file, '.sched' or '.sched2' respectively. However for *n* greater than nine, the output is always printed to standard error.

For *n* greater than zero, '-fsched-verbose' outputs the same information as '-dRS'. For *n* greater than one, it also output basic block probabilities, detailed ready list information and unit/insn info. For *n* greater than two, it includes RTL at abort point, control-flow and regions info. And for *n* over four, '-fsched-verbose' also includes dependence info.

`-save-temps`

Store the usual "temporary" intermediate files permanently; place them in the current directory and name them based on the source file. Thus, compiling 'foo.c' with '-c -save-temps' would produce files 'foo.i' and 'foo.s', as well as 'foo.o'. This creates a preprocessed 'foo.i' output file even though the compiler now normally uses an integrated preprocessor.

When used in combination with the '-x' command line option, '-save-temps' is sensible enough to avoid over writing an input source file with the same extension as an intermediate file. The corresponding intermediate file may be obtained by renaming the source file before using '-save-temps'.

`-time`

Report the CPU time taken by each subprocess in the compilation sequence. For C source files, this is the compiler proper and assembler (plus the linker if linking is done). The output looks like this:

```
# cc1 0.12 0.01
# as 0.00 0.01
```

The first number on each line is the "user time", that is time spent executing the program itself. The second number is "system time", time spent executing operating system routines on behalf of the program. Both numbers are in seconds.

`-fvar-tracking`

Run variable tracking pass. It computes where variables are stored at each position in code. Better debugging information is then generated (if the debugging information format supports this information).

It is enabled by default when compiling with optimization ('-Os', '-O', '-O2', ...), debugging information ('-g') and the debug info format supports it.

`-print-file-name=library`

Print the full absolute name of the library file *library* that would be used when linking—and don't do anything else. With this option, GCC does not compile or link anything; it just prints the file name.

`-print-multi-directory`

Print the directory name corresponding to the multilib selected by any other switches present in the command line. This directory is supposed to exist in GCC_EXEC_PREFIX.

`-print-multi-lib`

Print the mapping from multilib directory names to compiler switches that enable them. The directory name is separated from the switches by ';', and

Chapter 3: GCC Command Options   77

each switch starts with an '@' instead of the '-', without spaces between multiple switches. This is supposed to ease shell-processing.

`-print-prog-name=program`

Like '-print-file-name', but searches for a program such as 'cpp'.

`-print-libgcc-file-name`

Same as '-print-file-name=libgcc.a'.

This is useful when you use '-nostdlib' or '-nodefaultlibs' but you do want to link with 'libgcc.a'. You can do

```
gcc -nostdlib files... `gcc -print-libgcc-file-name`
```

`-print-search-dirs`

Print the name of the configured installation directory and a list of program and library directories gcc will search—and don't do anything else.

This is useful when gcc prints the error message 'installation problem, cannot exec cpp0: No such file or directory'. To resolve this you either need to put 'cpp0' and the other compiler components where gcc expects to find them, or you can set the environment variable GCC_EXEC_PREFIX to the directory where you installed them. Don't forget the trailing '/'. See Section 3.19 [Environment Variables], page 229.

`-print-sysroot-headers-suffix`

Print the suffix added to the target sysroot when searching for headers, or give an error if the compiler is not configured with such a suffix—and don't do anything else.

`-dumpmachine`

Print the compiler's target machine (for example, 'i686-pc-linux-gnu')—and don't do anything else.

`-dumpversion`

Print the compiler version (for example, '3.0')—and don't do anything else.

`-dumpspecs`

Print the compiler's built-in specs—and don't do anything else. (This is used when GCC itself is being built.) See Section 3.15 [Spec Files], page 128.

`-feliminate-unused-debug-types`

Normally, when producing DWARF2 output, GCC will emit debugging information for all types declared in a compilation unit, regardless of whether or not they are actually used in that compilation unit. Sometimes this is useful, such as if, in the debugger, you want to cast a value to a type that is not actually used in your program (but is declared). More often, however, this results in a significant amount of wasted space. With this option, GCC will avoid producing debug symbol output for types that are nowhere used in the source file being compiled.

3.10 Options That Control Optimization

These options control various sorts of optimizations.

Without any optimization option, the compiler's goal is to reduce the cost of compilation and to make debugging produce the expected results. Statements are independent: if you stop the program with a breakpoint between statements, you can then assign a new value to any variable or change the program counter to any other statement in the function and get exactly the results you would expect from the source code.

Turning on optimization flags makes the compiler attempt to improve the performance and/or code size at the expense of compilation time and possibly the ability to debug the program.

The compiler performs optimization based on the knowledge it has of the program. Optimization levels '-O' and above, in particular, enable *unit-at-a-time* mode, which allows the compiler to consider information gained from later functions in the file when compiling a function. Compiling multiple files at once to a single output file in *unit-at-a-time* mode allows the compiler to use information gained from all of the files when compiling each of them.

Not all optimizations are controlled directly by a flag. Only optimizations that have a flag are listed.

-O
-O1 Optimize. Optimizing compilation takes somewhat more time, and a lot more memory for a large function.

With '-O', the compiler tries to reduce code size and execution time, without performing any optimizations that take a great deal of compilation time.

'-O' turns on the following optimization flags:

```
-fauto-inc-dec
-fcprop-registers
-fdce
-fdefer-pop
-fdelayed-branch
-fdse
-fguess-branch-probability
-fif-conversion2
-fif-conversion
-finline-small-functions
-fipa-pure-const
-fipa-reference
-fmerge-constants -fsplit-wide-types
-ftree-ccp
-ftree-ch
-ftree-copyrename
-ftree-dce
-ftree-dominator-opts
-ftree-dse
-ftree-fre
-ftree-sra
-ftree-ter
-funit-at-a-time
```

'-O' also turns on '-fomit-frame-pointer' on machines where doing so does not interfere with debugging.

-O2 Optimize even more. GCC performs nearly all supported optimizations that do not involve a space-speed tradeoff. The compiler does not perform loop

Chapter 3: GCC Command Options   79

unrolling or function inlining when you specify '-O2'. As compared to '-O', this option increases both compilation time and the performance of the generated code.

'-O2' turns on all optimization flags specified by '-O'. It also turns on the following optimization flags:

```
-fthread-jumps
-falign-functions  -falign-jumps
-falign-loops  -falign-labels
-fcaller-saves
-fcrossjumping
-fcse-follow-jumps  -fcse-skip-blocks
-fdelete-null-pointer-checks
-fexpensive-optimizations
-fgcse  -fgcse-lm
-foptimize-sibling-calls
-fpeephole2
-fregmove
-freorder-blocks  -freorder-functions
-frerun-cse-after-loop
-fsched-interblock  -fsched-spec
-fschedule-insns  -fschedule-insns2
-fstrict-aliasing  -fstrict-overflow
-ftree-pre
-ftree-vrp
```

Please note the warning under '-fgcse' about invoking '-O2' on programs that use computed gotos.

-O3   Optimize yet more. '-O3' turns on all optimizations specified by '-O2' and also turns on the '-finline-functions', '-funswitch-loops', '-fpredictive-commoning', '-fgcse-after-reload' and '-ftree-vectorize' options.

-O0   Reduce compilation time and make debugging produce the expected results. This is the default.

-Os   Optimize for size. '-Os' enables all '-O2' optimizations that do not typically increase code size. It also performs further optimizations designed to reduce code size.

'-Os' disables the following optimization flags:

```
-falign-functions  -falign-jumps  -falign-loops
-falign-labels  -freorder-blocks  -freorder-blocks-and-partition
-fprefetch-loop-arrays  -ftree-vect-loop-version
```

If you use multiple '-O' options, with or without level numbers, the last such option is the one that is effective.

Options of the form '-fflag' specify machine-independent flags. Most flags have both positive and negative forms; the negative form of '-ffoo' would be '-fno-foo'. In the table below, only one of the forms is listed—the one you typically will use. You can figure out the other form by either removing 'no-' or adding it.

The following options control specific optimizations. They are either activated by '-O' options or are related to ones that are. You can use the following flags in the rare cases when "fine-tuning" of optimizations to be performed is desired.

`-fno-default-inline`
> Do not make member functions inline by default merely because they are defined inside the class scope (C++ only). Otherwise, when you specify '-O', member functions defined inside class scope are compiled inline by default; i.e., you don't need to add 'inline' in front of the member function name.

`-fno-defer-pop`
> Always pop the arguments to each function call as soon as that function returns. For machines which must pop arguments after a function call, the compiler normally lets arguments accumulate on the stack for several function calls and pops them all at once.
>
> Disabled at levels '-O', '-O2', '-O3', '-Os'.

`-fforward-propagate`
> Perform a forward propagation pass on RTL. The pass tries to combine two instructions and checks if the result can be simplified. If loop unrolling is active, two passes are performed and the second is scheduled after loop unrolling.
>
> This option is enabled by default at optimization levels '-O2', '-O3', '-Os'.

`-fomit-frame-pointer`
> Don't keep the frame pointer in a register for functions that don't need one. This avoids the instructions to save, set up and restore frame pointers; it also makes an extra register available in many functions. **It also makes debugging impossible on some machines.**
>
> On some machines, such as the VAX, this flag has no effect, because the standard calling sequence automatically handles the frame pointer and nothing is saved by pretending it doesn't exist. The machine-description macro `FRAME_POINTER_REQUIRED` controls whether a target machine supports this flag. See Section "Register Usage" in *GNU Compiler Collection (GCC) Internals*.
>
> Enabled at levels '-O', '-O2', '-O3', '-Os'.

`-foptimize-sibling-calls`
> Optimize sibling and tail recursive calls.
>
> Enabled at levels '-O2', '-O3', '-Os'.

`-fno-inline`
> Don't pay attention to the `inline` keyword. Normally this option is used to keep the compiler from expanding any functions inline. Note that if you are not optimizing, no functions can be expanded inline.

`-finline-small-functions`
> Integrate functions into their callers when their body is smaller than expected function call code (so overall size of program gets smaller). The compiler heuristically decides which functions are simple enough to be worth integrating in this way.
>
> Enabled at level '-O2'.

`-finline-functions`
> Integrate all simple functions into their callers. The compiler heuristically decides which functions are simple enough to be worth integrating in this way.

Chapter 3: GCC Command Options

> If all calls to a given function are integrated, and the function is declared `static`, then the function is normally not output as assembler code in its own right.
>
> Enabled at level '-O3'.

`-finline-functions-called-once`
> Consider all `static` functions called once for inlining into their caller even if they are not marked `inline`. If a call to a given function is integrated, then the function is not output as assembler code in its own right.
>
> Enabled if '-funit-at-a-time' is enabled.

`-fearly-inlining`
> Inline functions marked by `always_inline` and functions whose body seems smaller than the function call overhead early before doing '-fprofile-generate' instrumentation and real inlining pass. Doing so makes profiling significantly cheaper and usually inlining faster on programs having large chains of nested wrapper functions.
>
> Enabled by default.

`-finline-limit=n`
> By default, GCC limits the size of functions that can be inlined. This flag allows coarse control of this limit. n is the size of functions that can be inlined in number of pseudo instructions.
>
> Inlining is actually controlled by a number of parameters, which may be specified individually by using '--param name=value'. The '-finline-limit=n' option sets some of these parameters as follows:
>
> `max-inline-insns-single`
> > is set to $n/2$.
>
> `max-inline-insns-auto`
> > is set to $n/2$.
>
> See below for a documentation of the individual parameters controlling inlining and for the defaults of these parameters.
>
> *Note:* there may be no value to '-finline-limit' that results in default behavior.
>
> *Note:* pseudo instruction represents, in this particular context, an abstract measurement of function's size. In no way does it represent a count of assembly instructions and as such its exact meaning might change from one release to an another.

`-fkeep-inline-functions`
> In C, emit `static` functions that are declared `inline` into the object file, even if the function has been inlined into all of its callers. This switch does not affect functions using the `extern inline` extension in GNU C89. In C++, emit any and all inline functions into the object file.

`-fkeep-static-consts`
> Emit variables declared `static const` when optimization isn't turned on, even if the variables aren't referenced.

GCC enables this option by default. If you want to force the compiler to check if the variable was referenced, regardless of whether or not optimization is turned on, use the '`-fno-keep-static-consts`' option.

`-fmerge-constants`

Attempt to merge identical constants (string constants and floating point constants) across compilation units.

This option is the default for optimized compilation if the assembler and linker support it. Use '`-fno-merge-constants`' to inhibit this behavior.

Enabled at levels '`-O`', '`-O2`', '`-O3`', '`-Os`'.

`-fmerge-all-constants`

Attempt to merge identical constants and identical variables.

This option implies '`-fmerge-constants`'. In addition to '`-fmerge-constants`' this considers e.g. even constant initialized arrays or initialized constant variables with integral or floating point types. Languages like C or C++ require each non-automatic variable to have distinct location, so using this option will result in non-conforming behavior.

`-fmodulo-sched`

Perform swing modulo scheduling immediately before the first scheduling pass. This pass looks at innermost loops and reorders their instructions by overlapping different iterations.

`-fmodulo-sched-allow-regmoves`

Perform more aggressive SMS based modulo scheduling with register moves allowed. By setting this flag certain anti-dependences edges will be deleted which will trigger the generation of reg-moves based on the life-range analysis. This option is effective only with '`-fmodulo-sched`' enabled.

`-fno-branch-count-reg`

Do not use "decrement and branch" instructions on a count register, but instead generate a sequence of instructions that decrement a register, compare it against zero, then branch based upon the result. This option is only meaningful on architectures that support such instructions, which include x86, PowerPC, IA-64 and S/390.

The default is '`-fbranch-count-reg`'.

`-fno-function-cse`

Do not put function addresses in registers; make each instruction that calls a constant function contain the function's address explicitly.

This option results in less efficient code, but some strange hacks that alter the assembler output may be confused by the optimizations performed when this option is not used.

The default is '`-ffunction-cse`'

`-fno-zero-initialized-in-bss`

If the target supports a BSS section, GCC by default puts variables that are initialized to zero into BSS. This can save space in the resulting code.

Chapter 3: GCC Command Options   83

This option turns off this behavior because some programs explicitly rely on variables going to the data section. E.g., so that the resulting executable can find the beginning of that section and/or make assumptions based on that.

The default is '-fzero-initialized-in-bss'.

`-fmudflap -fmudflapth -fmudflapir`

For front-ends that support it (C and C++), instrument all risky pointer/array dereferencing operations, some standard library string/heap functions, and some other associated constructs with range/validity tests. Modules so instrumented should be immune to buffer overflows, invalid heap use, and some other classes of C/C++ programming errors. The instrumentation relies on a separate runtime library ('libmudflap'), which will be linked into a program if '-fmudflap' is given at link time. Run-time behavior of the instrumented program is controlled by the MUDFLAP_OPTIONS environment variable. See env MUDFLAP_OPTIONS=-help a.out for its options.

Use '-fmudflapth' instead of '-fmudflap' to compile and to link if your program is multi-threaded. Use '-fmudflapir', in addition to '-fmudflap' or '-fmudflapth', if instrumentation should ignore pointer reads. This produces less instrumentation (and therefore faster execution) and still provides some protection against outright memory corrupting writes, but allows erroneously read data to propagate within a program.

`-fthread-jumps`

Perform optimizations where we check to see if a jump branches to a location where another comparison subsumed by the first is found. If so, the first branch is redirected to either the destination of the second branch or a point immediately following it, depending on whether the condition is known to be true or false.

Enabled at levels '-O2', '-O3', '-Os'.

`-fsplit-wide-types`

When using a type that occupies multiple registers, such as `long long` on a 32-bit system, split the registers apart and allocate them independently. This normally generates better code for those types, but may make debugging more difficult.

Enabled at levels '-O', '-O2', '-O3', '-Os'.

`-fcse-follow-jumps`

In common subexpression elimination (CSE), scan through jump instructions when the target of the jump is not reached by any other path. For example, when CSE encounters an `if` statement with an `else` clause, CSE will follow the jump when the condition tested is false.

Enabled at levels '-O2', '-O3', '-Os'.

`-fcse-skip-blocks`

This is similar to '-fcse-follow-jumps', but causes CSE to follow jumps which conditionally skip over blocks. When CSE encounters a simple `if` statement with no else clause, '-fcse-skip-blocks' causes CSE to follow the jump around the body of the `if`.

Enabled at levels '-O2', '-O3', '-Os'.

`-frerun-cse-after-loop`
: Re-run common subexpression elimination after loop optimizations has been performed.

    Enabled at levels '-O2', '-O3', '-Os'.

`-fgcse`
: Perform a global common subexpression elimination pass. This pass also performs global constant and copy propagation.

    Note: When compiling a program using computed gotos, a GCC extension, you may get better runtime performance if you disable the global common subexpression elimination pass by adding '`-fno-gcse`' to the command line.

    Enabled at levels '-O2', '-O3', '-Os'.

`-fgcse-lm`
: When '`-fgcse-lm`' is enabled, global common subexpression elimination will attempt to move loads which are only killed by stores into themselves. This allows a loop containing a load/store sequence to be changed to a load outside the loop, and a copy/store within the loop.

    Enabled by default when gcse is enabled.

`-fgcse-sm`
: When '`-fgcse-sm`' is enabled, a store motion pass is run after global common subexpression elimination. This pass will attempt to move stores out of loops. When used in conjunction with '`-fgcse-lm`', loops containing a load/store sequence can be changed to a load before the loop and a store after the loop.

    Not enabled at any optimization level.

`-fgcse-las`
: When '`-fgcse-las`' is enabled, the global common subexpression elimination pass eliminates redundant loads that come after stores to the same memory location (both partial and full redundancies).

    Not enabled at any optimization level.

`-fgcse-after-reload`
: When '`-fgcse-after-reload`' is enabled, a redundant load elimination pass is performed after reload. The purpose of this pass is to cleanup redundant spilling.

`-funsafe-loop-optimizations`
: If given, the loop optimizer will assume that loop indices do not overflow, and that the loops with nontrivial exit condition are not infinite. This enables a wider range of loop optimizations even if the loop optimizer itself cannot prove that these assumptions are valid. Using '`-Wunsafe-loop-optimizations`', the compiler will warn you if it finds this kind of loop.

`-fcrossjumping`
: Perform cross-jumping transformation. This transformation unifies equivalent code and save code size. The resulting code may or may not perform better than without cross-jumping.

    Enabled at levels '-O2', '-O3', '-Os'.

Chapter 3: GCC Command Options   85

`-fauto-inc-dec`
           Combine increments or decrements of addresses with memory accesses. This
           pass is always skipped on architectures that do not have instructions to support
           this. Enabled by default at '-O' and higher on architectures that support this.

`-fdce`   Perform dead code elimination (DCE) on RTL. Enabled by default at '-O' and
           higher.

`-fdse`   Perform dead store elimination (DSE) on RTL. Enabled by default at '-O' and
           higher.

`-fif-conversion`
           Attempt to transform conditional jumps into branch-less equivalents. This
           include use of conditional moves, min, max, set flags and abs instructions, and
           some tricks doable by standard arithmetics. The use of conditional execution
           on chips where it is available is controlled by `if-conversion2`.

           Enabled at levels '-O', '-O2', '-O3', '-Os'.

`-fif-conversion2`
           Use conditional execution (where available) to transform conditional jumps into
           branch-less equivalents.

           Enabled at levels '-O', '-O2', '-O3', '-Os'.

`-fdelete-null-pointer-checks`
           Use global dataflow analysis to identify and eliminate useless checks for null
           pointers. The compiler assumes that dereferencing a null pointer would have
           halted the program. If a pointer is checked after it has already been derefer-
           enced, it cannot be null.

           In some environments, this assumption is not true, and programs can safely
           dereference null pointers. Use '-fno-delete-null-pointer-checks' to disable
           this optimization for programs which depend on that behavior.

           Enabled at levels '-O2', '-O3', '-Os'.

`-fexpensive-optimizations`
           Perform a number of minor optimizations that are relatively expensive.

           Enabled at levels '-O2', '-O3', '-Os'.

`-foptimize-register-move`
`-fregmove`
           Attempt to reassign register numbers in move instructions and as operands of
           other simple instructions in order to maximize the amount of register tying.
           This is especially helpful on machines with two-operand instructions.

           Note '-fregmove' and '-foptimize-register-move' are the same optimiza-
           tion.

           Enabled at levels '-O2', '-O3', '-Os'.

`-fdelayed-branch`
           If supported for the target machine, attempt to reorder instructions to exploit
           instruction slots available after delayed branch instructions.

           Enabled at levels '-O', '-O2', '-O3', '-Os'.

`-fschedule-insns`
> If supported for the target machine, attempt to reorder instructions to eliminate execution stalls due to required data being unavailable. This helps machines that have slow floating point or memory load instructions by allowing other instructions to be issued until the result of the load or floating point instruction is required.
>
> Enabled at levels '-O2', '-O3', '-Os'.

`-fschedule-insns2`
> Similar to '-fschedule-insns', but requests an additional pass of instruction scheduling after register allocation has been done. This is especially useful on machines with a relatively small number of registers and where memory load instructions take more than one cycle.
>
> Enabled at levels '-O2', '-O3', '-Os'.

`-fno-sched-interblock`
> Don't schedule instructions across basic blocks. This is normally enabled by default when scheduling before register allocation, i.e. with '-fschedule-insns' or at '-O2' or higher.

`-fno-sched-spec`
> Don't allow speculative motion of non-load instructions. This is normally enabled by default when scheduling before register allocation, i.e. with '-fschedule-insns' or at '-O2' or higher.

`-fsched-spec-load`
> Allow speculative motion of some load instructions. This only makes sense when scheduling before register allocation, i.e. with '-fschedule-insns' or at '-O2' or higher.

`-fsched-spec-load-dangerous`
> Allow speculative motion of more load instructions. This only makes sense when scheduling before register allocation, i.e. with '-fschedule-insns' or at '-O2' or higher.

`-fsched-stalled-insns`
`-fsched-stalled-insns=n`
> Define how many insns (if any) can be moved prematurely from the queue of stalled insns into the ready list, during the second scheduling pass. '-fno-sched-stalled-insns' means that no insns will be moved prematurely, '-fsched-stalled-insns=0' means there is no limit on how many queued insns can be moved prematurely. '-fsched-stalled-insns' without a value is equivalent to '-fsched-stalled-insns=1'.

`-fsched-stalled-insns-dep`
`-fsched-stalled-insns-dep=n`
> Define how many insn groups (cycles) will be examined for a dependency on a stalled insn that is candidate for premature removal from the queue of stalled insns. This has an effect only during the second scheduling pass, and only if '-fsched-stalled-insns'

Chapter 3: GCC Command Options 87

is used. '-fno-sched-stalled-insns-dep' is equivalent to '-fsched-stalled-insns-dep=0'. '-fsched-stalled-insns-dep' without a value is equivalent to '-fsched-stalled-insns-dep=1'.

`-fsched2-use-superblocks`
When scheduling after register allocation, do use superblock scheduling algorithm. Superblock scheduling allows motion across basic block boundaries resulting on faster schedules. This option is experimental, as not all machine descriptions used by GCC model the CPU closely enough to avoid unreliable results from the algorithm.

This only makes sense when scheduling after register allocation, i.e. with '-fschedule-insns2' or at '-O2' or higher.

`-fsched2-use-traces`
Use '-fsched2-use-superblocks' algorithm when scheduling after register allocation and additionally perform code duplication in order to increase the size of superblocks using tracer pass. See '-ftracer' for details on trace formation.

This mode should produce faster but significantly longer programs. Also without '-fbranch-probabilities' the traces constructed may not match the reality and hurt the performance. This only makes sense when scheduling after register allocation, i.e. with '-fschedule-insns2' or at '-O2' or higher.

`-fsee` Eliminate redundant sign extension instructions and move the non-redundant ones to optimal placement using lazy code motion (LCM).

`-freschedule-modulo-scheduled-loops`
The modulo scheduling comes before the traditional scheduling, if a loop was modulo scheduled we may want to prevent the later scheduling passes from changing its schedule, we use this option to control that.

`-fcaller-saves`
Enable values to be allocated in registers that will be clobbered by function calls, by emitting extra instructions to save and restore the registers around such calls. Such allocation is done only when it seems to result in better code than would otherwise be produced.

This option is always enabled by default on certain machines, usually those which have no call-preserved registers to use instead.

Enabled at levels '-O2', '-O3', '-Os'.

`-ftree-reassoc`
Perform reassociation on trees. This flag is enabled by default at '-O' and higher.

`-ftree-pre`
Perform partial redundancy elimination (PRE) on trees. This flag is enabled by default at '-O2' and '-O3'.

`-ftree-fre`
Perform full redundancy elimination (FRE) on trees. The difference between FRE and PRE is that FRE only considers expressions that are computed on

all paths leading to the redundant computation. This analysis is faster than PRE, though it exposes fewer redundancies. This flag is enabled by default at '-O' and higher.

`-ftree-copy-prop`
: Perform copy propagation on trees. This pass eliminates unnecessary copy operations. This flag is enabled by default at '-O' and higher.

`-ftree-salias`
: Perform structural alias analysis on trees. This flag is enabled by default at '-O' and higher.

`-fipa-pure-const`
: Discover which functions are pure or constant. Enabled by default at '-O' and higher.

`-fipa-reference`
: Discover which static variables do not escape cannot escape the compilation unit. Enabled by default at '-O' and higher.

`-fipa-struct-reorg`
: Perform structure reorganization optimization, that change C-like structures layout in order to better utilize spatial locality. This transformation is affective for programs containing arrays of structures. Available in two compilation modes: profile-based (enabled with '-fprofile-generate') or static (which uses built-in heuristics). Require '-fipa-type-escape' to provide the safety of this transformation. It works only in whole program mode, so it requires '-fwhole-program' and '-combine' to be enabled. Structures considered 'cold' by this transformation are not affected (see '--param struct-reorg-cold-struct-ratio=value').

With this flag, the program debug info reflects a new structure layout.

`-fipa-pta`
: Perform interprocedural pointer analysis.

`-fipa-cp`
: Perform interprocedural constant propagation. This optimization analyzes the program to determine when values passed to functions are constants and then optimizes accordingly. This optimization can substantially increase performance if the application has constants passed to functions, but because this optimization can create multiple copies of functions, it may significantly increase code size.

`-fipa-matrix-reorg`
: Perform matrix flattening and transposing. Matrix flattening tries to replace a m-dimensional matrix with its equivalent n-dimensional matrix, where n < m. This reduces the level of indirection needed for accessing the elements of the matrix. The second optimization is matrix transposing that attemps to change the order of the matrix's dimensions in order to improve cache locality. Both optimizations need fwhole-program flag. Transposing is enabled only if profiling information is avaliable.

`-ftree-sink`
> Perform forward store motion on trees. This flag is enabled by default at '-O' and higher.

`-ftree-ccp`
> Perform sparse conditional constant propagation (CCP) on trees. This pass only operates on local scalar variables and is enabled by default at '-O' and higher.

`-ftree-store-ccp`
> Perform sparse conditional constant propagation (CCP) on trees. This pass operates on both local scalar variables and memory stores and loads (global variables, structures, arrays, etc). This flag is enabled by default at '-O2' and higher.

`-ftree-dce`
> Perform dead code elimination (DCE) on trees. This flag is enabled by default at '-O' and higher.

`-ftree-dominator-opts`
> Perform a variety of simple scalar cleanups (constant/copy propagation, redundancy elimination, range propagation and expression simplification) based on a dominator tree traversal. This also performs jump threading (to reduce jumps to jumps). This flag is enabled by default at '-O' and higher.

`-ftree-dse`
> Perform dead store elimination (DSE) on trees. A dead store is a store into a memory location which will later be overwritten by another store without any intervening loads. In this case the earlier store can be deleted. This flag is enabled by default at '-O' and higher.

`-ftree-ch`
> Perform loop header copying on trees. This is beneficial since it increases effectiveness of code motion optimizations. It also saves one jump. This flag is enabled by default at '-O' and higher. It is not enabled for '-Os', since it usually increases code size.

`-ftree-loop-optimize`
> Perform loop optimizations on trees. This flag is enabled by default at '-O' and higher.

`-ftree-loop-linear`
> Perform linear loop transformations on tree. This flag can improve cache performance and allow further loop optimizations to take place.

`-fcheck-data-deps`
> Compare the results of several data dependence analyzers. This option is used for debugging the data dependence analyzers.

`-ftree-loop-im`
> Perform loop invariant motion on trees. This pass moves only invariants that would be hard to handle at RTL level (function calls, operations that expand

to nontrivial sequences of insns). With '`-funswitch-loops`' it also moves operands of conditions that are invariant out of the loop, so that we can use just trivial invariantness analysis in loop unswitching. The pass also includes store motion.

`-ftree-loop-ivcanon`
: Create a canonical counter for number of iterations in the loop for that determining number of iterations requires complicated analysis. Later optimizations then may determine the number easily. Useful especially in connection with unrolling.

`-fivopts`
: Perform induction variable optimizations (strength reduction, induction variable merging and induction variable elimination) on trees.

`-ftree-parallelize-loops=n`
: Parallelize loops, i.e., split their iteration space to run in n threads. This is only possible for loops whose iterations are independent and can be arbitrarily reordered. The optimization is only profitable on multiprocessor machines, for loops that are CPU-intensive, rather than constrained e.g. by memory bandwidth. This option implies '`-pthread`', and thus is only supported on targets that have support for '`-pthread`'.

`-ftree-sra`
: Perform scalar replacement of aggregates. This pass replaces structure references with scalars to prevent committing structures to memory too early. This flag is enabled by default at '`-O`' and higher.

`-ftree-copyrename`
: Perform copy renaming on trees. This pass attempts to rename compiler temporaries to other variables at copy locations, usually resulting in variable names which more closely resemble the original variables. This flag is enabled by default at '`-O`' and higher.

`-ftree-ter`
: Perform temporary expression replacement during the SSA->normal phase. Single use/single def temporaries are replaced at their use location with their defining expression. This results in non-GIMPLE code, but gives the expanders much more complex trees to work on resulting in better RTL generation. This is enabled by default at '`-O`' and higher.

`-ftree-vectorize`
: Perform loop vectorization on trees. This flag is enabled by default at '`-O3`'.

`-ftree-vect-loop-version`
: Perform loop versioning when doing loop vectorization on trees. When a loop appears to be vectorizable except that data alignment or data dependence cannot be determined at compile time then vectorized and non-vectorized versions of the loop are generated along with runtime checks for alignment or dependence to control which version is executed. This option is enabled by default except at level '`-Os`' where it is disabled.

`-fvect-cost-model`
: Enable cost model for vectorization.

Chapter 3: GCC Command Options   91

`-ftree-vrp`
> Perform Value Range Propagation on trees. This is similar to the constant propagation pass, but instead of values, ranges of values are propagated. This allows the optimizers to remove unnecessary range checks like array bound checks and null pointer checks. This is enabled by default at '-O2' and higher. Null pointer check elimination is only done if '`-fdelete-null-pointer-checks`' is enabled.

`-ftracer` Perform tail duplication to enlarge superblock size. This transformation simplifies the control flow of the function allowing other optimizations to do better job.

`-funroll-loops`
> Unroll loops whose number of iterations can be determined at compile time or upon entry to the loop. '`-funroll-loops`' implies '`-frerun-cse-after-loop`'. This option makes code larger, and may or may not make it run faster.

`-funroll-all-loops`
> Unroll all loops, even if their number of iterations is uncertain when the loop is entered. This usually makes programs run more slowly. '`-funroll-all-loops`' implies the same options as '`-funroll-loops`',

`-fsplit-ivs-in-unroller`
> Enables expressing of values of induction variables in later iterations of the unrolled loop using the value in the first iteration. This breaks long dependency chains, thus improving efficiency of the scheduling passes.
>
> Combination of '`-fweb`' and CSE is often sufficient to obtain the same effect. However in cases the loop body is more complicated than a single basic block, this is not reliable. It also does not work at all on some of the architectures due to restrictions in the CSE pass.
>
> This optimization is enabled by default.

`-fvariable-expansion-in-unroller`
> With this option, the compiler will create multiple copies of some local variables when unrolling a loop which can result in superior code.

`-fpredictive-commoning`
> Perform predictive commoning optimization, i.e., reusing computations (especially memory loads and stores) performed in previous iterations of loops.
>
> This option is enabled at level '-O3'.

`-fprefetch-loop-arrays`
> If supported by the target machine, generate instructions to prefetch memory to improve the performance of loops that access large arrays.
>
> This option may generate better or worse code; results are highly dependent on the structure of loops within the source code.
>
> Disabled at level '-Os'.

`-fno-peephole`
`-fno-peephole2`
> Disable any machine-specific peephole optimizations. The difference between '`-fno-peephole`' and '`-fno-peephole2`' is in how they are implemented in the compiler; some targets use one, some use the other, a few use both.
>
> '`-fpeephole`' is enabled by default. '`-fpeephole2`' enabled at levels '`-O2`', '`-O3`', '`-Os`'.

`-fno-guess-branch-probability`
> Do not guess branch probabilities using heuristics.
>
> GCC will use heuristics to guess branch probabilities if they are not provided by profiling feedback ('`-fprofile-arcs`'). These heuristics are based on the control flow graph. If some branch probabilities are specified by '`__builtin_expect`', then the heuristics will be used to guess branch probabilities for the rest of the control flow graph, taking the '`__builtin_expect`' info into account. The interactions between the heuristics and '`__builtin_expect`' can be complex, and in some cases, it may be useful to disable the heuristics so that the effects of '`__builtin_expect`' are easier to understand.
>
> The default is '`-fguess-branch-probability`' at levels '`-O`', '`-O2`', '`-O3`', '`-Os`'.

`-freorder-blocks`
> Reorder basic blocks in the compiled function in order to reduce number of taken branches and improve code locality.
>
> Enabled at levels '`-O2`', '`-O3`'.

`-freorder-blocks-and-partition`
> In addition to reordering basic blocks in the compiled function, in order to reduce number of taken branches, partitions hot and cold basic blocks into separate sections of the assembly and .o files, to improve paging and cache locality performance.
>
> This optimization is automatically turned off in the presence of exception handling, for linkonce sections, for functions with a user-defined section attribute and on any architecture that does not support named sections.

`-freorder-functions`
> Reorder functions in the object file in order to improve code locality. This is implemented by using special subsections `.text.hot` for most frequently executed functions and `.text.unlikely` for unlikely executed functions. Reordering is done by the linker so object file format must support named sections and linker must place them in a reasonable way.
>
> Also profile feedback must be available in to make this option effective. See '`-fprofile-arcs`' for details.
>
> Enabled at levels '`-O2`', '`-O3`', '`-Os`'.

`-fstrict-aliasing`
> Allows the compiler to assume the strictest aliasing rules applicable to the language being compiled. For C (and C++), this activates optimizations based

on the type of expressions. In particular, an object of one type is assumed never to reside at the same address as an object of a different type, unless the types are almost the same. For example, an `unsigned int` can alias an `int`, but not a `void*` or a `double`. A character type may alias any other type.

Pay special attention to code like this:

```
union a_union {
  int i;
  double d;
};

int f() {
  a_union t;
  t.d = 3.0;
  return t.i;
}
```

The practice of reading from a different union member than the one most recently written to (called "type-punning") is common. Even with '-fstrict-aliasing', type-punning is allowed, provided the memory is accessed through the union type. So, the code above will work as expected. See Section 4.9 [Structures unions enumerations and bit-fields implementation], page 241. However, this code might not:

```
int f() {
  a_union t;
  int* ip;
  t.d = 3.0;
  ip = &t.i;
  return *ip;
}
```

Similarly, access by taking the address, casting the resulting pointer and dereferencing the result has undefined behavior, even if the cast uses a union type, e.g.:

```
int f() {
  double d = 3.0;
  return ((union a_union *) &d)->i;
}
```

The '-fstrict-aliasing' option is enabled at levels '-O2', '-O3', '-Os'.

`-fstrict-overflow`

Allow the compiler to assume strict signed overflow rules, depending on the language being compiled. For C (and C++) this means that overflow when doing arithmetic with signed numbers is undefined, which means that the compiler may assume that it will not happen. This permits various optimizations. For example, the compiler will assume that an expression like `i + 10 > i` will always be true for signed `i`. This assumption is only valid if signed overflow is undefined, as the expression is false if `i + 10` overflows when using twos complement arithmetic. When this option is in effect any attempt to determine whether an operation on signed numbers will overflow must be written carefully to not actually involve overflow.

This option also allows the compiler to assume strict pointer semantics: given a pointer to an object, if adding an offset to that pointer does not produce a pointer to the same object, the addition is undefined. This permits the compiler to conclude that `p + u > p` is always true for a pointer p and unsigned integer u. This assumption is only valid because pointer wraparound is undefined, as the expression is false if `p + u` overflows using twos complement arithmetic.

See also the '-fwrapv' option. Using '-fwrapv' means that integer signed overflow is fully defined: it wraps. When '-fwrapv' is used, there is no difference between '-fstrict-overflow' and '-fno-strict-overflow' for integers. With '-fwrapv' certain types of overflow are permitted. For example, if the compiler gets an overflow when doing arithmetic on constants, the overflowed value can still be used with '-fwrapv', but not otherwise.

The '-fstrict-overflow' option is enabled at levels '-O2', '-O3', '-Os'.

`-falign-functions`
`-falign-functions=n`

Align the start of functions to the next power-of-two greater than n, skipping up to n bytes. For instance, '-falign-functions=32' aligns functions to the next 32-byte boundary, but '-falign-functions=24' would align to the next 32-byte boundary only if this can be done by skipping 23 bytes or less.

'-fno-align-functions' and '-falign-functions=1' are equivalent and mean that functions will not be aligned.

Some assemblers only support this flag when n is a power of two; in that case, it is rounded up.

If n is not specified or is zero, use a machine-dependent default.

Enabled at levels '-O2', '-O3'.

`-falign-labels`
`-falign-labels=n`

Align all branch targets to a power-of-two boundary, skipping up to n bytes like '-falign-functions'. This option can easily make code slower, because it must insert dummy operations for when the branch target is reached in the usual flow of the code.

'-fno-align-labels' and '-falign-labels=1' are equivalent and mean that labels will not be aligned.

If '-falign-loops' or '-falign-jumps' are applicable and are greater than this value, then their values are used instead.

If n is not specified or is zero, use a machine-dependent default which is very likely to be '1', meaning no alignment.

Enabled at levels '-O2', '-O3'.

`-falign-loops`
`-falign-loops=n`

Align loops to a power-of-two boundary, skipping up to n bytes like '-falign-functions'. The hope is that the loop will be executed many times, which will make up for any execution of the dummy operations.

'-fno-align-loops' and '-falign-loops=1' are equivalent and mean that loops will not be aligned.

Chapter 3: GCC Command Options   95

If *n* is not specified or is zero, use a machine-dependent default.

Enabled at levels '-O2', '-O3'.

`-falign-jumps`
`-falign-jumps=n`

Align branch targets to a power-of-two boundary, for branch targets where the targets can only be reached by jumping, skipping up to *n* bytes like '`-falign-functions`'. In this case, no dummy operations need be executed.

'`-fno-align-jumps`' and '`-falign-jumps=1`' are equivalent and mean that loops will not be aligned.

If *n* is not specified or is zero, use a machine-dependent default.

Enabled at levels '-O2', '-O3'.

`-funit-at-a-time`

Parse the whole compilation unit before starting to produce code. This allows some extra optimizations to take place but consumes more memory (in general). There are some compatibility issues with *unit-at-a-time* mode:

- enabling *unit-at-a-time* mode may change the order in which functions, variables, and top-level `asm` statements are emitted, and will likely break code relying on some particular ordering. The majority of such top-level `asm` statements, though, can be replaced by `section` attributes. The '`fno-toplevel-reorder`' option may be used to keep the ordering used in the input file, at the cost of some optimizations.

- *unit-at-a-time* mode removes unreferenced static variables and functions. This may result in undefined references when an `asm` statement refers directly to variables or functions that are otherwise unused. In that case either the variable/function shall be listed as an operand of the `asm` statement operand or, in the case of top-level `asm` statements the attribute `used` shall be used on the declaration.

- Static functions now can use non-standard passing conventions that may break `asm` statements calling functions directly. Again, attribute `used` will prevent this behavior.

As a temporary workaround, '`-fno-unit-at-a-time`' can be used, but this scheme may not be supported by future releases of GCC.

Enabled at levels '-O', '-O2', '-O3', '-Os'.

`-fno-toplevel-reorder`

Do not reorder top-level functions, variables, and `asm` statements. Output them in the same order that they appear in the input file. When this option is used, unreferenced static variables will not be removed. This option is intended to support existing code which relies on a particular ordering. For new code, it is better to use attributes.

`-fweb`   Constructs webs as commonly used for register allocation purposes and assign each web individual pseudo register. This allows the register allocation pass to operate on pseudos directly, but also strengthens several other optimization passes, such as CSE, loop optimizer and trivial dead code remover. It can, however, make debugging impossible, since variables will no longer stay in a "home register".

Enabled by default with '-funroll-loops'.

-fwhole-program
Assume that the current compilation unit represents whole program being compiled. All public functions and variables with the exception of main and those merged by attribute externally_visible become static functions and in a affect gets more aggressively optimized by interprocedural optimizers. While this option is equivalent to proper use of static keyword for programs consisting of single file, in combination with option '--combine' this flag can be used to compile most of smaller scale C programs since the functions and variables become local for the whole combined compilation unit, not for the single source file itself.

This option is not supported for Fortran programs.

-fcprop-registers
After register allocation and post-register allocation instruction splitting, we perform a copy-propagation pass to try to reduce scheduling dependencies and occasionally eliminate the copy.

Enabled at levels '-O', '-O2', '-O3', '-Os'.

-fprofile-generate
Enable options usually used for instrumenting application to produce profile useful for later recompilation with profile feedback based optimization. You must use '-fprofile-generate' both when compiling and when linking your program.

The following options are enabled: -fprofile-arcs, -fprofile-values, -fvpt.

-fprofile-use
Enable profile feedback directed optimizations, and optimizations generally profitable only with profile feedback available.

The following options are enabled: -fbranch-probabilities, -fvpt, -funroll-loops, -fpeel-loops, -ftracer

By default, GCC emits an error message if the feedback profiles do not match the source code. This error can be turned into a warning by using '-Wcoverage-mismatch'. Note this may result in poorly optimized code.

The following options control compiler behavior regarding floating point arithmetic. These options trade off between speed and correctness. All must be specifically enabled.

-ffloat-store
Do not store floating point variables in registers, and inhibit other options that might change whether a floating point value is taken from a register or memory.

This option prevents undesirable excess precision on machines such as the 68000 where the floating registers (of the 68881) keep more precision than a double is supposed to have. Similarly for the x86 architecture. For most programs, the excess precision does only good, but a few programs rely on the precise

Chapter 3: GCC Command Options   97

definition of IEEE floating point. Use '-ffloat-store' for such programs, after modifying them to store all pertinent intermediate computations into variables.

`-ffast-math`
Sets '-fno-math-errno', '-funsafe-math-optimizations', '-ffinite-math-only', '-fno-rounding-math', '-fno-signaling-nans' and '-fcx-limited-range'.

This option causes the preprocessor macro `__FAST_MATH__` to be defined.

This option is not turned on by any '-O' option since it can result in incorrect output for programs which depend on an exact implementation of IEEE or ISO rules/specifications for math functions. It may, however, yield faster code for programs that do not require the guarantees of these specifications.

`-fno-math-errno`
Do not set ERRNO after calling math functions that are executed with a single instruction, e.g., sqrt. A program that relies on IEEE exceptions for math error handling may want to use this flag for speed while maintaining IEEE arithmetic compatibility.

This option is not turned on by any '-O' option since it can result in incorrect output for programs which depend on an exact implementation of IEEE or ISO rules/specifications for math functions. It may, however, yield faster code for programs that do not require the guarantees of these specifications.

The default is '-fmath-errno'.

On Darwin systems, the math library never sets **errno**. There is therefore no reason for the compiler to consider the possibility that it might, and '-fno-math-errno' is the default.

`-funsafe-math-optimizations`
Allow optimizations for floating-point arithmetic that (a) assume that arguments and results are valid and (b) may violate IEEE or ANSI standards. When used at link-time, it may include libraries or startup files that change the default FPU control word or other similar optimizations.

This option is not turned on by any '-O' option since it can result in incorrect output for programs which depend on an exact implementation of IEEE or ISO rules/specifications for math functions. It may, however, yield faster code for programs that do not require the guarantees of these specifications. Enables '-fno-signed-zeros', '-fno-trapping-math', '-fassociative-math' and '-freciprocal-math'.

The default is '-fno-unsafe-math-optimizations'.

`-fassociative-math`
Allow re-association of operands in series of floating-point operations. This violates the ISO C and C++ language standard by possibly changing computation result. NOTE: re-ordering may change the sign of zero as well as ignore NaNs and inhibit or create underflow or overflow (and thus cannot be used on a code which relies on rounding behavior like (x + 2**52) - 2**52). May also reorder floating-point comparisons and thus may not be used when ordered comparisons are required. This option requires that both '-fno-signed-zeros'

and '`-fno-trapping-math`' be in effect. Moreover, it doesn't make much sense with '`-frounding-math`'.

The default is '`-fno-associative-math`'.

`-freciprocal-math`
Allow the reciprocal of a value to be used instead of dividing by the value if this enables optimizations. For example x / y can be replaced with x * (1/y) which is useful if (1/y) is subject to common subexpression elimination. Note that this loses precision and increases the number of flops operating on the value.

The default is '`-fno-reciprocal-math`'.

`-ffinite-math-only`
Allow optimizations for floating-point arithmetic that assume that arguments and results are not NaNs or +-Infs.

This option is not turned on by any '`-O`' option since it can result in incorrect output for programs which depend on an exact implementation of IEEE or ISO rules/specifications for math functions. It may, however, yield faster code for programs that do not require the guarantees of these specifications.

The default is '`-fno-finite-math-only`'.

`-fno-signed-zeros`
Allow optimizations for floating point arithmetic that ignore the signedness of zero. IEEE arithmetic specifies the behavior of distinct +0.0 and −0.0 values, which then prohibits simplification of expressions such as x+0.0 or 0.0*x (even with '`-ffinite-math-only`'). This option implies that the sign of a zero result isn't significant.

The default is '`-fsigned-zeros`'.

`-fno-trapping-math`
Compile code assuming that floating-point operations cannot generate user-visible traps. These traps include division by zero, overflow, underflow, inexact result and invalid operation. This option requires that '`-fno-signaling-nans`' be in effect. Setting this option may allow faster code if one relies on "non-stop" IEEE arithmetic, for example.

This option should never be turned on by any '`-O`' option since it can result in incorrect output for programs which depend on an exact implementation of IEEE or ISO rules/specifications for math functions.

The default is '`-ftrapping-math`'.

`-frounding-math`
Disable transformations and optimizations that assume default floating point rounding behavior. This is round-to-zero for all floating point to integer conversions, and round-to-nearest for all other arithmetic truncations. This option should be specified for programs that change the FP rounding mode dynamically, or that may be executed with a non-default rounding mode. This option disables constant folding of floating point expressions at compile-time (which may be affected by rounding mode) and arithmetic transformations that are unsafe in the presence of sign-dependent rounding modes.

Chapter 3: GCC Command Options   99

> The default is '-fno-rounding-math'.
>
> This option is experimental and does not currently guarantee to disable all GCC optimizations that are affected by rounding mode. Future versions of GCC may provide finer control of this setting using C99's `FENV_ACCESS` pragma. This command line option will be used to specify the default state for `FENV_ACCESS`.

`-frtl-abstract-sequences`
> It is a size optimization method. This option is to find identical sequences of code, which can be turned into pseudo-procedures and then replace all occurrences with calls to the newly created subroutine. It is kind of an opposite of '-finline-functions'. This optimization runs at RTL level.

`-fsignaling-nans`
> Compile code assuming that IEEE signaling NaNs may generate user-visible traps during floating-point operations. Setting this option disables optimizations that may change the number of exceptions visible with signaling NaNs. This option implies '-ftrapping-math'.
>
> This option causes the preprocessor macro `__SUPPORT_SNAN__` to be defined.
>
> The default is '-fno-signaling-nans'.
>
> This option is experimental and does not currently guarantee to disable all GCC optimizations that affect signaling NaN behavior.

`-fsingle-precision-constant`
> Treat floating point constant as single precision constant instead of implicitly converting it to double precision constant.

`-fcx-limited-range`
> When enabled, this option states that a range reduction step is not needed when performing complex division. The default is '-fno-cx-limited-range', but is enabled by '-ffast-math'.
>
> This option controls the default setting of the ISO C99 `CX_LIMITED_RANGE` pragma. Nevertheless, the option applies to all languages.

The following options control optimizations that may improve performance, but are not enabled by any '-O' options. This section includes experimental options that may produce broken code.

`-fbranch-probabilities`
> After running a program compiled with '-fprofile-arcs' (see Section 3.9 [Options for Debugging Your Program or gcc], page 63), you can compile it a second time using '-fbranch-probabilities', to improve optimizations based on the number of times each branch was taken. When the program compiled with '-fprofile-arcs' exits it saves arc execution counts to a file called '*sourcename*.gcda' for each source file. The information in this data file is very dependent on the structure of the generated code, so you must use the same source code and the same optimization options for both compilations.
>
> With '-fbranch-probabilities', GCC puts a 'REG_BR_PROB' note on each 'JUMP_INSN' and 'CALL_INSN'. These can be used to improve optimization. Currently, they are only used in one place: in 'reorg.c', instead of guessing

which path a branch is mostly to take, the 'REG_BR_PROB' values are used to exactly determine which path is taken more often.

`-fprofile-values`

If combined with '`-fprofile-arcs`', it adds code so that some data about values of expressions in the program is gathered.

With '`-fbranch-probabilities`', it reads back the data gathered from profiling values of expressions and adds 'REG_VALUE_PROFILE' notes to instructions for their later usage in optimizations.

Enabled with '`-fprofile-generate`' and '`-fprofile-use`'.

`-fvpt`   If combined with '`-fprofile-arcs`', it instructs the compiler to add a code to gather information about values of expressions.

With '`-fbranch-probabilities`', it reads back the data gathered and actually performs the optimizations based on them. Currently the optimizations include specialization of division operation using the knowledge about the value of the denominator.

`-frename-registers`

Attempt to avoid false dependencies in scheduled code by making use of registers left over after register allocation. This optimization will most benefit processors with lots of registers. Depending on the debug information format adopted by the target, however, it can make debugging impossible, since variables will no longer stay in a "home register".

Enabled by default with '`-funroll-loops`'.

`-ftracer`   Perform tail duplication to enlarge superblock size. This transformation simplifies the control flow of the function allowing other optimizations to do better job.

Enabled with '`-fprofile-use`'.

`-funroll-loops`

Unroll loops whose number of iterations can be determined at compile time or upon entry to the loop. '`-funroll-loops`' implies '`-frerun-cse-after-loop`', '`-fweb`' and '`-frename-registers`'. It also turns on complete loop peeling (i.e. complete removal of loops with small constant number of iterations). This option makes code larger, and may or may not make it run faster.

Enabled with '`-fprofile-use`'.

`-funroll-all-loops`

Unroll all loops, even if their number of iterations is uncertain when the loop is entered. This usually makes programs run more slowly. '`-funroll-all-loops`' implies the same options as '`-funroll-loops`'.

`-fpeel-loops`

Peels the loops for that there is enough information that they do not roll much (from profile feedback). It also turns on complete loop peeling (i.e. complete removal of loops with small constant number of iterations).

Enabled with '`-fprofile-use`'.

Chapter 3: GCC Command Options   101

`-fmove-loop-invariants`
> Enables the loop invariant motion pass in the RTL loop optimizer. Enabled at level '-O1'

`-funswitch-loops`
> Move branches with loop invariant conditions out of the loop, with duplicates of the loop on both branches (modified according to result of the condition).

`-ffunction-sections`
`-fdata-sections`
> Place each function or data item into its own section in the output file if the target supports arbitrary sections. The name of the function or the name of the data item determines the section's name in the output file.
>
> Use these options on systems where the linker can perform optimizations to improve locality of reference in the instruction space. Most systems using the ELF object format and SPARC processors running Solaris 2 have linkers with such optimizations. AIX may have these optimizations in the future.
>
> Only use these options when there are significant benefits from doing so. When you specify these options, the assembler and linker will create larger object and executable files and will also be slower. You will not be able to use **gprof** on all systems if you specify this option and you may have problems with debugging if you specify both this option and '-g'.

`-fbranch-target-load-optimize`
> Perform branch target register load optimization before prologue / epilogue threading. The use of target registers can typically be exposed only during reload, thus hoisting loads out of loops and doing inter-block scheduling needs a separate optimization pass.

`-fbranch-target-load-optimize2`
> Perform branch target register load optimization after prologue / epilogue threading.

`-fbtr-bb-exclusive`
> When performing branch target register load optimization, don't reuse branch target registers in within any basic block.

`-fstack-protector`
> Emit extra code to check for buffer overflows, such as stack smashing attacks. This is done by adding a guard variable to functions with vulnerable objects. This includes functions that call alloca, and functions with buffers larger than 8 bytes. The guards are initialized when a function is entered and then checked when the function exits. If a guard check fails, an error message is printed and the program exits.

`-fstack-protector-all`
> Like '-fstack-protector' except that all functions are protected.

`-fsection-anchors`
> Try to reduce the number of symbolic address calculations by using shared "anchor" symbols to address nearby objects. This transformation can help to reduce the number of GOT entries and GOT accesses on some targets.

For example, the implementation of the following function `foo`:
```
static int a, b, c;
int foo (void) { return a + b + c; }
```
would usually calculate the addresses of all three variables, but if you compile it with '-fsection-anchors', it will access the variables from a common anchor point instead. The effect is similar to the following pseudocode (which isn't valid C):
```
int foo (void)
{
  register int *xr = &x;
  return xr[&a - &x] + xr[&b - &x] + xr[&c - &x];
}
```
Not all targets support this option.

`--param` *name*=*value*

In some places, GCC uses various constants to control the amount of optimization that is done. For example, GCC will not inline functions that contain more that a certain number of instructions. You can control some of these constants on the command-line using the '`--param`' option.

The names of specific parameters, and the meaning of the values, are tied to the internals of the compiler, and are subject to change without notice in future releases.

In each case, the *value* is an integer. The allowable choices for *name* are given in the following table:

`salias-max-implicit-fields`
: The maximum number of fields in a variable without direct structure accesses for which structure aliasing will consider trying to track each field. The default is 5

`salias-max-array-elements`
: The maximum number of elements an array can have and its elements still be tracked individually by structure aliasing. The default is 4

`sra-max-structure-size`
: The maximum structure size, in bytes, at which the scalar replacement of aggregates (SRA) optimization will perform block copies. The default value, 0, implies that GCC will select the most appropriate size itself.

`sra-field-structure-ratio`
: The threshold ratio (as a percentage) between instantiated fields and the complete structure size. We say that if the ratio of the number of bytes in instantiated fields to the number of bytes in the complete structure exceeds this parameter, then block copies are not used. The default is 75.

`struct-reorg-cold-struct-ratio`
: The threshold ratio (as a percentage) between a structure frequency and the frequency of the hottest structure in the

Chapter 3: GCC Command Options   103

program. This parameter is used by struct-reorg optimization enabled by '-fipa-struct-reorg'. We say that if the ratio of a structure frequency, calculated by profiling, to the hottest structure frequency in the program is less than this parameter, then structure reorganization is not applied to this structure. The default is 10.

`max-crossjump-edges`

The maximum number of incoming edges to consider for crossjumping. The algorithm used by '-fcrossjumping' is $O(N^2)$ in the number of edges incoming to each block. Increasing values mean more aggressive optimization, making the compile time increase with probably small improvement in executable size.

`min-crossjump-insns`

The minimum number of instructions which must be matched at the end of two blocks before crossjumping will be performed on them. This value is ignored in the case where all instructions in the block being crossjumped from are matched. The default value is 5.

`max-grow-copy-bb-insns`

The maximum code size expansion factor when copying basic blocks instead of jumping. The expansion is relative to a jump instruction. The default value is 8.

`max-goto-duplication-insns`

The maximum number of instructions to duplicate to a block that jumps to a computed goto. To avoid $O(N^2)$ behavior in a number of passes, GCC factors computed gotos early in the compilation process, and unfactors them as late as possible. Only computed jumps at the end of a basic blocks with no more than max-goto-duplication-insns are unfactored. The default value is 8.

`max-delay-slot-insn-search`

The maximum number of instructions to consider when looking for an instruction to fill a delay slot. If more than this arbitrary number of instructions is searched, the time savings from filling the delay slot will be minimal so stop searching. Increasing values mean more aggressive optimization, making the compile time increase with probably small improvement in executable run time.

`max-delay-slot-live-search`

When trying to fill delay slots, the maximum number of instructions to consider when searching for a block with valid live register information. Increasing this arbitrarily chosen value means more aggressive optimization, increasing the compile time. This parameter should be removed when the delay slot code is rewritten to maintain the control-flow graph.

`max-gcse-memory`
: The approximate maximum amount of memory that will be allocated in order to perform the global common subexpression elimination optimization. If more memory than specified is required, the optimization will not be done.

`max-gcse-passes`
: The maximum number of passes of GCSE to run. The default is 1.

`max-pending-list-length`
: The maximum number of pending dependencies scheduling will allow before flushing the current state and starting over. Large functions with few branches or calls can create excessively large lists which needlessly consume memory and resources.

`max-inline-insns-single`
: Several parameters control the tree inliner used in gcc. This number sets the maximum number of instructions (counted in GCC's internal representation) in a single function that the tree inliner will consider for inlining. This only affects functions declared inline and methods implemented in a class declaration (C++). The default value is 450.

`max-inline-insns-auto`
: When you use '-finline-functions' (included in '-O3'), a lot of functions that would otherwise not be considered for inlining by the compiler will be investigated. To those functions, a different (more restrictive) limit compared to functions declared inline can be applied. The default value is 90.

`large-function-insns`
: The limit specifying really large functions. For functions larger than this limit after inlining inlining is constrained by '--param large-function-growth'. This parameter is useful primarily to avoid extreme compilation time caused by non-linear algorithms used by the backend. This parameter is ignored when '-funit-at-a-time' is not used. The default value is 2700.

`large-function-growth`
: Specifies maximal growth of large function caused by inlining in percents. This parameter is ignored when '-funit-at-a-time' is not used. The default value is 100 which limits large function growth to 2.0 times the original size.

`large-unit-insns`
: The limit specifying large translation unit. Growth caused by inlining of units larger than this limit is limited by '--param inline-unit-growth'. For small units this might be too tight (consider unit consisting of function A that is inline and B that just calls A three time. If B is small relative to A, the growth of unit is 300\% and yet such inlining is very sane. For

very large units consisting of small inlineable functions however the overall unit growth limit is needed to avoid exponential explosion of code size. Thus for smaller units, the size is increased to '--param large-unit-insns' before applying '--param inline-unit-growth'. The default is 10000

`inline-unit-growth`
: Specifies maximal overall growth of the compilation unit caused by inlining. This parameter is ignored when '-funit-at-a-time' is not used. The default value is 30 which limits unit growth to 1.3 times the original size.

`large-stack-frame`
: The limit specifying large stack frames. While inlining the algorithm is trying to not grow past this limit too much. Default value is 256 bytes.

`large-stack-frame-growth`
: Specifies maximal growth of large stack frames caused by inlining in percents. The default value is 1000 which limits large stack frame growth to 11 times the original size.

`max-inline-insns-recursive`
`max-inline-insns-recursive-auto`
: Specifies maximum number of instructions out-of-line copy of self recursive inline function can grow into by performing recursive inlining.

  For functions declared inline '--param max-inline-insns-recursive' is taken into account. For function not declared inline, recursive inlining happens only when '-finline-functions' (included in '-O3') is enabled and '--param max-inline-insns-recursive-auto' is used. The default value is 450.

`max-inline-recursive-depth`
`max-inline-recursive-depth-auto`
: Specifies maximum recursion depth used by the recursive inlining.

  For functions declared inline '--param max-inline-recursive-depth' is taken into account. For function not declared inline, recursive inlining happens only when '-finline-functions' (included in '-O3') is enabled and '--param max-inline-recursive-depth-auto' is used. The default value is 8.

`min-inline-recursive-probability`
: Recursive inlining is profitable only for function having deep recursion in average and can hurt for function having little recursion depth by increasing the prologue size or complexity of function body to other optimizers.

  When profile feedback is available (see '-fprofile-generate') the actual recursion depth can be guessed from probability that function will recurse via given call expression. This parameter limits inlining only to call expression whose probability exceeds given threshold (in percents). The default value is 10.

`inline-call-cost`
: Specify cost of call instruction relative to simple arithmetics operations (having cost of 1). Increasing this cost disqualifies inlining of non-leaf functions and at the same time increases size of leaf function that is believed to reduce function size by being inlined. In effect it increases amount of inlining for code having large abstraction penalty (many functions that just pass the arguments to other functions) and decrease inlining for code with low abstraction penalty. The default value is 12.

`min-vect-loop-bound`
: The minimum number of iterations under which a loop will not get vectorized when '`-ftree-vectorize`' is used. The number of iterations after vectorization needs to be greater than the value specified by this option to allow vectorization. The default value is 0.

`max-unrolled-insns`
: The maximum number of instructions that a loop should have if that loop is unrolled, and if the loop is unrolled, it determines how many times the loop code is unrolled.

`max-average-unrolled-insns`
: The maximum number of instructions biased by probabilities of their execution that a loop should have if that loop is unrolled, and if the loop is unrolled, it determines how many times the loop code is unrolled.

`max-unroll-times`
: The maximum number of unrollings of a single loop.

`max-peeled-insns`
: The maximum number of instructions that a loop should have if that loop is peeled, and if the loop is peeled, it determines how many times the loop code is peeled.

`max-peel-times`
: The maximum number of peelings of a single loop.

`max-completely-peeled-insns`
: The maximum number of insns of a completely peeled loop.

`max-completely-peel-times`
: The maximum number of iterations of a loop to be suitable for complete peeling.

`max-unswitch-insns`
: The maximum number of insns of an unswitched loop.

`max-unswitch-level`
: The maximum number of branches unswitched in a single loop.

Chapter 3: GCC Command Options   107

`lim-expensive`
> The minimum cost of an expensive expression in the loop invariant motion.

`iv-consider-all-candidates-bound`
> Bound on number of candidates for induction variables below that all candidates are considered for each use in induction variable optimizations. Only the most relevant candidates are considered if there are more candidates, to avoid quadratic time complexity.

`iv-max-considered-uses`
> The induction variable optimizations give up on loops that contain more induction variable uses.

`iv-always-prune-cand-set-bound`
> If number of candidates in the set is smaller than this value, we always try to remove unnecessary ivs from the set during its optimization when a new iv is added to the set.

`scev-max-expr-size`
> Bound on size of expressions used in the scalar evolutions analyzer. Large expressions slow the analyzer.

`omega-max-vars`
> The maximum number of variables in an Omega constraint system. The default value is 128.

`omega-max-geqs`
> The maximum number of inequalities in an Omega constraint system. The default value is 256.

`omega-max-eqs`
> The maximum number of equalities in an Omega constraint system. The default value is 128.

`omega-max-wild-cards`
> The maximum number of wildcard variables that the Omega solver will be able to insert. The default value is 18.

`omega-hash-table-size`
> The size of the hash table in the Omega solver. The default value is 550.

`omega-max-keys`
> The maximal number of keys used by the Omega solver. The default value is 500.

`omega-eliminate-redundant-constraints`
> When set to 1, use expensive methods to eliminate all redundant constraints. The default value is 0.

`vect-max-version-for-alignment-checks`
> The maximum number of runtime checks that can be performed when doing loop versioning for alignment in the vectorizer. See option ftree-vect-loop-version for more information.

`vect-max-version-for-alias-checks`
> The maximum number of runtime checks that can be performed when doing loop versioning for alias in the vectorizer. See option ftree-vect-loop-version for more information.

`max-iterations-to-track`
> The maximum number of iterations of a loop the brute force algorithm for analysis of # of iterations of the loop tries to evaluate.

`hot-bb-count-fraction`
> Select fraction of the maximal count of repetitions of basic block in program given basic block needs to have to be considered hot.

`hot-bb-frequency-fraction`
> Select fraction of the maximal frequency of executions of basic block in function given basic block needs to have to be considered hot

`max-predicted-iterations`
> The maximum number of loop iterations we predict statically. This is useful in cases where function contain single loop with known bound and other loop with unknown. We predict the known number of iterations correctly, while the unknown number of iterations average to roughly 10. This means that the loop without bounds would appear artificially cold relative to the other one.

`align-threshold`
> Select fraction of the maximal frequency of executions of basic block in function given basic block will get aligned.

`align-loop-iterations`
> A loop expected to iterate at lest the selected number of iterations will get aligned.

`tracer-dynamic-coverage`
`tracer-dynamic-coverage-feedback`
> This value is used to limit superblock formation once the given percentage of executed instructions is covered. This limits unnecessary code size expansion.
>
> The '`tracer-dynamic-coverage-feedback`' is used only when profile feedback is available. The real profiles (as opposed to statically estimated ones) are much less balanced allowing the threshold to be larger value.

`tracer-max-code-growth`
> Stop tail duplication once code growth has reached given percentage. This is rather hokey argument, as most of the duplicates will be eliminated later in cross jumping, so it may be set to much higher values than is the desired code growth.

`tracer-min-branch-ratio`
> Stop reverse growth when the reverse probability of best edge is less than this threshold (in percent).

Chapter 3: GCC Command Options   109

`tracer-min-branch-ratio`
`tracer-min-branch-ratio-feedback`
: Stop forward growth if the best edge do have probability lower than this threshold.

    Similarly to '`tracer-dynamic-coverage`' two values are present, one for compilation for profile feedback and one for compilation without. The value for compilation with profile feedback needs to be more conservative (higher) in order to make tracer effective.

`max-cse-path-length`
: Maximum number of basic blocks on path that cse considers. The default is 10.

`max-cse-insns`
: The maximum instructions CSE process before flushing. The default is 1000.

`max-aliased-vops`
: Maximum number of virtual operands per function allowed to represent aliases before triggering the alias partitioning heuristic. Alias partitioning reduces compile times and memory consumption needed for aliasing at the expense of precision loss in alias information. The default value for this parameter is 100 for -O1, 500 for -O2 and 1000 for -O3.

    Notice that if a function contains more memory statements than the value of this parameter, it is not really possible to achieve this reduction. In this case, the compiler will use the number of memory statements as the value for '`max-aliased-vops`'.

`avg-aliased-vops`
: Average number of virtual operands per statement allowed to represent aliases before triggering the alias partitioning heuristic. This works in conjunction with '`max-aliased-vops`'. If a function contains more than '`max-aliased-vops`' virtual operators, then memory symbols will be grouped into memory partitions until either the total number of virtual operators is below '`max-aliased-vops`' or the average number of virtual operators per memory statement is below '`avg-aliased-vops`'. The default value for this parameter is 1 for -O1 and -O2, and 3 for -O3.

`ggc-min-expand`
: GCC uses a garbage collector to manage its own memory allocation. This parameter specifies the minimum percentage by which the garbage collector's heap should be allowed to expand between collections. Tuning this may improve compilation speed; it has no effect on code generation.

    The default is 30% + 70% * (RAM/1GB) with an upper bound of 100% when RAM >= 1GB. If `getrlimit` is available, the notion of "RAM" is the smallest of actual RAM and `RLIMIT_DATA` or

RLIMIT_AS. If GCC is not able to calculate RAM on a particular platform, the lower bound of 30% is used. Setting this parameter and 'ggc-min-heapsize' to zero causes a full collection to occur at every opportunity. This is extremely slow, but can be useful for debugging.

ggc-min-heapsize

Minimum size of the garbage collector's heap before it begins bothering to collect garbage. The first collection occurs after the heap expands by 'ggc-min-expand'% beyond 'ggc-min-heapsize'. Again, tuning this may improve compilation speed, and has no effect on code generation.

The default is the smaller of RAM/8, RLIMIT_RSS, or a limit which tries to ensure that RLIMIT_DATA or RLIMIT_AS are not exceeded, but with a lower bound of 4096 (four megabytes) and an upper bound of 131072 (128 megabytes). If GCC is not able to calculate RAM on a particular platform, the lower bound is used. Setting this parameter very large effectively disables garbage collection. Setting this parameter and 'ggc-min-expand' to zero causes a full collection to occur at every opportunity.

max-reload-search-insns

The maximum number of instruction reload should look backward for equivalent register. Increasing values mean more aggressive optimization, making the compile time increase with probably slightly better performance. The default value is 100.

max-cselib-memory-locations

The maximum number of memory locations cselib should take into account. Increasing values mean more aggressive optimization, making the compile time increase with probably slightly better performance. The default value is 500.

max-flow-memory-locations

Similar as 'max-cselib-memory-locations' but for dataflow liveness. The default value is 100.

reorder-blocks-duplicate
reorder-blocks-duplicate-feedback

Used by basic block reordering pass to decide whether to use unconditional branch or duplicate the code on its destination. Code is duplicated when its estimated size is smaller than this value multiplied by the estimated size of unconditional jump in the hot spots of the program.

The 'reorder-block-duplicate-feedback' is used only when profile feedback is available and may be set to higher values than 'reorder-block-duplicate' since information about the hot spots is more accurate.

Chapter 3: GCC Command Options   111

`max-sched-ready-insns`
: The maximum number of instructions ready to be issued the scheduler should consider at any given time during the first scheduling pass. Increasing values mean more thorough searches, making the compilation time increase with probably little benefit. The default value is 100.

`max-sched-region-blocks`
: The maximum number of blocks in a region to be considered for interblock scheduling. The default value is 10.

`max-sched-region-insns`
: The maximum number of insns in a region to be considered for interblock scheduling. The default value is 100.

`min-spec-prob`
: The minimum probability (in percents) of reaching a source block for interblock speculative scheduling. The default value is 40.

`max-sched-extend-regions-iters`
: The maximum number of iterations through CFG to extend regions. 0 - disable region extension, N - do at most N iterations. The default value is 0.

`max-sched-insn-conflict-delay`
: The maximum conflict delay for an insn to be considered for speculative motion. The default value is 3.

`sched-spec-prob-cutoff`
: The minimal probability of speculation success (in percents), so that speculative insn will be scheduled. The default value is 40.

`max-last-value-rtl`
: The maximum size measured as number of RTLs that can be recorded in an expression in combiner for a pseudo register as last known value of that register. The default is 10000.

`integer-share-limit`
: Small integer constants can use a shared data structure, reducing the compiler's memory usage and increasing its speed. This sets the maximum value of a shared integer constant. The default value is 256.

`min-virtual-mappings`
: Specifies the minimum number of virtual mappings in the incremental SSA updater that should be registered to trigger the virtual mappings heuristic defined by virtual-mappings-ratio. The default value is 100.

`virtual-mappings-ratio`
: If the number of virtual mappings is virtual-mappings-ratio bigger than the number of virtual symbols to be updated, then the incre-

mental SSA updater switches to a full update for those symbols. The default ratio is 3.

`ssp-buffer-size`
: The minimum size of buffers (i.e. arrays) that will receive stack smashing protection when '`-fstack-protection`' is used.

`max-jump-thread-duplication-stmts`
: Maximum number of statements allowed in a block that needs to be duplicated when threading jumps.

`max-fields-for-field-sensitive`
: Maximum number of fields in a structure we will treat in a field sensitive manner during pointer analysis. The default is zero for -O0, and -O1 and 100 for -Os, -O2, and -O3.

`prefetch-latency`
: Estimate on average number of instructions that are executed before prefetch finishes. The distance we prefetch ahead is proportional to this constant. Increasing this number may also lead to less streams being prefetched (see '`simultaneous-prefetches`').

`simultaneous-prefetches`
: Maximum number of prefetches that can run at the same time.

`l1-cache-line-size`
: The size of cache line in L1 cache, in bytes.

`l1-cache-size`
: The size of L1 cache, in kilobytes.

`l2-cache-size`
: The size of L2 cache, in kilobytes.

`use-canonical-types`
: Whether the compiler should use the "canonical" type system. By default, this should always be 1, which uses a more efficient internal mechanism for comparing types in C++ and Objective-C++. However, if bugs in the canonical type system are causing compilation failures, set this value to 0 to disable canonical types.

`max-partial-antic-length`
: Maximum length of the partial antic set computed during the tree partial redundancy elimination optimization ('`-ftree-pre`') when optimizing at '`-O3`' and above. For some sorts of source code the enhanced partial redundancy elimination optimization can run away, consuming all of the memory available on the host machine. This parameter sets a limit on the length of the sets that are computed, which prevents the runaway behaviour. Setting a value of 0 for this parameter will allow an unlimited set length.

`sccvn-max-scc-size`
: Maximum size of a strongly connected component (SCC) during SCCVN processing. If this limit is hit, SCCVN processing for the

Chapter 3: GCC Command Options   113

whole function will not be done and optimizations depending on it will be disabled. The default maximum SCC size is 10000.

3.11 Options Controlling the Preprocessor

These options control the C preprocessor, which is run on each C source file before actual compilation.

If you use the '-E' option, nothing is done except preprocessing. Some of these options make sense only together with '-E' because they cause the preprocessor output to be unsuitable for actual compilation.

> You can use '-Wp,*option*' to bypass the compiler driver and pass *option* directly through to the preprocessor. If *option* contains commas, it is split into multiple options at the commas. However, many options are modified, translated or interpreted by the compiler driver before being passed to the preprocessor, and '-Wp' forcibly bypasses this phase. The preprocessor's direct interface is undocumented and subject to change, so whenever possible you should avoid using '-Wp' and let the driver handle the options instead.

`-Xpreprocessor` *option*

> Pass *option* as an option to the preprocessor. You can use this to supply system-specific preprocessor options which GCC does not know how to recognize.
>
> If you want to pass an option that takes an argument, you must use '-Xpreprocessor' twice, once for the option and once for the argument.

`-D` *name*   Predefine *name* as a macro, with definition 1.

`-D` *name=definition*

> The contents of *definition* are tokenized and processed as if they appeared during translation phase three in a '#define' directive. In particular, the definition will be truncated by embedded newline characters.
>
> If you are invoking the preprocessor from a shell or shell-like program you may need to use the shell's quoting syntax to protect characters such as spaces that have a meaning in the shell syntax.
>
> If you wish to define a function-like macro on the command line, write its argument list with surrounding parentheses before the equals sign (if any). Parentheses are meaningful to most shells, so you will need to quote the option. With sh and csh, '-D'*name(args...)=definition*'' works.
>
> '-D' and '-U' options are processed in the order they are given on the command line. All '-imacros *file*' and '-include *file*' options are processed after all '-D' and '-U' options.

`-U` *name*   Cancel any previous definition of *name*, either built in or provided with a '-D' option.

`-undef`   Do not predefine any system-specific or GCC-specific macros. The standard predefined macros remain defined.

`-I` *dir*   Add the directory *dir* to the list of directories to be searched for header files. Directories named by '-I' are searched before the standard system include directories. If the directory *dir* is a standard system include directory, the option is ignored to ensure that the default search order for system directories and the special treatment of system headers are not defeated. If *dir* begins with =, then the = will be replaced by the sysroot prefix; see '`--sysroot`' and '`-isysroot`'.

`-o file` Write output to *file*. This is the same as specifying *file* as the second non-option argument to `cpp`. `gcc` has a different interpretation of a second non-option argument, so you must use '-o' to specify the output file.

`-Wall` Turns on all optional warnings which are desirable for normal code. At present this is '`-Wcomment`', '`-Wtrigraphs`', '`-Wmultichar`' and a warning about integer promotion causing a change of sign in `#if` expressions. Note that many of the preprocessor's warnings are on by default and have no options to control them.

`-Wcomment`
`-Wcomments`
Warn whenever a comment-start sequence '/*' appears in a '/*' comment, or whenever a backslash-newline appears in a '//' comment. (Both forms have the same effect.)

`-Wtrigraphs`
Most trigraphs in comments cannot affect the meaning of the program. However, a trigraph that would form an escaped newline ('??/' at the end of a line) can, by changing where the comment begins or ends. Therefore, only trigraphs that would form escaped newlines produce warnings inside a comment.

This option is implied by '`-Wall`'. If '`-Wall`' is not given, this option is still enabled unless trigraphs are enabled. To get trigraph conversion without warnings, but get the other '`-Wall`' warnings, use '`-trigraphs -Wall -Wno-trigraphs`'.

`-Wtraditional`
Warn about certain constructs that behave differently in traditional and ISO C. Also warn about ISO C constructs that have no traditional C equivalent, and problematic constructs which should be avoided.

`-Wimport` Warn the first time '`#import`' is used.

`-Wundef` Warn whenever an identifier which is not a macro is encountered in an '`#if`' directive, outside of '`defined`'. Such identifiers are replaced with zero.

`-Wunused-macros`
Warn about macros defined in the main file that are unused. A macro is *used* if it is expanded or tested for existence at least once. The preprocessor will also warn if the macro has not been used at the time it is redefined or undefined.

Built-in macros, macros defined on the command line, and macros defined in include files are not warned about.

Note: If a macro is actually used, but only used in skipped conditional blocks, then CPP will report it as unused. To avoid the warning in such a case, you might improve the scope of the macro's definition by, for example, moving it into the first skipped block. Alternatively, you could provide a dummy use with something like:

Chapter 3: GCC Command Options   115

```
#if defined the_macro_causing_the_warning
#endif
```

-Wendif-labels
: Warn whenever an '#else' or an '#endif' are followed by text. This usually happens in code of the form

```
#if FOO
 ...
#else FOO
 ...
#endif FOO
```

The second and third FOO should be in comments, but often are not in older programs. This warning is on by default.

-Werror
: Make all warnings into hard errors. Source code which triggers warnings will be rejected.

-Wsystem-headers
: Issue warnings for code in system headers. These are normally unhelpful in finding bugs in your own code, therefore suppressed. If you are responsible for the system library, you may want to see them.

-w
: Suppress all warnings, including those which GNU CPP issues by default.

-pedantic
: Issue all the mandatory diagnostics listed in the C standard. Some of them are left out by default, since they trigger frequently on harmless code.

-pedantic-errors
: Issue all the mandatory diagnostics, and make all mandatory diagnostics into errors. This includes mandatory diagnostics that GCC issues without '-pedantic' but treats as warnings.

-M
: Instead of outputting the result of preprocessing, output a rule suitable for make describing the dependencies of the main source file. The preprocessor outputs one make rule containing the object file name for that source file, a colon, and the names of all the included files, including those coming from '-include' or '-imacros' command line options.

Unless specified explicitly (with '-MT' or '-MQ'), the object file name consists of the name of the source file with any suffix replaced with object file suffix and with any leading directory parts removed. If there are many included files then the rule is split into several lines using '\'-newline. The rule has no commands.

This option does not suppress the preprocessor's debug output, such as '-dM'. To avoid mixing such debug output with the dependency rules you should explicitly specify the dependency output file with '-MF', or use an environment variable like DEPENDENCIES_OUTPUT (see Section 3.19 [Environment Variables], page 229). Debug output will still be sent to the regular output stream as normal.

Passing '-M' to the driver implies '-E', and suppresses warnings with an implicit '-w'.

`-MM` Like '`-M`' but do not mention header files that are found in system header directories, nor header files that are included, directly or indirectly, from such a header.

This implies that the choice of angle brackets or double quotes in an '`#include`' directive does not in itself determine whether that header will appear in '`-MM`' dependency output. This is a slight change in semantics from GCC versions 3.0 and earlier.

`-MF file` When used with '`-M`' or '`-MM`', specifies a file to write the dependencies to. If no '`-MF`' switch is given the preprocessor sends the rules to the same place it would have sent preprocessed output.

When used with the driver options '`-MD`' or '`-MMD`', '`-MF`' overrides the default dependency output file.

`-MG` In conjunction with an option such as '`-M`' requesting dependency generation, '`-MG`' assumes missing header files are generated files and adds them to the dependency list without raising an error. The dependency filename is taken directly from the `#include` directive without prepending any path. '`-MG`' also suppresses preprocessed output, as a missing header file renders this useless.

This feature is used in automatic updating of makefiles.

`-MP` This option instructs CPP to add a phony target for each dependency other than the main file, causing each to depend on nothing. These dummy rules work around errors `make` gives if you remove header files without updating the '`Makefile`' to match.

This is typical output:

```
test.o: test.c test.h

test.h:
```

`-MT target` Change the target of the rule emitted by dependency generation. By default CPP takes the name of the main input file, deletes any directory components and any file suffix such as '`.c`', and appends the platform's usual object suffix. The result is the target.

An '`-MT`' option will set the target to be exactly the string you specify. If you want multiple targets, you can specify them as a single argument to '`-MT`', or use multiple '`-MT`' options.

For example, '`-MT '$(objpfx)foo.o`'' might give

```
$(objpfx)foo.o: foo.c
```

`-MQ target` Same as '`-MT`', but it quotes any characters which are special to Make. '`-MQ '$(objpfx)foo.o`'' gives

```
$$(objpfx)foo.o: foo.c
```

The default target is automatically quoted, as if it were given with '`-MQ`'.

`-MD` '`-MD`' is equivalent to '`-M -MF file`', except that '`-E`' is not implied. The driver determines *file* based on whether an '`-o`' option is given. If it is, the driver uses

Chapter 3: GCC Command Options   117

its argument but with a suffix of '.d', otherwise it takes the name of the input file, removes any directory components and suffix, and applies a '.d' suffix.

If '-MD' is used in conjunction with '-E', any '-o' switch is understood to specify the dependency output file (see [-MF], page 116), but if used without '-E', each '-o' is understood to specify a target object file.

Since '-E' is not implied, '-MD' can be used to generate a dependency output file as a side-effect of the compilation process.

-MMD   Like '-MD' except mention only user header files, not system header files.

-fpch-deps
            When using precompiled headers (see Section 3.20 [Precompiled Headers], page 232), this flag will cause the dependency-output flags to also list the files from the precompiled header's dependencies. If not specified only the precompiled header would be listed and not the files that were used to create it because those files are not consulted when a precompiled header is used.

-fpch-preprocess
            This option allows use of a precompiled header (see Section 3.20 [Precompiled Headers], page 232) together with '-E'. It inserts a special #pragma, #pragma GCC pch_preprocess "<filename>" in the output to mark the place where the precompiled header was found, and its filename. When '-fpreprocessed' is in use, GCC recognizes this #pragma and loads the PCH.

            This option is off by default, because the resulting preprocessed output is only really suitable as input to GCC. It is switched on by '-save-temps'.

            You should not write this #pragma in your own code, but it is safe to edit the filename if the PCH file is available in a different location. The filename may be absolute or it may be relative to GCC's current directory.

-x c
-x c++
-x objective-c
-x assembler-with-cpp
            Specify the source language: C, C++, Objective-C, or assembly. This has nothing to do with standards conformance or extensions; it merely selects which base syntax to expect. If you give none of these options, cpp will deduce the language from the extension of the source file: '.c', '.cc', '.m', or '.S'. Some other common extensions for C++ and assembly are also recognized. If cpp does not recognize the extension, it will treat the file as C; this is the most generic mode.

            Note: Previous versions of cpp accepted a '-lang' option which selected both the language and the standards conformance level. This option has been removed, because it conflicts with the '-l' option.

-std=*standard*
-ansi   Specify the standard to which the code should conform. Currently CPP knows about C and C++ standards; others may be added in the future.

            standard may be one of:

iso9899:1990
c89   The ISO C standard from 1990. 'c89' is the customary shorthand for this version of the standard.

            The '-ansi' option is equivalent to '-std=c89'.

iso9899:199409
            The 1990 C standard, as amended in 1994.

iso9899:1999
c99
iso9899:199x
c9x   The revised ISO C standard, published in December 1999. Before publication, this was known as C9X.

gnu89   The 1990 C standard plus GNU extensions. This is the default.

gnu99
gnu9x   The 1999 C standard plus GNU extensions.

c++98   The 1998 ISO C++ standard plus amendments.

gnu++98   The same as '-std=c++98' plus GNU extensions. This is the default for C++ code.

-I-   Split the include path. Any directories specified with '-I' options before '-I-' are searched only for headers requested with #include "*file*"; they are not searched for #include <*file*>. If additional directories are specified with '-I' options after the '-I-', those directories are searched for all '#include' directives.

            In addition, '-I-' inhibits the use of the directory of the current file directory as the first search directory for #include "*file*". This option has been deprecated.

-nostdinc
            Do not search the standard system directories for header files. Only the directories you have specified with '-I' options (and the directory of the current file, if appropriate) are searched.

-nostdinc++
            Do not search for header files in the C++-specific standard directories, but do still search the other standard directories. (This option is used when building the C++ library.)

-include *file*
            Process *file* as if #include "file" appeared as the first line of the primary source file. However, the first directory searched for *file* is the preprocessor's working directory *instead of* the directory containing the main source file. If not found there, it is searched for in the remainder of the #include "..." search chain as normal.

            If multiple '-include' options are given, the files are included in the order they appear on the command line.

`-imacros file`
> Exactly like '`-include`', except that any output produced by scanning file is thrown away. Macros it defines remain defined. This allows you to acquire all the macros from a header without also processing its declarations.
>
> All files specified by '`-imacros`' are processed before all files specified by '`-include`'.

`-idirafter dir`
> Search *dir* for header files, but do it *after* all directories specified with '`-I`' and the standard system directories have been exhausted. *dir* is treated as a system include directory. If *dir* begins with =, then the = will be replaced by the sysroot prefix; see '`--sysroot`' and '`-isysroot`'.

`-iprefix prefix`
> Specify *prefix* as the prefix for subsequent '`-iwithprefix`' options. If the prefix represents a directory, you should include the final '`/`'.

`-iwithprefix dir`
`-iwithprefixbefore dir`
> Append *dir* to the prefix specified previously with '`-iprefix`', and add the resulting directory to the include search path. '`-iwithprefixbefore`' puts it in the same place '`-I`' would; '`-iwithprefix`' puts it where '`-idirafter`' would.

`-isysroot dir`
> This option is like the '`--sysroot`' option, but applies only to header files. See the '`--sysroot`' option for more information.

`-imultilib dir`
> Use *dir* as a subdirectory of the directory containing target-specific C++ headers.

`-isystem dir`
> Search *dir* for header files, after all directories specified by '`-I`' but before the standard system directories. Mark it as a system directory, so that it gets the same special treatment as is applied to the standard system directories. If *dir* begins with =, then the = will be replaced by the sysroot prefix; see '`--sysroot`' and '`-isysroot`'.

`-iquote dir`
> Search *dir* only for header files requested with `#include "file"`; they are not searched for `#include <file>`, before all directories specified by '`-I`' and before the standard system directories. If *dir* begins with =, then the = will be replaced by the sysroot prefix; see '`--sysroot`' and '`-isysroot`'.

`-fdirectives-only`
> When preprocessing, handle directives, but do not expand macros.
>
> The option's behavior depends on the '`-E`' and '`-fpreprocessed`' options.
>
> With '`-E`', preprocessing is limited to the handling of directives such as `#define`, `#ifdef`, and `#error`. Other preprocessor operations, such as macro expansion and trigraph conversion are not performed. In addition, the '`-dD`' option is implicitly enabled.

With '-fpreprocessed', predefinition of command line and most builtin macros is disabled. Macros such as __LINE__, which are contextually dependent, are handled normally. This enables compilation of files previously preprocessed with -E -fdirectives-only.

With both '-E' and '-fpreprocessed', the rules for '-fpreprocessed' take precedence. This enables full preprocessing of files previously preprocessed with -E -fdirectives-only.

-fdollars-in-identifiers
: Accept '$' in identifiers.

-fextended-identifiers
: Accept universal character names in identifiers. This option is experimental; in a future version of GCC, it will be enabled by default for C99 and C++.

-fpreprocessed
: Indicate to the preprocessor that the input file has already been preprocessed. This suppresses things like macro expansion, trigraph conversion, escaped newline splicing, and processing of most directives. The preprocessor still recognizes and removes comments, so that you can pass a file preprocessed with '-C' to the compiler without problems. In this mode the integrated preprocessor is little more than a tokenizer for the front ends.

    '-fpreprocessed' is implicit if the input file has one of the extensions '.i', '.ii' or '.mi'. These are the extensions that GCC uses for preprocessed files created by '-save-temps'.

-ftabstop=width
: Set the distance between tab stops. This helps the preprocessor report correct column numbers in warnings or errors, even if tabs appear on the line. If the value is less than 1 or greater than 100, the option is ignored. The default is 8.

-fexec-charset=charset
: Set the execution character set, used for string and character constants. The default is UTF-8. charset can be any encoding supported by the system's iconv library routine.

-fwide-exec-charset=charset
: Set the wide execution character set, used for wide string and character constants. The default is UTF-32 or UTF-16, whichever corresponds to the width of wchar_t. As with '-fexec-charset', charset can be any encoding supported by the system's iconv library routine; however, you will have problems with encodings that do not fit exactly in wchar_t.

-finput-charset=charset
: Set the input character set, used for translation from the character set of the input file to the source character set used by GCC. If the locale does not specify, or GCC cannot get this information from the locale, the default is UTF-8. This can be overridden by either the locale or this command line option. Currently the command line option takes precedence if there's a conflict. charset can be any encoding supported by the system's iconv library routine.

Chapter 3: GCC Command Options   121

`-fworking-directory`
> Enable generation of linemarkers in the preprocessor output that will let the compiler know the current working directory at the time of preprocessing. When this option is enabled, the preprocessor will emit, after the initial linemarker, a second linemarker with the current working directory followed by two slashes. GCC will use this directory, when it's present in the preprocessed input, as the directory emitted as the current working directory in some debugging information formats. This option is implicitly enabled if debugging information is enabled, but this can be inhibited with the negated form '`-fno-working-directory`'. If the '`-P`' flag is present in the command line, this option has no effect, since no `#line` directives are emitted whatsoever.

`-fno-show-column`
> Do not print column numbers in diagnostics. This may be necessary if diagnostics are being scanned by a program that does not understand the column numbers, such as `dejagnu`.

`-A predicate=answer`
> Make an assertion with the predicate *predicate* and answer *answer*. This form is preferred to the older form '`-A predicate(answer)`', which is still supported, because it does not use shell special characters.

`-A -predicate=answer`
> Cancel an assertion with the predicate *predicate* and answer *answer*.

`-dCHARS` *CHARS* is a sequence of one or more of the following characters, and must not be preceded by a space. Other characters are interpreted by the compiler proper, or reserved for future versions of GCC, and so are silently ignored. If you specify characters whose behavior conflicts, the result is undefined.

> 'M'
>> Instead of the normal output, generate a list of '`#define`' directives for all the macros defined during the execution of the preprocessor, including predefined macros. This gives you a way of finding out what is predefined in your version of the preprocessor. Assuming you have no file '`foo.h`', the command
>>
>> ```
>> touch foo.h; cpp -dM foo.h
>> ```
>>
>> will show all the predefined macros.
>>
>> If you use '`-dM`' without the '`-E`' option, '`-dM`' is interpreted as a synonym for '`-fdump-rtl-mach`'. See Section 3.9 [Debugging Options], page 63.

> 'D'
>> Like 'M' except in two respects: it does *not* include the predefined macros, and it outputs *both* the '`#define`' directives and the result of preprocessing. Both kinds of output go to the standard output file.

> 'N'
>> Like 'D', but emit only the macro names, not their expansions.

> 'I'
>> Output '`#include`' directives in addition to the result of preprocessing.

-P Inhibit generation of linemarkers in the output from the preprocessor. This might be useful when running the preprocessor on something that is not C code, and will be sent to a program which might be confused by the linemarkers.

-C Do not discard comments. All comments are passed through to the output file, except for comments in processed directives, which are deleted along with the directive.

You should be prepared for side effects when using '-C'; it causes the preprocessor to treat comments as tokens in their own right. For example, comments appearing at the start of what would be a directive line have the effect of turning that line into an ordinary source line, since the first token on the line is no longer a '#'.

-CC Do not discard comments, including during macro expansion. This is like '-C', except that comments contained within macros are also passed through to the output file where the macro is expanded.

In addition to the side-effects of the '-C' option, the '-CC' option causes all C++-style comments inside a macro to be converted to C-style comments. This is to prevent later use of that macro from inadvertently commenting out the remainder of the source line.

The '-CC' option is generally used to support lint comments.

-traditional-cpp
Try to imitate the behavior of old-fashioned C preprocessors, as opposed to ISO C preprocessors.

-trigraphs
Process trigraph sequences. These are three-character sequences, all starting with '??', that are defined by ISO C to stand for single characters. For example, '??/' stands for '\', so '??/n' is a character constant for a newline. By default, GCC ignores trigraphs, but in standard-conforming modes it converts them. See the '-std' and '-ansi' options.

The nine trigraphs and their replacements are

```
Trigraph:        ??(  ??)  ??<  ??>  ??=  ??/  ??'  ??!  ??-
Replacement:     [    ]    {    }    #    \    ^    |    ~
```

-remap Enable special code to work around file systems which only permit very short file names, such as MS-DOS.

--help
--target-help
Print text describing all the command line options instead of preprocessing anything.

-v Verbose mode. Print out GNU CPP's version number at the beginning of execution, and report the final form of the include path.

-H Print the name of each header file used, in addition to other normal activities. Each name is indented to show how deep in the '#include' stack it is. Precompiled header files are also printed, even if they are found to be invalid; an invalid precompiled header file is printed with '...x' and a valid one with '...!'.

Chapter 3: GCC Command Options   123

`-version`
`--version`
> Print out GNU CPP's version number. With one dash, proceed to preprocess as normal. With two dashes, exit immediately.

3.12 Passing Options to the Assembler

You can pass options to the assembler.

`-Wa,option`
> Pass *option* as an option to the assembler. If *option* contains commas, it is split into multiple options at the commas.

`-Xassembler option`
> Pass *option* as an option to the assembler. You can use this to supply system-specific assembler options which GCC does not know how to recognize.
>
> If you want to pass an option that takes an argument, you must use '`-Xassembler`' twice, once for the option and once for the argument.

3.13 Options for Linking

These options come into play when the compiler links object files into an executable output file. They are meaningless if the compiler is not doing a link step.

`object-file-name`
> A file name that does not end in a special recognized suffix is considered to name an object file or library. (Object files are distinguished from libraries by the linker according to the file contents.) If linking is done, these object files are used as input to the linker.

`-c`
`-S`
`-E`
> If any of these options is used, then the linker is not run, and object file names should not be used as arguments. See Section 3.2 [Overall Options], page 20.

`-llibrary`
`-l library`
> Search the library named *library* when linking. (The second alternative with the library as a separate argument is only for POSIX compliance and is not recommended.)
>
> It makes a difference where in the command you write this option; the linker searches and processes libraries and object files in the order they are specified. Thus, '`foo.o -lz bar.o`' searches library '`z`' after file '`foo.o`' but before '`bar.o`'. If '`bar.o`' refers to functions in '`z`', those functions may not be loaded.
>
> The linker searches a standard list of directories for the library, which is actually a file named '`liblibrary.a`'. The linker then uses this file as if it had been specified precisely by name.
>
> The directories searched include several standard system directories plus any that you specify with '`-L`'.

Normally the files found this way are library files—archive files whose members are object files. The linker handles an archive file by scanning through it for members which define symbols that have so far been referenced but not defined. But if the file that is found is an ordinary object file, it is linked in the usual fashion. The only difference between using an '-l' option and specifying a file name is that '-l' surrounds *library* with 'lib' and '.a' and searches several directories.

`-lobjc`
You need this special case of the '-l' option in order to link an Objective-C or Objective-C++ program.

`-nostartfiles`
Do not use the standard system startup files when linking. The standard system libraries are used normally, unless '-nostdlib' or '-nodefaultlibs' is used.

`-nodefaultlibs`
Do not use the standard system libraries when linking. Only the libraries you specify will be passed to the linker. The standard startup files are used normally, unless '-nostartfiles' is used. The compiler may generate calls to `memcmp`, `memset`, `memcpy` and `memmove`. These entries are usually resolved by entries in libc. These entry points should be supplied through some other mechanism when this option is specified.

`-nostdlib`
Do not use the standard system startup files or libraries when linking. No startup files and only the libraries you specify will be passed to the linker. The compiler may generate calls to `memcmp`, `memset`, `memcpy` and `memmove`. These entries are usually resolved by entries in libc. These entry points should be supplied through some other mechanism when this option is specified.

One of the standard libraries bypassed by '-nostdlib' and '-nodefaultlibs' is 'libgcc.a', a library of internal subroutines that GCC uses to overcome shortcomings of particular machines, or special needs for some languages. (See Section "Interfacing to GCC Output" in *GNU Compiler Collection (GCC) Internals*, for more discussion of 'libgcc.a'.) In most cases, you need 'libgcc.a' even when you want to avoid other standard libraries. In other words, when you specify '-nostdlib' or '-nodefaultlibs' you should usually specify '-lgcc' as well. This ensures that you have no unresolved references to internal GCC library subroutines. (For example, '`__main`', used to ensure C++ constructors will be called; see Section "collect2" in *GNU Compiler Collection (GCC) Internals*.)

`-pie`
Produce a position independent executable on targets which support it. For predictable results, you must also specify the same set of options that were used to generate code ('-fpie', '-fPIE', or model suboptions) when you specify this option.

`-rdynamic`
Pass the flag '-export-dynamic' to the ELF linker, on targets that support it. This instructs the linker to add all symbols, not only used ones, to the dynamic symbol table. This option is needed for some uses of `dlopen` or to allow obtaining backtraces from within a program.

Chapter 3: GCC Command Options   125

`-s`   Remove all symbol table and relocation information from the executable.

`-static`   On systems that support dynamic linking, this prevents linking with the shared libraries. On other systems, this option has no effect.

`-shared`   Produce a shared object which can then be linked with other objects to form an executable. Not all systems support this option. For predictable results, you must also specify the same set of options that were used to generate code ('`-fpic`', '`-fPIC`', or model suboptions) when you specify this option.[1]

`-shared-libgcc`
`-static-libgcc`

On systems that provide '`libgcc`' as a shared library, these options force the use of either the shared or static version respectively. If no shared version of '`libgcc`' was built when the compiler was configured, these options have no effect.

There are several situations in which an application should use the shared '`libgcc`' instead of the static version. The most common of these is when the application wishes to throw and catch exceptions across different shared libraries. In that case, each of the libraries as well as the application itself should use the shared '`libgcc`'.

Therefore, the G++ and GCJ drivers automatically add '`-shared-libgcc`' whenever you build a shared library or a main executable, because C++ and Java programs typically use exceptions, so this is the right thing to do.

If, instead, you use the GCC driver to create shared libraries, you may find that they will not always be linked with the shared '`libgcc`'. If GCC finds, at its configuration time, that you have a non-GNU linker or a GNU linker that does not support option '`--eh-frame-hdr`', it will link the shared version of '`libgcc`' into shared libraries by default. Otherwise, it will take advantage of the linker and optimize away the linking with the shared version of '`libgcc`', linking with the static version of libgcc by default. This allows exceptions to propagate through such shared libraries, without incurring relocation costs at library load time.

However, if a library or main executable is supposed to throw or catch exceptions, you must link it using the G++ or GCJ driver, as appropriate for the languages used in the program, or using the option '`-shared-libgcc`', such that it is linked with the shared '`libgcc`'.

`-symbolic`   Bind references to global symbols when building a shared object. Warn about any unresolved references (unless overridden by the link editor option '`-Xlinker -z -Xlinker defs`'). Only a few systems support this option.

---

[1] On some systems, '`gcc -shared`' needs to build supplementary stub code for constructors to work. On multi-libbed systems, '`gcc -shared`' must select the correct support libraries to link against. Failing to supply the correct flags may lead to subtle defects. Supplying them in cases where they are not necessary is innocuous.

`-Xlinker` *option*

    Pass *option* as an option to the linker. You can use this to supply system-specific linker options which GCC does not know how to recognize.

    If you want to pass an option that takes an argument, you must use '`-Xlinker`' twice, once for the option and once for the argument. For example, to pass '`-assert definitions`', you must write '`-Xlinker -assert -Xlinker definitions`'. It does not work to write '`-Xlinker "-assert definitions"`', because this passes the entire string as a single argument, which is not what the linker expects.

`-Wl,`*option*

    Pass *option* as an option to the linker. If *option* contains commas, it is split into multiple options at the commas.

`-u` *symbol*

    Pretend the symbol *symbol* is undefined, to force linking of library modules to define it. You can use '`-u`' multiple times with different symbols to force loading of additional library modules.

3.14 Options for Directory Search

These options specify directories to search for header files, for libraries and for parts of the compiler:

`-I`*dir*   Add the directory *dir* to the head of the list of directories to be searched for header files. This can be used to override a system header file, substituting your own version, since these directories are searched before the system header file directories. However, you should not use this option to add directories that contain vendor-supplied system header files (use '`-isystem`' for that). If you use more than one '`-I`' option, the directories are scanned in left-to-right order; the standard system directories come after.

    If a standard system include directory, or a directory specified with '`-isystem`', is also specified with '`-I`', the '`-I`' option will be ignored. The directory will still be searched but as a system directory at its normal position in the system include chain. This is to ensure that GCC's procedure to fix buggy system headers and the ordering for the include_next directive are not inadvertently changed. If you really need to change the search order for system directories, use the '`-nostdinc`' and/or '`-isystem`' options.

`-iquote`*dir*

    Add the directory *dir* to the head of the list of directories to be searched for header files only for the case of '`#include "file"`'; they are not searched for '`#include <file>`', otherwise just like '`-I`'.

`-L`*dir*   Add directory *dir* to the list of directories to be searched for '`-l`'.

`-B`*prefix*   This option specifies where to find the executables, libraries, include files, and data files of the compiler itself.

    The compiler driver program runs one or more of the subprograms '`cpp`', '`cc1`', '`as`' and '`ld`'. It tries *prefix* as a prefix for each program it tries to run, both with and without '`machine/version/`' (see Section 3.16 [Target Options], page 135).

Chapter 3: GCC Command Options   127

> For each subprogram to be run, the compiler driver first tries the '-B' prefix, if any. If that name is not found, or if '-B' was not specified, the driver tries two standard prefixes, which are '/usr/lib/gcc/' and '/usr/local/lib/gcc/'. If neither of those results in a file name that is found, the unmodified program name is searched for using the directories specified in your PATH environment variable.
>
> The compiler will check to see if the path provided by the '-B' refers to a directory, and if necessary it will add a directory separator character at the end of the path.
>
> '-B' prefixes that effectively specify directory names also apply to libraries in the linker, because the compiler translates these options into '-L' options for the linker. They also apply to includes files in the preprocessor, because the compiler translates these options into '-isystem' options for the preprocessor. In this case, the compiler appends 'include' to the prefix.
>
> The run-time support file 'libgcc.a' can also be searched for using the '-B' prefix, if needed. If it is not found there, the two standard prefixes above are tried, and that is all. The file is left out of the link if it is not found by those means.
>
> Another way to specify a prefix much like the '-B' prefix is to use the environment variable GCC_EXEC_PREFIX. See Section 3.19 [Environment Variables], page 229.
>
> As a special kludge, if the path provided by '-B' is '[dir/]stageN/', where N is a number in the range 0 to 9, then it will be replaced by '[dir/]include'. This is to help with boot-strapping the compiler.

`-specs=file`
> Process file after the compiler reads in the standard 'specs' file, in order to override the defaults that the 'gcc' driver program uses when determining what switches to pass to 'cc1', 'cc1plus', 'as', 'ld', etc. More than one '-specs=file' can be specified on the command line, and they are processed in order, from left to right.

`--sysroot=dir`
> Use dir as the logical root directory for headers and libraries. For example, if the compiler would normally search for headers in '/usr/include' and libraries in '/usr/lib', it will instead search 'dir/usr/include' and 'dir/usr/lib'.
>
> If you use both this option and the '-isysroot' option, then the '--sysroot' option will apply to libraries, but the '-isysroot' option will apply to header files.
>
> The GNU linker (beginning with version 2.16) has the necessary support for this option. If your linker does not support this option, the header file aspect of '--sysroot' will still work, but the library aspect will not.

`-I-`
> This option has been deprecated. Please use '-iquote' instead for '-I' directories before the '-I-' and remove the '-I-'. Any directories you specify with '-I' options before the '-I-' option are searched only for the case of '#include "file"'; they are not searched for '#include <file>'.

If additional directories are specified with '-I' options after the '-I-', these
directories are searched for all '#include' directives. (Ordinarily *all* '-I' directories are used this way.)

In addition, the '-I-' option inhibits the use of the current directory (where
the current input file came from) as the first search directory for '#include
"file"'. There is no way to override this effect of '-I-'. With '-I.' you
can specify searching the directory which was current when the compiler was
invoked. That is not exactly the same as what the preprocessor does by default,
but it is often satisfactory.

'-I-' does not inhibit the use of the standard system directories for header files.
Thus, '-I-' and '-nostdinc' are independent.

3.15 Specifying subprocesses and the switches to pass to them

gcc is a driver program. It performs its job by invoking a sequence of other programs to do the work of compiling, assembling and linking. GCC interprets its command-line parameters and uses these to deduce which programs it should invoke, and which command-line options it ought to place on their command lines. This behavior is controlled by *spec strings*. In most cases there is one spec string for each program that GCC can invoke, but a few programs have multiple spec strings to control their behavior. The spec strings built into GCC can be overridden by using the '-specs=' command-line switch to specify a spec file.

Spec files are plaintext files that are used to construct spec strings. They consist of a sequence of directives separated by blank lines. The type of directive is determined by the first non-whitespace character on the line and it can be one of the following:

%command   Issues a *command* to the spec file processor. The commands that can appear here are:

   %include <*file*>
             Search for *file* and insert its text at the current point in the specs file.

   %include_noerr <*file*>
             Just like '%include', but do not generate an error message if the include file cannot be found.

   %rename *old_name new_name*
             Rename the spec string *old_name* to *new_name*.

*[*spec_name*]:
             This tells the compiler to create, override or delete the named spec string. All lines after this directive up to the next directive or blank line are considered to be the text for the spec string. If this results in an empty string then the spec will be deleted. (Or, if the spec did not exist, then nothing will happened.) Otherwise, if the spec does not currently exist a new spec will be created. If the spec does exist then its contents will be overridden by the text of this directive, unless the first character of that text is the '+' character, in which case the text will be appended to the spec.

Chapter 3: GCC Command Options   129

[*suffix*]:
>   Creates a new '[*suffix*] spec' pair. All lines after this directive and up to the next directive or blank line are considered to make up the spec string for the indicated suffix. When the compiler encounters an input file with the named suffix, it will processes the spec string in order to work out how to compile that file. For example:
>
>   ```
>   .ZZ:
>   z-compile -input %i
>   ```
>
>   This says that any input file whose name ends in '.ZZ' should be passed to the program 'z-compile', which should be invoked with the command-line switch '-input' and with the result of performing the '%i' substitution. (See below.)
>
>   As an alternative to providing a spec string, the text that follows a suffix directive can be one of the following:
>
>   @*language*
>   >   This says that the suffix is an alias for a known *language*. This is similar to using the '-x' command-line switch to GCC to specify a language explicitly. For example:
>   >
>   >   ```
>   >   .ZZ:
>   >   @c++
>   >   ```
>   >
>   >   Says that .ZZ files are, in fact, C++ source files.
>
>   #*name*
>   >   This causes an error messages saying:
>   >
>   >   ```
>   >   name compiler not installed on this system.
>   >   ```
>
>   GCC already has an extensive list of suffixes built into it. This directive will add an entry to the end of the list of suffixes, but since the list is searched from the end backwards, it is effectively possible to override earlier entries using this technique.

GCC has the following spec strings built into it. Spec files can override these strings or create their own. Note that individual targets can also add their own spec strings to this list.

```
asm          Options to pass to the assembler
asm_final    Options to pass to the assembler post-processor
cpp          Options to pass to the C preprocessor
cc1          Options to pass to the C compiler
cc1plus      Options to pass to the C++ compiler
endfile      Object files to include at the end of the link
link         Options to pass to the linker
lib          Libraries to include on the command line to the linker
libgcc       Decides which GCC support library to pass to the linker
linker       Sets the name of the linker
predefines   Defines to be passed to the C preprocessor
signed_char  Defines to pass to CPP to say whether char is signed
             by default
startfile    Object files to include at the start of the link
```

Here is a small example of a spec file:

```
%rename lib              old_lib

*lib:
--start-group -lgcc -lc -leval1 --end-group %(old_lib)
```

This example renames the spec called 'lib' to 'old_lib' and then overrides the previous definition of 'lib' with a new one. The new definition adds in some extra command-line options before including the text of the old definition.

Spec strings are a list of command-line options to be passed to their corresponding program. In addition, the spec strings can contain '%'-prefixed sequences to substitute variable text or to conditionally insert text into the command line. Using these constructs it is possible to generate quite complex command lines.

Here is a table of all defined '%'-sequences for spec strings. Note that spaces are not generated automatically around the results of expanding these sequences. Therefore you can concatenate them together or combine them with constant text in a single argument.

%%
: Substitute one '%' into the program name or argument.

%i
: Substitute the name of the input file being processed.

%b
: Substitute the basename of the input file being processed. This is the substring up to (and not including) the last period and not including the directory.

%B
: This is the same as '%b', but include the file suffix (text after the last period).

%d
: Marks the argument containing or following the '%d' as a temporary file name, so that that file will be deleted if GCC exits successfully. Unlike '%g', this contributes no text to the argument.

%g*suffix*
: Substitute a file name that has suffix *suffix* and is chosen once per compilation, and mark the argument in the same way as '%d'. To reduce exposure to denial-of-service attacks, the file name is now chosen in a way that is hard to predict even when previously chosen file names are known. For example, '%g.s ... %g.o ... %g.s' might turn into 'ccUVUUAU.s ccXYAXZ12.o ccUVUUAU.s'. *suffix* matches the regexp '[.A-Za-z]*' or the special string '%O', which is treated exactly as if '%O' had been preprocessed. Previously, '%g' was simply substituted with a file name chosen once per compilation, without regard to any appended suffix (which was therefore treated just like ordinary text), making such attacks more likely to succeed.

%u*suffix*
: Like '%g', but generates a new temporary file name even if '%u*suffix*' was already seen.

%U*suffix*
: Substitutes the last file name generated with '%u*suffix*', generating a new one if there is no such last file name. In the absence of any '%u*suffix*', this is just like '%g*suffix*', except they don't share the same suffix *space*, so '%g.s ... %U.s ... %g.s ... %U.s' would involve the generation of two distinct file names, one for each '%g.s' and another for each '%U.s'. Previously, '%U' was simply substituted with a file name chosen for the previous '%u', without regard to any appended suffix.

%j*suffix*
: Substitutes the name of the HOST_BIT_BUCKET, if any, and if it is writable, and if save-temps is off; otherwise, substitute the name of a temporary file, just like '%u'. This temporary file is not meant for communication between processes, but rather as a junk disposal mechanism.

Chapter 3: GCC Command Options   131

`%|suffix`
`%msuffix`   Like '`%g`', except if '`-pipe`' is in effect. In that case '`%|`' substitutes a single dash and '`%m`' substitutes nothing at all. These are the two most common ways to instruct a program that it should read from standard input or write to standard output. If you need something more elaborate you can use an '`%{pipe:X}`' construct: see for example '`f/lang-specs.h`'.

`%.SUFFIX`   Substitutes .SUFFIX for the suffixes of a matched switch's args when it is subsequently output with '`%*`'. SUFFIX is terminated by the next space or %.

`%w`   Marks the argument containing or following the '`%w`' as the designated output file of this compilation. This puts the argument into the sequence of arguments that '`%o`' will substitute later.

`%o`   Substitutes the names of all the output files, with spaces automatically placed around them. You should write spaces around the '`%o`' as well or the results are undefined. '`%o`' is for use in the specs for running the linker. Input files whose names have no recognized suffix are not compiled at all, but they are included among the output files, so they will be linked.

`%O`   Substitutes the suffix for object files. Note that this is handled specially when it immediately follows '`%g, %u, or %U`', because of the need for those to form complete file names. The handling is such that '`%O`' is treated exactly as if it had already been substituted, except that '`%g, %u, and %U`' do not currently support additional suffix characters following '`%O`' as they would following, for example, '`.o`'.

`%p`   Substitutes the standard macro predefinitions for the current target machine. Use this when running `cpp`.

`%P`   Like '`%p`', but puts '`__`' before and after the name of each predefined macro, except for macros that start with '`__`' or with '`_L`', where L is an uppercase letter. This is for ISO C.

`%I`   Substitute any of '`-iprefix`' (made from `GCC_EXEC_PREFIX`), '`-isysroot`' (made from `TARGET_SYSTEM_ROOT`), '`-isystem`' (made from `COMPILER_PATH` and '`-B`' options) and '`-imultilib`' as necessary.

`%s`   Current argument is the name of a library or startup file of some sort. Search for that file in a standard list of directories and substitute the full name found.

`%estr`   Print str as an error message. str is terminated by a newline. Use this when inconsistent options are detected.

`%(name)`   Substitute the contents of spec string name at this point.

`%[name]`   Like '`%(...)`' but put '`__`' around '`-D`' arguments.

`%x{option}`
          Accumulate an option for '`%X`'.

`%X`   Output the accumulated linker options specified by '`-Wl`' or a '`%x`' spec string.

`%Y`   Output the accumulated assembler options specified by '`-Wa`'.

%Z   Output the accumulated preprocessor options specified by '-Wp'.

%a   Process the `asm` spec. This is used to compute the switches to be passed to the assembler.

%A   Process the `asm_final` spec. This is a spec string for passing switches to an assembler post-processor, if such a program is needed.

%l   Process the `link` spec. This is the spec for computing the command line passed to the linker. Typically it will make use of the '%L %G %S %D and %E' sequences.

%D   Dump out a '-L' option for each directory that GCC believes might contain startup files. If the target supports multilibs then the current multilib directory will be prepended to each of these paths.

%L   Process the `lib` spec. This is a spec string for deciding which libraries should be included on the command line to the linker.

%G   Process the `libgcc` spec. This is a spec string for deciding which GCC support library should be included on the command line to the linker.

%S   Process the `startfile` spec. This is a spec for deciding which object files should be the first ones passed to the linker. Typically this might be a file named 'crt0.o'.

%E   Process the `endfile` spec. This is a spec string that specifies the last object files that will be passed to the linker.

%C   Process the `cpp` spec. This is used to construct the arguments to be passed to the C preprocessor.

%1   Process the `cc1` spec. This is used to construct the options to be passed to the actual C compiler ('cc1').

%2   Process the `cc1plus` spec. This is used to construct the options to be passed to the actual C++ compiler ('cc1plus').

%*   Substitute the variable part of a matched option. See below. Note that each comma in the substituted string is replaced by a single space.

%<S   Remove all occurrences of -S from the command line. Note—this command is position dependent. '%' commands in the spec string before this one will see -S, '%' commands in the spec string after this one will not.

%:function(args)

Call the named function *function*, passing it *args*. *args* is first processed as a nested spec string, then split into an argument vector in the usual fashion. The function returns a string which is processed as if it had appeared literally as part of the current spec.

The following built-in spec functions are provided:

getenv   The `getenv` spec function takes two arguments: an environment variable name and a string. If the environment variable is not defined, a fatal error is issued. Otherwise, the return value is the value of the environment variable concatenated with the string. For example, if `TOPDIR` is defined as '/path/to/top', then:

Chapter 3: GCC Command Options 133

> %:getenv(TOPDIR /include)
>
> expands to '/path/to/top/include'.

if-exists
: The `if-exists` spec function takes one argument, an absolute pathname to a file. If the file exists, `if-exists` returns the pathname. Here is a small example of its usage:
```
*startfile:
crt0%O%s %:if-exists(crti%O%s) crtbegin%O%s
```

if-exists-else
: The `if-exists-else` spec function is similar to the `if-exists` spec function, except that it takes two arguments. The first argument is an absolute pathname to a file. If the file exists, `if-exists-else` returns the pathname. If it does not exist, it returns the second argument. This way, `if-exists-else` can be used to select one file or another, based on the existence of the first. Here is a small example of its usage:
```
*startfile:
crt0%O%s %:if-exists(crti%O%s) \
%:if-exists-else(crtbeginT%O%s crtbegin%O%s)
```

replace-outfile
: The `replace-outfile` spec function takes two arguments. It looks for the first argument in the outfiles array and replaces it with the second argument. Here is a small example of its usage:
```
%{fgnu-runtime:%:replace-outfile(-lobjc -lobjc-gnu)}
```

print-asm-header
: The `print-asm-header` function takes no arguments and simply prints a banner like:
```
Assembler options
=================

Use "-Wa,OPTION" to pass "OPTION" to the assembler.
```
It is used to separate compiler options from assembler options in the '--target-help' output.

%{S}
: Substitutes the -S switch, if that switch was given to GCC. If that switch was not specified, this substitutes nothing. Note that the leading dash is omitted when specifying this option, and it is automatically inserted if the substitution is performed. Thus the spec string '%{foo}' would match the command-line option '-foo' and would output the command line option '-foo'.

%W{S}
: Like %{S} but mark last argument supplied within as a file to be deleted on failure.

%{S*}
: Substitutes all the switches specified to GCC whose names start with -S, but which also take an argument. This is used for switches like '-o', '-D', '-I', etc. GCC considers '-o foo' as being one switch whose names starts with 'o'. %{o*} would substitute this text, including the space. Thus two arguments would be generated.

%{S*&T*}   Like %{S*}, but preserve order of S and T options (the order of S and T in the spec is not significant). There can be any number of ampersand-separated variables; for each the wild card is optional. Useful for CPP as '%{D*&U*&A*}'.

%{S:X}   Substitutes X, if the '-S' switch was given to GCC.

%{!S:X}   Substitutes X, if the '-S' switch was *not* given to GCC.

%{S*:X}   Substitutes X if one or more switches whose names start with -S are specified to GCC. Normally X is substituted only once, no matter how many such switches appeared. However, if %* appears somewhere in X, then X will be substituted once for each matching switch, with the %* replaced by the part of that switch that matched the *.

%{.S:X}   Substitutes X, if processing a file with suffix S.

%{!.S:X}   Substitutes X, if *not* processing a file with suffix S.

%{,S:X}   Substitutes X, if processing a file for language S.

%{!,S:X}   Substitutes X, if not processing a file for language S.

%{S|P:X}   Substitutes X if either -S or -P was given to GCC. This may be combined with '!', '.', ',', and * sequences as well, although they have a stronger binding than the '|'. If %* appears in X, all of the alternatives must be starred, and only the first matching alternative is substituted.

For example, a spec string like this:

```
%{.c:-foo} %{!.c:-bar} %{.c|d:-baz} %{!.c|d:-boggle}
```

will output the following command-line options from the following input command-line options:

```
fred.c      -foo -baz
jim.d       -bar -boggle
-d fred.c   -foo -baz -boggle
-d jim.d    -bar -baz -boggle
```

%{S:X; T:Y; :D}

If S was given to GCC, substitutes X; else if T was given to GCC, substitutes Y; else substitutes D. There can be as many clauses as you need. This may be combined with ., ,, !, |, and * as needed.

The conditional text X in a %{S:X} or similar construct may contain other nested '%' constructs or spaces, or even newlines. They are processed as usual, as described above. Trailing white space in X is ignored. White space may also appear anywhere on the left side of the colon in these constructs, except between . or * and the corresponding word.

The '-O', '-f', '-m', and '-W' switches are handled specifically in these constructs. If another value of '-O' or the negated form of a '-f', '-m', or '-W' switch is found later in the command line, the earlier switch value is ignored, except with {S*} where S is just one letter, which passes all matching options.

The character '|' at the beginning of the predicate text is used to indicate that a command should be piped to the following command, but only if '-pipe' is specified.

It is built into GCC which switches take arguments and which do not. (You might think it would be useful to generalize this to allow each compiler's spec to say which switches

Chapter 3: GCC Command Options   135

take arguments. But this cannot be done in a consistent fashion. GCC cannot even decide which input files have been specified without knowing which switches take arguments, and it must know which input files to compile in order to tell which compilers to run).

GCC also knows implicitly that arguments starting in '-l' are to be treated as compiler output files, and passed to the linker in their proper position among the other output files.

3.16 Specifying Target Machine and Compiler Version

The usual way to run GCC is to run the executable called 'gcc', or '<machine>-gcc' when cross-compiling, or '<machine>-gcc-<version>' to run a version other than the one that was installed last. Sometimes this is inconvenient, so GCC provides options that will switch to another cross-compiler or version.

-b *machine*
: The argument *machine* specifies the target machine for compilation.

    The value to use for *machine* is the same as was specified as the machine type when configuring GCC as a cross-compiler. For example, if a cross-compiler was configured with 'configure arm-elf', meaning to compile for an arm processor with elf binaries, then you would specify '-b arm-elf' to run that cross compiler. Because there are other options beginning with '-b', the configuration must contain a hyphen.

-V *version*
: The argument *version* specifies which version of GCC to run. This is useful when multiple versions are installed. For example, *version* might be '4.0', meaning to run GCC version 4.0.

The '-V' and '-b' options work by running the '<machine>-gcc-<version>' executable, so there's no real reason to use them if you can just run that directly.

3.17 Hardware Models and Configurations

Earlier we discussed the standard option '-b' which chooses among different installed compilers for completely different target machines, such as VAX vs. 68000 vs. 80386.

In addition, each of these target machine types can have its own special options, starting with '-m', to choose among various hardware models or configurations—for example, 68010 vs 68020, floating coprocessor or none. A single installed version of the compiler can compile for any model or configuration, according to the options specified.

Some configurations of the compiler also support additional special options, usually for compatibility with other compilers on the same platform.

3.17.1 ARC Options

These options are defined for ARC implementations:

-EL   Compile code for little endian mode. This is the default.

-EB   Compile code for big endian mode.

-mmangle-cpu
: Prepend the name of the cpu to all public symbol names. In multiple-processor systems, there are many ARC variants with different instruction and register

set characteristics. This flag prevents code compiled for one cpu to be linked with code compiled for another. No facility exists for handling variants that are "almost identical". This is an all or nothing option.

`-mcpu=cpu`
> Compile code for ARC variant *cpu*. Which variants are supported depend on the configuration. All variants support '`-mcpu=base`', this is the default.

`-mtext=text-section`
`-mdata=data-section`
`-mrodata=readonly-data-section`
> Put functions, data, and readonly data in *text-section*, *data-section*, and *readonly-data-section* respectively by default. This can be overridden with the section attribute. See Section 5.34 [Variable Attributes], page 286.

3.17.2 ARM Options

These '`-m`' options are defined for Advanced RISC Machines (ARM) architectures:

`-mabi=name`
> Generate code for the specified ABI. Permissible values are: '`apcs-gnu`', '`atpcs`', '`aapcs`', '`aapcs-linux`' and '`iwmmxt`'.

`-mapcs-frame`
> Generate a stack frame that is compliant with the ARM Procedure Call Standard for all functions, even if this is not strictly necessary for correct execution of the code. Specifying '`-fomit-frame-pointer`' with this option will cause the stack frames not to be generated for leaf functions. The default is '`-mno-apcs-frame`'.

`-mapcs`
> This is a synonym for '`-mapcs-frame`'.

`-mthumb-interwork`
> Generate code which supports calling between the ARM and Thumb instruction sets. Without this option the two instruction sets cannot be reliably used inside one program. The default is '`-mno-thumb-interwork`', since slightly larger code is generated when '`-mthumb-interwork`' is specified.

`-mno-sched-prolog`
> Prevent the reordering of instructions in the function prolog, or the merging of those instruction with the instructions in the function's body. This means that all functions will start with a recognizable set of instructions (or in fact one of a choice from a small set of different function prologues), and this information can be used to locate the start if functions inside an executable piece of code. The default is '`-msched-prolog`'.

`-mhard-float`
> Generate output containing floating point instructions. This is the default.

`-msoft-float`
> Generate output containing library calls for floating point. **Warning:** the requisite libraries are not available for all ARM targets. Normally the facilities of the machine's usual C compiler are used, but this cannot be done directly in

Chapter 3: GCC Command Options   137

cross-compilation. You must make your own arrangements to provide suitable library functions for cross-compilation.

'-msoft-float' changes the calling convention in the output file; therefore, it is only useful if you compile *all* of a program with this option. In particular, you need to compile 'libgcc.a', the library that comes with GCC, with '-msoft-float' in order for this to work.

`-mfloat-abi=name`
: Specifies which ABI to use for floating point values. Permissible values are: 'soft', 'softfp' and 'hard'.

    'soft' and 'hard' are equivalent to '-msoft-float' and '-mhard-float' respectively. 'softfp' allows the generation of floating point instructions, but still uses the soft-float calling conventions.

`-mlittle-endian`
: Generate code for a processor running in little-endian mode. This is the default for all standard configurations.

`-mbig-endian`
: Generate code for a processor running in big-endian mode; the default is to compile code for a little-endian processor.

`-mwords-little-endian`
: This option only applies when generating code for big-endian processors. Generate code for a little-endian word order but a big-endian byte order. That is, a byte order of the form '32107654'. Note: this option should only be used if you require compatibility with code for big-endian ARM processors generated by versions of the compiler prior to 2.8.

`-mcpu=name`
: This specifies the name of the target ARM processor. GCC uses this name to determine what kind of instructions it can emit when generating assembly code. Permissible names are: 'arm2', 'arm250', 'arm3', 'arm6', 'arm60', 'arm600', 'arm610', 'arm620', 'arm7', 'arm7m', 'arm7d', 'arm7dm', 'arm7di', 'arm7dmi', 'arm70', 'arm700', 'arm700i', 'arm710', 'arm710c', 'arm7100', 'arm7500', 'arm7500fe', 'arm7tdmi', 'arm7tdmi-s', 'arm8', 'strongarm', 'strongarm110', 'strongarm1100', 'arm8', 'arm810', 'arm9', 'arm9e', 'arm920', 'arm920t', 'arm922t', 'arm946e-s', 'arm966e-s', 'arm968e-s', 'arm926ej-s', 'arm940t', 'arm9tdmi', 'arm10tdmi', 'arm1020t', 'arm1026ej-s', 'arm10e', 'arm1020e', 'arm1022e', 'arm1136j-s', 'arm1136jf-s', 'mpcore', 'mpcorenovfp', 'arm1156t2-s', 'arm1176jz-s', 'arm1176jzf-s', 'cortex-a8', 'cortex-r4', 'cortex-m3', 'xscale', 'iwmmxt', 'ep9312'.

`-mtune=name`
: This option is very similar to the '-mcpu=' option, except that instead of specifying the actual target processor type, and hence restricting which instructions can be used, it specifies that GCC should tune the performance of the code as if the target were of the type specified in this option, but still choosing the instructions that it will generate based on the cpu specified by a '-mcpu=' option. For some ARM implementations better performance can be obtained by using this option.

`-march=`*name*
>   This specifies the name of the target ARM architecture. GCC uses this name to determine what kind of instructions it can emit when generating assembly code. This option can be used in conjunction with or instead of the '`-mcpu=`' option. Permissible names are: 'armv2', 'armv2a', 'armv3', 'armv3m', 'armv4', 'armv4t', 'armv5', 'armv5t', 'armv5te', 'armv6', 'armv6j', 'armv6t2', 'armv6z', 'armv6zk', 'armv7', 'armv7-a', 'armv7-r', 'armv7-m', 'iwmmxt', 'ep9312'.

`-mfpu=`*name*
`-mfpe=`*number*
`-mfp=`*number*
>   This specifies what floating point hardware (or hardware emulation) is available on the target. Permissible names are: 'fpa', 'fpe2', 'fpe3', 'maverick', 'vfp'. '-mfp' and '-mfpe' are synonyms for '-mfpu'='fpe'*number*, for compatibility with older versions of GCC.
>
>   If '-msoft-float' is specified this specifies the format of floating point values.

`-mstructure-size-boundary=`*n*
>   The size of all structures and unions will be rounded up to a multiple of the number of bits set by this option. Permissible values are 8, 32 and 64. The default value varies for different toolchains. For the COFF targeted toolchain the default value is 8. A value of 64 is only allowed if the underlying ABI supports it.
>
>   Specifying the larger number can produce faster, more efficient code, but can also increase the size of the program. Different values are potentially incompatible. Code compiled with one value cannot necessarily expect to work with code or libraries compiled with another value, if they exchange information using structures or unions.

`-mabort-on-noreturn`
>   Generate a call to the function **abort** at the end of a **noreturn** function. It will be executed if the function tries to return.

`-mlong-calls`
`-mno-long-calls`
>   Tells the compiler to perform function calls by first loading the address of the function into a register and then performing a subroutine call on this register. This switch is needed if the target function will lie outside of the 64 megabyte addressing range of the offset based version of subroutine call instruction.
>
>   Even if this switch is enabled, not all function calls will be turned into long calls. The heuristic is that static functions, functions which have the '`short-call`' attribute, functions that are inside the scope of a '`#pragma no_long_calls`' directive and functions whose definitions have already been compiled within the current compilation unit, will not be turned into long calls. The exception to this rule is that weak function definitions, functions with the '`long-call`' attribute or the '`section`' attribute, and functions that are within the scope of a '`#pragma long_calls`' directive, will always be turned into long calls.
>
>   This feature is not enabled by default. Specifying '-mno-long-calls' will restore the default behavior, as will placing the function calls within the scope of

Chapter 3: GCC Command Options   139

a '#pragma long_calls_off' directive. Note these switches have no effect on
how the compiler generates code to handle function calls via function pointers.

`-mnop-fun-dllimport`
> Disable support for the `dllimport` attribute.

`-msingle-pic-base`
> Treat the register used for PIC addressing as read-only, rather than loading
> it in the prologue for each function. The run-time system is responsible for
> initializing this register with an appropriate value before execution begins.

`-mpic-register=reg`
> Specify the register to be used for PIC addressing. The default is R10 unless
> stack-checking is enabled, when R9 is used.

`-mcirrus-fix-invalid-insns`
> Insert NOPs into the instruction stream to in order to work around problems
> with invalid Maverick instruction combinations. This option is only valid if the
> '-mcpu=ep9312' option has been used to enable generation of instructions for
> the Cirrus Maverick floating point co-processor. This option is not enabled by
> default, since the problem is only present in older Maverick implementations.
> The default can be re-enabled by use of the '-mno-cirrus-fix-invalid-insns'
> switch.

`-mpoke-function-name`
> Write the name of each function into the text section, directly preceding the
> function prologue. The generated code is similar to this:
>
> ```
> t0
>     .ascii "arm_poke_function_name", 0
>     .align
> t1
>     .word 0xff000000 + (t1 - t0)
> arm_poke_function_name
>     mov     ip, sp
>     stmfd   sp!, {fp, ip, lr, pc}
>     sub     fp, ip, #4
> ```

When performing a stack backtrace, code can inspect the value of `pc` stored at
`fp + 0`. If the trace function then looks at location `pc - 12` and the top 8 bits
are set, then we know that there is a function name embedded immediately
preceding this location and has length `((pc[-3]) & 0xff000000)`.

`-mthumb`   Generate code for the Thumb instruction set. The default is to use the 32-bit
ARM instruction set. This option automatically enables either 16-bit Thumb-
1 or mixed 16/32-bit Thumb-2 instructions based on the '-mcpu=name' and
'-march=name' options.

`-mtpcs-frame`
> Generate a stack frame that is compliant with the Thumb Procedure Call Stan-
> dard for all non-leaf functions. (A leaf function is one that does not call any
> other functions.) The default is '-mno-tpcs-frame'.

`-mtpcs-leaf-frame`
> Generate a stack frame that is compliant with the Thumb Procedure Call Standard for all leaf functions. (A leaf function is one that does not call any other functions.) The default is '`-mno-apcs-leaf-frame`'.

`-mcallee-super-interworking`
> Gives all externally visible functions in the file being compiled an ARM instruction set header which switches to Thumb mode before executing the rest of the function. This allows these functions to be called from non-interworking code.

`-mcaller-super-interworking`
> Allows calls via function pointers (including virtual functions) to execute correctly regardless of whether the target code has been compiled for interworking or not. There is a small overhead in the cost of executing a function pointer if this option is enabled.

`-mtp=name`
> Specify the access model for the thread local storage pointer. The valid models are '`soft`', which generates calls to `__aeabi_read_tp`, '`cp15`', which fetches the thread pointer from `cp15` directly (supported in the arm6k architecture), and '`auto`', which uses the best available method for the selected processor. The default setting is '`auto`'.

3.17.3 AVR Options

These options are defined for AVR implementations:

`-mmcu=mcu`
> Specify ATMEL AVR instruction set or MCU type.
>
> Instruction set avr1 is for the minimal AVR core, not supported by the C compiler, only for assembler programs (MCU types: at90s1200, attiny10, attiny11, attiny12, attiny15, attiny28).
>
> Instruction set avr2 (default) is for the classic AVR core with up to 8K program memory space (MCU types: at90s2313, at90s2323, attiny22, at90s2333, at90s2343, at90s4414, at90s4433, at90s4434, at90s8515, at90c8534, at90s8535).
>
> Instruction set avr3 is for the classic AVR core with up to 128K program memory space (MCU types: atmega103, atmega603, at43usb320, at76c711).
>
> Instruction set avr4 is for the enhanced AVR core with up to 8K program memory space (MCU types: atmega8, atmega83, atmega85).
>
> Instruction set avr5 is for the enhanced AVR core with up to 128K program memory space (MCU types: atmega16, atmega161, atmega163, atmega32, atmega323, atmega64, atmega128, at43usb355, at94k).

`-msize`   Output instruction sizes to the asm file.

`-minit-stack=N`
> Specify the initial stack address, which may be a symbol or numeric value, '`__stack`' is the default.

`-mno-interrupts`
> Generated code is not compatible with hardware interrupts. Code size will be smaller.

Chapter 3: GCC Command Options   141

`-mcall-prologues`
: Functions prologues/epilogues expanded as call to appropriate subroutines. Code size will be smaller.

`-mno-tablejump`
: Do not generate tablejump insns which sometimes increase code size.

`-mtiny-stack`
: Change only the low 8 bits of the stack pointer.

`-mint8` Assume int to be 8 bit integer. This affects the sizes of all types: A char will be 1 byte, an int will be 1 byte, an long will be 2 bytes and long long will be 4 bytes. Please note that this option does not comply to the C standards, but it will provide you with smaller code size.

3.17.4 Blackfin Options

`-mcpu=cpu[-sirevision]`
: Specifies the name of the target Blackfin processor. Currently, *cpu* can be one of 'bf522', 'bf523', 'bf524', 'bf525', 'bf526', 'bf527', 'bf531', 'bf532', 'bf533', 'bf534', 'bf536', 'bf537', 'bf538', 'bf539', 'bf542', 'bf544', 'bf547', 'bf548', 'bf549', 'bf561'. The optional *sirevision* specifies the silicon revision of the target Blackfin processor. Any workarounds available for the targeted silicon revision will be enabled. If *sirevision* is 'none', no workarounds are enabled. If *sirevision* is 'any', all workarounds for the targeted processor will be enabled. The __SILICON_REVISION__ macro is defined to two hexadecimal digits representing the major and minor numbers in the silicon revision. If *sirevision* is 'none', the __SILICON_REVISION__ is not defined. If *sirevision* is 'any', the __SILICON_REVISION__ is defined to be 0xffff. If this optional *sirevision* is not used, GCC assumes the latest known silicon revision of the targeted Blackfin processor.

   Support for 'bf561' is incomplete. For 'bf561', Only the processor macro is defined. Without this option, 'bf532' is used as the processor by default. The corresponding predefined processor macros for *cpu* is to be defined. And for 'bfin-elf' toolchain, this causes the hardware BSP provided by libgloss to be linked in if '-msim' is not given.

`-msim`   Specifies that the program will be run on the simulator. This causes the simulator BSP provided by libgloss to be linked in. This option has effect only for 'bfin-elf' toolchain. Certain other options, such as '-mid-shared-library' and '-mfdpic', imply '-msim'.

`-momit-leaf-frame-pointer`
: Don't keep the frame pointer in a register for leaf functions. This avoids the instructions to save, set up and restore frame pointers and makes an extra register available in leaf functions. The option '-fomit-frame-pointer' removes the frame pointer for all functions which might make debugging harder.

`-mspecld-anomaly`
> When enabled, the compiler will ensure that the generated code does not contain speculative loads after jump instructions. If this option is used, `__WORKAROUND_SPECULATIVE_LOADS` is defined.

`-mno-specld-anomaly`
> Don't generate extra code to prevent speculative loads from occurring.

`-mcsync-anomaly`
> When enabled, the compiler will ensure that the generated code does not contain CSYNC or SSYNC instructions too soon after conditional branches. If this option is used, `__WORKAROUND_SPECULATIVE_SYNCS` is defined.

`-mno-csync-anomaly`
> Don't generate extra code to prevent CSYNC or SSYNC instructions from occurring too soon after a conditional branch.

`-mlow-64k`
> When enabled, the compiler is free to take advantage of the knowledge that the entire program fits into the low 64k of memory.

`-mno-low-64k`
> Assume that the program is arbitrarily large. This is the default.

`-mstack-check-l1`
> Do stack checking using information placed into L1 scratchpad memory by the uClinux kernel.

`-mid-shared-library`
> Generate code that supports shared libraries via the library ID method. This allows for execute in place and shared libraries in an environment without virtual memory management. This option implies '-fPIC'. With a 'bfin-elf' target, this option implies '-msim'.

`-mno-id-shared-library`
> Generate code that doesn't assume ID based shared libraries are being used. This is the default.

`-mleaf-id-shared-library`
> Generate code that supports shared libraries via the library ID method, but assumes that this library or executable won't link against any other ID shared libraries. That allows the compiler to use faster code for jumps and calls.

`-mno-leaf-id-shared-library`
> Do not assume that the code being compiled won't link against any ID shared libraries. Slower code will be generated for jump and call insns.

`-mshared-library-id=n`
> Specified the identification number of the ID based shared library being compiled. Specifying a value of 0 will generate more compact code, specifying other values will force the allocation of that number to the current library but is no more space or time efficient than omitting this option.

Chapter 3: GCC Command Options   143

`-msep-data`
: Generate code that allows the data segment to be located in a different area of memory from the text segment. This allows for execute in place in an environment without virtual memory management by eliminating relocations against the text section.

`-mno-sep-data`
: Generate code that assumes that the data segment follows the text segment. This is the default.

`-mlong-calls`
`-mno-long-calls`
: Tells the compiler to perform function calls by first loading the address of the function into a register and then performing a subroutine call on this register. This switch is needed if the target function will lie outside of the 24 bit addressing range of the offset based version of subroutine call instruction.

  This feature is not enabled by default. Specifying '`-mno-long-calls`' will restore the default behavior. Note these switches have no effect on how the compiler generates code to handle function calls via function pointers.

`-mfast-fp`
: Link with the fast floating-point library. This library relaxes some of the IEEE floating-point standard's rules for checking inputs against Not-a-Number (NAN), in the interest of performance.

`-minline-plt`
: Enable inlining of PLT entries in function calls to functions that are not known to bind locally. It has no effect without '`-mfdpic`'.

3.17.5 CRIS Options

These options are defined specifically for the CRIS ports.

`-march=architecture-type`
`-mcpu=architecture-type`
: Generate code for the specified architecture. The choices for *architecture-type* are 'v3', 'v8' and 'v10' for respectively ETRAX 4, ETRAX 100, and ETRAX 100 LX. Default is 'v0' except for cris-axis-linux-gnu, where the default is 'v10'.

`-mtune=architecture-type`
: Tune to *architecture-type* everything applicable about the generated code, except for the ABI and the set of available instructions. The choices for *architecture-type* are the same as for '`-march=architecture-type`'.

`-mmax-stack-frame=n`
: Warn when the stack frame of a function exceeds *n* bytes.

`-melinux-stacksize=n`
: Only available with the '`cris-axis-aout`' target. Arranges for indications in the program to the kernel loader that the stack of the program should be set to *n* bytes.

`-metrax4`
`-metrax100`
: The options '`-metrax4`' and '`-metrax100`' are synonyms for '`-march=v3`' and '`-march=v8`' respectively.

`-mmul-bug-workaround`
`-mno-mul-bug-workaround`
: Work around a bug in the `muls` and `mulu` instructions for CPU models where it applies. This option is active by default.

`-mpdebug`
: Enable CRIS-specific verbose debug-related information in the assembly code. This option also has the effect to turn off the '`#NO_APP`' formatted-code indicator to the assembler at the beginning of the assembly file.

`-mcc-init`
: Do not use condition-code results from previous instruction; always emit compare and test instructions before use of condition codes.

`-mno-side-effects`
: Do not emit instructions with side-effects in addressing modes other than post-increment.

`-mstack-align`
`-mno-stack-align`
`-mdata-align`
`-mno-data-align`
`-mconst-align`
`-mno-const-align`
: These options (no-options) arranges (eliminate arrangements) for the stack-frame, individual data and constants to be aligned for the maximum single data access size for the chosen CPU model. The default is to arrange for 32-bit alignment. ABI details such as structure layout are not affected by these options.

`-m32-bit`
`-m16-bit`
`-m8-bit`
: Similar to the stack- data- and const-align options above, these options arrange for stack-frame, writable data and constants to all be 32-bit, 16-bit or 8-bit aligned. The default is 32-bit alignment.

`-mno-prologue-epilogue`
`-mprologue-epilogue`
: With '`-mno-prologue-epilogue`', the normal function prologue and epilogue that sets up the stack-frame are omitted and no return instructions or return sequences are generated in the code. Use this option only together with visual inspection of the compiled code: no warnings or errors are generated when call-saved registers must be saved, or storage for local variable needs to be allocated.

Chapter 3: GCC Command Options   145

`-mno-gotplt`
`-mgotplt`   With '`-fpic`' and '`-fPIC`', don't generate (do generate) instruction sequences that load addresses for functions from the PLT part of the GOT rather than (traditional on other architectures) calls to the PLT. The default is '`-mgotplt`'.

`-maout`   Legacy no-op option only recognized with the cris-axis-aout target.

`-melf`   Legacy no-op option only recognized with the cris-axis-elf and cris-axis-linux-gnu targets.

`-melinux`   Only recognized with the cris-axis-aout target, where it selects a GNU/linux-like multilib, include files and instruction set for '`-march=v8`'.

`-mlinux`   Legacy no-op option only recognized with the cris-axis-linux-gnu target.

`-sim`   This option, recognized for the cris-axis-aout and cris-axis-elf arranges to link with input-output functions from a simulator library. Code, initialized data and zero-initialized data are allocated consecutively.

`-sim2`   Like '`-sim`', but pass linker options to locate initialized data at 0x40000000 and zero-initialized data at 0x80000000.

3.17.6 CRX Options

These options are defined specifically for the CRX ports.

`-mmac`   Enable the use of multiply-accumulate instructions. Disabled by default.

`-mpush-args`
             Push instructions will be used to pass outgoing arguments when functions are called. Enabled by default.

3.17.7 Darwin Options

These options are defined for all architectures running the Darwin operating system.

FSF GCC on Darwin does not create "fat" object files; it will create an object file for the single architecture that it was built to target. Apple's GCC on Darwin does create "fat" files if multiple '`-arch`' options are used; it does so by running the compiler or linker multiple times and joining the results together with '`lipo`'.

The subtype of the file created (like '`ppc7400`' or '`ppc970`' or '`i686`') is determined by the flags that specify the ISA that GCC is targetting, like '`-mcpu`' or '`-march`'. The '`-force_cpusubtype_ALL`' option can be used to override this.

The Darwin tools vary in their behavior when presented with an ISA mismatch. The assembler, '`as`', will only permit instructions to be used that are valid for the subtype of the file it is generating, so you cannot put 64-bit instructions in an '`ppc750`' object file. The linker for shared libraries, '`/usr/bin/libtool`', will fail and print an error if asked to create a shared library with a less restrictive subtype than its input files (for instance, trying to put a '`ppc970`' object file in a '`ppc7400`' library). The linker for executables, '`ld`', will quietly give the executable the most restrictive subtype of any of its input files.

`-Fdir`   Add the framework directory *dir* to the head of the list of directories to be searched for header files. These directories are interleaved with those specified by '`-I`' options and are scanned in a left-to-right order.

A framework directory is a directory with frameworks in it. A framework is a directory with a '"Headers"' and/or '"PrivateHeaders"' directory contained directly in it that ends in '".framework"'. The name of a framework is the name of this directory excluding the '".framework"'. Headers associated with the framework are found in one of those two directories, with '"Headers"' being searched first. A subframework is a framework directory that is in a framework's '"Frameworks"' directory. Includes of subframework headers can only appear in a header of a framework that contains the subframework, or in a sibling subframework header. Two subframeworks are siblings if they occur in the same framework. A subframework should not have the same name as a framework, a warning will be issued if this is violated. Currently a subframework cannot have subframeworks, in the future, the mechanism may be extended to support this. The standard frameworks can be found in '"/System/Library/Frameworks"' and '"/Library/Frameworks"'. An example include looks like #include <Framework/header.h>, where 'Framework' denotes the name of the framework and header.h is found in the '"PrivateHeaders"' or '"Headers"' directory.

-iframework*dir*

Like '-F' except the directory is a treated as a system directory. The main difference between this '-iframework' and '-F' is that with '-iframework' the compiler does not warn about constructs contained within header files found via *dir*. This option is valid only for the C family of languages.

-gused   Emit debugging information for symbols that are used. For STABS debugging format, this enables '-feliminate-unused-debug-symbols'. This is by default ON.

-gfull   Emit debugging information for all symbols and types.

-mmacosx-version-min=*version*

The earliest version of MacOS X that this executable will run on is *version*. Typical values of *version* include 10.1, 10.2, and 10.3.9.

If the compiler was built to use the system's headers by default, then the default for this option is the system version on which the compiler is running, otherwise the default is to make choices which are compatible with as many systems and code bases as possible.

-mkernel   Enable kernel development mode. The '-mkernel' option sets '-static', '-fno-common', '-fno-cxa-atexit', '-fno-exceptions', '-fno-non-call-exceptions', '-fapple-kext', '-fno-weak' and '-fno-rtti' where applicable. This mode also sets '-mno-altivec', '-msoft-float', '-fno-builtin' and '-mlong-branch' for PowerPC targets.

-mone-byte-bool

Override the defaults for 'bool' so that 'sizeof(bool)==1'. By default 'sizeof(bool)' is '4' when compiling for Darwin/PowerPC and '1' when compiling for Darwin/x86, so this option has no effect on x86.

Warning: The '-mone-byte-bool' switch causes GCC to generate code that is not binary compatible with code generated without that switch. Using this

Chapter 3: GCC Command Options   147

switch may require recompiling all other modules in a program, including system libraries. Use this switch to conform to a non-default data model.

`-mfix-and-continue`
`-ffix-and-continue`
`-findirect-data`
    Generate code suitable for fast turn around development. Needed to enable gdb to dynamically load .o files into already running programs. '`-findirect-data`' and '`-ffix-and-continue`' are provided for backwards compatibility.

`-all_load`
    Loads all members of static archive libraries. See man ld(1) for more information.

`-arch_errors_fatal`
    Cause the errors having to do with files that have the wrong architecture to be fatal.

`-bind_at_load`
    Causes the output file to be marked such that the dynamic linker will bind all undefined references when the file is loaded or launched.

`-bundle` Produce a Mach-o bundle format file. See man ld(1) for more information.

`-bundle_loader` *executable*
    This option specifies the *executable* that will be loading the build output file being linked. See man ld(1) for more information.

`-dynamiclib`
    When passed this option, GCC will produce a dynamic library instead of an executable when linking, using the Darwin '`libtool`' command.

`-force_cpusubtype_ALL`
    This causes GCC's output file to have the *ALL* subtype, instead of one controlled by the '`-mcpu`' or '`-march`' option.

```
-allowable_client client_name
-client_name
-compatibility_version
-current_version
-dead_strip
-dependency-file
-dylib_file
-dylinker_install_name
-dynamic
-exported_symbols_list
-filelist
-flat_namespace
-force_flat_namespace
-headerpad_max_install_names
-image_base
-init
-install_name
-keep_private_externs
-multi_module
-multiply_defined
-multiply_defined_unused
-noall_load
-no_dead_strip_inits_and_terms
-nofixprebinding
-nomultidefs
-noprebind
-noseglinkedit
-pagezero_size
-prebind
-prebind_all_twolevel_modules
-private_bundle
-read_only_relocs
-sectalign
-sectobjectsymbols
-whyload
-seg1addr
-sectcreate
-sectobjectsymbols
-sectorder
-segaddr
-segs_read_only_addr
-segs_read_write_addr
-seg_addr_table
-seg_addr_table_filename
-seglinkedit
-segprot
-segs_read_only_addr
-segs_read_write_addr
-single_module
-static
-sub_library
```

3.17.8 DEC Alpha Options

These '-m' options are defined for the DEC Alpha implementations:

`-mno-soft-float`
`-msoft-float`

>Use (do not use) the hardware floating-point instructions for floating-point operations. When '-msoft-float' is specified, functions in 'libgcc.a' will be used to perform floating-point operations. Unless they are replaced by routines that emulate the floating-point operations, or compiled in such a way as to call such emulations routines, these routines will issue floating-point operations. If you are compiling for an Alpha without floating-point operations, you must ensure that the library is built so as not to call them.
>
>Note that Alpha implementations without floating-point operations are required to have floating-point registers.

`-mfp-reg`
`-mno-fp-regs`

>Generate code that uses (does not use) the floating-point register set. '-mno-fp-regs' implies '-msoft-float'. If the floating-point register set is not used, floating point operands are passed in integer registers as if they were integers and floating-point results are passed in $0 instead of $f0. This is a non-standard calling sequence, so any function with a floating-point argument or return value called by code compiled with '-mno-fp-regs' must also be compiled with that option.
>
>A typical use of this option is building a kernel that does not use, and hence need not save and restore, any floating-point registers.

`-mieee` The Alpha architecture implements floating-point hardware optimized for maximum performance. It is mostly compliant with the IEEE floating point standard. However, for full compliance, software assistance is required. This option generates code fully IEEE compliant code *except* that the *inexact-flag* is not maintained (see below). If this option is turned on, the preprocessor macro `_IEEE_FP` is defined during compilation. The resulting code is less efficient but is able to correctly support denormalized numbers and exceptional IEEE values such as not-a-number and plus/minus infinity. Other Alpha compilers call this option '-ieee_with_no_inexact'.

`-mieee-with-inexact`

>This is like '-mieee' except the generated code also maintains the IEEE *inexact-flag*. Turning on this option causes the generated code to implement fully-compliant IEEE math. In addition to `_IEEE_FP`, `_IEEE_FP_EXACT` is defined as a preprocessor macro. On some Alpha implementations the resulting code may execute significantly slower than the code generated by default. Since there is very little code that depends on the *inexact-flag*, you should normally not specify this option. Other Alpha compilers call this option '-ieee_with_inexact'.

`-mfp-trap-mode=trap-mode`
>   This option controls what floating-point related traps are enabled. Other Alpha compilers call this option '`-fptm trap-mode`'. The trap mode can be set to one of four values:
>
>   'n'
>   >   This is the default (normal) setting. The only traps that are enabled are the ones that cannot be disabled in software (e.g., division by zero trap).
>
>   'u'
>   >   In addition to the traps enabled by 'n', underflow traps are enabled as well.
>
>   'su'
>   >   Like 'u', but the instructions are marked to be safe for software completion (see Alpha architecture manual for details).
>
>   'sui'
>   >   Like 'su', but inexact traps are enabled as well.

`-mfp-rounding-mode=rounding-mode`
>   Selects the IEEE rounding mode. Other Alpha compilers call this option '`-fprm rounding-mode`'. The *rounding-mode* can be one of:
>
>   'n'
>   >   Normal IEEE rounding mode. Floating point numbers are rounded towards the nearest machine number or towards the even machine number in case of a tie.
>
>   'm'
>   >   Round towards minus infinity.
>
>   'c'
>   >   Chopped rounding mode. Floating point numbers are rounded towards zero.
>
>   'd'
>   >   Dynamic rounding mode. A field in the floating point control register (*fpcr*, see Alpha architecture reference manual) controls the rounding mode in effect. The C library initializes this register for rounding towards plus infinity. Thus, unless your program modifies the *fpcr*, 'd' corresponds to round towards plus infinity.

`-mtrap-precision=trap-precision`
>   In the Alpha architecture, floating point traps are imprecise. This means without software assistance it is impossible to recover from a floating trap and program execution normally needs to be terminated. GCC can generate code that can assist operating system trap handlers in determining the exact location that caused a floating point trap. Depending on the requirements of an application, different levels of precisions can be selected:
>
>   'p'
>   >   Program precision. This option is the default and means a trap handler can only identify which program caused a floating point exception.
>
>   'f'
>   >   Function precision. The trap handler can determine the function that caused a floating point exception.
>
>   'i'
>   >   Instruction precision. The trap handler can determine the exact instruction that caused a floating point exception.

Chapter 3: GCC Command Options   151

`-mieee-conformant`
> This option marks the generated code as IEEE conformant. You must not use this option unless you also specify '`-mtrap-precision=i`' and either '`-mfp-trap-mode=su`' or '`-mfp-trap-mode=sui`'. Its only effect is to emit the line '`.eflag 48`' in the function prologue of the generated assembly file. Under DEC Unix, this has the effect that IEEE-conformant math library routines will be linked in.

`-mbuild-constants`
> Normally GCC examines a 32- or 64-bit integer constant to see if it can construct it from smaller constants in two or three instructions. If it cannot, it will output the constant as a literal and generate code to load it from the data segment at runtime.
>
> Use this option to require GCC to construct *all* integer constants using code, even if it takes more instructions (the maximum is six).
>
> You would typically use this option to build a shared library dynamic loader. Itself a shared library, it must relocate itself in memory before it can find the variables and constants in its own data segment.

`-malpha-as`
`-mgas`
>   Select whether to generate code to be assembled by the vendor-supplied assembler ('`-malpha-as`') or by the GNU assembler '`-mgas`'.

`-mbwx`
`-mno-bwx`
`-mcix`
`-mno-cix`
`-mfix`
`-mno-fix`
`-mmax`
`-mno-max`
>   Indicate whether GCC should generate code to use the optional BWX, CIX, FIX and MAX instruction sets. The default is to use the instruction sets supported by the CPU type specified via '`-mcpu=`' option or that of the CPU on which GCC was built if none was specified.

`-mfloat-vax`
`-mfloat-ieee`
> Generate code that uses (does not use) VAX F and G floating point arithmetic instead of IEEE single and double precision.

`-mexplicit-relocs`
`-mno-explicit-relocs`
> Older Alpha assemblers provided no way to generate symbol relocations except via assembler macros. Use of these macros does not allow optimal instruction scheduling. GNU binutils as of version 2.12 supports a new syntax that allows the compiler to explicitly mark which relocations should apply to which

instructions. This option is mostly useful for debugging, as GCC detects the capabilities of the assembler when it is built and sets the default accordingly.

`-msmall-data`
`-mlarge-data`

When '`-mexplicit-relocs`' is in effect, static data is accessed via *gp-relative* relocations. When '`-msmall-data`' is used, objects 8 bytes long or smaller are placed in a *small data area* (the `.sdata` and `.sbss` sections) and are accessed via 16-bit relocations off of the `$gp` register. This limits the size of the small data area to 64KB, but allows the variables to be directly accessed via a single instruction.

The default is '`-mlarge-data`'. With this option the data area is limited to just below 2GB. Programs that require more than 2GB of data must use `malloc` or `mmap` to allocate the data in the heap instead of in the program's data segment.

When generating code for shared libraries, '`-fpic`' implies '`-msmall-data`' and '`-fPIC`' implies '`-mlarge-data`'.

`-msmall-text`
`-mlarge-text`

When '`-msmall-text`' is used, the compiler assumes that the code of the entire program (or shared library) fits in 4MB, and is thus reachable with a branch instruction. When '`-msmall-data`' is used, the compiler can assume that all local symbols share the same `$gp` value, and thus reduce the number of instructions required for a function call from 4 to 1.

The default is '`-mlarge-text`'.

`-mcpu=cpu_type`

Set the instruction set and instruction scheduling parameters for machine type *cpu_type*. You can specify either the 'EV' style name or the corresponding chip number. GCC supports scheduling parameters for the EV4, EV5 and EV6 family of processors and will choose the default values for the instruction set from the processor you specify. If you do not specify a processor type, GCC will default to the processor on which the compiler was built.

Supported values for *cpu_type* are

'ev4'
'ev45'
'21064'   Schedules as an EV4 and has no instruction set extensions.

'ev5'
'21164'   Schedules as an EV5 and has no instruction set extensions.

'ev56'
'21164a'   Schedules as an EV5 and supports the BWX extension.

'pca56'
'21164pc'
'21164PC' Schedules as an EV5 and supports the BWX and MAX extensions.

Chapter 3: GCC Command Options   153

> 'ev6'
> '21264'   Schedules as an EV6 and supports the BWX, FIX, and MAX extensions.
>
> 'ev67'
> '21264a'   Schedules as an EV6 and supports the BWX, CIX, FIX, and MAX extensions.

`-mtune=cpu_type`
> Set only the instruction scheduling parameters for machine type *cpu_type*. The instruction set is not changed.

`-mmemory-latency=time`
> Sets the latency the scheduler should assume for typical memory references as seen by the application. This number is highly dependent on the memory access patterns used by the application and the size of the external cache on the machine.
>
> Valid options for *time* are
>
> 'number'   A decimal number representing clock cycles.
>
> 'L1'
> 'L2'
> 'L3'
> 'main'   The compiler contains estimates of the number of clock cycles for "typical" EV4 & EV5 hardware for the Level 1, 2 & 3 caches (also called Dcache, Scache, and Bcache), as well as to main memory. Note that L3 is only valid for EV5.

3.17.9 DEC Alpha/VMS Options

These '-m' options are defined for the DEC Alpha/VMS implementations:

`-mvms-return-codes`
> Return VMS condition codes from main. The default is to return POSIX style condition (e.g. error) codes.

3.17.10 FRV Options

`-mgpr-32`
> Only use the first 32 general purpose registers.

`-mgpr-64`
> Use all 64 general purpose registers.

`-mfpr-32`
> Use only the first 32 floating point registers.

`-mfpr-64`
> Use all 64 floating point registers

`-mhard-float`
> Use hardware instructions for floating point operations.

`-msoft-float`
: Use library routines for floating point operations.

`-malloc-cc`
: Dynamically allocate condition code registers.

`-mfixed-cc`
: Do not try to dynamically allocate condition code registers, only use `icc0` and `fcc0`.

`-mdword`
: Change ABI to use double word insns.

`-mno-dword`
: Do not use double word instructions.

`-mdouble`
: Use floating point double instructions.

`-mno-double`
: Do not use floating point double instructions.

`-mmedia`
: Use media instructions.

`-mno-media`
: Do not use media instructions.

`-mmuladd`
: Use multiply and add/subtract instructions.

`-mno-muladd`
: Do not use multiply and add/subtract instructions.

`-mfdpic`
: Select the FDPIC ABI, that uses function descriptors to represent pointers to functions. Without any PIC/PIE-related options, it implies '-fPIE'. With '-fpic' or '-fpie', it assumes GOT entries and small data are within a 12-bit range from the GOT base address; with '-fPIC' or '-fPIE', GOT offsets are computed with 32 bits. With a 'bfin-elf' target, this option implies '-msim'.

`-minline-plt`
: Enable inlining of PLT entries in function calls to functions that are not known to bind locally. It has no effect without '-mfdpic'. It's enabled by default if optimizing for speed and compiling for shared libraries (i.e., '-fPIC' or '-fpic'), or when an optimization option such as '-O3' or above is present in the command line.

`-mTLS`
: Assume a large TLS segment when generating thread-local code.

`-mtls`
: Do not assume a large TLS segment when generating thread-local code.

Chapter 3: GCC Command Options 155

`-mgprel-ro`
: Enable the use of `GPREL` relocations in the FDPIC ABI for data that is known to be in read-only sections. It's enabled by default, except for '`-fpic`' or '`-fpie`': even though it may help make the global offset table smaller, it trades 1 instruction for 4. With '`-fPIC`' or '`-fPIE`', it trades 3 instructions for 4, one of which may be shared by multiple symbols, and it avoids the need for a GOT entry for the referenced symbol, so it's more likely to be a win. If it is not, '`-mno-gprel-ro`' can be used to disable it.

`-multilib-library-pic`
: Link with the (library, not FD) pic libraries. It's implied by '`-mlibrary-pic`', as well as by '`-fPIC`' and '`-fpic`' without '`-mfdpic`'. You should never have to use it explicitly.

`-mlinked-fp`
: Follow the EABI requirement of always creating a frame pointer whenever a stack frame is allocated. This option is enabled by default and can be disabled with '`-mno-linked-fp`'.

`-mlong-calls`
: Use indirect addressing to call functions outside the current compilation unit. This allows the functions to be placed anywhere within the 32-bit address space.

`-malign-labels`
: Try to align labels to an 8-byte boundary by inserting nops into the previous packet. This option only has an effect when VLIW packing is enabled. It doesn't create new packets; it merely adds nops to existing ones.

`-mlibrary-pic`
: Generate position-independent EABI code.

`-macc-4`
: Use only the first four media accumulator registers.

`-macc-8`
: Use all eight media accumulator registers.

`-mpack`
: Pack VLIW instructions.

`-mno-pack`
: Do not pack VLIW instructions.

`-mno-eflags`
: Do not mark ABI switches in e_flags.

`-mcond-move`
: Enable the use of conditional-move instructions (default).

  This switch is mainly for debugging the compiler and will likely be removed in a future version.

`-mno-cond-move`
: Disable the use of conditional-move instructions.

This switch is mainly for debugging the compiler and will likely be removed in a future version.

`-mscc`
    Enable the use of conditional set instructions (default).

    This switch is mainly for debugging the compiler and will likely be removed in a future version.

`-mno-scc`
    Disable the use of conditional set instructions.

    This switch is mainly for debugging the compiler and will likely be removed in a future version.

`-mcond-exec`
    Enable the use of conditional execution (default).

    This switch is mainly for debugging the compiler and will likely be removed in a future version.

`-mno-cond-exec`
    Disable the use of conditional execution.

    This switch is mainly for debugging the compiler and will likely be removed in a future version.

`-mvliw-branch`
    Run a pass to pack branches into VLIW instructions (default).

    This switch is mainly for debugging the compiler and will likely be removed in a future version.

`-mno-vliw-branch`
    Do not run a pass to pack branches into VLIW instructions.

    This switch is mainly for debugging the compiler and will likely be removed in a future version.

`-mmulti-cond-exec`
    Enable optimization of && and || in conditional execution (default).

    This switch is mainly for debugging the compiler and will likely be removed in a future version.

`-mno-multi-cond-exec`
    Disable optimization of && and || in conditional execution.

    This switch is mainly for debugging the compiler and will likely be removed in a future version.

`-mnested-cond-exec`
    Enable nested conditional execution optimizations (default).

    This switch is mainly for debugging the compiler and will likely be removed in a future version.

`-mno-nested-cond-exec`
    Disable nested conditional execution optimizations.

Chapter 3: GCC Command Options   157

This switch is mainly for debugging the compiler and will likely be removed in a future version.

`-moptimize-membar`
: This switch removes redundant `membar` instructions from the compiler generated code. It is enabled by default.

`-mno-optimize-membar`
: This switch disables the automatic removal of redundant `membar` instructions from the generated code.

`-mtomcat-stats`
: Cause gas to print out tomcat statistics.

`-mcpu=`*cpu*
: Select the processor type for which to generate code. Possible values are 'frv', 'fr550', 'tomcat', 'fr500', 'fr450', 'fr405', 'fr400', 'fr300' and 'simple'.

3.17.11 GNU/Linux Options

These '-m' options are defined for GNU/Linux targets:

`-mglibc`
: Use the GNU C library instead of uClibc. This is the default except on '*-*-linux-*uclibc*' targets.

`-muclibc`
: Use uClibc instead of the GNU C library. This is the default on '*-*-linux-*uclibc*' targets.

3.17.12 H8/300 Options

These '-m' options are defined for the H8/300 implementations:

`-mrelax`
: Shorten some address references at link time, when possible; uses the linker option '-relax'. See Section "ld and the H8/300" in Using ld, for a fuller description.

`-mh`
: Generate code for the H8/300H.

`-ms`
: Generate code for the H8S.

`-mn`
: Generate code for the H8S and H8/300H in the normal mode. This switch must be used either with '-mh' or '-ms'.

`-ms2600`
: Generate code for the H8S/2600. This switch must be used with '-ms'.

`-mint32`
: Make `int` data 32 bits by default.

`-malign-300`
: On the H8/300H and H8S, use the same alignment rules as for the H8/300. The default for the H8/300H and H8S is to align longs and floats on 4 byte boundaries. '-malign-300' causes them to be aligned on 2 byte boundaries. This option has no effect on the H8/300.

3.17.13 HPPA Options

These '-m' options are defined for the HPPA family of computers:

-march=*architecture-type*
: Generate code for the specified architecture. The choices for *architecture-type* are '1.0' for PA 1.0, '1.1' for PA 1.1, and '2.0' for PA 2.0 processors. Refer to '/usr/lib/sched.models' on an HP-UX system to determine the proper architecture option for your machine. Code compiled for lower numbered architectures will run on higher numbered architectures, but not the other way around.

-mpa-risc-1-0
-mpa-risc-1-1
-mpa-risc-2-0
: Synonyms for '-march=1.0', '-march=1.1', and '-march=2.0' respectively.

-mbig-switch
: Generate code suitable for big switch tables. Use this option only if the assembler/linker complain about out of range branches within a switch table.

-mjump-in-delay
: Fill delay slots of function calls with unconditional jump instructions by modifying the return pointer for the function call to be the target of the conditional jump.

-mdisable-fpregs
: Prevent floating point registers from being used in any manner. This is necessary for compiling kernels which perform lazy context switching of floating point registers. If you use this option and attempt to perform floating point operations, the compiler will abort.

-mdisable-indexing
: Prevent the compiler from using indexing address modes. This avoids some rather obscure problems when compiling MIG generated code under MACH.

-mno-space-regs
: Generate code that assumes the target has no space registers. This allows GCC to generate faster indirect calls and use unscaled index address modes.

  Such code is suitable for level 0 PA systems and kernels.

-mfast-indirect-calls
: Generate code that assumes calls never cross space boundaries. This allows GCC to emit code which performs faster indirect calls.

  This option will not work in the presence of shared libraries or nested functions.

-mfixed-range=*register-range*
: Generate code treating the given register range as fixed registers. A fixed register is one that the register allocator can not use. This is useful when compiling kernel code. A register range is specified as two registers separated by a dash. Multiple register ranges can be specified separated by a comma.

Chapter 3: GCC Command Options 159

`-mlong-load-store`
> Generate 3-instruction load and store sequences as sometimes required by the HP-UX 10 linker. This is equivalent to the '+k' option to the HP compilers.

`-mportable-runtime`
> Use the portable calling conventions proposed by HP for ELF systems.

`-mgas`   Enable the use of assembler directives only GAS understands.

`-mschedule=cpu-type`
> Schedule code according to the constraints for the machine type *cpu-type*. The choices for *cpu-type* are '700' '7100', '7100LC', '7200', '7300' and '8000'. Refer to '/usr/lib/sched.models' on an HP-UX system to determine the proper scheduling option for your machine. The default scheduling is '8000'.

`-mlinker-opt`
> Enable the optimization pass in the HP-UX linker. Note this makes symbolic debugging impossible. It also triggers a bug in the HP-UX 8 and HP-UX 9 linkers in which they give bogus error messages when linking some programs.

`-msoft-float`
> Generate output containing library calls for floating point. **Warning:** the requisite libraries are not available for all HPPA targets. Normally the facilities of the machine's usual C compiler are used, but this cannot be done directly in cross-compilation. You must make your own arrangements to provide suitable library functions for cross-compilation. The embedded target 'hppa1.1-*-pro' does provide software floating point support.
>
> '-msoft-float' changes the calling convention in the output file; therefore, it is only useful if you compile *all* of a program with this option. In particular, you need to compile 'libgcc.a', the library that comes with GCC, with '-msoft-float' in order for this to work.

`-msio`   Generate the predefine, _SIO, for server IO. The default is '-mwsio'. This generates the predefines, __hp9000s700, __hp9000s700__ and _WSIO, for workstation IO. These options are available under HP-UX and HI-UX.

`-mgnu-ld`   Use GNU ld specific options. This passes '-shared' to ld when building a shared library. It is the default when GCC is configured, explicitly or implicitly, with the GNU linker. This option does not have any affect on which ld is called, it only changes what parameters are passed to that ld. The ld that is called is determined by the '--with-ld' configure option, GCC's program search path, and finally by the user's PATH. The linker used by GCC can be printed using 'which `gcc -print-prog-name=ld`'. This option is only available on the 64 bit HP-UX GCC, i.e. configured with 'hppa*64*-*-hpux*'.

`-mhp-ld`   Use HP ld specific options. This passes '-b' to ld when building a shared library and passes '+Accept TypeMismatch' to ld on all links. It is the default when GCC is configured, explicitly or implicitly, with the HP linker. This option does not have any affect on which ld is called, it only changes what parameters are passed to that ld. The ld that is called is determined by the '--with-ld' configure option, GCC's program search path, and finally by the user's PATH. The linker used by GCC can be printed using 'which `gcc -print-prog-name=ld`'. This option is only available on the 64 bit HP-UX GCC, i.e. configured with 'hppa*64*-*-hpux*'.

`-mlong-calls`

Generate code that uses long call sequences. This ensures that a call is always able to reach linker generated stubs. The default is to generate long calls only when the distance from the call site to the beginning of the function or translation unit, as the case may be, exceeds a predefined limit set by the branch type being used. The limits for normal calls are 7,600,000 and 240,000 bytes, respectively for the PA 2.0 and PA 1.X architectures. Sibcalls are always limited at 240,000 bytes.

Distances are measured from the beginning of functions when using the '-ffunction-sections' option, or when using the '-mgas' and '-mno-portable-runtime' options together under HP-UX with the SOM linker.

It is normally not desirable to use this option as it will degrade performance. However, it may be useful in large applications, particularly when partial linking is used to build the application.

The types of long calls used depends on the capabilities of the assembler and linker, and the type of code being generated. The impact on systems that support long absolute calls, and long pic symbol-difference or pc-relative calls should be relatively small. However, an indirect call is used on 32-bit ELF systems in pic code and it is quite long.

`-munix=`*unix-std*

Generate compiler predefines and select a startfile for the specified UNIX standard. The choices for *unix-std* are '93', '95' and '98'. '93' is supported on all HP-UX versions. '95' is available on HP-UX 10.10 and later. '98' is available on HP-UX 11.11 and later. The default values are '93' for HP-UX 10.00, '95' for HP-UX 10.10 though to 11.00, and '98' for HP-UX 11.11 and later.

'-munix=93' provides the same predefines as GCC 3.3 and 3.4. '-munix=95' provides additional predefines for XOPEN_UNIX and _XOPEN_SOURCE_EXTENDED, and the startfile 'unix95.o'. '-munix=98' provides additional predefines for _XOPEN_UNIX, _XOPEN_SOURCE_EXTENDED, _INCLUDE__STDC_A1_SOURCE and _INCLUDE_XOPEN_SOURCE_500, and the startfile 'unix98.o'.

It is *important* to note that this option changes the interfaces for various library routines. It also affects the operational behavior of the C library. Thus, *extreme* care is needed in using this option.

Library code that is intended to operate with more than one UNIX standard must test, set and restore the variable *__xpg4_extended_mask* as appropriate. Most GNU software doesn't provide this capability.

`-nolibdld`

Suppress the generation of link options to search libdld.sl when the '-static' option is specified on HP-UX 10 and later.

Chapter 3: GCC Command Options   161

`-static`   The HP-UX implementation of setlocale in libc has a dependency on libdld.sl. There isn't an archive version of libdld.sl. Thus, when the '`-static`' option is specified, special link options are needed to resolve this dependency.

On HP-UX 10 and later, the GCC driver adds the necessary options to link with libdld.sl when the '`-static`' option is specified. This causes the resulting binary to be dynamic. On the 64-bit port, the linkers generate dynamic binaries by default in any case. The '`-nolibdld`' option can be used to prevent the GCC driver from adding these link options.

`-threads`   Add support for multithreading with the *dce thread* library under HP-UX. This option sets flags for both the preprocessor and linker.

3.17.14 Intel 386 and AMD x86-64 Options

These '`-m`' options are defined for the i386 and x86-64 family of computers:

`-mtune=`*cpu-type*

Tune to *cpu-type* everything applicable about the generated code, except for the ABI and the set of available instructions. The choices for *cpu-type* are:

generic   Produce code optimized for the most common IA32/AMD64/EM64T processors. If you know the CPU on which your code will run, then you should use the corresponding '`-mtune`' option instead of '`-mtune=generic`'. But, if you do not know exactly what CPU users of your application will have, then you should use this option.

As new processors are deployed in the marketplace, the behavior of this option will change. Therefore, if you upgrade to a newer version of GCC, the code generated option will change to reflect the processors that were most common when that version of GCC was released.

There is no '`-march=generic`' option because '`-march`' indicates the instruction set the compiler can use, and there is no generic instruction set applicable to all processors. In contrast, '`-mtune`' indicates the processor (or, in this case, collection of processors) for which the code is optimized.

native   This selects the CPU to tune for at compilation time by determining the processor type of the compiling machine. Using '`-mtune=native`' will produce code optimized for the local machine under the constraints of the selected instruction set. Using '`-march=native`' will enable all instruction subsets supported by the local machine (hence the result might not run on different machines).

i386   Original Intel's i386 CPU.

i486   Intel's i486 CPU. (No scheduling is implemented for this chip.)

i586, pentium

Intel Pentium CPU with no MMX support.

pentium-mmx
: Intel PentiumMMX CPU based on Pentium core with MMX instruction set support.

pentiumpro
: Intel PentiumPro CPU.

i686
: Same as `generic`, but when used as `march` option, PentiumPro instruction set will be used, so the code will run on all i686 family chips.

pentium2
: Intel Pentium2 CPU based on PentiumPro core with MMX instruction set support.

pentium3, pentium3m
: Intel Pentium3 CPU based on PentiumPro core with MMX and SSE instruction set support.

pentium-m
: Low power version of Intel Pentium3 CPU with MMX, SSE and SSE2 instruction set support. Used by Centrino notebooks.

pentium4, pentium4m
: Intel Pentium4 CPU with MMX, SSE and SSE2 instruction set support.

prescott
: Improved version of Intel Pentium4 CPU with MMX, SSE, SSE2 and SSE3 instruction set support.

nocona
: Improved version of Intel Pentium4 CPU with 64-bit extensions, MMX, SSE, SSE2 and SSE3 instruction set support.

core2
: Intel Core2 CPU with 64-bit extensions, MMX, SSE, SSE2, SSE3 and SSSE3 instruction set support.

k6
: AMD K6 CPU with MMX instruction set support.

k6-2, k6-3
: Improved versions of AMD K6 CPU with MMX and 3dNOW! instruction set support.

athlon, athlon-tbird
: AMD Athlon CPU with MMX, 3dNOW!, enhanced 3dNOW! and SSE prefetch instructions support.

athlon-4, athlon-xp, athlon-mp
: Improved AMD Athlon CPU with MMX, 3dNOW!, enhanced 3dNOW! and full SSE instruction set support.

k8, opteron, athlon64, athlon-fx
: AMD K8 core based CPUs with x86-64 instruction set support. (This supersets MMX, SSE, SSE2, 3dNOW!, enhanced 3dNOW! and 64-bit instruction set extensions.)

k8-sse3, opteron-sse3, athlon64-sse3
: Improved versions of k8, opteron and athlon64 with SSE3 instruction set support.

Chapter 3: GCC Command Options   163

> *amdfam10, barcelona*
> > AMD Family 10h core based CPUs with x86-64 instruction set support. (This supersets MMX, SSE, SSE2, SSE3, SSE4A, 3dNOW!, enhanced 3dNOW!, ABM and 64-bit instruction set extensions.)
>
> *winchip-c6*
> > IDT Winchip C6 CPU, dealt in same way as i486 with additional MMX instruction set support.
>
> *winchip2* IDT Winchip2 CPU, dealt in same way as i486 with additional MMX and 3dNOW! instruction set support.
>
> *c3* Via C3 CPU with MMX and 3dNOW! instruction set support. (No scheduling is implemented for this chip.)
>
> *c3-2* Via C3-2 CPU with MMX and SSE instruction set support. (No scheduling is implemented for this chip.)
>
> *geode* Embedded AMD CPU with MMX and 3dNOW! instruction set support.
>
> While picking a specific *cpu-type* will schedule things appropriately for that particular chip, the compiler will not generate any code that does not run on the i386 without the '-march=*cpu-type*' option being used.

-march=*cpu-type*
> Generate instructions for the machine type *cpu-type*. The choices for *cpu-type* are the same as for '-mtune'. Moreover, specifying '-march=*cpu-type*' implies '-mtune=*cpu-type*'.

-mcpu=*cpu-type*
> A deprecated synonym for '-mtune'.

-mfpmath=*unit*
> Generate floating point arithmetics for selected unit *unit*. The choices for *unit* are:
>
> > '387' Use the standard 387 floating point coprocessor present majority of chips and emulated otherwise. Code compiled with this option will run almost everywhere. The temporary results are computed in 80bit precision instead of precision specified by the type resulting in slightly different results compared to most of other chips. See '-ffloat-store' for more detailed description.
> >
> > This is the default choice for i386 compiler.
> >
> > 'sse' Use scalar floating point instructions present in the SSE instruction set. This instruction set is supported by Pentium3 and newer chips, in the AMD line by Athlon-4, Athlon-xp and Athlon-mp chips. The earlier version of SSE instruction set supports only single precision arithmetics, thus the double and extended precision arithmetics is still done using 387. Later version, present only in Pentium4 and the future AMD x86-64 chips supports double precision arithmetics too.

For the i386 compiler, you need to use '`-march=cpu-type`', '`-msse`' or '`-msse2`' switches to enable SSE extensions and make this option effective. For the x86-64 compiler, these extensions are enabled by default.

The resulting code should be considerably faster in the majority of cases and avoid the numerical instability problems of 387 code, but may break some existing code that expects temporaries to be 80bit.

This is the default choice for the x86-64 compiler.

'sse,387'
: Attempt to utilize both instruction sets at once. This effectively double the amount of available registers and on chips with separate execution units for 387 and SSE the execution resources too. Use this option with care, as it is still experimental, because the GCC register allocator does not model separate functional units well resulting in instable performance.

`-masm=dialect`
: Output asm instructions using selected *dialect*. Supported choices are '`intel`' or '`att`' (the default one). Darwin does not support '`intel`'.

`-mieee-fp`
`-mno-ieee-fp`
: Control whether or not the compiler uses IEEE floating point comparisons. These handle correctly the case where the result of a comparison is unordered.

`-msoft-float`
: Generate output containing library calls for floating point. **Warning:** the requisite libraries are not part of GCC. Normally the facilities of the machine's usual C compiler are used, but this can't be done directly in cross-compilation. You must make your own arrangements to provide suitable library functions for cross-compilation.

  On machines where a function returns floating point results in the 80387 register stack, some floating point opcodes may be emitted even if '`-msoft-float`' is used.

`-mno-fp-ret-in-387`
: Do not use the FPU registers for return values of functions.

  The usual calling convention has functions return values of types `float` and `double` in an FPU register, even if there is no FPU. The idea is that the operating system should emulate an FPU.

  The option '`-mno-fp-ret-in-387`' causes such values to be returned in ordinary CPU registers instead.

`-mno-fancy-math-387`
: Some 387 emulators do not support the `sin`, `cos` and `sqrt` instructions for the 387. Specify this option to avoid generating those instructions. This option is the default on FreeBSD, OpenBSD and NetBSD. This option is overridden when '`-march`' indicates that the target cpu will always have an FPU and so the

Chapter 3: GCC Command Options							165

instruction will not need emulation. As of revision 2.6.1, these instructions are not generated unless you also use the '-funsafe-math-optimizations' switch.

`-malign-double`
`-mno-align-double`
> Control whether GCC aligns `double`, `long double`, and `long long` variables on a two word boundary or a one word boundary. Aligning `double` variables on a two word boundary will produce code that runs somewhat faster on a 'Pentium' at the expense of more memory.
>
> On x86-64, '-malign-double' is enabled by default.
>
> **Warning:** if you use the '-malign-double' switch, structures containing the above types will be aligned differently than the published application binary interface specifications for the 386 and will not be binary compatible with structures in code compiled without that switch.

`-m96bit-long-double`
`-m128bit-long-double`
> These switches control the size of `long double` type. The i386 application binary interface specifies the size to be 96 bits, so '-m96bit-long-double' is the default in 32 bit mode.
>
> Modern architectures (Pentium and newer) would prefer `long double` to be aligned to an 8 or 16 byte boundary. In arrays or structures conforming to the ABI, this would not be possible. So specifying a '-m128bit-long-double' will align `long double` to a 16 byte boundary by padding the `long double` with an additional 32 bit zero.
>
> In the x86-64 compiler, '-m128bit-long-double' is the default choice as its ABI specifies that `long double` is to be aligned on 16 byte boundary.
>
> Notice that neither of these options enable any extra precision over the x87 standard of 80 bits for a `long double`.
>
> **Warning:** if you override the default value for your target ABI, the structures and arrays containing `long double` variables will change their size as well as function calling convention for function taking `long double` will be modified. Hence they will not be binary compatible with arrays or structures in code compiled without that switch.

`-mmlarge-data-threshold=number`
> When '-mcmodel=medium' is specified, the data greater than *threshold* are placed in large data section. This value must be the same across all object linked into the binary and defaults to 65535.

`-mrtd`
> Use a different function-calling convention, in which functions that take a fixed number of arguments return with the `ret` *num* instruction, which pops their arguments while returning. This saves one instruction in the caller since there is no need to pop the arguments there.
>
> You can specify that an individual function is called with this calling sequence with the function attribute 'stdcall'. You can also override the '-mrtd' option by using the function attribute 'cdecl'. See Section 5.27 [Function Attributes], page 264.

Warning: this calling convention is incompatible with the one normally used on Unix, so you cannot use it if you need to call libraries compiled with the Unix compiler.

Also, you must provide function prototypes for all functions that take variable numbers of arguments (including `printf`); otherwise incorrect code will be generated for calls to those functions.

In addition, seriously incorrect code will result if you call a function with too many arguments. (Normally, extra arguments are harmlessly ignored.)

`-mregparm=num`

Control how many registers are used to pass integer arguments. By default, no registers are used to pass arguments, and at most 3 registers can be used. You can control this behavior for a specific function by using the function attribute '`regparm`'. See Section 5.27 [Function Attributes], page 264.

Warning: if you use this switch, and *num* is nonzero, then you must build all modules with the same value, including any libraries. This includes the system libraries and startup modules.

`-msseregparm`

Use SSE register passing conventions for float and double arguments and return values. You can control this behavior for a specific function by using the function attribute '`sseregparm`'. See Section 5.27 [Function Attributes], page 264.

Warning: if you use this switch then you must build all modules with the same value, including any libraries. This includes the system libraries and startup modules.

`-mpc32`
`-mpc64`
`-mpc80`

Set 80387 floating-point precision to 32, 64 or 80 bits. When '`-mpc32`' is specified, the significands of results of floating-point operations are rounded to 24 bits (single precision); '`-mpc64`' rounds the the significands of results of floating-point operations to 53 bits (double precision) and '`-mpc80`' rounds the significands of results of floating-point operations to 64 bits (extended double precision), which is the default. When this option is used, floating-point operations in higher precisions are not available to the programmer without setting the FPU control word explicitly.

Setting the rounding of floating-point operations to less than the default 80 bits can speed some programs by 2% or more. Note that some mathematical libraries assume that extended precision (80 bit) floating-point operations are enabled by default; routines in such libraries could suffer significant loss of accuracy, typically through so-called "catastrophic cancellation", when this option is used to set the precision to less than extended precision.

`-mstackrealign`

Realign the stack at entry. On the Intel x86, the '`-mstackrealign`' option will generate an alternate prologue and epilogue that realigns the runtime stack. This supports mixing legacy codes that keep a 4-byte aligned stack with modern

Chapter 3: GCC Command Options   167

codes that keep a 16-byte stack for SSE compatibility. The alternate prologue and epilogue are slower and bigger than the regular ones, and the alternate prologue requires an extra scratch register; this lowers the number of registers available if used in conjunction with the `regparm` attribute. The '-mstackrealign' option is incompatible with the nested function prologue; this is considered a hard error. See also the attribute `force_align_arg_pointer`, applicable to individual functions.

`-mpreferred-stack-boundary=num`

Attempt to keep the stack boundary aligned to a 2 raised to *num* byte boundary. If '-mpreferred-stack-boundary' is not specified, the default is 4 (16 bytes or 128 bits).

On Pentium and PentiumPro, `double` and `long double` values should be aligned to an 8 byte boundary (see '-malign-double') or suffer significant run time performance penalties. On Pentium III, the Streaming SIMD Extension (SSE) data type `__m128` may not work properly if it is not 16 byte aligned.

To ensure proper alignment of this values on the stack, the stack boundary must be as aligned as that required by any value stored on the stack. Further, every function must be generated such that it keeps the stack aligned. Thus calling a function compiled with a higher preferred stack boundary from a function compiled with a lower preferred stack boundary will most likely misalign the stack. It is recommended that libraries that use callbacks always use the default setting.

This extra alignment does consume extra stack space, and generally increases code size. Code that is sensitive to stack space usage, such as embedded systems and operating system kernels, may want to reduce the preferred alignment to '-mpreferred-stack-boundary=2'.

`-mmmx`
`-mno-mmx`

`-msse`
`-mno-sse`

`-msse2`
`-mno-sse2`
`-msse3`
`-mno-sse3`
`-mssse3`
`-mno-ssse3`
`-msse4.1`
`-mno-sse4.1`
`-msse4.2`
`-mno-sse4.2`
`-msse4`
`-mno-sse4`
`-msse4a`

`-mno-sse4a`
`-msse5`
`-mno-sse5`
`-m3dnow`
`-mno-3dnow`
`-mpopcnt`
`-mno-popcnt`
`-mabm`
`-mno-abm`   These switches enable or disable the use of instructions in the MMX, SSE, SSE2, SSE3, SSSE3, SSE4.1, SSE4A, SSE5, ABM or 3DNow! extended instruction sets. These extensions are also available as built-in functions: see Section 5.50.6 [X86 Built-in Functions], page 439, for details of the functions enabled and disabled by these switches.

To have SSE/SSE2 instructions generated automatically from floating-point code (as opposed to 387 instructions), see '`-mfpmath=sse`'.

These options will enable GCC to use these extended instructions in generated code, even without '`-mfpmath=sse`'. Applications which perform runtime CPU detection must compile separate files for each supported architecture, using the appropriate flags. In particular, the file containing the CPU detection code should be compiled without these options.

`-mcld`   This option instructs GCC to emit a `cld` instruction in the prologue of functions that use string instructions. String instructions depend on the DF flag to select between autoincrement or autodecrement mode. While the ABI specifies the DF flag to be cleared on function entry, some operating systems violate this specification by not clearing the DF flag in their exception dispatchers. The exception handler can be invoked with the DF flag set which leads to wrong direction mode, when string instructions are used. This option can be enabled by default on 32-bit x86 targets by configuring GCC with the '`--enable-cld`' configure option. Generation of `cld` instructions can be suppressed with the '`-mno-cld`' compiler option in this case.

`-mcx16`   This option will enable GCC to use CMPXCHG16B instruction in generated code. CMPXCHG16B allows for atomic operations on 128-bit double quadword (or oword) data types. This is useful for high resolution counters that could be updated by multiple processors (or cores). This instruction is generated as part of atomic built-in functions: see Section 5.47 [Atomic Builtins], page 333 for details.

`-msahf`   This option will enable GCC to use SAHF instruction in generated 64-bit code. Early Intel CPUs with Intel 64 lacked LAHF and SAHF instructions supported by AMD64 until introduction of Pentium 4 G1 step in December 2005. LAHF and SAHF are load and store instructions, respectively, for certain status flags. In 64-bit mode, SAHF instruction is used to optimize `fmod`, `drem` or `remainder` built-in functions: see Section 5.49 [Other Builtins], page 337 for details.

`-mrecip`   This option will enable GCC to use RCPSS and RSQRTSS instructions (and their vectorized variants RCPPS and RSQRTPS) with an additional Newton-Rhapson step to increase precision instead of DIVSS and SQRTSS (and their

Chapter 3: GCC Command Options   169

>   vectorized variants) for single precision floating point arguments. These in-
>   structions are generated only when '-funsafe-math-optimizations' is en-
>   abled together with '-finite-math-only' and '-fno-trapping-math'. Note
>   that while the throughput of the sequence is higher than the throughput of the
>   non-reciprocal instruction, the precision of the sequence can be decreased by
>   up to 2 ulp (i.e. the inverse of 1.0 equals 0.99999994).

`-mveclibabi=`*type*
>   Specifies the ABI type to use for vectorizing intrinsics using an external library.
>   Supported types are `acml` for the AMD math core library style of interfacing.
>   GCC will currently emit calls to `__vrd2_sin`, `__vrd2_cos`, `__vrd2_exp`, `__vrd2_log`, `__vrd2_log2`, `__vrd2_log10`, `__vrs4_sinf`, `__vrs4_cosf`, `__vrs4_expf`, `__vrs4_logf`, `__vrs4_log2f`, `__vrs4_log10f` and `__vrs4_powf` when
>   using this type and '-ftree-vectorize' is enabled. A ACML ABI compatible
>   library will have to be specified at link time.

`-mpush-args`
`-mno-push-args`
>   Use PUSH operations to store outgoing parameters. This method is shorter
>   and usually equally fast as method using SUB/MOV operations and is enabled
>   by default. In some cases disabling it may improve performance because of
>   improved scheduling and reduced dependencies.

`-maccumulate-outgoing-args`
>   If enabled, the maximum amount of space required for outgoing arguments will
>   be computed in the function prologue. This is faster on most modern CPUs
>   because of reduced dependencies, improved scheduling and reduced stack usage
>   when preferred stack boundary is not equal to 2. The drawback is a notable
>   increase in code size. This switch implies '-mno-push-args'.

`-mthreads`
>   Support thread-safe exception handling on 'Mingw32'. Code that relies on
>   thread-safe exception handling must compile and link all code with the
>   '-mthreads' option. When compiling, '-mthreads' defines '-D_MT'; when
>   linking, it links in a special thread helper library '-lmingwthrd' which cleans
>   up per thread exception handling data.

`-mno-align-stringops`
>   Do not align destination of inlined string operations. This switch reduces code
>   size and improves performance in case the destination is already aligned, but
>   GCC doesn't know about it.

`-minline-all-stringops`
>   By default GCC inlines string operations only when destination is known to be
>   aligned at least to 4 byte boundary. This enables more inlining, increase code
>   size, but may improve performance of code that depends on fast memcpy, strlen
>   and memset for short lengths.

`-minline-stringops-dynamically`
>   For string operation of unknown size, inline runtime checks so for small blocks
>   inline code is used, while for large blocks library call is used.

`-mstringop-strategy=`*alg*
> Overwrite internal decision heuristic about particular algorithm to inline string operation with. The allowed values are `rep_byte`, `rep_4byte`, `rep_8byte` for expanding using i386 `rep` prefix of specified size, `byte_loop`, `loop`, `unrolled_loop` for expanding inline loop, `libcall` for always expanding library call.

`-momit-leaf-frame-pointer`
> Don't keep the frame pointer in a register for leaf functions. This avoids the instructions to save, set up and restore frame pointers and makes an extra register available in leaf functions. The option '`-fomit-frame-pointer`' removes the frame pointer for all functions which might make debugging harder.

`-mtls-direct-seg-refs`
`-mno-tls-direct-seg-refs`
> Controls whether TLS variables may be accessed with offsets from the TLS segment register (`%gs` for 32-bit, `%fs` for 64-bit), or whether the thread base pointer must be added. Whether or not this is legal depends on the operating system, and whether it maps the segment to cover the entire TLS area.
>
> For systems that use GNU libc, the default is on.

`-mfused-madd`
`-mno-fused-madd`
> Enable automatic generation of fused floating point multiply-add instructions if the ISA supports such instructions. The -mfused-madd option is on by default. The fused multiply-add instructions have a different rounding behavior compared to executing a multiply followed by an add.

These '-m' switches are supported in addition to the above on AMD x86-64 processors in 64-bit environments.

`-m32`
`-m64`
> Generate code for a 32-bit or 64-bit environment. The 32-bit environment sets int, long and pointer to 32 bits and generates code that runs on any i386 system. The 64-bit environment sets int to 32 bits and long and pointer to 64 bits and generates code for AMD's x86-64 architecture. For darwin only the -m64 option turns off the '`-fno-pic`' and '`-mdynamic-no-pic`' options.

`-mno-red-zone`
> Do not use a so called red zone for x86-64 code. The red zone is mandated by the x86-64 ABI, it is a 128-byte area beyond the location of the stack pointer that will not be modified by signal or interrupt handlers and therefore can be used for temporary data without adjusting the stack pointer. The flag '`-mno-red-zone`' disables this red zone.

`-mcmodel=small`
> Generate code for the small code model: the program and its symbols must be linked in the lower 2 GB of the address space. Pointers are 64 bits. Programs can be statically or dynamically linked. This is the default code model.

`-mcmodel=kernel`
> Generate code for the kernel code model. The kernel runs in the negative 2 GB of the address space. This model has to be used for Linux kernel code.

`-mcmodel=medium`
: Generate code for the medium model: The program is linked in the lower 2 GB of the address space but symbols can be located anywhere in the address space. Programs can be statically or dynamically linked, but building of shared libraries are not supported with the medium model.

`-mcmodel=large`
: Generate code for the large model: This model makes no assumptions about addresses and sizes of sections.

3.17.15 IA-64 Options

These are the '-m' options defined for the Intel IA-64 architecture.

`-mbig-endian`
: Generate code for a big endian target. This is the default for HP-UX.

`-mlittle-endian`
: Generate code for a little endian target. This is the default for AIX5 and GNU/Linux.

`-mgnu-as`
`-mno-gnu-as`
: Generate (or don't) code for the GNU assembler. This is the default.

`-mgnu-ld`
`-mno-gnu-ld`
: Generate (or don't) code for the GNU linker. This is the default.

`-mno-pic`
: Generate code that does not use a global pointer register. The result is not position independent code, and violates the IA-64 ABI.

`-mvolatile-asm-stop`
`-mno-volatile-asm-stop`
: Generate (or don't) a stop bit immediately before and after volatile asm statements.

`-mregister-names`
`-mno-register-names`
: Generate (or don't) 'in', 'loc', and 'out' register names for the stacked registers. This may make assembler output more readable.

`-mno-sdata`
`-msdata`
: Disable (or enable) optimizations that use the small data section. This may be useful for working around optimizer bugs.

`-mconstant-gp`
: Generate code that uses a single constant global pointer value. This is useful when compiling kernel code.

`-mauto-pic`
: Generate code that is self-relocatable. This implies '-mconstant-gp'. This is useful when compiling firmware code.

`-minline-float-divide-min-latency`
: Generate code for inline divides of floating point values using the minimum latency algorithm.

`-minline-float-divide-max-throughput`
: Generate code for inline divides of floating point values using the maximum throughput algorithm.

`-minline-int-divide-min-latency`
: Generate code for inline divides of integer values using the minimum latency algorithm.

`-minline-int-divide-max-throughput`
: Generate code for inline divides of integer values using the maximum throughput algorithm.

`-minline-sqrt-min-latency`
: Generate code for inline square roots using the minimum latency algorithm.

`-minline-sqrt-max-throughput`
: Generate code for inline square roots using the maximum throughput algorithm.

`-mno-dwarf2-asm`
`-mdwarf2-asm`
: Don't (or do) generate assembler code for the DWARF2 line number debugging info. This may be useful when not using the GNU assembler.

`-mearly-stop-bits`
`-mno-early-stop-bits`
: Allow stop bits to be placed earlier than immediately preceding the instruction that triggered the stop bit. This can improve instruction scheduling, but does not always do so.

`-mfixed-range=register-range`
: Generate code treating the given register range as fixed registers. A fixed register is one that the register allocator can not use. This is useful when compiling kernel code. A register range is specified as two registers separated by a dash. Multiple register ranges can be specified separated by a comma.

`-mtls-size=tls-size`
: Specify bit size of immediate TLS offsets. Valid values are 14, 22, and 64.

`-mtune=cpu-type`
: Tune the instruction scheduling for a particular CPU, Valid values are itanium, itanium1, merced, itanium2, and mckinley.

`-mt`
`-pthread`
: Add support for multithreading using the POSIX threads library. This option sets flags for both the preprocessor and linker. It does not affect the thread safety of object code produced by the compiler or that of libraries supplied with it. These are HP-UX specific flags.

Chapter 3: GCC Command Options   173

`-milp32`
`-mlp64`   Generate code for a 32-bit or 64-bit environment. The 32-bit environment sets int, long and pointer to 32 bits. The 64-bit environment sets int to 32 bits and long and pointer to 64 bits. These are HP-UX specific flags.

`-mno-sched-br-data-spec`
`-msched-br-data-spec`
                    (Dis/En)able data speculative scheduling before reload. This will result in generation of the ld.a instructions and the corresponding check instructions (ld.c / chk.a). The default is 'disable'.

`-msched-ar-data-spec`
`-mno-sched-ar-data-spec`
                    (En/Dis)able data speculative scheduling after reload. This will result in generation of the ld.a instructions and the corresponding check instructions (ld.c / chk.a). The default is 'enable'.

`-mno-sched-control-spec`
`-msched-control-spec`
                    (Dis/En)able control speculative scheduling. This feature is available only during region scheduling (i.e. before reload). This will result in generation of the ld.s instructions and the corresponding check instructions chk.s . The default is 'disable'.

`-msched-br-in-data-spec`
`-mno-sched-br-in-data-spec`
                    (En/Dis)able speculative scheduling of the instructions that are dependent on the data speculative loads before reload. This is effective only with '-msched-br-data-spec' enabled. The default is 'enable'.

`-msched-ar-in-data-spec`
`-mno-sched-ar-in-data-spec`
                    (En/Dis)able speculative scheduling of the instructions that are dependent on the data speculative loads after reload. This is effective only with '-msched-ar-data-spec' enabled. The default is 'enable'.

`-msched-in-control-spec`
`-mno-sched-in-control-spec`
                    (En/Dis)able speculative scheduling of the instructions that are dependent on the control speculative loads. This is effective only with '-msched-control-spec' enabled. The default is 'enable'.

`-msched-ldc`
`-mno-sched-ldc`
                    (En/Dis)able use of simple data speculation checks ld.c . If disabled, only chk.a instructions will be emitted to check data speculative loads. The default is 'enable'.

`-mno-sched-control-ldc`
`-msched-control-ldc`
                    (Dis/En)able use of ld.c instructions to check control speculative loads. If enabled, in case of control speculative load with no speculatively scheduled

dependent instructions this load will be emitted as ld.sa and ld.c will be used to check it. The default is 'disable'.

`-mno-sched-spec-verbose`
`-msched-spec-verbose`
> (Dis/En)able printing of the information about speculative motions.

`-mno-sched-prefer-non-data-spec-insns`
`-msched-prefer-non-data-spec-insns`
> If enabled, data speculative instructions will be chosen for schedule only if there are no other choices at the moment. This will make the use of the data speculation much more conservative. The default is 'disable'.

`-mno-sched-prefer-non-control-spec-insns`
`-msched-prefer-non-control-spec-insns`
> If enabled, control speculative instructions will be chosen for schedule only if there are no other choices at the moment. This will make the use of the control speculation much more conservative. The default is 'disable'.

`-mno-sched-count-spec-in-critical-path`
`-msched-count-spec-in-critical-path`
> If enabled, speculative dependencies will be considered during computation of the instructions priorities. This will make the use of the speculation a bit more conservative. The default is 'disable'.

3.17.16 M32C Options

`-mcpu=name`
> Select the CPU for which code is generated. *name* may be one of 'r8c' for the R8C/Tiny series, 'm16c' for the M16C (up to /60) series, 'm32cm' for the M16C/80 series, or 'm32c' for the M32C/80 series.

`-msim`
> Specifies that the program will be run on the simulator. This causes an alternate runtime library to be linked in which supports, for example, file I/O. You must not use this option when generating programs that will run on real hardware; you must provide your own runtime library for whatever I/O functions are needed.

`-memregs=number`
> Specifies the number of memory-based pseudo-registers GCC will use during code generation. These pseudo-registers will be used like real registers, so there is a tradeoff between GCC's ability to fit the code into available registers, and the performance penalty of using memory instead of registers. Note that all modules in a program must be compiled with the same value for this option. Because of that, you must not use this option with the default runtime libraries gcc builds.

3.17.17 M32R/D Options

These '-m' options are defined for Renesas M32R/D architectures:

`-m32r2` Generate code for the M32R/2.

Chapter 3: GCC Command Options

`-m32rx` Generate code for the M32R/X.

`-m32r` Generate code for the M32R. This is the default.

`-mmodel=small`
> Assume all objects live in the lower 16MB of memory (so that their addresses can be loaded with the `ld24` instruction), and assume all subroutines are reachable with the `bl` instruction. This is the default.
>
> The addressability of a particular object can be set with the `model` attribute.

`-mmodel=medium`
> Assume objects may be anywhere in the 32-bit address space (the compiler will generate `seth/add3` instructions to load their addresses), and assume all subroutines are reachable with the `bl` instruction.

`-mmodel=large`
> Assume objects may be anywhere in the 32-bit address space (the compiler will generate `seth/add3` instructions to load their addresses), and assume subroutines may not be reachable with the `bl` instruction (the compiler will generate the much slower `seth/add3/jl` instruction sequence).

`-msdata=none`
> Disable use of the small data area. Variables will be put into one of '.data', 'bss', or '.rodata' (unless the `section` attribute has been specified). This is the default.
>
> The small data area consists of sections '.sdata' and '.sbss'. Objects may be explicitly put in the small data area with the `section` attribute using one of these sections.

`-msdata=sdata`
> Put small global and static data in the small data area, but do not generate special code to reference them.

`-msdata=use`
> Put small global and static data in the small data area, and generate special instructions to reference them.

`-G num`
> Put global and static objects less than or equal to *num* bytes into the small data or bss sections instead of the normal data or bss sections. The default value of *num* is 8. The '-msdata' option must be set to one of 'sdata' or 'use' for this option to have any effect.
>
> All modules should be compiled with the same '-G *num*' value. Compiling with different values of *num* may or may not work; if it doesn't the linker will give an error message—incorrect code will not be generated.

`-mdebug` Makes the M32R specific code in the compiler display some statistics that might help in debugging programs.

`-malign-loops`
> Align all loops to a 32-byte boundary.

`-mno-align-loops`
> Do not enforce a 32-byte alignment for loops. This is the default.

`-missue-rate=number`
>   Issue *number* instructions per cycle. *number* can only be 1 or 2.

`-mbranch-cost=number`
>   *number* can only be 1 or 2. If it is 1 then branches will be preferred over conditional code, if it is 2, then the opposite will apply.

`-mflush-trap=number`
>   Specifies the trap number to use to flush the cache. The default is 12. Valid numbers are between 0 and 15 inclusive.

`-mno-flush-trap`
>   Specifies that the cache cannot be flushed by using a trap.

`-mflush-func=name`
>   Specifies the name of the operating system function to call to flush the cache. The default is *_flush_cache*, but a function call will only be used if a trap is not available.

`-mno-flush-func`
>   Indicates that there is no OS function for flushing the cache.

3.17.18 M680x0 Options

These are the '-m' options defined for M680x0 and ColdFire processors. The default settings depend on which architecture was selected when the compiler was configured; the defaults for the most common choices are given below.

`-march=arch`
>   Generate code for a specific M680x0 or ColdFire instruction set architecture. Permissible values of *arch* for M680x0 architectures are: '68000', '68010', '68020', '68030', '68040', '68060' and 'cpu32'. ColdFire architectures are selected according to Freescale's ISA classification and the permissible values are: 'isaa', 'isaaplus', 'isab' and 'isac'.
>
>   gcc defines a macro '`__mcfarch__`' whenever it is generating code for a ColdFire target. The *arch* in this macro is one of the '-march' arguments given above.
>
>   When used together, '-march' and '-mtune' select code that runs on a family of similar processors but that is optimized for a particular microarchitecture.

`-mcpu=cpu`
>   Generate code for a specific M680x0 or ColdFire processor. The M680x0 *cpus* are: '68000', '68010', '68020', '68030', '68040', '68060', '68302', '68332' and 'cpu32'. The ColdFire *cpus* are given by the table below, which also classifies the CPUs into families:

Family	'-mcpu' arguments
'51qe'	'51qe'
'5206'	'5202' '5204' '5206'
'5206e'	'5206e'
'5208'	'5207' '5208'
'5211a'	'5210a' '5211a'
'5213'	'5211' '5212' '5213'

Chapter 3: GCC Command Options   177

'5216'	'5214' '5216'
'52235'	'52230' '52231' '52232' '52233' '52234' '52235'
'5225'	'5224' '5225'
'5235'	'5232' '5233' '5234' '5235' '523x'
'5249'	'5249'
'5250'	'5250'
'5271'	'5270' '5271'
'5272'	'5272'
'5275'	'5274' '5275'
'5282'	'5280' '5281' '5282' '528x'
'5307'	'5307'
'5329'	'5327' '5328' '5329' '532x'
'5373'	'5372' '5373' '537x'
'5407'	'5407'
'5475'	'5470' '5471' '5472' '5473' '5474' '5475' '547x' '5480' '5481' '548 '5483' '5484' '5485'

'-mcpu=cpu' overrides '-march=arch' if arch is compatible with cpu. Other combinations of '-mcpu' and '-march' are rejected.

gcc defines the macro '__mcf_cpu_cpu' when ColdFire target cpu is selected. It also defines '__mcf_family_family', where the value of family is given by the table above.

-mtune=tune

Tune the code for a particular microarchitecture, within the constraints set by '-march' and '-mcpu'. The M680x0 microarchitectures are: '68000', '68010', '68020', '68030', '68040', '68060' and 'cpu32'. The ColdFire microarchitectures are: 'cfv1', 'cfv2', 'cfv3', 'cfv4' and 'cfv4e'.

You can also use '-mtune=68020-40' for code that needs to run relatively well on 68020, 68030 and 68040 targets. '-mtune=68020-60' is similar but includes 68060 targets as well. These two options select the same tuning decisions as '-m68020-40' and '-m68020-60' respectively.

gcc defines the macros '__mcarch' and '__mcarch__' when tuning for 680x0 architecture arch. It also defines 'mcarch' unless either '-ansi' or a non-GNU '-std' option is used. If gcc is tuning for a range of architectures, as selected by '-mtune=68020-40' or '-mtune=68020-60', it defines the macros for every architecture in the range.

gcc also defines the macro '__muarch__' when tuning for ColdFire microarchitecture uarch, where uarch is one of the arguments given above.

-m68000
-mc68000   Generate output for a 68000. This is the default when the compiler is configured for 68000-based systems. It is equivalent to '-march=68000'.

Use this option for microcontrollers with a 68000 or EC000 core, including the 68008, 68302, 68306, 68307, 68322, 68328 and 68356.

-m68010   Generate output for a 68010. This is the default when the compiler is configured for 68010-based systems. It is equivalent to '-march=68010'.

`-m68020`
`-mc68020` Generate output for a 68020. This is the default when the compiler is configured for 68020-based systems. It is equivalent to '`-march=68020`'.

`-m68030` Generate output for a 68030. This is the default when the compiler is configured for 68030-based systems. It is equivalent to '`-march=68030`'.

`-m68040` Generate output for a 68040. This is the default when the compiler is configured for 68040-based systems. It is equivalent to '`-march=68040`'.

This option inhibits the use of 68881/68882 instructions that have to be emulated by software on the 68040. Use this option if your 68040 does not have code to emulate those instructions.

`-m68060` Generate output for a 68060. This is the default when the compiler is configured for 68060-based systems. It is equivalent to '`-march=68060`'.

This option inhibits the use of 68020 and 68881/68882 instructions that have to be emulated by software on the 68060. Use this option if your 68060 does not have code to emulate those instructions.

`-mcpu32` Generate output for a CPU32. This is the default when the compiler is configured for CPU32-based systems. It is equivalent to '`-march=cpu32`'.

Use this option for microcontrollers with a CPU32 or CPU32+ core, including the 68330, 68331, 68332, 68333, 68334, 68336, 68340, 68341, 68349 and 68360.

`-m5200` Generate output for a 520X ColdFire CPU. This is the default when the compiler is configured for 520X-based systems. It is equivalent to '`-mcpu=5206`', and is now deprecated in favor of that option.

Use this option for microcontroller with a 5200 core, including the MCF5202, MCF5203, MCF5204 and MCF5206.

`-m5206e` Generate output for a 5206e ColdFire CPU. The option is now deprecated in favor of the equivalent '`-mcpu=5206e`'.

`-m528x` Generate output for a member of the ColdFire 528X family. The option is now deprecated in favor of the equivalent '`-mcpu=528x`'.

`-m5307` Generate output for a ColdFire 5307 CPU. The option is now deprecated in favor of the equivalent '`-mcpu=5307`'.

`-m5407` Generate output for a ColdFire 5407 CPU. The option is now deprecated in favor of the equivalent '`-mcpu=5407`'.

`-mcfv4e` Generate output for a ColdFire V4e family CPU (e.g. 547x/548x). This includes use of hardware floating point instructions. The option is equivalent to '`-mcpu=547x`', and is now deprecated in favor of that option.

`-m68020-40`
Generate output for a 68040, without using any of the new instructions. This results in code which can run relatively efficiently on either a 68020/68881 or a 68030 or a 68040. The generated code does use the 68881 instructions that are emulated on the 68040.

The option is equivalent to '`-march=68020`' '`-mtune=68020-40`'.

Chapter 3: GCC Command Options   179

`-m68020-60`
Generate output for a 68060, without using any of the new instructions. This results in code which can run relatively efficiently on either a 68020/68881 or a 68030 or a 68040. The generated code does use the 68881 instructions that are emulated on the 68060.

The option is equivalent to '`-march=68020`' '`-mtune=68020-60`'.

`-mhard-float`
`-m68881`
Generate floating-point instructions. This is the default for 68020 and above, and for ColdFire devices that have an FPU. It defines the macro '`__HAVE_68881__`' on M680x0 targets and '`__mcffpu__`' on ColdFire targets.

`-msoft-float`
Do not generate floating-point instructions; use library calls instead. This is the default for 68000, 68010, and 68832 targets. It is also the default for ColdFire devices that have no FPU.

`-mdiv`
`-mno-div`
Generate (do not generate) ColdFire hardware divide and remainder instructions. If '`-march`' is used without '`-mcpu`', the default is "on" for ColdFire architectures and "off" for M680x0 architectures. Otherwise, the default is taken from the target CPU (either the default CPU, or the one specified by '`-mcpu`'). For example, the default is "off" for '`-mcpu=5206`' and "on" for '`-mcpu=5206e`'.

gcc defines the macro '`__mcfhwdiv__`' when this option is enabled.

`-mshort`
Consider type `int` to be 16 bits wide, like `short int`. Additionally, parameters passed on the stack are also aligned to a 16-bit boundary even on targets whose API mandates promotion to 32-bit.

`-mno-short`
Do not consider type `int` to be 16 bits wide. This is the default.

`-mnobitfield`
`-mno-bitfield`
Do not use the bit-field instructions. The '`-m68000`', '`-mcpu32`' and '`-m5200`' options imply '`-mnobitfield`'.

`-mbitfield`
Do use the bit-field instructions. The '`-m68020`' option implies '`-mbitfield`'. This is the default if you use a configuration designed for a 68020.

`-mrtd`
Use a different function-calling convention, in which functions that take a fixed number of arguments return with the `rtd` instruction, which pops their arguments while returning. This saves one instruction in the caller since there is no need to pop the arguments there.

This calling convention is incompatible with the one normally used on Unix, so you cannot use it if you need to call libraries compiled with the Unix compiler.

Also, you must provide function prototypes for all functions that take variable numbers of arguments (including `printf`); otherwise incorrect code will be generated for calls to those functions.

In addition, seriously incorrect code will result if you call a function with too many arguments. (Normally, extra arguments are harmlessly ignored.)

The `rtd` instruction is supported by the 68010, 68020, 68030, 68040, 68060 and CPU32 processors, but not by the 68000 or 5200.

`-mno-rtd` Do not use the calling conventions selected by '`-mrtd`'. This is the default.

`-malign-int`
`-mno-align-int`
Control whether GCC aligns `int`, `long`, `long long`, `float`, `double`, and `long double` variables on a 32-bit boundary ('`-malign-int`') or a 16-bit boundary ('`-mno-align-int`'). Aligning variables on 32-bit boundaries produces code that runs somewhat faster on processors with 32-bit busses at the expense of more memory.

Warning: if you use the '`-malign-int`' switch, GCC will align structures containing the above types differently than most published application binary interface specifications for the m68k.

`-mpcrel` Use the pc-relative addressing mode of the 68000 directly, instead of using a global offset table. At present, this option implies '`-fpic`', allowing at most a 16-bit offset for pc-relative addressing. '`-fPIC`' is not presently supported with '`-mpcrel`', though this could be supported for 68020 and higher processors.

`-mno-strict-align`
`-mstrict-align`
Do not (do) assume that unaligned memory references will be handled by the system.

`-msep-data`
Generate code that allows the data segment to be located in a different area of memory from the text segment. This allows for execute in place in an environment without virtual memory management. This option implies '`-fPIC`'.

`-mno-sep-data`
Generate code that assumes that the data segment follows the text segment. This is the default.

`-mid-shared-library`
Generate code that supports shared libraries via the library ID method. This allows for execute in place and shared libraries in an environment without virtual memory management. This option implies '`-fPIC`'.

`-mno-id-shared-library`
Generate code that doesn't assume ID based shared libraries are being used. This is the default.

`-mshared-library-id=n`
Specified the identification number of the ID based shared library being compiled. Specifying a value of 0 will generate more compact code, specifying other values will force the allocation of that number to the current library but is no more space or time efficient than omitting this option.

Chapter 3: GCC Command Options   181

3.17.19 M68hc1x Options

These are the '-m' options defined for the 68hc11 and 68hc12 microcontrollers. The default values for these options depends on which style of microcontroller was selected when the compiler was configured; the defaults for the most common choices are given below.

`-m6811`
`-m68hc11` Generate output for a 68HC11. This is the default when the compiler is configured for 68HC11-based systems.

`-m6812`
`-m68hc12` Generate output for a 68HC12. This is the default when the compiler is configured for 68HC12-based systems.

`-m68S12`
`-m68hcs12`
    Generate output for a 68HCS12.

`-mauto-incdec`
    Enable the use of 68HC12 pre and post auto-increment and auto-decrement addressing modes.

`-minmax`
`-nominmax`
    Enable the use of 68HC12 min and max instructions.

`-mlong-calls`
`-mno-long-calls`
    Treat all calls as being far away (near). If calls are assumed to be far away, the compiler will use the `call` instruction to call a function and the `rtc` instruction for returning.

`-mshort` Consider type `int` to be 16 bits wide, like `short int`.

`-msoft-reg-count=`*count*
    Specify the number of pseudo-soft registers which are used for the code generation. The maximum number is 32. Using more pseudo-soft register may or may not result in better code depending on the program. The default is 4 for 68HC11 and 2 for 68HC12.

3.17.20 MCore Options

These are the '-m' options defined for the Motorola M*Core processors.

`-mhardlit`
`-mno-hardlit`
    Inline constants into the code stream if it can be done in two instructions or less.

`-mdiv`
`-mno-div` Use the divide instruction. (Enabled by default).

`-mrelax-immediate`
`-mno-relax-immediate`
    Allow arbitrary sized immediates in bit operations.

`-mwide-bitfields`
`-mno-wide-bitfields`
     Always treat bit-fields as int-sized.

`-m4byte-functions`
`-mno-4byte-functions`
     Force all functions to be aligned to a four byte boundary.

`-mcallgraph-data`
`-mno-callgraph-data`
     Emit callgraph information.

`-mslow-bytes`
`-mno-slow-bytes`
     Prefer word access when reading byte quantities.

`-mlittle-endian`
`-mbig-endian`
     Generate code for a little endian target.

`-m210`
`-m340`   Generate code for the 210 processor.

3.17.21 MIPS Options

`-EB`   Generate big-endian code.

`-EL`   Generate little-endian code. This is the default for 'mips*el-*-*' configurations.

`-march=arch`
     Generate code that will run on *arch*, which can be the name of a generic MIPS ISA, or the name of a particular processor. The ISA names are: 'mips1', 'mips2', 'mips3', 'mips4', 'mips32', 'mips32r2', and 'mips64'. The processor names are: '4kc', '4km', '4kp', '4ksc', '4kec', '4kem', '4kep', '4ksd', '5kc', '5kf', '20kc', '24kc', '24kf2_1', '24kf1_1', '24kec', '24kef2_1', '24kef1_1', '34kc', '34kf2_1', '34kf1_1', '74kc', '74kf2_1', '74kf1_1', '74kf3_2', 'm4k', 'orion', 'r2000', 'r3000', 'r3900', 'r4000', 'r4400', 'r4600', 'r4650', 'r6000', 'r8000', 'rm7000', 'rm9000', 'sb1', 'sr71000', 'vr4100', 'vr4111', 'vr4120', 'vr4130', 'vr4300', 'vr5000', 'vr5400' and 'vr5500'. The special value 'from-abi' selects the most compatible architecture for the selected ABI (that is, 'mips1' for 32-bit ABIs and 'mips3' for 64-bit ABIs).

     In processor names, a final '000' can be abbreviated as 'k' (for example, '-march=r2k'). Prefixes are optional, and 'vr' may be written 'r'.

     Names of the form 'nf2_1' refer to processors with FPUs clocked at half the rate of the core, names of the form 'nf1_1' refer to processors with FPUs clocked at the same rate as the core, and names of the form 'nf3_2' refer to processors with FPUs clocked a ratio of 3:2 with respect to the core. For compatibility reasons, 'nf' is accepted as a synonym for 'nf2_1' while 'nx' and 'bfx' are accepted as synonyms for 'nf1_1'.

Chapter 3: GCC Command Options   183

GCC defines two macros based on the value of this option. The first is '_MIPS_ARCH', which gives the name of target architecture, as a string. The second has the form '_MIPS_ARCH_foo', where foo is the capitalized value of '_MIPS_ARCH'. For example, '-march=r2000' will set '_MIPS_ARCH' to '"r2000"' and define the macro '_MIPS_ARCH_R2000'.

Note that the '_MIPS_ARCH' macro uses the processor names given above. In other words, it will have the full prefix and will not abbreviate '000' as 'k'. In the case of 'from-abi', the macro names the resolved architecture (either '"mips1"' or '"mips3"'). It names the default architecture when no '-march' option is given.

`-mtune=arch`
: Optimize for *arch*. Among other things, this option controls the way instructions are scheduled, and the perceived cost of arithmetic operations. The list of *arch* values is the same as for '-march'.

  When this option is not used, GCC will optimize for the processor specified by '-march'. By using '-march' and '-mtune' together, it is possible to generate code that will run on a family of processors, but optimize the code for one particular member of that family.

  '-mtune' defines the macros '_MIPS_TUNE' and '_MIPS_TUNE_foo', which work in the same way as the '-march' ones described above.

`-mips1`
: Equivalent to '-march=mips1'.

`-mips2`
: Equivalent to '-march=mips2'.

`-mips3`
: Equivalent to '-march=mips3'.

`-mips4`
: Equivalent to '-march=mips4'.

`-mips32`
: Equivalent to '-march=mips32'.

`-mips32r2`
: Equivalent to '-march=mips32r2'.

`-mips64`
: Equivalent to '-march=mips64'.

`-mips16`
`-mno-mips16`
: Generate (do not generate) MIPS16 code. If GCC is targetting a MIPS32 or MIPS64 architecture, it will make use of the MIPS16e ASE.

  MIPS16 code generation can also be controlled on a per-function basis by means of `mips16` and `nomips16` attributes. See Section 5.27 [Function Attributes], page 264, for more information.

`-mflip-mips16`
: Generate MIPS16 code on alternating functions. This option is provided for regression testing of mixed MIPS16/non-MIPS16 code generation, and is not intended for ordinary use in compiling user code.

`-minterlink-mips16`
`-mno-interlink-mips16`
: Require (do not require) that non-MIPS16 code be link-compatible with MIPS16 code.

For example, non-MIPS16 code cannot jump directly to MIPS16 code; it must either use a call or an indirect jump. '-minterlink-mips16' therefore disables direct jumps unless GCC knows that the target of the jump is not MIPS16.

`-mabi=32`
`-mabi=o64`
`-mabi=n32`
`-mabi=64`
`-mabi=eabi`

Generate code for the given ABI.

Note that the EABI has a 32-bit and a 64-bit variant. GCC normally generates 64-bit code when you select a 64-bit architecture, but you can use '-mgp32' to get 32-bit code instead.

For information about the O64 ABI, see http://gcc.gnu.org/projects/mipso64-abi

GCC supports a variant of the o32 ABI in which floating-point registers are 64 rather than 32 bits wide. You can select this combination with '-mabi=32' '-mfp64'. This ABI relies on the 'mthc1' and 'mfhc1' instructions and is therefore only supported for MIPS32R2 processors.

The register assignments for arguments and return values remain the same, but each scalar value is passed in a single 64-bit register rather than a pair of 32-bit registers. For example, scalar floating-point values are returned in '$f0' only, not a '$f0'/'$f1' pair. The set of call-saved registers also remains the same, but all 64 bits are saved.

`-mabicalls`
`-mno-abicalls`

Generate (do not generate) code that is suitable for SVR4-style dynamic objects. '-mabicalls' is the default for SVR4-based systems.

`-mshared`
`-mno-shared`

Generate (do not generate) code that is fully position-independent, and that can therefore be linked into shared libraries. This option only affects '-mabicalls'.

All '-mabicalls' code has traditionally been position-independent, regardless of options like '-fPIC' and '-fpic'. However, as an extension, the GNU toolchain allows executables to use absolute accesses for locally-binding symbols. It can also use shorter GP initialization sequences and generate direct calls to locally-defined functions. This mode is selected by '-mno-shared'.

'-mno-shared' depends on binutils 2.16 or higher and generates objects that can only be linked by the GNU linker. However, the option does not affect the ABI of the final executable; it only affects the ABI of relocatable objects. Using '-mno-shared' will generally make executables both smaller and quicker.

'-mshared' is the default.

`-mxgot`
`-mno-xgot`

Lift (do not lift) the usual restrictions on the size of the global offset table.

Chapter 3: GCC Command Options 185

GCC normally uses a single instruction to load values from the GOT. While this is relatively efficient, it will only work if the GOT is smaller than about 64k. Anything larger will cause the linker to report an error such as:

```
relocation truncated to fit: R_MIPS_GOT16 foobar
```

If this happens, you should recompile your code with '-mxgot'. It should then work with very large GOTs, although it will also be less efficient, since it will take three instructions to fetch the value of a global symbol.

Note that some linkers can create multiple GOTs. If you have such a linker, you should only need to use '-mxgot' when a single object file accesses more than 64k's worth of GOT entries. Very few do.

These options have no effect unless GCC is generating position independent code.

-mgp32 Assume that general-purpose registers are 32 bits wide.

-mgp64 Assume that general-purpose registers are 64 bits wide.

-mfp32 Assume that floating-point registers are 32 bits wide.

-mfp64 Assume that floating-point registers are 64 bits wide.

-mhard-float
    Use floating-point coprocessor instructions.

-msoft-float
    Do not use floating-point coprocessor instructions. Implement floating-point calculations using library calls instead.

-msingle-float
    Assume that the floating-point coprocessor only supports single-precision operations.

-mdouble-float
    Assume that the floating-point coprocessor supports double-precision operations. This is the default.

-mllsc
-mno-llsc
    Use (do not use) 'll', 'sc', and 'sync' instructions to implement atomic memory built-in functions. When neither option is specified, GCC will use the instructions if the target architecture supports them.

    '-mllsc' is useful if the runtime environment can emulate the instructions and '-mno-llsc' can be useful when compiling for nonstandard ISAs. You can make either option the default by configuring GCC with '--with-llsc' and '--without-llsc' respectively. '--with-llsc' is the default for some configurations; see the installation documentation for details.

-mdsp
-mno-dsp
    Use (do not use) revision 1 of the MIPS DSP ASE. See Section 5.50.7 [MIPS DSP Built-in Functions], page 452. This option defines the preprocessor macro '__mips_dsp'. It also defines '__mips_dsp_rev' to 1.

`-mdspr2`
`-mno-dspr2`
> Use (do not use) revision 2 of the MIPS DSP ASE. See Section 5.50.7 [MIPS DSP Built-in Functions], page 452. This option defines the preprocessor macros '`__mips_dsp`' and '`__mips_dspr2`'. It also defines '`__mips_dsp_rev`' to 2.

`-msmartmips`
`-mno-smartmips`
> Use (do not use) the MIPS SmartMIPS ASE.

`-mpaired-single`
`-mno-paired-single`
> Use (do not use) paired-single floating-point instructions. See Section 5.50.8 [MIPS Paired-Single Support], page 456. This option requires hardware floating-point support to be enabled.

`-mdmx`
`-mno-mdmx`
> Use (do not use) MIPS Digital Media Extension instructions. This option can only be used when generating 64-bit code and requires hardware floating-point support to be enabled.

`-mips3d`
`-mno-mips3d`
> Use (do not use) the MIPS-3D ASE. See Section 5.50.8.3 [MIPS-3D Built-in Functions], page 458. The option '`-mips3d`' implies '`-mpaired-single`'.

`-mmt`
`-mno-mt` Use (do not use) MT Multithreading instructions.

`-mlong64` Force `long` types to be 64 bits wide. See '`-mlong32`' for an explanation of the default and the way that the pointer size is determined.

`-mlong32` Force `long`, `int`, and pointer types to be 32 bits wide.

> The default size of `int`s, `long`s and pointers depends on the ABI. All the supported ABIs use 32-bit `int`s. The n64 ABI uses 64-bit `long`s, as does the 64-bit EABI; the others use 32-bit `long`s. Pointers are the same size as `long`s, or the same size as integer registers, whichever is smaller.

`-msym32`
`-mno-sym32`
> Assume (do not assume) that all symbols have 32-bit values, regardless of the selected ABI. This option is useful in combination with '`-mabi=64`' and '`-mno-abicalls`' because it allows GCC to generate shorter and faster references to symbolic addresses.

`-G num` Put definitions of externally-visible data in a small data section if that data is no bigger than *num* bytes. GCC can then access the data more efficiently; see '`-mgpopt`' for details.

> The default '`-G`' option depends on the configuration.

Chapter 3: GCC Command Options   187

`-mlocal-sdata`
`-mno-local-sdata`

> Extend (do not extend) the '-G' behavior to local data too, such as to static variables in C. '`-mlocal-sdata`' is the default for all configurations.
>
> If the linker complains that an application is using too much small data, you might want to try rebuilding the less performance-critical parts with '`-mno-local-sdata`'. You might also want to build large libraries with '`-mno-local-sdata`', so that the libraries leave more room for the main program.

`-mextern-sdata`
`-mno-extern-sdata`

> Assume (do not assume) that externally-defined data will be in a small data section if that data is within the '-G' limit. '`-mextern-sdata`' is the default for all configurations.
>
> If you compile a module *Mod* with '`-mextern-sdata`' '-G *num*' '-mgpopt', and *Mod* references a variable *Var* that is no bigger than *num* bytes, you must make sure that *Var* is placed in a small data section. If *Var* is defined by another module, you must either compile that module with a high-enough '-G' setting or attach a `section` attribute to *Var*'s definition. If *Var* is common, you must link the application with a high-enough '-G' setting.
>
> The easiest way of satisfying these restrictions is to compile and link every module with the same '-G' option. However, you may wish to build a library that supports several different small data limits. You can do this by compiling the library with the highest supported '-G' setting and additionally using '`-mno-extern-sdata`' to stop the library from making assumptions about externally-defined data.

`-mgpopt`
`-mno-gpopt`

> Use (do not use) GP-relative accesses for symbols that are known to be in a small data section; see '-G', '`-mlocal-sdata`' and '`-mextern-sdata`'. '`-mgpopt`' is the default for all configurations.
>
> '`-mno-gpopt`' is useful for cases where the $gp register might not hold the value of _gp. For example, if the code is part of a library that might be used in a boot monitor, programs that call boot monitor routines will pass an unknown value in $gp. (In such situations, the boot monitor itself would usually be compiled with '-G0'.)
>
> '`-mno-gpopt`' implies '`-mno-local-sdata`' and '`-mno-extern-sdata`'.

`-membedded-data`
`-mno-embedded-data`

> Allocate variables to the read-only data section first if possible, then next in the small data section if possible, otherwise in data. This gives slightly slower code than the default, but reduces the amount of RAM required when executing, and thus may be preferred for some embedded systems.

`-muninit-const-in-rodata`
`-mno-uninit-const-in-rodata`
> Put uninitialized `const` variables in the read-only data section. This option is only meaningful in conjunction with '`-membedded-data`'.

`-mcode-readable=setting`
> Specify whether GCC may generate code that reads from executable sections. There are three possible settings:
>
> `-mcode-readable=yes`
>> Instructions may freely access executable sections. This is the default setting.
>
> `-mcode-readable=pcrel`
>> MIPS16 PC-relative load instructions can access executable sections, but other instructions must not do so. This option is useful on 4KSc and 4KSd processors when the code TLBs have the Read Inhibit bit set. It is also useful on processors that can be configured to have a dual instruction/data SRAM interface and that, like the M4K, automatically redirect PC-relative loads to the instruction RAM.
>
> `-mcode-readable=no`
>> Instructions must not access executable sections. This option can be useful on targets that are configured to have a dual instruction/data SRAM interface but that (unlike the M4K) do not automatically redirect PC-relative loads to the instruction RAM.

`-msplit-addresses`
`-mno-split-addresses`
> Enable (disable) use of the `%hi()` and `%lo()` assembler relocation operators. This option has been superseded by '`-mexplicit-relocs`' but is retained for backwards compatibility.

`-mexplicit-relocs`
`-mno-explicit-relocs`
> Use (do not use) assembler relocation operators when dealing with symbolic addresses. The alternative, selected by '`-mno-explicit-relocs`', is to use assembler macros instead.
>
> '`-mexplicit-relocs`' is the default if GCC was configured to use an assembler that supports relocation operators.

`-mcheck-zero-division`
`-mno-check-zero-division`
> Trap (do not trap) on integer division by zero.
>
> The default is '`-mcheck-zero-division`'.

`-mdivide-traps`
`-mdivide-breaks`
> MIPS systems check for division by zero by generating either a conditional trap or a break instruction. Using traps results in smaller code, but is only

Chapter 3: GCC Command Options   189

supported on MIPS II and later. Also, some versions of the Linux kernel have
a bug that prevents trap from generating the proper signal (SIGFPE). Use
'-mdivide-traps' to allow conditional traps on architectures that support them
and '-mdivide-breaks' to force the use of breaks.

The default is usually '-mdivide-traps', but this can be overridden at configure
time using '--with-divide=breaks'. Divide-by-zero checks can be completely
disabled using '-mno-check-zero-division'.

`-mmemcpy`
`-mno-memcpy`
: Force (do not force) the use of memcpy() for non-trivial block moves. The default is '-mno-memcpy', which allows GCC to inline most constant-sized copies.

`-mlong-calls`
`-mno-long-calls`
: Disable (do not disable) use of the jal instruction. Calling functions using jal is more efficient but requires the caller and callee to be in the same 256 megabyte segment.

This option has no effect on abicalls code. The default is '-mno-long-calls'.

`-mmad`
`-mno-mad`
: Enable (disable) use of the mad, madu and mul instructions, as provided by the R4650 ISA.

`-mfused-madd`
`-mno-fused-madd`
: Enable (disable) use of the floating point multiply-accumulate instructions, when they are available. The default is '-mfused-madd'.

When multiply-accumulate instructions are used, the intermediate product is calculated to infinite precision and is not subject to the FCSR Flush to Zero bit. This may be undesirable in some circumstances.

`-nocpp`
: Tell the MIPS assembler to not run its preprocessor over user assembler files (with a '.s' suffix) when assembling them.

`-mfix-r4000`
`-mno-fix-r4000`
: Work around certain R4000 CPU errata:
    - A double-word or a variable shift may give an incorrect result if executed immediately after starting an integer division.
    - A double-word or a variable shift may give an incorrect result if executed while an integer multiplication is in progress.
    - An integer division may give an incorrect result if started in a delay slot of a taken branch or a jump.

`-mfix-r4400`
`-mno-fix-r4400`
: Work around certain R4400 CPU errata:
    - A double-word or a variable shift may give an incorrect result if executed immediately after starting an integer division.

`-mfix-vr4120`
`-mno-fix-vr4120`

> Work around certain VR4120 errata:
>
> - `dmultu` does not always produce the correct result.
> - `div` and `ddiv` do not always produce the correct result if one of the operands is negative.
>
> The workarounds for the division errata rely on special functions in 'libgcc.a'. At present, these functions are only provided by the `mips64vr*-elf` configurations.
>
> Other VR4120 errata require a nop to be inserted between certain pairs of instructions. These errata are handled by the assembler, not by GCC itself.

`-mfix-vr4130`

> Work around the VR4130 `mflo`/`mfhi` errata. The workarounds are implemented by the assembler rather than by GCC, although GCC will avoid using `mflo` and `mfhi` if the VR4130 `macc`, `macchi`, `dmacc` and `dmacchi` instructions are available instead.

`-mfix-sb1`
`-mno-fix-sb1`

> Work around certain SB-1 CPU core errata. (This flag currently works around the SB-1 revision 2 "F1" and "F2" floating point errata.)

`-mflush-func=func`
`-mno-flush-func`

> Specifies the function to call to flush the I and D caches, or to not call any such function. If called, the function must take the same arguments as the common `_flush_func()`, that is, the address of the memory range for which the cache is being flushed, the size of the memory range, and the number 3 (to flush both caches). The default depends on the target GCC was configured for, but commonly is either '`_flush_func`' or '`__cpu_flush`'.

`mbranch-cost=num`

> Set the cost of branches to roughly *num* "simple" instructions. This cost is only a heuristic and is not guaranteed to produce consistent results across releases. A zero cost redundantly selects the default, which is based on the '-mtune' setting.

`-mbranch-likely`
`-mno-branch-likely`

> Enable or disable use of Branch Likely instructions, regardless of the default for the selected architecture. By default, Branch Likely instructions may be generated if they are supported by the selected architecture. An exception is for the MIPS32 and MIPS64 architectures and processors which implement those architectures; for those, Branch Likely instructions will not be generated by default because the MIPS32 and MIPS64 architectures specifically deprecate their use.

Chapter 3: GCC Command Options   191

`-mfp-exceptions`
`-mno-fp-exceptions`

> Specifies whether FP exceptions are enabled. This affects how we schedule FP instructions for some processors. The default is that FP exceptions are enabled.
>
> For instance, on the SB-1, if FP exceptions are disabled, and we are emitting 64-bit code, then we can use both FP pipes. Otherwise, we can only use one FP pipe.

`-mvr4130-align`
`-mno-vr4130-align`

> The VR4130 pipeline is two-way superscalar, but can only issue two instructions together if the first one is 8-byte aligned. When this option is enabled, GCC will align pairs of instructions that it thinks should execute in parallel.
>
> This option only has an effect when optimizing for the VR4130. It normally makes code faster, but at the expense of making it bigger. It is enabled by default at optimization level '-O3'.

3.17.22 MMIX Options

These options are defined for the MMIX:

`-mlibfuncs`
`-mno-libfuncs`

> Specify that intrinsic library functions are being compiled, passing all values in registers, no matter the size.

`-mepsilon`
`-mno-epsilon`

> Generate floating-point comparison instructions that compare with respect to the rE epsilon register.

`-mabi=mmixware`
`-mabi=gnu`

> Generate code that passes function parameters and return values that (in the called function) are seen as registers $0 and up, as opposed to the GNU ABI which uses global registers $231 and up.

`-mzero-extend`
`-mno-zero-extend`

> When reading data from memory in sizes shorter than 64 bits, use (do not use) zero-extending load instructions by default, rather than sign-extending ones.

`-mknuthdiv`
`-mno-knuthdiv`

> Make the result of a division yielding a remainder have the same sign as the divisor. With the default, '-mno-knuthdiv', the sign of the remainder follows the sign of the dividend. Both methods are arithmetically valid, the latter being almost exclusively used.

`-mtoplevel-symbols`
`-mno-toplevel-symbols`
> Prepend (do not prepend) a ':' to all global symbols, so the assembly code can be used with the `PREFIX` assembly directive.

`-melf`   Generate an executable in the ELF format, rather than the default 'mmo' format used by the `mmix` simulator.

`-mbranch-predict`
`-mno-branch-predict`
> Use (do not use) the probable-branch instructions, when static branch prediction indicates a probable branch.

`-mbase-addresses`
`-mno-base-addresses`
> Generate (do not generate) code that uses *base addresses*. Using a base address automatically generates a request (handled by the assembler and the linker) for a constant to be set up in a global register. The register is used for one or more base address requests within the range 0 to 255 from the value held in the register. The generally leads to short and fast code, but the number of different data items that can be addressed is limited. This means that a program that uses lots of static data may require '`-mno-base-addresses`'.

`-msingle-exit`
`-mno-single-exit`
> Force (do not force) generated code to have a single exit point in each function.

3.17.23 MN10300 Options

These '-m' options are defined for Matsushita MN10300 architectures:

`-mmult-bug`
> Generate code to avoid bugs in the multiply instructions for the MN10300 processors. This is the default.

`-mno-mult-bug`
> Do not generate code to avoid bugs in the multiply instructions for the MN10300 processors.

`-mam33`   Generate code which uses features specific to the AM33 processor.

`-mno-am33`
> Do not generate code which uses features specific to the AM33 processor. This is the default.

`-mreturn-pointer-on-d0`
> When generating a function which returns a pointer, return the pointer in both a0 and d0. Otherwise, the pointer is returned only in a0, and attempts to call such functions without a prototype would result in errors. Note that this option is on by default; use '`-mno-return-pointer-on-d0`' to disable it.

`-mno-crt0`
> Do not link in the C run-time initialization object file.

Chapter 3: GCC Command Options   193

-mrelax   Indicate to the linker that it should perform a relaxation optimization pass to
             shorten branches, calls and absolute memory addresses. This option only has
             an effect when used on the command line for the final link step.

             This option makes symbolic debugging impossible.

3.17.24 MT Options

These '-m' options are defined for Morpho MT architectures:

-march=*cpu-type*
             Generate code that will run on *cpu-type*, which is the name of a system repre-
             senting a certain processor type. Possible values for *cpu-type* are 'ms1-64-001',
             'ms1-16-002', 'ms1-16-003' and 'ms2'.

             When this option is not used, the default is '-march=ms1-16-002'.

-mbacc   Use byte loads and stores when generating code.

-mno-bacc
             Do not use byte loads and stores when generating code.

-msim   Use simulator runtime

-mno-crt0
             Do not link in the C run-time initialization object file 'crti.o'. Other run-time
             initialization and termination files such as 'startup.o' and 'exit.o' are still
             included on the linker command line.

3.17.25 PDP-11 Options

These options are defined for the PDP-11:

-mfpu   Use hardware FPP floating point. This is the default. (FIS floating point on
             the PDP-11/40 is not supported.)

-msoft-float
             Do not use hardware floating point.

-mac0   Return floating-point results in ac0 (fr0 in Unix assembler syntax).

-mno-ac0   Return floating-point results in memory. This is the default.

-m40   Generate code for a PDP-11/40.

-m45   Generate code for a PDP-11/45. This is the default.

-m10   Generate code for a PDP-11/10.

-mbcopy-builtin
             Use inline movmemhi patterns for copying memory. This is the default.

-mbcopy   Do not use inline movmemhi patterns for copying memory.

-mint16
-mno-int32
             Use 16-bit int. This is the default.

`-mint32`
`-mno-int16`
> Use 32-bit `int`.

`-mfloat64`
`-mno-float32`
> Use 64-bit `float`. This is the default.

`-mfloat32`
`-mno-float64`
> Use 32-bit `float`.

`-mabshi` Use `abshi2` pattern. This is the default.

`-mno-abshi`
> Do not use `abshi2` pattern.

`-mbranch-expensive`
> Pretend that branches are expensive. This is for experimenting with code generation only.

`-mbranch-cheap`
> Do not pretend that branches are expensive. This is the default.

`-msplit` Generate code for a system with split I&D.

`-mno-split`
> Generate code for a system without split I&D. This is the default.

`-munix-asm`
> Use Unix assembler syntax. This is the default when configured for 'pdp11-*-bsd'.

`-mdec-asm`
> Use DEC assembler syntax. This is the default when configured for any PDP-11 target other than 'pdp11-*-bsd'.

3.17.26 PowerPC Options

These are listed under See Section 3.17.27 [RS/6000 and PowerPC Options], page 194.

3.17.27 IBM RS/6000 and PowerPC Options

These '-m' options are defined for the IBM RS/6000 and PowerPC:

Chapter 3: GCC Command Options   195

```
-mpower
-mno-power
-mpower2
-mno-power2
-mpowerpc
-mno-powerpc
-mpowerpc-gpopt
-mno-powerpc-gpopt
-mpowerpc-gfxopt
-mno-powerpc-gfxopt
-mpowerpc64
-mno-powerpc64
-mmfcrf
-mno-mfcrf
-mpopcntb
-mno-popcntb
-mfprnd
-mno-fprnd
-mcmpb
-mno-cmpb
-mmfpgpr
-mno-mfpgpr
-mhard-dfp
-mno-hard-dfp
```
GCC supports two related instruction set architectures for the RS/6000 and PowerPC. The *POWER* instruction set are those instructions supported by the 'rios' chip set used in the original RS/6000 systems and the *PowerPC* instruction set is the architecture of the Freescale MPC5xx, MPC6xx, MPC8xx microprocessors, and the IBM 4xx, 6xx, and follow-on microprocessors.

Neither architecture is a subset of the other. However there is a large common subset of instructions supported by both. An MQ register is included in processors supporting the POWER architecture.

You use these options to specify which instructions are available on the processor you are using. The default value of these options is determined when configuring GCC. Specifying the '-mcpu=*cpu_type*' overrides the specification of these options. We recommend you use the '-mcpu=*cpu_type*' option rather than the options listed above.

The '-mpower' option allows GCC to generate instructions that are found only in the POWER architecture and to use the MQ register. Specifying '-mpower2' implies '-power' and also allows GCC to generate instructions that are present in the POWER2 architecture but not the original POWER architecture.

The '-mpowerpc' option allows GCC to generate instructions that are found only in the 32-bit subset of the PowerPC architecture. Specifying '-mpowerpc-gpopt' implies '-mpowerpc' and also allows GCC to use the optional PowerPC architecture instructions in the General Purpose group, including floating-point square root. Specifying '-mpowerpc-gfxopt' implies

'-mpowerpc' and also allows GCC to use the optional PowerPC architecture instructions in the Graphics group, including floating-point select.

The '-mmfcrf' option allows GCC to generate the move from condition register field instruction implemented on the POWER4 processor and other processors that support the PowerPC V2.01 architecture. The '-mpopcntb' option allows GCC to generate the popcount and double precision FP reciprocal estimate instruction implemented on the POWER5 processor and other processors that support the PowerPC V2.02 architecture. The '-mfprnd' option allows GCC to generate the FP round to integer instructions implemented on the POWER5+ processor and other processors that support the PowerPC V2.03 architecture. The '-mcmpb' option allows GCC to generate the compare bytes instruction implemented on the POWER6 processor and other processors that support the PowerPC V2.05 architecture. The '-mmfpgpr' option allows GCC to generate the FP move to/from general purpose register instructions implemented on the POWER6X processor and other processors that support the extended PowerPC V2.05 architecture. The '-mhard-dfp' option allows GCC to generate the decimal floating point instructions implemented on some POWER processors.

The '-mpowerpc64' option allows GCC to generate the additional 64-bit instructions that are found in the full PowerPC64 architecture and to treat GPRs as 64-bit, doubleword quantities. GCC defaults to '-mno-powerpc64'.

If you specify both '-mno-power' and '-mno-powerpc', GCC will use only the instructions in the common subset of both architectures plus some special AIX common-mode calls, and will not use the MQ register. Specifying both '-mpower' and '-mpowerpc' permits GCC to use any instruction from either architecture and to allow use of the MQ register; specify this for the Motorola MPC601.

`-mnew-mnemonics`
`-mold-mnemonics`

    Select which mnemonics to use in the generated assembler code. With '-mnew-mnemonics', GCC uses the assembler mnemonics defined for the PowerPC architecture. With '-mold-mnemonics' it uses the assembler mnemonics defined for the POWER architecture. Instructions defined in only one architecture have only one mnemonic; GCC uses that mnemonic irrespective of which of these options is specified.

    GCC defaults to the mnemonics appropriate for the architecture in use. Specifying '-mcpu=cpu_type' sometimes overrides the value of these option. Unless you are building a cross-compiler, you should normally not specify either '-mnew-mnemonics' or '-mold-mnemonics', but should instead accept the default.

`-mcpu=cpu_type`

    Set architecture type, register usage, choice of mnemonics, and instruction scheduling parameters for machine type cpu_type. Supported values for cpu_type are '401', '403', '405', '405fp', '440', '440fp', '505', '601', '602', '603', '603e', '604', '604e', '620', '630', '740', '7400', '7450', '750', '801', '821', '823', '860', '970', '8540', 'ec603e', 'G3', 'G4', 'G5', 'power', 'power2', 'power3',

Chapter 3: GCC Command Options   197

'power4', 'power5', 'power5+', 'power6', 'power6x', 'common', 'powerpc', 'powerpc64', 'rios', 'rios1', 'rios2', 'rsc', and 'rs64'.

'-mcpu=common' selects a completely generic processor. Code generated under this option will run on any POWER or PowerPC processor. GCC will use only the instructions in the common subset of both architectures, and will not use the MQ register. GCC assumes a generic processor model for scheduling purposes.

'-mcpu=power', '-mcpu=power2', '-mcpu=powerpc', and '-mcpu=powerpc64' specify generic POWER, POWER2, pure 32-bit PowerPC (i.e., not MPC601), and 64-bit PowerPC architecture machine types, with an appropriate, generic processor model assumed for scheduling purposes.

The other options specify a specific processor. Code generated under those options will run best on that processor, and may not run at all on others.

The '-mcpu' options automatically enable or disable the following options:

```
-maltivec -mfprnd -mhard-float -mmfcrf -mmultiple
-mnew-mnemonics -mpopcntb -mpower -mpower2 -mpowerpc64
-mpowerpc-gpopt -mpowerpc-gfxopt -mstring -mmulhw -mdlmzb -mmfpgpr
```

The particular options set for any particular CPU will vary between compiler versions, depending on what setting seems to produce optimal code for that CPU; it doesn't necessarily reflect the actual hardware's capabilities. If you wish to set an individual option to a particular value, you may specify it after the '-mcpu' option, like '-mcpu=970 -mno-altivec'.

On AIX, the '-maltivec' and '-mpowerpc64' options are not enabled or disabled by the '-mcpu' option at present because AIX does not have full support for these options. You may still enable or disable them individually if you're sure it'll work in your environment.

-mtune=cpu_type
> Set the instruction scheduling parameters for machine type cpu_type, but do not set the architecture type, register usage, or choice of mnemonics, as '-mcpu=cpu_type' would. The same values for cpu_type are used for '-mtune' as for '-mcpu'. If both are specified, the code generated will use the architecture, registers, and mnemonics set by '-mcpu', but the scheduling parameters set by '-mtune'.

-mswdiv
-mno-swdiv
> Generate code to compute division as reciprocal estimate and iterative refinement, creating opportunities for increased throughput. This feature requires: optional PowerPC Graphics instruction set for single precision and FRE instruction for double precision, assuming divides cannot generate user-visible traps, and the domain values not include Infinities, denormals or zero denominator.

-maltivec
-mno-altivec
> Generate code that uses (does not use) AltiVec instructions, and also enable the use of built-in functions that allow more direct access to the AltiVec instruction

set. You may also need to set '`-mabi=altivec`' to adjust the current ABI with AltiVec ABI enhancements.

`-mvrsave`

`-mno-vrsave`

Generate VRSAVE instructions when generating AltiVec code.

`-msecure-plt`

Generate code that allows ld and ld.so to build executables and shared libraries with non-exec .plt and .got sections. This is a PowerPC 32-bit SYSV ABI option.

`-mbss-plt`

Generate code that uses a BSS .plt section that ld.so fills in, and requires .plt and .got sections that are both writable and executable. This is a PowerPC 32-bit SYSV ABI option.

`-misel`

`-mno-isel`

This switch enables or disables the generation of ISEL instructions.

`-misel=yes/no`

This switch has been deprecated. Use '`-misel`' and '`-mno-isel`' instead.

`-mspe`

`-mno-spe` This switch enables or disables the generation of SPE simd instructions.

`-mpaired`

`-mno-paired`

This switch enables or disables the generation of PAIRED simd instructions.

`-mspe=yes/no`

This option has been deprecated. Use '`-mspe`' and '`-mno-spe`' instead.

`-mfloat-gprs=yes/single/double/no`

`-mfloat-gprs`

This switch enables or disables the generation of floating point operations on the general purpose registers for architectures that support it.

The argument *yes* or *single* enables the use of single-precision floating point operations.

The argument *double* enables the use of single and double-precision floating point operations.

The argument *no* disables floating point operations on the general purpose registers.

This option is currently only available on the MPC854x.

`-m32`

`-m64` Generate code for 32-bit or 64-bit environments of Darwin and SVR4 targets (including GNU/Linux). The 32-bit environment sets int, long and pointer to 32 bits and generates code that runs on any PowerPC variant. The 64-bit environment sets int to 32 bits and long and pointer to 64 bits, and generates code for PowerPC64, as for '`-mpowerpc64`'.

Chapter 3: GCC Command Options   199

`-mfull-toc`
`-mno-fp-in-toc`
`-mno-sum-in-toc`
`-mminimal-toc`

        Modify generation of the TOC (Table Of Contents), which is created for every executable file. The '`-mfull-toc`' option is selected by default. In that case, GCC will allocate at least one TOC entry for each unique non-automatic variable reference in your program. GCC will also place floating-point constants in the TOC. However, only 16,384 entries are available in the TOC.

        If you receive a linker error message that saying you have overflowed the available TOC space, you can reduce the amount of TOC space used with the '`-mno-fp-in-toc`' and '`-mno-sum-in-toc`' options. '`-mno-fp-in-toc`' prevents GCC from putting floating-point constants in the TOC and '`-mno-sum-in-toc`' forces GCC to generate code to calculate the sum of an address and a constant at run-time instead of putting that sum into the TOC. You may specify one or both of these options. Each causes GCC to produce very slightly slower and larger code at the expense of conserving TOC space.

        If you still run out of space in the TOC even when you specify both of these options, specify '`-mminimal-toc`' instead. This option causes GCC to make only one TOC entry for every file. When you specify this option, GCC will produce code that is slower and larger but which uses extremely little TOC space. You may wish to use this option only on files that contain less frequently executed code.

`-maix64`
`-maix32`   Enable 64-bit AIX ABI and calling convention: 64-bit pointers, 64-bit **long** type, and the infrastructure needed to support them. Specifying '`-maix64`' implies '`-mpowerpc64`' and '`-mpowerpc`', while '`-maix32`' disables the 64-bit ABI and implies '`-mno-powerpc64`'. GCC defaults to '`-maix32`'.

`-mxl-compat`
`-mno-xl-compat`

        Produce code that conforms more closely to IBM XL compiler semantics when using AIX-compatible ABI. Pass floating-point arguments to prototyped functions beyond the register save area (RSA) on the stack in addition to argument FPRs. Do not assume that most significant double in 128-bit long double value is properly rounded when comparing values and converting to double. Use XL symbol names for long double support routines.

        The AIX calling convention was extended but not initially documented to handle an obscure K&R C case of calling a function that takes the address of its arguments with fewer arguments than declared. IBM XL compilers access floating point arguments which do not fit in the RSA from the stack when a subroutine is compiled without optimization. Because always storing floating-point arguments on the stack is inefficient and rarely needed, this option is not enabled by default and only is necessary when calling subroutines compiled by IBM XL compilers without optimization.

`-mpe`
Support *IBM RS/6000 SP Parallel Environment* (PE). Link an application written to use message passing with special startup code to enable the application to run. The system must have PE installed in the standard location ('/usr/lpp/ppe.poe/'), or the 'specs' file must be overridden with the '-specs=' option to specify the appropriate directory location. The Parallel Environment does not support threads, so the '-mpe' option and the '-pthread' option are incompatible.

`-malign-natural`
`-malign-power`
On AIX, 32-bit Darwin, and 64-bit PowerPC GNU/Linux, the option '-malign-natural' overrides the ABI-defined alignment of larger types, such as floating-point doubles, on their natural size-based boundary. The option '-malign-power' instructs GCC to follow the ABI-specified alignment rules. GCC defaults to the standard alignment defined in the ABI.

On 64-bit Darwin, natural alignment is the default, and '-malign-power' is not supported.

`-msoft-float`
`-mhard-float`
Generate code that does not use (uses) the floating-point register set. Software floating point emulation is provided if you use the '-msoft-float' option, and pass the option to GCC when linking.

`-mmultiple`
`-mno-multiple`
Generate code that uses (does not use) the load multiple word instructions and the store multiple word instructions. These instructions are generated by default on POWER systems, and not generated on PowerPC systems. Do not use '-mmultiple' on little endian PowerPC systems, since those instructions do not work when the processor is in little endian mode. The exceptions are PPC740 and PPC750 which permit the instructions usage in little endian mode.

`-mstring`
`-mno-string`
Generate code that uses (does not use) the load string instructions and the store string word instructions to save multiple registers and do small block moves. These instructions are generated by default on POWER systems, and not generated on PowerPC systems. Do not use '-mstring' on little endian PowerPC systems, since those instructions do not work when the processor is in little endian mode. The exceptions are PPC740 and PPC750 which permit the instructions usage in little endian mode.

`-mupdate`
`-mno-update`
Generate code that uses (does not use) the load or store instructions that update the base register to the address of the calculated memory location. These instructions are generated by default. If you use '-mno-update', there is a small window between the time that the stack pointer is updated and the address of

Chapter 3: GCC Command Options   201

            the previous frame is stored, which means code that walks the stack frame
            across interrupts or signals may get corrupted data.

`-mfused-madd`
`-mno-fused-madd`
            Generate code that uses (does not use) the floating point multiply and accumulate instructions. These instructions are generated by default if hardware floating is used.

`-mmulhw`
`-mno-mulhw`
            Generate code that uses (does not use) the half-word multiply and multiply-accumulate instructions on the IBM 405 and 440 processors. These instructions are generated by default when targetting those processors.

`-mdlmzb`
`-mno-dlmzb`
            Generate code that uses (does not use) the string-search 'dlmzb' instruction on the IBM 405 and 440 processors. This instruction is generated by default when targetting those processors.

`-mno-bit-align`
`-mbit-align`
            On System V.4 and embedded PowerPC systems do not (do) force structures and unions that contain bit-fields to be aligned to the base type of the bit-field.

            For example, by default a structure containing nothing but 8 `unsigned` bit-fields of length 1 would be aligned to a 4 byte boundary and have a size of 4 bytes. By using '-mno-bit-align', the structure would be aligned to a 1 byte boundary and be one byte in size.

`-mno-strict-align`
`-mstrict-align`
            On System V.4 and embedded PowerPC systems do not (do) assume that unaligned memory references will be handled by the system.

`-mrelocatable`
`-mno-relocatable`
            On embedded PowerPC systems generate code that allows (does not allow) the program to be relocated to a different address at runtime. If you use '-mrelocatable' on any module, all objects linked together must be compiled with '-mrelocatable' or '-mrelocatable-lib'.

`-mrelocatable-lib`
`-mno-relocatable-lib`
            On embedded PowerPC systems generate code that allows (does not allow) the program to be relocated to a different address at runtime. Modules compiled with '-mrelocatable-lib' can be linked with either modules compiled without '-mrelocatable' and '-mrelocatable-lib' or with modules compiled with the '-mrelocatable' options.

`-mno-toc`
`-mtoc`
>   On System V.4 and embedded PowerPC systems do not (do) assume that register 2 contains a pointer to a global area pointing to the addresses used in the program.

`-mlittle`
`-mlittle-endian`
>   On System V.4 and embedded PowerPC systems compile code for the processor in little endian mode. The '`-mlittle-endian`' option is the same as '`-mlittle`'.

`-mbig`
`-mbig-endian`
>   On System V.4 and embedded PowerPC systems compile code for the processor in big endian mode. The '`-mbig-endian`' option is the same as '`-mbig`'.

`-mdynamic-no-pic`
>   On Darwin and Mac OS X systems, compile code so that it is not relocatable, but that its external references are relocatable. The resulting code is suitable for applications, but not shared libraries.

`-mprioritize-restricted-insns=priority`
>   This option controls the priority that is assigned to dispatch-slot restricted instructions during the second scheduling pass. The argument *priority* takes the value *0/1/2* to assign *no/highest/second-highest* priority to dispatch slot restricted instructions.

`-msched-costly-dep=dependence_type`
>   This option controls which dependences are considered costly by the target during instruction scheduling. The argument *dependence_type* takes one of the following values: *no*: no dependence is costly, *all*: all dependences are costly, *true_store_to_load*: a true dependence from store to load is costly, *store_to_load*: any dependence from store to load is costly, *number*: any dependence which latency >= *number* is costly.

`-minsert-sched-nops=scheme`
>   This option controls which nop insertion scheme will be used during the second scheduling pass. The argument *scheme* takes one of the following values: *no*: Don't insert nops. *pad*: Pad with nops any dispatch group which has vacant issue slots, according to the scheduler's grouping. *regroup_exact*: Insert nops to force costly dependent insns into separate groups. Insert exactly as many nops as needed to force an insn to a new group, according to the estimated processor grouping. *number*: Insert nops to force costly dependent insns into separate groups. Insert *number* nops to force an insn to a new group.

`-mcall-sysv`
>   On System V.4 and embedded PowerPC systems compile code using calling conventions that adheres to the March 1995 draft of the System V Application Binary Interface, PowerPC processor supplement. This is the default unless you configured GCC using '`powerpc-*-eabiaix`'.

`-mcall-sysv-eabi`
>   Specify both '`-mcall-sysv`' and '`-meabi`' options.

Chapter 3: GCC Command Options   203

-mcall-sysv-noeabi
: Specify both '-mcall-sysv' and '-mno-eabi' options.

-mcall-solaris
: On System V.4 and embedded PowerPC systems compile code for the Solaris operating system.

-mcall-linux
: On System V.4 and embedded PowerPC systems compile code for the Linux-based GNU system.

-mcall-gnu
: On System V.4 and embedded PowerPC systems compile code for the Hurd-based GNU system.

-mcall-netbsd
: On System V.4 and embedded PowerPC systems compile code for the NetBSD operating system.

-maix-struct-return
: Return all structures in memory (as specified by the AIX ABI).

-msvr4-struct-return
: Return structures smaller than 8 bytes in registers (as specified by the SVR4 ABI).

-mabi=abi-type
: Extend the current ABI with a particular extension, or remove such extension. Valid values are *altivec, no-altivec, spe, no-spe, ibmlongdouble, ieeelongdouble*.

-mabi=spe
: Extend the current ABI with SPE ABI extensions. This does not change the default ABI, instead it adds the SPE ABI extensions to the current ABI.

-mabi=no-spe
: Disable Booke SPE ABI extensions for the current ABI.

-mabi=ibmlongdouble
: Change the current ABI to use IBM extended precision long double. This is a PowerPC 32-bit SYSV ABI option.

-mabi=ieeelongdouble
: Change the current ABI to use IEEE extended precision long double. This is a PowerPC 32-bit Linux ABI option.

-mprototype
-mno-prototype
: On System V.4 and embedded PowerPC systems assume that all calls to variable argument functions are properly prototyped. Otherwise, the compiler must insert an instruction before every non prototyped call to set or clear bit 6 of the condition code register (*CR*) to indicate whether floating point values were passed in the floating point registers in case the function takes a variable arguments. With '-mprototype', only calls to prototyped variable argument functions will set or clear the bit.

-msim   On embedded PowerPC systems, assume that the startup module is called
                'sim-crt0.o' and that the standard C libraries are 'libsim.a' and 'libc.a'.
                This is the default for 'powerpc-*-eabisim' configurations.

-mmvme   On embedded PowerPC systems, assume that the startup module is called
                'crt0.o' and the standard C libraries are 'libmvme.a' and 'libc.a'.

-mads   On embedded PowerPC systems, assume that the startup module is called
                'crt0.o' and the standard C libraries are 'libads.a' and 'libc.a'.

-myellowknife
                On embedded PowerPC systems, assume that the startup module is called
                'crt0.o' and the standard C libraries are 'libyk.a' and 'libc.a'.

-mvxworks
                On System V.4 and embedded PowerPC systems, specify that you are compiling
                for a VxWorks system.

-mwindiss
                Specify that you are compiling for the WindISS simulation environment.

-memb   On embedded PowerPC systems, set the *PPC_EMB* bit in the ELF flags header
                to indicate that 'eabi' extended relocations are used.

-meabi
-mno-eabi
                On System V.4 and embedded PowerPC systems do (do not) adhere to the
                Embedded Applications Binary Interface (eabi) which is a set of modifications
                to the System V.4 specifications. Selecting '-meabi' means that the stack is
                aligned to an 8 byte boundary, a function __eabi is called to from main to set
                up the eabi environment, and the '-msdata' option can use both r2 and r13
                to point to two separate small data areas. Selecting '-mno-eabi' means that
                the stack is aligned to a 16 byte boundary, do not call an initialization function
                from main, and the '-msdata' option will only use r13 to point to a single small
                data area. The '-meabi' option is on by default if you configured GCC using
                one of the 'powerpc*-*-eabi*' options.

-msdata=eabi
                On System V.4 and embedded PowerPC systems, put small initialized const
                global and static data in the '.sdata2' section, which is pointed to by register
                r2. Put small initialized non-const global and static data in the '.sdata'
                section, which is pointed to by register r13. Put small uninitialized global and
                static data in the '.sbss' section, which is adjacent to the '.sdata' section.
                The '-msdata=eabi' option is incompatible with the '-mrelocatable' option.
                The '-msdata=eabi' option also sets the '-memb' option.

-msdata=sysv
                On System V.4 and embedded PowerPC systems, put small global and static
                data in the '.sdata' section, which is pointed to by register r13. Put small
                uninitialized global and static data in the '.sbss' section, which is adjacent
                to the '.sdata' section. The '-msdata=sysv' option is incompatible with the
                '-mrelocatable' option.

Chapter 3: GCC Command Options   205

`-msdata=default`
`-msdata`   On System V.4 and embedded PowerPC systems, if '-meabi' is used, compile code the same as '-msdata=eabi', otherwise compile code the same as '-msdata=sysv'.

`-msdata-data`
            On System V.4 and embedded PowerPC systems, put small global data in the '.sdata' section. Put small uninitialized global data in the '.sbss' section. Do not use register r13 to address small data however. This is the default behavior unless other '-msdata' options are used.

`-msdata=none`
`-mno-sdata`
            On embedded PowerPC systems, put all initialized global and static data in the '.data' section, and all uninitialized data in the '.bss' section.

`-G num`   On embedded PowerPC systems, put global and static items less than or equal to num bytes into the small data or bss sections instead of the normal data or bss section. By default, num is 8. The '-G num' switch is also passed to the linker. All modules should be compiled with the same '-G num' value.

`-mregnames`
`-mno-regnames`
            On System V.4 and embedded PowerPC systems do (do not) emit register names in the assembly language output using symbolic forms.

`-mlongcall`
`-mno-longcall`
            By default assume that all calls are far away so that a longer more expensive calling sequence is required. This is required for calls further than 32 megabytes (33,554,432 bytes) from the current location. A short call will be generated if the compiler knows the call cannot be that far away. This setting can be overridden by the shortcall function attribute, or by #pragma longcall(0).

            Some linkers are capable of detecting out-of-range calls and generating glue code on the fly. On these systems, long calls are unnecessary and generate slower code. As of this writing, the AIX linker can do this, as can the GNU linker for PowerPC/64. It is planned to add this feature to the GNU linker for 32-bit PowerPC systems as well.

            On Darwin/PPC systems, #pragma longcall will generate "jbsr callee, L42", plus a "branch island" (glue code). The two target addresses represent the callee and the "branch island". The Darwin/PPC linker will prefer the first address and generate a "bl callee" if the PPC "bl" instruction will reach the callee directly; otherwise, the linker will generate "bl L42" to call the "branch island". The "branch island" is appended to the body of the calling function; it computes the full 32-bit address of the callee and jumps to it.

            On Mach-O (Darwin) systems, this option directs the compiler emit to the glue for every direct call, and the Darwin linker decides whether to use or discard it.

In the future, we may cause GCC to ignore all longcall specifications when the linker is known to generate glue.

`-pthread` Adds support for multithreading with the *pthreads* library. This option sets flags for both the preprocessor and linker.

3.17.28 S/390 and zSeries Options

These are the '-m' options defined for the S/390 and zSeries architecture.

`-mhard-float`
`-msoft-float`
> Use (do not use) the hardware floating-point instructions and registers for floating-point operations. When '-msoft-float' is specified, functions in 'libgcc.a' will be used to perform floating-point operations. When '-mhard-float' is specified, the compiler generates IEEE floating-point instructions. This is the default.

`-mhard-dfp`
`-mno-hard-dfp`
> Use (do not use) the hardware decimal-floating-point instructions for decimal-floating-point operations. When '-mno-hard-dfp' is specified, functions in 'libgcc.a' will be used to perform decimal-floating-point operations. When '-mhard-dfp' is specified, the compiler generates decimal-floating-point hardware instructions. This is the default for '-march=z9-ec' or higher.

`-mlong-double-64`
`-mlong-double-128`
> These switches control the size of `long double` type. A size of 64bit makes the `long double` type equivalent to the `double` type. This is the default.

`-mbackchain`
`-mno-backchain`
> Store (do not store) the address of the caller's frame as backchain pointer into the callee's stack frame. A backchain may be needed to allow debugging using tools that do not understand DWARF-2 call frame information. When '-mno-packed-stack' is in effect, the backchain pointer is stored at the bottom of the stack frame; when '-mpacked-stack' is in effect, the backchain is placed into the topmost word of the 96/160 byte register save area.
>
> In general, code compiled with '-mbackchain' is call-compatible with code compiled with '-mmo-backchain'; however, use of the backchain for debugging purposes usually requires that the whole binary is built with '-mbackchain'. Note that the combination of '-mbackchain', '-mpacked-stack' and '-mhard-float' is not supported. In order to build a linux kernel use '-msoft-float'.
>
> The default is to not maintain the backchain.

`-mpacked-stack`
`-mno-packed-stack`
> Use (do not use) the packed stack layout. When '-mno-packed-stack' is specified, the compiler uses the all fields of the 96/160 byte register save area only for their default purpose; unused fields still take up stack space. When

Chapter 3: GCC Command Options   207

'`-mpacked-stack`' is specified, register save slots are densely packed at the top of the register save area; unused space is reused for other purposes, allowing for more efficient use of the available stack space. However, when '`-mbackchain`' is also in effect, the topmost word of the save area is always used to store the backchain, and the return address register is always saved two words below the backchain.

As long as the stack frame backchain is not used, code generated with '`-mpacked-stack`' is call-compatible with code generated with '`-mno-packed-stack`'. Note that some non-FSF releases of GCC 2.95 for S/390 or zSeries generated code that uses the stack frame backchain at run time, not just for debugging purposes. Such code is not call-compatible with code compiled with '`-mpacked-stack`'. Also, note that the combination of '`-mbackchain`', '`-mpacked-stack`' and '`-mhard-float`' is not supported. In order to build a linux kernel use '`-msoft-float`'.

The default is to not use the packed stack layout.

`-msmall-exec`
`-mno-small-exec`
> Generate (or do not generate) code using the `bras` instruction to do subroutine calls. This only works reliably if the total executable size does not exceed 64k. The default is to use the `basr` instruction instead, which does not have this limitation.

`-m64`
`-m31`
> When '`-m31`' is specified, generate code compliant to the GNU/Linux for S/390 ABI. When '`-m64`' is specified, generate code compliant to the GNU/Linux for zSeries ABI. This allows GCC in particular to generate 64-bit instructions. For the 's390' targets, the default is '`-m31`', while the 's390x' targets default to '`-m64`'.

`-mzarch`
`-mesa`
> When '`-mzarch`' is specified, generate code using the instructions available on z/Architecture. When '`-mesa`' is specified, generate code using the instructions available on ESA/390. Note that '`-mesa`' is not possible with '`-m64`'. When generating code compliant to the GNU/Linux for S/390 ABI, the default is '`-mesa`'. When generating code compliant to the GNU/Linux for zSeries ABI, the default is '`-mzarch`'.

`-mmvcle`
`-mno-mvcle`
> Generate (or do not generate) code using the `mvcle` instruction to perform block moves. When '`-mno-mvcle`' is specified, use a `mvc` loop instead. This is the default unless optimizing for size.

`-mdebug`
`-mno-debug`
> Print (or do not print) additional debug information when compiling. The default is to not print debug information.

`-march=cpu-type`
> Generate code that will run on *cpu-type*, which is the name of a system representing a certain processor type. Possible values for *cpu-type* are 'g5', 'g6', 'z900', 'z990', 'z9-109' and 'z9-ec'. When generating code using the instructions available on z/Architecture, the default is '-march=z900'. Otherwise, the default is '-march=g5'.

`-mtune=cpu-type`
> Tune to *cpu-type* everything applicable about the generated code, except for the ABI and the set of available instructions. The list of *cpu-type* values is the same as for '-march'. The default is the value used for '-march'.

`-mtpf-trace`
`-mno-tpf-trace`
> Generate code that adds (does not add) in TPF OS specific branches to trace routines in the operating system. This option is off by default, even when compiling for the TPF OS.

`-mfused-madd`
`-mno-fused-madd`
> Generate code that uses (does not use) the floating point multiply and accumulate instructions. These instructions are generated by default if hardware floating point is used.

`-mwarn-framesize=framesize`
> Emit a warning if the current function exceeds the given frame size. Because this is a compile time check it doesn't need to be a real problem when the program runs. It is intended to identify functions which most probably cause a stack overflow. It is useful to be used in an environment with limited stack size e.g. the linux kernel.

`-mwarn-dynamicstack`
> Emit a warning if the function calls alloca or uses dynamically sized arrays. This is generally a bad idea with a limited stack size.

`-mstack-guard=stack-guard`
`-mstack-size=stack-size`
> If these options are provided the s390 back end emits additional instructions in the function prologue which trigger a trap if the stack size is *stack-guard* bytes above the *stack-size* (remember that the stack on s390 grows downward). If the *stack-guard* option is omitted the smallest power of 2 larger than the frame size of the compiled function is chosen. These options are intended to be used to help debugging stack overflow problems. The additionally emitted code causes only little overhead and hence can also be used in production like systems without greater performance degradation. The given values have to be exact powers of 2 and *stack-size* has to be greater than *stack-guard* without exceeding 64k. In order to be efficient the extra code makes the assumption that the stack starts at an address aligned to the value given by *stack-size*. The *stack-guard* option can only be used in conjunction with *stack-size*.

Chapter 3: GCC Command Options   209

3.17.29 Score Options

These options are defined for Score implementations:

`-meb`   Compile code for big endian mode. This is the default.

`-mel`   Compile code for little endian mode.

`-mnhwloop`
               Disable generate bcnz instruction.

`-muls`   Enable generate unaligned load and store instruction.

`-mmac`   Enable the use of multiply-accumulate instructions. Disabled by default.

`-mscore5`   Specify the SCORE5 as the target architecture.

`-mscore5u`
               Specify the SCORE5U of the target architecture.

`-mscore7`   Specify the SCORE7 as the target architecture. This is the default.

`-mscore7d`
               Specify the SCORE7D as the target architecture.

3.17.30 SH Options

These '-m' options are defined for the SH implementations:

`-m1`   Generate code for the SH1.

`-m2`   Generate code for the SH2.

`-m2e`   Generate code for the SH2e.

`-m3`   Generate code for the SH3.

`-m3e`   Generate code for the SH3e.

`-m4-nofpu`
               Generate code for the SH4 without a floating-point unit.

`-m4-single-only`
               Generate code for the SH4 with a floating-point unit that only supports single-precision arithmetic.

`-m4-single`
               Generate code for the SH4 assuming the floating-point unit is in single-precision mode by default.

`-m4`   Generate code for the SH4.

`-m4a-nofpu`
               Generate code for the SH4al-dsp, or for a SH4a in such a way that the floating-point unit is not used.

`-m4a-single-only`
               Generate code for the SH4a, in such a way that no double-precision floating point operations are used.

`-m4a-single`
: Generate code for the SH4a assuming the floating-point unit is in single-precision mode by default.

`-m4a`
: Generate code for the SH4a.

`-m4al`
: Same as '`-m4a-nofpu`', except that it implicitly passes '`-dsp`' to the assembler. GCC doesn't generate any DSP instructions at the moment.

`-mb`
: Compile code for the processor in big endian mode.

`-ml`
: Compile code for the processor in little endian mode.

`-mdalign`
: Align doubles at 64-bit boundaries. Note that this changes the calling conventions, and thus some functions from the standard C library will not work unless you recompile it first with '`-mdalign`'.

`-mrelax`
: Shorten some address references at link time, when possible; uses the linker option '`-relax`'.

`-mbigtable`
: Use 32-bit offsets in `switch` tables. The default is to use 16-bit offsets.

`-mfmovd`
: Enable the use of the instruction `fmovd`.

`-mhitachi`
: Comply with the calling conventions defined by Renesas.

`-mrenesas`
: Comply with the calling conventions defined by Renesas.

`-mno-renesas`
: Comply with the calling conventions defined for GCC before the Renesas conventions were available. This option is the default for all targets of the SH toolchain except for '`sh-symbianelf`'.

`-mnomacsave`
: Mark the `MAC` register as call-clobbered, even if '`-mhitachi`' is given.

`-mieee`
: Increase IEEE-compliance of floating-point code. At the moment, this is equivalent to '`-fno-finite-math-only`'. When generating 16 bit SH opcodes, getting IEEE-conforming results for comparisons of NANs / infinities incurs extra overhead in every floating point comparison, therefore the default is set to '`-ffinite-math-only`'.

`-minline-ic_invalidate`
: Inline code to invalidate instruction cache entries after setting up nested function trampolines. This option has no effect if -musermode is in effect and the selected code generation option (e.g. -m4) does not allow the use of the icbi instruction. If the selected code generation option does not allow the use of the icbi instruction, and -musermode is not in effect, the inlined code will manipulate the instruction cache address array directly with an associative write. This not only requires privileged mode, but it will also fail if the cache line had been mapped via the TLB and has become unmapped.

Chapter 3: GCC Command Options   211

-misize   Dump instruction size and location in the assembly code.

-mpadstruct
            This option is deprecated. It pads structures to multiple of 4 bytes, which is
            incompatible with the SH ABI.

-mspace   Optimize for space instead of speed. Implied by '-Os'.

-mprefergot
            When generating position-independent code, emit function calls using the
            Global Offset Table instead of the Procedure Linkage Table.

-musermode
            Don't generate privileged mode only code; implies -mno-inline-ic_invalidate if
            the inlined code would not work in user mode. This is the default when the
            target is sh-*-linux*.

-multcost=*number*
            Set the cost to assume for a multiply insn.

-mdiv=*strategy*
            Set the division strategy to use for SHmedia code. *strategy* must be one of:
            call, call2, fp, inv, inv:minlat, inv20u, inv20l, inv:call, inv:call2, inv:fp . "fp"
            performs the operation in floating point. This has a very high latency, but
            needs only a few instructions, so it might be a good choice if your code has
            enough easily exploitable ILP to allow the compiler to schedule the floating
            point instructions together with other instructions. Division by zero causes a
            floating point exception. "inv" uses integer operations to calculate the inverse
            of the divisor, and then multiplies the dividend with the inverse. This strategy
            allows cse and hoisting of the inverse calculation. Division by zero calculates an
            unspecified result, but does not trap. "inv:minlat" is a variant of "inv" where
            if no cse / hoisting opportunities have been found, or if the entire operation
            has been hoisted to the same place, the last stages of the inverse calculation are
            intertwined with the final multiply to reduce the overall latency, at the expense
            of using a few more instructions, and thus offering fewer scheduling opportuni-
            ties with other code. "call" calls a library function that usually implements the
            inv:minlat strategy. This gives high code density for m5-*media-nofpu compila-
            tions. "call2" uses a different entry point of the same library function, where it
            assumes that a pointer to a lookup table has already been set up, which exposes
            the pointer load to cse / code hoisting optimizations. "inv:call", "inv:call2" and
            "inv:fp" all use the "inv" algorithm for initial code generation, but if the code
            stays unoptimized, revert to the "call", "call2", or "fp" strategies, respectively.
            Note that the potentially-trapping side effect of division by zero is carried by a
            separate instruction, so it is possible that all the integer instructions are hoisted
            out, but the marker for the side effect stays where it is. A recombination to
            fp operations or a call is not possible in that case. "inv20u" and "inv20l" are
            variants of the "inv:minlat" strategy. In the case that the inverse calculation
            was nor separated from the multiply, they speed up division where the dividend
            fits into 20 bits (plus sign where applicable), by inserting a test to skip a num-
            ber of operations in this case; this test slows down the case of larger dividends.

inv20u assumes the case of a such a small dividend to be unlikely, and inv20l assumes it to be likely.

`-mdivsi3_libfunc=`*name*
> Set the name of the library function used for 32 bit signed division to *name*. This only affect the name used in the call and inv:call division strategies, and the compiler will still expect the same sets of input/output/clobbered registers as if this option was not present.

`-madjust-unroll`
> Throttle unrolling to avoid thrashing target registers. This option only has an effect if the gcc code base supports the TARGET_ADJUST_UNROLL_MAX target hook.

`-mindexed-addressing`
> Enable the use of the indexed addressing mode for SHmedia32/SHcompact. This is only safe if the hardware and/or OS implement 32 bit wrap-around semantics for the indexed addressing mode. The architecture allows the implementation of processors with 64 bit MMU, which the OS could use to get 32 bit addressing, but since no current hardware implementation supports this or any other way to make the indexed addressing mode safe to use in the 32 bit ABI, the default is -mno-indexed-addressing.

`-mgettrcost=`*number*
> Set the cost assumed for the gettr instruction to *number*. The default is 2 if '`-mpt-fixed`' is in effect, 100 otherwise.

`-mpt-fixed`
> Assume pt* instructions won't trap. This will generally generate better scheduled code, but is unsafe on current hardware. The current architecture definition says that ptabs and ptrel trap when the target anded with 3 is 3. This has the unintentional effect of making it unsafe to schedule ptabs / ptrel before a branch, or hoist it out of a loop. For example, __do_global_ctors, a part of libgcc that runs constructors at program startup, calls functions in a list which is delimited by −1. With the -mpt-fixed option, the ptabs will be done before testing against −1. That means that all the constructors will be run a bit quicker, but when the loop comes to the end of the list, the program crashes because ptabs loads −1 into a target register. Since this option is unsafe for any hardware implementing the current architecture specification, the default is -mno-pt-fixed. Unless the user specifies a specific cost with '`-mgettrcost`', -mno-pt-fixed also implies '`-mgettrcost=100`'; this deters register allocation using target registers for storing ordinary integers.

`-minvalid-symbols`
> Assume symbols might be invalid. Ordinary function symbols generated by the compiler will always be valid to load with movi/shori/ptabs or movi/shori/ptrel, but with assembler and/or linker tricks it is possible to generate symbols that will cause ptabs / ptrel to trap. This option is only meaningful when '`-mno-pt-fixed`' is in effect. It will then prevent cross-basic-block cse, hoisting and most scheduling of symbol loads. The default is '`-mno-invalid-symbols`'.

Chapter 3: GCC Command Options 213

3.17.31 SPARC Options

These '-m' options are supported on the SPARC:

`-mno-app-regs`
`-mapp-regs`

>Specify '-mapp-regs' to generate output using the global registers 2 through 4, which the SPARC SVR4 ABI reserves for applications. This is the default.
>
>To be fully SVR4 ABI compliant at the cost of some performance loss, specify '-mno-app-regs'. You should compile libraries and system software with this option.

`-mfpu`
`-mhard-float`

>Generate output containing floating point instructions. This is the default.

`-mno-fpu`
`-msoft-float`

>Generate output containing library calls for floating point. **Warning:** the requisite libraries are not available for all SPARC targets. Normally the facilities of the machine's usual C compiler are used, but this cannot be done directly in cross-compilation. You must make your own arrangements to provide suitable library functions for cross-compilation. The embedded targets 'sparc-*-aout' and 'sparclite-*-*' do provide software floating point support.
>
>'-msoft-float' changes the calling convention in the output file; therefore, it is only useful if you compile *all* of a program with this option. In particular, you need to compile 'libgcc.a', the library that comes with GCC, with '-msoft-float' in order for this to work.

`-mhard-quad-float`

>Generate output containing quad-word (long double) floating point instructions.

`-msoft-quad-float`

>Generate output containing library calls for quad-word (long double) floating point instructions. The functions called are those specified in the SPARC ABI. This is the default.
>
>As of this writing, there are no SPARC implementations that have hardware support for the quad-word floating point instructions. They all invoke a trap handler for one of these instructions, and then the trap handler emulates the effect of the instruction. Because of the trap handler overhead, this is much slower than calling the ABI library routines. Thus the '-msoft-quad-float' option is the default.

`-mno-unaligned-doubles`
`-munaligned-doubles`

>Assume that doubles have 8 byte alignment. This is the default.
>
>With '-munaligned-doubles', GCC assumes that doubles have 8 byte alignment only if they are contained in another type, or if they have an absolute address. Otherwise, it assumes they have 4 byte alignment. Specifying this option avoids some rare compatibility problems with code generated by other

compilers. It is not the default because it results in a performance loss, especially for floating point code.

`-mno-faster-structs`
`-mfaster-structs`

With '`-mfaster-structs`', the compiler assumes that structures should have 8 byte alignment. This enables the use of pairs of `ldd` and `std` instructions for copies in structure assignment, in place of twice as many `ld` and `st` pairs. However, the use of this changed alignment directly violates the SPARC ABI. Thus, it's intended only for use on targets where the developer acknowledges that their resulting code will not be directly in line with the rules of the ABI.

`-mimpure-text`

'`-mimpure-text`', used in addition to '`-shared`', tells the compiler to not pass '`-z text`' to the linker when linking a shared object. Using this option, you can link position-dependent code into a shared object.

'`-mimpure-text`' suppresses the "relocations remain against allocatable but non-writable sections" linker error message. However, the necessary relocations will trigger copy-on-write, and the shared object is not actually shared across processes. Instead of using '`-mimpure-text`', you should compile all source code with '`-fpic`' or '`-fPIC`'.

This option is only available on SunOS and Solaris.

`-mcpu=cpu_type`

Set the instruction set, register set, and instruction scheduling parameters for machine type *cpu_type*. Supported values for *cpu_type* are '`v7`', '`cypress`', '`v8`', '`supersparc`', '`sparclite`', '`f930`', '`f934`', '`hypersparc`', '`sparclite86x`', '`sparclet`', '`tsc701`', '`v9`', '`ultrasparc`', '`ultrasparc3`', '`niagara`' and '`niagara2`'.

Default instruction scheduling parameters are used for values that select an architecture and not an implementation. These are '`v7`', '`v8`', '`sparclite`', '`sparclet`', '`v9`'.

Here is a list of each supported architecture and their supported implementations.

```
v7:         cypress
v8:         supersparc, hypersparc
sparclite:  f930, f934, sparclite86x
sparclet:   tsc701
v9:         ultrasparc, ultrasparc3, niagara, niagara2
```

By default (unless configured otherwise), GCC generates code for the V7 variant of the SPARC architecture. With '`-mcpu=cypress`', the compiler additionally optimizes it for the Cypress CY7C602 chip, as used in the SPARCStation/SPARCServer 3xx series. This is also appropriate for the older SPARCStation 1, 2, IPX etc.

With '`-mcpu=v8`', GCC generates code for the V8 variant of the SPARC architecture. The only difference from V7 code is that the compiler emits the integer multiply and integer divide instructions which exist in SPARC-V8 but not in SPARC-V7. With '`-mcpu=supersparc`', the compiler additionally optimizes it

Chapter 3: GCC Command Options   215

for the SuperSPARC chip, as used in the SPARCStation 10, 1000 and 2000 series.

With '-mcpu=sparclite', GCC generates code for the SPARClite variant of the SPARC architecture. This adds the integer multiply, integer divide step and scan (ffs) instructions which exist in SPARClite but not in SPARC-V7. With '-mcpu=f930', the compiler additionally optimizes it for the Fujitsu MB86930 chip, which is the original SPARClite, with no FPU. With '-mcpu=f934', the compiler additionally optimizes it for the Fujitsu MB86934 chip, which is the more recent SPARClite with FPU.

With '-mcpu=sparclet', GCC generates code for the SPARClet variant of the SPARC architecture. This adds the integer multiply, multiply/accumulate, integer divide step and scan (ffs) instructions which exist in SPARClet but not in SPARC-V7. With '-mcpu=tsc701', the compiler additionally optimizes it for the TEMIC SPARClet chip.

With '-mcpu=v9', GCC generates code for the V9 variant of the SPARC architecture. This adds 64-bit integer and floating-point move instructions, 3 additional floating-point condition code registers and conditional move instructions. With '-mcpu=ultrasparc', the compiler additionally optimizes it for the Sun UltraSPARC I/II/IIi chips. With '-mcpu=ultrasparc3', the compiler additionally optimizes it for the Sun UltraSPARC III/III+/IIIi/IIIi+/IV/IV+ chips. With '-mcpu=niagara', the compiler additionally optimizes it for Sun UltraSPARC T1 chips. With '-mcpu=niagara2', the compiler additionally optimizes it for Sun UltraSPARC T2 chips.

-mtune=*cpu_type*
Set the instruction scheduling parameters for machine type *cpu_type*, but do not set the instruction set or register set that the option '-mcpu=*cpu_type*' would.

The same values for '-mcpu=*cpu_type*' can be used for '-mtune=*cpu_type*', but the only useful values are those that select a particular cpu implementation. Those are 'cypress', 'supersparc', 'hypersparc', 'f930', 'f934', 'sparclite86x', 'tsc701', 'ultrasparc', 'ultrasparc3', 'niagara', and 'niagara2'.

-mv8plus
-mno-v8plus
With '-mv8plus', GCC generates code for the SPARC-V8+ ABI. The difference from the V8 ABI is that the global and out registers are considered 64-bit wide. This is enabled by default on Solaris in 32-bit mode for all SPARC-V9 processors.

-mvis
-mno-vis   With '-mvis', GCC generates code that takes advantage of the UltraSPARC Visual Instruction Set extensions. The default is '-mno-vis'.

These '-m' options are supported in addition to the above on SPARC-V9 processors in 64-bit environments:

`-mlittle-endian`
: Generate code for a processor running in little-endian mode. It is only available for a few configurations and most notably not on Solaris and Linux.

`-m32`
`-m64`
: Generate code for a 32-bit or 64-bit environment. The 32-bit environment sets int, long and pointer to 32 bits. The 64-bit environment sets int to 32 bits and long and pointer to 64 bits.

`-mcmodel=medlow`
: Generate code for the Medium/Low code model: 64-bit addresses, programs must be linked in the low 32 bits of memory. Programs can be statically or dynamically linked.

`-mcmodel=medmid`
: Generate code for the Medium/Middle code model: 64-bit addresses, programs must be linked in the low 44 bits of memory, the text and data segments must be less than 2GB in size and the data segment must be located within 2GB of the text segment.

`-mcmodel=medany`
: Generate code for the Medium/Anywhere code model: 64-bit addresses, programs may be linked anywhere in memory, the text and data segments must be less than 2GB in size and the data segment must be located within 2GB of the text segment.

`-mcmodel=embmedany`
: Generate code for the Medium/Anywhere code model for embedded systems: 64-bit addresses, the text and data segments must be less than 2GB in size, both starting anywhere in memory (determined at link time). The global register %g4 points to the base of the data segment. Programs are statically linked and PIC is not supported.

`-mstack-bias`
`-mno-stack-bias`
: With '`-mstack-bias`', GCC assumes that the stack pointer, and frame pointer if present, are offset by -2047 which must be added back when making stack frame references. This is the default in 64-bit mode. Otherwise, assume no such offset is present.

These switches are supported in addition to the above on Solaris:

`-threads`
: Add support for multithreading using the Solaris threads library. This option sets flags for both the preprocessor and linker. This option does not affect the thread safety of object code produced by the compiler or that of libraries supplied with it.

`-pthreads`
: Add support for multithreading using the POSIX threads library. This option sets flags for both the preprocessor and linker. This option does not affect the thread safety of object code produced by the compiler or that of libraries supplied with it.

Chapter 3: GCC Command Options   217

`-pthread`   This is a synonym for '`-pthreads`'.

3.17.32 SPU Options

These '-m' options are supported on the SPU:

`-mwarn-reloc`
`-merror-reloc`
> The loader for SPU does not handle dynamic relocations. By default, GCC will give an error when it generates code that requires a dynamic relocation. '`-mno-error-reloc`' disables the error, '`-mwarn-reloc`' will generate a warning instead.

`-msafe-dma`
`-munsafe-dma`
> Instructions which initiate or test completion of DMA must not be reordered with respect to loads and stores of the memory which is being accessed. Users typically address this problem using the volatile keyword, but that can lead to inefficient code in places where the memory is known to not change. Rather than mark the memory as volatile we treat the DMA instructions as potentially effecting all memory. With '`-munsafe-dma`' users must use the volatile keyword to protect memory accesses.

`-mbranch-hints`
> By default, GCC will generate a branch hint instruction to avoid pipeline stalls for always taken or probably taken branches. A hint will not be generated closer than 8 instructions away from its branch. There is little reason to disable them, except for debugging purposes, or to make an object a little bit smaller.

`-msmall-mem`
`-mlarge-mem`
> By default, GCC generates code assuming that addresses are never larger than 18 bits. With '`-mlarge-mem`' code is generated that assumes a full 32 bit address.

`-mstdmain`
> By default, GCC links against startup code that assumes the SPU-style main function interface (which has an unconventional parameter list). With '`-mstdmain`', GCC will link your program against startup code that assumes a C99-style interface to main, including a local copy of argv strings.

`-mfixed-range=register-range`
> Generate code treating the given register range as fixed registers. A fixed register is one that the register allocator can not use. This is useful when compiling kernel code. A register range is specified as two registers separated by a dash. Multiple register ranges can be specified separated by a comma.

`-mdual-nops`
`-mdual-nops=n`
> By default, GCC will insert nops to increase dual issue when it expects it to increase performance. n can be a value from 0 to 10. A smaller n will insert

fewer nops. 10 is the default, 0 is the same as '-mno-dual-nops'. Disabled with '-Os'.

`-mhint-max-nops=n`
> Maximum number of nops to insert for a branch hint. A branch hint must be at least 8 instructions away from the branch it is effecting. GCC will insert up to *n* nops to enforce this, otherwise it will not generate the branch hint.

`-mhint-max-distance=n`
> The encoding of the branch hint instruction limits the hint to be within 256 instructions of the branch it is effecting. By default, GCC makes sure it is within 125.

`-msafe-hints`
> Work around a hardware bug which causes the SPU to stall indefinitely. By default, GCC will insert the `hbrp` instruction to make sure this stall won't happen.

3.17.33 Options for System V

These additional options are available on System V Release 4 for compatibility with other compilers on those systems:

`-G`
> Create a shared object. It is recommended that '-symbolic' or '-shared' be used instead.

`-Qy`
> Identify the versions of each tool used by the compiler, in a `.ident` assembler directive in the output.

`-Qn`
> Refrain from adding `.ident` directives to the output file (this is the default).

`-YP,dirs`
> Search the directories *dirs*, and no others, for libraries specified with '-l'.

`-Ym,dir`
> Look in the directory *dir* to find the M4 preprocessor. The assembler uses this option.

3.17.34 V850 Options

These '-m' options are defined for V850 implementations:

`-mlong-calls`
`-mno-long-calls`
> Treat all calls as being far away (near). If calls are assumed to be far away, the compiler will always load the functions address up into a register, and call indirect through the pointer.

`-mno-ep`
`-mep`
> Do not optimize (do optimize) basic blocks that use the same index pointer 4 or more times to copy pointer into the `ep` register, and use the shorter `sld` and `sst` instructions. The '-mep' option is on by default if you optimize.

`-mno-prolog-function`
`-mprolog-function`
> Do not use (do use) external functions to save and restore registers at the prologue and epilogue of a function. The external functions are slower, but use

less code space if more than one function saves the same number of registers. The '-mprolog-function' option is on by default if you optimize.

-mspace   Try to make the code as small as possible. At present, this just turns on the '-mep' and '-mprolog-function' options.

-mtda=n   Put static or global variables whose size is *n* bytes or less into the tiny data area that register **ep** points to. The tiny data area can hold up to 256 bytes in total (128 bytes for byte references).

-msda=n   Put static or global variables whose size is *n* bytes or less into the small data area that register **gp** points to. The small data area can hold up to 64 kilobytes.

-mzda=n   Put static or global variables whose size is *n* bytes or less into the first 32 kilobytes of memory.

-mv850   Specify that the target processor is the V850.

-mbig-switch
           Generate code suitable for big switch tables. Use this option only if the assembler/linker complain about out of range branches within a switch table.

-mapp-regs
           This option will cause r2 and r5 to be used in the code generated by the compiler. This setting is the default.

-mno-app-regs
           This option will cause r2 and r5 to be treated as fixed registers.

-mv850e1   Specify that the target processor is the V850E1. The preprocessor constants '__v850e1__' and '__v850e__' will be defined if this option is used.

-mv850e   Specify that the target processor is the V850E. The preprocessor constant '__v850e__' will be defined if this option is used.

           If neither '-mv850' nor '-mv850e' nor '-mv850e1' are defined then a default target processor will be chosen and the relevant '__v850*__' preprocessor constant will be defined.

           The preprocessor constants '__v850' and '__v851__' are always defined, regardless of which processor variant is the target.

-mdisable-callt
           This option will suppress generation of the CALLT instruction for the v850e and v850e1 flavors of the v850 architecture. The default is '-mno-disable-callt' which allows the CALLT instruction to be used.

3.17.35 VAX Options

These '-m' options are defined for the VAX:

-munix   Do not output certain jump instructions (**aobleq** and so on) that the Unix assembler for the VAX cannot handle across long ranges.

-mgnu   Do output those jump instructions, on the assumption that you will assemble with the GNU assembler.

-mg   Output code for g-format floating point numbers instead of d-format.

3.17.36 VxWorks Options

The options in this section are defined for all VxWorks targets. Options specific to the target hardware are listed with the other options for that target.

-mrtp GCC can generate code for both VxWorks kernels and real time processes (RTPs). This option switches from the former to the latter. It also defines the preprocessor macro __RTP__.

-non-static

Link an RTP executable against shared libraries rather than static libraries. The options '-static' and '-shared' can also be used for RTPs (see Section 3.13 [Link Options], page 123); '-static' is the default.

-Bstatic
-Bdynamic

These options are passed down to the linker. They are defined for compatibility with Diab.

-Xbind-lazy

Enable lazy binding of function calls. This option is equivalent to '-Wl,-z,now' and is defined for compatibility with Diab.

-Xbind-now

Disable lazy binding of function calls. This option is the default and is defined for compatibility with Diab.

3.17.37 x86-64 Options

These are listed under See Section 3.17.14 [i386 and x86-64 Options], page 161.

3.17.38 Xstormy16 Options

These options are defined for Xstormy16:

-msim Choose startup files and linker script suitable for the simulator.

3.17.39 Xtensa Options

These options are supported for Xtensa targets:

-mconst16
-mno-const16

Enable or disable use of CONST16 instructions for loading constant values. The CONST16 instruction is currently not a standard option from Tensilica. When enabled, CONST16 instructions are always used in place of the standard L32R instructions. The use of CONST16 is enabled by default only if the L32R instruction is not available.

-mfused-madd
-mno-fused-madd

Enable or disable use of fused multiply/add and multiply/subtract instructions in the floating-point option. This has no effect if the floating-point option is not also enabled. Disabling fused multiply/add and multiply/subtract instructions forces the compiler to use separate instructions for the multiply and

Chapter 3: GCC Command Options   221

add/subtract operations. This may be desirable in some cases where strict
IEEE 754-compliant results are required: the fused multiply add/subtract instructions do not round the intermediate result, thereby producing results with
more bits of precision than specified by the IEEE standard. Disabling fused
multiply add/subtract instructions also ensures that the program output is not
sensitive to the compiler's ability to combine multiply and add/subtract operations.

`-mtext-section-literals`
`-mno-text-section-literals`

Control the treatment of literal pools. The default is '`-mno-text-section-literals`',
which places literals in a separate section in the output file. This allows the
literal pool to be placed in a data RAM/ROM, and it also allows the linker to
combine literal pools from separate object files to remove redundant literals
and improve code size. With '`-mtext-section-literals`', the literals are
interspersed in the text section in order to keep them as close as possible to
their references. This may be necessary for large assembly files.

`-mtarget-align`
`-mno-target-align`

When this option is enabled, GCC instructs the assembler to automatically align
instructions to reduce branch penalties at the expense of some code density. The
assembler attempts to widen density instructions to align branch targets and
the instructions following call instructions. If there are not enough preceding
safe density instructions to align a target, no widening will be performed. The
default is '`-mtarget-align`'. These options do not affect the treatment of auto-
aligned instructions like `LOOP`, which the assembler will always align, either by
widening density instructions or by inserting no-op instructions.

`-mlongcalls`
`-mno-longcalls`

When this option is enabled, GCC instructs the assembler to translate direct
calls to indirect calls unless it can determine that the target of a direct call is
in the range allowed by the call instruction. This translation typically occurs
for calls to functions in other source files. Specifically, the assembler translates
a direct `CALL` instruction into an `L32R` followed by a `CALLX` instruction. The
default is '`-mno-longcalls`'. This option should be used in programs where
the call target can potentially be out of range. This option is implemented in
the assembler, not the compiler, so the assembly code generated by GCC will
still show direct call instructions—look at the disassembled object code to see
the actual instructions. Note that the assembler will use an indirect call for
every cross-file call, not just those that really will be out of range.

3.17.40 zSeries Options

These are listed under See Section 3.17.28 [S/390 and zSeries Options], page 206.

3.18 Options for Code Generation Conventions

These machine-independent options control the interface conventions used in code generation.

Most of them have both positive and negative forms; the negative form of '-ffoo' would be '-fno-foo'. In the table below, only one of the forms is listed—the one which is not the default. You can figure out the other form by either removing 'no-' or adding it.

-fbounds-check
: For front-ends that support it, generate additional code to check that indices used to access arrays are within the declared range. This is currently only supported by the Java and Fortran front-ends, where this option defaults to true and false respectively.

-ftrapv
: This option generates traps for signed overflow on addition, subtraction, multiplication operations.

-fwrapv
: This option instructs the compiler to assume that signed arithmetic overflow of addition, subtraction and multiplication wraps around using twos-complement representation. This flag enables some optimizations and disables others. This option is enabled by default for the Java front-end, as required by the Java language specification.

-fexceptions
: Enable exception handling. Generates extra code needed to propagate exceptions. For some targets, this implies GCC will generate frame unwind information for all functions, which can produce significant data size overhead, although it does not affect execution. If you do not specify this option, GCC will enable it by default for languages like C++ which normally require exception handling, and disable it for languages like C that do not normally require it. However, you may need to enable this option when compiling C code that needs to interoperate properly with exception handlers written in C++. You may also wish to disable this option if you are compiling older C++ programs that don't use exception handling.

-fnon-call-exceptions
: Generate code that allows trapping instructions to throw exceptions. Note that this requires platform-specific runtime support that does not exist everywhere. Moreover, it only allows *trapping* instructions to throw exceptions, i.e. memory references or floating point instructions. It does not allow exceptions to be thrown from arbitrary signal handlers such as SIGALRM.

-funwind-tables
: Similar to '-fexceptions', except that it will just generate any needed static data, but will not affect the generated code in any other way. You will normally not enable this option; instead, a language processor that needs this handling would enable it on your behalf.

-fasynchronous-unwind-tables
: Generate unwind table in dwarf2 format, if supported by target machine. The table is exact at each instruction boundary, so it can be used for stack unwinding from asynchronous events (such as debugger or garbage collector).

Chapter 3: GCC Command Options   223

`-fpcc-struct-return`

> Return "short" `struct` and `union` values in memory like longer ones, rather than in registers. This convention is less efficient, but it has the advantage of allowing intercallability between GCC-compiled files and files compiled with other compilers, particularly the Portable C Compiler (pcc).
>
> The precise convention for returning structures in memory depends on the target configuration macros.
>
> Short structures and unions are those whose size and alignment match that of some integer type.
>
> **Warning:** code compiled with the '`-fpcc-struct-return`' switch is not binary compatible with code compiled with the '`-freg-struct-return`' switch. Use it to conform to a non-default application binary interface.

`-freg-struct-return`

> Return `struct` and `union` values in registers when possible. This is more efficient for small structures than '`-fpcc-struct-return`'.
>
> If you specify neither '`-fpcc-struct-return`' nor '`-freg-struct-return`', GCC defaults to whichever convention is standard for the target. If there is no standard convention, GCC defaults to '`-fpcc-struct-return`', except on targets where GCC is the principal compiler. In those cases, we can choose the standard, and we chose the more efficient register return alternative.
>
> **Warning:** code compiled with the '`-freg-struct-return`' switch is not binary compatible with code compiled with the '`-fpcc-struct-return`' switch. Use it to conform to a non-default application binary interface.

`-fshort-enums`

> Allocate to an `enum` type only as many bytes as it needs for the declared range of possible values. Specifically, the `enum` type will be equivalent to the smallest integer type which has enough room.
>
> **Warning:** the '`-fshort-enums`' switch causes GCC to generate code that is not binary compatible with code generated without that switch. Use it to conform to a non-default application binary interface.

`-fshort-double`

> Use the same size for `double` as for `float`.
>
> **Warning:** the '`-fshort-double`' switch causes GCC to generate code that is not binary compatible with code generated without that switch. Use it to conform to a non-default application binary interface.

`-fshort-wchar`

> Override the underlying type for '`wchar_t`' to be '`short unsigned int`' instead of the default for the target. This option is useful for building programs to run under WINE.
>
> **Warning:** the '`-fshort-wchar`' switch causes GCC to generate code that is not binary compatible with code generated without that switch. Use it to conform to a non-default application binary interface.

`-fno-common`
> In C, allocate even uninitialized global variables in the data section of the object file, rather than generating them as common blocks. This has the effect that if the same variable is declared (without `extern`) in two different compilations, you will get an error when you link them. The only reason this might be useful is if you wish to verify that the program will work on other systems which always work this way.

`-fno-ident`
> Ignore the '`#ident`' directive.

`-finhibit-size-directive`
> Don't output a `.size` assembler directive, or anything else that would cause trouble if the function is split in the middle, and the two halves are placed at locations far apart in memory. This option is used when compiling '`crtstuff.c`'; you should not need to use it for anything else.

`-fverbose-asm`
> Put extra commentary information in the generated assembly code to make it more readable. This option is generally only of use to those who actually need to read the generated assembly code (perhaps while debugging the compiler itself).
>
> '`-fno-verbose-asm`', the default, causes the extra information to be omitted and is useful when comparing two assembler files.

`-frecord-gcc-switches`
> This switch causes the command line that was used to invoke the compiler to be recorded into the object file that is being created. This switch is only implemented on some targets and the exact format of the recording is target and binary file format dependent, but it usually takes the form of a section containing ASCII text. This switch is related to the '`-fverbose-asm`' switch, but that switch only records information in the assembler output file as comments, so it never reaches the object file.

`-fpic`
> Generate position-independent code (PIC) suitable for use in a shared library, if supported for the target machine. Such code accesses all constant addresses through a global offset table (GOT). The dynamic loader resolves the GOT entries when the program starts (the dynamic loader is not part of GCC; it is part of the operating system). If the GOT size for the linked executable exceeds a machine-specific maximum size, you get an error message from the linker indicating that '`-fpic`' does not work; in that case, recompile with '`-fPIC`' instead. (These maximums are 8k on the SPARC and 32k on the m68k and RS/6000. The 386 has no such limit.)
>
> Position-independent code requires special support, and therefore works only on certain machines. For the 386, GCC supports PIC for System V but not for the Sun 386i. Code generated for the IBM RS/6000 is always position-independent.
>
> When this flag is set, the macros `__pic__` and `__PIC__` are defined to 1.

Chapter 3: GCC Command Options   225

-fPIC   If supported for the target machine, emit position-independent code, suitable for dynamic linking and avoiding any limit on the size of the global offset table. This option makes a difference on the m68k, PowerPC and SPARC.

            Position-independent code requires special support, and therefore works only on certain machines.

            When this flag is set, the macros __pic__ and __PIC__ are defined to 2.

-fpie
-fPIE   These options are similar to '-fpic' and '-fPIC', but generated position independent code can be only linked into executables. Usually these options are used when '-pie' GCC option will be used during linking.

            '-fpie' and '-fPIE' both define the macros __pie__ and __PIE__. The macros have the value 1 for '-fpie' and 2 for '-fPIE'.

-fno-jump-tables
            Do not use jump tables for switch statements even where it would be more efficient than other code generation strategies. This option is of use in conjunction with '-fpic' or '-fPIC' for building code which forms part of a dynamic linker and cannot reference the address of a jump table. On some targets, jump tables do not require a GOT and this option is not needed.

-ffixed-*reg*
            Treat the register named *reg* as a fixed register; generated code should never refer to it (except perhaps as a stack pointer, frame pointer or in some other fixed role).

            reg must be the name of a register. The register names accepted are machine-specific and are defined in the REGISTER_NAMES macro in the machine description macro file.

            This flag does not have a negative form, because it specifies a three-way choice.

-fcall-used-*reg*
            Treat the register named *reg* as an allocable register that is clobbered by function calls. It may be allocated for temporaries or variables that do not live across a call. Functions compiled this way will not save and restore the register *reg*.

            It is an error to used this flag with the frame pointer or stack pointer. Use of this flag for other registers that have fixed pervasive roles in the machine's execution model will produce disastrous results.

            This flag does not have a negative form, because it specifies a three-way choice.

-fcall-saved-*reg*
            Treat the register named *reg* as an allocable register saved by functions. It may be allocated even for temporaries or variables that live across a call. Functions compiled this way will save and restore the register *reg* if they use it.

            It is an error to used this flag with the frame pointer or stack pointer. Use of this flag for other registers that have fixed pervasive roles in the machine's execution model will produce disastrous results.

A different sort of disaster will result from the use of this flag for a register in which function values may be returned.

This flag does not have a negative form, because it specifies a three-way choice.

`-fpack-struct[=n]`

Without a value specified, pack all structure members together without holes. When a value is specified (which must be a small power of two), pack structure members according to this value, representing the maximum alignment (that is, objects with default alignment requirements larger than this will be output potentially unaligned at the next fitting location.

Warning: the '`-fpack-struct`' switch causes GCC to generate code that is not binary compatible with code generated without that switch. Additionally, it makes the code suboptimal. Use it to conform to a non-default application binary interface.

`-finstrument-functions`

Generate instrumentation calls for entry and exit to functions. Just after function entry and just before function exit, the following profiling functions will be called with the address of the current function and its call site. (On some platforms, `__builtin_return_address` does not work beyond the current function, so the call site information may not be available to the profiling functions otherwise.)

```
void __cyg_profile_func_enter (void *this_fn,
                               void *call_site);
void __cyg_profile_func_exit  (void *this_fn,
                               void *call_site);
```

The first argument is the address of the start of the current function, which may be looked up exactly in the symbol table.

This instrumentation is also done for functions expanded inline in other functions. The profiling calls will indicate where, conceptually, the inline function is entered and exited. This means that addressable versions of such functions must be available. If all your uses of a function are expanded inline, this may mean an additional expansion of code size. If you use '`extern inline`' in your C code, an addressable version of such functions must be provided. (This is normally the case anyways, but if you get lucky and the optimizer always expands the functions inline, you might have gotten away without providing static copies.)

A function may be given the attribute `no_instrument_function`, in which case this instrumentation will not be done. This can be used, for example, for the profiling functions listed above, high-priority interrupt routines, and any functions from which the profiling functions cannot safely be called (perhaps signal handlers, if the profiling routines generate output or allocate memory).

`-finstrument-functions-exclude-file-list=file,file,...`

Set the list of functions that are excluded from instrumentation (see the description of `-finstrument-functions`). If the file that contains a function definition matches with one of *file*, then that function is not instrumented. The match is done on substrings: if the *file* parameter is a substring of the file name, it is considered to be a match.

Chapter 3: GCC Command Options   227

> For example, `-finstrument-functions-exclude-file-list=/bits/stl,include/sys` will exclude any inline function defined in files whose pathnames contain /bits/stl or include/sys.
>
> If, for some reason, you want to include letter ',' in one of sym, write '\,'. For example, `-finstrument-functions-exclude-file-list='\,\,tmp'` (note the single quote surrounding the option).

`-finstrument-functions-exclude-function-list=sym,sym,...`
> This is similar to `-finstrument-functions-exclude-file-list`, but this option sets the list of function names to be excluded from instrumentation. The function name to be matched is its user-visible name, such as `vector<int> blah(const vector<int> &)`, not the internal mangled name (e.g., `_Z4blahRSt6vectorIiSaIiEE`). The match is done on substrings: if the sym parameter is a substring of the function name, it is considered to be a match.

`-fstack-check`
> Generate code to verify that you do not go beyond the boundary of the stack. You should specify this flag if you are running in an environment with multiple threads, but only rarely need to specify it in a single-threaded environment since stack overflow is automatically detected on nearly all systems if there is only one stack.
>
> Note that this switch does not actually cause checking to be done; the operating system must do that. The switch causes generation of code to ensure that the operating system sees the stack being extended.

`-fstack-limit-register=reg`
`-fstack-limit-symbol=sym`
`-fno-stack-limit`
> Generate code to ensure that the stack does not grow beyond a certain value, either the value of a register or the address of a symbol. If the stack would grow beyond the value, a signal is raised. For most targets, the signal is raised before the stack overruns the boundary, so it is possible to catch the signal without taking special precautions.
>
> For instance, if the stack starts at absolute address '0x80000000' and grows downwards, you can use the flags '`-fstack-limit-symbol=__stack_limit`' and '`-Wl,--defsym,__stack_limit=0x7ffe0000`' to enforce a stack limit of 128KB. Note that this may only work with the GNU linker.

`-fargument-alias`
`-fargument-noalias`
`-fargument-noalias-global`
`-fargument-noalias-anything`
> Specify the possible relationships among parameters and between parameters and global data.
>
> '`-fargument-alias`' specifies that arguments (parameters) may alias each other and may alias global storage.
>
> '`-fargument-noalias`' specifies that arguments do not alias each other, but

may alias global storage.

'-fargument-noalias-global' specifies that arguments do not alias each other and do not alias global storage. '-fargument-noalias-anything' specifies that arguments do not alias any other storage.

Each language will automatically use whatever option is required by the language standard. You should not need to use these options yourself.

-fleading-underscore

This option and its counterpart, '-fno-leading-underscore', forcibly change the way C symbols are represented in the object file. One use is to help link with legacy assembly code.

Warning: the '-fleading-underscore' switch causes GCC to generate code that is not binary compatible with code generated without that switch. Use it to conform to a non-default application binary interface. Not all targets provide complete support for this switch.

-ftls-model=*model*

Alter the thread-local storage model to be used (see Section 5.54 [Thread-Local], page 499). The *model* argument should be one of global-dynamic, local-dynamic, initial-exec or local-exec.

The default without '-fpic' is initial-exec; with '-fpic' the default is global-dynamic.

-fvisibility=*default|internal|hidden|protected*

Set the default ELF image symbol visibility to the specified option—all symbols will be marked with this unless overridden within the code. Using this feature can very substantially improve linking and load times of shared object libraries, produce more optimized code, provide near-perfect API export and prevent symbol clashes. It is **strongly** recommended that you use this in any shared objects you distribute.

Despite the nomenclature, default always means public ie; available to be linked against from outside the shared object. protected and internal are pretty useless in real-world usage so the only other commonly used option will be hidden. The default if '-fvisibility' isn't specified is default, i.e., make every symbol public—this causes the same behavior as previous versions of GCC.

A good explanation of the benefits offered by ensuring ELF symbols have the correct visibility is given by "How To Write Shared Libraries" by Ulrich Drepper (which can be found at http://people.redhat.com/~drepper/)—however a superior solution made possible by this option to marking things hidden when the default is public is to make the default hidden and mark things public. This is the norm with DLL's on Windows and with '-fvisibility=hidden' and __attribute__ ((visibility("default"))) instead of __declspec(dllexport) you get almost identical semantics with identical syntax. This is a great boon to those working with cross-platform projects.

For those adding visibility support to existing code, you may find '#pragma GCC visibility' of use. This works by you enclosing the declarations you wish to

Chapter 3: GCC Command Options   229

set visibility for with (for example) '`#pragma GCC visibility push(hidden)`' and '`#pragma GCC visibility pop`'. Bear in mind that symbol visibility should be viewed **as part of the API interface contract** and thus all new code should always specify visibility when it is not the default ie; declarations only for use within the local DSO should **always** be marked explicitly as hidden as so to avoid PLT indirection overheads—making this abundantly clear also aids readability and self-documentation of the code. Note that due to ISO C++ specification requirements, operator new and operator delete must always be of default visibility.

Be aware that headers from outside your project, in particular system headers and headers from any other library you use, may not be expecting to be compiled with visibility other than the default. You may need to explicitly say '`#pragma GCC visibility push(default)`' before including any such headers.

'`extern`' declarations are not affected by '`-fvisibility`', so a lot of code can be recompiled with '`-fvisibility=hidden`' with no modifications. However, this means that calls to '`extern`' functions with no explicit visibility will use the PLT, so it is more effective to use '`__attribute ((visibility))`' and/or '`#pragma GCC visibility`' to tell the compiler which '`extern`' declarations should be treated as hidden.

Note that '`-fvisibility`' does affect C++ vague linkage entities. This means that, for instance, an exception class that will be thrown between DSOs must be explicitly marked with default visibility so that the '`type_info`' nodes will be unified between the DSOs.

An overview of these techniques, their benefits and how to use them is at http://gcc.gnu.org/wiki/Visibility.

3.19 Environment Variables Affecting GCC

This section describes several environment variables that affect how GCC operates. Some of them work by specifying directories or prefixes to use when searching for various kinds of files. Some are used to specify other aspects of the compilation environment.

Note that you can also specify places to search using options such as '-B', '-I' and '-L' (see Section 3.14 [Directory Options], page 126). These take precedence over places specified using environment variables, which in turn take precedence over those specified by the configuration of GCC. See Section "Controlling the Compilation Driver 'gcc'" in *GNU Compiler Collection (GCC) Internals*.

`LANG`
`LC_CTYPE`
`LC_MESSAGES`
`LC_ALL`   These environment variables control the way that GCC uses localization information that allow GCC to work with different national conventions. GCC inspects the locale categories `LC_CTYPE` and `LC_MESSAGES` if it has been configured to do so. These locale categories can be set to any value supported by your installation. A typical value is '`en_GB.UTF-8`' for English in the United Kingdom encoded in UTF-8.

The LC_CTYPE environment variable specifies character classification. GCC uses it to determine the character boundaries in a string; this is needed for some multibyte encodings that contain quote and escape characters that would otherwise be interpreted as a string end or escape.

The LC_MESSAGES environment variable specifies the language to use in diagnostic messages.

If the LC_ALL environment variable is set, it overrides the value of LC_CTYPE and LC_MESSAGES; otherwise, LC_CTYPE and LC_MESSAGES default to the value of the LANG environment variable. If none of these variables are set, GCC defaults to traditional C English behavior.

TMPDIR If TMPDIR is set, it specifies the directory to use for temporary files. GCC uses temporary files to hold the output of one stage of compilation which is to be used as input to the next stage: for example, the output of the preprocessor, which is the input to the compiler proper.

GCC_EXEC_PREFIX

If GCC_EXEC_PREFIX is set, it specifies a prefix to use in the names of the subprograms executed by the compiler. No slash is added when this prefix is combined with the name of a subprogram, but you can specify a prefix that ends with a slash if you wish.

If GCC_EXEC_PREFIX is not set, GCC will attempt to figure out an appropriate prefix to use based on the pathname it was invoked with.

If GCC cannot find the subprogram using the specified prefix, it tries looking in the usual places for the subprogram.

The default value of GCC_EXEC_PREFIX is 'prefix/lib/gcc/' where prefix is the prefix to the installed compiler. In many cases prefix is the value of prefix when you ran the 'configure' script.

Other prefixes specified with '-B' take precedence over this prefix.

This prefix is also used for finding files such as 'crt0.o' that are used for linking.

In addition, the prefix is used in an unusual way in finding the directories to search for header files. For each of the standard directories whose name normally begins with '/usr/local/lib/gcc' (more precisely, with the value of GCC_INCLUDE_DIR), GCC tries replacing that beginning with the specified prefix to produce an alternate directory name. Thus, with '-Bfoo/', GCC will search 'foo/bar' where it would normally search '/usr/local/lib/bar'. These alternate directories are searched first; the standard directories come next. If a standard directory begins with the configured prefix then the value of prefix is replaced by GCC_EXEC_PREFIX when looking for header files.

COMPILER_PATH

The value of COMPILER_PATH is a colon-separated list of directories, much like PATH. GCC tries the directories thus specified when searching for subprograms, if it can't find the subprograms using GCC_EXEC_PREFIX.

LIBRARY_PATH

The value of LIBRARY_PATH is a colon-separated list of directories, much like PATH. When configured as a native compiler, GCC tries the directories thus

Chapter 3: GCC Command Options 231

> specified when searching for special linker files, if it can't find them using `GCC_EXEC_PREFIX`. Linking using GCC also uses these directories when searching for ordinary libraries for the '`-l`' option (but directories specified with '`-L`' come first).

`LANG`   This variable is used to pass locale information to the compiler. One way in which this information is used is to determine the character set to be used when character literals, string literals and comments are parsed in C and C++. When the compiler is configured to allow multibyte characters, the following values for `LANG` are recognized:

> '`C-JIS`'   Recognize JIS characters.
>
> '`C-SJIS`'   Recognize SJIS characters.
>
> '`C-EUCJP`'   Recognize EUCJP characters.
>
> If `LANG` is not defined, or if it has some other value, then the compiler will use mblen and mbtowc as defined by the default locale to recognize and translate multibyte characters.

Some additional environments variables affect the behavior of the preprocessor.

`CPATH`
`C_INCLUDE_PATH`
`CPLUS_INCLUDE_PATH`
`OBJC_INCLUDE_PATH`

> Each variable's value is a list of directories separated by a special character, much like `PATH`, in which to look for header files. The special character, `PATH_SEPARATOR`, is target-dependent and determined at GCC build time. For Microsoft Windows-based targets it is a semicolon, and for almost all other targets it is a colon.
>
> `CPATH` specifies a list of directories to be searched as if specified with '`-I`', but after any paths given with '`-I`' options on the command line. This environment variable is used regardless of which language is being preprocessed.
>
> The remaining environment variables apply only when preprocessing the particular language indicated. Each specifies a list of directories to be searched as if specified with '`-isystem`', but after any paths given with '`-isystem`' options on the command line.
>
> In all these variables, an empty element instructs the compiler to search its current working directory. Empty elements can appear at the beginning or end of a path. For instance, if the value of `CPATH` is `:/special/include`, that has the same effect as '`-I. -I/special/include`'.

`DEPENDENCIES_OUTPUT`

> If this variable is set, its value specifies how to output dependencies for Make based on the non-system header files processed by the compiler. System header files are ignored in the dependency output.
>
> The value of `DEPENDENCIES_OUTPUT` can be just a file name, in which case the Make rules are written to that file, guessing the target name from the source

file name. Or the value can have the form '*file target*', in which case the rules are written to file *file* using *target* as the target name.

In other words, this environment variable is equivalent to combining the options '-MM' and '-MF' (see Section 3.11 [Preprocessor Options], page 113), with an optional '-MT' switch too.

SUNPRO_DEPENDENCIES

This variable is the same as DEPENDENCIES_OUTPUT (see above), except that system header files are not ignored, so it implies '-M' rather than '-MM'. However, the dependence on the main input file is omitted. See Section 3.11 [Preprocessor Options], page 113.

3.20 Using Precompiled Headers

Often large projects have many header files that are included in every source file. The time the compiler takes to process these header files over and over again can account for nearly all of the time required to build the project. To make builds faster, GCC allows users to 'precompile' a header file; then, if builds can use the precompiled header file they will be much faster.

To create a precompiled header file, simply compile it as you would any other file, if necessary using the '-x' option to make the driver treat it as a C or C++ header file. You will probably want to use a tool like make to keep the precompiled header up-to-date when the headers it contains change.

A precompiled header file will be searched for when #include is seen in the compilation. As it searches for the included file (see Section "Search Path" in *The C Preprocessor*) the compiler looks for a precompiled header in each directory just before it looks for the include file in that directory. The name searched for is the name specified in the #include with '.gch' appended. If the precompiled header file can't be used, it is ignored.

For instance, if you have #include "all.h", and you have 'all.h.gch' in the same directory as 'all.h', then the precompiled header file will be used if possible, and the original header will be used otherwise.

Alternatively, you might decide to put the precompiled header file in a directory and use '-I' to ensure that directory is searched before (or instead of) the directory containing the original header. Then, if you want to check that the precompiled header file is always used, you can put a file of the same name as the original header in this directory containing an #error command.

This also works with '-include'. So yet another way to use precompiled headers, good for projects not designed with precompiled header files in mind, is to simply take most of the header files used by a project, include them from another header file, precompile that header file, and '-include' the precompiled header. If the header files have guards against multiple inclusion, they will be skipped because they've already been included (in the precompiled header).

If you need to precompile the same header file for different languages, targets, or compiler options, you can instead make a *directory* named like 'all.h.gch', and put each precompiled header in the directory, perhaps using '-o'. It doesn't matter what you call the files in the directory, every precompiled header in the directory will be considered. The first

Chapter 3: GCC Command Options   233

precompiled header encountered in the directory that is valid for this compilation will be used; they're searched in no particular order.

There are many other possibilities, limited only by your imagination, good sense, and the constraints of your build system.

A precompiled header file can be used only when these conditions apply:

- Only one precompiled header can be used in a particular compilation.
- A precompiled header can't be used once the first C token is seen. You can have preprocessor directives before a precompiled header; you can even include a precompiled header from inside another header, so long as there are no C tokens before the `#include`.
- The precompiled header file must be produced for the same language as the current compilation. You can't use a C precompiled header for a C++ compilation.
- The precompiled header file must have been produced by the same compiler binary as the current compilation is using.
- Any macros defined before the precompiled header is included must either be defined in the same way as when the precompiled header was generated, or must not affect the precompiled header, which usually means that they don't appear in the precompiled header at all.

  The '-D' option is one way to define a macro before a precompiled header is included; using a `#define` can also do it. There are also some options that define macros implicitly, like '-O' and '-Wdeprecated'; the same rule applies to macros defined this way.
- If debugging information is output when using the precompiled header, using '-g' or similar, the same kind of debugging information must have been output when building the precompiled header. However, a precompiled header built using '-g' can be used in a compilation when no debugging information is being output.
- The same '-m' options must generally be used when building and using the precompiled header. See Section 3.17 [Submodel Options], page 135, for any cases where this rule is relaxed.
- Each of the following options must be the same when building and using the precompiled header:

    `-fexceptions -funit-at-a-time`
- Some other command-line options starting with '-f', '-p', or '-O' must be defined in the same way as when the precompiled header was generated. At present, it's not clear which options are safe to change and which are not; the safest choice is to use exactly the same options when generating and using the precompiled header. The following are known to be safe:

    `-fmessage-length= -fpreprocessed -fsched-interblock`
    `-fsched-spec -fsched-spec-load -fsched-spec-load-dangerous`
    `-fsched-verbose=<number> -fschedule-insns -fvisibility=`
    `-pedantic-errors`

For all of these except the last, the compiler will automatically ignore the precompiled header if the conditions aren't met. If you find an option combination that doesn't work and doesn't cause the precompiled header to be ignored, please consider filing a bug report, see Chapter 11 [Bugs], page 551.

If you do use differing options when generating and using the precompiled header, the actual behavior will be a mixture of the behavior for the options. For instance, if you use '-g' to generate the precompiled header but not when using it, you may or may not get debugging information for routines in the precompiled header.

3.21 Running Protoize

The program `protoize` is an optional part of GCC. You can use it to add prototypes to a program, thus converting the program to ISO C in one respect. The companion program `unprotoize` does the reverse: it removes argument types from any prototypes that are found.

When you run these programs, you must specify a set of source files as command line arguments. The conversion programs start out by compiling these files to see what functions they define. The information gathered about a file *foo* is saved in a file named '*foo*.X'.

After scanning comes actual conversion. The specified files are all eligible to be converted; any files they include (whether sources or just headers) are eligible as well.

But not all the eligible files are converted. By default, `protoize` and `unprotoize` convert only source and header files in the current directory. You can specify additional directories whose files should be converted with the '-d *directory*' option. You can also specify particular files to exclude with the '-x *file*' option. A file is converted if it is eligible, its directory name matches one of the specified directory names, and its name within the directory has not been excluded.

Basic conversion with `protoize` consists of rewriting most function definitions and function declarations to specify the types of the arguments. The only ones not rewritten are those for varargs functions.

`protoize` optionally inserts prototype declarations at the beginning of the source file, to make them available for any calls that precede the function's definition. Or it can insert prototype declarations with block scope in the blocks where undeclared functions are called.

Basic conversion with `unprotoize` consists of rewriting most function declarations to remove any argument types, and rewriting function definitions to the old-style pre-ISO form.

Both conversion programs print a warning for any function declaration or definition that they can't convert. You can suppress these warnings with '-q'.

The output from `protoize` or `unprotoize` replaces the original source file. The original file is renamed to a name ending with '.save' (for DOS, the saved filename ends in '.sav' without the original '.c' suffix). If the '.save' ('.sav' for DOS) file already exists, then the source file is simply discarded.

`protoize` and `unprotoize` both depend on GCC itself to scan the program and collect information about the functions it uses. So neither of these programs will work until GCC is installed.

Here is a table of the options you can use with `protoize` and `unprotoize`. Each option works with both programs unless otherwise stated.

Chapter 3: GCC Command Options 235

-B *directory*
: Look for the file 'SYSCALLS.c.X' in *directory*, instead of the usual directory (normally '/usr/local/lib'). This file contains prototype information about standard system functions. This option applies only to **protoize**.

-c *compilation-options*
: Use *compilation-options* as the options when running **gcc** to produce the '.X' files. The special option '-aux-info' is always passed in addition, to tell **gcc** to write a '.X' file.

  Note that the compilation options must be given as a single argument to **protoize** or **unprotoize**. If you want to specify several **gcc** options, you must quote the entire set of compilation options to make them a single word in the shell.

  There are certain **gcc** arguments that you cannot use, because they would produce the wrong kind of output. These include '-g', '-O', '-c', '-S', and '-o' If you include these in the *compilation-options*, they are ignored.

-C
: Rename files to end in '.C' ('.cc' for DOS-based file systems) instead of '.c'. This is convenient if you are converting a C program to C++. This option applies only to **protoize**.

-g
: Add explicit global declarations. This means inserting explicit declarations at the beginning of each source file for each function that is called in the file and was not declared. These declarations precede the first function definition that contains a call to an undeclared function. This option applies only to **protoize**.

-i *string*
: Indent old-style parameter declarations with the string *string*. This option applies only to **protoize**.

  unprotoize converts prototyped function definitions to old-style function definitions, where the arguments are declared between the argument list and the initial '{'. By default, **unprotoize** uses five spaces as the indentation. If you want to indent with just one space instead, use '-i " "'.

-k
: Keep the '.X' files. Normally, they are deleted after conversion is finished.

-l
: Add explicit local declarations. **protoize** with '-l' inserts a prototype declaration for each function in each block which calls the function without any declaration. This option applies only to **protoize**.

-n
: Make no real changes. This mode just prints information about the conversions that would have been done without '-n'.

-N
: Make no '.save' files. The original files are simply deleted. Use this option with caution.

-p *program*
: Use the program *program* as the compiler. Normally, the name 'gcc' is used.

-q
: Work quietly. Most warnings are suppressed.

-v
: Print the version number, just like '-v' for **gcc**.

If you need special compiler options to compile one of your program's source files, then you should generate that file's '.X' file specially, by running gcc on that source file with the appropriate options and the option '-aux-info'. Then run protoize on the entire set of files. protoize will use the existing '.X' file because it is newer than the source file. For example:

```
gcc -Dfoo=bar file1.c -aux-info file1.X
protoize *.c
```

You need to include the special files along with the rest in the protoize command, even though their '.X' files already exist, because otherwise they won't get converted.

See Section 10.9 [Protoize Caveats], page 544, for more information on how to use protoize successfully.

4 C Implementation-defined behavior

A conforming implementation of ISO C is required to document its choice of behavior in each of the areas that are designated "implementation defined". The following lists all such areas, along with the section numbers from the ISO/IEC 9899:1990 and ISO/IEC 9899:1999 standards. Some areas are only implementation-defined in one version of the standard.

Some choices depend on the externally determined ABI for the platform (including standard character encodings) which GCC follows; these are listed as "determined by ABI" below. See Chapter 8 [Binary Compatibility], page 521, and http://gcc.gnu.org/readings.html. Some choices are documented in the preprocessor manual. See Section "Implementation-defined behavior" in The C Preprocessor. Some choices are made by the library and operating system (or other environment when compiling for a freestanding environment); refer to their documentation for details.

4.1 Translation

- *How a diagnostic is identified (C90 3.7, C99 3.10, C90 and C99 5.1.1.3).*

  Diagnostics consist of all the output sent to stderr by GCC.

- *Whether each nonempty sequence of white-space characters other than new-line is retained or replaced by one space character in translation phase 3 (C90 and C99 5.1.1.2).*

  See Section "Implementation-defined behavior" in The C Preprocessor.

4.2 Environment

The behavior of most of these points are dependent on the implementation of the C library, and are not defined by GCC itself.

- *The mapping between physical source file multibyte characters and the source character set in translation phase 1 (C90 and C99 5.1.1.2).*

  See Section "Implementation-defined behavior" in The C Preprocessor.

4.3 Identifiers

- *Which additional multibyte characters may appear in identifiers and their correspondence to universal character names (C99 6.4.2).*

  See Section "Implementation-defined behavior" in The C Preprocessor.

- *The number of significant initial characters in an identifier (C90 6.1.2, C90 and C99 5.2.4.1, C99 6.4.2).*

  For internal names, all characters are significant. For external names, the number of significant characters are defined by the linker; for almost all targets, all characters are significant.

- *Whether case distinctions are significant in an identifier with external linkage (C90 6.1.2).*

  This is a property of the linker. C99 requires that case distinctions are always significant in identifiers with external linkage and systems without this property are not supported by GCC.

4.4 Characters

- *The number of bits in a byte (C90 3.4, C99 3.6).*
  Determined by ABI.
- *The values of the members of the execution character set (C90 and C99 5.2.1).*
  Determined by ABI.
- *The unique value of the member of the execution character set produced for each of the standard alphabetic escape sequences (C90 and C99 5.2.2).*
  Determined by ABI.
- *The value of a* char *object into which has been stored any character other than a member of the basic execution character set (C90 6.1.2.5, C99 6.2.5).*
  Determined by ABI.
- *Which of* signed char *or* unsigned char *has the same range, representation, and behavior as "plain" char (C90 6.1.2.5, C90 6.2.1.1, C99 6.2.5, C99 6.3.1.1).*
  Determined by ABI. The options '-funsigned-char' and '-fsigned-char' change the default. See Section 3.4 [Options Controlling C Dialect], page 26.
- *The mapping of members of the source character set (in character constants and string literals) to members of the execution character set (C90 6.1.3.4, C99 6.4.4.4, C90 and C99 5.1.1.2).*
  Determined by ABI.
- *The value of an integer character constant containing more than one character or containing a character or escape sequence that does not map to a single-byte execution character (C90 6.1.3.4, C99 6.4.4.4).*
  See Section "Implementation-defined behavior" in The C Preprocessor.
- *The value of a wide character constant containing more than one multibyte character, or containing a multibyte character or escape sequence not represented in the extended execution character set (C90 6.1.3.4, C99 6.4.4.4).*
  See Section "Implementation-defined behavior" in The C Preprocessor.
- *The current locale used to convert a wide character constant consisting of a single multibyte character that maps to a member of the extended execution character set into a corresponding wide character code (C90 6.1.3.4, C99 6.4.4.4).*
  See Section "Implementation-defined behavior" in The C Preprocessor.
- *The current locale used to convert a wide string literal into corresponding wide character codes (C90 6.1.4, C99 6.4.5).*
  See Section "Implementation-defined behavior" in The C Preprocessor.
- *The value of a string literal containing a multibyte character or escape sequence not represented in the execution character set (C90 6.1.4, C99 6.4.5).*
  See Section "Implementation-defined behavior" in The C Preprocessor.

4.5 Integers

- *Any extended integer types that exist in the implementation (C99 6.2.5).*
  GCC does not support any extended integer types.

Chapter 4: C Implementation-defined behavior   239

- *Whether signed integer types are represented using sign and magnitude, two's complement, or one's complement, and whether the extraordinary value is a trap representation or an ordinary value (C99 6.2.6.2).*

  GCC supports only two's complement integer types, and all bit patterns are ordinary values.

- *The rank of any extended integer type relative to another extended integer type with the same precision (C99 6.3.1.1).*

  GCC does not support any extended integer types.

- *The result of, or the signal raised by, converting an integer to a signed integer type when the value cannot be represented in an object of that type (C90 6.2.1.2, C99 6.3.1.3).*

  For conversion to a type of width N, the value is reduced modulo 2^N to be within range of the type; no signal is raised.

- *The results of some bitwise operations on signed integers (C90 6.3, C99 6.5).*

  Bitwise operators act on the representation of the value including both the sign and value bits, where the sign bit is considered immediately above the highest-value value bit. Signed '>>' acts on negative numbers by sign extension.

  GCC does not use the latitude given in C99 only to treat certain aspects of signed '<<' as undefined, but this is subject to change.

- *The sign of the remainder on integer division (C90 6.3.5).*

  GCC always follows the C99 requirement that the result of division is truncated towards zero.

4.6 Floating point

- *The accuracy of the floating-point operations and of the library functions in <math.h> and <complex.h> that return floating-point results (C90 and C99 5.2.4.2.2).*

  The accuracy is unknown.

- *The rounding behaviors characterized by non-standard values of* FLT_ROUNDS *(C90 and C99 5.2.4.2.2).*

  GCC does not use such values.

- *The evaluation methods characterized by non-standard negative values of* FLT_EVAL_METHOD *(C99 5.2.4.2.2).*

  GCC does not use such values.

- *The direction of rounding when an integer is converted to a floating-point number that cannot exactly represent the original value (C90 6.2.1.3, C99 6.3.1.4).*

  C99 Annex F is followed.

- *The direction of rounding when a floating-point number is converted to a narrower floating-point number (C90 6.2.1.4, C99 6.3.1.5).*

  C99 Annex F is followed.

- *How the nearest representable value or the larger or smaller representable value immediately adjacent to the nearest representable value is chosen for certain floating constants (C90 6.1.3.1, C99 6.4.4.2).*

  C99 Annex F is followed.

- *Whether and how floating expressions are contracted when not disallowed by the* `FP_CONTRACT` *pragma (C99 6.5).*

  Expressions are currently only contracted if '`-funsafe-math-optimizations`' or '`-ffast-math`' are used. This is subject to change.

- *The default state for the* `FENV_ACCESS` *pragma (C99 7.6.1).*

  This pragma is not implemented, but the default is to "off" unless '`-frounding-math`' is used in which case it is "on".

- *Additional floating-point exceptions, rounding modes, environments, and classifications, and their macro names (C99 7.6, C99 7.12).*

  This is dependent on the implementation of the C library, and is not defined by GCC itself.

- *The default state for the* `FP_CONTRACT` *pragma (C99 7.12.2).*

  This pragma is not implemented. Expressions are currently only contracted if '`-funsafe-math-optimizations`' or '`-ffast-math`' are used. This is subject to change.

- *Whether the "inexact" floating-point exception can be raised when the rounded result actually does equal the mathematical result in an IEC 60559 conformant implementation (C99 F.9).*

  This is dependent on the implementation of the C library, and is not defined by GCC itself.

- *Whether the "underflow" (and "inexact") floating-point exception can be raised when a result is tiny but not inexact in an IEC 60559 conformant implementation (C99 F.9).*

  This is dependent on the implementation of the C library, and is not defined by GCC itself.

4.7 Arrays and pointers

- *The result of converting a pointer to an integer or vice versa (C90 6.3.4, C99 6.3.2.3).*

  A cast from pointer to integer discards most-significant bits if the pointer representation is larger than the integer type, sign-extends[1] if the pointer representation is smaller than the integer type, otherwise the bits are unchanged.

  A cast from integer to pointer discards most-significant bits if the pointer representation is smaller than the integer type, extends according to the signedness of the integer type if the pointer representation is larger than the integer type, otherwise the bits are unchanged.

  When casting from pointer to integer and back again, the resulting pointer must reference the same object as the original pointer, otherwise the behavior is undefined. That is, one may not use integer arithmetic to avoid the undefined behavior of pointer arithmetic as proscribed in C99 6.5.6/8.

- *The size of the result of subtracting two pointers to elements of the same array (C90 6.3.6, C99 6.5.6).*

  The value is as specified in the standard and the type is determined by the ABI.

---

[1] Future versions of GCC may zero-extend, or use a target-defined `ptr_extend` pattern. Do not rely on sign extension.

Chapter 4: C Implementation-defined behavior   241

4.8 Hints

- *The extent to which suggestions made by using the* `register` *storage-class specifier are effective (C90 6.5.1, C99 6.7.1).*

  The `register` specifier affects code generation only in these ways:
  - When used as part of the register variable extension, see Section 5.40 [Explicit Reg Vars], page 327.
  - When '-O0' is in use, the compiler allocates distinct stack memory for all variables that do not have the `register` storage-class specifier; if `register` is specified, the variable may have a shorter lifespan than the code would indicate and may never be placed in memory.
  - On some rare x86 targets, `setjmp` doesn't save the registers in all circumstances. In those cases, GCC doesn't allocate any variables in registers unless they are marked `register`.

- *The extent to which suggestions made by using the inline function specifier are effective (C99 6.7.4).*

  GCC will not inline any functions if the '-fno-inline' option is used or if '-O0' is used. Otherwise, GCC may still be unable to inline a function for many reasons; the '-Winline' option may be used to determine if a function has not been inlined and why not.

4.9 Structures, unions, enumerations, and bit-fields

- *A member of a union object is accessed using a member of a different type (C90 6.3.2.3).*

  The relevant bytes of the representation of the object are treated as an object of the type used for the access. See [Type-punning], page 93. This may be a trap representation.

- *Whether a "plain"* int *bit-field is treated as a* `signed int` *bit-field or as an* `unsigned int` *bit-field (C90 6.5.2, C90 6.5.2.1, C99 6.7.2, C99 6.7.2.1).*

  By default it is treated as `signed int` but this may be changed by the '-funsigned-bitfields' option.

- *Allowable bit-field types other than* `_Bool`, `signed int`, *and* `unsigned int` *(C99 6.7.2.1).*

  No other types are permitted in strictly conforming mode.

- *Whether a bit-field can straddle a storage-unit boundary (C90 6.5.2.1, C99 6.7.2.1).*

  Determined by ABI.

- *The order of allocation of bit-fields within a unit (C90 6.5.2.1, C99 6.7.2.1).*

  Determined by ABI.

- *The alignment of non-bit-field members of structures (C90 6.5.2.1, C99 6.7.2.1).*

  Determined by ABI.

- *The integer type compatible with each enumerated type (C90 6.5.2.2, C99 6.7.2.2).*

  Normally, the type is `unsigned int` if there are no negative values in the enumeration, otherwise `int`. If '-fshort-enums' is specified, then if there are negative values it is the first of `signed char`, `short` and `int` that can represent all the values, otherwise it is the first of `unsigned char`, `unsigned short` and `unsigned int` that can represent all the values.

On some targets, '`-fshort-enums`' is the default; this is determined by the ABI.

4.10 Qualifiers

- *What constitutes an access to an object that has volatile-qualified type (C90 6.5.3, C99 6.7.3).*

  Such an object is normally accessed by pointers and used for accessing hardware. In most expressions, it is intuitively obvious what is a read and what is a write. For example

  ```
  volatile int *dst = somevalue;
  volatile int *src = someothervalue;
  *dst = *src;
  ```

  will cause a read of the volatile object pointed to by *src* and store the value into the volatile object pointed to by *dst*. There is no guarantee that these reads and writes are atomic, especially for objects larger than `int`.

  However, if the volatile storage is not being modified, and the value of the volatile storage is not used, then the situation is less obvious. For example

  ```
  volatile int *src = somevalue;
  *src;
  ```

  According to the C standard, such an expression is an rvalue whose type is the unqualified version of its original type, i.e. `int`. Whether GCC interprets this as a read of the volatile object being pointed to or only as a request to evaluate the expression for its side-effects depends on this type.

  If it is a scalar type, or on most targets an aggregate type whose only member object is of a scalar type, or a union type whose member objects are of scalar types, the expression is interpreted by GCC as a read of the volatile object; in the other cases, the expression is only evaluated for its side-effects.

4.11 Declarators

- *The maximum number of declarators that may modify an arithmetic, structure or union type (C90 6.5.4).*

  GCC is only limited by available memory.

4.12 Statements

- *The maximum number of `case` values in a `switch` statement (C90 6.6.4.2).*

  GCC is only limited by available memory.

4.13 Preprocessing directives

See Section "Implementation-defined behavior" in *The C Preprocessor*, for details of these aspects of implementation-defined behavior.

- *How sequences in both forms of header names are mapped to headers or external source file names (C90 6.1.7, C99 6.4.7).*

Chapter 4: C Implementation-defined behavior   243

- Whether the value of a character constant in a constant expression that controls conditional inclusion matches the value of the same character constant in the execution character set (C90 6.8.1, C99 6.10.1).
- Whether the value of a single-character character constant in a constant expression that controls conditional inclusion may have a negative value (C90 6.8.1, C99 6.10.1).
- The places that are searched for an included '<>' delimited header, and how the places are specified or the header is identified (C90 6.8.2, C99 6.10.2).
- How the named source file is searched for in an included '""' delimited header (C90 6.8.2, C99 6.10.2).
- The method by which preprocessing tokens (possibly resulting from macro expansion) in a #include directive are combined into a header name (C90 6.8.2, C99 6.10.2).
- The nesting limit for #include processing (C90 6.8.2, C99 6.10.2).
- Whether the '#' operator inserts a '\' character before the '\' character that begins a universal character name in a character constant or string literal (C99 6.10.3.2).
- The behavior on each recognized non-STDC #pragma directive (C90 6.8.6, C99 6.10.6).

    See Section "Pragmas" in The C Preprocessor, for details of pragmas accepted by GCC on all targets. See Section 5.52 [Pragmas Accepted by GCC], page 494, for details of target-specific pragmas.

- The definitions for __DATE__ and __TIME__ when respectively, the date and time of translation are not available (C90 6.8.8, C99 6.10.8).

4.14 Library functions

The behavior of most of these points are dependent on the implementation of the C library, and are not defined by GCC itself.

- The null pointer constant to which the macro NULL expands (C90 7.1.6, C99 7.17).

    In <stddef.h>, NULL expands to ((void *)0). GCC does not provide the other headers which define NULL and some library implementations may use other definitions in those headers.

4.15 Architecture

- The values or expressions assigned to the macros specified in the headers <float.h>, <limits.h>, and <stdint.h> (C90 and C99 5.2.4.2, C99 7.18.2, C99 7.18.3).

    Determined by ABI.

- The number, order, and encoding of bytes in any object (when not explicitly specified in this International Standard) (C99 6.2.6.1).

    Determined by ABI.

- The value of the result of the sizeof operator (C90 6.3.3.4, C99 6.5.3.4).

    Determined by ABI.

4.16 Locale-specific behavior

The behavior of these points are dependent on the implementation of the C library, and are not defined by GCC itself.

5 Extensions to the C Language Family

GNU C provides several language features not found in ISO standard C. (The '-pedantic' option directs GCC to print a warning message if any of these features is used.) To test for the availability of these features in conditional compilation, check for a predefined macro __GNUC__, which is always defined under GCC.

These extensions are available in C and Objective-C. Most of them are also available in C++. See Chapter 6 [Extensions to the C++ Language], page 503, for extensions that apply *only* to C++.

Some features that are in ISO C99 but not C89 or C++ are also, as extensions, accepted by GCC in C89 mode and in C++.

5.1 Statements and Declarations in Expressions

A compound statement enclosed in parentheses may appear as an expression in GNU C. This allows you to use loops, switches, and local variables within an expression.

Recall that a compound statement is a sequence of statements surrounded by braces; in this construct, parentheses go around the braces. For example:

```
({ int y = foo (); int z;
   if (y > 0) z = y;
   else z = - y;
   z; })
```

is a valid (though slightly more complex than necessary) expression for the absolute value of `foo ()`.

The last thing in the compound statement should be an expression followed by a semicolon; the value of this subexpression serves as the value of the entire construct. (If you use some other kind of statement last within the braces, the construct has type void, and thus effectively no value.)

This feature is especially useful in making macro definitions "safe" (so that they evaluate each operand exactly once). For example, the "maximum" function is commonly defined as a macro in standard C as follows:

```
#define max(a,b) ((a) > (b) ? (a) : (b))
```

But this definition computes either *a* or *b* twice, with bad results if the operand has side effects. In GNU C, if you know the type of the operands (here taken as int), you can define the macro safely as follows:

```
#define maxint(a,b) \
  ({int _a = (a), _b = (b); _a > _b ? _a : _b; })
```

Embedded statements are not allowed in constant expressions, such as the value of an enumeration constant, the width of a bit-field, or the initial value of a static variable.

If you don't know the type of the operand, you can still do this, but you must use typeof (see Section 5.6 [Typeof], page 252).

In G++, the result value of a statement expression undergoes array and function pointer decay, and is returned by value to the enclosing expression. For instance, if A is a class, then

```
A a;

({a;}).Foo ()
```
will construct a temporary A object to hold the result of the statement expression, and that will be used to invoke Foo. Therefore the `this` pointer observed by Foo will not be the address of a.

Any temporaries created within a statement within a statement expression will be destroyed at the statement's end. This makes statement expressions inside macros slightly different from function calls. In the latter case temporaries introduced during argument evaluation will be destroyed at the end of the statement that includes the function call. In the statement expression case they will be destroyed during the statement expression. For instance,

```
#define macro(a)  ({__typeof__(a) b = (a); b + 3; })
template<typename T> T function(T a) { T b = a; return b + 3; }

void foo ()
{
  macro (X ());
  function (X ());
}
```

will have different places where temporaries are destroyed. For the `macro` case, the temporary X will be destroyed just after the initialization of b. In the `function` case that temporary will be destroyed when the function returns.

These considerations mean that it is probably a bad idea to use statement-expressions of this form in header files that are designed to work with C++. (Note that some versions of the GNU C Library contained header files using statement-expression that lead to precisely this bug.)

Jumping into a statement expression with `goto` or using a `switch` statement outside the statement expression with a `case` or `default` label inside the statement expression is not permitted. Jumping into a statement expression with a computed `goto` (see Section 5.3 [Labels as Values], page 247) yields undefined behavior. Jumping out of a statement expression is permitted, but if the statement expression is part of a larger expression then it is unspecified which other subexpressions of that expression have been evaluated except where the language definition requires certain subexpressions to be evaluated before or after the statement expression. In any case, as with a function call the evaluation of a statement expression is not interleaved with the evaluation of other parts of the containing expression. For example,

```
foo (), (({ bar1 (); goto a; 0; }) + bar2 ()), baz();
```

will call foo and bar1 and will not call baz but may or may not call bar2. If bar2 is called, it will be called after foo and before bar1

5.2 Locally Declared Labels

GCC allows you to declare *local labels* in any nested block scope. A local label is just like an ordinary label, but you can only reference it (with a `goto` statement, or by taking its address) within the block in which it was declared.

A local label declaration looks like this:

Chapter 5: Extensions to the C Language Family   247

```
    __label__ label;
```
or
```
    __label__ label1, label2, /* ... */;
```

Local label declarations must come at the beginning of the block, before any ordinary declarations or statements.

The label declaration defines the label *name*, but does not define the label itself. You must do this in the usual way, with `label:`, within the statements of the statement expression.

The local label feature is useful for complex macros. If a macro contains nested loops, a `goto` can be useful for breaking out of them. However, an ordinary label whose scope is the whole function cannot be used: if the macro can be expanded several times in one function, the label will be multiply defined in that function. A local label avoids this problem. For example:

```
#define SEARCH(value, array, target)              \
do {                                              \
  __label__ found;                                \
  typeof (target) _SEARCH_target = (target);      \
  typeof (*(array)) *_SEARCH_array = (array);     \
  int i, j;                                       \
  int value;                                      \
  for (i = 0; i < max; i++)                       \
    for (j = 0; j < max; j++)                     \
      if (_SEARCH_array[i][j] == _SEARCH_target)  \
        { (value) = i; goto found; }              \
  (value) = -1;                                   \
 found:;                                          \
} while (0)
```

This could also be written using a statement-expression:

```
#define SEARCH(array, target)                     \
({                                                \
  __label__ found;                                \
  typeof (target) _SEARCH_target = (target);      \
  typeof (*(array)) *_SEARCH_array = (array);     \
  int i, j;                                       \
  int value;                                      \
  for (i = 0; i < max; i++)                       \
    for (j = 0; j < max; j++)                     \
      if (_SEARCH_array[i][j] == _SEARCH_target)  \
        { value = i; goto found; }                \
  value = -1;                                     \
 found:                                           \
  value;                                          \
})
```

Local label declarations also make the labels they declare visible to nested functions, if there are any. See Section 5.4 [Nested Functions], page 248, for details.

5.3 Labels as Values

You can get the address of a label defined in the current function (or a containing function) with the unary operator '&&'. The value has type `void *`. This value is a constant and can be used wherever a constant of that type is valid. For example:

```
    void *ptr;
```

```
/* ... */
ptr = &&foo;
```

To use these values, you need to be able to jump to one. This is done with the computed goto statement[1], goto *exp;. For example,

```
goto *ptr;
```

Any expression of type void * is allowed.

One way of using these constants is in initializing a static array that will serve as a jump table:

```
static void *array[] = { &&foo, &&bar, &&hack };
```

Then you can select a label with indexing, like this:

```
goto *array[i];
```

Note that this does not check whether the subscript is in bounds—array indexing in C never does that.

Such an array of label values serves a purpose much like that of the switch statement. The switch statement is cleaner, so use that rather than an array unless the problem does not fit a switch statement very well.

Another use of label values is in an interpreter for threaded code. The labels within the interpreter function can be stored in the threaded code for super-fast dispatching.

You may not use this mechanism to jump to code in a different function. If you do that, totally unpredictable things will happen. The best way to avoid this is to store the label address only in automatic variables and never pass it as an argument.

An alternate way to write the above example is

```
static const int array[] = { &&foo - &&foo, &&bar - &&foo,
                             &&hack - &&foo };
goto *(&&foo + array[i]);
```

This is more friendly to code living in shared libraries, as it reduces the number of dynamic relocations that are needed, and by consequence, allows the data to be read-only.

The &&foo expressions for the same label might have different values if the containing function is inlined or cloned. If a program relies on them being always the same, __attribute__((__noinline__)) should be used to prevent inlining. If &&foo is used in a static variable initializer, inlining is forbidden.

5.4 Nested Functions

A *nested function* is a function defined inside another function. (Nested functions are not supported for GNU C++.) The nested function's name is local to the block where it is defined. For example, here we define a nested function named square, and call it twice:

```
foo (double a, double b)
{
  double square (double z) { return z * z; }

  return square (a) + square (b);
}
```

---

[1] The analogous feature in Fortran is called an assigned goto, but that name seems inappropriate in C, where one can do more than simply store label addresses in label variables.

Chapter 5: Extensions to the C Language Family   249

The nested function can access all the variables of the containing function that are visible at the point of its definition. This is called *lexical scoping*. For example, here we show a nested function which uses an inherited variable named `offset`:

```
bar (int *array, int offset, int size)
{
  int access (int *array, int index)
    { return array[index + offset]; }
  int i;
  /* ... */
  for (i = 0; i < size; i++)
    /* ... */ access (array, i) /* ... */
}
```

Nested function definitions are permitted within functions in the places where variable definitions are allowed; that is, in any block, mixed with the other declarations and statements in the block.

It is possible to call the nested function from outside the scope of its name by storing its address or passing the address to another function:

```
hack (int *array, int size)
{
  void store (int index, int value)
    { array[index] = value; }

  intermediate (store, size);
}
```

Here, the function `intermediate` receives the address of `store` as an argument. If `intermediate` calls `store`, the arguments given to `store` are used to store into `array`. But this technique works only so long as the containing function (`hack`, in this example) does not exit.

If you try to call the nested function through its address after the containing function has exited, all hell will break loose. If you try to call it after a containing scope level has exited, and if it refers to some of the variables that are no longer in scope, you may be lucky, but it's not wise to take the risk. If, however, the nested function does not refer to anything that has gone out of scope, you should be safe.

GCC implements taking the address of a nested function using a technique called *trampolines*. A paper describing them is available as

http://people.debian.org/~aaronl/Usenix88-lexic.pdf.

A nested function can jump to a label inherited from a containing function, provided the label was explicitly declared in the containing function (see Section 5.2 [Local Labels], page 246). Such a jump returns instantly to the containing function, exiting the nested function which did the `goto` and any intermediate functions as well. Here is an example:

```
bar (int *array, int offset, int size)
{
  __label__ failure;
  int access (int *array, int index)
    {
      if (index > size)
        goto failure;
      return array[index + offset];
    }
  int i;
  /* ... */
  for (i = 0; i < size; i++)
    /* ... */ access (array, i) /* ... */
  /* ... */
  return 0;

 /* Control comes here from access
    if it detects an error.  */
 failure:
  return -1;
}
```

A nested function always has no linkage. Declaring one with `extern` or `static` is erroneous. If you need to declare the nested function before its definition, use `auto` (which is otherwise meaningless for function declarations).

```
bar (int *array, int offset, int size)
{
  __label__ failure;
  auto int access (int *, int);
  /* ... */
  int access (int *array, int index)
    {
      if (index > size)
        goto failure;
      return array[index + offset];
    }
  /* ... */
}
```

5.5 Constructing Function Calls

Using the built-in functions described below, you can record the arguments a function received, and call another function with the same arguments, without knowing the number or types of the arguments.

You can also record the return value of that function call, and later return that value, without knowing what data type the function tried to return (as long as your caller expects that data type).

However, these built-in functions may interact badly with some sophisticated features or other extensions of the language. It is, therefore, not recommended to use them outside very simple functions acting as mere forwarders for their arguments.

void * __builtin_apply_args () [Built-in Function]
> This built-in function returns a pointer to data describing how to perform a call with the same arguments as were passed to the current function.

Chapter 5: Extensions to the C Language Family   251

The function saves the arg pointer register, structure value address, and all registers that might be used to pass arguments to a function into a block of memory allocated on the stack. Then it returns the address of that block.

void * __builtin_apply (*void* (**function*)(), *void* [Built-in Function]
        **arguments*, *size_t size*)
This built-in function invokes *function* with a copy of the parameters described by *arguments* and *size*.

The value of *arguments* should be the value returned by __builtin_apply_args. The argument *size* specifies the size of the stack argument data, in bytes.

This function returns a pointer to data describing how to return whatever value was returned by *function*. The data is saved in a block of memory allocated on the stack.

It is not always simple to compute the proper value for *size*. The value is used by __builtin_apply to compute the amount of data that should be pushed on the stack and copied from the incoming argument area.

void __builtin_return (*void *result*) [Built-in Function]
This built-in function returns the value described by *result* from the containing function. You should specify, for *result*, a value returned by __builtin_apply.

__builtin_va_arg_pack () [Built-in Function]
This built-in function represents all anonymous arguments of an inline function. It can be used only in inline functions which will be always inlined, never compiled as a separate function, such as those using __attribute__ ((__always_inline__)) or __attribute__ ((__gnu_inline__)) extern inline functions. It must be only passed as last argument to some other function with variable arguments. This is useful for writing small wrapper inlines for variable argument functions, when using preprocessor macros is undesirable. For example:

```
extern int myprintf (FILE *f, const char *format, ...);
extern inline __attribute__ ((__gnu_inline__)) int
myprintf (FILE *f, const char *format, ...)
{
  int r = fprintf (f, "myprintf: ");
  if (r < 0)
    return r;
  int s = fprintf (f, format, __builtin_va_arg_pack ());
  if (s < 0)
    return s;
  return r + s;
}
```

__builtin_va_arg_pack_len () [Built-in Function]
This built-in function returns the number of anonymous arguments of an inline function. It can be used only in inline functions which will be always inlined, never compiled as a separate function, such as those using __attribute__ ((__always_inline__)) or __attribute__ ((__gnu_inline__)) extern inline functions. For example following will do link or runtime checking of open arguments for optimized code:

```
#ifdef __OPTIMIZE__
extern inline __attribute__((__gnu_inline__)) int
```

```
      myopen (const char *path, int oflag, ...)
      {
        if (__builtin_va_arg_pack_len () > 1)
          warn_open_too_many_arguments ();

        if (__builtin_constant_p (oflag))
          {
            if ((oflag & O_CREAT) != 0 && __builtin_va_arg_pack_len () < 1)
              {
                warn_open_missing_mode ();
                return __open_2 (path, oflag);
              }
            return open (path, oflag, __builtin_va_arg_pack ());
          }

        if (__builtin_va_arg_pack_len () < 1)
          return __open_2 (path, oflag);

        return open (path, oflag, __builtin_va_arg_pack ());
      }
      #endif
```

5.6 Referring to a Type with typeof

Another way to refer to the type of an expression is with **typeof**. The syntax of using of this keyword looks like **sizeof**, but the construct acts semantically like a type name defined with **typedef**.

There are two ways of writing the argument to **typeof**: with an expression or with a type. Here is an example with an expression:

     typeof (x[0](1))

This assumes that x is an array of pointers to functions; the type described is that of the values of the functions.

Here is an example with a typename as the argument:

     typeof (int *)

Here the type described is that of pointers to **int**.

If you are writing a header file that must work when included in ISO C programs, write **__typeof__** instead of **typeof**. See Section 5.41 [Alternate Keywords], page 329.

A **typeof**-construct can be used anywhere a typedef name could be used. For example, you can use it in a declaration, in a cast, or inside of **sizeof** or **typeof**.

typeof is often useful in conjunction with the statements-within-expressions feature. Here is how the two together can be used to define a safe "maximum" macro that operates on any arithmetic type and evaluates each of its arguments exactly once:

```
     #define max(a,b) \
       ({ typeof (a) _a = (a); \
           typeof (b) _b = (b); \
         _a > _b ? _a : _b; })
```

The reason for using names that start with underscores for the local variables is to avoid conflicts with variable names that occur within the expressions that are substituted for a and b. Eventually we hope to design a new form of declaration syntax that allows you to

Chapter 5: Extensions to the C Language Family   253

declare variables whose scopes start only after their initializers; this will be a more reliable way to prevent such conflicts.

Some more examples of the use of `typeof`:

- This declares y with the type of what x points to.
    ```
    typeof (*x) y;
    ```
- This declares y as an array of such values.
    ```
    typeof (*x) y[4];
    ```
- This declares y as an array of pointers to characters:
    ```
    typeof (typeof (char *)[4]) y;
    ```
    It is equivalent to the following traditional C declaration:
    ```
    char *y[4];
    ```

To see the meaning of the declaration using `typeof`, and why it might be a useful way to write, rewrite it with these macros:

```
#define pointer(T)  typeof(T *)
#define array(T, N) typeof(T [N])
```

Now the declaration can be rewritten this way:

```
array (pointer (char), 4) y;
```

Thus, `array (pointer (char), 4)` is the type of arrays of 4 pointers to `char`.

Compatibility Note: In addition to `typeof`, GCC 2 supported a more limited extension which permitted one to write

```
typedef T = expr;
```

with the effect of declaring `T` to have the type of the expression *expr*. This extension does not work with GCC 3 (versions between 3.0 and 3.2 will crash; 3.2.1 and later give an error). Code which relies on it should be rewritten to use `typeof`:

```
typedef typeof(expr) T;
```

This will work with all versions of GCC.

5.7 Conditionals with Omitted Operands

The middle operand in a conditional expression may be omitted. Then if the first operand is nonzero, its value is the value of the conditional expression.

Therefore, the expression

```
x ? : y
```

has the value of x if that is nonzero; otherwise, the value of y.

This example is perfectly equivalent to

```
x ? x : y
```

In this simple case, the ability to omit the middle operand is not especially useful. When it becomes useful is when the first operand does, or may (if it is a macro argument), contain a side effect. Then repeating the operand in the middle would perform the side effect twice. Omitting the middle operand uses the value already computed without the undesirable effects of recomputing it.

5.8 Double-Word Integers

ISO C99 supports data types for integers that are at least 64 bits wide, and as an extension GCC supports them in C89 mode and in C++. Simply write `long long int` for a signed integer, or `unsigned long long int` for an unsigned integer. To make an integer constant of type `long long int`, add the suffix 'LL' to the integer. To make an integer constant of type `unsigned long long int`, add the suffix 'ULL' to the integer.

You can use these types in arithmetic like any other integer types. Addition, subtraction, and bitwise boolean operations on these types are open-coded on all types of machines. Multiplication is open-coded if the machine supports fullword-to-doubleword a widening multiply instruction. Division and shifts are open-coded only on machines that provide special support. The operations that are not open-coded use special library routines that come with GCC.

There may be pitfalls when you use `long long` types for function arguments, unless you declare function prototypes. If a function expects type `int` for its argument, and you pass a value of type `long long int`, confusion will result because the caller and the subroutine will disagree about the number of bytes for the argument. Likewise, if the function expects `long long int` and you pass `int`. The best way to avoid such problems is to use prototypes.

5.9 Complex Numbers

ISO C99 supports complex floating data types, and as an extension GCC supports them in C89 mode and in C++, and supports complex integer data types which are not part of ISO C99. You can declare complex types using the keyword `_Complex`. As an extension, the older GNU keyword `__complex__` is also supported.

For example, '`_Complex double x;`' declares x as a variable whose real part and imaginary part are both of type `double`. '`_Complex short int y;`' declares y to have real and imaginary parts of type `short int`; this is not likely to be useful, but it shows that the set of complex types is complete.

To write a constant with a complex data type, use the suffix 'i' or 'j' (either one; they are equivalent). For example, `2.5fi` has type `_Complex float` and `3i` has type `_Complex int`. Such a constant always has a pure imaginary value, but you can form any complex value you like by adding one to a real constant. This is a GNU extension; if you have an ISO C99 conforming C library (such as GNU libc), and want to construct complex constants of floating type, you should include `<complex.h>` and use the macros `I` or `_Complex_I` instead.

To extract the real part of a complex-valued expression *exp*, write `__real__` *exp*. Likewise, use `__imag__` to extract the imaginary part. This is a GNU extension; for values of floating type, you should use the ISO C99 functions `crealf`, `creal`, `creall`, `cimagf`, `cimag` and `cimagl`, declared in `<complex.h>` and also provided as built-in functions by GCC.

The operator '~' performs complex conjugation when used on a value with a complex type. This is a GNU extension; for values of floating type, you should use the ISO C99 functions `conjf`, `conj` and `conjl`, declared in `<complex.h>` and also provided as built-in functions by GCC.

GCC can allocate complex automatic variables in a noncontiguous fashion; it's even possible for the real part to be in a register while the imaginary part is on the stack (or vice-versa). Only the DWARF2 debug info format can represent this, so use of DWARF2 is

Chapter 5: Extensions to the C Language Family   255

recommended. If you are using the stabs debug info format, GCC describes a noncontiguous complex variable as if it were two separate variables of noncomplex type. If the variable's actual name is `foo`, the two fictitious variables are named `foo$real` and `foo$imag`. You can examine and set these two fictitious variables with your debugger.

5.10 Additional Floating Types

As an extension, the GNU C compiler supports additional floating types, `__float80` and `__float128` to support 80bit (`XFmode`) and 128 bit (`TFmode`) floating types. Support for additional types includes the arithmetic operators: add, subtract, multiply, divide; unary arithmetic operators; relational operators; equality operators; and conversions to and from integer and other floating types. Use a suffix 'w' or 'W' in a literal constant of type `__float80` and 'q' or 'Q' for `_float128`. You can declare complex types using the corresponding internal complex type, `XCmode` for `__float80` type and `TCmode` for `__float128` type:

```
typedef _Complex float __attribute__((mode(TC))) _Complex128;
typedef _Complex float __attribute__((mode(XC))) _Complex80;
```

Not all targets support additional floating point types. `__float80` is supported on i386, x86_64 and ia64 targets and target `__float128` is supported on x86_64 and ia64 targets.

5.11 Decimal Floating Types

As an extension, the GNU C compiler supports decimal floating types as defined in the N1176 draft of ISO/IEC WDTR24732. Support for decimal floating types in GCC will evolve as the draft technical report changes. Calling conventions for any target might also change. Not all targets support decimal floating types.

The decimal floating types are `_Decimal32`, `_Decimal64`, and `_Decimal128`. They use a radix of ten, unlike the floating types `float`, `double`, and `long double` whose radix is not specified by the C standard but is usually two.

Support for decimal floating types includes the arithmetic operators add, subtract, multiply, divide; unary arithmetic operators; relational operators; equality operators; and conversions to and from integer and other floating types. Use a suffix 'df' or 'DF' in a literal constant of type `_Decimal32`, 'dd' or 'DD' for `_Decimal64`, and 'dl' or 'DL' for `_Decimal128`.

GCC support of decimal float as specified by the draft technical report is incomplete:

- Translation time data type (TTDT) is not supported.
- When the value of a decimal floating type cannot be represented in the integer type to which it is being converted, the result is undefined rather than the result value specified by the draft technical report.

Types `_Decimal32`, `_Decimal64`, and `_Decimal128` are supported by the DWARF2 debug information format.

5.12 Hex Floats

ISO C99 supports floating-point numbers written not only in the usual decimal notation, such as `1.55e1`, but also numbers such as `0x1.fp3` written in hexadecimal format. As a GNU extension, GCC supports this in C89 mode (except in some cases when strictly conforming) and in C++. In that format the '0x' hex introducer and the 'p' or 'P' exponent field are mandatory. The exponent is a decimal number that indicates the power of 2 by which the significant part will be multiplied. Thus '0x1.f' is $1\frac{15}{16}$, 'p3' multiplies it by 8, and the value of 0x1.fp3 is the same as 1.55e1.

Unlike for floating-point numbers in the decimal notation the exponent is always required in the hexadecimal notation. Otherwise the compiler would not be able to resolve the ambiguity of, e.g., 0x1.f. This could mean 1.0f or 1.9375 since 'f' is also the extension for floating-point constants of type float.

5.13 Fixed-Point Types

As an extension, the GNU C compiler supports fixed-point types as defined in the N1169 draft of ISO/IEC DTR 18037. Support for fixed-point types in GCC will evolve as the draft technical report changes. Calling conventions for any target might also change. Not all targets support fixed-point types.

The fixed-point types are short _Fract, _Fract, long _Fract, long long _Fract, unsigned short _Fract, unsigned _Fract, unsigned long _Fract, unsigned long long _Fract, _Sat short _Fract, _Sat _Fract, _Sat long _Fract, _Sat long long _Fract, _Sat unsigned short _Fract, _Sat unsigned _Fract, _Sat unsigned long _Fract, _Sat unsigned long long _Fract, short _Accum, _Accum, long _Accum, long long _Accum, unsigned short _Accum, unsigned _Accum, unsigned long _Accum, unsigned long long _Accum, _Sat short _Accum, _Sat _Accum, _Sat long _Accum, _Sat long long _Accum, _Sat unsigned short _Accum, _Sat unsigned _Accum, _Sat unsigned long _Accum, _Sat unsigned long long _Accum. Fixed-point data values contain fractional and optional integral parts. The format of fixed-point data varies and depends on the target machine.

Support for fixed-point types includes prefix and postfix increment and decrement operators (++, --); unary arithmetic operators (+, -, !); binary arithmetic operators (+, -, *, /); binary shift operators (<<, >>); relational operators (<, <=, >=, >); equality operators (==, !=); assignment operators (+=, -=, *=, /=, <<=, >>=); and conversions to and from integer, floating-point, or fixed-point types.

Use a suffix 'hr' or 'HR' in a literal constant of type short _Fract and _Sat short _Fract, 'r' or 'R' for _Fract and _Sat _Fract, 'lr' or 'LR' for long _Fract and _Sat long _Fract, 'llr' or 'LLR' for long long _Fract and _Sat long long _Fract, 'uhr' or 'UHR' for unsigned short _Fract and _Sat unsigned short _Fract, 'ur' or 'UR' for unsigned _Fract and _Sat unsigned _Fract, 'ulr' or 'ULR' for unsigned long _Fract and _Sat unsigned long _Fract, 'ullr' or 'ULLR' for unsigned long long _Fract and _Sat unsigned long long _Fract, 'hk' or 'HK' for short _Accum and _Sat short _Accum, 'k' or 'K' for _Accum and _Sat _Accum, 'lk' or 'LK' for long _Accum and _Sat long _Accum, 'llk' or 'LLK' for long long _Accum and _Sat long long _Accum, 'uhk' or 'UHK' for unsigned short _Accum and _Sat unsigned short _Accum, 'uk' or 'UK' for unsigned _Accum and _Sat unsigned _Accum, 'ulk' or 'ULK' for unsigned long _Accum and _Sat unsigned long _Accum, and 'ullk' or 'ULLK' for unsigned long long _Accum and _Sat unsigned long long _Accum.

GCC support of fixed-point types as specified by the draft technical report is incomplete:

- Pragmas to control overflow and rounding behaviors are not implemented.

Fixed-point types are supported by the DWARF2 debug information format.

Chapter 5: Extensions to the C Language Family   257

5.14 Arrays of Length Zero

Zero-length arrays are allowed in GNU C. They are very useful as the last element of a structure which is really a header for a variable-length object:

```
struct line {
  int length;
  char contents[0];
};

struct line *thisline = (struct line *)
  malloc (sizeof (struct line) + this_length);
thisline->length = this_length;
```

In ISO C90, you would have to give `contents` a length of 1, which means either you waste space or complicate the argument to `malloc`.

In ISO C99, you would use a *flexible array member*, which is slightly different in syntax and semantics:

- Flexible array members are written as `contents[]` without the 0.
- Flexible array members have incomplete type, and so the `sizeof` operator may not be applied. As a quirk of the original implementation of zero-length arrays, `sizeof` evaluates to zero.
- Flexible array members may only appear as the last member of a `struct` that is otherwise non-empty.
- A structure containing a flexible array member, or a union containing such a structure (possibly recursively), may not be a member of a structure or an element of an array. (However, these uses are permitted by GCC as extensions.)

GCC versions before 3.0 allowed zero-length arrays to be statically initialized, as if they were flexible arrays. In addition to those cases that were useful, it also allowed initializations in situations that would corrupt later data. Non-empty initialization of zero-length arrays is now treated like any case where there are more initializer elements than the array holds, in that a suitable warning about "excess elements in array" is given, and the excess elements (all of them, in this case) are ignored.

Instead GCC allows static initialization of flexible array members. This is equivalent to defining a new structure containing the original structure followed by an array of sufficient size to contain the data. I.e. in the following, `f1` is constructed as if it were declared like `f2`.

```
struct f1 {
  int x; int y[];
} f1 = { 1, { 2, 3, 4 } };

struct f2 {
  struct f1 f1; int data[3];
} f2 = { { 1 }, { 2, 3, 4 } };
```

The convenience of this extension is that `f1` has the desired type, eliminating the need to consistently refer to `f2.f1`.

This has symmetry with normal static arrays, in that an array of unknown size is also written with `[]`.

Of course, this extension only makes sense if the extra data comes at the end of a top-level object, as otherwise we would be overwriting data at subsequent offsets. To avoid undue complication and confusion with initialization of deeply nested arrays, we simply disallow any non-empty initialization except when the structure is the top-level object. For example:

```
struct foo { int x; int y[]; };
struct bar { struct foo z; };

struct foo a = { 1, { 2, 3, 4 } };          // Valid.
struct bar b = { { 1, { 2, 3, 4 } } };      // Invalid.
struct bar c = { { 1, { } } };              // Valid.
struct foo d[1] = { { 1 { 2, 3, 4 } } };    // Invalid.
```

5.15 Structures With No Members

GCC permits a C structure to have no members:

```
struct empty {
};
```

The structure will have size zero. In C++, empty structures are part of the language. G++ treats empty structures as if they had a single member of type `char`.

5.16 Arrays of Variable Length

Variable-length automatic arrays are allowed in ISO C99, and as an extension GCC accepts them in C89 mode and in C++. (However, GCC's implementation of variable-length arrays does not yet conform in detail to the ISO C99 standard.) These arrays are declared like any other automatic arrays, but with a length that is not a constant expression. The storage is allocated at the point of declaration and deallocated when the brace-level is exited. For example:

```
FILE *
concat_fopen (char *s1, char *s2, char *mode)
{
  char str[strlen (s1) + strlen (s2) + 1];
  strcpy (str, s1);
  strcat (str, s2);
  return fopen (str, mode);
}
```

Jumping or breaking out of the scope of the array name deallocates the storage. Jumping into the scope is not allowed; you get an error message for it.

You can use the function `alloca` to get an effect much like variable-length arrays. The function `alloca` is available in many other C implementations (but not in all). On the other hand, variable-length arrays are more elegant.

There are other differences between these two methods. Space allocated with `alloca` exists until the containing *function* returns. The space for a variable-length array is deallocated as soon as the array name's scope ends. (If you use both variable-length arrays and `alloca` in the same function, deallocation of a variable-length array will also deallocate anything more recently allocated with `alloca`.)

You can also use variable-length arrays as arguments to functions:

```
struct entry
tester (int len, char data[len][len])
{
  /* ... */
}
```

Chapter 5: Extensions to the C Language Family   259

The length of an array is computed once when the storage is allocated and is remembered for the scope of the array in case you access it with `sizeof`.

If you want to pass the array first and the length afterward, you can use a forward declaration in the parameter list—another GNU extension.

```
struct entry
tester (int len; char data[len][len], int len)
{
  /* ... */
}
```

The '`int len`' before the semicolon is a *parameter forward declaration*, and it serves the purpose of making the name `len` known when the declaration of `data` is parsed.

You can write any number of such parameter forward declarations in the parameter list. They can be separated by commas or semicolons, but the last one must end with a semicolon, which is followed by the "real" parameter declarations. Each forward declaration must match a "real" declaration in parameter name and data type. ISO C99 does not support parameter forward declarations.

5.17 Macros with a Variable Number of Arguments.

In the ISO C standard of 1999, a macro can be declared to accept a variable number of arguments much as a function can. The syntax for defining the macro is similar to that of a function. Here is an example:

```
#define debug(format, ...) fprintf (stderr, format, __VA_ARGS__)
```

Here '`...`' is a *variable argument*. In the invocation of such a macro, it represents the zero or more tokens until the closing parenthesis that ends the invocation, including any commas. This set of tokens replaces the identifier `__VA_ARGS__` in the macro body wherever it appears. See the CPP manual for more information.

GCC has long supported variadic macros, and used a different syntax that allowed you to give a name to the variable arguments just like any other argument. Here is an example:

```
#define debug(format, args...) fprintf (stderr, format, args)
```

This is in all ways equivalent to the ISO C example above, but arguably more readable and descriptive.

GNU CPP has two further variadic macro extensions, and permits them to be used with either of the above forms of macro definition.

In standard C, you are not allowed to leave the variable argument out entirely; but you are allowed to pass an empty argument. For example, this invocation is invalid in ISO C, because there is no comma after the string:

```
debug ("A message")
```

GNU CPP permits you to completely omit the variable arguments in this way. In the above examples, the compiler would complain, though since the expansion of the macro still has the extra comma after the format string.

To help solve this problem, CPP behaves specially for variable arguments used with the token paste operator, '`##`'. If instead you write

```
#define debug(format, ...) fprintf (stderr, format, ## __VA_ARGS__)
```

and if the variable arguments are omitted or empty, the '`##`' operator causes the preprocessor to remove the comma before it. If you do provide some variable arguments in your macro invocation, GNU CPP does not complain about the paste operation and instead places the variable arguments after the comma. Just like any other pasted macro argument, these arguments are not macro expanded.

5.18 Slightly Looser Rules for Escaped Newlines

Recently, the preprocessor has relaxed its treatment of escaped newlines. Previously, the newline had to immediately follow a backslash. The current implementation allows whitespace in the form of spaces, horizontal and vertical tabs, and form feeds between the backslash and the subsequent newline. The preprocessor issues a warning, but treats it as a valid escaped newline and combines the two lines to form a single logical line. This works within comments and tokens, as well as between tokens. Comments are *not* treated as whitespace for the purposes of this relaxation, since they have not yet been replaced with spaces.

5.19 Non-Lvalue Arrays May Have Subscripts

In ISO C99, arrays that are not lvalues still decay to pointers, and may be subscripted, although they may not be modified or used after the next sequence point and the unary '&' operator may not be applied to them. As an extension, GCC allows such arrays to be subscripted in C89 mode, though otherwise they do not decay to pointers outside C99 mode. For example, this is valid in GNU C though not valid in C89:

```
struct foo {int a[4];};

struct foo f();

bar (int index)
{
  return f().a[index];
}
```

5.20 Arithmetic on `void`- and Function-Pointers

In GNU C, addition and subtraction operations are supported on pointers to `void` and on pointers to functions. This is done by treating the size of a `void` or of a function as 1.

A consequence of this is that `sizeof` is also allowed on `void` and on function types, and returns 1.

The option '-Wpointer-arith' requests a warning if these extensions are used.

5.21 Non-Constant Initializers

As in standard C++ and ISO C99, the elements of an aggregate initializer for an automatic variable are not required to be constant expressions in GNU C. Here is an example of an initializer with run-time varying elements:

```
foo (float f, float g)
{
  float beat_freqs[2] = { f-g, f+g };
  /* ... */
}
```

Chapter 5: Extensions to the C Language Family   261

5.22 Compound Literals

ISO C99 supports compound literals. A compound literal looks like a cast containing an initializer. Its value is an object of the type specified in the cast, containing the elements specified in the initializer; it is an lvalue. As an extension, GCC supports compound literals in C89 mode and in C++.

Usually, the specified type is a structure. Assume that `struct foo` and `structure` are declared as shown:

```
struct foo {int a; char b[2];} structure;
```

Here is an example of constructing a `struct foo` with a compound literal:

```
structure = ((struct foo) {x + y, 'a', 0});
```

This is equivalent to writing the following:

```
{
  struct foo temp = {x + y, 'a', 0};
  structure = temp;
}
```

You can also construct an array. If all the elements of the compound literal are (made up of) simple constant expressions, suitable for use in initializers of objects of static storage duration, then the compound literal can be coerced to a pointer to its first element and used in such an initializer, as shown here:

```
char **foo = (char *[]) { "x", "y", "z" };
```

Compound literals for scalar types and union types are is also allowed, but then the compound literal is equivalent to a cast.

As a GNU extension, GCC allows initialization of objects with static storage duration by compound literals (which is not possible in ISO C99, because the initializer is not a constant). It is handled as if the object was initialized only with the bracket enclosed list if the types of the compound literal and the object match. The initializer list of the compound literal must be constant. If the object being initialized has array type of unknown size, the size is determined by compound literal size.

```
static struct foo x = (struct foo) {1, 'a', 'b'};
static int y[] = (int []) {1, 2, 3};
static int z[] = (int [3]) {1};
```

The above lines are equivalent to the following:

```
static struct foo x = {1, 'a', 'b'};
static int y[] = {1, 2, 3};
static int z[] = {1, 0, 0};
```

5.23 Designated Initializers

Standard C89 requires the elements of an initializer to appear in a fixed order, the same as the order of the elements in the array or structure being initialized.

In ISO C99 you can give the elements in any order, specifying the array indices or structure field names they apply to, and GNU C allows this as an extension in C89 mode as well. This extension is not implemented in GNU C++.

To specify an array index, write '`[index] =`' before the element value. For example,

```
int a[6] = { [4] = 29, [2] = 15 };
```

is equivalent to

```
int a[6] = { 0, 0, 15, 0, 29, 0 };
```
The index values must be constant expressions, even if the array being initialized is automatic.

An alternative syntax for this which has been obsolete since GCC 2.5 but GCC still accepts is to write '`[index]`' before the element value, with no '`=`'.

To initialize a range of elements to the same value, write '`[first ... last] = value`'. This is a GNU extension. For example,
```
int widths[] = { [0 ... 9] = 1, [10 ... 99] = 2, [100] = 3 };
```
If the value in it has side-effects, the side-effects will happen only once, not for each initialized field by the range initializer.

Note that the length of the array is the highest value specified plus one.

In a structure initializer, specify the name of a field to initialize with '`.fieldname =`' before the element value. For example, given the following structure,
```
struct point { int x, y; };
```
the following initialization
```
struct point p = { .y = yvalue, .x = xvalue };
```
is equivalent to
```
struct point p = { xvalue, yvalue };
```
Another syntax which has the same meaning, obsolete since GCC 2.5, is '`fieldname:`', as shown here:
```
struct point p = { y: yvalue, x: xvalue };
```
The '`[index]`' or '`.fieldname`' is known as a *designator*. You can also use a designator (or the obsolete colon syntax) when initializing a union, to specify which element of the union should be used. For example,
```
union foo { int i; double d; };

union foo f = { .d = 4 };
```
will convert 4 to a **double** to store it in the union using the second element. By contrast, casting 4 to type **union foo** would store it into the union as the integer i, since it is an integer. (See Section 5.25 [Cast to Union], page 263.)

You can combine this technique of naming elements with ordinary C initialization of successive elements. Each initializer element that does not have a designator applies to the next consecutive element of the array or structure. For example,
```
int a[6] = { [1] = v1, v2, [4] = v4 };
```
is equivalent to
```
int a[6] = { 0, v1, v2, 0, v4, 0 };
```
Labeling the elements of an array initializer is especially useful when the indices are characters or belong to an **enum** type. For example:
```
int whitespace[256]
    = { [' '] = 1, ['\t'] = 1, ['\h'] = 1,
        ['\f'] = 1, ['\n'] = 1, ['\r'] = 1 };
```
You can also write a series of '`.fieldname`' and '`[index]`' designators before an '`=`' to specify a nested subobject to initialize; the list is taken relative to the subobject corresponding to the closest surrounding brace pair. For example, with the '**struct point**' declaration above:

Chapter 5: Extensions to the C Language Family   263

```
struct point ptarray[10] = { [2].y = yv2, [2].x = xv2, [0].x = xv0 };
```

If the same field is initialized multiple times, it will have value from the last initialization. If any such overridden initialization has side-effect, it is unspecified whether the side-effect happens or not. Currently, GCC will discard them and issue a warning.

5.24 Case Ranges

You can specify a range of consecutive values in a single `case` label, like this:

```
case low ... high:
```

This has the same effect as the proper number of individual `case` labels, one for each integer value from *low* to *high*, inclusive.

This feature is especially useful for ranges of ASCII character codes:

```
case 'A' ... 'Z':
```

Be careful: Write spaces around the ..., for otherwise it may be parsed wrong when you use it with integer values. For example, write this:

```
case 1 ... 5:
```

rather than this:

```
case 1...5:
```

5.25 Cast to a Union Type

A cast to union type is similar to other casts, except that the type specified is a union type. You can specify the type either with `union tag` or with a typedef name. A cast to union is actually a constructor though, not a cast, and hence does not yield an lvalue like normal casts. (See Section 5.22 [Compound Literals], page 261.)

The types that may be cast to the union type are those of the members of the union. Thus, given the following union and variables:

```
union foo { int i; double d; };
int x;
double y;
```

both x and y can be cast to type `union foo`.

Using the cast as the right-hand side of an assignment to a variable of union type is equivalent to storing in a member of the union:

```
union foo u;
/* ... */
u = (union foo) x  ≡  u.i = x
u = (union foo) y  ≡  u.d = y
```

You can also use the union cast as a function argument:

```
void hack (union foo);
/* ... */
hack ((union foo) x);
```

5.26 Mixed Declarations and Code

ISO C99 and ISO C++ allow declarations and code to be freely mixed within compound statements. As an extension, GCC also allows this in C89 mode. For example, you could do:

```
int i;
/* ... */
i++;
int j = i + 2;
```

Each identifier is visible from where it is declared until the end of the enclosing block.

5.27 Declaring Attributes of Functions

In GNU C, you declare certain things about functions called in your program which help the compiler optimize function calls and check your code more carefully.

The keyword `__attribute__` allows you to specify special attributes when making a declaration. This keyword is followed by an attribute specification inside double parentheses. The following attributes are currently defined for functions on all targets: `aligned`, `alloc_size`, `noreturn`, `returns_twice`, `noinline`, `always_inline`, `flatten`, `pure`, `const`, `nothrow`, `sentinel`, `format`, `format_arg`, `no_instrument_function`, `section`, `constructor`, `destructor`, `used`, `unused`, `deprecated`, `weak`, `malloc`, `alias`, `warn_unused_result`, `nonnull`, `gnu_inline`, `externally_visible`, `hot`, `cold`, `artificial`, `error` and `warning`. Several other attributes are defined for functions on particular target systems. Other attributes, including `section` are supported for variables declarations (see Section 5.34 [Variable Attributes], page 286) and for types (see Section 5.35 [Type Attributes], page 293).

You may also specify attributes with '`__`' preceding and following each keyword. This allows you to use them in header files without being concerned about a possible macro of the same name. For example, you may use `__noreturn__` instead of `noreturn`.

See Section 5.28 [Attribute Syntax], page 281, for details of the exact syntax for using attributes.

`alias ("target")`
> The `alias` attribute causes the declaration to be emitted as an alias for another symbol, which must be specified. For instance,
>
> ```
> void __f () { /* Do something. */; }
> void f () __attribute__ ((weak, alias ("__f")));
> ```
>
> defines 'f' to be a weak alias for '`__f`'. In C++, the mangled name for the target must be used. It is an error if '`__f`' is not defined in the same translation unit.
>
> Not all target machines support this attribute.

`aligned (alignment)`
> This attribute specifies a minimum alignment for the function, measured in bytes.
>
> You cannot use this attribute to decrease the alignment of a function, only to increase it. However, when you explicitly specify a function alignment this will override the effect of the '`-falign-functions`' (see Section 3.10 [Optimize Options], page 77) option for this function.

Chapter 5: Extensions to the C Language Family 265

Note that the effectiveness of `aligned` attributes may be limited by inherent limitations in your linker. On many systems, the linker is only able to arrange for functions to be aligned up to a certain maximum alignment. (For some linkers, the maximum supported alignment may be very very small.) See your linker documentation for further information.

The `aligned` attribute can also be used for variables and fields (see Section 5.34 [Variable Attributes], page 286.)

`alloc_size`
The `alloc_size` attribute is used to tell the compiler that the function return value points to memory, where the size is given by one or two of the functions parameters. GCC uses this information to improve the correctness of `__builtin_object_size`.

The function parameter(s) denoting the allocated size are specified by one or two integer arguments supplied to the attribute. The allocated size is either the value of the single function argument specified or the product of the two function arguments specified. Argument numbering starts at one.

For instance,
```
void* my_calloc(size_t, size_t) __attribute__((alloc_size(1,2)))
void my_realloc(void* size_t) __attribute__((alloc_size(2)))
```
declares that my_calloc will return memory of the size given by the product of parameter 1 and 2 and that my_realloc will return memory of the size given by parameter 2.

`always_inline`
Generally, functions are not inlined unless optimization is specified. For functions declared inline, this attribute inlines the function even if no optimization level was specified.

`gnu_inline`
This attribute should be used with a function which is also declared with the `inline` keyword. It directs GCC to treat the function as if it were defined in gnu89 mode even when compiling in C99 or gnu99 mode.

If the function is declared `extern`, then this definition of the function is used only for inlining. In no case is the function compiled as a standalone function, not even if you take its address explicitly. Such an address becomes an external reference, as if you had only declared the function, and had not defined it. This has almost the effect of a macro. The way to use this is to put a function definition in a header file with this attribute, and put another copy of the function, without `extern`, in a library file. The definition in the header file will cause most calls to the function to be inlined. If any uses of the function remain, they will refer to the single copy in the library. Note that the two definitions of the functions need not be precisely the same, although if they do not have the same effect your program may behave oddly.

In C, if the function is neither `extern` nor `static`, then the function is compiled as a standalone function, as well as being inlined where possible.

This is how GCC traditionally handled functions declared `inline`. Since ISO C99 specifies a different semantics for `inline`, this function attribute is provided as a transition measure and as a useful feature in its own right. This attribute is available in GCC 4.1.3 and later. It is available if either of the preprocessor macros `__GNUC_GNU_INLINE__` or `__GNUC_STDC_INLINE__` are defined. See Section 5.36 [An Inline Function is As Fast As a Macro], page 299.

In C++, this attribute does not depend on `extern` in any way, but it still requires the `inline` keyword to enable its special behavior.

`artificial`
: This attribute is useful for small inline wrappers which if possible should appear during debugging as a unit, depending on the debug info format it will either mean marking the function as artificial or using the caller location for all instructions within the inlined body.

`flatten`
: Generally, inlining into a function is limited. For a function marked with this attribute, every call inside this function will be inlined, if possible. Whether the function itself is considered for inlining depends on its size and the current inlining parameters. The `flatten` attribute only works reliably in unit-at-a-time mode.

`error ("message")`
: If this attribute is used on a function declaration and a call to such a function is not eliminated through dead code elimination or other optimizations, an error which will include *message* will be diagnosed. This is useful for compile time checking, especially together with `__builtin_constant_p` and inline functions where checking the inline function arguments is not possible through `extern char [(condition) ? 1 : -1];` tricks. While it is possible to leave the function undefined and thus invoke a link failure, when using this attribute the problem will be diagnosed earlier and with exact location of the call even in presence of inline functions or when not emitting debugging information.

`warning ("message")`
: If this attribute is used on a function declaration and a call to such a function is not eliminated through dead code elimination or other optimizations, a warning which will include *message* will be diagnosed. This is useful for compile time checking, especially together with `__builtin_constant_p` and inline functions. While it is possible to define the function with a message in `.gnu.warning*` section, when using this attribute the problem will be diagnosed earlier and with exact location of the call even in presence of inline functions or when not emitting debugging information.

`cdecl`
: On the Intel 386, the `cdecl` attribute causes the compiler to assume that the calling function will pop off the stack space used to pass arguments. This is useful to override the effects of the '-mrtd' switch.

`const`
: Many functions do not examine any values except their arguments, and have no effects except the return value. Basically this is just slightly more strict class than the `pure` attribute below, since function is not allowed to read global memory.

Note that a function that has pointer arguments and examines the data pointed to must *not* be declared `const`. Likewise, a function that calls a non-`const`

Chapter 5: Extensions to the C Language Family 267

function usually must not be `const`. It does not make sense for a `const` function to return `void`.

The attribute `const` is not implemented in GCC versions earlier than 2.5. An alternative way to declare that a function has no side effects, which works in the current version and in some older versions, is as follows:

```
typedef int intfn ();

extern const intfn square;
```

This approach does not work in GNU C++ from 2.6.0 on, since the language specifies that the 'const' must be attached to the return value.

`constructor`
`destructor`
`constructor (priority)`
`destructor (priority)`

The `constructor` attribute causes the function to be called automatically before execution enters `main ()`. Similarly, the `destructor` attribute causes the function to be called automatically after `main ()` has completed or `exit ()` has been called. Functions with these attributes are useful for initializing data that will be used implicitly during the execution of the program.

You may provide an optional integer priority to control the order in which constructor and destructor functions are run. A constructor with a smaller priority number runs before a constructor with a larger priority number; the opposite relationship holds for destructors. So, if you have a constructor that allocates a resource and a destructor that deallocates the same resource, both functions typically have the same priority. The priorities for constructor and destructor functions are the same as those specified for namespace-scope C++ objects (see Section 6.7 [C++ Attributes], page 509).

These attributes are not currently implemented for Objective-C.

`deprecated`

The `deprecated` attribute results in a warning if the function is used anywhere in the source file. This is useful when identifying functions that are expected to be removed in a future version of a program. The warning also includes the location of the declaration of the deprecated function, to enable users to easily find further information about why the function is deprecated, or what they should do instead. Note that the warnings only occurs for uses:

```
int old_fn () __attribute__ ((deprecated));
int old_fn ();
int (*fn_ptr)() = old_fn;
```

results in a warning on line 3 but not line 2.

The `deprecated` attribute can also be used for variables and types (see Section 5.34 [Variable Attributes], page 286, see Section 5.35 [Type Attributes], page 293.)

`dllexport`

On Microsoft Windows targets and Symbian OS targets the `dllexport` attribute causes the compiler to provide a global pointer to a pointer in a DLL, so that it can be referenced with the `dllimport` attribute. On Microsoft Windows targets, the pointer name is formed by combining `_imp__` and the function or variable name.

You can use `__declspec(dllexport)` as a synonym for `__attribute__ ((dllexport))` for compatibility with other compilers.

On systems that support the `visibility` attribute, this attribute also implies "default" visibility. It is an error to explicitly specify any other visibility.

Currently, the `dllexport` attribute is ignored for inlined functions, unless the '-fkeep-inline-functions' flag has been used. The attribute is also ignored for undefined symbols.

When applied to C++ classes, the attribute marks defined non-inlined member functions and static data members as exports. Static consts initialized in-class are not marked unless they are also defined out-of-class.

For Microsoft Windows targets there are alternative methods for including the symbol in the DLL's export table such as using a '.def' file with an `EXPORTS` section or, with GNU ld, using the '--export-all' linker flag.

`dllimport`

On Microsoft Windows and Symbian OS targets, the `dllimport` attribute causes the compiler to reference a function or variable via a global pointer to a pointer that is set up by the DLL exporting the symbol. The attribute implies `extern`. On Microsoft Windows targets, the pointer name is formed by combining `_imp__` and the function or variable name.

You can use `__declspec(dllimport)` as a synonym for `__attribute__ ((dllimport))` for compatibility with other compilers.

On systems that support the `visibility` attribute, this attribute also implies "default" visibility. It is an error to explicitly specify any other visibility.

Currently, the attribute is ignored for inlined functions. If the attribute is applied to a symbol *definition*, an error is reported. If a symbol previously declared `dllimport` is later defined, the attribute is ignored in subsequent references, and a warning is emitted. The attribute is also overridden by a subsequent declaration as `dllexport`.

When applied to C++ classes, the attribute marks non-inlined member functions and static data members as imports. However, the attribute is ignored for virtual methods to allow creation of vtables using thunks.

On the SH Symbian OS target the `dllimport` attribute also has another affect—it can cause the vtable and run-time type information for a class to be exported. This happens when the class has a dllimport'ed constructor or a non-inline, non-pure virtual function and, for either of those two conditions, the class also has a inline constructor or destructor and has a key function that is defined in the current translation unit.

For Microsoft Windows based targets the use of the `dllimport` attribute on functions is not necessary, but provides a small performance benefit by eliminating a thunk in the DLL. The use of the `dllimport` attribute on imported variables was required on older versions of the GNU linker, but can now be

Chapter 5: Extensions to the C Language Family   269

avoided by passing the '--enable-auto-import' switch to the GNU linker. As with functions, using the attribute for a variable eliminates a thunk in the DLL.

One drawback to using this attribute is that a pointer to a *variable* marked as `dllimport` cannot be used as a constant address. However, a pointer to a *function* with the `dllimport` attribute can be used as a constant initializer; in this case, the address of a stub function in the import lib is referenced. On Microsoft Windows targets, the attribute can be disabled for functions by setting the '-mnop-fun-dllimport' flag.

`eightbit_data`
Use this attribute on the H8/300, H8/300H, and H8S to indicate that the specified variable should be placed into the eight bit data section. The compiler will generate more efficient code for certain operations on data in the eight bit data area. Note the eight bit data area is limited to 256 bytes of data.

You must use GAS and GLD from GNU binutils version 2.7 or later for this attribute to work correctly.

`exception_handler`
Use this attribute on the Blackfin to indicate that the specified function is an exception handler. The compiler will generate function entry and exit sequences suitable for use in an exception handler when this attribute is present.

`far`
On 68HC11 and 68HC12 the `far` attribute causes the compiler to use a calling convention that takes care of switching memory banks when entering and leaving a function. This calling convention is also the default when using the '-mlong-calls' option.

On 68HC12 the compiler will use the `call` and `rtc` instructions to call and return from a function.

On 68HC11 the compiler will generate a sequence of instructions to invoke a board-specific routine to switch the memory bank and call the real function. The board-specific routine simulates a `call`. At the end of a function, it will jump to a board-specific routine instead of using `rts`. The board-specific return routine simulates the `rtc`.

`fastcall`
On the Intel 386, the `fastcall` attribute causes the compiler to pass the first argument (if of integral type) in the register ECX and the second argument (if of integral type) in the register EDX. Subsequent and other typed arguments are passed on the stack. The called function will pop the arguments off the stack. If the number of arguments is variable all arguments are pushed on the stack.

`format (archetype, string-index, first-to-check)`
The `format` attribute specifies that a function takes `printf`, `scanf`, `strftime` or `strfmon` style arguments which should be type-checked against a format string. For example, the declaration:

```
extern int
my_printf (void *my_object, const char *my_format, ...)
     __attribute__ ((format (printf, 2, 3)));
```

causes the compiler to check the arguments in calls to `my_printf` for consistency with the `printf` style format string argument `my_format`.

The parameter *archetype* determines how the format string is interpreted, and should be `printf`, `scanf`, `strftime` or `strfmon`. (You can also use `__printf__`, `__scanf__`, `__strftime__` or `__strfmon__`.) The parameter *string-index* specifies which argument is the format string argument (starting from 1), while *first-to-check* is the number of the first argument to check against the format string. For functions where the arguments are not available to be checked (such as `vprintf`), specify the third parameter as zero. In this case the compiler only checks the format string for consistency. For `strftime` formats, the third parameter is required to be zero. Since non-static C++ methods have an implicit `this` argument, the arguments of such methods should be counted from two, not one, when giving values for *string-index* and *first-to-check*.

In the example above, the format string (`my_format`) is the second argument of the function `my_print`, and the arguments to check start with the third argument, so the correct parameters for the format attribute are 2 and 3.

The `format` attribute allows you to identify your own functions which take format strings as arguments, so that GCC can check the calls to these functions for errors. The compiler always (unless '`-ffreestanding`' or '`-fno-builtin`' is used) checks formats for the standard library functions `printf`, `fprintf`, `sprintf`, `scanf`, `fscanf`, `sscanf`, `strftime`, `vprintf`, `vfprintf` and `vsprintf` whenever such warnings are requested (using '`-Wformat`'), so there is no need to modify the header file '`stdio.h`'. In C99 mode, the functions `snprintf`, `vsnprintf`, `vscanf`, `vfscanf` and `vsscanf` are also checked. Except in strictly conforming C standard modes, the X/Open function `strfmon` is also checked as are `printf_unlocked` and `fprintf_unlocked`. See Section 3.4 [Options Controlling C Dialect], page 26.

The target may provide additional types of format checks. See Section 5.51 [Format Checks Specific to Particular Target Machines], page 494.

`format_arg (string-index)`

The `format_arg` attribute specifies that a function takes a format string for a `printf`, `scanf`, `strftime` or `strfmon` style function and modifies it (for example, to translate it into another language), so the result can be passed to a `printf`, `scanf`, `strftime` or `strfmon` style function (with the remaining arguments to the format function the same as they would have been for the unmodified string). For example, the declaration:

```
extern char *
my_dgettext (char *my_domain, const char *my_format)
     __attribute__ ((format_arg (2)));
```

causes the compiler to check the arguments in calls to a `printf`, `scanf`, `strftime` or `strfmon` type function, whose format string argument is a call to the `my_dgettext` function, for consistency with the format string argument `my_format`. If the `format_arg` attribute had not been specified, all the compiler could tell in such calls to format functions would be that the format string argument is not constant; this would generate a warning when '`-Wformat-nonliteral`' is used, but the calls could not be checked without the attribute.

Chapter 5: Extensions to the C Language Family 271

The parameter *string-index* specifies which argument is the format string argument (starting from one). Since non-static C++ methods have an implicit `this` argument, the arguments of such methods should be counted from two.

The `format-arg` attribute allows you to identify your own functions which modify format strings, so that GCC can check the calls to `printf`, `scanf`, `strftime` or `strfmon` type function whose operands are a call to one of your own function. The compiler always treats `gettext`, `dgettext`, and `dcgettext` in this manner except when strict ISO C support is requested by '-ansi' or an appropriate '-std' option, or '-ffreestanding' or '-fno-builtin' is used. See Section 3.4 [Options Controlling C Dialect], page 26.

`function_vector`

Use this attribute on the H8/300, H8/300H, and H8S to indicate that the specified function should be called through the function vector. Calling a function through the function vector will reduce code size, however; the function vector has a limited size (maximum 128 entries on the H8/300 and 64 entries on the H8/300H and H8S) and shares space with the interrupt vector.

You must use GAS and GLD from GNU binutils version 2.7 or later for this attribute to work correctly.

On M16C/M32C targets, the `function_vector` attribute declares a special page subroutine call function. Use of this attribute reduces the code size by 2 bytes for each call generated to the subroutine. The argument to the attribute is the vector number entry from the special page vector table which contains the 16 low-order bits of the subroutine's entry address. Each vector table has special page number (18 to 255) which are used in `jsrs` instruction. Jump addresses of the routines are generated by adding 0x0F0000 (in case of M16C targets) or 0xFF0000 (in case of M32C targets), to the 2 byte addresses set in the vector table. Therefore you need to ensure that all the special page vector routines should get mapped within the address range 0x0F0000 to 0x0FFFFF (for M16C) and 0xFF0000 to 0xFFFFFF (for M32C).

In the following example 2 bytes will be saved for each call to function `foo`.

```
void foo (void) __attribute__((function_vector(0x18)));
void foo (void)
{
}

void bar (void)
{
    foo();
}
```

If functions are defined in one file and are called in another file, then be sure to write this declaration in both files.

This attribute is ignored for R8C target.

`interrupt`

Use this attribute on the ARM, AVR, CRX, M32C, M32R/D, m68k, MS1, and Xstormy16 ports to indicate that the specified function is an interrupt handler. The compiler will generate function entry and exit sequences suitable for use in an interrupt handler when this attribute is present.

Note, interrupt handlers for the Blackfin, H8/300, H8/300H, H8S, and SH processors can be specified via the `interrupt_handler` attribute.

Note, on the AVR, interrupts will be enabled inside the function.

Note, for the ARM, you can specify the kind of interrupt to be handled by adding an optional parameter to the interrupt attribute like this:

```
void f () __attribute__ ((interrupt ("IRQ")));
```

Permissible values for this parameter are: IRQ, FIQ, SWI, ABORT and UNDEF.

On ARMv7-M the interrupt type is ignored, and the attribute means the function may be called with a word aligned stack pointer.

`interrupt_handler`
: Use this attribute on the Blackfin, m68k, H8/300, H8/300H, H8S, and SH to indicate that the specified function is an interrupt handler. The compiler will generate function entry and exit sequences suitable for use in an interrupt handler when this attribute is present.

`interrupt_thread`
: Use this attribute on fido, a subarchitecture of the m68k, to indicate that the specified function is an interrupt handler that is designed to run as a thread. The compiler omits generate prologue/epilogue sequences and replaces the return instruction with a `sleep` instruction. This attribute is available only on fido.

`kspisusp`
: When used together with `interrupt_handler`, `exception_handler` or `nmi_handler`, code will be generated to load the stack pointer from the USP register in the function prologue.

`l1_text`
: This attribute specifies a function to be placed into L1 Instruction SRAM. The function will be put into a specific section named `.l1.text`. With '-mfdpic', function calls with a such function as the callee or caller will use inlined PLT.

`long_call/short_call`
: This attribute specifies how a particular function is called on ARM. Both attributes override the '-mlong-calls' (see Section 3.17.2 [ARM Options], page 136) command line switch and `#pragma long_calls` settings. The `long_call` attribute indicates that the function might be far away from the call site and require a different (more expensive) calling sequence. The `short_call` attribute always places the offset to the function from the call site into the 'BL' instruction directly.

`longcall/shortcall`
: On the Blackfin, RS/6000 and PowerPC, the `longcall` attribute indicates that the function might be far away from the call site and require a different (more expensive) calling sequence. The `shortcall` attribute indicates that the function is always close enough for the shorter calling sequence to be used. These attributes override both the '-mlongcall' switch and, on the RS/6000 and PowerPC, the `#pragma longcall` setting.

See Section 3.17.27 [RS/6000 and PowerPC Options], page 194, for more information on whether long calls are necessary.

Chapter 5: Extensions to the C Language Family 273

`long_call`/`near`/`far`
: These attributes specify how a particular function is called on MIPS. The attributes override the '`-mlong-calls`' (see Section 3.17.21 [MIPS Options], page 182) command-line switch. The `long_call` and `far` attributes are synonyms, and cause the compiler to always call the function by first loading its address into a register, and then using the contents of that register. The `near` attribute has the opposite effect; it specifies that non-PIC calls should be made using the more efficient `jal` instruction.

`malloc`
: The `malloc` attribute is used to tell the compiler that a function may be treated as if any non-`NULL` pointer it returns cannot alias any other pointer valid when the function returns. This will often improve optimization. Standard functions with this property include `malloc` and `calloc`. `realloc`-like functions have this property as long as the old pointer is never referred to (including comparing it to the new pointer) after the function returns a non-`NULL` value.

`mips16`/`nomips16`
: On MIPS targets, you can use the `mips16` and `nomips16` function attributes to locally select or turn off MIPS16 code generation. A function with the `mips16` attribute is emitted as MIPS16 code, while MIPS16 code generation is disabled for functions with the `nomips16` attribute. These attributes override the '`-mips16`' and '`-mno-mips16`' options on the command line (see Section 3.17.21 [MIPS Options], page 182).

    When compiling files containing mixed MIPS16 and non-MIPS16 code, the preprocessor symbol `__mips16` reflects the setting on the command line, not that within individual functions. Mixed MIPS16 and non-MIPS16 code may interact badly with some GCC extensions such as `__builtin_apply` (see Section 5.5 [Constructing Calls], page 250).

`model (model-name)`
: On the M32R/D, use this attribute to set the addressability of an object, and of the code generated for a function. The identifier *model-name* is one of `small`, `medium`, or `large`, representing each of the code models.

    Small model objects live in the lower 16MB of memory (so that their addresses can be loaded with the `ld24` instruction), and are callable with the `bl` instruction.

    Medium model objects may live anywhere in the 32-bit address space (the compiler will generate `seth/add3` instructions to load their addresses), and are callable with the `bl` instruction.

    Large model objects may live anywhere in the 32-bit address space (the compiler will generate `seth/add3` instructions to load their addresses), and may not be reachable with the `bl` instruction (the compiler will generate the much slower `seth/add3/jl` instruction sequence).

    On IA-64, use this attribute to set the addressability of an object. At present, the only supported identifier for *model-name* is `small`, indicating addressability via "small" (22-bit) addresses (so that their addresses can be loaded with the `addl` instruction). Caveat: such addressing is by definition not position independent and hence this attribute must not be used for objects defined by shared libraries.

naked Use this attribute on the ARM, AVR, IP2K and SPU ports to indicate that the specified function does not need prologue/epilogue sequences generated by the compiler. It is up to the programmer to provide these sequences.

near On 68HC11 and 68HC12 the `near` attribute causes the compiler to use the normal calling convention based on `jsr` and `rts`. This attribute can be used to cancel the effect of the '-mlong-calls' option.

nesting Use this attribute together with `interrupt_handler`, `exception_handler` or `nmi_handler` to indicate that the function entry code should enable nested interrupts or exceptions.

nmi_handler
Use this attribute on the Blackfin to indicate that the specified function is an NMI handler. The compiler will generate function entry and exit sequences suitable for use in an NMI handler when this attribute is present.

no_instrument_function
If '-finstrument-functions' is given, profiling function calls will be generated at entry and exit of most user-compiled functions. Functions with this attribute will not be so instrumented.

noinline This function attribute prevents a function from being considered for inlining. If the function does not have side-effects, there are optimizations other than inlining that causes function calls to be optimized away, although the function call is live. To keep such calls from being optimized away, put

```
asm ("");
```

(see Section 5.37 [Extended Asm], page 300) in the called function, to serve as a special side-effect.

nonnull (arg-index, ...)
The `nonnull` attribute specifies that some function parameters should be non-null pointers. For instance, the declaration:

```
extern void *
my_memcpy (void *dest, const void *src, size_t len)
        __attribute__((nonnull (1, 2)));
```

causes the compiler to check that, in calls to `my_memcpy`, arguments *dest* and *src* are non-null. If the compiler determines that a null pointer is passed in an argument slot marked as non-null, and the '-Wnonnull' option is enabled, a warning is issued. The compiler may also choose to make optimizations based on the knowledge that certain function arguments will not be null.

If no argument index list is given to the `nonnull` attribute, all pointer arguments are marked as non-null. To illustrate, the following declaration is equivalent to the previous example:

```
extern void *
my_memcpy (void *dest, const void *src, size_t len)
        __attribute__((nonnull));
```

Chapter 5: Extensions to the C Language Family   275

noreturn   A few standard library functions, such as **abort** and **exit**, cannot return. GCC knows this automatically. Some programs define their own functions that never return. You can declare them **noreturn** to tell the compiler this fact. For example,
```
void fatal () __attribute__ ((noreturn));

void
fatal (/* ... */)
{
  /* ... */ /* Print error message. */ /* ... */
  exit (1);
}
```
The **noreturn** keyword tells the compiler to assume that **fatal** cannot return. It can then optimize without regard to what would happen if **fatal** ever did return. This makes slightly better code. More importantly, it helps avoid spurious warnings of uninitialized variables.

The **noreturn** keyword does not affect the exceptional path when that applies: a **noreturn**-marked function may still return to the caller by throwing an exception or calling **longjmp**.

Do not assume that registers saved by the calling function are restored before calling the **noreturn** function.

It does not make sense for a **noreturn** function to have a return type other than **void**.

The attribute **noreturn** is not implemented in GCC versions earlier than 2.5. An alternative way to declare that a function does not return, which works in the current version and in some older versions, is as follows:
```
typedef void voidfn ();

volatile voidfn fatal;
```
This approach does not work in GNU C++.

nothrow   The **nothrow** attribute is used to inform the compiler that a function cannot throw an exception. For example, most functions in the standard C library can be guaranteed not to throw an exception with the notable exceptions of **qsort** and **bsearch** that take function pointer arguments. The **nothrow** attribute is not implemented in GCC versions earlier than 3.3.

pure   Many functions have no effects except the return value and their return value depends only on the parameters and/or global variables. Such a function can be subject to common subexpression elimination and loop optimization just as an arithmetic operator would be. These functions should be declared with the attribute **pure**. For example,
```
int square (int) __attribute__ ((pure));
```
says that the hypothetical function **square** is safe to call fewer times than the program says.

Some of common examples of pure functions are **strlen** or **memcmp**. Interesting non-pure functions are functions with infinite loops or those depending on volatile memory or other system resource, that may change between two consecutive calls (such as **feof** in a multithreading environment).

hot
The attribute pure is not implemented in GCC versions earlier than 2.96.

The hot attribute is used to inform the compiler that a function is a hot spot of the compiled program. The function is optimized more aggressively and on many target it is placed into special subsection of the text section so all hot functions appears close together improving locality.

When profile feedback is available, via '-fprofile-use', hot functions are automatically detected and this attribute is ignored.

The hot attribute is not implemented in GCC versions earlier than 4.3.

cold
The cold attribute is used to inform the compiler that a function is unlikely executed. The function is optimized for size rather than speed and on many targets it is placed into special subsection of the text section so all cold functions appears close together improving code locality of non-cold parts of program. The paths leading to call of cold functions within code are marked as unlikely by the branch prediction mechanism. It is thus useful to mark functions used to handle unlikely conditions, such as perror, as cold to improve optimization of hot functions that do call marked functions in rare occasions.

When profile feedback is available, via '-fprofile-use', hot functions are automatically detected and this attribute is ignored.

The hot attribute is not implemented in GCC versions earlier than 4.3.

regparm (number)
On the Intel 386, the regparm attribute causes the compiler to pass arguments number one to number if they are of integral type in registers EAX, EDX, and ECX instead of on the stack. Functions that take a variable number of arguments will continue to be passed all of their arguments on the stack.

Beware that on some ELF systems this attribute is unsuitable for global functions in shared libraries with lazy binding (which is the default). Lazy binding will send the first call via resolving code in the loader, which might assume EAX, EDX and ECX can be clobbered, as per the standard calling conventions. Solaris 8 is affected by this. GNU systems with GLIBC 2.1 or higher, and FreeBSD, are believed to be safe since the loaders there save all registers. (Lazy binding can be disabled with the linker or the loader if desired, to avoid the problem.)

sseregparm
On the Intel 386 with SSE support, the sseregparm attribute causes the compiler to pass up to 3 floating point arguments in SSE registers instead of on the stack. Functions that take a variable number of arguments will continue to pass all of their floating point arguments on the stack.

force_align_arg_pointer
On the Intel x86, the force_align_arg_pointer attribute may be applied to individual function definitions, generating an alternate prologue and epilogue that realigns the runtime stack. This supports mixing legacy codes that run with a 4-byte aligned stack with modern codes that keep a 16-byte stack for SSE compatibility. The alternate prologue and epilogue are slower and bigger than the regular ones, and the alternate prologue requires a scratch register;

Chapter 5: Extensions to the C Language Family   277

>   this lowers the number of registers available if used in conjunction with the
>   `regparm` attribute. The `force_align_arg_pointer` attribute is incompatible
>   with nested functions; this is considered a hard error.

`returns_twice`
>   The `returns_twice` attribute tells the compiler that a function may return
>   more than one time. The compiler will ensure that all registers are dead before
>   calling such a function and will emit a warning about the variables that may be
>   clobbered after the second return from the function. Examples of such functions
>   are `setjmp` and `vfork`. The `longjmp`-like counterpart of such function, if any,
>   might need to be marked with the `noreturn` attribute.

`saveall`   Use this attribute on the Blackfin, H8/300, H8/300H, and H8S to indicate that
>   all registers except the stack pointer should be saved in the prologue regardless
>   of whether they are used or not.

`section ("section-name")`
>   Normally, the compiler places the code it generates in the `text` section. Sometimes, however, you need additional sections, or you need certain particular
>   functions to appear in special sections. The `section` attribute specifies that a
>   function lives in a particular section. For example, the declaration:
>
>                   ```
>                   extern void foobar (void) __attribute__ ((section ("bar")));
>                   ```
>
>   puts the function `foobar` in the `bar` section.
>
>   Some file formats do not support arbitrary sections so the `section` attribute
>   is not available on all platforms. If you need to map the entire contents of a
>   module to a particular section, consider using the facilities of the linker instead.

`sentinel`   This function attribute ensures that a parameter in a function call is an explicit
>   NULL. The attribute is only valid on variadic functions. By default, the sentinel
>   is located at position zero, the last parameter of the function call. If an optional
>   integer position argument P is supplied to the attribute, the sentinel must be
>   located at position P counting backwards from the end of the argument list.
>
>                   ```
>                   __attribute__ ((sentinel))
>                   is equivalent to
>                   __attribute__ ((sentinel(0)))
>                   ```
>
>   The attribute is automatically set with a position of 0 for the built-in functions
>   `execl` and `execlp`. The built-in function `execle` has the attribute set with a
>   position of 1.
>
>   A valid NULL in this context is defined as zero with any pointer type. If your
>   system defines the NULL macro with an integer type then you need to add
>   an explicit cast. GCC replaces `stddef.h` with a copy that redefines NULL
>   appropriately.
>
>   The warnings for missing or incorrect sentinels are enabled with '`-Wformat`'.

`short_call`
>   See long_call/short_call.

`shortcall`
>   See longcall/shortcall.

signal
: Use this attribute on the AVR to indicate that the specified function is a signal handler. The compiler will generate function entry and exit sequences suitable for use in a signal handler when this attribute is present. Interrupts will be disabled inside the function.

sp_switch
: Use this attribute on the SH to indicate an `interrupt_handler` function should switch to an alternate stack. It expects a string argument that names a global variable holding the address of the alternate stack.

    ```
    void *alt_stack;
    void f () __attribute__ ((interrupt_handler,
                             sp_switch ("alt_stack")));
    ```

stdcall
: On the Intel 386, the `stdcall` attribute causes the compiler to assume that the called function will pop off the stack space used to pass arguments, unless it takes a variable number of arguments.

tiny_data
: Use this attribute on the H8/300H and H8S to indicate that the specified variable should be placed into the tiny data section. The compiler will generate more efficient code for loads and stores on data in the tiny data section. Note the tiny data area is limited to slightly under 32kbytes of data.

trap_exit
: Use this attribute on the SH for an `interrupt_handler` to return using `trapa` instead of `rte`. This attribute expects an integer argument specifying the trap number to be used.

unused
: This attribute, attached to a function, means that the function is meant to be possibly unused. GCC will not produce a warning for this function.

used
: This attribute, attached to a function, means that code must be emitted for the function even if it appears that the function is not referenced. This is useful, for example, when the function is referenced only in inline assembly.

version_id
: This attribute, attached to a global variable or function, renames a symbol to contain a version string, thus allowing for function level versioning. HP-UX system header files may use version level functioning for some system calls.

    ```
    extern int foo () __attribute__((version_id ("20040821")));
    ```

    Calls to *foo* will be mapped to calls to *foo{20040821}*.

visibility ("*visibility_type*")
: This attribute affects the linkage of the declaration to which it is attached. There are four supported *visibility_type* values: default, hidden, protected or internal visibility.

    ```
    void __attribute__ ((visibility ("protected")))
    f () { /* Do something. */; }
    int i __attribute__ ((visibility ("hidden")));
    ```

    The possible values of *visibility_type* correspond to the visibility settings in the ELF gABI.

Chapter 5: Extensions to the C Language Family

default Default visibility is the normal case for the object file format. This value is available for the visibility attribute to override other options that may change the assumed visibility of entities.

On ELF, default visibility means that the declaration is visible to other modules and, in shared libraries, means that the declared entity may be overridden.

On Darwin, default visibility means that the declaration is visible to other modules.

Default visibility corresponds to "external linkage" in the language.

hidden Hidden visibility indicates that the entity declared will have a new form of linkage, which we'll call "hidden linkage". Two declarations of an object with hidden linkage refer to the same object if they are in the same shared object.

internal Internal visibility is like hidden visibility, but with additional processor specific semantics. Unless otherwise specified by the psABI, GCC defines internal visibility to mean that a function is *never* called from another module. Compare this with hidden functions which, while they cannot be referenced directly by other modules, can be referenced indirectly via function pointers. By indicating that a function cannot be called from outside the module, GCC may for instance omit the load of a PIC register since it is known that the calling function loaded the correct value.

protected Protected visibility is like default visibility except that it indicates that references within the defining module will bind to the definition in that module. That is, the declared entity cannot be overridden by another module.

All visibilities are supported on many, but not all, ELF targets (supported when the assembler supports the '.visibility' pseudo-op). Default visibility is supported everywhere. Hidden visibility is supported on Darwin targets.

The visibility attribute should be applied only to declarations which would otherwise have external linkage. The attribute should be applied consistently, so that the same entity should not be declared with different settings of the attribute.

In C++, the visibility attribute applies to types as well as functions and objects, because in C++ types have linkage. A class must not have greater visibility than its non-static data member types and bases, and class members default to the visibility of their class. Also, a declaration without explicit visibility is limited to the visibility of its type.

In C++, you can mark member functions and static member variables of a class with the visibility attribute. This is useful if if you know a particular method or static member variable should only be used from one shared object, then you can mark it hidden while the rest of the class has default visibility. Care must be taken to avoid breaking the One Definition Rule; for example, it is usually not useful to mark an inline method as hidden without marking the whole class as hidden.

A C++ namespace declaration can also have the visibility attribute. This attribute applies only to the particular namespace body, not to other definitions of the same namespace; it is equivalent to using '#pragma GCC visibility' before and after the namespace definition (see Section 5.52.10 [Visibility Pragmas], page 498).

In C++, if a template argument has limited visibility, this restriction is implicitly propagated to the template instantiation. Otherwise, template instantiations and specializations default to the visibility of their template.

If both the template and enclosing class have explicit visibility, the visibility from the template is used.

`warn_unused_result`

The `warn_unused_result` attribute causes a warning to be emitted if a caller of the function with this attribute does not use its return value. This is useful for functions where not checking the result is either a security problem or always a bug, such as `realloc`.

```
int fn () __attribute__ ((warn_unused_result));
int foo ()
{
  if (fn () < 0) return -1;
  fn ();
  return 0;
}
```

results in warning on line 5.

`weak`   The `weak` attribute causes the declaration to be emitted as a weak symbol rather than a global. This is primarily useful in defining library functions which can be overridden in user code, though it can also be used with non-function declarations. Weak symbols are supported for ELF targets, and also for a.out targets when using the GNU assembler and linker.

`weakref`
`weakref ("target")`

The `weakref` attribute marks a declaration as a weak reference. Without arguments, it should be accompanied by an `alias` attribute naming the target symbol. Optionally, the *target* may be given as an argument to `weakref` itself. In either case, `weakref` implicitly marks the declaration as `weak`. Without a *target*, given as an argument to `weakref` or to `alias`, `weakref` is equivalent to `weak`.

```
static int x() __attribute__ ((weakref ("y")));
/* is equivalent to... */
static int x() __attribute__ ((weak, weakref, alias ("y")));
/* and to... */
static int x() __attribute__ ((weakref));
static int x() __attribute__ ((alias ("y")));
```

A weak reference is an alias that does not by itself require a definition to be given for the target symbol. If the target symbol is only referenced through weak references, then the becomes a `weak` undefined symbol. If it is directly referenced, however, then such strong references prevail, and a definition will be required for the symbol, not necessarily in the same translation unit.

The effect is equivalent to moving all references to the alias to a separate translation unit, renaming the alias to the aliased symbol, declaring it as weak, compiling the two separate translation units and performing a reloadable link on them.

At present, a declaration to which `weakref` is attached can only be `static`.

`externally_visible`
This attribute, attached to a global variable or function nullify effect of '`-fwhole-program`' command line option, so the object remain visible outside the current compilation unit

You can specify multiple attributes in a declaration by separating them by commas within the double parentheses or by immediately following an attribute declaration with another attribute declaration.

Some people object to the `__attribute__` feature, suggesting that ISO C's `#pragma` should be used instead. At the time `__attribute__` was designed, there were two reasons for not doing this.

1. It is impossible to generate `#pragma` commands from a macro.
2. There is no telling what the same `#pragma` might mean in another compiler.

These two reasons applied to almost any application that might have been proposed for `#pragma`. It was basically a mistake to use `#pragma` for *anything*.

The ISO C99 standard includes `_Pragma`, which now allows pragmas to be generated from macros. In addition, a `#pragma GCC` namespace is now in use for GCC-specific pragmas. However, it has been found convenient to use `__attribute__` to achieve a natural attachment of attributes to their corresponding declarations, whereas `#pragma GCC` is of use for constructs that do not naturally form part of the grammar. See Section "Miscellaneous Preprocessing Directives" in *The GNU C Preprocessor*.

5.28 Attribute Syntax

This section describes the syntax with which `__attribute__` may be used, and the constructs to which attribute specifiers bind, for the C language. Some details may vary for C++ and Objective-C. Because of infelicities in the grammar for attributes, some forms described here may not be successfully parsed in all cases.

There are some problems with the semantics of attributes in C++. For example, there are no manglings for attributes, although they may affect code generation, so problems may arise when attributed types are used in conjunction with templates or overloading. Similarly, `typeid` does not distinguish between types with different attributes. Support for attributes in C++ may be restricted in future to attributes on declarations only, but not on nested declarators.

See Section 5.27 [Function Attributes], page 264, for details of the semantics of attributes applying to functions. See Section 5.34 [Variable Attributes], page 286, for details of the semantics of attributes applying to variables. See Section 5.35 [Type Attributes], page 293, for details of the semantics of attributes applying to structure, union and enumerated types.

An *attribute specifier* is of the form `__attribute__ ((attribute-list))`. An *attribute list* is a possibly empty comma-separated sequence of *attributes*, where each attribute is one of the following:

- Empty. Empty attributes are ignored.
- A word (which may be an identifier such as `unused`, or a reserved word such as `const`).
- A word, followed by, in parentheses, parameters for the attribute. These parameters take one of the following forms:
  - An identifier. For example, `mode` attributes use this form.
  - An identifier followed by a comma and a non-empty comma-separated list of expressions. For example, `format` attributes use this form.
  - A possibly empty comma-separated list of expressions. For example, `format_arg` attributes use this form with the list being a single integer constant expression, and `alias` attributes use this form with the list being a single string constant.

An *attribute specifier list* is a sequence of one or more attribute specifiers, not separated by any other tokens.

In GNU C, an attribute specifier list may appear after the colon following a label, other than a `case` or `default` label. The only attribute it makes sense to use after a label is `unused`. This feature is intended for code generated by programs which contains labels that may be unused but which is compiled with '-Wall'. It would not normally be appropriate to use in it human-written code, though it could be useful in cases where the code that jumps to the label is contained within an `#ifdef` conditional. GNU C++ does not permit such placement of attribute lists, as it is permissible for a declaration, which could begin with an attribute list, to be labelled in C++. Declarations cannot be labelled in C90 or C99, so the ambiguity does not arise there.

An attribute specifier list may appear as part of a `struct`, `union` or `enum` specifier. It may go either immediately after the `struct`, `union` or `enum` keyword, or after the closing brace. The former syntax is preferred. Where attribute specifiers follow the closing brace, they are considered to relate to the structure, union or enumerated type defined, not to any enclosing declaration the type specifier appears in, and the type defined is not complete until after the attribute specifiers.

Otherwise, an attribute specifier appears as part of a declaration, counting declarations of unnamed parameters and type names, and relates to that declaration (which may be nested in another declaration, for example in the case of a parameter declaration), or to a particular declarator within a declaration. Where an attribute specifier is applied to a parameter declared as a function or an array, it should apply to the function or array rather than the pointer to which the parameter is implicitly converted, but this is not yet correctly implemented.

Any list of specifiers and qualifiers at the start of a declaration may contain attribute specifiers, whether or not such a list may in that context contain storage class specifiers. (Some attributes, however, are essentially in the nature of storage class specifiers, and only make sense where storage class specifiers may be used; for example, `section`.) There is one necessary limitation to this syntax: the first old-style parameter declaration in a function definition cannot begin with an attribute specifier, because such an attribute applies to the function instead by syntax described below (which, however, is not yet implemented in this case). In some other cases, attribute specifiers are permitted by this grammar but not yet supported by the compiler. All attribute specifiers in this place relate to the declaration as a whole. In the obsolescent usage where a type of int is implied by the absence of type specifiers, such a list of specifiers and qualifiers may be an attribute specifier list with no other specifiers or qualifiers.

At present, the first parameter in a function prototype must have some type specifier which is not an attribute specifier; this resolves an ambiguity in the interpretation of void f(int (__attribute__((foo)) x)), but is subject to change. At present, if the parentheses of a function declarator contain only attributes then those attributes are ignored, rather than yielding an error or warning or implying a single parameter of type int, but this is subject to change.

An attribute specifier list may appear immediately before a declarator (other than the first) in a comma-separated list of declarators in a declaration of more than one identifier using a single list of specifiers and qualifiers. Such attribute specifiers apply only to the identifier before whose declarator they appear. For example, in

```
__attribute__((noreturn)) void d0 (void),
    __attribute__((format(printf, 1, 2))) d1 (const char *, ...),
     d2 (void)
```

the noreturn attribute applies to all the functions declared; the format attribute only applies to d1.

An attribute specifier list may appear immediately before the comma, = or semicolon terminating the declaration of an identifier other than a function definition. Such attribute specifiers apply to the declared object or function. Where an assembler name for an object or function is specified (see Section 5.39 [Asm Labels], page 326), the attribute must follow the asm specification.

An attribute specifier list may, in future, be permitted to appear after the declarator in a function definition (before any old-style parameter declarations or the function body).

Attribute specifiers may be mixed with type qualifiers appearing inside the [] of a parameter array declarator, in the C99 construct by which such qualifiers are applied to the pointer to which the array is implicitly converted. Such attribute specifiers apply to the pointer, not to the array, but at present this is not implemented and they are ignored.

An attribute specifier list may appear at the start of a nested declarator. At present, there are some limitations in this usage: the attributes correctly apply to the declarator, but for most individual attributes the semantics this implies are not implemented. When attribute specifiers follow the * of a pointer declarator, they may be mixed with any type qualifiers present. The following describes the formal semantics of this syntax. It will make the most sense if you are familiar with the formal specification of declarators in the ISO C standard.

Consider (as in C99 subclause 6.7.5 paragraph 4) a declaration T D1, where T contains declaration specifiers that specify a type *Type* (such as int) and D1 is a declarator that contains an identifier *ident*. The type specified for *ident* for derived declarators whose type does not include an attribute specifier is as in the ISO C standard.

If D1 has the form (*attribute-specifier-list* D), and the declaration T D specifies the type "*derived-declarator-type-list Type*" for *ident*, then T D1 specifies the type "*derived-declarator-type-list attribute-specifier-list Type*" for *ident*.

If D1 has the form * *type-qualifier-and-attribute-specifier-list* D, and the declaration T D specifies the type "*derived-declarator-type-list Type*" for *ident*, then T D1 specifies the type "*derived-declarator-type-list type-qualifier-and-attribute-specifier-list Type*" for *ident*.

For example,

```
void (__attribute__((noreturn)) ****f) (void);
```

specifies the type "pointer to pointer to pointer to pointer to non-returning function returning void". As another example,

```
char *__attribute__((aligned(8))) *f;
```

specifies the type "pointer to 8-byte-aligned pointer to char". Note again that this does not work with most attributes; for example, the usage of 'aligned' and 'noreturn' attributes given above is not yet supported.

For compatibility with existing code written for compiler versions that did not implement attributes on nested declarators, some laxity is allowed in the placing of attributes. If an attribute that only applies to types is applied to a declaration, it will be treated as applying to the type of that declaration. If an attribute that only applies to declarations is applied to the type of a declaration, it will be treated as applying to that declaration; and, for compatibility with code placing the attributes immediately before the identifier declared, such an attribute applied to a function return type will be treated as applying to the function type, and such an attribute applied to an array element type will be treated as applying to the array type. If an attribute that only applies to function types is applied to a pointer-to-function type, it will be treated as applying to the pointer target type; if such an attribute is applied to a function return type that is not a pointer-to-function type, it will be treated as applying to the function type.

5.29 Prototypes and Old-Style Function Definitions

GNU C extends ISO C to allow a function prototype to override a later old-style non-prototype definition. Consider the following example:

```
/* Use prototypes unless the compiler is old-fashioned.  */
#ifdef __STDC__
#define P(x) x
#else
#define P(x) ()
#endif

/* Prototype function declaration.  */
int isroot P((uid_t));

/* Old-style function definition.  */
int
isroot (x)   /* ??? lossage here ??? */
     uid_t x;
{
  return x == 0;
}
```

Suppose the type uid_t happens to be short. ISO C does not allow this example, because subword arguments in old-style non-prototype definitions are promoted. Therefore in this example the function definition's argument is really an int, which does not match the prototype argument type of short.

Chapter 5: Extensions to the C Language Family   285

This restriction of ISO C makes it hard to write code that is portable to traditional C compilers, because the programmer does not know whether the `uid_t` type is `short`, `int`, or `long`. Therefore, in cases like these GNU C allows a prototype to override a later old-style definition. More precisely, in GNU C, a function prototype argument type overrides the argument type specified by a later old-style definition if the former type is the same as the latter type before promotion. Thus in GNU C the above example is equivalent to the following:

```
int isroot (uid_t);

int
isroot (uid_t x)
{
  return x == 0;
}
```

GNU C++ does not support old-style function definitions, so this extension is irrelevant.

5.30 C++ Style Comments

In GNU C, you may use C++ style comments, which start with '//' and continue until the end of the line. Many other C implementations allow such comments, and they are included in the 1999 C standard. However, C++ style comments are not recognized if you specify an '-std' option specifying a version of ISO C before C99, or '-ansi' (equivalent to '-std=c89').

5.31 Dollar Signs in Identifier Names

In GNU C, you may normally use dollar signs in identifier names. This is because many traditional C implementations allow such identifiers. However, dollar signs in identifiers are not supported on a few target machines, typically because the target assembler does not allow them.

5.32 The Character ESC in Constants

You can use the sequence '\e' in a string or character constant to stand for the ASCII character ESC.

5.33 Inquiring on Alignment of Types or Variables

The keyword `__alignof__` allows you to inquire about how an object is aligned, or the minimum alignment usually required by a type. Its syntax is just like `sizeof`.

For example, if the target machine requires a `double` value to be aligned on an 8-byte boundary, then `__alignof__ (double)` is 8. This is true on many RISC machines. On more traditional machine designs, `__alignof__ (double)` is 4 or even 2.

Some machines never actually require alignment; they allow reference to any data type even at an odd address. For these machines, `__alignof__` reports the smallest alignment that GCC will give the data type, usually as mandated by the target ABI.

If the operand of `__alignof__` is an lvalue rather than a type, its value is the required alignment for its type, taking into account any minimum alignment specified with GCC's `__attribute__` extension (see Section 5.34 [Variable Attributes], page 286). For example, after this declaration:

```
struct foo { int x; char y; } foo1;
```

the value of `__alignof__ (foo1.y)` is 1, even though its actual alignment is probably 2 or 4, the same as `__alignof__ (int)`.

It is an error to ask for the alignment of an incomplete type.

5.34 Specifying Attributes of Variables

The keyword `__attribute__` allows you to specify special attributes of variables or structure fields. This keyword is followed by an attribute specification inside double parentheses. Some attributes are currently defined generically for variables. Other attributes are defined for variables on particular target systems. Other attributes are available for functions (see Section 5.27 [Function Attributes], page 264) and for types (see Section 5.35 [Type Attributes], page 293). Other front ends might define more attributes (see Chapter 6 [Extensions to the C++ Language], page 503).

You may also specify attributes with '__' preceding and following each keyword. This allows you to use them in header files without being concerned about a possible macro of the same name. For example, you may use `__aligned__` instead of `aligned`.

See Section 5.28 [Attribute Syntax], page 281, for details of the exact syntax for using attributes.

aligned (*alignment*)

> This attribute specifies a minimum alignment for the variable or structure field, measured in bytes. For example, the declaration:
>
> ```
> int x __attribute__ ((aligned (16))) = 0;
> ```
>
> causes the compiler to allocate the global variable x on a 16-byte boundary. On a 68040, this could be used in conjunction with an `asm` expression to access the `move16` instruction which requires 16-byte aligned operands.
>
> You can also specify the alignment of structure fields. For example, to create a double-word aligned `int` pair, you could write:
>
> ```
> struct foo { int x[2] __attribute__ ((aligned (8))); };
> ```
>
> This is an alternative to creating a union with a **double** member that forces the union to be double-word aligned.
>
> As in the preceding examples, you can explicitly specify the alignment (in bytes) that you wish the compiler to use for a given variable or structure field. Alternatively, you can leave out the alignment factor and just ask the compiler to align a variable or field to the maximum useful alignment for the target machine you are compiling for. For example, you could write:
>
> ```
> short array[3] __attribute__ ((aligned));
> ```
>
> Whenever you leave out the alignment factor in an **aligned** attribute specification, the compiler automatically sets the alignment for the declared variable or field to the largest alignment which is ever used for any data type on the target machine you are compiling for. Doing this can often make copy operations more efficient, because the compiler can use whatever instructions copy the biggest

Chapter 5: Extensions to the C Language Family 287

chunks of memory when performing copies to or from the variables or fields that you have aligned this way.

When used on a struct, or struct member, the `aligned` attribute can only increase the alignment; in order to decrease it, the `packed` attribute must be specified as well. When used as part of a typedef, the `aligned` attribute can both increase and decrease alignment, and specifying the `packed` attribute will generate a warning.

Note that the effectiveness of `aligned` attributes may be limited by inherent limitations in your linker. On many systems, the linker is only able to arrange for variables to be aligned up to a certain maximum alignment. (For some linkers, the maximum supported alignment may be very very small.) If your linker is only able to align variables up to a maximum of 8 byte alignment, then specifying `aligned(16)` in an `__attribute__` will still only provide you with 8 byte alignment. See your linker documentation for further information.

The `aligned` attribute can also be used for functions (see Section 5.27 [Function Attributes], page 264.)

`cleanup (cleanup_function)`
The `cleanup` attribute runs a function when the variable goes out of scope. This attribute can only be applied to auto function scope variables; it may not be applied to parameters or variables with static storage duration. The function must take one parameter, a pointer to a type compatible with the variable. The return value of the function (if any) is ignored.

If '`-fexceptions`' is enabled, then *cleanup_function* will be run during the stack unwinding that happens during the processing of the exception. Note that the `cleanup` attribute does not allow the exception to be caught, only to perform an action. It is undefined what happens if *cleanup_function* does not return normally.

`common`
`nocommon`
The `common` attribute requests GCC to place a variable in "common" storage. The `nocommon` attribute requests the opposite—to allocate space for it directly.

These attributes override the default chosen by the '`-fno-common`' and '`-fcommon`' flags respectively.

`deprecated`
The `deprecated` attribute results in a warning if the variable is used anywhere in the source file. This is useful when identifying variables that are expected to be removed in a future version of a program. The warning also includes the location of the declaration of the deprecated variable, to enable users to easily find further information about why the variable is deprecated, or what they should do instead. Note that the warning only occurs for uses:

```
extern int old_var __attribute__ ((deprecated));
extern int old_var;
int new_fn () { return old_var; }
```

results in a warning on line 3 but not line 2.

The `deprecated` attribute can also be used for functions and types (see Section 5.27 [Function Attributes], page 264, see Section 5.35 [Type Attributes], page 293.)

`mode (mode)`
> This attribute specifies the data type for the declaration—whichever type corresponds to the mode *mode*. This in effect lets you request an integer or floating point type according to its width.
>
> You may also specify a mode of 'byte' or '__byte__' to indicate the mode corresponding to a one-byte integer, 'word' or '__word__' for the mode of a one-word integer, and 'pointer' or '__pointer__' for the mode used to represent pointers.

`packed`
> The `packed` attribute specifies that a variable or structure field should have the smallest possible alignment—one byte for a variable, and one bit for a field, unless you specify a larger value with the `aligned` attribute.
>
> Here is a structure in which the field x is packed, so that it immediately follows a:
>
> ```
> struct foo
> {
>   char a;
>   int x[2] __attribute__ ((packed));
> };
> ```

`section ("section-name")`
> Normally, the compiler places the objects it generates in sections like data and bss. Sometimes, however, you need additional sections, or you need certain particular variables to appear in special sections, for example to map to special hardware. The `section` attribute specifies that a variable (or function) lives in a particular section. For example, this small program uses several specific section names:
>
> ```
> struct duart a __attribute__ ((section ("DUART_A"))) = { 0 };
> struct duart b __attribute__ ((section ("DUART_B"))) = { 0 };
> char stack[10000] __attribute__ ((section ("STACK"))) = { 0 };
> int init_data __attribute__ ((section ("INITDATA"))) = 0;
>
> main()
> {
>   /* Initialize stack pointer */
>   init_sp (stack + sizeof (stack));
>
>   /* Initialize initialized data */
>   memcpy (&init_data, &data, &edata - &data);
>
>   /* Turn on the serial ports */
>   init_duart (&a);
>   init_duart (&b);
> }
> ```
>
> Use the `section` attribute with an *initialized* definition of a *global* variable, as shown in the example. GCC issues a warning and otherwise ignores the `section` attribute in uninitialized variable declarations.

Chapter 5: Extensions to the C Language Family   289

You may only use the `section` attribute with a fully initialized global definition because of the way linkers work. The linker requires each object be defined once, with the exception that uninitialized variables tentatively go in the `common` (or `bss`) section and can be multiply "defined". You can force a variable to be initialized with the '-fno-common' flag or the `nocommon` attribute.

Some file formats do not support arbitrary sections so the `section` attribute is not available on all platforms. If you need to map the entire contents of a module to a particular section, consider using the facilities of the linker instead.

`shared`   On Microsoft Windows, in addition to putting variable definitions in a named section, the section can also be shared among all running copies of an executable or DLL. For example, this small program defines shared data by putting it in a named section `shared` and marking the section shareable:

```
int foo __attribute__((section ("shared"), shared)) = 0;

int
main()
{
  /* Read and write foo.  All running
     copies see the same value.  */
  return 0;
}
```

You may only use the `shared` attribute along with `section` attribute with a fully initialized global definition because of the way linkers work. See `section` attribute for more information.

The `shared` attribute is only available on Microsoft Windows.

`tls_model ("tls_model")`

The `tls_model` attribute sets thread-local storage model (see Section 5.54 [Thread-Local], page 499) of a particular `__thread` variable, overriding '-ftls-model=' command line switch on a per-variable basis. The *tls_model* argument should be one of `global-dynamic`, `local-dynamic`, `initial-exec` or `local-exec`.

Not all targets support this attribute.

`unused`   This attribute, attached to a variable, means that the variable is meant to be possibly unused. GCC will not produce a warning for this variable.

`used`   This attribute, attached to a variable, means that the variable must be emitted even if it appears that the variable is not referenced.

`vector_size (bytes)`

This attribute specifies the vector size for the variable, measured in bytes. For example, the declaration:

```
int foo __attribute__ ((vector_size (16)));
```

causes the compiler to set the mode for `foo`, to be 16 bytes, divided into `int` sized units. Assuming a 32-bit int (a vector of 4 units of 4 bytes), the corresponding mode of `foo` will be V4SI.

This attribute is only applicable to integral and float scalars, although arrays, pointers, and function return values are allowed in conjunction with this construct.

Aggregates with this attribute are invalid, even if they are of the same size as a corresponding scalar. For example, the declaration:

```
struct S { int a; };
struct S  __attribute__ ((vector_size (16))) foo;
```

is invalid even if the size of the structure is the same as the size of the `int`.

`selectany`

The `selectany` attribute causes an initialized global variable to have link-once semantics. When multiple definitions of the variable are encountered by the linker, the first is selected and the remainder are discarded. Following usage by the Microsoft compiler, the linker is told *not* to warn about size or content differences of the multiple definitions.

Although the primary usage of this attribute is for POD types, the attribute can also be applied to global C++ objects that are initialized by a constructor. In this case, the static initialization and destruction code for the object is emitted in each translation defining the object, but the calls to the constructor and destructor are protected by a link-once guard variable.

The `selectany` attribute is only available on Microsoft Windows targets. You can use `__declspec (selectany)` as a synonym for `__attribute__ ((selectany))` for compatibility with other compilers.

`weak`

The `weak` attribute is described in See Section 5.27 [Function Attributes], page 264.

`dllimport`

The `dllimport` attribute is described in See Section 5.27 [Function Attributes], page 264.

`dllexport`

The `dllexport` attribute is described in See Section 5.27 [Function Attributes], page 264.

5.34.1 Blackfin Variable Attributes

Three attributes are currently defined for the Blackfin.

`l1_data`

`l1_data_A`
`l1_data_B`

Use these attributes on the Blackfin to place the variable into L1 Data SRAM. Variables with `l1_data` attribute will be put into the specific section named `.l1.data`. Those with `l1_data_A` attribute will be put into the specific section named `.l1.data.A`. Those with `l1_data_B` attribute will be put into the specific section named `.l1.data.B`.

5.34.2 M32R/D Variable Attributes

One attribute is currently defined for the M32R/D.

Chapter 5: Extensions to the C Language Family   291

`model (model-name)`
> Use this attribute on the M32R/D to set the addressability of an object. The identifier *model-name* is one of `small`, `medium`, or `large`, representing each of the code models.
>
> Small model objects live in the lower 16MB of memory (so that their addresses can be loaded with the `ld24` instruction).
>
> Medium and large model objects may live anywhere in the 32-bit address space (the compiler will generate `seth/add3` instructions to load their addresses).

5.34.3 i386 Variable Attributes

Two attributes are currently defined for i386 configurations: `ms_struct` and `gcc_struct`

`ms_struct`
`gcc_struct`
> If `packed` is used on a structure, or if bit-fields are used it may be that the Microsoft ABI packs them differently than GCC would normally pack them. Particularly when moving packed data between functions compiled with GCC and the native Microsoft compiler (either via function call or as data in a file), it may be necessary to access either format.
>
> Currently '`-m[no-]ms-bitfields`' is provided for the Microsoft Windows X86 compilers to match the native Microsoft compiler.
>
> The Microsoft structure layout algorithm is fairly simple with the exception of the bitfield packing:
>
> The padding and alignment of members of structures and whether a bit field can straddle a storage-unit boundary
>
> 1. Structure members are stored sequentially in the order in which they are declared: the first member has the lowest memory address and the last member the highest.
> 2. Every data object has an alignment-requirement. The alignment-requirement for all data except structures, unions, and arrays is either the size of the object or the current packing size (specified with either the aligned attribute or the pack pragma), whichever is less. For structures, unions, and arrays, the alignment-requirement is the largest alignment-requirement of its members. Every object is allocated an offset so that:
>
>   offset % alignment-requirement == 0
> 3. Adjacent bit fields are packed into the same 1-, 2-, or 4-byte allocation unit if the integral types are the same size and if the next bit field fits into the current allocation unit without crossing the boundary imposed by the common alignment requirements of the bit fields.
>
> Handling of zero-length bitfields:
>
> MSVC interprets zero-length bitfields in the following ways:
>
> 1. If a zero-length bitfield is inserted between two bitfields that would normally be coalesced, the bitfields will not be coalesced.
>
>   For example:

```
struct
{
  unsigned long bf_1 : 12;
  unsigned long : 0;
  unsigned long bf_2 : 12;
} t1;
```

The size of `t1` would be 8 bytes with the zero-length bitfield. If the zero-length bitfield were removed, `t1`'s size would be 4 bytes.

2. If a zero-length bitfield is inserted after a bitfield, `foo`, and the alignment of the zero-length bitfield is greater than the member that follows it, `bar`, `bar` will be aligned as the type of the zero-length bitfield.

   For example:
   ```
   struct
   {
     char foo : 4;
     short : 0;
     char bar;
   } t2;

   struct
   {
     char foo : 4;
     short : 0;
     double bar;
   } t3;
   ```

   For `t2`, `bar` will be placed at offset 2, rather than offset 1. Accordingly, the size of `t2` will be 4. For `t3`, the zero-length bitfield will not affect the alignment of `bar` or, as a result, the size of the structure.

   Taking this into account, it is important to note the following:

   1. If a zero-length bitfield follows a normal bitfield, the type of the zero-length bitfield may affect the alignment of the structure as whole. For example, `t2` has a size of 4 bytes, since the zero-length bitfield follows a normal bitfield, and is of type short.

   2. Even if a zero-length bitfield is not followed by a normal bitfield, it may still affect the alignment of the structure:
      ```
      struct
      {
        char foo : 6;
        long : 0;
      } t4;
      ```
      Here, `t4` will take up 4 bytes.

   3. Zero-length bitfields following non-bitfield members are ignored:
      ```
      struct
      {
        char foo;
        long : 0;
        char bar;
      } t5;
      ```
      Here, `t5` will take up 2 bytes.

Chapter 5: Extensions to the C Language Family   293

5.34.4 PowerPC Variable Attributes

Three attributes currently are defined for PowerPC configurations: `altivec`, `ms_struct` and `gcc_struct`.

For full documentation of the struct attributes please see the documentation in the See [i386 Variable Attributes], page 291, section.

For documentation of `altivec` attribute please see the documentation in the See [PowerPC Type Attributes], page 298, section.

5.34.5 SPU Variable Attributes

The SPU supports the `spu_vector` attribute for variables. For documentation of this attribute please see the documentation in the See [SPU Type Attributes], page 298, section.

5.34.6 Xstormy16 Variable Attributes

One attribute is currently defined for xstormy16 configurations: `below100`

`below100`
> If a variable has the `below100` attribute (`BELOW100` is allowed also), GCC will place the variable in the first 0x100 bytes of memory and use special opcodes to access it. Such variables will be placed in either the `.bss_below100` section or the `.data_below100` section.

5.34.7 AVR Variable Attributes

`progmem`   The `progmem` attribute is used on the AVR to place data in the Program Memory address space. The AVR is a Harvard Architecture processor and data normally resides in the Data Memory address space.

5.35 Specifying Attributes of Types

The keyword `__attribute__` allows you to specify special attributes of `struct` and `union` types when you define such types. This keyword is followed by an attribute specification inside double parentheses. Seven attributes are currently defined for types: `aligned`, `packed`, `transparent_union`, `unused`, `deprecated`, `visibility`, and `may_alias`. Other attributes are defined for functions (see Section 5.27 [Function Attributes], page 264) and for variables (see Section 5.34 [Variable Attributes], page 286).

You may also specify any one of these attributes with '`__`' preceding and following its keyword. This allows you to use these attributes in header files without being concerned about a possible macro of the same name. For example, you may use `__aligned__` instead of `aligned`.

You may specify type attributes in an enum, struct or union type declaration or definition, or for other types in a `typedef` declaration.

For an enum, struct or union type, you may specify attributes either between the enum, struct or union tag and the name of the type, or just past the closing curly brace of the *definition*. The former syntax is preferred.

See Section 5.28 [Attribute Syntax], page 281, for details of the exact syntax for using attributes.

`aligned (`*`alignment`*`)`

> This attribute specifies a minimum alignment (in bytes) for variables of the specified type. For example, the declarations:
>
> ```
> struct S { short f[3]; } __attribute__ ((aligned (8)));
> typedef int more_aligned_int __attribute__ ((aligned (8)));
> ```
>
> force the compiler to insure (as far as it can) that each variable whose type is `struct S` or `more_aligned_int` will be allocated and aligned *at least* on a 8-byte boundary. On a SPARC, having all variables of type `struct S` aligned to 8-byte boundaries allows the compiler to use the `ldd` and `std` (doubleword load and store) instructions when copying one variable of type `struct S` to another, thus improving run-time efficiency.
>
> Note that the alignment of any given `struct` or `union` type is required by the ISO C standard to be at least a perfect multiple of the lowest common multiple of the alignments of all of the members of the `struct` or `union` in question. This means that you *can* effectively adjust the alignment of a `struct` or `union` type by attaching an `aligned` attribute to any one of the members of such a type, but the notation illustrated in the example above is a more obvious, intuitive, and readable way to request the compiler to adjust the alignment of an entire `struct` or `union` type.
>
> As in the preceding example, you can explicitly specify the alignment (in bytes) that you wish the compiler to use for a given `struct` or `union` type. Alternatively, you can leave out the alignment factor and just ask the compiler to align a type to the maximum useful alignment for the target machine you are compiling for. For example, you could write:
>
> ```
> struct S { short f[3]; } __attribute__ ((aligned));
> ```
>
> Whenever you leave out the alignment factor in an `aligned` attribute specification, the compiler automatically sets the alignment for the type to the largest alignment which is ever used for any data type on the target machine you are compiling for. Doing this can often make copy operations more efficient, because the compiler can use whatever instructions copy the biggest chunks of memory when performing copies to or from the variables which have types that you have aligned this way.
>
> In the example above, if the size of each `short` is 2 bytes, then the size of the entire `struct S` type is 6 bytes. The smallest power of two which is greater than or equal to that is 8, so the compiler sets the alignment for the entire `struct S` type to 8 bytes.
>
> Note that although you can ask the compiler to select a time-efficient alignment for a given type and then declare only individual stand-alone objects of that type, the compiler's ability to select a time-efficient alignment is primarily useful only when you plan to create arrays of variables having the relevant (efficiently aligned) type. If you declare or use arrays of variables of an efficiently-aligned type, then it is likely that your program will also be doing pointer arithmetic (or subscripting, which amounts to the same thing) on pointers to the relevant type, and the code that the compiler generates for these pointer arithmetic operations will often be more efficient for efficiently-aligned types than for other types.

Chapter 5: Extensions to the C Language Family

The `aligned` attribute can only increase the alignment; but you can decrease it by specifying `packed` as well. See below.

Note that the effectiveness of `aligned` attributes may be limited by inherent limitations in your linker. On many systems, the linker is only able to arrange for variables to be aligned up to a certain maximum alignment. (For some linkers, the maximum supported alignment may be very very small.) If your linker is only able to align variables up to a maximum of 8 byte alignment, then specifying `aligned(16)` in an `__attribute__` will still only provide you with 8 byte alignment. See your linker documentation for further information.

`packed`
This attribute, attached to `struct` or `union` type definition, specifies that each member (other than zero-width bitfields) of the structure or union is placed to minimize the memory required. When attached to an `enum` definition, it indicates that the smallest integral type should be used.

Specifying this attribute for `struct` and `union` types is equivalent to specifying the `packed` attribute on each of the structure or union members. Specifying the '-fshort-enums' flag on the line is equivalent to specifying the `packed` attribute on all `enum` definitions.

In the following example struct `my_packed_struct`'s members are packed closely together, but the internal layout of its s member is not packed—to do that, struct `my_unpacked_struct` would need to be packed too.

```
struct my_unpacked_struct
 {
    char c;
    int i;
 };

struct __attribute__ ((__packed__)) my_packed_struct
 {
    char c;
    int  i;
    struct my_unpacked_struct s;
 };
```

You may only specify this attribute on the definition of a `enum`, `struct` or `union`, not on a `typedef` which does not also define the enumerated type, structure or union.

`transparent_union`
This attribute, attached to a `union` type definition, indicates that any function parameter having that union type causes calls to that function to be treated in a special way.

First, the argument corresponding to a transparent union type can be of any type in the union; no cast is required. Also, if the union contains a pointer type, the corresponding argument can be a null pointer constant or a void pointer expression; and if the union contains a void pointer type, the corresponding argument can be any pointer expression. If the union member type is a pointer, qualifiers like `const` on the referenced type must be respected, just as with normal pointer conversions.

Second, the argument is passed to the function using the calling conventions of the first member of the transparent union, not the calling conventions of the union itself. All members of the union must have the same machine representation; this is necessary for this argument passing to work properly.

Transparent unions are designed for library functions that have multiple interfaces for compatibility reasons. For example, suppose the `wait` function must accept either a value of type `int *` to comply with Posix, or a value of type `union wait *` to comply with the 4.1BSD interface. If `wait`'s parameter were `void *`, `wait` would accept both kinds of arguments, but it would also accept any other pointer type and this would make argument type checking less useful. Instead, `<sys/wait.h>` might define the interface as follows:

```
typedef union __attribute__ ((__transparent_union__))
  {
    int *__ip;
    union wait *__up;
  } wait_status_ptr_t;

pid_t wait (wait_status_ptr_t);
```

This interface allows either `int *` or `union wait *` arguments to be passed, using the `int *` calling convention. The program can call `wait` with arguments of either type:

```
int w1 () { int w; return wait (&w); }
int w2 () { union wait w; return wait (&w); }
```

With this interface, `wait`'s implementation might look like this:

```
pid_t wait (wait_status_ptr_t p)
{
  return waitpid (-1, p.__ip, 0);
}
```

`unused`   When attached to a type (including a `union` or a `struct`), this attribute means that variables of that type are meant to appear possibly unused. GCC will not produce a warning for any variables of that type, even if the variable appears to do nothing. This is often the case with lock or thread classes, which are usually defined and then not referenced, but contain constructors and destructors that have nontrivial bookkeeping functions.

`deprecated`

The `deprecated` attribute results in a warning if the type is used anywhere in the source file. This is useful when identifying types that are expected to be removed in a future version of a program. If possible, the warning also includes the location of the declaration of the deprecated type, to enable users to easily find further information about why the type is deprecated, or what they should do instead. Note that the warnings only occur for uses and then only if the type is being applied to an identifier that itself is not being declared as deprecated.

```
typedef int T1 __attribute__ ((deprecated));
T1 x;
typedef T1 T2;
T2 y;
typedef T1 T3 __attribute__ ((deprecated));
T3 z __attribute__ ((deprecated));
```

Chapter 5: Extensions to the C Language Family   297

results in a warning on line 2 and 3 but not lines 4, 5, or 6. No warning is issued for line 4 because T2 is not explicitly deprecated. Line 5 has no warning because T3 is explicitly deprecated. Similarly for line 6.

The `deprecated` attribute can also be used for functions and variables (see Section 5.27 [Function Attributes], page 264, see Section 5.34 [Variable Attributes], page 286.)

`may_alias`

Accesses through pointers to types with this attribute are not subject to type-based alias analysis, but are instead assumed to be able to alias any other type of objects. In the context of 6.5/7 an lvalue expression dereferencing such a pointer is treated like having a character type. See '-fstrict-aliasing' for more information on aliasing issues. This extension exists to support some vector APIs, in which pointers to one vector type are permitted to alias pointers to a different vector type.

Note that an object of a type with this attribute does not have any special semantics.

Example of use:

```
typedef short __attribute__((__may_alias__)) short_a;

int
main (void)
{
  int a = 0x12345678;
  short_a *b = (short_a *) &a;

  b[1] = 0;

  if (a == 0x12345678)
    abort();

  exit(0);
}
```

If you replaced `short_a` with `short` in the variable declaration, the above program would abort when compiled with '-fstrict-aliasing', which is on by default at '-O2' or above in recent GCC versions.

`visibility`

In C++, attribute visibility (see Section 5.27 [Function Attributes], page 264) can also be applied to class, struct, union and enum types. Unlike other type attributes, the attribute must appear between the initial keyword and the name of the type; it cannot appear after the body of the type.

Note that the type visibility is applied to vague linkage entities associated with the class (vtable, typeinfo node, etc.). In particular, if a class is thrown as an exception in one shared object and caught in another, the class must have default visibility. Otherwise the two shared objects will be unable to use the same typeinfo node and exception handling will break.

5.35.1 ARM Type Attributes

On those ARM targets that support `dllimport` (such as Symbian OS), you can use the `notshared` attribute to indicate that the virtual table and other similar data for a class should not be exported from a DLL. For example:

```
class __declspec(notshared) C {
public:
  __declspec(dllimport) C();
  virtual void f();
}

__declspec(dllexport)
C::C() {}
```

In this code, `C::C` is exported from the current DLL, but the virtual table for C is not exported. (You can use `__attribute__` instead of `__declspec` if you prefer, but most Symbian OS code uses `__declspec`.)

5.35.2 i386 Type Attributes

Two attributes are currently defined for i386 configurations: `ms_struct` and `gcc_struct`.

`ms_struct`
`gcc_struct`

> If `packed` is used on a structure, or if bit-fields are used it may be that the Microsoft ABI packs them differently than GCC would normally pack them. Particularly when moving packed data between functions compiled with GCC and the native Microsoft compiler (either via function call or as data in a file), it may be necessary to access either format.
>
> Currently '-m[no-]ms-bitfields' is provided for the Microsoft Windows X86 compilers to match the native Microsoft compiler.

To specify multiple attributes, separate them by commas within the double parentheses: for example, '`__attribute__ ((aligned (16), packed))`'.

5.35.3 PowerPC Type Attributes

Three attributes currently are defined for PowerPC configurations: `altivec`, `ms_struct` and `gcc_struct`.

For full documentation of the struct attributes please see the documentation in the See [i386 Type Attributes], page 298, section.

The `altivec` attribute allows one to declare AltiVec vector data types supported by the AltiVec Programming Interface Manual. The attribute requires an argument to specify one of three vector types: `vector__`, `pixel__` (always followed by unsigned short), and `bool__` (always followed by unsigned).

```
__attribute__((altivec(vector__)))
__attribute__((altivec(pixel__))) unsigned short
__attribute__((altivec(bool__))) unsigned
```

These attributes mainly are intended to support the `__vector`, `__pixel`, and `__bool` AltiVec keywords.

5.35.4 SPU Type Attributes

The SPU supports the `spu_vector` attribute for types. This attribute allows one to declare vector data types supported by the Sony/Toshiba/IBM SPU Language Extensions Specification. It is intended to support the `__vector` keyword.

5.36 An Inline Function is As Fast As a Macro

By declaring a function inline, you can direct GCC to make calls to that function faster. One way GCC can achieve this is to integrate that function's code into the code for its callers. This makes execution faster by eliminating the function-call overhead; in addition, if any of the actual argument values are constant, their known values may permit simplifications at compile time so that not all of the inline function's code needs to be included. The effect on code size is less predictable; object code may be larger or smaller with function inlining, depending on the particular case. You can also direct GCC to try to integrate all "simple enough" functions into their callers with the option '-finline-functions'.

GCC implements three different semantics of declaring a function inline. One is available with '-std=gnu89' or '-fgnu89-inline' or when `gnu_inline` attribute is present on all inline declarations, another when '-std=c99' or '-std=gnu99' (without '-fgnu89-inline'), and the third is used when compiling C++.

To declare a function inline, use the `inline` keyword in its declaration, like this:

```
static inline int
inc (int *a)
{
  (*a)++;
}
```

If you are writing a header file to be included in ISO C89 programs, write `__inline__` instead of `inline`. See Section 5.41 [Alternate Keywords], page 329.

The three types of inlining behave similarly in two important cases: when the `inline` keyword is used on a `static` function, like the example above, and when a function is first declared without using the `inline` keyword and then is defined with `inline`, like this:

```
extern int inc (int *a);
inline int
inc (int *a)
{
  (*a)++;
}
```

In both of these common cases, the program behaves the same as if you had not used the `inline` keyword, except for its speed.

When a function is both inline and `static`, if all calls to the function are integrated into the caller, and the function's address is never used, then the function's own assembler code is never referenced. In this case, GCC does not actually output assembler code for the function, unless you specify the option '-fkeep-inline-functions'. Some calls cannot be integrated for various reasons (in particular, calls that precede the function's definition cannot be integrated, and neither can recursive calls within the definition). If there is a nonintegrated call, then the function is compiled to assembler code as usual. The function must also be compiled as usual if the program refers to its address, because that can't be inlined.

Note that certain usages in a function definition can make it unsuitable for inline substitution. Among these usages are: use of varargs, use of alloca, use of variable sized data types (see Section 5.16 [Variable Length], page 258), use of computed goto (see Section 5.3 [Labels as Values], page 247), use of nonlocal goto, and nested functions (see Section 5.4 [Nested Functions], page 248). Using '-Winline' will warn when a function marked `inline` could not be substituted, and will give the reason for the failure.

As required by ISO C++, GCC considers member functions defined within the body of a class to be marked inline even if they are not explicitly declared with the `inline` keyword. You can override this with '-fno-default-inline'; see Section 3.5 [Options Controlling C++ Dialect], page 31.

GCC does not inline any functions when not optimizing unless you specify the 'always_inline' attribute for the function, like this:

```
/* Prototype.  */
inline void foo (const char) __attribute__((always_inline));
```

The remainder of this section is specific to GNU C89 inlining.

When an inline function is not `static`, then the compiler must assume that there may be calls from other source files; since a global symbol can be defined only once in any program, the function must not be defined in the other source files, so the calls therein cannot be integrated. Therefore, a non-`static` inline function is always compiled on its own in the usual fashion.

If you specify both `inline` and `extern` in the function definition, then the definition is used only for inlining. In no case is the function compiled on its own, not even if you refer to its address explicitly. Such an address becomes an external reference, as if you had only declared the function, and had not defined it.

This combination of `inline` and `extern` has almost the effect of a macro. The way to use it is to put a function definition in a header file with these keywords, and put another copy of the definition (lacking `inline` and `extern`) in a library file. The definition in the header file will cause most calls to the function to be inlined. If any uses of the function remain, they will refer to the single copy in the library.

5.37 Assembler Instructions with C Expression Operands

In an assembler instruction using `asm`, you can specify the operands of the instruction using C expressions. This means you need not guess which registers or memory locations will contain the data you want to use.

You must specify an assembler instruction template much like what appears in a machine description, plus an operand constraint string for each operand.

For example, here is how to use the 68881's `fsinx` instruction:

```
asm ("fsinx %1,%0" : "=f" (result) : "f" (angle));
```

Here `angle` is the C expression for the input operand while `result` is that of the output operand. Each has '"f"' as its operand constraint, saying that a floating point register is required. The '=' in '=f' indicates that the operand is an output; all output operands' constraints must use '='. The constraints use the same language used in the machine description (see Section 5.38 [Constraints], page 306).

Each operand is described by an operand-constraint string followed by the C expression in parentheses. A colon separates the assembler template from the first output operand and

Chapter 5: Extensions to the C Language Family   301

another separates the last output operand from the first input, if any. Commas separate the operands within each group. The total number of operands is currently limited to 30; this limitation may be lifted in some future version of GCC.

If there are no output operands but there are input operands, you must place two consecutive colons surrounding the place where the output operands would go.

As of GCC version 3.1, it is also possible to specify input and output operands using symbolic names which can be referenced within the assembler code. These names are specified inside square brackets preceding the constraint string, and can be referenced inside the assembler code using %[name] instead of a percentage sign followed by the operand number. Using named operands the above example could look like:

```
asm ("fsinx %[angle],%[output]"
     : [output] "=f" (result)
     : [angle] "f" (angle));
```

Note that the symbolic operand names have no relation whatsoever to other C identifiers. You may use any name you like, even those of existing C symbols, but you must ensure that no two operands within the same assembler construct use the same symbolic name.

Output operand expressions must be lvalues; the compiler can check this. The input operands need not be lvalues. The compiler cannot check whether the operands have data types that are reasonable for the instruction being executed. It does not parse the assembler instruction template and does not know what it means or even whether it is valid assembler input. The extended **asm** feature is most often used for machine instructions the compiler itself does not know exist. If the output expression cannot be directly addressed (for example, it is a bit-field), your constraint must allow a register. In that case, GCC will use the register as the output of the **asm**, and then store that register into the output.

The ordinary output operands must be write-only; GCC will assume that the values in these operands before the instruction are dead and need not be generated. Extended asm supports input-output or read-write operands. Use the constraint character '+' to indicate such an operand and list it with the output operands. You should only use read-write operands when the constraints for the operand (or the operand in which only some of the bits are to be changed) allow a register.

You may, as an alternative, logically split its function into two separate operands, one input operand and one write-only output operand. The connection between them is expressed by constraints which say they need to be in the same location when the instruction executes. You can use the same C expression for both operands, or different expressions. For example, here we write the (fictitious) '**combine**' instruction with **bar** as its read-only source operand and **foo** as its read-write destination:

```
asm ("combine %2,%0" : "=r" (foo) : "0" (foo), "g" (bar));
```

The constraint '"0"' for operand 1 says that it must occupy the same location as operand 0. A number in constraint is allowed only in an input operand and it must refer to an output operand.

Only a number in the constraint can guarantee that one operand will be in the same place as another. The mere fact that **foo** is the value of both operands is not enough to guarantee that they will be in the same place in the generated assembler code. The following would not work reliably:

```
asm ("combine %2,%0" : "=r" (foo) : "r" (foo), "g" (bar));
```

Various optimizations or reloading could cause operands 0 and 1 to be in different registers; GCC knows no reason not to do so. For example, the compiler might find a copy of the value of foo in one register and use it for operand 1, but generate the output operand 0 in a different register (copying it afterward to foo's own address). Of course, since the register for operand 1 is not even mentioned in the assembler code, the result will not work, but GCC can't tell that.

As of GCC version 3.1, one may write [*name*] instead of the operand number for a matching constraint. For example:

```
asm ("cmoveq %1,%2,%[result]"
     : [result] "=r"(result)
     : "r" (test), "r"(new), "[result]"(old));
```

Sometimes you need to make an asm operand be a specific register, but there's no matching constraint letter for that register *by itself*. To force the operand into that register, use a local variable for the operand and specify the register in the variable declaration. See Section 5.40 [Explicit Reg Vars], page 327. Then for the asm operand, use any register constraint letter that matches the register:

```
register int *p1 asm ("r0") = ...;
register int *p2 asm ("r1") = ...;
register int *result asm ("r0");
asm ("sysint" : "=r" (result) : "0" (p1), "r" (p2));
```

In the above example, beware that a register that is call-clobbered by the target ABI will be overwritten by any function call in the assignment, including library calls for arithmetic operators. Assuming it is a call-clobbered register, this may happen to r0 above by the assignment to p2. If you have to use such a register, use temporary variables for expressions between the register assignment and use:

```
int t1 = ...;
register int *p1 asm ("r0") = ...;
register int *p2 asm ("r1") = t1;
register int *result asm ("r0");
asm ("sysint" : "=r" (result) : "0" (p1), "r" (p2));
```

Some instructions clobber specific hard registers. To describe this, write a third colon after the input operands, followed by the names of the clobbered hard registers (given as strings). Here is a realistic example for the VAX:

```
asm volatile ("movc3 %0,%1,%2"
              : /* no outputs */
              : "g" (from), "g" (to), "g" (count)
              : "r0", "r1", "r2", "r3", "r4", "r5");
```

You may not write a clobber description in a way that overlaps with an input or output operand. For example, you may not have an operand describing a register class with one member if you mention that register in the clobber list. Variables declared to live in specific registers (see Section 5.40 [Explicit Reg Vars], page 327), and used as asm input or output operands must have no part mentioned in the clobber description. There is no way for you to specify that an input operand is modified without also specifying it as an output operand. Note that if all the output operands you specify are for this purpose (and hence unused), you will then also need to specify volatile for the asm construct, as described below, to prevent GCC from deleting the asm statement as unused.

If you refer to a particular hardware register from the assembler code, you will probably have to list the register after the third colon to tell the compiler the register's value is

Chapter 5: Extensions to the C Language Family   303

modified. In some assemblers, the register names begin with '%'; to produce one '%' in the assembler code, you must write '%%' in the input.

If your assembler instruction can alter the condition code register, add 'cc' to the list of clobbered registers. GCC on some machines represents the condition codes as a specific hardware register; 'cc' serves to name this register. On other machines, the condition code is handled differently, and specifying 'cc' has no effect. But it is valid no matter what the machine.

If your assembler instructions access memory in an unpredictable fashion, add 'memory' to the list of clobbered registers. This will cause GCC to not keep memory values cached in registers across the assembler instruction and not optimize stores or loads to that memory. You will also want to add the **volatile** keyword if the memory affected is not listed in the inputs or outputs of the **asm**, as the 'memory' clobber does not count as a side-effect of the **asm**. If you know how large the accessed memory is, you can add it as input or output but if this is not known, you should add 'memory'. As an example, if you access ten bytes of a string, you can use a memory input like:

```
{"m"( ({ struct { char x[10]; } *p = (void *)ptr ; *p; }) )}.
```

Note that in the following example the memory input is necessary, otherwise GCC might optimize the store to x away:

```
int foo ()
{
  int x = 42;
  int *y = &x;
  int result;
  asm ("magic stuff accessing an 'int' pointed to by '%1'"
        "=&d" (r) : "a" (y), "m" (*y));
  return result;
}
```

You can put multiple assembler instructions together in a single **asm** template, separated by the characters normally used in assembly code for the system. A combination that works in most places is a newline to break the line, plus a tab character to move to the instruction field (written as '\n\t'). Sometimes semicolons can be used, if the assembler allows semicolons as a line-breaking character. Note that some assembler dialects use semicolons to start a comment. The input operands are guaranteed not to use any of the clobbered registers, and neither will the output operands' addresses, so you can read and write the clobbered registers as many times as you like. Here is an example of multiple instructions in a template; it assumes the subroutine _foo accepts arguments in registers 9 and 10:

```
asm ("movl %0,r9\n\tmovl %1,r10\n\tcall _foo"
     : /* no outputs */
     : "g" (from), "g" (to)
     : "r9", "r10");
```

Unless an output operand has the '&' constraint modifier, GCC may allocate it in the same register as an unrelated input operand, on the assumption the inputs are consumed before the outputs are produced. This assumption may be false if the assembler code actually consists of more than one instruction. In such a case, use '&' for each output operand that may not overlap an input. See Section 5.38.3 [Modifiers], page 309.

If you want to test the condition code produced by an assembler instruction, you must include a branch and a label in the **asm** construct, as follows:

```
asm ("clr %0\n\tfrob %1\n\tbeq 0f\n\tmov #1,%0\n0:"
    : "g" (result)
    : "g" (input));
```

This assumes your assembler supports local labels, as the GNU assembler and most Unix assemblers do.

Speaking of labels, jumps from one `asm` to another are not supported. The compiler's optimizers do not know about these jumps, and therefore they cannot take account of them when deciding how to optimize.

Usually the most convenient way to use these `asm` instructions is to encapsulate them in macros that look like functions. For example,

```
#define sin(x)       \
({ double __value, __arg = (x);   \
   asm ("fsinx %1,%0": "=f" (__value): "f" (__arg));   \
   __value; })
```

Here the variable `__arg` is used to make sure that the instruction operates on a proper `double` value, and to accept only those arguments `x` which can convert automatically to a `double`.

Another way to make sure the instruction operates on the correct data type is to use a cast in the `asm`. This is different from using a variable `__arg` in that it converts more different types. For example, if the desired type were `int`, casting the argument to `int` would accept a pointer with no complaint, while assigning the argument to an `int` variable named `__arg` would warn about using a pointer unless the caller explicitly casts it.

If an `asm` has output operands, GCC assumes for optimization purposes the instruction has no side effects except to change the output operands. This does not mean instructions with a side effect cannot be used, but you must be careful, because the compiler may eliminate them if the output operands aren't used, or move them out of loops, or replace two with one if they constitute a common subexpression. Also, if your instruction does have a side effect on a variable that otherwise appears not to change, the old value of the variable may be reused later if it happens to be found in a register.

You can prevent an `asm` instruction from being deleted by writing the keyword `volatile` after the `asm`. For example:

```
#define get_and_set_priority(new)            \
({ int __old;                                \
   asm volatile ("get_and_set_priority %0, %1" \
                 : "=g" (__old) : "g" (new));  \
   __old; })
```

The `volatile` keyword indicates that the instruction has important side-effects. GCC will not delete a volatile `asm` if it is reachable. (The instruction can still be deleted if GCC can prove that control-flow will never reach the location of the instruction.) Note that even a volatile `asm` instruction can be moved relative to other code, including across jump instructions. For example, on many targets there is a system register which can be set to control the rounding mode of floating point operations. You might try setting it with a volatile `asm`, like this PowerPC example:

```
        asm volatile("mtfsf 255,%0" : : "f" (fpenv));
        sum = x + y;
```

Chapter 5: Extensions to the C Language Family   305

This will not work reliably, as the compiler may move the addition back before the volatile
asm. To make it work you need to add an artificial dependency to the **asm** referencing a
variable in the code you don't want moved, for example:

```
asm volatile ("mtfsf 255,%1" : "=X"(sum): "f"(fpenv));
sum = x + y;
```

Similarly, you can't expect a sequence of volatile **asm** instructions to remain perfectly
consecutive. If you want consecutive output, use a single **asm**. Also, GCC will perform
some optimizations across a volatile **asm** instruction; GCC does not "forget everything"
when it encounters a volatile **asm** instruction the way some other compilers do.

An **asm** instruction without any output operands will be treated identically to a volatile
asm instruction.

It is a natural idea to look for a way to give access to the condition code left by the
assembler instruction. However, when we attempted to implement this, we found no way
to make it work reliably. The problem is that output operands might need reloading,
which would result in additional following "store" instructions. On most machines, these
instructions would alter the condition code before there was time to test it. This problem
doesn't arise for ordinary "test" and "compare" instructions because they don't have any
output operands.

For reasons similar to those described above, it is not possible to give an assembler
instruction access to the condition code left by previous instructions.

If you are writing a header file that should be includable in ISO C programs, write
__asm__ instead of **asm**. See Section 5.41 [Alternate Keywords], page 329.

5.37.1 Size of an asm

Some targets require that GCC track the size of each instruction used in order to generate
correct code. Because the final length of an **asm** is only known by the assembler, GCC
must make an estimate as to how big it will be. The estimate is formed by counting the
number of statements in the pattern of the **asm** and multiplying that by the length of
the longest instruction on that processor. Statements in the **asm** are identified by newline
characters and whatever statement separator characters are supported by the assembler; on
most processors this is the ';' character.

Normally, GCC's estimate is perfectly adequate to ensure that correct code is generated,
but it is possible to confuse the compiler if you use pseudo instructions or assembler macros
that expand into multiple real instructions or if you use assembler directives that expand to
more space in the object file than would be needed for a single instruction. If this happens
then the assembler will produce a diagnostic saying that a label is unreachable.

5.37.2 i386 floating point asm operands

There are several rules on the usage of stack-like regs in asm_operands insns. These rules
apply only to the operands that are stack-like regs:

1. Given a set of input regs that die in an asm_operands, it is necessary to know which
   are implicitly popped by the asm, and which must be explicitly popped by gcc.

   An input reg that is implicitly popped by the asm must be explicitly clobbered, unless
   it is constrained to match an output operand.

2. For any input reg that is implicitly popped by an asm, it is necessary to know how to adjust the stack to compensate for the pop. If any non-popped input is closer to the top of the reg-stack than the implicitly popped reg, it would not be possible to know what the stack looked like—it's not clear how the rest of the stack "slides up".

   All implicitly popped input regs must be closer to the top of the reg-stack than any input that is not implicitly popped.

   It is possible that if an input dies in an insn, reload might use the input reg for an output reload. Consider this example:

   ```
   asm ("foo" : "=t" (a) : "f" (b));
   ```

   This asm says that input B is not popped by the asm, and that the asm pushes a result onto the reg-stack, i.e., the stack is one deeper after the asm than it was before. But, it is possible that reload will think that it can use the same reg for both the input and the output, if input B dies in this insn.

   If any input operand uses the f constraint, all output reg constraints must use the & earlyclobber.

   The asm above would be written as

   ```
   asm ("foo" : "=&t" (a) : "f" (b));
   ```

3. Some operands need to be in particular places on the stack. All output operands fall in this category—there is no other way to know which regs the outputs appear in unless the user indicates this in the constraints.

   Output operands must specifically indicate which reg an output appears in after an asm. =f is not allowed: the operand constraints must select a class with a single reg.

4. Output operands may not be "inserted" between existing stack regs. Since no 387 opcode uses a read/write operand, all output operands are dead before the asm_operands, and are pushed by the asm_operands. It makes no sense to push anywhere but the top of the reg-stack.

   Output operands must start at the top of the reg-stack: output operands may not "skip" a reg.

5. Some asm statements may need extra stack space for internal calculations. This can be guaranteed by clobbering stack registers unrelated to the inputs and outputs.

Here are a couple of reasonable asms to want to write. This asm takes one input, which is internally popped, and produces two outputs.

```
asm ("fsincos" : "=t" (cos), "=u" (sin) : "0" (inp));
```

This asm takes two inputs, which are popped by the fyl2xp1 opcode, and replaces them with one output. The user must code the st(1) clobber for reg-stack.c to know that fyl2xp1 pops both inputs.

```
asm ("fyl2xp1" : "=t" (result) : "0" (x), "u" (y) : "st(1)");
```

5.38 Constraints for asm Operands

Here are specific details on what constraint letters you can use with asm operands. Constraints can say whether an operand may be in a register, and which kinds of register; whether the operand can be a memory reference, and which kinds of address; whether the operand may be an immediate constant, and which possible values it may have. Constraints can also require two operands to match.

Chapter 5: Extensions to the C Language Family 307

5.38.1 Simple Constraints

The simplest kind of constraint is a string full of letters, each of which describes one kind of operand that is permitted. Here are the letters that are allowed:

whitespace
> Whitespace characters are ignored and can be inserted at any position except the first. This enables each alternative for different operands to be visually aligned in the machine description even if they have different number of constraints and modifiers.

'm'
> A memory operand is allowed, with any kind of address that the machine supports in general.

'o'
> A memory operand is allowed, but only if the address is *offsettable*. This means that adding a small integer (actually, the width in bytes of the operand, as determined by its machine mode) may be added to the address and the result is also a valid memory address.
>
> For example, an address which is constant is offsettable; so is an address that is the sum of a register and a constant (as long as a slightly larger constant is also within the range of address-offsets supported by the machine); but an autoincrement or autodecrement address is not offsettable. More complicated indirect/indexed addresses may or may not be offsettable depending on the other addressing modes that the machine supports.
>
> Note that in an output operand which can be matched by another operand, the constraint letter 'o' is valid only when accompanied by both '<' (if the target machine has predecrement addressing) and '>' (if the target machine has preincrement addressing).

'V'
> A memory operand that is not offsettable. In other words, anything that would fit the 'm' constraint but not the 'o' constraint.

'<'
> A memory operand with autodecrement addressing (either predecrement or postdecrement) is allowed.

'>'
> A memory operand with autoincrement addressing (either preincrement or postincrement) is allowed.

'r'
> A register operand is allowed provided that it is in a general register.

'i'
> An immediate integer operand (one with constant value) is allowed. This includes symbolic constants whose values will be known only at assembly time or later.

'n'
> An immediate integer operand with a known numeric value is allowed. Many systems cannot support assembly-time constants for operands less than a word wide. Constraints for these operands should use 'n' rather than 'i'.

'I', 'J', 'K', ... 'P'
> Other letters in the range 'I' through 'P' may be defined in a machine-dependent fashion to permit immediate integer operands with explicit integer values in specified ranges. For example, on the 68000, 'I' is defined to stand for the range of values 1 to 8. This is the range permitted as a shift count in the shift instructions.

'E' An immediate floating operand (expression code `const_double`) is allowed, but only if the target floating point format is the same as that of the host machine (on which the compiler is running).

'F' An immediate floating operand (expression code `const_double` or `const_vector`) is allowed.

'G', 'H' 'G' and 'H' may be defined in a machine-dependent fashion to permit immediate floating operands in particular ranges of values.

's' An immediate integer operand whose value is not an explicit integer is allowed.

This might appear strange; if an insn allows a constant operand with a value not known at compile time, it certainly must allow any known value. So why use 's' instead of 'i'? Sometimes it allows better code to be generated.

For example, on the 68000 in a fullword instruction it is possible to use an immediate operand; but if the immediate value is between -128 and 127, better code results from loading the value into a register and using the register. This is because the load into the register can be done with a 'moveq' instruction. We arrange for this to happen by defining the letter 'K' to mean "any integer outside the range -128 to 127", and then specifying 'Ks' in the operand constraints.

'g' Any register, memory or immediate integer operand is allowed, except for registers that are not general registers.

'X' Any operand whatsoever is allowed.

'0', '1', '2', ... '9'
An operand that matches the specified operand number is allowed. If a digit is used together with letters within the same alternative, the digit should come last.

This number is allowed to be more than a single digit. If multiple digits are encountered consecutively, they are interpreted as a single decimal integer. There is scant chance for ambiguity, since to-date it has never been desirable that '10' be interpreted as matching either operand 1 *or* operand 0. Should this be desired, one can use multiple alternatives instead.

This is called a *matching constraint* and what it really means is that the assembler has only a single operand that fills two roles which `asm` distinguishes. For example, an add instruction uses two input operands and an output operand, but on most CISC machines an add instruction really has only two operands, one of them an input-output operand:

```
addl #35,r12
```

Matching constraints are used in these circumstances. More precisely, the two operands that match must include one input-only operand and one output-only operand. Moreover, the digit must be a smaller number than the number of the operand that uses it in the constraint.

'p' An operand that is a valid memory address is allowed. This is for "load address" and "push address" instructions.

'p' in the constraint must be accompanied by `address_operand` as the predicate in the `match_operand`. This predicate interprets the mode specified in the

Chapter 5: Extensions to the C Language Family   309

> `match_operand` as the mode of the memory reference for which the address would be valid.

other-letters
> Other letters can be defined in machine-dependent fashion to stand for particular classes of registers or other arbitrary operand types. 'd', 'a' and 'f' are defined on the 68000/68020 to stand for data, address and floating point registers.

5.38.2 Multiple Alternative Constraints

Sometimes a single instruction has multiple alternative sets of possible operands. For example, on the 68000, a logical-or instruction can combine register or an immediate value into memory, or it can combine any kind of operand into a register; but it cannot combine one memory location into another.

These constraints are represented as multiple alternatives. An alternative can be described by a series of letters for each operand. The overall constraint for an operand is made from the letters for this operand from the first alternative, a comma, the letters for this operand from the second alternative, a comma, and so on until the last alternative.

If all the operands fit any one alternative, the instruction is valid. Otherwise, for each alternative, the compiler counts how many instructions must be added to copy the operands so that that alternative applies. The alternative requiring the least copying is chosen. If two alternatives need the same amount of copying, the one that comes first is chosen. These choices can be altered with the '?' and '!' characters:

?
> Disparage slightly the alternative that the '?' appears in, as a choice when no alternative applies exactly. The compiler regards this alternative as one unit more costly for each '?' that appears in it.

!
> Disparage severely the alternative that the '!' appears in. This alternative can still be used if it fits without reloading, but if reloading is needed, some other alternative will be used.

5.38.3 Constraint Modifier Characters

Here are constraint modifier characters.

'='
> Means that this operand is write-only for this instruction: the previous value is discarded and replaced by output data.

'+'
> Means that this operand is both read and written by the instruction.
>
> When the compiler fixes up the operands to satisfy the constraints, it needs to know which operands are inputs to the instruction and which are outputs from it. '=' identifies an output; '+' identifies an operand that is both input and output; all other operands are assumed to be input only.
>
> If you specify '=' or '+' in a constraint, you put it in the first character of the constraint string.

'&'
> Means (in a particular alternative) that this operand is an *earlyclobber* operand, which is modified before the instruction is finished using the input operands.

Therefore, this operand may not lie in a register that is used as an input operand or as part of any memory address.

'&' applies only to the alternative in which it is written. In constraints with multiple alternatives, sometimes one alternative requires '&' while others do not. See, for example, the 'movdf' insn of the 68000.

An input operand can be tied to an earlyclobber operand if its only use as an input occurs before the early result is written. Adding alternatives of this form often allows GCC to produce better code when only some of the inputs can be affected by the earlyclobber. See, for example, the 'mulsi3' insn of the ARM.

'&' does not obviate the need to write '='.

'%' Declares the instruction to be commutative for this operand and the following operand. This means that the compiler may interchange the two operands if that is the cheapest way to make all operands fit the constraints. GCC can only handle one commutative pair in an asm; if you use more, the compiler may fail. Note that you need not use the modifier if the two alternatives are strictly identical; this would only waste time in the reload pass. The modifier is not operational after register allocation, so the result of define_peephole2 and define_splits performed after reload cannot rely on '%' to make the intended insn match.

'#' Says that all following characters, up to the next comma, are to be ignored as a constraint. They are significant only for choosing register preferences.

'*' Says that the following character should be ignored when choosing register preferences. '*' has no effect on the meaning of the constraint as a constraint, and no effect on reloading.

5.38.4 Constraints for Particular Machines

Whenever possible, you should use the general-purpose constraint letters in asm arguments, since they will convey meaning more readily to people reading your code. Failing that, use the constraint letters that usually have very similar meanings across architectures. The most commonly used constraints are 'm' and 'r' (for memory and general-purpose registers respectively; see Section 5.38.1 [Simple Constraints], page 307), and 'I', usually the letter indicating the most common immediate-constant format.

Each architecture defines additional constraints. These constraints are used by the compiler itself for instruction generation, as well as for asm statements; therefore, some of the constraints are not particularly useful for asm. Here is a summary of some of the machine-dependent constraints available on some particular machines; it includes both constraints that are useful for asm and constraints that aren't. The compiler source file mentioned in the table heading for each architecture is the definitive reference for the meanings of that architecture's constraints.

ARM family—'config/arm/arm.h'

f   Floating-point register

w   VFP floating-point register

F   One of the floating-point constants 0.0, 0.5, 1.0, 2.0, 3.0, 4.0, 5.0 or 10.0

Chapter 5: Extensions to the C Language Family   311

G	Floating-point constant that would satisfy the constraint 'F' if it were negated
I	Integer that is valid as an immediate operand in a data processing instruction. That is, an integer in the range 0 to 255 rotated by a multiple of 2
J	Integer in the range −4095 to 4095
K	Integer that satisfies constraint 'I' when inverted (ones complement)
L	Integer that satisfies constraint 'I' when negated (twos complement)
M	Integer in the range 0 to 32
Q	A memory reference where the exact address is in a single register ("m" is preferable for asm statements)
R	An item in the constant pool
S	A symbol in the text segment of the current file
Uv	A memory reference suitable for VFP load/store insns (reg+constant offset)
Uy	A memory reference suitable for iWMMXt load/store instructions.
Uq	A memory reference suitable for the ARMv4 ldrsb instruction.

AVR family—'config/avr/constraints.md'

l	Registers from r0 to r15
a	Registers from r16 to r23
d	Registers from r16 to r31
w	Registers from r24 to r31. These registers can be used in 'adiw' command
e	Pointer register (r26–r31)
b	Base pointer register (r28–r31)
q	Stack pointer register (SPH:SPL)
t	Temporary register r0
x	Register pair X (r27:r26)
y	Register pair Y (r29:r28)
z	Register pair Z (r31:r30)
I	Constant greater than −1, less than 64
J	Constant greater than −64, less than 1
K	Constant integer 2

L	Constant integer 0
M	Constant that fits in 8 bits
N	Constant integer −1
O	Constant integer 8, 16, or 24
P	Constant integer 1
G	A floating point constant 0.0
R	Integer constant in the range -6 ... 5.
Q	A memory address based on Y or Z pointer with displacement.

CRX Architecture—'config/crx/crx.h'

b	Registers from r0 to r14 (registers without stack pointer)
l	Register r16 (64-bit accumulator lo register)
h	Register r17 (64-bit accumulator hi register)
k	Register pair r16-r17. (64-bit accumulator lo-hi pair)
I	Constant that fits in 3 bits
J	Constant that fits in 4 bits
K	Constant that fits in 5 bits
L	Constant that is one of -1, 4, -4, 7, 8, 12, 16, 20, 32, 48
G	Floating point constant that is legal for store immediate

Hewlett-Packard PA-RISC—'config/pa/pa.h'

a	General register 1
f	Floating point register
q	Shift amount register
x	Floating point register (deprecated)
y	Upper floating point register (32-bit), floating point register (64-bit)
Z	Any register
I	Signed 11-bit integer constant
J	Signed 14-bit integer constant
K	Integer constant that can be deposited with a `zdepi` instruction
L	Signed 5-bit integer constant
M	Integer constant 0
N	Integer constant that can be loaded with a `ldil` instruction
O	Integer constant whose value plus one is a power of 2

Chapter 5: Extensions to the C Language Family   313

P	Integer constant that can be used for **and** operations in **depi** and **extru** instructions
S	Integer constant 31
U	Integer constant 63
G	Floating-point constant 0.0
A	A `lo_sum` data-linkage-table memory operand
Q	A memory operand that can be used as the destination operand of an integer store instruction
R	A scaled or unscaled indexed memory operand
T	A memory operand for floating-point loads and stores
W	A register indirect memory operand

PowerPC and IBM RS6000—'config/rs6000/rs6000.h'

b	Address base register
f	Floating point register
v	Vector register
h	'MQ', 'CTR', or 'LINK' register
q	'MQ' register
c	'CTR' register
l	'LINK' register
x	'CR' register (condition register) number 0
y	'CR' register (condition register)
z	'FPMEM' stack memory for FPR-GPR transfers
I	Signed 16-bit constant
J	Unsigned 16-bit constant shifted left 16 bits (use 'L' instead for **SImode** constants)
K	Unsigned 16-bit constant
L	Signed 16-bit constant shifted left 16 bits
M	Constant larger than 31
N	Exact power of 2
O	Zero
P	Constant whose negation is a signed 16-bit constant
G	Floating point constant that can be loaded into a register with one instruction per word
H	Integer/Floating point constant that can be loaded into a register using three instructions

Q	Memory operand that is an offset from a register ('m' is preferable for asm statements)
Z	Memory operand that is an indexed or indirect from a register ('m' is preferable for asm statements)
R	AIX TOC entry
a	Address operand that is an indexed or indirect from a register ('p' is preferable for asm statements)
S	Constant suitable as a 64-bit mask operand
T	Constant suitable as a 32-bit mask operand
U	System V Release 4 small data area reference
t	AND masks that can be performed by two rldic{l, r} instructions
W	Vector constant that does not require memory

MorphoTech family—'config/mt/mt.h'

I	Constant for an arithmetic insn (16-bit signed integer).
J	The constant 0.
K	Constant for a logical insn (16-bit zero-extended integer).
L	A constant that can be loaded with lui (i.e. the bottom 16 bits are zero).
M	A constant that takes two words to load (i.e. not matched by I, K, or L).
N	Negative 16-bit constants other than -65536.
O	A 15-bit signed integer constant.
P	A positive 16-bit constant.

Intel 386—'config/i386/constraints.md'

R	Legacy register—the eight integer registers available on all i386 processors (a, b, c, d, si, di, bp, sp).
q	Any register accessible as rl. In 32-bit mode, a, b, c, and d; in 64-bit mode, any integer register.
Q	Any register accessible as rh: a, b, c, and d.
a	The a register.
b	The b register.
c	The c register.
d	The d register.
S	The si register.
D	The di register.

Chapter 5: Extensions to the C Language Family   315

A		The a and d registers, as a pair (for instructions that return half the result in one and half in the other).
f		Any 80387 floating-point (stack) register.
t		Top of 80387 floating-point stack (%st(0)).
u		Second from top of 80387 floating-point stack (%st(1)).
y		Any MMX register.
x		Any SSE register.
Yz		First SSE register (%xmm0).
I		Integer constant in the range 0 ... 31, for 32-bit shifts.
J		Integer constant in the range 0 ... 63, for 64-bit shifts.
K		Signed 8-bit integer constant.
L		0xFF or 0xFFFF, for andsi as a zero-extending move.
M		0, 1, 2, or 3 (shifts for the lea instruction).
N		Unsigned 8-bit integer constant (for in and out instructions).
G		Standard 80387 floating point constant.
C		Standard SSE floating point constant.
e		32-bit signed integer constant, or a symbolic reference known to fit that range (for immediate operands in sign-extending x86-64 instructions).
Z		32-bit unsigned integer constant, or a symbolic reference known to fit that range (for immediate operands in zero-extending x86-64 instructions).

Intel IA-64—'config/ia64/ia64.h'

a	General register r0 to r3 for addl instruction
b	Branch register
c	Predicate register ('c' as in "conditional")
d	Application register residing in M-unit
e	Application register residing in I-unit
f	Floating-point register
m	Memory operand. Remember that 'm' allows postincrement and postdecrement which require printing with '%Pn' on IA-64. Use 'S' to disallow postincrement and postdecrement.
G	Floating-point constant 0.0 or 1.0
I	14-bit signed integer constant
J	22-bit signed integer constant

K	8-bit signed integer constant for logical instructions
L	8-bit adjusted signed integer constant for compare pseudo-ops
M	6-bit unsigned integer constant for shift counts
N	9-bit signed integer constant for load and store postincrements
O	The constant zero
P	0 or −1 for dep instruction
Q	Non-volatile memory for floating-point loads and stores
R	Integer constant in the range 1 to 4 for shladd instruction
S	Memory operand except postincrement and postdecrement

FRV—'config/frv/frv.h'

a	Register in the class ACC_REGS (acc0 to acc7).
b	Register in the class EVEN_ACC_REGS (acc0 to acc7).
c	Register in the class CC_REGS (fcc0 to fcc3 and icc0 to icc3).
d	Register in the class GPR_REGS (gr0 to gr63).
e	Register in the class EVEN_REGS (gr0 to gr63). Odd registers are excluded not in the class but through the use of a machine mode larger than 4 bytes.
f	Register in the class FPR_REGS (fr0 to fr63).
h	Register in the class FEVEN_REGS (fr0 to fr63). Odd registers are excluded not in the class but through the use of a machine mode larger than 4 bytes.
l	Register in the class LR_REG (the lr register).
q	Register in the class QUAD_REGS (gr2 to gr63). Register numbers not divisible by 4 are excluded not in the class but through the use of a machine mode larger than 8 bytes.
t	Register in the class ICC_REGS (icc0 to icc3).
u	Register in the class FCC_REGS (fcc0 to fcc3).
v	Register in the class ICR_REGS (cc4 to cc7).
w	Register in the class FCR_REGS (cc0 to cc3).
x	Register in the class QUAD_FPR_REGS (fr0 to fr63). Register numbers not divisible by 4 are excluded not in the class but through the use of a machine mode larger than 8 bytes.
z	Register in the class SPR_REGS (lcr and lr).
A	Register in the class QUAD_ACC_REGS (acc0 to acc7).
B	Register in the class ACCG_REGS (accg0 to accg7).

Chapter 5: Extensions to the C Language Family   317

C		Register in the class `CR_REGS` (`cc0` to `cc7`).
G		Floating point constant zero
I		6-bit signed integer constant
J		10-bit signed integer constant
L		16-bit signed integer constant
M		16-bit unsigned integer constant
N		12-bit signed integer constant that is negative—i.e. in the range of -2048 to -1
O		Constant zero
P		12-bit signed integer constant that is greater than zero—i.e. in the range of 1 to 2047.

Blackfin family—'`config/bfin/bfin.h`'

a	P register
d	D register
z	A call clobbered P register.
q*n*	A single register. If *n* is in the range 0 to 7, the corresponding D register. If it is `A`, then the register P0.
D	Even-numbered D register
W	Odd-numbered D register
e	Accumulator register.
A	Even-numbered accumulator register.
B	Odd-numbered accumulator register.
b	I register
v	B register
f	M register
c	Registers used for circular buffering, i.e. I, B, or L registers.
C	The CC register.
t	LT0 or LT1.
k	LC0 or LC1.
u	LB0 or LB1.
x	Any D, P, B, M, I or L register.
y	Additional registers typically used only in prologues and epilogues: RETS, RETN, RETI, RETX, RETE, ASTAT, SEQSTAT and USP.
w	Any register except accumulators or CC.

Ksh	Signed 16 bit integer (in the range -32768 to 32767)
Kuh	Unsigned 16 bit integer (in the range 0 to 65535)
Ks7	Signed 7 bit integer (in the range -64 to 63)
Ku7	Unsigned 7 bit integer (in the range 0 to 127)
Ku5	Unsigned 5 bit integer (in the range 0 to 31)
Ks4	Signed 4 bit integer (in the range -8 to 7)
Ks3	Signed 3 bit integer (in the range -3 to 4)
Ku3	Unsigned 3 bit integer (in the range 0 to 7)
Pn	Constant n, where n is a single-digit constant in the range 0 to 4.
PA	An integer equal to one of the MACFLAG_XXX constants that is suitable for use with either accumulator.
PB	An integer equal to one of the MACFLAG_XXX constants that is suitable for use only with accumulator A1.
M1	Constant 255.
M2	Constant 65535.
J	An integer constant with exactly a single bit set.
L	An integer constant with all bits set except exactly one.
H	
Q	Any SYMBOL_REF.

M32C—'config/m32c/m32c.c'

Rsp	
Rfb	
Rsb	'$sp', '$fb', '$sb'.
Rcr	Any control register, when they're 16 bits wide (nothing if control registers are 24 bits wide)
Rcl	Any control register, when they're 24 bits wide.
R0w	
R1w	
R2w	
R3w	$r0, $r1, $r2, $r3.
R02	$r0 or $r2, or $r2r0 for 32 bit values.
R13	$r1 or $r3, or $r3r1 for 32 bit values.
Rdi	A register that can hold a 64 bit value.
Rhl	$r0 or $r1 (registers with addressable high/low bytes)
R23	$r2 or $r3

Chapter 5: Extensions to the C Language Family   319

Raa	Address registers
Raw	Address registers when they're 16 bits wide.
Ral	Address registers when they're 24 bits wide.
Rqi	Registers that can hold QI values.
Rad	Registers that can be used with displacements ($a0, $a1, $sb).
Rsi	Registers that can hold 32 bit values.
Rhi	Registers that can hold 16 bit values.
Rhc	Registers chat can hold 16 bit values, including all control registers.
Rra	$r0 through R1, plus $a0 and $a1.
Rfl	The flags register.
Rmm	The memory-based pseudo-registers $mem0 through $mem15.
Rpi	Registers that can hold pointers (16 bit registers for r8c, m16c; 24 bit registers for m32cm, m32c).
Rpa	Matches multiple registers in a PARALLEL to form a larger register. Used to match function return values.
Is3	-8 ... 7
IS1	-128 ... 127
IS2	-32768 ... 32767
IU2	0 ... 65535
In4	-8 ... -1 or 1 ... 8
In5	-16 ... -1 or 1 ... 16
In6	-32 ... -1 or 1 ... 32
IM2	-65536 ... -1
Ilb	An 8 bit value with exactly one bit set.
Ilw	A 16 bit value with exactly one bit set.
Sd	The common src/dest memory addressing modes.
Sa	Memory addressed using $a0 or $a1.
Si	Memory addressed with immediate addresses.
Ss	Memory addressed using the stack pointer ($sp).
Sf	Memory addressed using the frame base register ($fb).
Ss	Memory addressed using the small base register ($sb).
S1	$r1h

MIPS— 'config/mips/constraints.md'

d	An address register. This is equivalent to r unless generating MIPS16 code.

f	A floating-point register (if available).
h	The `hi` register.
l	The `lo` register.
x	The `hi` and `lo` registers.
c	A register suitable for use in an indirect jump. This will always be `$25` for '-mabicalls'.
v	Register `$3`. Do not use this constraint in new code; it is retained only for compatibility with glibc.
y	Equivalent to `r`; retained for backwards compatibility.
z	A floating-point condition code register.
I	A signed 16-bit constant (for arithmetic instructions).
J	Integer zero.
K	An unsigned 16-bit constant (for logic instructions).
L	A signed 32-bit constant in which the lower 16 bits are zero. Such constants can be loaded using `lui`.
M	A constant that cannot be loaded using `lui`, `addiu` or `ori`.
N	A constant in the range -65535 to -1 (inclusive).
O	A signed 15-bit constant.
P	A constant in the range 1 to 65535 (inclusive).
G	Floating-point zero.
R	An address that can be used in a non-macro load or store.

Motorola 680x0—'`config/m68k/constraints.md`'

a	Address register
d	Data register
f	68881 floating-point register, if available
I	Integer in the range 1 to 8
J	16-bit signed number
K	Signed number whose magnitude is greater than 0x80
L	Integer in the range −8 to −1
M	Signed number whose magnitude is greater than 0x100
N	Range 24 to 31, rotatert:SI 8 to 1 expressed as rotate
O	16 (for rotate using swap)
P	Range 8 to 15, rotatert:HI 8 to 1 expressed as rotate
R	Numbers that mov3q can handle

Chapter 5: Extensions to the C Language Family 321

G		Floating point constant that is not a 68881 constant
S		Operands that satisfy 'm' when -mpcrel is in effect
T		Operands that satisfy 's' when -mpcrel is not in effect
Q		Address register indirect addressing mode
U		Register offset addressing
W		const_call_operand
Cs		symbol_ref or const
Ci		const_int
C0		const_int 0
Cj		Range of signed numbers that don't fit in 16 bits
Cmvq		Integers valid for mvq
Capsw		Integers valid for a moveq followed by a swap
Cmvz		Integers valid for mvz
Cmvs		Integers valid for mvs
Ap		push_operand
Ac		Non-register operands allowed in clr

Motorola 68HC11 & 68HC12 families—'`config/m68hc11/m68hc11.h`'

a		Register 'a'
b		Register 'b'
d		Register 'd'
q		An 8-bit register
t		Temporary soft register _.tmp
u		A soft register _.d1 to _.d31
w		Stack pointer register
x		Register 'x'
y		Register 'y'
z		Pseudo register 'z' (replaced by 'x' or 'y' at the end)
A		An address register: x, y or z
B		An address register: x or y
D		Register pair (x:d) to form a 32-bit value
L		Constants in the range −65536 to 65535
M		Constants whose 16-bit low part is zero
N		Constant integer 1 or −1

O	Constant integer 16
P	Constants in the range −8 to 2

SPARC—`config/sparc/sparc.h`

f	Floating-point register on the SPARC-V8 architecture and lower floating-point register on the SPARC-V9 architecture.
e	Floating-point register. It is equivalent to 'f' on the SPARC-V8 architecture and contains both lower and upper floating-point registers on the SPARC-V9 architecture.
c	Floating-point condition code register.
d	Lower floating-point register. It is only valid on the SPARC-V9 architecture when the Visual Instruction Set is available.
b	Floating-point register. It is only valid on the SPARC-V9 architecture when the Visual Instruction Set is available.
h	64-bit global or out register for the SPARC-V8+ architecture.
D	A vector constant
I	Signed 13-bit constant
J	Zero
K	32-bit constant with the low 12 bits clear (a constant that can be loaded with the `sethi` instruction)
L	A constant in the range supported by `movcc` instructions
M	A constant in the range supported by `movrcc` instructions
N	Same as 'K', except that it verifies that bits that are not in the lower 32-bit range are all zero. Must be used instead of 'K' for modes wider than `SImode`
O	The constant 4096
G	Floating-point zero
H	Signed 13-bit constant, sign-extended to 32 or 64 bits
Q	Floating-point constant whose integral representation can be moved into an integer register using a single sethi instruction
R	Floating-point constant whose integral representation can be moved into an integer register using a single mov instruction
S	Floating-point constant whose integral representation can be moved into an integer register using a high/lo_sum instruction sequence
T	Memory address aligned to an 8-byte boundary
U	Even register
W	Memory address for 'e' constraint registers

Chapter 5: Extensions to the C Language Family   323

Y	Vector zero

SPU—`config/spu/spu.h`

a	An immediate which can be loaded with the il/ila/ilh/ilhu instructions. const_int is treated as a 64 bit value.
c	An immediate for and/xor/or instructions. const_int is treated as a 64 bit value.
d	An immediate for the `iohl` instruction. const_int is treated as a 64 bit value.
f	An immediate which can be loaded with `fsmbi`.
A	An immediate which can be loaded with the il/ila/ilh/ilhu instructions. const_int is treated as a 32 bit value.
B	An immediate for most arithmetic instructions. const_int is treated as a 32 bit value.
C	An immediate for and/xor/or instructions. const_int is treated as a 32 bit value.
D	An immediate for the `iohl` instruction. const_int is treated as a 32 bit value.
I	A constant in the range [-64, 63] for shift/rotate instructions.
J	An unsigned 7-bit constant for conversion/nop/channel instructions.
K	A signed 10-bit constant for most arithmetic instructions.
M	A signed 16 bit immediate for `stop`.
N	An unsigned 16-bit constant for `iohl` and `fsmbi`.
O	An unsigned 7-bit constant whose 3 least significant bits are 0.
P	An unsigned 3-bit constant for 16-byte rotates and shifts
R	Call operand, reg, for indirect calls
S	Call operand, symbol, for relative calls.
T	Call operand, const_int, for absolute calls.
U	An immediate which can be loaded with the il/ila/ilh/ilhu instructions. const_int is sign extended to 128 bit.
W	An immediate for shift and rotate instructions. const_int is treated as a 32 bit value.
Y	An immediate for and/xor/or instructions. const_int is sign extended as a 128 bit.
Z	An immediate for the `iohl` instruction. const_int is sign extended to 128 bit.

S/390 and zSeries—'config/s390/s390.h'

a	Address register (general purpose register except r0)
c	Condition code register
d	Data register (arbitrary general purpose register)
f	Floating-point register
I	Unsigned 8-bit constant (0–255)
J	Unsigned 12-bit constant (0–4095)
K	Signed 16-bit constant (−32768–32767)
L	Value appropriate as displacement.

>   (0..4095)
>   for short displacement
>
>   (-524288..524287)
>   for long displacement

M	Constant integer with a value of 0x7fffffff.
N	Multiple letter constraint followed by 4 parameter letters.

>   0..9: number of the part counting from most to least significant
>   H,Q: mode of the part
>   D,S,H: mode of the containing operand
>   0,F: value of the other parts (F—all bits set)
>
>   The constraint matches if the specified part of a constant has a value different from its other parts.

Q	Memory reference without index register and with short displacement.
R	Memory reference with index register and short displacement.
S	Memory reference without index register but with long displacement.
T	Memory reference with index register and long displacement.
U	Pointer with short displacement.
W	Pointer with long displacement.
Y	Shift count operand.

Score family—'config/score/score.h'

d	Registers from r0 to r32.
e	Registers from r0 to r16.
t	r8—r11 or r22—r27 registers.

Chapter 5: Extensions to the C Language Family   325

h	hi register.	
l	lo register.	
x	hi + lo register.	
q	cnt register.	
y	lcb register.	
z	scb register.	
a	cnt + lcb + scb register.	
c	cr0—cr15 register.	
b	cp1 registers.	
f	cp2 registers.	
i	cp3 registers.	
j	cp1 + cp2 + cp3 registers.	
I	High 16-bit constant (32-bit constant with 16 LSBs zero).	
J	Unsigned 5 bit integer (in the range 0 to 31).	
K	Unsigned 16 bit integer (in the range 0 to 65535).	
L	Signed 16 bit integer (in the range −32768 to 32767).	
M	Unsigned 14 bit integer (in the range 0 to 16383).	
N	Signed 14 bit integer (in the range −8192 to 8191).	
Z	Any SYMBOL_REF.	

Xstormy16—'config/stormy16/stormy16.h'

a	Register r0.
b	Register r1.
c	Register r2.
d	Register r8.
e	Registers r0 through r7.
t	Registers r0 and r1.
y	The carry register.
z	Registers r8 and r9.
I	A constant between 0 and 3 inclusive.
J	A constant that has exactly one bit set.
K	A constant that has exactly one bit clear.
L	A constant between 0 and 255 inclusive.
M	A constant between −255 and 0 inclusive.

N	A constant between −3 and 0 inclusive.
O	A constant between 1 and 4 inclusive.
P	A constant between −4 and −1 inclusive.
Q	A memory reference that is a stack push.
R	A memory reference that is a stack pop.
S	A memory reference that refers to a constant address of known value.
T	The register indicated by Rx (not implemented yet).
U	A constant that is not between 2 and 15 inclusive.
Z	The constant 0.

Xtensa—'config/xtensa/constraints.md'

a	General-purpose 32-bit register
b	One-bit boolean register
A	MAC16 40-bit accumulator register
I	Signed 12-bit integer constant, for use in MOVI instructions
J	Signed 8-bit integer constant, for use in ADDI instructions
K	Integer constant valid for BccI instructions
L	Unsigned constant valid for BccUI instructions

5.39 Controlling Names Used in Assembler Code

You can specify the name to be used in the assembler code for a C function or variable by writing the asm (or __asm__) keyword after the declarator as follows:

    int foo asm ("myfoo") = 2;

This specifies that the name to be used for the variable foo in the assembler code should be 'myfoo' rather than the usual '_foo'.

On systems where an underscore is normally prepended to the name of a C function or variable, this feature allows you to define names for the linker that do not start with an underscore.

It does not make sense to use this feature with a non-static local variable since such variables do not have assembler names. If you are trying to put the variable in a particular register, see Section 5.40 [Explicit Reg Vars], page 327. GCC presently accepts such code with a warning, but will probably be changed to issue an error, rather than a warning, in the future.

You cannot use asm in this way in a function *definition*; but you can get the same effect by writing a declaration for the function before its definition and putting asm there, like this:

Chapter 5: Extensions to the C Language Family 327

```
extern func () asm ("FUNC");

func (x, y)
    int x, y;
/* ... */
```

It is up to you to make sure that the assembler names you choose do not conflict with any other assembler symbols. Also, you must not use a register name; that would produce completely invalid assembler code. GCC does not as yet have the ability to store static variables in registers. Perhaps that will be added.

5.40 Variables in Specified Registers

GNU C allows you to put a few global variables into specified hardware registers. You can also specify the register in which an ordinary register variable should be allocated.

- Global register variables reserve registers throughout the program. This may be useful in programs such as programming language interpreters which have a couple of global variables that are accessed very often.
- Local register variables in specific registers do not reserve the registers, except at the point where they are used as input or output operands in an asm statement and the asm statement itself is not deleted. The compiler's data flow analysis is capable of determining where the specified registers contain live values, and where they are available for other uses. Stores into local register variables may be deleted when they appear to be dead according to dataflow analysis. References to local register variables may be deleted or moved or simplified.

These local variables are sometimes convenient for use with the extended asm feature (see Section 5.37 [Extended Asm], page 300), if you want to write one output of the assembler instruction directly into a particular register. (This will work provided the register you specify fits the constraints specified for that operand in the asm.)

5.40.1 Defining Global Register Variables

You can define a global register variable in GNU C like this:

```
register int *foo asm ("a5");
```

Here a5 is the name of the register which should be used. Choose a register which is normally saved and restored by function calls on your machine, so that library routines will not clobber it.

Naturally the register name is cpu-dependent, so you would need to conditionalize your program according to cpu type. The register a5 would be a good choice on a 68000 for a variable of pointer type. On machines with register windows, be sure to choose a "global" register that is not affected magically by the function call mechanism.

In addition, operating systems on one type of cpu may differ in how they name the registers; then you would need additional conditionals. For example, some 68000 operating systems call this register %a5.

Eventually there may be a way of asking the compiler to choose a register automatically, but first we need to figure out how it should choose and how to enable you to guide the choice. No solution is evident.

Defining a global register variable in a certain register reserves that register entirely for this use, at least within the current compilation. The register will not be allocated for any other purpose in the functions in the current compilation. The register will not be saved and restored by these functions. Stores into this register are never deleted even if they would appear to be dead, but references may be deleted or moved or simplified.

It is not safe to access the global register variables from signal handlers, or from more than one thread of control, because the system library routines may temporarily use the register for other things (unless you recompile them specially for the task at hand).

It is not safe for one function that uses a global register variable to call another such function `foo` by way of a third function `lose` that was compiled without knowledge of this variable (i.e. in a different source file in which the variable wasn't declared). This is because `lose` might save the register and put some other value there. For example, you can't expect a global register variable to be available in the comparison-function that you pass to `qsort`, since `qsort` might have put something else in that register. (If you are prepared to recompile `qsort` with the same global register variable, you can solve this problem.)

If you want to recompile `qsort` or other source files which do not actually use your global register variable, so that they will not use that register for any other purpose, then it suffices to specify the compiler option '`-ffixed-reg`'. You need not actually add a global register declaration to their source code.

A function which can alter the value of a global register variable cannot safely be called from a function compiled without this variable, because it could clobber the value the caller expects to find there on return. Therefore, the function which is the entry point into the part of the program that uses the global register variable must explicitly save and restore the value which belongs to its caller.

On most machines, `longjmp` will restore to each global register variable the value it had at the time of the `setjmp`. On some machines, however, `longjmp` will not change the value of global register variables. To be portable, the function that called `setjmp` should make other arrangements to save the values of the global register variables, and to restore them in a `longjmp`. This way, the same thing will happen regardless of what `longjmp` does.

All global register variable declarations must precede all function definitions. If such a declaration could appear after function definitions, the declaration would be too late to prevent the register from being used for other purposes in the preceding functions.

Global register variables may not have initial values, because an executable file has no means to supply initial contents for a register.

On the SPARC, there are reports that g3 ... g7 are suitable registers, but certain library functions, such as `getwd`, as well as the subroutines for division and remainder, modify g3 and g4. g1 and g2 are local temporaries.

On the 68000, a2 ... a5 should be suitable, as should d2 ... d7. Of course, it will not do to use more than a few of those.

5.40.2 Specifying Registers for Local Variables

You can define a local register variable with a specified register like this:

```
register int *foo asm ("a5");
```

Chapter 5: Extensions to the C Language Family   329

Here a5 is the name of the register which should be used. Note that this is the same syntax used for defining global register variables, but for a local variable it would appear within a function.

Naturally the register name is cpu-dependent, but this is not a problem, since specific registers are most often useful with explicit assembler instructions (see Section 5.37 [Extended Asm], page 300). Both of these things generally require that you conditionalize your program according to cpu type.

In addition, operating systems on one type of cpu may differ in how they name the registers; then you would need additional conditionals. For example, some 68000 operating systems call this register %a5.

Defining such a register variable does not reserve the register; it remains available for other uses in places where flow control determines the variable's value is not live.

This option does not guarantee that GCC will generate code that has this variable in the register you specify at all times. You may not code an explicit reference to this register in the *assembler instruction template* part of an asm statement and assume it will always refer to this variable. However, using the variable as an asm *operand* guarantees that the specified register is used for the operand.

Stores into local register variables may be deleted when they appear to be dead according to dataflow analysis. References to local register variables may be deleted or moved or simplified.

As for global register variables, it's recommended that you choose a register which is normally saved and restored by function calls on your machine, so that library routines will not clobber it. A common pitfall is to initialize multiple call-clobbered registers with arbitrary expressions, where a function call or library call for an arithmetic operator will overwrite a register value from a previous assignment, for example r0 below:

```
register int *p1 asm ("r0") = ...;
register int *p2 asm ("r1") = ...;
```

In those cases, a solution is to use a temporary variable for each arbitrary expression. See [Example of asm with clobbered asm reg], page 302.

5.41 Alternate Keywords

'-ansi' and the various '-std' options disable certain keywords. This causes trouble when you want to use GNU C extensions, or a general-purpose header file that should be usable by all programs, including ISO C programs. The keywords asm, typeof and inline are not available in programs compiled with '-ansi' or '-std' (although inline can be used in a program compiled with '-std=c99'). The ISO C99 keyword restrict is only available when '-std=gnu99' (which will eventually be the default) or '-std=c99' (or the equivalent '-std=iso9899:1999') is used.

The way to solve these problems is to put '__' at the beginning and end of each problematical keyword. For example, use __asm__ instead of asm, and __inline__ instead of inline.

Other C compilers won't accept these alternative keywords; if you want to compile with another compiler, you can define the alternate keywords as macros to replace them with the customary keywords. It looks like this:

```
#ifndef __GNUC__
#define __asm__ asm
#endif
```

'`-pedantic`' and other options cause warnings for many GNU C extensions. You can prevent such warnings within one expression by writing `__extension__` before the expression. `__extension__` has no effect aside from this.

5.42 Incomplete `enum` Types

You can define an `enum` tag without specifying its possible values. This results in an incomplete type, much like what you get if you write `struct foo` without describing the elements. A later declaration which does specify the possible values completes the type.

You can't allocate variables or storage using the type while it is incomplete. However, you can work with pointers to that type.

This extension may not be very useful, but it makes the handling of `enum` more consistent with the way `struct` and `union` are handled.

This extension is not supported by GNU C++.

5.43 Function Names as Strings

GCC provides three magic variables which hold the name of the current function, as a string. The first of these is `__func__`, which is part of the C99 standard:

> The identifier `__func__` is implicitly declared by the translator
> as if, immediately following the opening brace of each function
> definition, the declaration
>
> ```
> static const char __func__[] = "function-name";
> ```
>
> appeared, where function-name is the name of the lexically-enclosing
> function. This name is the unadorned name of the function.

`__FUNCTION__` is another name for `__func__`. Older versions of GCC recognize only this name. However, it is not standardized. For maximum portability, we recommend you use `__func__`, but provide a fallback definition with the preprocessor:

```
#if __STDC_VERSION__ < 199901L
# if __GNUC__ >= 2
#  define __func__ __FUNCTION__
# else
#  define __func__ "<unknown>"
# endif
#endif
```

In C, `__PRETTY_FUNCTION__` is yet another name for `__func__`. However, in C++, `__PRETTY_FUNCTION__` contains the type signature of the function as well as its bare name. For example, this program:

```
extern "C" {
extern int printf (char *, ...);
}

class a {
 public:
```

Chapter 5: Extensions to the C Language Family 331

```
        void sub (int i)
          {
            printf ("__FUNCTION__ = %s\n", __FUNCTION__);
            printf ("__PRETTY_FUNCTION__ = %s\n", __PRETTY_FUNCTION__);
          }
      };

      int
      main (void)
      {
        a ax;
        ax.sub (0);
        return 0;
      }
```

gives this output:

```
    __FUNCTION__ = sub
    __PRETTY_FUNCTION__ = void a::sub(int)
```

These identifiers are not preprocessor macros. In GCC 3.3 and earlier, in C only, `__FUNCTION__` and `__PRETTY_FUNCTION__` were treated as string literals; they could be used to initialize `char` arrays, and they could be concatenated with other string literals. GCC 3.4 and later treat them as variables, like `__func__`. In C++, `__FUNCTION__` and `__PRETTY_FUNCTION__` have always been variables.

5.44 Getting the Return or Frame Address of a Function

These functions may be used to get information about the callers of a function.

`void * __builtin_return_address (`*unsigned int* `level)`   [Built-in Function]

This function returns the return address of the current function, or of one of its callers. The *level* argument is number of frames to scan up the call stack. A value of 0 yields the return address of the current function, a value of 1 yields the return address of the caller of the current function, and so forth. When inlining the expected behavior is that the function will return the address of the function that will be returned to. To work around this behavior use the `noinline` function attribute.

The *level* argument must be a constant integer.

On some machines it may be impossible to determine the return address of any function other than the current one; in such cases, or when the top of the stack has been reached, this function will return 0 or a random value. In addition, `__builtin_frame_address` may be used to determine if the top of the stack has been reached.

This function should only be used with a nonzero argument for debugging purposes.

`void * __builtin_frame_address (`*unsigned int* `level)`   [Built-in Function]

This function is similar to `__builtin_return_address`, but it returns the address of the function frame rather than the return address of the function. Calling `__builtin_frame_address` with a value of 0 yields the frame address of the current function, a value of 1 yields the frame address of the caller of the current function, and so forth.

The frame is the area on the stack which holds local variables and saved registers. The frame address is normally the address of the first word pushed on to the stack by the function. However, the exact definition depends upon the processor and the calling convention. If the processor has a dedicated frame pointer register, and the function has a frame, then `__builtin_frame_address` will return the value of the frame pointer register.

On some machines it may be impossible to determine the frame address of any function other than the current one; in such cases, or when the top of the stack has been reached, this function will return 0 if the first frame pointer is properly initialized by the startup code.

This function should only be used with a nonzero argument for debugging purposes.

5.45 Using vector instructions through built-in functions

On some targets, the instruction set contains SIMD vector instructions that operate on multiple values contained in one large register at the same time. For example, on the i386 the MMX, 3Dnow! and SSE extensions can be used this way.

The first step in using these extensions is to provide the necessary data types. This should be done using an appropriate `typedef`:

```
typedef int v4si __attribute__ ((vector_size (16)));
```

The `int` type specifies the base type, while the attribute specifies the vector size for the variable, measured in bytes. For example, the declaration above causes the compiler to set the mode for the `v4si` type to be 16 bytes wide and divided into `int` sized units. For a 32-bit `int` this means a vector of 4 units of 4 bytes, and the corresponding mode of `foo` will be V4SI.

The `vector_size` attribute is only applicable to integral and float scalars, although arrays, pointers, and function return values are allowed in conjunction with this construct.

All the basic integer types can be used as base types, both as signed and as unsigned: `char`, `short`, `int`, `long`, `long long`. In addition, `float` and `double` can be used to build floating-point vector types.

Specifying a combination that is not valid for the current architecture will cause GCC to synthesize the instructions using a narrower mode. For example, if you specify a variable of type `V4SI` and your architecture does not allow for this specific SIMD type, GCC will produce code that uses 4 `SI`s.

The types defined in this manner can be used with a subset of normal C operations. Currently, GCC will allow using the following operators on these types: +, -, *, /, unary minus, ^, |, &, ~.

The operations behave like C++ `valarrays`. Addition is defined as the addition of the corresponding elements of the operands. For example, in the code below, each of the 4 elements in a will be added to the corresponding 4 elements in b and the resulting vector will be stored in c.

```
typedef int v4si __attribute__ ((vector_size (16)));

v4si a, b, c;

c = a + b;
```

Subtraction, multiplication, division, and the logical operations operate in a similar manner. Likewise, the result of using the unary minus or complement operators on a vector type

Chapter 5: Extensions to the C Language Family 333

is a vector whose elements are the negative or complemented values of the corresponding elements in the operand.

You can declare variables and use them in function calls and returns, as well as in assignments and some casts. You can specify a vector type as a return type for a function. Vector types can also be used as function arguments. It is possible to cast from one vector type to another, provided they are of the same size (in fact, you can also cast vectors to and from other datatypes of the same size).

You cannot operate between vectors of different lengths or different signedness without a cast.

A port that supports hardware vector operations, usually provides a set of built-in functions that can be used to operate on vectors. For example, a function to add two vectors and multiply the result by a third could look like this:

```
v4si f (v4si a, v4si b, v4si c)
{
  v4si tmp = __builtin_addv4si (a, b);
  return __builtin_mulv4si (tmp, c);
}
```

5.46 Offsetof

GCC implements for both C and C++ a syntactic extension to implement the `offsetof` macro.

```
primary:
"__builtin_offsetof" "(" typename "," offsetof_member_designator ")"

offsetof_member_designator:
  identifier
| offsetof_member_designator "." identifier
| offsetof_member_designator "[" expr "]"
```

This extension is sufficient such that

```
#define offsetof(type, member)  __builtin_offsetof (type, member)
```

is a suitable definition of the `offsetof` macro. In C++, *type* may be dependent. In either case, *member* may consist of a single identifier, or a sequence of member accesses and array references.

5.47 Built-in functions for atomic memory access

The following builtins are intended to be compatible with those described in the *Intel Itanium Processor-specific Application Binary Interface*, section 7.4. As such, they depart from the normal GCC practice of using the "`__builtin_`" prefix, and further that they are overloaded such that they work on multiple types.

The definition given in the Intel documentation allows only for the use of the types `int`, `long`, `long long` as well as their unsigned counterparts. GCC will allow any integral scalar or pointer type that is 1, 2, 4 or 8 bytes in length.

Not all operations are supported by all target processors. If a particular operation cannot be implemented on the target processor, a warning will be generated and a call an external function will be generated. The external function will carry the same name as the builtin, with an additional suffix '`_n`' where n is the size of the data type.

In most cases, these builtins are considered a *full barrier*. That is, no memory operand will be moved across the operation, either forward or backward. Further, instructions will be issued as necessary to prevent the processor from speculating loads across the operation and from queuing stores after the operation.

All of the routines are are described in the Intel documentation to take "an optional list of variables protected by the memory barrier". It's not clear what is meant by that; it could mean that *only* the following variables are protected, or it could mean that these variables should in addition be protected. At present GCC ignores this list and protects all variables which are globally accessible. If in the future we make some use of this list, an empty list will continue to mean all globally accessible variables.

type __sync_fetch_and_add (*type* *ptr, *type* value, ...)
type __sync_fetch_and_sub (*type* *ptr, *type* value, ...)
type __sync_fetch_and_or (*type* *ptr, *type* value, ...)
type __sync_fetch_and_and (*type* *ptr, *type* value, ...)
type __sync_fetch_and_xor (*type* *ptr, *type* value, ...)
type __sync_fetch_and_nand (*type* *ptr, *type* value, ...)

> These builtins perform the operation suggested by the name, and returns the value that had previously been in memory. That is,
>
> > { tmp = *ptr; *ptr op= value; return tmp; }
> > { tmp = *ptr; *ptr = ~tmp & value; return tmp; }   // nand

type __sync_add_and_fetch (*type* *ptr, *type* value, ...)
type __sync_sub_and_fetch (*type* *ptr, *type* value, ...)
type __sync_or_and_fetch (*type* *ptr, *type* value, ...)
type __sync_and_and_fetch (*type* *ptr, *type* value, ...)
type __sync_xor_and_fetch (*type* *ptr, *type* value, ...)
type __sync_nand_and_fetch (*type* *ptr, *type* value, ...)

> These builtins perform the operation suggested by the name, and return the new value. That is,
>
> > { *ptr op= value; return *ptr; }
> > { *ptr = ~*ptr & value; return *ptr; }   // nand

bool __sync_bool_compare_and_swap (*type* *ptr, *type* oldval *type* newval, ...)
type __sync_val_compare_and_swap (*type* *ptr, *type* oldval *type* newval, ...)

> These builtins perform an atomic compare and swap. That is, if the current value of *ptr is *oldval*, then write *newval* into *ptr.
>
> The "bool" version returns true if the comparison is successful and *newval* was written. The "val" version returns the contents of *ptr before the operation.

__sync_synchronize (...)

> This builtin issues a full memory barrier.

type __sync_lock_test_and_set (*type* *ptr, *type* value, ...)

> This builtin, as described by Intel, is not a traditional test-and-set operation, but rather an atomic exchange operation. It writes *value* into *ptr, and returns the previous contents of *ptr.
>
> Many targets have only minimal support for such locks, and do not support a full exchange operation. In this case, a target may support reduced functionality

Chapter 5: Extensions to the C Language Family   335

>here by which the *only* valid value to store is the immediate constant 1. The
>exact value actually stored in *ptr is implementation defined.
>
>This builtin is not a full barrier, but rather an *acquire barrier*. This means
>that references after the builtin cannot move to (or be speculated to) before
>the builtin, but previous memory stores may not be globally visible yet, and
>previous memory loads may not yet be satisfied.

void __sync_lock_release (*type* *ptr, ...)
>This builtin releases the lock acquired by __sync_lock_test_and_set. Normally this means writing the constant 0 to *ptr.
>
>This builtin is not a full barrier, but rather a *release barrier*. This means that
>all previous memory stores are globally visible, and all previous memory loads
>have been satisfied, but following memory reads are not prevented from being
>speculated to before the barrier.

5.48 Object Size Checking Builtins

GCC implements a limited buffer overflow protection mechanism that can prevent some
buffer overflow attacks.

size_t __builtin_object_size (*void* * *ptr*, *int* *type*)   [Built-in Function]
>is a built-in construct that returns a constant number of bytes from *ptr* to the end of
>the object *ptr* pointer points to (if known at compile time). __builtin_object_size
>never evaluates its arguments for side-effects. If there are any side-effects in them,
>it returns (size_t) -1 for *type* 0 or 1 and (size_t) 0 for *type* 2 or 3. If there are
>multiple objects *ptr* can point to and all of them are known at compile time, the
>returned number is the maximum of remaining byte counts in those objects if *type*
>& 2 is 0 and minimum if nonzero. If it is not possible to determine which objects *ptr*
>points to at compile time, __builtin_object_size should return (size_t) -1 for
>*type* 0 or 1 and (size_t) 0 for *type* 2 or 3.
>
>*type* is an integer constant from 0 to 3. If the least significant bit is clear, objects are
>whole variables, if it is set, a closest surrounding subobject is considered the object a
>pointer points to. The second bit determines if maximum or minimum of remaining
>bytes is computed.
>
>```
>struct V { char buf1[10]; int b; char buf2[10]; } var;
>char *p = &var.buf1[1], *q = &var.b;
>
>/* Here the object p points to is var.  */
>assert (__builtin_object_size (p, 0) == sizeof (var) - 1);
>/* The subobject p points to is var.buf1.  */
>assert (__builtin_object_size (p, 1) == sizeof (var.buf1) - 1);
>/* The object q points to is var.  */
>assert (__builtin_object_size (q, 0)
>        == (char *) (&var + 1) - (char *) &var.b);
>/* The subobject q points to is var.b.  */
>assert (__builtin_object_size (q, 1) == sizeof (var.b));
>```

There are built-in functions added for many common string operation functions, e.g., for
memcpy __builtin___memcpy_chk built-in is provided. This built-in has an additional last
argument, which is the number of bytes remaining in object the *dest* argument points to or
(size_t) -1 if the size is not known.

The built-in functions are optimized into the normal string functions like `memcpy` if the last argument is `(size_t) -1` or if it is known at compile time that the destination object will not be overflown. If the compiler can determine at compile time the object will be always overflown, it issues a warning.

The intended use can be e.g.

```
#undef memcpy
#define bos0(dest) __builtin_object_size (dest, 0)
#define memcpy(dest, src, n) \
  __builtin___memcpy_chk (dest, src, n, bos0 (dest))

char *volatile p;
char buf[10];
/* It is unknown what object p points to, so this is optimized
   into plain memcpy - no checking is possible.  */
memcpy (p, "abcde", n);
/* Destination is known and length too.  It is known at compile
   time there will be no overflow.  */
memcpy (&buf[5], "abcde", 5);
/* Destination is known, but the length is not known at compile time.
   This will result in __memcpy_chk call that can check for overflow
   at runtime.  */
memcpy (&buf[5], "abcde", n);
/* Destination is known and it is known at compile time there will
   be overflow.  There will be a warning and __memcpy_chk call that
   will abort the program at runtime.  */
memcpy (&buf[6], "abcde", 5);
```

Such built-in functions are provided for `memcpy`, `mempcpy`, `memmove`, `memset`, `strcpy`, `stpcpy`, `strncpy`, `strcat` and `strncat`.

There are also checking built-in functions for formatted output functions.

```
int __builtin___sprintf_chk (char *s, int flag, size_t os, const char *fmt, ...);
int __builtin___snprintf_chk (char *s, size_t maxlen, int flag, size_t os,
    const char *fmt, ...);
int __builtin___vsprintf_chk (char *s, int flag, size_t os, const char *fmt,
    va_list ap);
int __builtin___vsnprintf_chk (char *s, size_t maxlen, int flag, size_t os,
    const char *fmt, va_list ap);
```

The added *flag* argument is passed unchanged to `__sprintf_chk` etc. functions and can contain implementation specific flags on what additional security measures the checking function might take, such as handling %n differently.

The *os* argument is the object size *s* points to, like in the other built-in functions. There is a small difference in the behavior though, if *os* is `(size_t) -1`, the built-in functions are optimized into the non-checking functions only if *flag* is 0, otherwise the checking function is called with *os* argument set to `(size_t) -1`.

In addition to this, there are checking built-in functions `__builtin___printf_chk`, `__builtin___vprintf_chk`, `__builtin___fprintf_chk` and `__builtin___vfprintf_chk`. These have just one additional argument, *flag*, right before format string *fmt*. If the compiler is able to optimize them to `fputc` etc. functions, it will, otherwise the checking function should be called and the *flag* argument passed to it.

5.49 Other built-in functions provided by GCC

GCC provides a large number of built-in functions other than the ones mentioned above. Some of these are for internal use in the processing of exceptions or variable-length argument lists and will not be documented here because they may change from time to time; we do not recommend general use of these functions.

The remaining functions are provided for optimization purposes.

GCC includes built-in versions of many of the functions in the standard C library. The versions prefixed with __builtin_ will always be treated as having the same meaning as the C library function even if you specify the '-fno-builtin' option. (see Section 3.4 [C Dialect Options], page 26) Many of these functions are only optimized in certain cases; if they are not optimized in a particular case, a call to the library function will be emitted.

Outside strict ISO C mode ('-ansi', '-std=c89' or '-std=c99'), the functions _exit, alloca, bcmp, bzero, dcgettext, dgettext, dremf, dreml, drem, exp10f, exp10l, exp10, ffsll, ffsl, ffs, fprintf_unlocked, fputs_unlocked, gammaf, gammal, gamma, gammaf_r, gammal_r, gamma_r, gettext, index, isascii, j0f, j0l, j0, j1f, j1l, j1, jnf, jnl, jn, lgammaf_r, lgammal_r, lgamma_r, mempcpy, pow10f, pow10l, pow10, printf_unlocked, rindex, scalbf, scalbl, scalb, signbit, signbitf, signbitl, signbitd32, signbitd64, signbitd128, significandf, significandl, significand, sincosf, sincosl, sincos, stpcpy, stpncpy, strcasecmp, strdup, strfmon, strncasecmp, strndup, toascii, y0f, y0l, y0, y1f, y1l, y1, ynf, ynl and yn may be handled as built-in functions. All these functions have corresponding versions prefixed with __builtin_, which may be used even in strict C89 mode.

The ISO C99 functions _Exit, acoshf, acoshl, acosh, asinhf, asinhl, asinh, atanhf, atanhl, atanh, cabsf, cabsl, cabs, cacosf, cacoshf, cacoshl, cacosh, cacosl, cacos, cargf, cargl, carg, casinf, casinhf, casinhl, casinh, casinl, casin, catanf, catanhf, catanhl, catanh, catanl, catan, cbrtf, cbrtl, cbrt, ccosf, ccoshf, ccoshl, ccosh, ccosl, ccos, cexpf, cexpl, cexp, cimagf, cimagl, cimag, clogf, clogl, clog, conjf, conjl, conj, copysignf, copysignl, copysign, cpowf, cpowl, cpow, cprojf, cprojl, cproj, crealf, creall, creal, csinf, csinhf, csinhl, csinh, csinl, csin, csqrtf, csqrtl, csqrt, ctanf, ctanhf, ctanhl, ctanh, ctanl, ctan, erfcf, erfcl, erfc, erff, erfl, erf, exp2f, exp2l, exp2, expm1f, expm1l, expm1, fdimf, fdiml, fdim, fmaf, fmal, fmaxf, fmaxl, fmax, fma, fminf, fminl, fmin, hypotf, hypotl, hypot, ilogbf, ilogbl, ilogb, imaxabs, isblank, iswblank, lgammaf, lgammal, lgamma, llabs, llrintf, llrintl, llrint, llroundf, llroundl, llround, log1pf, log1pl, log1p, log2f, log2l, log2, logbf, logbl, logb, lrintf, lrintl, lrint, lroundf, lroundl, lround, nearbyintf, nearbyintl, nearbyint, nextafterf, nextafterl, nextafter, nexttowardf, nexttowardl, nexttoward, remainderf, remainderl, remainder, remquof, remquol, remquo, rintf, rintl, rint, roundf, roundl, round, scalblnf, scalblnl, scalbln, scalbnf, scalbnl, scalbn, snprintf, tgammaf, tgammal, tgamma, truncf, truncl, trunc, vfscanf, vscanf, vsnprintf and vsscanf are handled as built-in functions except in strict ISO C90 mode ('-ansi' or '-std=c89').

There are also built-in versions of the ISO C99 functions acosf, acosl, asinf, asinl, atan2f, atan2l, atanf, atanl, ceilf, ceill, cosf, coshf, coshl, cosl, expf, expl, fabsf, fabsl, floorf, floorl, fmodf, fmodl, frexpf, frexpl, ldexpf, ldexpl, log10f, log10l, logf, logl, modfl, modf, powf, powl, sinf, sinhf, sinhl, sinl, sqrtf, sqrtl, tanf, tanhf, tanhl and tanl that are recognized in any mode since ISO C90 reserves these names for the purpose to which ISO C99 puts them. All these functions have corresponding versions prefixed with __builtin_.

The ISO C94 functions iswalnum, iswalpha, iswcntrl, iswdigit, iswgraph, iswlower, iswprint, iswpunct, iswspace, iswupper, iswxdigit, towlower and towupper are handled as built-in functions except in strict ISO C90 mode ('-ansi' or '-std=c89').

The ISO C90 functions abort, abs, acos, asin, atan2, atan, calloc, ceil, cosh, cos, exit, exp, fabs, floor, fmod, fprintf, fputs, frexp, fscanf, isalnum, isalpha, iscntrl, isdigit, isgraph, islower, isprint, ispunct, isspace, isupper, isxdigit, tolower, toupper, labs, ldexp, log10, log, malloc, memchr, memcmp, memcpy, memset, modf, pow, printf, putchar, puts, scanf, sinh, sin, snprintf, sprintf, sqrt, sscanf, strcat, strchr, strcmp, strcpy, strcspn, strlen, strncat, strncmp, strncpy, strpbrk, strrchr, strspn, strstr, tanh, tan, vfprintf, vprintf and vsprintf are all recognized as built-in functions unless '-fno-builtin' is specified (or '-fno-builtin-*function*' is specified for an individual function). All of these functions have corresponding versions prefixed with __builtin_.

GCC provides built-in versions of the ISO C99 floating point comparison macros that avoid raising exceptions for unordered operands. They have the same names as the standard macros (isgreater, isgreaterequal, isless, islessequal, islessgreater, and isunordered) , with __builtin_ prefixed. We intend for a library implementor to be able to simply #define each standard macro to its built-in equivalent. In the same fashion, GCC provides isfinite and isnormal built-ins used with __builtin_ prefixed.

int __builtin_types_compatible_p (*type1*, *type2*)　　　　　　[Built-in Function]

　　You can use the built-in function __builtin_types_compatible_p to determine whether two types are the same.

　　This built-in function returns 1 if the unqualified versions of the types *type1* and *type2* (which are types, not expressions) are compatible, 0 otherwise. The result of this built-in function can be used in integer constant expressions.

　　This built-in function ignores top level qualifiers (e.g., const, volatile). For example, int is equivalent to const int.

　　The type int[] and int[5] are compatible. On the other hand, int and char * are not compatible, even if the size of their types, on the particular architecture are the same. Also, the amount of pointer indirection is taken into account when determining similarity. Consequently, short * is not similar to short **. Furthermore, two types that are typedefed are considered compatible if their underlying types are compatible.

　　An enum type is not considered to be compatible with another enum type even if both are compatible with the same integer type; this is what the C standard specifies. For example, enum {foo, bar} is not similar to enum {hot, dog}.

　　You would typically use this function in code whose execution varies depending on the arguments' types. For example:

```
#define foo(x)                                                  \
  ({                                                            \
    typeof (x) tmp = (x);                                       \
    if (__builtin_types_compatible_p (typeof (x), long double)) \
      tmp = foo_long_double (tmp);                              \
```

Chapter 5: Extensions to the C Language Family   339

```
        else if (__builtin_types_compatible_p (typeof (x), double)) \
          tmp = foo_double (tmp);                                   \
        else if (__builtin_types_compatible_p (typeof (x), float))  \
          tmp = foo_float (tmp);                                    \
        else                                                        \
          abort ();                                                 \
        tmp;                                                        \
      })
```

Note: This construct is only available for C.

type __builtin_choose_expr (*const_exp, exp1, exp2*)   [Built-in Function]

You can use the built-in function __builtin_choose_expr to evaluate code depending on the value of a constant expression. This built-in function returns *exp1* if *const_exp*, which is a constant expression that must be able to be determined at compile time, is nonzero. Otherwise it returns 0.

This built-in function is analogous to the '? :' operator in C, except that the expression returned has its type unaltered by promotion rules. Also, the built-in function does not evaluate the expression that was not chosen. For example, if *const_exp* evaluates to true, *exp2* is not evaluated even if it has side-effects.

This built-in function can return an lvalue if the chosen argument is an lvalue.

If *exp1* is returned, the return type is the same as *exp1*'s type. Similarly, if *exp2* is returned, its return type is the same as *exp2*.

Example:
```
        #define foo(x)                                                       \
          __builtin_choose_expr (                                            \
            __builtin_types_compatible_p (typeof (x), double),               \
            foo_double (x),                                                  \
            __builtin_choose_expr (                                          \
              __builtin_types_compatible_p (typeof (x), float),              \
              foo_float (x),                                                 \
              /* The void expression results in a compile-time error   \
                 when assigning the result to something.   */          \
              (void)0))
```

Note: This construct is only available for C. Furthermore, the unused expression (*exp1* or *exp2* depending on the value of *const_exp*) may still generate syntax errors. This may change in future revisions.

int __builtin_constant_p (*exp*)   [Built-in Function]

You can use the built-in function __builtin_constant_p to determine if a value is known to be constant at compile-time and hence that GCC can perform constant-folding on expressions involving that value. The argument of the function is the value to test. The function returns the integer 1 if the argument is known to be a compile-time constant and 0 if it is not known to be a compile-time constant. A return of 0 does not indicate that the value is *not* a constant, but merely that GCC cannot prove it is a constant with the specified value of the '-O' option.

You would typically use this function in an embedded application where memory was a critical resource. If you have some complex calculation, you may want it to be folded if it involves constants, but need to call a function if it does not. For example:

```
#define Scale_Value(X)      \
  (__builtin_constant_p (X) \
  ? ((X) * SCALE + OFFSET) : Scale (X))
```

You may use this built-in function in either a macro or an inline function. However, if you use it in an inlined function and pass an argument of the function as the argument to the built-in, GCC will never return 1 when you call the inline function with a string constant or compound literal (see Section 5.22 [Compound Literals], page 261) and will not return 1 when you pass a constant numeric value to the inline function unless you specify the '-O' option.

You may also use __builtin_constant_p in initializers for static data. For instance, you can write

```
static const int table[] = {
   __builtin_constant_p (EXPRESSION) ? (EXPRESSION) : -1,
   /* ... */
};
```

This is an acceptable initializer even if *EXPRESSION* is not a constant expression. GCC must be more conservative about evaluating the built-in in this case, because it has no opportunity to perform optimization.

Previous versions of GCC did not accept this built-in in data initializers. The earliest version where it is completely safe is 3.0.1.

long __builtin_expect (*long exp, long c*)   [Built-in Function]
You may use __builtin_expect to provide the compiler with branch prediction information. In general, you should prefer to use actual profile feedback for this ('-fprofile-arcs'), as programmers are notoriously bad at predicting how their programs actually perform. However, there are applications in which this data is hard to collect.

The return value is the value of *exp*, which should be an integral expression. The semantics of the built-in are that it is expected that *exp* == *c*. For example:

```
if (__builtin_expect (x, 0))
   foo ();
```

would indicate that we do not expect to call `foo`, since we expect `x` to be zero. Since you are limited to integral expressions for *exp*, you should use constructions such as

```
if (__builtin_expect (ptr != NULL, 1))
   error ();
```

when testing pointer or floating-point values.

void __builtin_trap (*void*)   [Built-in Function]
This function causes the program to exit abnormally. GCC implements this function by using a target-dependent mechanism (such as intentionally executing an illegal instruction) or by calling `abort`. The mechanism used may vary from release to release so you should not rely on any particular implementation.

void __builtin___clear_cache (*char *begin, char *end*)   [Built-in Function]
This function is used to flush the processor's instruction cache for the region of memory between *begin* inclusive and *end* exclusive. Some targets require that the instruction cache be flushed, after modifying memory containing code, in order to obtain deterministic behavior.

Chapter 5: Extensions to the C Language Family   341

If the target does not require instruction cache flushes, `__builtin___clear_cache` has no effect. Otherwise either instructions are emitted in-line to clear the instruction cache or a call to the `__clear_cache` function in libgcc is made.

`void __builtin_prefetch (const void *addr, ...)`   [Built-in Function]
This function is used to minimize cache-miss latency by moving data into a cache before it is accessed. You can insert calls to `__builtin_prefetch` into code for which you know addresses of data in memory that is likely to be accessed soon. If the target supports them, data prefetch instructions will be generated. If the prefetch is done early enough before the access then the data will be in the cache by the time it is accessed.

The value of *addr* is the address of the memory to prefetch. There are two optional arguments, *rw* and *locality*. The value of *rw* is a compile-time constant one or zero; one means that the prefetch is preparing for a write to the memory address and zero, the default, means that the prefetch is preparing for a read. The value *locality* must be a compile-time constant integer between zero and three. A value of zero means that the data has no temporal locality, so it need not be left in the cache after the access. A value of three means that the data has a high degree of temporal locality and should be left in all levels of cache possible. Values of one and two mean, respectively, a low or moderate degree of temporal locality. The default is three.

```
for (i = 0; i < n; i++)
  {
    a[i] = a[i] + b[i];
    __builtin_prefetch (&a[i+j], 1, 1);
    __builtin_prefetch (&b[i+j], 0, 1);
    /* ... */
  }
```

Data prefetch does not generate faults if *addr* is invalid, but the address expression itself must be valid. For example, a prefetch of `p->next` will not fault if `p->next` is not a valid address, but evaluation will fault if `p` is not a valid address.

If the target does not support data prefetch, the address expression is evaluated if it includes side effects but no other code is generated and GCC does not issue a warning.

`double __builtin_huge_val (void)`   [Built-in Function]
Returns a positive infinity, if supported by the floating-point format, else `DBL_MAX`. This function is suitable for implementing the ISO C macro `HUGE_VAL`.

`float __builtin_huge_valf (void)`   [Built-in Function]
Similar to `__builtin_huge_val`, except the return type is `float`.

`long double __builtin_huge_vall (void)`   [Built-in Function]
Similar to `__builtin_huge_val`, except the return type is `long double`.

`double __builtin_inf (void)`   [Built-in Function]
Similar to `__builtin_huge_val`, except a warning is generated if the target floating-point format does not support infinities.

`_Decimal32 __builtin_infd32 (void)`   [Built-in Function]
Similar to `__builtin_inf`, except the return type is `_Decimal32`.

_Decimal64 __builtin_infd64 (*void*)   [Built-in Function]
    Similar to `__builtin_inf`, except the return type is `_Decimal64`.

_Decimal128 __builtin_infd128 (*void*)   [Built-in Function]
    Similar to `__builtin_inf`, except the return type is `_Decimal128`.

float __builtin_inff (*void*)   [Built-in Function]
    Similar to `__builtin_inf`, except the return type is `float`. This function is suitable for implementing the ISO C99 macro `INFINITY`.

long double __builtin_infl (*void*)   [Built-in Function]
    Similar to `__builtin_inf`, except the return type is `long double`.

double __builtin_nan (*const char *str*)   [Built-in Function]
    This is an implementation of the ISO C99 function `nan`.

    Since ISO C99 defines this function in terms of `strtod`, which we do not implement, a description of the parsing is in order. The string is parsed as by `strtol`; that is, the base is recognized by leading '0' or '0x' prefixes. The number parsed is placed in the significand such that the least significant bit of the number is at the least significant bit of the significand. The number is truncated to fit the significand field provided. The significand is forced to be a quiet NaN.

    This function, if given a string literal all of which would have been consumed by strtol, is evaluated early enough that it is considered a compile-time constant.

_Decimal32 __builtin_nand32 (*const char *str*)   [Built-in Function]
    Similar to `__builtin_nan`, except the return type is `_Decimal32`.

_Decimal64 __builtin_nand64 (*const char *str*)   [Built-in Function]
    Similar to `__builtin_nan`, except the return type is `_Decimal64`.

_Decimal128 __builtin_nand128 (*const char *str*)   [Built-in Function]
    Similar to `__builtin_nan`, except the return type is `_Decimal128`.

float __builtin_nanf (*const char *str*)   [Built-in Function]
    Similar to `__builtin_nan`, except the return type is `float`.

long double __builtin_nanl (*const char *str*)   [Built-in Function]
    Similar to `__builtin_nan`, except the return type is `long double`.

double __builtin_nans (*const char *str*)   [Built-in Function]
    Similar to `__builtin_nan`, except the significand is forced to be a signaling NaN. The `nans` function is proposed by WG14 N965.

float __builtin_nansf (*const char *str*)   [Built-in Function]
    Similar to `__builtin_nans`, except the return type is `float`.

long double __builtin_nansl (*const char *str*)   [Built-in Function]
    Similar to `__builtin_nans`, except the return type is `long double`.

int __builtin_ffs (*unsigned int x*)   [Built-in Function]
    Returns one plus the index of the least significant 1-bit of x, or if x is zero, returns zero.

`int __builtin_clz (`*unsigned int x*`)` [Built-in Function]
> Returns the number of leading 0-bits in *x*, starting at the most significant bit position. If *x* is 0, the result is undefined.

`int __builtin_ctz (`*unsigned int x*`)` [Built-in Function]
> Returns the number of trailing 0-bits in *x*, starting at the least significant bit position. If *x* is 0, the result is undefined.

`int __builtin_popcount (`*unsigned int x*`)` [Built-in Function]
> Returns the number of 1-bits in *x*.

`int __builtin_parity (`*unsigned int x*`)` [Built-in Function]
> Returns the parity of *x*, i.e. the number of 1-bits in *x* modulo 2.

`int __builtin_ffsl (`*unsigned long*`)` [Built-in Function]
> Similar to `__builtin_ffs`, except the argument type is `unsigned long`.

`int __builtin_clzl (`*unsigned long*`)` [Built-in Function]
> Similar to `__builtin_clz`, except the argument type is `unsigned long`.

`int __builtin_ctzl (`*unsigned long*`)` [Built-in Function]
> Similar to `__builtin_ctz`, except the argument type is `unsigned long`.

`int __builtin_popcountl (`*unsigned long*`)` [Built-in Function]
> Similar to `__builtin_popcount`, except the argument type is `unsigned long`.

`int __builtin_parityl (`*unsigned long*`)` [Built-in Function]
> Similar to `__builtin_parity`, except the argument type is `unsigned long`.

`int __builtin_ffsll (`*unsigned long long*`)` [Built-in Function]
> Similar to `__builtin_ffs`, except the argument type is `unsigned long long`.

`int __builtin_clzll (`*unsigned long long*`)` [Built-in Function]
> Similar to `__builtin_clz`, except the argument type is `unsigned long long`.

`int __builtin_ctzll (`*unsigned long long*`)` [Built-in Function]
> Similar to `__builtin_ctz`, except the argument type is `unsigned long long`.

`int __builtin_popcountll (`*unsigned long long*`)` [Built-in Function]
> Similar to `__builtin_popcount`, except the argument type is `unsigned long long`.

`int __builtin_parityll (`*unsigned long long*`)` [Built-in Function]
> Similar to `__builtin_parity`, except the argument type is `unsigned long long`.

`double __builtin_powi (`*double, int*`)` [Built-in Function]
> Returns the first argument raised to the power of the second. Unlike the `pow` function no guarantees about precision and rounding are made.

`float __builtin_powif (`*float, int*`)` [Built-in Function]
> Similar to `__builtin_powi`, except the argument and return types are `float`.

`long double __builtin_powil (`*long double, int*`)` [Built-in Function]
> Similar to `__builtin_powi`, except the argument and return types are `long double`.

int32_t __builtin_bswap32 (*int32_t x*) [Built-in Function]
: Returns x with the order of the bytes reversed; for example, 0xaabbccdd becomes 0xddccbbaa. Byte here always means exactly 8 bits.

int64_t __builtin_bswap64 (*int64_t x*) [Built-in Function]
: Similar to __builtin_bswap32, except the argument and return types are 64-bit.

5.50 Built-in Functions Specific to Particular Target Machines

On some target machines, GCC supports many built-in functions specific to those machines. Generally these generate calls to specific machine instructions, but allow the compiler to schedule those calls.

5.50.1 Alpha Built-in Functions

These built-in functions are available for the Alpha family of processors, depending on the command-line switches used.

The following built-in functions are always available. They all generate the machine instruction that is part of the name.

```
long __builtin_alpha_implver (void)
long __builtin_alpha_rpcc (void)
long __builtin_alpha_amask (long)
long __builtin_alpha_cmpbge (long, long)
long __builtin_alpha_extbl (long, long)
long __builtin_alpha_extwl (long, long)
long __builtin_alpha_extll (long, long)
long __builtin_alpha_extql (long, long)
long __builtin_alpha_extwh (long, long)
long __builtin_alpha_extlh (long, long)
long __builtin_alpha_extqh (long, long)
long __builtin_alpha_insbl (long, long)
long __builtin_alpha_inswl (long, long)
long __builtin_alpha_insll (long, long)
long __builtin_alpha_insql (long, long)
long __builtin_alpha_inswh (long, long)
long __builtin_alpha_inslh (long, long)
long __builtin_alpha_insqh (long, long)
long __builtin_alpha_mskbl (long, long)
long __builtin_alpha_mskwl (long, long)
long __builtin_alpha_mskll (long, long)
long __builtin_alpha_mskql (long, long)
long __builtin_alpha_mskwh (long, long)
long __builtin_alpha_msklh (long, long)
long __builtin_alpha_mskqh (long, long)
long __builtin_alpha_umulh (long, long)
long __builtin_alpha_zap (long, long)
long __builtin_alpha_zapnot (long, long)
```

The following built-in functions are always with '-mmax' or '-mcpu=*cpu*' where *cpu* is pca56 or later. They all generate the machine instruction that is part of the name.

```
long __builtin_alpha_pklb (long)
long __builtin_alpha_pkwb (long)
long __builtin_alpha_unpkbl (long)
long __builtin_alpha_unpkbw (long)
```

Chapter 5: Extensions to the C Language Family   345

```
long __builtin_alpha_minub8 (long, long)
long __builtin_alpha_minsb8 (long, long)
long __builtin_alpha_minuw4 (long, long)
long __builtin_alpha_minsw4 (long, long)
long __builtin_alpha_maxub8 (long, long)
long __builtin_alpha_maxsb8 (long, long)
long __builtin_alpha_maxuw4 (long, long)
long __builtin_alpha_maxsw4 (long, long)
long __builtin_alpha_perr (long, long)
```

The following built-in functions are always with '-mcix' or '-mcpu=cpu' where cpu is ev67 or later. They all generate the machine instruction that is part of the name.

```
long __builtin_alpha_cttz (long)
long __builtin_alpha_ctlz (long)
long __builtin_alpha_ctpop (long)
```

The following builtins are available on systems that use the OSF/1 PALcode. Normally they invoke the rduniq and wruniq PAL calls, but when invoked with '-mtls-kernel', they invoke rdval and wrval.

```
void *__builtin_thread_pointer (void)
void __builtin_set_thread_pointer (void *)
```

5.50.2 ARM iWMMXt Built-in Functions

These built-in functions are available for the ARM family of processors when the '-mcpu=iwmmxt' switch is used:

```
typedef int v2si __attribute__ ((vector_size (8)));
typedef short v4hi __attribute__ ((vector_size (8)));
typedef char v8qi __attribute__ ((vector_size (8)));

int __builtin_arm_getwcx (int)
void __builtin_arm_setwcx (int, int)
int __builtin_arm_textrmsb (v8qi, int)
int __builtin_arm_textrmsh (v4hi, int)
int __builtin_arm_textrmsw (v2si, int)
int __builtin_arm_textrmub (v8qi, int)
int __builtin_arm_textrmuh (v4hi, int)
int __builtin_arm_textrmuw (v2si, int)
v8qi __builtin_arm_tinsrb (v8qi, int)
v4hi __builtin_arm_tinsrh (v4hi, int)
v2si __builtin_arm_tinsrw (v2si, int)
long long __builtin_arm_tmia (long long, int, int)
long long __builtin_arm_tmiabb (long long, int, int)
long long __builtin_arm_tmiabt (long long, int, int)
long long __builtin_arm_tmiaph (long long, int, int)
long long __builtin_arm_tmiatb (long long, int, int)
long long __builtin_arm_tmiatt (long long, int, int)
int __builtin_arm_tmovmskb (v8qi)
int __builtin_arm_tmovmskh (v4hi)
int __builtin_arm_tmovmskw (v2si)
long long __builtin_arm_waccb (v8qi)
long long __builtin_arm_wacch (v4hi)
long long __builtin_arm_waccw (v2si)
v8qi __builtin_arm_waddb (v8qi, v8qi)
v8qi __builtin_arm_waddbss (v8qi, v8qi)
v8qi __builtin_arm_waddbus (v8qi, v8qi)
v4hi __builtin_arm_waddh (v4hi, v4hi)
v4hi __builtin_arm_waddhss (v4hi, v4hi)
```

```
v4hi __builtin_arm_waddhus (v4hi, v4hi)
v2si __builtin_arm_waddw (v2si, v2si)
v2si __builtin_arm_waddwss (v2si, v2si)
v2si __builtin_arm_waddwus (v2si, v2si)
v8qi __builtin_arm_walign (v8qi, v8qi, int)
long long __builtin_arm_wand(long long, long long)
long long __builtin_arm_wandn (long long, long long)
v8qi __builtin_arm_wavg2b (v8qi, v8qi)
v8qi __builtin_arm_wavg2br (v8qi, v8qi)
v4hi __builtin_arm_wavg2h (v4hi, v4hi)
v4hi __builtin_arm_wavg2hr (v4hi, v4hi)
v8qi __builtin_arm_wcmpeqb (v8qi, v8qi)
v4hi __builtin_arm_wcmpeqh (v4hi, v4hi)
v2si __builtin_arm_wcmpeqw (v2si, v2si)
v8qi __builtin_arm_wcmpgtsb (v8qi, v8qi)
v4hi __builtin_arm_wcmpgtsh (v4hi, v4hi)
v2si __builtin_arm_wcmpgtsw (v2si, v2si)
v8qi __builtin_arm_wcmpgtub (v8qi, v8qi)
v4hi __builtin_arm_wcmpgtuh (v4hi, v4hi)
v2si __builtin_arm_wcmpgtuw (v2si, v2si)
long long __builtin_arm_wmacs (long long, v4hi, v4hi)
long long __builtin_arm_wmacsz (v4hi, v4hi)
long long __builtin_arm_wmacu (long long, v4hi, v4hi)
long long __builtin_arm_wmacuz (v4hi, v4hi)
v4hi __builtin_arm_wmadds (v4hi, v4hi)
v4hi __builtin_arm_wmaddu (v4hi, v4hi)
v8qi __builtin_arm_wmaxsb (v8qi, v8qi)
v4hi __builtin_arm_wmaxsh (v4hi, v4hi)
v2si __builtin_arm_wmaxsw (v2si, v2si)
v8qi __builtin_arm_wmaxub (v8qi, v8qi)
v4hi __builtin_arm_wmaxuh (v4hi, v4hi)
v2si __builtin_arm_wmaxuw (v2si, v2si)
v8qi __builtin_arm_wminsb (v8qi, v8qi)
v4hi __builtin_arm_wminsh (v4hi, v4hi)
v2si __builtin_arm_wminsw (v2si, v2si)
v8qi __builtin_arm_wminub (v8qi, v8qi)
v4hi __builtin_arm_wminuh (v4hi, v4hi)
v2si __builtin_arm_wminuw (v2si, v2si)
v4hi __builtin_arm_wmulsm (v4hi, v4hi)
v4hi __builtin_arm_wmulul (v4hi, v4hi)
v4hi __builtin_arm_wmulum (v4hi, v4hi)
long long __builtin_arm_wor (long long, long long)
v2si __builtin_arm_wpackdss (long long, long long)
v2si __builtin_arm_wpackdus (long long, long long)
v8qi __builtin_arm_wpackhss (v4hi, v4hi)
v8qi __builtin_arm_wpackhus (v4hi, v4hi)
v4hi __builtin_arm_wpackwss (v2si, v2si)
v4hi __builtin_arm_wpackwus (v2si, v2si)
long long __builtin_arm_wrord (long long, long long)
long long __builtin_arm_wrordi (long long, int)
v4hi __builtin_arm_wrorh (v4hi, long long)
v4hi __builtin_arm_wrorhi (v4hi, int)
v2si __builtin_arm_wrorw (v2si, long long)
v2si __builtin_arm_wrorwi (v2si, int)
v2si __builtin_arm_wsadb (v8qi, v8qi)
v2si __builtin_arm_wsadbz (v8qi, v8qi)
v2si __builtin_arm_wsadh (v4hi, v4hi)
v2si __builtin_arm_wsadhz (v4hi, v4hi)
```

Chapter 5: Extensions to the C Language Family   347

```
v4hi __builtin_arm_wshufh (v4hi, int)
long long __builtin_arm_wslld (long long, long long)
long long __builtin_arm_wslldi (long long, int)
v4hi __builtin_arm_wsllh (v4hi, long long)
v4hi __builtin_arm_wsllhi (v4hi, int)
v2si __builtin_arm_wsllw (v2si, long long)
v2si __builtin_arm_wsllwi (v2si, int)
long long __builtin_arm_wsrad (long long, long long)
long long __builtin_arm_wsradi (long long, int)
v4hi __builtin_arm_wsrah (v4hi, long long)
v4hi __builtin_arm_wsrahi (v4hi, int)
v2si __builtin_arm_wsraw (v2si, long long)
v2si __builtin_arm_wsrawi (v2si, int)
long long __builtin_arm_wsrld (long long, long long)
long long __builtin_arm_wsrldi (long long, int)
v4hi __builtin_arm_wsrlh (v4hi, long long)
v4hi __builtin_arm_wsrlhi (v4hi, int)
v2si __builtin_arm_wsrlw (v2si, long long)
v2si __builtin_arm_wsrlwi (v2si, int)
v8qi __builtin_arm_wsubb (v8qi, v8qi)
v8qi __builtin_arm_wsubbss (v8qi, v8qi)
v8qi __builtin_arm_wsubbus (v8qi, v8qi)
v4hi __builtin_arm_wsubh (v4hi, v4hi)
v4hi __builtin_arm_wsubhss (v4hi, v4hi)
v4hi __builtin_arm_wsubhus (v4hi, v4hi)
v2si __builtin_arm_wsubw (v2si, v2si)
v2si __builtin_arm_wsubwss (v2si, v2si)
v2si __builtin_arm_wsubwus (v2si, v2si)
v4hi __builtin_arm_wunpckehsb (v8qi)
v2si __builtin_arm_wunpckehsh (v4hi)
long long __builtin_arm_wunpckehsw (v2si)
v4hi __builtin_arm_wunpckehub (v8qi)
v2si __builtin_arm_wunpckehuh (v4hi)
long long __builtin_arm_wunpckehuw (v2si)
v4hi __builtin_arm_wunpckelsb (v8qi)
v2si __builtin_arm_wunpckelsh (v4hi)
long long __builtin_arm_wunpckelsw (v2si)
v4hi __builtin_arm_wunpckelub (v8qi)
v2si __builtin_arm_wunpckeluh (v4hi)
long long __builtin_arm_wunpckeluw (v2si)
v8qi __builtin_arm_wunpckihb (v8qi, v8qi)
v4hi __builtin_arm_wunpckihh (v4hi, v4hi)
v2si __builtin_arm_wunpckihw (v2si, v2si)
v8qi __builtin_arm_wunpckilb (v8qi, v8qi)
v4hi __builtin_arm_wunpckilh (v4hi, v4hi)
v2si __builtin_arm_wunpckilw (v2si, v2si)
long long __builtin_arm_wxor (long long, long long)
long long __builtin_arm_wzero ()
```

5.50.3 ARM NEON Intrinsics

These built-in intrinsics for the ARM Advanced SIMD extension are available when the '-mfpu=neon' switch is used:

5.50.3.1 Addition

- uint32x2_t vadd_u32 (uint32x2_t, uint32x2_t)
  Form of expected instruction(s): `vadd.i32 d0, d0, d0`

- uint16x4_t vadd_u16 (uint16x4_t, uint16x4_t)
  Form of expected instruction(s): `vadd.i16 d0, d0, d0`
- uint8x8_t vadd_u8 (uint8x8_t, uint8x8_t)
  Form of expected instruction(s): `vadd.i8 d0, d0, d0`
- int32x2_t vadd_s32 (int32x2_t, int32x2_t)
  Form of expected instruction(s): `vadd.i32 d0, d0, d0`
- int16x4_t vadd_s16 (int16x4_t, int16x4_t)
  Form of expected instruction(s): `vadd.i16 d0, d0, d0`
- int8x8_t vadd_s8 (int8x8_t, int8x8_t)
  Form of expected instruction(s): `vadd.i8 d0, d0, d0`
- uint64x1_t vadd_u64 (uint64x1_t, uint64x1_t)
  Form of expected instruction(s): `vadd.i64 d0, d0, d0`
- int64x1_t vadd_s64 (int64x1_t, int64x1_t)
  Form of expected instruction(s): `vadd.i64 d0, d0, d0`
- float32x2_t vadd_f32 (float32x2_t, float32x2_t)
  Form of expected instruction(s): `vadd.f32 d0, d0, d0`
- uint32x4_t vaddq_u32 (uint32x4_t, uint32x4_t)
  Form of expected instruction(s): `vadd.i32 q0, q0, q0`
- uint16x8_t vaddq_u16 (uint16x8_t, uint16x8_t)
  Form of expected instruction(s): `vadd.i16 q0, q0, q0`
- uint8x16_t vaddq_u8 (uint8x16_t, uint8x16_t)
  Form of expected instruction(s): `vadd.i8 q0, q0, q0`
- int32x4_t vaddq_s32 (int32x4_t, int32x4_t)
  Form of expected instruction(s): `vadd.i32 q0, q0, q0`
- int16x8_t vaddq_s16 (int16x8_t, int16x8_t)
  Form of expected instruction(s): `vadd.i16 q0, q0, q0`
- int8x16_t vaddq_s8 (int8x16_t, int8x16_t)
  Form of expected instruction(s): `vadd.i8 q0, q0, q0`
- uint64x2_t vaddq_u64 (uint64x2_t, uint64x2_t)
  Form of expected instruction(s): `vadd.i64 q0, q0, q0`
- int64x2_t vaddq_s64 (int64x2_t, int64x2_t)
  Form of expected instruction(s): `vadd.i64 q0, q0, q0`
- float32x4_t vaddq_f32 (float32x4_t, float32x4_t)
  Form of expected instruction(s): `vadd.f32 q0, q0, q0`
- uint64x2_t vaddl_u32 (uint32x2_t, uint32x2_t)
  Form of expected instruction(s): `vaddl.u32 q0, d0, d0`
- uint32x4_t vaddl_u16 (uint16x4_t, uint16x4_t)
  Form of expected instruction(s): `vaddl.u16 q0, d0, d0`
- uint16x8_t vaddl_u8 (uint8x8_t, uint8x8_t)
  Form of expected instruction(s): `vaddl.u8 q0, d0, d0`
- int64x2_t vaddl_s32 (int32x2_t, int32x2_t)
  Form of expected instruction(s): `vaddl.s32 q0, d0, d0`

Chapter 5: Extensions to the C Language Family 349

- int32x4_t vaddl_s16 (int16x4_t, int16x4_t)
  Form of expected instruction(s): **vaddl.s16** *q0, d0, d0*
- int16x8_t vaddl_s8 (int8x8_t, int8x8_t)
  Form of expected instruction(s): **vaddl.s8** *q0, d0, d0*
- uint64x2_t vaddw_u32 (uint64x2_t, uint32x2_t)
  Form of expected instruction(s): **vaddw.u32** *q0, q0, d0*
- uint32x4_t vaddw_u16 (uint32x4_t, uint16x4_t)
  Form of expected instruction(s): **vaddw.u16** *q0, q0, d0*
- uint16x8_t vaddw_u8 (uint16x8_t, uint8x8_t)
  Form of expected instruction(s): **vaddw.u8** *q0, q0, d0*
- int64x2_t vaddw_s32 (int64x2_t, int32x2_t)
  Form of expected instruction(s): **vaddw.s32** *q0, q0, d0*
- int32x4_t vaddw_s16 (int32x4_t, int16x4_t)
  Form of expected instruction(s): **vaddw.s16** *q0, q0, d0*
- int16x8_t vaddw_s8 (int16x8_t, int8x8_t)
  Form of expected instruction(s): **vaddw.s8** *q0, q0, d0*
- uint32x2_t vhadd_u32 (uint32x2_t, uint32x2_t)
  Form of expected instruction(s): **vhadd.u32** *d0, d0, d0*
- uint16x4_t vhadd_u16 (uint16x4_t, uint16x4_t)
  Form of expected instruction(s): **vhadd.u16** *d0, d0, d0*
- uint8x8_t vhadd_u8 (uint8x8_t, uint8x8_t)
  Form of expected instruction(s): **vhadd.u8** *d0, d0, d0*
- int32x2_t vhadd_s32 (int32x2_t, int32x2_t)
  Form of expected instruction(s): **vhadd.s32** *d0, d0, d0*
- int16x4_t vhadd_s16 (int16x4_t, int16x4_t)
  Form of expected instruction(s): **vhadd.s16** *d0, d0, d0*
- int8x8_t vhadd_s8 (int8x8_t, int8x8_t)
  Form of expected instruction(s): **vhadd.s8** *d0, d0, d0*
- uint32x4_t vhaddq_u32 (uint32x4_t, uint32x4_t)
  Form of expected instruction(s): **vhadd.u32** *q0, q0, q0*
- uint16x8_t vhaddq_u16 (uint16x8_t, uint16x8_t)
  Form of expected instruction(s): **vhadd.u16** *q0, q0, q0*
- uint8x16_t vhaddq_u8 (uint8x16_t, uint8x16_t)
  Form of expected instruction(s): **vhadd.u8** *q0, q0, q0*
- int32x4_t vhaddq_s32 (int32x4_t, int32x4_t)
  Form of expected instruction(s): **vhadd.s32** *q0, q0, q0*
- int16x8_t vhaddq_s16 (int16x8_t, int16x8_t)
  Form of expected instruction(s): **vhadd.s16** *q0, q0, q0*
- int8x16_t vhaddq_s8 (int8x16_t, int8x16_t)
  Form of expected instruction(s): **vhadd.s8** *q0, q0, q0*
- uint32x2_t vrhadd_u32 (uint32x2_t, uint32x2_t)
  Form of expected instruction(s): **vrhadd.u32** *d0, d0, d0*

- uint16x4_t vrhadd_u16 (uint16x4_t, uint16x4_t)
  Form of expected instruction(s): **vrhadd.u16** *d0, d0, d0*
- uint8x8_t vrhadd_u8 (uint8x8_t, uint8x8_t)
  Form of expected instruction(s): **vrhadd.u8** *d0, d0, d0*
- int32x2_t vrhadd_s32 (int32x2_t, int32x2_t)
  Form of expected instruction(s): **vrhadd.s32** *d0, d0, d0*
- int16x4_t vrhadd_s16 (int16x4_t, int16x4_t)
  Form of expected instruction(s): **vrhadd.s16** *d0, d0, d0*
- int8x8_t vrhadd_s8 (int8x8_t, int8x8_t)
  Form of expected instruction(s): **vrhadd.s8** *d0, d0, d0*
- uint32x4_t vrhaddq_u32 (uint32x4_t, uint32x4_t)
  Form of expected instruction(s): **vrhadd.u32** *q0, q0, q0*
- uint16x8_t vrhaddq_u16 (uint16x8_t, uint16x8_t)
  Form of expected instruction(s): **vrhadd.u16** *q0, q0, q0*
- uint8x16_t vrhaddq_u8 (uint8x16_t, uint8x16_t)
  Form of expected instruction(s): **vrhadd.u8** *q0, q0, q0*
- int32x4_t vrhaddq_s32 (int32x4_t, int32x4_t)
  Form of expected instruction(s): **vrhadd.s32** *q0, q0, q0*
- int16x8_t vrhaddq_s16 (int16x8_t, int16x8_t)
  Form of expected instruction(s): **vrhadd.s16** *q0, q0, q0*
- int8x16_t vrhaddq_s8 (int8x16_t, int8x16_t)
  Form of expected instruction(s): **vrhadd.s8** *q0, q0, q0*
- uint32x2_t vqadd_u32 (uint32x2_t, uint32x2_t)
  Form of expected instruction(s): **vqadd.u32** *d0, d0, d0*
- uint16x4_t vqadd_u16 (uint16x4_t, uint16x4_t)
  Form of expected instruction(s): **vqadd.u16** *d0, d0, d0*
- uint8x8_t vqadd_u8 (uint8x8_t, uint8x8_t)
  Form of expected instruction(s): **vqadd.u8** *d0, d0, d0*
- int32x2_t vqadd_s32 (int32x2_t, int32x2_t)
  Form of expected instruction(s): **vqadd.s32** *d0, d0, d0*
- int16x4_t vqadd_s16 (int16x4_t, int16x4_t)
  Form of expected instruction(s): **vqadd.s16** *d0, d0, d0*
- int8x8_t vqadd_s8 (int8x8_t, int8x8_t)
  Form of expected instruction(s): **vqadd.s8** *d0, d0, d0*
- uint64x1_t vqadd_u64 (uint64x1_t, uint64x1_t)
  Form of expected instruction(s): **vqadd.u64** *d0, d0, d0*
- int64x1_t vqadd_s64 (int64x1_t, int64x1_t)
  Form of expected instruction(s): **vqadd.s64** *d0, d0, d0*
- uint32x4_t vqaddq_u32 (uint32x4_t, uint32x4_t)
  Form of expected instruction(s): **vqadd.u32** *q0, q0, q0*
- uint16x8_t vqaddq_u16 (uint16x8_t, uint16x8_t)
  Form of expected instruction(s): **vqadd.u16** *q0, q0, q0*

Chapter 5: Extensions to the C Language Family   351

- uint8x16_t vqaddq_u8 (uint8x16_t, uint8x16_t)
  Form of expected instruction(s): `vqadd.u8` *q0, q0, q0*
- int32x4_t vqaddq_s32 (int32x4_t, int32x4_t)
  Form of expected instruction(s): `vqadd.s32` *q0, q0, q0*
- int16x8_t vqaddq_s16 (int16x8_t, int16x8_t)
  Form of expected instruction(s): `vqadd.s16` *q0, q0, q0*
- int8x16_t vqaddq_s8 (int8x16_t, int8x16_t)
  Form of expected instruction(s): `vqadd.s8` *q0, q0, q0*
- uint64x2_t vqaddq_u64 (uint64x2_t, uint64x2_t)
  Form of expected instruction(s): `vqadd.u64` *q0, q0, q0*
- int64x2_t vqaddq_s64 (int64x2_t, int64x2_t)
  Form of expected instruction(s): `vqadd.s64` *q0, q0, q0*
- uint32x2_t vaddhn_u64 (uint64x2_t, uint64x2_t)
  Form of expected instruction(s): `vaddhn.i64` *d0, q0, q0*
- uint16x4_t vaddhn_u32 (uint32x4_t, uint32x4_t)
  Form of expected instruction(s): `vaddhn.i32` *d0, q0, q0*
- uint8x8_t vaddhn_u16 (uint16x8_t, uint16x8_t)
  Form of expected instruction(s): `vaddhn.i16` *d0, q0, q0*
- int32x2_t vaddhn_s64 (int64x2_t, int64x2_t)
  Form of expected instruction(s): `vaddhn.i64` *d0, q0, q0*
- int16x4_t vaddhn_s32 (int32x4_t, int32x4_t)
  Form of expected instruction(s): `vaddhn.i32` *d0, q0, q0*
- int8x8_t vaddhn_s16 (int16x8_t, int16x8_t)
  Form of expected instruction(s): `vaddhn.i16` *d0, q0, q0*
- uint32x2_t vraddhn_u64 (uint64x2_t, uint64x2_t)
  Form of expected instruction(s): `vraddhn.i64` *d0, q0, q0*
- uint16x4_t vraddhn_u32 (uint32x4_t, uint32x4_t)
  Form of expected instruction(s): `vraddhn.i32` *d0, q0, q0*
- uint8x8_t vraddhn_u16 (uint16x8_t, uint16x8_t)
  Form of expected instruction(s): `vraddhn.i16` *d0, q0, q0*
- int32x2_t vraddhn_s64 (int64x2_t, int64x2_t)
  Form of expected instruction(s): `vraddhn.i64` *d0, q0, q0*
- int16x4_t vraddhn_s32 (int32x4_t, int32x4_t)
  Form of expected instruction(s): `vraddhn.i32` *d0, q0, q0*
- int8x8_t vraddhn_s16 (int16x8_t, int16x8_t)
  Form of expected instruction(s): `vraddhn.i16` *d0, q0, q0*

5.50.3.2 Multiplication

- uint32x2_t vmul_u32 (uint32x2_t, uint32x2_t)
  Form of expected instruction(s): `vmul.i32` *d0, d0, d0*
- uint16x4_t vmul_u16 (uint16x4_t, uint16x4_t)
  Form of expected instruction(s): `vmul.i16` *d0, d0, d0*

- uint8x8_t vmul_u8 (uint8x8_t, uint8x8_t)
  Form of expected instruction(s): `vmul.i8 d0, d0, d0`
- int32x2_t vmul_s32 (int32x2_t, int32x2_t)
  Form of expected instruction(s): `vmul.i32 d0, d0, d0`
- int16x4_t vmul_s16 (int16x4_t, int16x4_t)
  Form of expected instruction(s): `vmul.i16 d0, d0, d0`
- int8x8_t vmul_s8 (int8x8_t, int8x8_t)
  Form of expected instruction(s): `vmul.i8 d0, d0, d0`
- float32x2_t vmul_f32 (float32x2_t, float32x2_t)
  Form of expected instruction(s): `vmul.f32 d0, d0, d0`
- poly8x8_t vmul_p8 (poly8x8_t, poly8x8_t)
  Form of expected instruction(s): `vmul.p8 d0, d0, d0`
- uint32x4_t vmulq_u32 (uint32x4_t, uint32x4_t)
  Form of expected instruction(s): `vmul.i32 q0, q0, q0`
- uint16x8_t vmulq_u16 (uint16x8_t, uint16x8_t)
  Form of expected instruction(s): `vmul.i16 q0, q0, q0`
- uint8x16_t vmulq_u8 (uint8x16_t, uint8x16_t)
  Form of expected instruction(s): `vmul.i8 q0, q0, q0`
- int32x4_t vmulq_s32 (int32x4_t, int32x4_t)
  Form of expected instruction(s): `vmul.i32 q0, q0, q0`
- int16x8_t vmulq_s16 (int16x8_t, int16x8_t)
  Form of expected instruction(s): `vmul.i16 q0, q0, q0`
- int8x16_t vmulq_s8 (int8x16_t, int8x16_t)
  Form of expected instruction(s): `vmul.i8 q0, q0, q0`
- float32x4_t vmulq_f32 (float32x4_t, float32x4_t)
  Form of expected instruction(s): `vmul.f32 q0, q0, q0`
- poly8x16_t vmulq_p8 (poly8x16_t, poly8x16_t)
  Form of expected instruction(s): `vmul.p8 q0, q0, q0`
- int32x2_t vqdmulh_s32 (int32x2_t, int32x2_t)
  Form of expected instruction(s): `vqdmulh.s32 d0, d0, d0`
- int16x4_t vqdmulh_s16 (int16x4_t, int16x4_t)
  Form of expected instruction(s): `vqdmulh.s16 d0, d0, d0`
- int32x4_t vqdmulhq_s32 (int32x4_t, int32x4_t)
  Form of expected instruction(s): `vqdmulh.s32 q0, q0, q0`
- int16x8_t vqdmulhq_s16 (int16x8_t, int16x8_t)
  Form of expected instruction(s): `vqdmulh.s16 q0, q0, q0`
- int32x2_t vqrdmulh_s32 (int32x2_t, int32x2_t)
  Form of expected instruction(s): `vqrdmulh.s32 d0, d0, d0`
- int16x4_t vqrdmulh_s16 (int16x4_t, int16x4_t)
  Form of expected instruction(s): `vqrdmulh.s16 d0, d0, d0`
- int32x4_t vqrdmulhq_s32 (int32x4_t, int32x4_t)
  Form of expected instruction(s): `vqrdmulh.s32 q0, q0, q0`

Chapter 5: Extensions to the C Language Family   353

- int16x8_t vqrdmulhq_s16 (int16x8_t, int16x8_t)
  Form of expected instruction(s): `vqrdmulh.s16 q0, q0, q0`
- uint64x2_t vmull_u32 (uint32x2_t, uint32x2_t)
  Form of expected instruction(s): `vmull.u32 q0, d0, d0`
- uint32x4_t vmull_u16 (uint16x4_t, uint16x4_t)
  Form of expected instruction(s): `vmull.u16 q0, d0, d0`
- uint16x8_t vmull_u8 (uint8x8_t, uint8x8_t)
  Form of expected instruction(s): `vmull.u8 q0, d0, d0`
- int64x2_t vmull_s32 (int32x2_t, int32x2_t)
  Form of expected instruction(s): `vmull.s32 q0, d0, d0`
- int32x4_t vmull_s16 (int16x4_t, int16x4_t)
  Form of expected instruction(s): `vmull.s16 q0, d0, d0`
- int16x8_t vmull_s8 (int8x8_t, int8x8_t)
  Form of expected instruction(s): `vmull.s8 q0, d0, d0`
- poly16x8_t vmull_p8 (poly8x8_t, poly8x8_t)
  Form of expected instruction(s): `vmull.p8 q0, d0, d0`
- int64x2_t vqdmull_s32 (int32x2_t, int32x2_t)
  Form of expected instruction(s): `vqdmull.s32 q0, d0, d0`
- int32x4_t vqdmull_s16 (int16x4_t, int16x4_t)
  Form of expected instruction(s): `vqdmull.s16 q0, d0, d0`

5.50.3.3 Multiply-accumulate

- uint32x2_t vmla_u32 (uint32x2_t, uint32x2_t, uint32x2_t)
  Form of expected instruction(s): `vmla.i32 d0, d0, d0`
- uint16x4_t vmla_u16 (uint16x4_t, uint16x4_t, uint16x4_t)
  Form of expected instruction(s): `vmla.i16 d0, d0, d0`
- uint8x8_t vmla_u8 (uint8x8_t, uint8x8_t, uint8x8_t)
  Form of expected instruction(s): `vmla.i8 d0, d0, d0`
- int32x2_t vmla_s32 (int32x2_t, int32x2_t, int32x2_t)
  Form of expected instruction(s): `vmla.i32 d0, d0, d0`
- int16x4_t vmla_s16 (int16x4_t, int16x4_t, int16x4_t)
  Form of expected instruction(s): `vmla.i16 d0, d0, d0`
- int8x8_t vmla_s8 (int8x8_t, int8x8_t, int8x8_t)
  Form of expected instruction(s): `vmla.i8 d0, d0, d0`
- float32x2_t vmla_f32 (float32x2_t, float32x2_t, float32x2_t)
  Form of expected instruction(s): `vmla.f32 d0, d0, d0`
- uint32x4_t vmlaq_u32 (uint32x4_t, uint32x4_t, uint32x4_t)
  Form of expected instruction(s): `vmla.i32 q0, q0, q0`
- uint16x8_t vmlaq_u16 (uint16x8_t, uint16x8_t, uint16x8_t)
  Form of expected instruction(s): `vmla.i16 q0, q0, q0`
- uint8x16_t vmlaq_u8 (uint8x16_t, uint8x16_t, uint8x16_t)
  Form of expected instruction(s): `vmla.i8 q0, q0, q0`

- int32x4_t vmlaq_s32 (int32x4_t, int32x4_t, int32x4_t)
  Form of expected instruction(s): `vmla.i32 q0, q0, q0`
- int16x8_t vmlaq_s16 (int16x8_t, int16x8_t, int16x8_t)
  Form of expected instruction(s): `vmla.i16 q0, q0, q0`
- int8x16_t vmlaq_s8 (int8x16_t, int8x16_t, int8x16_t)
  Form of expected instruction(s): `vmla.i8 q0, q0, q0`
- float32x4_t vmlaq_f32 (float32x4_t, float32x4_t, float32x4_t)
  Form of expected instruction(s): `vmla.f32 q0, q0, q0`
- uint64x2_t vmlal_u32 (uint64x2_t, uint32x2_t, uint32x2_t)
  Form of expected instruction(s): `vmlal.u32 q0, d0, d0`
- uint32x4_t vmlal_u16 (uint32x4_t, uint16x4_t, uint16x4_t)
  Form of expected instruction(s): `vmlal.u16 q0, d0, d0`
- uint16x8_t vmlal_u8 (uint16x8_t, uint8x8_t, uint8x8_t)
  Form of expected instruction(s): `vmlal.u8 q0, d0, d0`
- int64x2_t vmlal_s32 (int64x2_t, int32x2_t, int32x2_t)
  Form of expected instruction(s): `vmlal.s32 q0, d0, d0`
- int32x4_t vmlal_s16 (int32x4_t, int16x4_t, int16x4_t)
  Form of expected instruction(s): `vmlal.s16 q0, d0, d0`
- int16x8_t vmlal_s8 (int16x8_t, int8x8_t, int8x8_t)
  Form of expected instruction(s): `vmlal.s8 q0, d0, d0`
- int64x2_t vqdmlal_s32 (int64x2_t, int32x2_t, int32x2_t)
  Form of expected instruction(s): `vqdmlal.s32 q0, d0, d0`
- int32x4_t vqdmlal_s16 (int32x4_t, int16x4_t, int16x4_t)
  Form of expected instruction(s): `vqdmlal.s16 q0, d0, d0`

5.50.3.4 Multiply-subtract

- uint32x2_t vmls_u32 (uint32x2_t, uint32x2_t, uint32x2_t)
  Form of expected instruction(s): `vmls.i32 d0, d0, d0`
- uint16x4_t vmls_u16 (uint16x4_t, uint16x4_t, uint16x4_t)
  Form of expected instruction(s): `vmls.i16 d0, d0, d0`
- uint8x8_t vmls_u8 (uint8x8_t, uint8x8_t, uint8x8_t)
  Form of expected instruction(s): `vmls.i8 d0, d0, d0`
- int32x2_t vmls_s32 (int32x2_t, int32x2_t, int32x2_t)
  Form of expected instruction(s): `vmls.i32 d0, d0, d0`
- int16x4_t vmls_s16 (int16x4_t, int16x4_t, int16x4_t)
  Form of expected instruction(s): `vmls.i16 d0, d0, d0`
- int8x8_t vmls_s8 (int8x8_t, int8x8_t, int8x8_t)
  Form of expected instruction(s): `vmls.i8 d0, d0, d0`
- float32x2_t vmls_f32 (float32x2_t, float32x2_t, float32x2_t)
  Form of expected instruction(s): `vmls.f32 d0, d0, d0`
- uint32x4_t vmlsq_u32 (uint32x4_t, uint32x4_t, uint32x4_t)
  Form of expected instruction(s): `vmls.i32 q0, q0, q0`

Chapter 5: Extensions to the C Language Family   355

- uint16x8_t vmlsq_u16 (uint16x8_t, uint16x8_t, uint16x8_t)
  Form of expected instruction(s): `vmls.i16 q0, q0, q0`
- uint8x16_t vmlsq_u8 (uint8x16_t, uint8x16_t, uint8x16_t)
  Form of expected instruction(s): `vmls.i8 q0, q0, q0`
- int32x4_t vmlsq_s32 (int32x4_t, int32x4_t, int32x4_t)
  Form of expected instruction(s): `vmls.i32 q0, q0, q0`
- int16x8_t vmlsq_s16 (int16x8_t, int16x8_t, int16x8_t)
  Form of expected instruction(s): `vmls.i16 q0, q0, q0`
- int8x16_t vmlsq_s8 (int8x16_t, int8x16_t, int8x16_t)
  Form of expected instruction(s): `vmls.i8 q0, q0, q0`
- float32x4_t vmlsq_f32 (float32x4_t, float32x4_t, float32x4_t)
  Form of expected instruction(s): `vmls.f32 q0, q0, q0`
- uint64x2_t vmlsl_u32 (uint64x2_t, uint32x2_t, uint32x2_t)
  Form of expected instruction(s): `vmlsl.u32 q0, d0, d0`
- uint32x4_t vmlsl_u16 (uint32x4_t, uint16x4_t, uint16x4_t)
  Form of expected instruction(s): `vmlsl.u16 q0, d0, d0`
- uint16x8_t vmlsl_u8 (uint16x8_t, uint8x8_t, uint8x8_t)
  Form of expected instruction(s): `vmlsl.u8 q0, d0, d0`
- int64x2_t vmlsl_s32 (int64x2_t, int32x2_t, int32x2_t)
  Form of expected instruction(s): `vmlsl.s32 q0, d0, d0`
- int32x4_t vmlsl_s16 (int32x4_t, int16x4_t, int16x4_t)
  Form of expected instruction(s): `vmlsl.s16 q0, d0, d0`
- int16x8_t vmlsl_s8 (int16x8_t, int8x8_t, int8x8_t)
  Form of expected instruction(s): `vmlsl.s8 q0, d0, d0`
- int64x2_t vqdmlsl_s32 (int64x2_t, int32x2_t, int32x2_t)
  Form of expected instruction(s): `vqdmlsl.s32 q0, d0, d0`
- int32x4_t vqdmlsl_s16 (int32x4_t, int16x4_t, int16x4_t)
  Form of expected instruction(s): `vqdmlsl.s16 q0, d0, d0`

5.50.3.5 Subtraction

- uint32x2_t vsub_u32 (uint32x2_t, uint32x2_t)
  Form of expected instruction(s): `vsub.i32 d0, d0, d0`
- uint16x4_t vsub_u16 (uint16x4_t, uint16x4_t)
  Form of expected instruction(s): `vsub.i16 d0, d0, d0`
- uint8x8_t vsub_u8 (uint8x8_t, uint8x8_t)
  Form of expected instruction(s): `vsub.i8 d0, d0, d0`
- int32x2_t vsub_s32 (int32x2_t, int32x2_t)
  Form of expected instruction(s): `vsub.i32 d0, d0, d0`
- int16x4_t vsub_s16 (int16x4_t, int16x4_t)
  Form of expected instruction(s): `vsub.i16 d0, d0, d0`
- int8x8_t vsub_s8 (int8x8_t, int8x8_t)
  Form of expected instruction(s): `vsub.i8 d0, d0, d0`

- uint64x1_t vsub_u64 (uint64x1_t, uint64x1_t)
  Form of expected instruction(s): vsub.i64 *d0, d0, d0*
- int64x1_t vsub_s64 (int64x1_t, int64x1_t)
  Form of expected instruction(s): vsub.i64 *d0, d0, d0*
- float32x2_t vsub_f32 (float32x2_t, float32x2_t)
  Form of expected instruction(s): vsub.f32 *d0, d0, d0*
- uint32x4_t vsubq_u32 (uint32x4_t, uint32x4_t)
  Form of expected instruction(s): vsub.i32 *q0, q0, q0*
- uint16x8_t vsubq_u16 (uint16x8_t, uint16x8_t)
  Form of expected instruction(s): vsub.i16 *q0, q0, q0*
- uint8x16_t vsubq_u8 (uint8x16_t, uint8x16_t)
  Form of expected instruction(s): vsub.i8 *q0, q0, q0*
- int32x4_t vsubq_s32 (int32x4_t, int32x4_t)
  Form of expected instruction(s): vsub.i32 *q0, q0, q0*
- int16x8_t vsubq_s16 (int16x8_t, int16x8_t)
  Form of expected instruction(s): vsub.i16 *q0, q0, q0*
- int8x16_t vsubq_s8 (int8x16_t, int8x16_t)
  Form of expected instruction(s): vsub.i8 *q0, q0, q0*
- uint64x2_t vsubq_u64 (uint64x2_t, uint64x2_t)
  Form of expected instruction(s): vsub.i64 *q0, q0, q0*
- int64x2_t vsubq_s64 (int64x2_t, int64x2_t)
  Form of expected instruction(s): vsub.i64 *q0, q0, q0*
- float32x4_t vsubq_f32 (float32x4_t, float32x4_t)
  Form of expected instruction(s): vsub.f32 *q0, q0, q0*
- uint64x2_t vsubl_u32 (uint32x2_t, uint32x2_t)
  Form of expected instruction(s): vsubl.u32 *q0, d0, d0*
- uint32x4_t vsubl_u16 (uint16x4_t, uint16x4_t)
  Form of expected instruction(s): vsubl.u16 *q0, d0, d0*
- uint16x8_t vsubl_u8 (uint8x8_t, uint8x8_t)
  Form of expected instruction(s): vsubl.u8 *q0, d0, d0*
- int64x2_t vsubl_s32 (int32x2_t, int32x2_t)
  Form of expected instruction(s): vsubl.s32 *q0, d0, d0*
- int32x4_t vsubl_s16 (int16x4_t, int16x4_t)
  Form of expected instruction(s): vsubl.s16 *q0, d0, d0*
- int16x8_t vsubl_s8 (int8x8_t, int8x8_t)
  Form of expected instruction(s): vsubl.s8 *q0, d0, d0*
- uint64x2_t vsubw_u32 (uint64x2_t, uint32x2_t)
  Form of expected instruction(s): vsubw.u32 *q0, q0, d0*
- uint32x4_t vsubw_u16 (uint32x4_t, uint16x4_t)
  Form of expected instruction(s): vsubw.u16 *q0, q0, d0*
- uint16x8_t vsubw_u8 (uint16x8_t, uint8x8_t)
  Form of expected instruction(s): vsubw.u8 *q0, q0, d0*

Chapter 5: Extensions to the C Language Family 357

- int64x2_t vsubw_s32 (int64x2_t, int32x2_t)
  Form of expected instruction(s): vsubw.s32 q0, q0, d0
- int32x4_t vsubw_s16 (int32x4_t, int16x4_t)
  Form of expected instruction(s): vsubw.s16 q0, q0, d0
- int16x8_t vsubw_s8 (int16x8_t, int8x8_t)
  Form of expected instruction(s): vsubw.s8 q0, q0, d0
- uint32x2_t vhsub_u32 (uint32x2_t, uint32x2_t)
  Form of expected instruction(s): vhsub.u32 d0, d0, d0
- uint16x4_t vhsub_u16 (uint16x4_t, uint16x4_t)
  Form of expected instruction(s): vhsub.u16 d0, d0, d0
- uint8x8_t vhsub_u8 (uint8x8_t, uint8x8_t)
  Form of expected instruction(s): vhsub.u8 d0, d0, d0
- int32x2_t vhsub_s32 (int32x2_t, int32x2_t)
  Form of expected instruction(s): vhsub.s32 d0, d0, d0
- int16x4_t vhsub_s16 (int16x4_t, int16x4_t)
  Form of expected instruction(s): vhsub.s16 d0, d0, d0
- int8x8_t vhsub_s8 (int8x8_t, int8x8_t)
  Form of expected instruction(s): vhsub.s8 d0, d0, d0
- uint32x4_t vhsubq_u32 (uint32x4_t, uint32x4_t)
  Form of expected instruction(s): vhsub.u32 q0, q0, q0
- uint16x8_t vhsubq_u16 (uint16x8_t, uint16x8_t)
  Form of expected instruction(s): vhsub.u16 q0, q0, q0
- uint8x16_t vhsubq_u8 (uint8x16_t, uint8x16_t)
  Form of expected instruction(s): vhsub.u8 q0, q0, q0
- int32x4_t vhsubq_s32 (int32x4_t, int32x4_t)
  Form of expected instruction(s): vhsub.s32 q0, q0, q0
- int16x8_t vhsubq_s16 (int16x8_t, int16x8_t)
  Form of expected instruction(s): vhsub.s16 q0, q0, q0
- int8x16_t vhsubq_s8 (int8x16_t, int8x16_t)
  Form of expected instruction(s): vhsub.s8 q0, q0, q0
- uint32x2_t vqsub_u32 (uint32x2_t, uint32x2_t)
  Form of expected instruction(s): vqsub.u32 d0, d0, d0
- uint16x4_t vqsub_u16 (uint16x4_t, uint16x4_t)
  Form of expected instruction(s): vqsub.u16 d0, d0, d0
- uint8x8_t vqsub_u8 (uint8x8_t, uint8x8_t)
  Form of expected instruction(s): vqsub.u8 d0, d0, d0
- int32x2_t vqsub_s32 (int32x2_t, int32x2_t)
  Form of expected instruction(s): vqsub.s32 d0, d0, d0
- int16x4_t vqsub_s16 (int16x4_t, int16x4_t)
  Form of expected instruction(s): vqsub.s16 d0, d0, d0
- int8x8_t vqsub_s8 (int8x8_t, int8x8_t)
  Form of expected instruction(s): vqsub.s8 d0, d0, d0

- uint64x1_t vqsub_u64 (uint64x1_t, uint64x1_t)
  Form of expected instruction(s): **vqsub.u64** *d0, d0, d0*
- int64x1_t vqsub_s64 (int64x1_t, int64x1_t)
  Form of expected instruction(s): **vqsub.s64** *d0, d0, d0*
- uint32x4_t vqsubq_u32 (uint32x4_t, uint32x4_t)
  Form of expected instruction(s): **vqsub.u32** *q0, q0, q0*
- uint16x8_t vqsubq_u16 (uint16x8_t, uint16x8_t)
  Form of expected instruction(s): **vqsub.u16** *q0, q0, q0*
- uint8x16_t vqsubq_u8 (uint8x16_t, uint8x16_t)
  Form of expected instruction(s): **vqsub.u8** *q0, q0, q0*
- int32x4_t vqsubq_s32 (int32x4_t, int32x4_t)
  Form of expected instruction(s): **vqsub.s32** *q0, q0, q0*
- int16x8_t vqsubq_s16 (int16x8_t, int16x8_t)
  Form of expected instruction(s): **vqsub.s16** *q0, q0, q0*
- int8x16_t vqsubq_s8 (int8x16_t, int8x16_t)
  Form of expected instruction(s): **vqsub.s8** *q0, q0, q0*
- uint64x2_t vqsubq_u64 (uint64x2_t, uint64x2_t)
  Form of expected instruction(s): **vqsub.u64** *q0, q0, q0*
- int64x2_t vqsubq_s64 (int64x2_t, int64x2_t)
  Form of expected instruction(s): **vqsub.s64** *q0, q0, q0*
- uint32x2_t vsubhn_u64 (uint64x2_t, uint64x2_t)
  Form of expected instruction(s): **vsubhn.i64** *d0, q0, q0*
- uint16x4_t vsubhn_u32 (uint32x4_t, uint32x4_t)
  Form of expected instruction(s): **vsubhn.i32** *d0, q0, q0*
- uint8x8_t vsubhn_u16 (uint16x8_t, uint16x8_t)
  Form of expected instruction(s): **vsubhn.i16** *d0, q0, q0*
- int32x2_t vsubhn_s64 (int64x2_t, int64x2_t)
  Form of expected instruction(s): **vsubhn.i64** *d0, q0, q0*
- int16x4_t vsubhn_s32 (int32x4_t, int32x4_t)
  Form of expected instruction(s): **vsubhn.i32** *d0, q0, q0*
- int8x8_t vsubhn_s16 (int16x8_t, int16x8_t)
  Form of expected instruction(s): **vsubhn.i16** *d0, q0, q0*
- uint32x2_t vrsubhn_u64 (uint64x2_t, uint64x2_t)
  Form of expected instruction(s): **vrsubhn.i64** *d0, q0, q0*
- uint16x4_t vrsubhn_u32 (uint32x4_t, uint32x4_t)
  Form of expected instruction(s): **vrsubhn.i32** *d0, q0, q0*
- uint8x8_t vrsubhn_u16 (uint16x8_t, uint16x8_t)
  Form of expected instruction(s): **vrsubhn.i16** *d0, q0, q0*
- int32x2_t vrsubhn_s64 (int64x2_t, int64x2_t)
  Form of expected instruction(s): **vrsubhn.i64** *d0, q0, q0*
- int16x4_t vrsubhn_s32 (int32x4_t, int32x4_t)
  Form of expected instruction(s): **vrsubhn.i32** *d0, q0, q0*

Chapter 5: Extensions to the C Language Family 359

- int8x8_t vrsubhn_s16 (int16x8_t, int16x8_t)
  Form of expected instruction(s): vrsubhn.i16 *d0, q0, q0*

5.50.3.6 Comparison (equal-to)

- uint32x2_t vceq_u32 (uint32x2_t, uint32x2_t)
  Form of expected instruction(s): vceq.i32 *d0, d0, d0*
- uint16x4_t vceq_u16 (uint16x4_t, uint16x4_t)
  Form of expected instruction(s): vceq.i16 *d0, d0, d0*
- uint8x8_t vceq_u8 (uint8x8_t, uint8x8_t)
  Form of expected instruction(s): vceq.i8 *d0, d0, d0*
- uint32x2_t vceq_s32 (int32x2_t, int32x2_t)
  Form of expected instruction(s): vceq.i32 *d0, d0, d0*
- uint16x4_t vceq_s16 (int16x4_t, int16x4_t)
  Form of expected instruction(s): vceq.i16 *d0, d0, d0*
- uint8x8_t vceq_s8 (int8x8_t, int8x8_t)
  Form of expected instruction(s): vceq.i8 *d0, d0, d0*
- uint32x2_t vceq_f32 (float32x2_t, float32x2_t)
  Form of expected instruction(s): vceq.f32 *d0, d0, d0*
- uint8x8_t vceq_p8 (poly8x8_t, poly8x8_t)
  Form of expected instruction(s): vceq.i8 *d0, d0, d0*
- uint32x4_t vceqq_u32 (uint32x4_t, uint32x4_t)
  Form of expected instruction(s): vceq.i32 *q0, q0, q0*
- uint16x8_t vceqq_u16 (uint16x8_t, uint16x8_t)
  Form of expected instruction(s): vceq.i16 *q0, q0, q0*
- uint8x16_t vceqq_u8 (uint8x16_t, uint8x16_t)
  Form of expected instruction(s): vceq.i8 *q0, q0, q0*
- uint32x4_t vceqq_s32 (int32x4_t, int32x4_t)
  Form of expected instruction(s): vceq.i32 *q0, q0, q0*
- uint16x8_t vceqq_s16 (int16x8_t, int16x8_t)
  Form of expected instruction(s): vceq.i16 *q0, q0, q0*
- uint8x16_t vceqq_s8 (int8x16_t, int8x16_t)
  Form of expected instruction(s): vceq.i8 *q0, q0, q0*
- uint32x4_t vceqq_f32 (float32x4_t, float32x4_t)
  Form of expected instruction(s): vceq.f32 *q0, q0, q0*
- uint8x16_t vceqq_p8 (poly8x16_t, poly8x16_t)
  Form of expected instruction(s): vceq.i8 *q0, q0, q0*

5.50.3.7 Comparison (greater-than-or-equal-to)

- uint32x2_t vcge_u32 (uint32x2_t, uint32x2_t)
  Form of expected instruction(s): vcge.u32 *d0, d0, d0*
- uint16x4_t vcge_u16 (uint16x4_t, uint16x4_t)
  Form of expected instruction(s): vcge.u16 *d0, d0, d0*

- uint8x8_t vcge_u8 (uint8x8_t, uint8x8_t)
  Form of expected instruction(s): `vcge.u8 d0, d0, d0`
- uint32x2_t vcge_s32 (int32x2_t, int32x2_t)
  Form of expected instruction(s): `vcge.s32 d0, d0, d0`
- uint16x4_t vcge_s16 (int16x4_t, int16x4_t)
  Form of expected instruction(s): `vcge.s16 d0, d0, d0`
- uint8x8_t vcge_s8 (int8x8_t, int8x8_t)
  Form of expected instruction(s): `vcge.s8 d0, d0, d0`
- uint32x2_t vcge_f32 (float32x2_t, float32x2_t)
  Form of expected instruction(s): `vcge.f32 d0, d0, d0`
- uint32x4_t vcgeq_u32 (uint32x4_t, uint32x4_t)
  Form of expected instruction(s): `vcge.u32 q0, q0, q0`
- uint16x8_t vcgeq_u16 (uint16x8_t, uint16x8_t)
  Form of expected instruction(s): `vcge.u16 q0, q0, q0`
- uint8x16_t vcgeq_u8 (uint8x16_t, uint8x16_t)
  Form of expected instruction(s): `vcge.u8 q0, q0, q0`
- uint32x4_t vcgeq_s32 (int32x4_t, int32x4_t)
  Form of expected instruction(s): `vcge.s32 q0, q0, q0`
- uint16x8_t vcgeq_s16 (int16x8_t, int16x8_t)
  Form of expected instruction(s): `vcge.s16 q0, q0, q0`
- uint8x16_t vcgeq_s8 (int8x16_t, int8x16_t)
  Form of expected instruction(s): `vcge.s8 q0, q0, q0`
- uint32x4_t vcgeq_f32 (float32x4_t, float32x4_t)
  Form of expected instruction(s): `vcge.f32 q0, q0, q0`

5.50.3.8 Comparison (less-than-or-equal-to)

- uint32x2_t vcle_u32 (uint32x2_t, uint32x2_t)
  Form of expected instruction(s): `vcge.u32 d0, d0, d0`
- uint16x4_t vcle_u16 (uint16x4_t, uint16x4_t)
  Form of expected instruction(s): `vcge.u16 d0, d0, d0`
- uint8x8_t vcle_u8 (uint8x8_t, uint8x8_t)
  Form of expected instruction(s): `vcge.u8 d0, d0, d0`
- uint32x2_t vcle_s32 (int32x2_t, int32x2_t)
  Form of expected instruction(s): `vcge.s32 d0, d0, d0`
- uint16x4_t vcle_s16 (int16x4_t, int16x4_t)
  Form of expected instruction(s): `vcge.s16 d0, d0, d0`
- uint8x8_t vcle_s8 (int8x8_t, int8x8_t)
  Form of expected instruction(s): `vcge.s8 d0, d0, d0`
- uint32x2_t vcle_f32 (float32x2_t, float32x2_t)
  Form of expected instruction(s): `vcge.f32 d0, d0, d0`
- uint32x4_t vcleq_u32 (uint32x4_t, uint32x4_t)
  Form of expected instruction(s): `vcge.u32 q0, q0, q0`

- uint16x8_t vcleq_u16 (uint16x8_t, uint16x8_t)
  Form of expected instruction(s): **vcge.u16** *q0, q0, q0*
- uint8x16_t vcleq_u8 (uint8x16_t, uint8x16_t)
  Form of expected instruction(s): **vcge.u8** *q0, q0, q0*
- uint32x4_t vcleq_s32 (int32x4_t, int32x4_t)
  Form of expected instruction(s): **vcge.s32** *q0, q0, q0*
- uint16x8_t vcleq_s16 (int16x8_t, int16x8_t)
  Form of expected instruction(s): **vcge.s16** *q0, q0, q0*
- uint8x16_t vcleq_s8 (int8x16_t, int8x16_t)
  Form of expected instruction(s): **vcge.s8** *q0, q0, q0*
- uint32x4_t vcleq_f32 (float32x4_t, float32x4_t)
  Form of expected instruction(s): **vcge.f32** *q0, q0, q0*

5.50.3.9 Comparison (greater-than)

- uint32x2_t vcgt_u32 (uint32x2_t, uint32x2_t)
  Form of expected instruction(s): **vcgt.u32** *d0, d0, d0*
- uint16x4_t vcgt_u16 (uint16x4_t, uint16x4_t)
  Form of expected instruction(s): **vcgt.u16** *d0, d0, d0*
- uint8x8_t vcgt_u8 (uint8x8_t, uint8x8_t)
  Form of expected instruction(s): **vcgt.u8** *d0, d0, d0*
- uint32x2_t vcgt_s32 (int32x2_t, int32x2_t)
  Form of expected instruction(s): **vcgt.s32** *d0, d0, d0*
- uint16x4_t vcgt_s16 (int16x4_t, int16x4_t)
  Form of expected instruction(s): **vcgt.s16** *d0, d0, d0*
- uint8x8_t vcgt_s8 (int8x8_t, int8x8_t)
  Form of expected instruction(s): **vcgt.s8** *d0, d0, d0*
- uint32x2_t vcgt_f32 (float32x2_t, float32x2_t)
  Form of expected instruction(s): **vcgt.f32** *d0, d0, d0*
- uint32x4_t vcgtq_u32 (uint32x4_t, uint32x4_t)
  Form of expected instruction(s): **vcgt.u32** *q0, q0, q0*
- uint16x8_t vcgtq_u16 (uint16x8_t, uint16x8_t)
  Form of expected instruction(s): **vcgt.u16** *q0, q0, q0*
- uint8x16_t vcgtq_u8 (uint8x16_t, uint8x16_t)
  Form of expected instruction(s): **vcgt.u8** *q0, q0, q0*
- uint32x4_t vcgtq_s32 (int32x4_t, int32x4_t)
  Form of expected instruction(s): **vcgt.s32** *q0, q0, q0*
- uint16x8_t vcgtq_s16 (int16x8_t, int16x8_t)
  Form of expected instruction(s): **vcgt.s16** *q0, q0, q0*
- uint8x16_t vcgtq_s8 (int8x16_t, int8x16_t)
  Form of expected instruction(s): **vcgt.s8** *q0, q0, q0*
- uint32x4_t vcgtq_f32 (float32x4_t, float32x4_t)
  Form of expected instruction(s): **vcgt.f32** *q0, q0, q0*

5.50.3.10 Comparison (less-than)

- uint32x2_t vclt_u32 (uint32x2_t, uint32x2_t)
  Form of expected instruction(s): `vcgt.u32` *d0, d0, d0*
- uint16x4_t vclt_u16 (uint16x4_t, uint16x4_t)
  Form of expected instruction(s): `vcgt.u16` *d0, d0, d0*
- uint8x8_t vclt_u8 (uint8x8_t, uint8x8_t)
  Form of expected instruction(s): `vcgt.u8` *d0, d0, d0*
- uint32x2_t vclt_s32 (int32x2_t, int32x2_t)
  Form of expected instruction(s): `vcgt.s32` *d0, d0, d0*
- uint16x4_t vclt_s16 (int16x4_t, int16x4_t)
  Form of expected instruction(s): `vcgt.s16` *d0, d0, d0*
- uint8x8_t vclt_s8 (int8x8_t, int8x8_t)
  Form of expected instruction(s): `vcgt.s8` *d0, d0, d0*
- uint32x2_t vclt_f32 (float32x2_t, float32x2_t)
  Form of expected instruction(s): `vcgt.f32` *d0, d0, d0*
- uint32x4_t vcltq_u32 (uint32x4_t, uint32x4_t)
  Form of expected instruction(s): `vcgt.u32` *q0, q0, q0*
- uint16x8_t vcltq_u16 (uint16x8_t, uint16x8_t)
  Form of expected instruction(s): `vcgt.u16` *q0, q0, q0*
- uint8x16_t vcltq_u8 (uint8x16_t, uint8x16_t)
  Form of expected instruction(s): `vcgt.u8` *q0, q0, q0*
- uint32x4_t vcltq_s32 (int32x4_t, int32x4_t)
  Form of expected instruction(s): `vcgt.s32` *q0, q0, q0*
- uint16x8_t vcltq_s16 (int16x8_t, int16x8_t)
  Form of expected instruction(s): `vcgt.s16` *q0, q0, q0*
- uint8x16_t vcltq_s8 (int8x16_t, int8x16_t)
  Form of expected instruction(s): `vcgt.s8` *q0, q0, q0*
- uint32x4_t vcltq_f32 (float32x4_t, float32x4_t)
  Form of expected instruction(s): `vcgt.f32` *q0, q0, q0*

5.50.3.11 Comparison (absolute greater-than-or-equal-to)

- uint32x2_t vcage_f32 (float32x2_t, float32x2_t)
  Form of expected instruction(s): `vacge.f32` *d0, d0, d0*
- uint32x4_t vcageq_f32 (float32x4_t, float32x4_t)
  Form of expected instruction(s): `vacge.f32` *q0, q0, q0*

5.50.3.12 Comparison (absolute less-than-or-equal-to)

- uint32x2_t vcale_f32 (float32x2_t, float32x2_t)
  Form of expected instruction(s): `vacge.f32` *d0, d0, d0*
- uint32x4_t vcaleq_f32 (float32x4_t, float32x4_t)
  Form of expected instruction(s): `vacge.f32` *q0, q0, q0*

5.50.3.13 Comparison (absolute greater-than)
- uint32x2_t vcagt_f32 (float32x2_t, float32x2_t)
  Form of expected instruction(s): `vacgt.f32 d0, d0, d0`
- uint32x4_t vcagtq_f32 (float32x4_t, float32x4_t)
  Form of expected instruction(s): `vacgt.f32 q0, q0, q0`

5.50.3.14 Comparison (absolute less-than)
- uint32x2_t vcalt_f32 (float32x2_t, float32x2_t)
  Form of expected instruction(s): `vacgt.f32 d0, d0, d0`
- uint32x4_t vcaltq_f32 (float32x4_t, float32x4_t)
  Form of expected instruction(s): `vacgt.f32 q0, q0, q0`

5.50.3.15 Test bits
- uint32x2_t vtst_u32 (uint32x2_t, uint32x2_t)
  Form of expected instruction(s): `vtst.32 d0, d0, d0`
- uint16x4_t vtst_u16 (uint16x4_t, uint16x4_t)
  Form of expected instruction(s): `vtst.16 d0, d0, d0`
- uint8x8_t vtst_u8 (uint8x8_t, uint8x8_t)
  Form of expected instruction(s): `vtst.8 d0, d0, d0`
- uint32x2_t vtst_s32 (int32x2_t, int32x2_t)
  Form of expected instruction(s): `vtst.32 d0, d0, d0`
- uint16x4_t vtst_s16 (int16x4_t, int16x4_t)
  Form of expected instruction(s): `vtst.16 d0, d0, d0`
- uint8x8_t vtst_s8 (int8x8_t, int8x8_t)
  Form of expected instruction(s): `vtst.8 d0, d0, d0`
- uint8x8_t vtst_p8 (poly8x8_t, poly8x8_t)
  Form of expected instruction(s): `vtst.8 d0, d0, d0`
- uint32x4_t vtstq_u32 (uint32x4_t, uint32x4_t)
  Form of expected instruction(s): `vtst.32 q0, q0, q0`
- uint16x8_t vtstq_u16 (uint16x8_t, uint16x8_t)
  Form of expected instruction(s): `vtst.16 q0, q0, q0`
- uint8x16_t vtstq_u8 (uint8x16_t, uint8x16_t)
  Form of expected instruction(s): `vtst.8 q0, q0, q0`
- uint32x4_t vtstq_s32 (int32x4_t, int32x4_t)
  Form of expected instruction(s): `vtst.32 q0, q0, q0`
- uint16x8_t vtstq_s16 (int16x8_t, int16x8_t)
  Form of expected instruction(s): `vtst.16 q0, q0, q0`
- uint8x16_t vtstq_s8 (int8x16_t, int8x16_t)
  Form of expected instruction(s): `vtst.8 q0, q0, q0`
- uint8x16_t vtstq_p8 (poly8x16_t, poly8x16_t)
  Form of expected instruction(s): `vtst.8 q0, q0, q0`

5.50.3.16 Absolute difference

- uint32x2_t vabd_u32 (uint32x2_t, uint32x2_t)
  Form of expected instruction(s): `vabd.u32 d0, d0, d0`
- uint16x4_t vabd_u16 (uint16x4_t, uint16x4_t)
  Form of expected instruction(s): `vabd.u16 d0, d0, d0`
- uint8x8_t vabd_u8 (uint8x8_t, uint8x8_t)
  Form of expected instruction(s): `vabd.u8 d0, d0, d0`
- int32x2_t vabd_s32 (int32x2_t, int32x2_t)
  Form of expected instruction(s): `vabd.s32 d0, d0, d0`
- int16x4_t vabd_s16 (int16x4_t, int16x4_t)
  Form of expected instruction(s): `vabd.s16 d0, d0, d0`
- int8x8_t vabd_s8 (int8x8_t, int8x8_t)
  Form of expected instruction(s): `vabd.s8 d0, d0, d0`
- float32x2_t vabd_f32 (float32x2_t, float32x2_t)
  Form of expected instruction(s): `vabd.f32 d0, d0, d0`
- uint32x4_t vabdq_u32 (uint32x4_t, uint32x4_t)
  Form of expected instruction(s): `vabd.u32 q0, q0, q0`
- uint16x8_t vabdq_u16 (uint16x8_t, uint16x8_t)
  Form of expected instruction(s): `vabd.u16 q0, q0, q0`
- uint8x16_t vabdq_u8 (uint8x16_t, uint8x16_t)
  Form of expected instruction(s): `vabd.u8 q0, q0, q0`
- int32x4_t vabdq_s32 (int32x4_t, int32x4_t)
  Form of expected instruction(s): `vabd.s32 q0, q0, q0`
- int16x8_t vabdq_s16 (int16x8_t, int16x8_t)
  Form of expected instruction(s): `vabd.s16 q0, q0, q0`
- int8x16_t vabdq_s8 (int8x16_t, int8x16_t)
  Form of expected instruction(s): `vabd.s8 q0, q0, q0`
- float32x4_t vabdq_f32 (float32x4_t, float32x4_t)
  Form of expected instruction(s): `vabd.f32 q0, q0, q0`
- uint64x2_t vabdl_u32 (uint32x2_t, uint32x2_t)
  Form of expected instruction(s): `vabdl.u32 q0, d0, d0`
- uint32x4_t vabdl_u16 (uint16x4_t, uint16x4_t)
  Form of expected instruction(s): `vabdl.u16 q0, d0, d0`
- uint16x8_t vabdl_u8 (uint8x8_t, uint8x8_t)
  Form of expected instruction(s): `vabdl.u8 q0, d0, d0`
- int64x2_t vabdl_s32 (int32x2_t, int32x2_t)
  Form of expected instruction(s): `vabdl.s32 q0, d0, d0`
- int32x4_t vabdl_s16 (int16x4_t, int16x4_t)
  Form of expected instruction(s): `vabdl.s16 q0, d0, d0`
- int16x8_t vabdl_s8 (int8x8_t, int8x8_t)
  Form of expected instruction(s): `vabdl.s8 q0, d0, d0`

Chapter 5: Extensions to the C Language Family   365

5.50.3.17 Absolute difference and accumulate

- uint32x2_t vaba_u32 (uint32x2_t, uint32x2_t, uint32x2_t)
  Form of expected instruction(s): `vaba.u32 d0, d0, d0`
- uint16x4_t vaba_u16 (uint16x4_t, uint16x4_t, uint16x4_t)
  Form of expected instruction(s): `vaba.u16 d0, d0, d0`
- uint8x8_t vaba_u8 (uint8x8_t, uint8x8_t, uint8x8_t)
  Form of expected instruction(s): `vaba.u8 d0, d0, d0`
- int32x2_t vaba_s32 (int32x2_t, int32x2_t, int32x2_t)
  Form of expected instruction(s): `vaba.s32 d0, d0, d0`
- int16x4_t vaba_s16 (int16x4_t, int16x4_t, int16x4_t)
  Form of expected instruction(s): `vaba.s16 d0, d0, d0`
- int8x8_t vaba_s8 (int8x8_t, int8x8_t, int8x8_t)
  Form of expected instruction(s): `vaba.s8 d0, d0, d0`
- uint32x4_t vabaq_u32 (uint32x4_t, uint32x4_t, uint32x4_t)
  Form of expected instruction(s): `vaba.u32 q0, q0, q0`
- uint16x8_t vabaq_u16 (uint16x8_t, uint16x8_t, uint16x8_t)
  Form of expected instruction(s): `vaba.u16 q0, q0, q0`
- uint8x16_t vabaq_u8 (uint8x16_t, uint8x16_t, uint8x16_t)
  Form of expected instruction(s): `vaba.u8 q0, q0, q0`
- int32x4_t vabaq_s32 (int32x4_t, int32x4_t, int32x4_t)
  Form of expected instruction(s): `vaba.s32 q0, q0, q0`
- int16x8_t vabaq_s16 (int16x8_t, int16x8_t, int16x8_t)
  Form of expected instruction(s): `vaba.s16 q0, q0, q0`
- int8x16_t vabaq_s8 (int8x16_t, int8x16_t, int8x16_t)
  Form of expected instruction(s): `vaba.s8 q0, q0, q0`
- uint64x2_t vabal_u32 (uint64x2_t, uint32x2_t, uint32x2_t)
  Form of expected instruction(s): `vabal.u32 q0, d0, d0`
- uint32x4_t vabal_u16 (uint32x4_t, uint16x4_t, uint16x4_t)
  Form of expected instruction(s): `vabal.u16 q0, d0, d0`
- uint16x8_t vabal_u8 (uint16x8_t, uint8x8_t, uint8x8_t)
  Form of expected instruction(s): `vabal.u8 q0, d0, d0`
- int64x2_t vabal_s32 (int64x2_t, int32x2_t, int32x2_t)
  Form of expected instruction(s): `vabal.s32 q0, d0, d0`
- int32x4_t vabal_s16 (int32x4_t, int16x4_t, int16x4_t)
  Form of expected instruction(s): `vabal.s16 q0, d0, d0`
- int16x8_t vabal_s8 (int16x8_t, int8x8_t, int8x8_t)
  Form of expected instruction(s): `vabal.s8 q0, d0, d0`

5.50.3.18 Maximum

- uint32x2_t vmax_u32 (uint32x2_t, uint32x2_t)
  Form of expected instruction(s): `vmax.u32 d0, d0, d0`
- uint16x4_t vmax_u16 (uint16x4_t, uint16x4_t)
  Form of expected instruction(s): `vmax.u16 d0, d0, d0`

- uint8x8_t vmax_u8 (uint8x8_t, uint8x8_t)
  Form of expected instruction(s): `vmax.u8 d0, d0, d0`
- int32x2_t vmax_s32 (int32x2_t, int32x2_t)
  Form of expected instruction(s): `vmax.s32 d0, d0, d0`
- int16x4_t vmax_s16 (int16x4_t, int16x4_t)
  Form of expected instruction(s): `vmax.s16 d0, d0, d0`
- int8x8_t vmax_s8 (int8x8_t, int8x8_t)
  Form of expected instruction(s): `vmax.s8 d0, d0, d0`
- float32x2_t vmax_f32 (float32x2_t, float32x2_t)
  Form of expected instruction(s): `vmax.f32 d0, d0, d0`
- uint32x4_t vmaxq_u32 (uint32x4_t, uint32x4_t)
  Form of expected instruction(s): `vmax.u32 q0, q0, q0`
- uint16x8_t vmaxq_u16 (uint16x8_t, uint16x8_t)
  Form of expected instruction(s): `vmax.u16 q0, q0, q0`
- uint8x16_t vmaxq_u8 (uint8x16_t, uint8x16_t)
  Form of expected instruction(s): `vmax.u8 q0, q0, q0`
- int32x4_t vmaxq_s32 (int32x4_t, int32x4_t)
  Form of expected instruction(s): `vmax.s32 q0, q0, q0`
- int16x8_t vmaxq_s16 (int16x8_t, int16x8_t)
  Form of expected instruction(s): `vmax.s16 q0, q0, q0`
- int8x16_t vmaxq_s8 (int8x16_t, int8x16_t)
  Form of expected instruction(s): `vmax.s8 q0, q0, q0`
- float32x4_t vmaxq_f32 (float32x4_t, float32x4_t)
  Form of expected instruction(s): `vmax.f32 q0, q0, q0`

5.50.3.19 Minimum

- uint32x2_t vmin_u32 (uint32x2_t, uint32x2_t)
  Form of expected instruction(s): `vmin.u32 d0, d0, d0`
- uint16x4_t vmin_u16 (uint16x4_t, uint16x4_t)
  Form of expected instruction(s): `vmin.u16 d0, d0, d0`
- uint8x8_t vmin_u8 (uint8x8_t, uint8x8_t)
  Form of expected instruction(s): `vmin.u8 d0, d0, d0`
- int32x2_t vmin_s32 (int32x2_t, int32x2_t)
  Form of expected instruction(s): `vmin.s32 d0, d0, d0`
- int16x4_t vmin_s16 (int16x4_t, int16x4_t)
  Form of expected instruction(s): `vmin.s16 d0, d0, d0`
- int8x8_t vmin_s8 (int8x8_t, int8x8_t)
  Form of expected instruction(s): `vmin.s8 d0, d0, d0`
- float32x2_t vmin_f32 (float32x2_t, float32x2_t)
  Form of expected instruction(s): `vmin.f32 d0, d0, d0`
- uint32x4_t vminq_u32 (uint32x4_t, uint32x4_t)
  Form of expected instruction(s): `vmin.u32 q0, q0, q0`

Chapter 5: Extensions to the C Language Family   367

- uint16x8_t vminq_u16 (uint16x8_t, uint16x8_t)
  Form of expected instruction(s): `vmin.u16 q0, q0, q0`
- uint8x16_t vminq_u8 (uint8x16_t, uint8x16_t)
  Form of expected instruction(s): `vmin.u8 q0, q0, q0`
- int32x4_t vminq_s32 (int32x4_t, int32x4_t)
  Form of expected instruction(s): `vmin.s32 q0, q0, q0`
- int16x8_t vminq_s16 (int16x8_t, int16x8_t)
  Form of expected instruction(s): `vmin.s16 q0, q0, q0`
- int8x16_t vminq_s8 (int8x16_t, int8x16_t)
  Form of expected instruction(s): `vmin.s8 q0, q0, q0`
- float32x4_t vminq_f32 (float32x4_t, float32x4_t)
  Form of expected instruction(s): `vmin.f32 q0, q0, q0`

5.50.3.20 Pairwise add

- uint32x2_t vpadd_u32 (uint32x2_t, uint32x2_t)
  Form of expected instruction(s): `vpadd.i32 d0, d0, d0`
- uint16x4_t vpadd_u16 (uint16x4_t, uint16x4_t)
  Form of expected instruction(s): `vpadd.i16 d0, d0, d0`
- uint8x8_t vpadd_u8 (uint8x8_t, uint8x8_t)
  Form of expected instruction(s): `vpadd.i8 d0, d0, d0`
- int32x2_t vpadd_s32 (int32x2_t, int32x2_t)
  Form of expected instruction(s): `vpadd.i32 d0, d0, d0`
- int16x4_t vpadd_s16 (int16x4_t, int16x4_t)
  Form of expected instruction(s): `vpadd.i16 d0, d0, d0`
- int8x8_t vpadd_s8 (int8x8_t, int8x8_t)
  Form of expected instruction(s): `vpadd.i8 d0, d0, d0`
- float32x2_t vpadd_f32 (float32x2_t, float32x2_t)
  Form of expected instruction(s): `vpadd.f32 d0, d0, d0`
- uint64x1_t vpaddl_u32 (uint32x2_t)
  Form of expected instruction(s): `vpaddl.u32 d0, d0`
- uint32x2_t vpaddl_u16 (uint16x4_t)
  Form of expected instruction(s): `vpaddl.u16 d0, d0`
- uint16x4_t vpaddl_u8 (uint8x8_t)
  Form of expected instruction(s): `vpaddl.u8 d0, d0`
- int64x1_t vpaddl_s32 (int32x2_t)
  Form of expected instruction(s): `vpaddl.s32 d0, d0`
- int32x2_t vpaddl_s16 (int16x4_t)
  Form of expected instruction(s): `vpaddl.s16 d0, d0`
- int16x4_t vpaddl_s8 (int8x8_t)
  Form of expected instruction(s): `vpaddl.s8 d0, d0`
- uint64x2_t vpaddlq_u32 (uint32x4_t)
  Form of expected instruction(s): `vpaddl.u32 q0, q0`

- uint32x4_t vpaddlq_u16 (uint16x8_t)
  Form of expected instruction(s): vpaddl.u16 q0, q0
- uint16x8_t vpaddlq_u8 (uint8x16_t)
  Form of expected instruction(s): vpaddl.u8 q0, q0
- int64x2_t vpaddlq_s32 (int32x4_t)
  Form of expected instruction(s): vpaddl.s32 q0, q0
- int32x4_t vpaddlq_s16 (int16x8_t)
  Form of expected instruction(s): vpaddl.s16 q0, q0
- int16x8_t vpaddlq_s8 (int8x16_t)
  Form of expected instruction(s): vpaddl.s8 q0, q0

5.50.3.21 Pairwise add, single_opcode widen and accumulate

- uint64x1_t vpadal_u32 (uint64x1_t, uint32x2_t)
  Form of expected instruction(s): vpadal.u32 d0, d0
- uint32x2_t vpadal_u16 (uint32x2_t, uint16x4_t)
  Form of expected instruction(s): vpadal.u16 d0, d0
- uint16x4_t vpadal_u8 (uint16x4_t, uint8x8_t)
  Form of expected instruction(s): vpadal.u8 d0, d0
- int64x1_t vpadal_s32 (int64x1_t, int32x2_t)
  Form of expected instruction(s): vpadal.s32 d0, d0
- int32x2_t vpadal_s16 (int32x2_t, int16x4_t)
  Form of expected instruction(s): vpadal.s16 d0, d0
- int16x4_t vpadal_s8 (int16x4_t, int8x8_t)
  Form of expected instruction(s): vpadal.s8 d0, d0
- uint64x2_t vpadalq_u32 (uint64x2_t, uint32x4_t)
  Form of expected instruction(s): vpadal.u32 q0, q0
- uint32x4_t vpadalq_u16 (uint32x4_t, uint16x8_t)
  Form of expected instruction(s): vpadal.u16 q0, q0
- uint16x8_t vpadalq_u8 (uint16x8_t, uint8x16_t)
  Form of expected instruction(s): vpadal.u8 q0, q0
- int64x2_t vpadalq_s32 (int64x2_t, int32x4_t)
  Form of expected instruction(s): vpadal.s32 q0, q0
- int32x4_t vpadalq_s16 (int32x4_t, int16x8_t)
  Form of expected instruction(s): vpadal.s16 q0, q0
- int16x8_t vpadalq_s8 (int16x8_t, int8x16_t)
  Form of expected instruction(s): vpadal.s8 q0, q0

5.50.3.22 Folding maximum

- uint32x2_t vpmax_u32 (uint32x2_t, uint32x2_t)
  Form of expected instruction(s): vpmax.u32 d0, d0, d0
- uint16x4_t vpmax_u16 (uint16x4_t, uint16x4_t)
  Form of expected instruction(s): vpmax.u16 d0, d0, d0

Chapter 5: Extensions to the C Language Family   369

- uint8x8_t vpmax_u8 (uint8x8_t, uint8x8_t)
  Form of expected instruction(s): **vpmax.u8** *d0, d0, d0*
- int32x2_t vpmax_s32 (int32x2_t, int32x2_t)
  Form of expected instruction(s): **vpmax.s32** *d0, d0, d0*
- int16x4_t vpmax_s16 (int16x4_t, int16x4_t)
  Form of expected instruction(s): **vpmax.s16** *d0, d0, d0*
- int8x8_t vpmax_s8 (int8x8_t, int8x8_t)
  Form of expected instruction(s): **vpmax.s8** *d0, d0, d0*
- float32x2_t vpmax_f32 (float32x2_t, float32x2_t)
  Form of expected instruction(s): **vpmax.f32** *d0, d0, d0*

5.50.3.23 Folding minimum

- uint32x2_t vpmin_u32 (uint32x2_t, uint32x2_t)
  Form of expected instruction(s): **vpmin.u32** *d0, d0, d0*
- uint16x4_t vpmin_u16 (uint16x4_t, uint16x4_t)
  Form of expected instruction(s): **vpmin.u16** *d0, d0, d0*
- uint8x8_t vpmin_u8 (uint8x8_t, uint8x8_t)
  Form of expected instruction(s): **vpmin.u8** *d0, d0, d0*
- int32x2_t vpmin_s32 (int32x2_t, int32x2_t)
  Form of expected instruction(s): **vpmin.s32** *d0, d0, d0*
- int16x4_t vpmin_s16 (int16x4_t, int16x4_t)
  Form of expected instruction(s): **vpmin.s16** *d0, d0, d0*
- int8x8_t vpmin_s8 (int8x8_t, int8x8_t)
  Form of expected instruction(s): **vpmin.s8** *d0, d0, d0*
- float32x2_t vpmin_f32 (float32x2_t, float32x2_t)
  Form of expected instruction(s): **vpmin.f32** *d0, d0, d0*

5.50.3.24 Reciprocal step

- float32x2_t vrecps_f32 (float32x2_t, float32x2_t)
  Form of expected instruction(s): **vrecps.f32** *d0, d0, d0*
- float32x4_t vrecpsq_f32 (float32x4_t, float32x4_t)
  Form of expected instruction(s): **vrecps.f32** *q0, q0, q0*
- float32x2_t vrsqrts_f32 (float32x2_t, float32x2_t)
  Form of expected instruction(s): **vrsqrts.f32** *d0, d0, d0*
- float32x4_t vrsqrtsq_f32 (float32x4_t, float32x4_t)
  Form of expected instruction(s): **vrsqrts.f32** *q0, q0, q0*

5.50.3.25 Vector shift left

- uint32x2_t vshl_u32 (uint32x2_t, int32x2_t)
  Form of expected instruction(s): **vshl.u32** *d0, d0, d0*
- uint16x4_t vshl_u16 (uint16x4_t, int16x4_t)
  Form of expected instruction(s): **vshl.u16** *d0, d0, d0*
- uint8x8_t vshl_u8 (uint8x8_t, int8x8_t)
  Form of expected instruction(s): **vshl.u8** *d0, d0, d0*

- int32x2_t vshl_s32 (int32x2_t, int32x2_t)
  Form of expected instruction(s): `vshl.s32 d0, d0, d0`
- int16x4_t vshl_s16 (int16x4_t, int16x4_t)
  Form of expected instruction(s): `vshl.s16 d0, d0, d0`
- int8x8_t vshl_s8 (int8x8_t, int8x8_t)
  Form of expected instruction(s): `vshl.s8 d0, d0, d0`
- uint64x1_t vshl_u64 (uint64x1_t, int64x1_t)
  Form of expected instruction(s): `vshl.u64 d0, d0, d0`
- int64x1_t vshl_s64 (int64x1_t, int64x1_t)
  Form of expected instruction(s): `vshl.s64 d0, d0, d0`
- uint32x4_t vshlq_u32 (uint32x4_t, int32x4_t)
  Form of expected instruction(s): `vshl.u32 q0, q0, q0`
- uint16x8_t vshlq_u16 (uint16x8_t, int16x8_t)
  Form of expected instruction(s): `vshl.u16 q0, q0, q0`
- uint8x16_t vshlq_u8 (uint8x16_t, int8x16_t)
  Form of expected instruction(s): `vshl.u8 q0, q0, q0`
- int32x4_t vshlq_s32 (int32x4_t, int32x4_t)
  Form of expected instruction(s): `vshl.s32 q0, q0, q0`
- int16x8_t vshlq_s16 (int16x8_t, int16x8_t)
  Form of expected instruction(s): `vshl.s16 q0, q0, q0`
- int8x16_t vshlq_s8 (int8x16_t, int8x16_t)
  Form of expected instruction(s): `vshl.s8 q0, q0, q0`
- uint64x2_t vshlq_u64 (uint64x2_t, int64x2_t)
  Form of expected instruction(s): `vshl.u64 q0, q0, q0`
- int64x2_t vshlq_s64 (int64x2_t, int64x2_t)
  Form of expected instruction(s): `vshl.s64 q0, q0, q0`
- uint32x2_t vrshl_u32 (uint32x2_t, int32x2_t)
  Form of expected instruction(s): `vrshl.u32 d0, d0, d0`
- uint16x4_t vrshl_u16 (uint16x4_t, int16x4_t)
  Form of expected instruction(s): `vrshl.u16 d0, d0, d0`
- uint8x8_t vrshl_u8 (uint8x8_t, int8x8_t)
  Form of expected instruction(s): `vrshl.u8 d0, d0, d0`
- int32x2_t vrshl_s32 (int32x2_t, int32x2_t)
  Form of expected instruction(s): `vrshl.s32 d0, d0, d0`
- int16x4_t vrshl_s16 (int16x4_t, int16x4_t)
  Form of expected instruction(s): `vrshl.s16 d0, d0, d0`
- int8x8_t vrshl_s8 (int8x8_t, int8x8_t)
  Form of expected instruction(s): `vrshl.s8 d0, d0, d0`
- uint64x1_t vrshl_u64 (uint64x1_t, int64x1_t)
  Form of expected instruction(s): `vrshl.u64 d0, d0, d0`
- int64x1_t vrshl_s64 (int64x1_t, int64x1_t)
  Form of expected instruction(s): `vrshl.s64 d0, d0, d0`

Chapter 5: Extensions to the C Language Family   371

- uint32x4_t vrshlq_u32 (uint32x4_t, int32x4_t)
  Form of expected instruction(s): `vrshl.u32 q0, q0, q0`
- uint16x8_t vrshlq_u16 (uint16x8_t, int16x8_t)
  Form of expected instruction(s): `vrshl.u16 q0, q0, q0`
- uint8x16_t vrshlq_u8 (uint8x16_t, int8x16_t)
  Form of expected instruction(s): `vrshl.u8 q0, q0, q0`
- int32x4_t vrshlq_s32 (int32x4_t, int32x4_t)
  Form of expected instruction(s): `vrshl.s32 q0, q0, q0`
- int16x8_t vrshlq_s16 (int16x8_t, int16x8_t)
  Form of expected instruction(s): `vrshl.s16 q0, q0, q0`
- int8x16_t vrshlq_s8 (int8x16_t, int8x16_t)
  Form of expected instruction(s): `vrshl.s8 q0, q0, q0`
- uint64x2_t vrshlq_u64 (uint64x2_t, int64x2_t)
  Form of expected instruction(s): `vrshl.u64 q0, q0, q0`
- int64x2_t vrshlq_s64 (int64x2_t, int64x2_t)
  Form of expected instruction(s): `vrshl.s64 q0, q0, q0`
- uint32x2_t vqshl_u32 (uint32x2_t, int32x2_t)
  Form of expected instruction(s): `vqshl.u32 d0, d0, d0`
- uint16x4_t vqshl_u16 (uint16x4_t, int16x4_t)
  Form of expected instruction(s): `vqshl.u16 d0, d0, d0`
- uint8x8_t vqshl_u8 (uint8x8_t, int8x8_t)
  Form of expected instruction(s): `vqshl.u8 d0, d0, d0`
- int32x2_t vqshl_s32 (int32x2_t, int32x2_t)
  Form of expected instruction(s): `vqshl.s32 d0, d0, d0`
- int16x4_t vqshl_s16 (int16x4_t, int16x4_t)
  Form of expected instruction(s): `vqshl.s16 d0, d0, d0`
- int8x8_t vqshl_s8 (int8x8_t, int8x8_t)
  Form of expected instruction(s): `vqshl.s8 d0, d0, d0`
- uint64x1_t vqshl_u64 (uint64x1_t, int64x1_t)
  Form of expected instruction(s): `vqshl.u64 d0, d0, d0`
- int64x1_t vqshl_s64 (int64x1_t, int64x1_t)
  Form of expected instruction(s): `vqshl.s64 d0, d0, d0`
- uint32x4_t vqshlq_u32 (uint32x4_t, int32x4_t)
  Form of expected instruction(s): `vqshl.u32 q0, q0, q0`
- uint16x8_t vqshlq_u16 (uint16x8_t, int16x8_t)
  Form of expected instruction(s): `vqshl.u16 q0, q0, q0`
- uint8x16_t vqshlq_u8 (uint8x16_t, int8x16_t)
  Form of expected instruction(s): `vqshl.u8 q0, q0, q0`
- int32x4_t vqshlq_s32 (int32x4_t, int32x4_t)
  Form of expected instruction(s): `vqshl.s32 q0, q0, q0`
- int16x8_t vqshlq_s16 (int16x8_t, int16x8_t)
  Form of expected instruction(s): `vqshl.s16 q0, q0, q0`

- int8x16_t vqshlq_s8 (int8x16_t, int8x16_t)
  Form of expected instruction(s): `vqshl.s8 q0, q0, q0`
- uint64x2_t vqshlq_u64 (uint64x2_t, int64x2_t)
  Form of expected instruction(s): `vqshl.u64 q0, q0, q0`
- int64x2_t vqshlq_s64 (int64x2_t, int64x2_t)
  Form of expected instruction(s): `vqshl.s64 q0, q0, q0`
- uint32x2_t vqrshl_u32 (uint32x2_t, int32x2_t)
  Form of expected instruction(s): `vqrshl.u32 d0, d0, d0`
- uint16x4_t vqrshl_u16 (uint16x4_t, int16x4_t)
  Form of expected instruction(s): `vqrshl.u16 d0, d0, d0`
- uint8x8_t vqrshl_u8 (uint8x8_t, int8x8_t)
  Form of expected instruction(s): `vqrshl.u8 d0, d0, d0`
- int32x2_t vqrshl_s32 (int32x2_t, int32x2_t)
  Form of expected instruction(s): `vqrshl.s32 d0, d0, d0`
- int16x4_t vqrshl_s16 (int16x4_t, int16x4_t)
  Form of expected instruction(s): `vqrshl.s16 d0, d0, d0`
- int8x8_t vqrshl_s8 (int8x8_t, int8x8_t)
  Form of expected instruction(s): `vqrshl.s8 d0, d0, d0`
- uint64x1_t vqrshl_u64 (uint64x1_t, int64x1_t)
  Form of expected instruction(s): `vqrshl.u64 d0, d0, d0`
- int64x1_t vqrshl_s64 (int64x1_t, int64x1_t)
  Form of expected instruction(s): `vqrshl.s64 d0, d0, d0`
- uint32x4_t vqrshlq_u32 (uint32x4_t, int32x4_t)
  Form of expected instruction(s): `vqrshl.u32 q0, q0, q0`
- uint16x8_t vqrshlq_u16 (uint16x8_t, int16x8_t)
  Form of expected instruction(s): `vqrshl.u16 q0, q0, q0`
- uint8x16_t vqrshlq_u8 (uint8x16_t, int8x16_t)
  Form of expected instruction(s): `vqrshl.u8 q0, q0, q0`
- int32x4_t vqrshlq_s32 (int32x4_t, int32x4_t)
  Form of expected instruction(s): `vqrshl.s32 q0, q0, q0`
- int16x8_t vqrshlq_s16 (int16x8_t, int16x8_t)
  Form of expected instruction(s): `vqrshl.s16 q0, q0, q0`
- int8x16_t vqrshlq_s8 (int8x16_t, int8x16_t)
  Form of expected instruction(s): `vqrshl.s8 q0, q0, q0`
- uint64x2_t vqrshlq_u64 (uint64x2_t, int64x2_t)
  Form of expected instruction(s): `vqrshl.u64 q0, q0, q0`
- int64x2_t vqrshlq_s64 (int64x2_t, int64x2_t)
  Form of expected instruction(s): `vqrshl.s64 q0, q0, q0`

5.50.3.26 Vector shift left by constant

- uint32x2_t vshl_n_u32 (uint32x2_t, const int)
  Form of expected instruction(s): `vshl.i32 d0, d0, #0`

Chapter 5: Extensions to the C Language Family   373

- uint16x4_t vshl_n_u16 (uint16x4_t, const int)
  Form of expected instruction(s): `vshl.i16 d0, d0, #0`
- uint8x8_t vshl_n_u8 (uint8x8_t, const int)
  Form of expected instruction(s): `vshl.i8 d0, d0, #0`
- int32x2_t vshl_n_s32 (int32x2_t, const int)
  Form of expected instruction(s): `vshl.i32 d0, d0, #0`
- int16x4_t vshl_n_s16 (int16x4_t, const int)
  Form of expected instruction(s): `vshl.i16 d0, d0, #0`
- int8x8_t vshl_n_s8 (int8x8_t, const int)
  Form of expected instruction(s): `vshl.i8 d0, d0, #0`
- uint64x1_t vshl_n_u64 (uint64x1_t, const int)
  Form of expected instruction(s): `vshl.i64 d0, d0, #0`
- int64x1_t vshl_n_s64 (int64x1_t, const int)
  Form of expected instruction(s): `vshl.i64 d0, d0, #0`
- uint32x4_t vshlq_n_u32 (uint32x4_t, const int)
  Form of expected instruction(s): `vshl.i32 q0, q0, #0`
- uint16x8_t vshlq_n_u16 (uint16x8_t, const int)
  Form of expected instruction(s): `vshl.i16 q0, q0, #0`
- uint8x16_t vshlq_n_u8 (uint8x16_t, const int)
  Form of expected instruction(s): `vshl.i8 q0, q0, #0`
- int32x4_t vshlq_n_s32 (int32x4_t, const int)
  Form of expected instruction(s): `vshl.i32 q0, q0, #0`
- int16x8_t vshlq_n_s16 (int16x8_t, const int)
  Form of expected instruction(s): `vshl.i16 q0, q0, #0`
- int8x16_t vshlq_n_s8 (int8x16_t, const int)
  Form of expected instruction(s): `vshl.i8 q0, q0, #0`
- uint64x2_t vshlq_n_u64 (uint64x2_t, const int)
  Form of expected instruction(s): `vshl.i64 q0, q0, #0`
- int64x2_t vshlq_n_s64 (int64x2_t, const int)
  Form of expected instruction(s): `vshl.i64 q0, q0, #0`
- uint32x2_t vqshl_n_u32 (uint32x2_t, const int)
  Form of expected instruction(s): `vqshl.u32 d0, d0, #0`
- uint16x4_t vqshl_n_u16 (uint16x4_t, const int)
  Form of expected instruction(s): `vqshl.u16 d0, d0, #0`
- uint8x8_t vqshl_n_u8 (uint8x8_t, const int)
  Form of expected instruction(s): `vqshl.u8 d0, d0, #0`
- int32x2_t vqshl_n_s32 (int32x2_t, const int)
  Form of expected instruction(s): `vqshl.s32 d0, d0, #0`
- int16x4_t vqshl_n_s16 (int16x4_t, const int)
  Form of expected instruction(s): `vqshl.s16 d0, d0, #0`
- int8x8_t vqshl_n_s8 (int8x8_t, const int)
  Form of expected instruction(s): `vqshl.s8 d0, d0, #0`

- uint64x1_t vqshl_n_u64 (uint64x1_t, const int)
  Form of expected instruction(s): `vqshl.u64 d0, d0, #0`
- int64x1_t vqshl_n_s64 (int64x1_t, const int)
  Form of expected instruction(s): `vqshl.s64 d0, d0, #0`
- uint32x4_t vqshlq_n_u32 (uint32x4_t, const int)
  Form of expected instruction(s): `vqshl.u32 q0, q0, #0`
- uint16x8_t vqshlq_n_u16 (uint16x8_t, const int)
  Form of expected instruction(s): `vqshl.u16 q0, q0, #0`
- uint8x16_t vqshlq_n_u8 (uint8x16_t, const int)
  Form of expected instruction(s): `vqshl.u8 q0, q0, #0`
- int32x4_t vqshlq_n_s32 (int32x4_t, const int)
  Form of expected instruction(s): `vqshl.s32 q0, q0, #0`
- int16x8_t vqshlq_n_s16 (int16x8_t, const int)
  Form of expected instruction(s): `vqshl.s16 q0, q0, #0`
- int8x16_t vqshlq_n_s8 (int8x16_t, const int)
  Form of expected instruction(s): `vqshl.s8 q0, q0, #0`
- uint64x2_t vqshlq_n_u64 (uint64x2_t, const int)
  Form of expected instruction(s): `vqshl.u64 q0, q0, #0`
- int64x2_t vqshlq_n_s64 (int64x2_t, const int)
  Form of expected instruction(s): `vqshl.s64 q0, q0, #0`
- uint64x1_t vqshlu_n_s64 (int64x1_t, const int)
  Form of expected instruction(s): `vqshlu.s64 d0, d0, #0`
- uint32x2_t vqshlu_n_s32 (int32x2_t, const int)
  Form of expected instruction(s): `vqshlu.s32 d0, d0, #0`
- uint16x4_t vqshlu_n_s16 (int16x4_t, const int)
  Form of expected instruction(s): `vqshlu.s16 d0, d0, #0`
- uint8x8_t vqshlu_n_s8 (int8x8_t, const int)
  Form of expected instruction(s): `vqshlu.s8 d0, d0, #0`
- uint64x2_t vqshluq_n_s64 (int64x2_t, const int)
  Form of expected instruction(s): `vqshlu.s64 q0, q0, #0`
- uint32x4_t vqshluq_n_s32 (int32x4_t, const int)
  Form of expected instruction(s): `vqshlu.s32 q0, q0, #0`
- uint16x8_t vqshluq_n_s16 (int16x8_t, const int)
  Form of expected instruction(s): `vqshlu.s16 q0, q0, #0`
- uint8x16_t vqshluq_n_s8 (int8x16_t, const int)
  Form of expected instruction(s): `vqshlu.s8 q0, q0, #0`
- uint64x2_t vshll_n_u32 (uint32x2_t, const int)
  Form of expected instruction(s): `vshll.u32 q0, d0, #0`
- uint32x4_t vshll_n_u16 (uint16x4_t, const int)
  Form of expected instruction(s): `vshll.u16 q0, d0, #0`
- uint16x8_t vshll_n_u8 (uint8x8_t, const int)
  Form of expected instruction(s): `vshll.u8 q0, d0, #0`

Chapter 5: Extensions to the C Language Family 375

- int64x2_t vshll_n_s32 (int32x2_t, const int)
  Form of expected instruction(s): **vshll.s32** *q0, d0, #0*
- int32x4_t vshll_n_s16 (int16x4_t, const int)
  Form of expected instruction(s): **vshll.s16** *q0, d0, #0*
- int16x8_t vshll_n_s8 (int8x8_t, const int)
  Form of expected instruction(s): **vshll.s8** *q0, d0, #0*

5.50.3.27 Vector shift right by constant

- uint32x2_t vshr_n_u32 (uint32x2_t, const int)
  Form of expected instruction(s): **vshr.u32** *d0, d0, #0*
- uint16x4_t vshr_n_u16 (uint16x4_t, const int)
  Form of expected instruction(s): **vshr.u16** *d0, d0, #0*
- uint8x8_t vshr_n_u8 (uint8x8_t, const int)
  Form of expected instruction(s): **vshr.u8** *d0, d0, #0*
- int32x2_t vshr_n_s32 (int32x2_t, const int)
  Form of expected instruction(s): **vshr.s32** *d0, d0, #0*
- int16x4_t vshr_n_s16 (int16x4_t, const int)
  Form of expected instruction(s): **vshr.s16** *d0, d0, #0*
- int8x8_t vshr_n_s8 (int8x8_t, const int)
  Form of expected instruction(s): **vshr.s8** *d0, d0, #0*
- uint64x1_t vshr_n_u64 (uint64x1_t, const int)
  Form of expected instruction(s): **vshr.u64** *d0, d0, #0*
- int64x1_t vshr_n_s64 (int64x1_t, const int)
  Form of expected instruction(s): **vshr.s64** *d0, d0, #0*
- uint32x4_t vshrq_n_u32 (uint32x4_t, const int)
  Form of expected instruction(s): **vshr.u32** *q0, q0, #0*
- uint16x8_t vshrq_n_u16 (uint16x8_t, const int)
  Form of expected instruction(s): **vshr.u16** *q0, q0, #0*
- uint8x16_t vshrq_n_u8 (uint8x16_t, const int)
  Form of expected instruction(s): **vshr.u8** *q0, q0, #0*
- int32x4_t vshrq_n_s32 (int32x4_t, const int)
  Form of expected instruction(s): **vshr.s32** *q0, q0, #0*
- int16x8_t vshrq_n_s16 (int16x8_t, const int)
  Form of expected instruction(s): **vshr.s16** *q0, q0, #0*
- int8x16_t vshrq_n_s8 (int8x16_t, const int)
  Form of expected instruction(s): **vshr.s8** *q0, q0, #0*
- uint64x2_t vshrq_n_u64 (uint64x2_t, const int)
  Form of expected instruction(s): **vshr.u64** *q0, q0, #0*
- int64x2_t vshrq_n_s64 (int64x2_t, const int)
  Form of expected instruction(s): **vshr.s64** *q0, q0, #0*
- uint32x2_t vrshr_n_u32 (uint32x2_t, const int)
  Form of expected instruction(s): **vrshr.u32** *d0, d0, #0*

- uint16x4_t vrshr_n_u16 (uint16x4_t, const int)
  Form of expected instruction(s): **vrshr.u16** *d0, d0, #0*
- uint8x8_t vrshr_n_u8 (uint8x8_t, const int)
  Form of expected instruction(s): **vrshr.u8** *d0, d0, #0*
- int32x2_t vrshr_n_s32 (int32x2_t, const int)
  Form of expected instruction(s): **vrshr.s32** *d0, d0, #0*
- int16x4_t vrshr_n_s16 (int16x4_t, const int)
  Form of expected instruction(s): **vrshr.s16** *d0, d0, #0*
- int8x8_t vrshr_n_s8 (int8x8_t, const int)
  Form of expected instruction(s): **vrshr.s8** *d0, d0, #0*
- uint64x1_t vrshr_n_u64 (uint64x1_t, const int)
  Form of expected instruction(s): **vrshr.u64** *d0, d0, #0*
- int64x1_t vrshr_n_s64 (int64x1_t, const int)
  Form of expected instruction(s): **vrshr.s64** *d0, d0, #0*
- uint32x4_t vrshrq_n_u32 (uint32x4_t, const int)
  Form of expected instruction(s): **vrshr.u32** *q0, q0, #0*
- uint16x8_t vrshrq_n_u16 (uint16x8_t, const int)
  Form of expected instruction(s): **vrshr.u16** *q0, q0, #0*
- uint8x16_t vrshrq_n_u8 (uint8x16_t, const int)
  Form of expected instruction(s): **vrshr.u8** *q0, q0, #0*
- int32x4_t vrshrq_n_s32 (int32x4_t, const int)
  Form of expected instruction(s): **vrshr.s32** *q0, q0, #0*
- int16x8_t vrshrq_n_s16 (int16x8_t, const int)
  Form of expected instruction(s): **vrshr.s16** *q0, q0, #0*
- int8x16_t vrshrq_n_s8 (int8x16_t, const int)
  Form of expected instruction(s): **vrshr.s8** *q0, q0, #0*
- uint64x2_t vrshrq_n_u64 (uint64x2_t, const int)
  Form of expected instruction(s): **vrshr.u64** *q0, q0, #0*
- int64x2_t vrshrq_n_s64 (int64x2_t, const int)
  Form of expected instruction(s): **vrshr.s64** *q0, q0, #0*
- uint32x2_t vshrn_n_u64 (uint64x2_t, const int)
  Form of expected instruction(s): **vshrn.i64** *d0, q0, #0*
- uint16x4_t vshrn_n_u32 (uint32x4_t, const int)
  Form of expected instruction(s): **vshrn.i32** *d0, q0, #0*
- uint8x8_t vshrn_n_u16 (uint16x8_t, const int)
  Form of expected instruction(s): **vshrn.i16** *d0, q0, #0*
- int32x2_t vshrn_n_s64 (int64x2_t, const int)
  Form of expected instruction(s): **vshrn.i64** *d0, q0, #0*
- int16x4_t vshrn_n_s32 (int32x4_t, const int)
  Form of expected instruction(s): **vshrn.i32** *d0, q0, #0*
- int8x8_t vshrn_n_s16 (int16x8_t, const int)
  Form of expected instruction(s): **vshrn.i16** *d0, q0, #0*

Chapter 5: Extensions to the C Language Family 377

- uint32x2_t vrshrn_n_u64 (uint64x2_t, const int)
  Form of expected instruction(s): **vrshrn.i64** *d0, q0, #0*
- uint16x4_t vrshrn_n_u32 (uint32x4_t, const int)
  Form of expected instruction(s): **vrshrn.i32** *d0, q0, #0*
- uint8x8_t vrshrn_n_u16 (uint16x8_t, const int)
  Form of expected instruction(s): **vrshrn.i16** *d0, q0, #0*
- int32x2_t vrshrn_n_s64 (int64x2_t, const int)
  Form of expected instruction(s): **vrshrn.i64** *d0, q0, #0*
- int16x4_t vrshrn_n_s32 (int32x4_t, const int)
  Form of expected instruction(s): **vrshrn.i32** *d0, q0, #0*
- int8x8_t vrshrn_n_s16 (int16x8_t, const int)
  Form of expected instruction(s): **vrshrn.i16** *d0, q0, #0*
- uint32x2_t vqshrn_n_u64 (uint64x2_t, const int)
  Form of expected instruction(s): **vqshrn.u64** *d0, q0, #0*
- uint16x4_t vqshrn_n_u32 (uint32x4_t, const int)
  Form of expected instruction(s): **vqshrn.u32** *d0, q0, #0*
- uint8x8_t vqshrn_n_u16 (uint16x8_t, const int)
  Form of expected instruction(s): **vqshrn.u16** *d0, q0, #0*
- int32x2_t vqshrn_n_s64 (int64x2_t, const int)
  Form of expected instruction(s): **vqshrn.s64** *d0, q0, #0*
- int16x4_t vqshrn_n_s32 (int32x4_t, const int)
  Form of expected instruction(s): **vqshrn.s32** *d0, q0, #0*
- int8x8_t vqshrn_n_s16 (int16x8_t, const int)
  Form of expected instruction(s): **vqshrn.s16** *d0, q0, #0*
- uint32x2_t vqrshrn_n_u64 (uint64x2_t, const int)
  Form of expected instruction(s): **vqrshrn.u64** *d0, q0, #0*
- uint16x4_t vqrshrn_n_u32 (uint32x4_t, const int)
  Form of expected instruction(s): **vqrshrn.u32** *d0, q0, #0*
- uint8x8_t vqrshrn_n_u16 (uint16x8_t, const int)
  Form of expected instruction(s): **vqrshrn.u16** *d0, q0, #0*
- int32x2_t vqrshrn_n_s64 (int64x2_t, const int)
  Form of expected instruction(s): **vqrshrn.s64** *d0, q0, #0*
- int16x4_t vqrshrn_n_s32 (int32x4_t, const int)
  Form of expected instruction(s): **vqrshrn.s32** *d0, q0, #0*
- int8x8_t vqrshrn_n_s16 (int16x8_t, const int)
  Form of expected instruction(s): **vqrshrn.s16** *d0, q0, #0*
- uint32x2_t vqshrun_n_s64 (int64x2_t, const int)
  Form of expected instruction(s): **vqshrun.s64** *d0, q0, #0*
- uint16x4_t vqshrun_n_s32 (int32x4_t, const int)
  Form of expected instruction(s): **vqshrun.s32** *d0, q0, #0*
- uint8x8_t vqshrun_n_s16 (int16x8_t, const int)
  Form of expected instruction(s): **vqshrun.s16** *d0, q0, #0*

- uint32x2_t vqrshrun_n_s64 (int64x2_t, const int)
  Form of expected instruction(s): `vqrshrun.s64 d0, q0, #0`
- uint16x4_t vqrshrun_n_s32 (int32x4_t, const int)
  Form of expected instruction(s): `vqrshrun.s32 d0, q0, #0`
- uint8x8_t vqrshrun_n_s16 (int16x8_t, const int)
  Form of expected instruction(s): `vqrshrun.s16 d0, q0, #0`

5.50.3.28 Vector shift right by constant and accumulate

- uint32x2_t vsra_n_u32 (uint32x2_t, uint32x2_t, const int)
  Form of expected instruction(s): `vsra.u32 d0, d0, #0`
- uint16x4_t vsra_n_u16 (uint16x4_t, uint16x4_t, const int)
  Form of expected instruction(s): `vsra.u16 d0, d0, #0`
- uint8x8_t vsra_n_u8 (uint8x8_t, uint8x8_t, const int)
  Form of expected instruction(s): `vsra.u8 d0, d0, #0`
- int32x2_t vsra_n_s32 (int32x2_t, int32x2_t, const int)
  Form of expected instruction(s): `vsra.s32 d0, d0, #0`
- int16x4_t vsra_n_s16 (int16x4_t, int16x4_t, const int)
  Form of expected instruction(s): `vsra.s16 d0, d0, #0`
- int8x8_t vsra_n_s8 (int8x8_t, int8x8_t, const int)
  Form of expected instruction(s): `vsra.s8 d0, d0, #0`
- uint64x1_t vsra_n_u64 (uint64x1_t, uint64x1_t, const int)
  Form of expected instruction(s): `vsra.u64 d0, d0, #0`
- int64x1_t vsra_n_s64 (int64x1_t, int64x1_t, const int)
  Form of expected instruction(s): `vsra.s64 d0, d0, #0`
- uint32x4_t vsraq_n_u32 (uint32x4_t, uint32x4_t, const int)
  Form of expected instruction(s): `vsra.u32 q0, q0, #0`
- uint16x8_t vsraq_n_u16 (uint16x8_t, uint16x8_t, const int)
  Form of expected instruction(s): `vsra.u16 q0, q0, #0`
- uint8x16_t vsraq_n_u8 (uint8x16_t, uint8x16_t, const int)
  Form of expected instruction(s): `vsra.u8 q0, q0, #0`
- int32x4_t vsraq_n_s32 (int32x4_t, int32x4_t, const int)
  Form of expected instruction(s): `vsra.s32 q0, q0, #0`
- int16x8_t vsraq_n_s16 (int16x8_t, int16x8_t, const int)
  Form of expected instruction(s): `vsra.s16 q0, q0, #0`
- int8x16_t vsraq_n_s8 (int8x16_t, int8x16_t, const int)
  Form of expected instruction(s): `vsra.s8 q0, q0, #0`
- uint64x2_t vsraq_n_u64 (uint64x2_t, uint64x2_t, const int)
  Form of expected instruction(s): `vsra.u64 q0, q0, #0`
- int64x2_t vsraq_n_s64 (int64x2_t, int64x2_t, const int)
  Form of expected instruction(s): `vsra.s64 q0, q0, #0`
- uint32x2_t vrsra_n_u32 (uint32x2_t, uint32x2_t, const int)
  Form of expected instruction(s): `vrsra.u32 d0, d0, #0`

Chapter 5: Extensions to the C Language Family   379

- uint16x4_t vrsra_n_u16 (uint16x4_t, uint16x4_t, const int)
  Form of expected instruction(s): vrsra.u16 d0, d0, #0
- uint8x8_t vrsra_n_u8 (uint8x8_t, uint8x8_t, const int)
  Form of expected instruction(s): vrsra.u8 d0, d0, #0
- int32x2_t vrsra_n_s32 (int32x2_t, int32x2_t, const int)
  Form of expected instruction(s): vrsra.s32 d0, d0, #0
- int16x4_t vrsra_n_s16 (int16x4_t, int16x4_t, const int)
  Form of expected instruction(s): vrsra.s16 d0, d0, #0
- int8x8_t vrsra_n_s8 (int8x8_t, int8x8_t, const int)
  Form of expected instruction(s): vrsra.s8 d0, d0, #0
- uint64x1_t vrsra_n_u64 (uint64x1_t, uint64x1_t, const int)
  Form of expected instruction(s): vrsra.u64 d0, d0, #0
- int64x1_t vrsra_n_s64 (int64x1_t, int64x1_t, const int)
  Form of expected instruction(s): vrsra.s64 d0, d0, #0
- uint32x4_t vrsraq_n_u32 (uint32x4_t, uint32x4_t, const int)
  Form of expected instruction(s): vrsra.u32 q0, q0, #0
- uint16x8_t vrsraq_n_u16 (uint16x8_t, uint16x8_t, const int)
  Form of expected instruction(s): vrsra.u16 q0, q0, #0
- uint8x16_t vrsraq_n_u8 (uint8x16_t, uint8x16_t, const int)
  Form of expected instruction(s): vrsra.u8 q0, q0, #0
- int32x4_t vrsraq_n_s32 (int32x4_t, int32x4_t, const int)
  Form of expected instruction(s): vrsra.s32 q0, q0, #0
- int16x8_t vrsraq_n_s16 (int16x8_t, int16x8_t, const int)
  Form of expected instruction(s): vrsra.s16 q0, q0, #0
- int8x16_t vrsraq_n_s8 (int8x16_t, int8x16_t, const int)
  Form of expected instruction(s): vrsra.s8 q0, q0, #0
- uint64x2_t vrsraq_n_u64 (uint64x2_t, uint64x2_t, const int)
  Form of expected instruction(s): vrsra.u64 q0, q0, #0
- int64x2_t vrsraq_n_s64 (int64x2_t, int64x2_t, const int)
  Form of expected instruction(s): vrsra.s64 q0, q0, #0

5.50.3.29 Vector shift right and insert

- uint32x2_t vsri_n_u32 (uint32x2_t, uint32x2_t, const int)
  Form of expected instruction(s): vsri.32 d0, d0, #0
- uint16x4_t vsri_n_u16 (uint16x4_t, uint16x4_t, const int)
  Form of expected instruction(s): vsri.16 d0, d0, #0
- uint8x8_t vsri_n_u8 (uint8x8_t, uint8x8_t, const int)
  Form of expected instruction(s): vsri.8 d0, d0, #0
- int32x2_t vsri_n_s32 (int32x2_t, int32x2_t, const int)
  Form of expected instruction(s): vsri.32 d0, d0, #0
- int16x4_t vsri_n_s16 (int16x4_t, int16x4_t, const int)
  Form of expected instruction(s): vsri.16 d0, d0, #0

- int8x8_t vsri_n_s8 (int8x8_t, int8x8_t, const int)
  Form of expected instruction(s): **vsri.8** *d0, d0, #0*
- uint64x1_t vsri_n_u64 (uint64x1_t, uint64x1_t, const int)
  Form of expected instruction(s): **vsri.64** *d0, d0, #0*
- int64x1_t vsri_n_s64 (int64x1_t, int64x1_t, const int)
  Form of expected instruction(s): **vsri.64** *d0, d0, #0*
- poly16x4_t vsri_n_p16 (poly16x4_t, poly16x4_t, const int)
  Form of expected instruction(s): **vsri.16** *d0, d0, #0*
- poly8x8_t vsri_n_p8 (poly8x8_t, poly8x8_t, const int)
  Form of expected instruction(s): **vsri.8** *d0, d0, #0*
- uint32x4_t vsriq_n_u32 (uint32x4_t, uint32x4_t, const int)
  Form of expected instruction(s): **vsri.32** *q0, q0, #0*
- uint16x8_t vsriq_n_u16 (uint16x8_t, uint16x8_t, const int)
  Form of expected instruction(s): **vsri.16** *q0, q0, #0*
- uint8x16_t vsriq_n_u8 (uint8x16_t, uint8x16_t, const int)
  Form of expected instruction(s): **vsri.8** *q0, q0, #0*
- int32x4_t vsriq_n_s32 (int32x4_t, int32x4_t, const int)
  Form of expected instruction(s): **vsri.32** *q0, q0, #0*
- int16x8_t vsriq_n_s16 (int16x8_t, int16x8_t, const int)
  Form of expected instruction(s): **vsri.16** *q0, q0, #0*
- int8x16_t vsriq_n_s8 (int8x16_t, int8x16_t, const int)
  Form of expected instruction(s): **vsri.8** *q0, q0, #0*
- uint64x2_t vsriq_n_u64 (uint64x2_t, uint64x2_t, const int)
  Form of expected instruction(s): **vsri.64** *q0, q0, #0*
- int64x2_t vsriq_n_s64 (int64x2_t, int64x2_t, const int)
  Form of expected instruction(s): **vsri.64** *q0, q0, #0*
- poly16x8_t vsriq_n_p16 (poly16x8_t, poly16x8_t, const int)
  Form of expected instruction(s): **vsri.16** *q0, q0, #0*
- poly8x16_t vsriq_n_p8 (poly8x16_t, poly8x16_t, const int)
  Form of expected instruction(s): **vsri.8** *q0, q0, #0*

5.50.3.30 Vector shift left and insert

- uint32x2_t vsli_n_u32 (uint32x2_t, uint32x2_t, const int)
  Form of expected instruction(s): **vsli.32** *d0, d0, #0*
- uint16x4_t vsli_n_u16 (uint16x4_t, uint16x4_t, const int)
  Form of expected instruction(s): **vsli.16** *d0, d0, #0*
- uint8x8_t vsli_n_u8 (uint8x8_t, uint8x8_t, const int)
  Form of expected instruction(s): **vsli.8** *d0, d0, #0*
- int32x2_t vsli_n_s32 (int32x2_t, int32x2_t, const int)
  Form of expected instruction(s): **vsli.32** *d0, d0, #0*
- int16x4_t vsli_n_s16 (int16x4_t, int16x4_t, const int)
  Form of expected instruction(s): **vsli.16** *d0, d0, #0*

- int8x8_t vsli_n_s8 (int8x8_t, int8x8_t, const int)
  Form of expected instruction(s): `vsli.8 d0, d0, #0`
- uint64x1_t vsli_n_u64 (uint64x1_t, uint64x1_t, const int)
  Form of expected instruction(s): `vsli.64 d0, d0, #0`
- int64x1_t vsli_n_s64 (int64x1_t, int64x1_t, const int)
  Form of expected instruction(s): `vsli.64 d0, d0, #0`
- poly16x4_t vsli_n_p16 (poly16x4_t, poly16x4_t, const int)
  Form of expected instruction(s): `vsli.16 d0, d0, #0`
- poly8x8_t vsli_n_p8 (poly8x8_t, poly8x8_t, const int)
  Form of expected instruction(s): `vsli.8 d0, d0, #0`
- uint32x4_t vsliq_n_u32 (uint32x4_t, uint32x4_t, const int)
  Form of expected instruction(s): `vsli.32 q0, q0, #0`
- uint16x8_t vsliq_n_u16 (uint16x8_t, uint16x8_t, const int)
  Form of expected instruction(s): `vsli.16 q0, q0, #0`
- uint8x16_t vsliq_n_u8 (uint8x16_t, uint8x16_t, const int)
  Form of expected instruction(s): `vsli.8 q0, q0, #0`
- int32x4_t vsliq_n_s32 (int32x4_t, int32x4_t, const int)
  Form of expected instruction(s): `vsli.32 q0, q0, #0`
- int16x8_t vsliq_n_s16 (int16x8_t, int16x8_t, const int)
  Form of expected instruction(s): `vsli.16 q0, q0, #0`
- int8x16_t vsliq_n_s8 (int8x16_t, int8x16_t, const int)
  Form of expected instruction(s): `vsli.8 q0, q0, #0`
- uint64x2_t vsliq_n_u64 (uint64x2_t, uint64x2_t, const int)
  Form of expected instruction(s): `vsli.64 q0, q0, #0`
- int64x2_t vsliq_n_s64 (int64x2_t, int64x2_t, const int)
  Form of expected instruction(s): `vsli.64 q0, q0, #0`
- poly16x8_t vsliq_n_p16 (poly16x8_t, poly16x8_t, const int)
  Form of expected instruction(s): `vsli.16 q0, q0, #0`
- poly8x16_t vsliq_n_p8 (poly8x16_t, poly8x16_t, const int)
  Form of expected instruction(s): `vsli.8 q0, q0, #0`

5.50.3.31 Absolute value

- float32x2_t vabs_f32 (float32x2_t)
  Form of expected instruction(s): `vabs.f32 d0, d0`
- int32x2_t vabs_s32 (int32x2_t)
  Form of expected instruction(s): `vabs.s32 d0, d0`
- int16x4_t vabs_s16 (int16x4_t)
  Form of expected instruction(s): `vabs.s16 d0, d0`
- int8x8_t vabs_s8 (int8x8_t)
  Form of expected instruction(s): `vabs.s8 d0, d0`
- float32x4_t vabsq_f32 (float32x4_t)
  Form of expected instruction(s): `vabs.f32 q0, q0`

- int32x4_t vabsq_s32 (int32x4_t)
  Form of expected instruction(s): vabs.s32 q0, q0
- int16x8_t vabsq_s16 (int16x8_t)
  Form of expected instruction(s): vabs.s16 q0, q0
- int8x16_t vabsq_s8 (int8x16_t)
  Form of expected instruction(s): vabs.s8 q0, q0
- int32x2_t vqabs_s32 (int32x2_t)
  Form of expected instruction(s): vqabs.s32 d0, d0
- int16x4_t vqabs_s16 (int16x4_t)
  Form of expected instruction(s): vqabs.s16 d0, d0
- int8x8_t vqabs_s8 (int8x8_t)
  Form of expected instruction(s): vqabs.s8 d0, d0
- int32x4_t vqabsq_s32 (int32x4_t)
  Form of expected instruction(s): vqabs.s32 q0, q0
- int16x8_t vqabsq_s16 (int16x8_t)
  Form of expected instruction(s): vqabs.s16 q0, q0
- int8x16_t vqabsq_s8 (int8x16_t)
  Form of expected instruction(s): vqabs.s8 q0, q0

5.50.3.32 Negation

- float32x2_t vneg_f32 (float32x2_t)
  Form of expected instruction(s): vneg.f32 d0, d0
- int32x2_t vneg_s32 (int32x2_t)
  Form of expected instruction(s): vneg.s32 d0, d0
- int16x4_t vneg_s16 (int16x4_t)
  Form of expected instruction(s): vneg.s16 d0, d0
- int8x8_t vneg_s8 (int8x8_t)
  Form of expected instruction(s): vneg.s8 d0, d0
- float32x4_t vnegq_f32 (float32x4_t)
  Form of expected instruction(s): vneg.f32 q0, q0
- int32x4_t vnegq_s32 (int32x4_t)
  Form of expected instruction(s): vneg.s32 q0, q0
- int16x8_t vnegq_s16 (int16x8_t)
  Form of expected instruction(s): vneg.s16 q0, q0
- int8x16_t vnegq_s8 (int8x16_t)
  Form of expected instruction(s): vneg.s8 q0, q0
- int32x2_t vqneg_s32 (int32x2_t)
  Form of expected instruction(s): vqneg.s32 d0, d0
- int16x4_t vqneg_s16 (int16x4_t)
  Form of expected instruction(s): vqneg.s16 d0, d0
- int8x8_t vqneg_s8 (int8x8_t)
  Form of expected instruction(s): vqneg.s8 d0, d0

Chapter 5: Extensions to the C Language Family   383

- int32x4_t vqnegq_s32 (int32x4_t)
  Form of expected instruction(s): `vqneg.s32 q0, q0`
- int16x8_t vqnegq_s16 (int16x8_t)
  Form of expected instruction(s): `vqneg.s16 q0, q0`
- int8x16_t vqnegq_s8 (int8x16_t)
  Form of expected instruction(s): `vqneg.s8 q0, q0`

5.50.3.33 Bitwise not

- uint32x2_t vmvn_u32 (uint32x2_t)
  Form of expected instruction(s): `vmvn d0, d0`
- uint16x4_t vmvn_u16 (uint16x4_t)
  Form of expected instruction(s): `vmvn d0, d0`
- uint8x8_t vmvn_u8 (uint8x8_t)
  Form of expected instruction(s): `vmvn d0, d0`
- int32x2_t vmvn_s32 (int32x2_t)
  Form of expected instruction(s): `vmvn d0, d0`
- int16x4_t vmvn_s16 (int16x4_t)
  Form of expected instruction(s): `vmvn d0, d0`
- int8x8_t vmvn_s8 (int8x8_t)
  Form of expected instruction(s): `vmvn d0, d0`
- poly8x8_t vmvn_p8 (poly8x8_t)
  Form of expected instruction(s): `vmvn d0, d0`
- uint32x4_t vmvnq_u32 (uint32x4_t)
  Form of expected instruction(s): `vmvn q0, q0`
- uint16x8_t vmvnq_u16 (uint16x8_t)
  Form of expected instruction(s): `vmvn q0, q0`
- uint8x16_t vmvnq_u8 (uint8x16_t)
  Form of expected instruction(s): `vmvn q0, q0`
- int32x4_t vmvnq_s32 (int32x4_t)
  Form of expected instruction(s): `vmvn q0, q0`
- int16x8_t vmvnq_s16 (int16x8_t)
  Form of expected instruction(s): `vmvn q0, q0`
- int8x16_t vmvnq_s8 (int8x16_t)
  Form of expected instruction(s): `vmvn q0, q0`
- poly8x16_t vmvnq_p8 (poly8x16_t)
  Form of expected instruction(s): `vmvn q0, q0`

5.50.3.34 Count leading sign bits

- int32x2_t vcls_s32 (int32x2_t)
  Form of expected instruction(s): `vcls.s32 d0, d0`
- int16x4_t vcls_s16 (int16x4_t)
  Form of expected instruction(s): `vcls.s16 d0, d0`

- int8x8_t vcls_s8 (int8x8_t)
  Form of expected instruction(s): vcls.s8 d0, d0
- int32x4_t vclsq_s32 (int32x4_t)
  Form of expected instruction(s): vcls.s32 q0, q0
- int16x8_t vclsq_s16 (int16x8_t)
  Form of expected instruction(s): vcls.s16 q0, q0
- int8x16_t vclsq_s8 (int8x16_t)
  Form of expected instruction(s): vcls.s8 q0, q0

5.50.3.35 Count leading zeros

- uint32x2_t vclz_u32 (uint32x2_t)
  Form of expected instruction(s): vclz.i32 d0, d0
- uint16x4_t vclz_u16 (uint16x4_t)
  Form of expected instruction(s): vclz.i16 d0, d0
- uint8x8_t vclz_u8 (uint8x8_t)
  Form of expected instruction(s): vclz.i8 d0, d0
- int32x2_t vclz_s32 (int32x2_t)
  Form of expected instruction(s): vclz.i32 d0, d0
- int16x4_t vclz_s16 (int16x4_t)
  Form of expected instruction(s): vclz.i16 d0, d0
- int8x8_t vclz_s8 (int8x8_t)
  Form of expected instruction(s): vclz.i8 d0, d0
- uint32x4_t vclzq_u32 (uint32x4_t)
  Form of expected instruction(s): vclz.i32 q0, q0
- uint16x8_t vclzq_u16 (uint16x8_t)
  Form of expected instruction(s): vclz.i16 q0, q0
- uint8x16_t vclzq_u8 (uint8x16_t)
  Form of expected instruction(s): vclz.i8 q0, q0
- int32x4_t vclzq_s32 (int32x4_t)
  Form of expected instruction(s): vclz.i32 q0, q0
- int16x8_t vclzq_s16 (int16x8_t)
  Form of expected instruction(s): vclz.i16 q0, q0
- int8x16_t vclzq_s8 (int8x16_t)
  Form of expected instruction(s): vclz.i8 q0, q0

5.50.3.36 Count number of set bits

- uint8x8_t vcnt_u8 (uint8x8_t)
  Form of expected instruction(s): vcnt.8 d0, d0
- int8x8_t vcnt_s8 (int8x8_t)
  Form of expected instruction(s): vcnt.8 d0, d0
- poly8x8_t vcnt_p8 (poly8x8_t)
  Form of expected instruction(s): vcnt.8 d0, d0

Chapter 5: Extensions to the C Language Family   385

- uint8x16_t vcntq_u8 (uint8x16_t)
  Form of expected instruction(s): vcnt.8 q0, q0
- int8x16_t vcntq_s8 (int8x16_t)
  Form of expected instruction(s): vcnt.8 q0, q0
- poly8x16_t vcntq_p8 (poly8x16_t)
  Form of expected instruction(s): vcnt.8 q0, q0

5.50.3.37 Reciprocal estimate

- float32x2_t vrecpe_f32 (float32x2_t)
  Form of expected instruction(s): vrecpe.f32 d0, d0
- uint32x2_t vrecpe_u32 (uint32x2_t)
  Form of expected instruction(s): vrecpe.u32 d0, d0
- float32x4_t vrecpeq_f32 (float32x4_t)
  Form of expected instruction(s): vrecpe.f32 q0, q0
- uint32x4_t vrecpeq_u32 (uint32x4_t)
  Form of expected instruction(s): vrecpe.u32 q0, q0

5.50.3.38 Reciprocal square-root estimate

- float32x2_t vrsqrte_f32 (float32x2_t)
  Form of expected instruction(s): vrsqrte.f32 d0, d0
- uint32x2_t vrsqrte_u32 (uint32x2_t)
  Form of expected instruction(s): vrsqrte.u32 d0, d0
- float32x4_t vrsqrteq_f32 (float32x4_t)
  Form of expected instruction(s): vrsqrte.f32 q0, q0
- uint32x4_t vrsqrteq_u32 (uint32x4_t)
  Form of expected instruction(s): vrsqrte.u32 q0, q0

5.50.3.39 Get lanes from a vector

- uint32_t vget_lane_u32 (uint32x2_t, const int)
  Form of expected instruction(s): vmov.u32 r0, d0[0]
- uint16_t vget_lane_u16 (uint16x4_t, const int)
  Form of expected instruction(s): vmov.u16 r0, d0[0]
- uint8_t vget_lane_u8 (uint8x8_t, const int)
  Form of expected instruction(s): vmov.u8 r0, d0[0]
- int32_t vget_lane_s32 (int32x2_t, const int)
  Form of expected instruction(s): vmov.s32 r0, d0[0]
- int16_t vget_lane_s16 (int16x4_t, const int)
  Form of expected instruction(s): vmov.s16 r0, d0[0]
- int8_t vget_lane_s8 (int8x8_t, const int)
  Form of expected instruction(s): vmov.s8 r0, d0[0]
- float32_t vget_lane_f32 (float32x2_t, const int)
  Form of expected instruction(s): vmov.f32 r0, d0[0]
- poly16_t vget_lane_p16 (poly16x4_t, const int)
  Form of expected instruction(s): vmov.u16 r0, d0[0]

- poly8_t vget_lane_p8 (poly8x8_t, const int)
  Form of expected instruction(s): `vmov.u8 r0, d0[0]`
- uint64_t vget_lane_u64 (uint64x1_t, const int)
  Form of expected instruction(s): `vmov r0, r0, d0`
- int64_t vget_lane_s64 (int64x1_t, const int)
  Form of expected instruction(s): `vmov r0, r0, d0`
- uint32_t vgetq_lane_u32 (uint32x4_t, const int)
  Form of expected instruction(s): `vmov.u32 r0, d0[0]`
- uint16_t vgetq_lane_u16 (uint16x8_t, const int)
  Form of expected instruction(s): `vmov.u16 r0, d0[0]`
- uint8_t vgetq_lane_u8 (uint8x16_t, const int)
  Form of expected instruction(s): `vmov.u8 r0, d0[0]`
- int32_t vgetq_lane_s32 (int32x4_t, const int)
  Form of expected instruction(s): `vmov.s32 r0, d0[0]`
- int16_t vgetq_lane_s16 (int16x8_t, const int)
  Form of expected instruction(s): `vmov.s16 r0, d0[0]`
- int8_t vgetq_lane_s8 (int8x16_t, const int)
  Form of expected instruction(s): `vmov.s8 r0, d0[0]`
- float32_t vgetq_lane_f32 (float32x4_t, const int)
  Form of expected instruction(s): `vmov.f32 r0, d0[0]`
- poly16_t vgetq_lane_p16 (poly16x8_t, const int)
  Form of expected instruction(s): `vmov.u16 r0, d0[0]`
- poly8_t vgetq_lane_p8 (poly8x16_t, const int)
  Form of expected instruction(s): `vmov.u8 r0, d0[0]`
- uint64_t vgetq_lane_u64 (uint64x2_t, const int)
  Form of expected instruction(s): `vmov r0, r0, d0`
- int64_t vgetq_lane_s64 (int64x2_t, const int)
  Form of expected instruction(s): `vmov r0, r0, d0`

5.50.3.40 Set lanes in a vector

- uint32x2_t vset_lane_u32 (uint32_t, uint32x2_t, const int)
  Form of expected instruction(s): `vmov.32 d0[0], r0`
- uint16x4_t vset_lane_u16 (uint16_t, uint16x4_t, const int)
  Form of expected instruction(s): `vmov.16 d0[0], r0`
- uint8x8_t vset_lane_u8 (uint8_t, uint8x8_t, const int)
  Form of expected instruction(s): `vmov.8 d0[0], r0`
- int32x2_t vset_lane_s32 (int32_t, int32x2_t, const int)
  Form of expected instruction(s): `vmov.32 d0[0], r0`
- int16x4_t vset_lane_s16 (int16_t, int16x4_t, const int)
  Form of expected instruction(s): `vmov.16 d0[0], r0`
- int8x8_t vset_lane_s8 (int8_t, int8x8_t, const int)
  Form of expected instruction(s): `vmov.8 d0[0], r0`

Chapter 5: Extensions to the C Language Family 387

- float32x2_t vset_lane_f32 (float32_t, float32x2_t, const int)
  Form of expected instruction(s): `vmov.32 d0[0], r0`
- poly16x4_t vset_lane_p16 (poly16_t, poly16x4_t, const int)
  Form of expected instruction(s): `vmov.16 d0[0], r0`
- poly8x8_t vset_lane_p8 (poly8_t, poly8x8_t, const int)
  Form of expected instruction(s): `vmov.8 d0[0], r0`
- uint64x1_t vset_lane_u64 (uint64_t, uint64x1_t, const int)
  Form of expected instruction(s): `vmov d0, r0, r0`
- int64x1_t vset_lane_s64 (int64_t, int64x1_t, const int)
  Form of expected instruction(s): `vmov d0, r0, r0`
- uint32x4_t vsetq_lane_u32 (uint32_t, uint32x4_t, const int)
  Form of expected instruction(s): `vmov.32 d0[0], r0`
- uint16x8_t vsetq_lane_u16 (uint16_t, uint16x8_t, const int)
  Form of expected instruction(s): `vmov.16 d0[0], r0`
- uint8x16_t vsetq_lane_u8 (uint8_t, uint8x16_t, const int)
  Form of expected instruction(s): `vmov.8 d0[0], r0`
- int32x4_t vsetq_lane_s32 (int32_t, int32x4_t, const int)
  Form of expected instruction(s): `vmov.32 d0[0], r0`
- int16x8_t vsetq_lane_s16 (int16_t, int16x8_t, const int)
  Form of expected instruction(s): `vmov.16 d0[0], r0`
- int8x16_t vsetq_lane_s8 (int8_t, int8x16_t, const int)
  Form of expected instruction(s): `vmov.8 d0[0], r0`
- float32x4_t vsetq_lane_f32 (float32_t, float32x4_t, const int)
  Form of expected instruction(s): `vmov.32 d0[0], r0`
- poly16x8_t vsetq_lane_p16 (poly16_t, poly16x8_t, const int)
  Form of expected instruction(s): `vmov.16 d0[0], r0`
- poly8x16_t vsetq_lane_p8 (poly8_t, poly8x16_t, const int)
  Form of expected instruction(s): `vmov.8 d0[0], r0`
- uint64x2_t vsetq_lane_u64 (uint64_t, uint64x2_t, const int)
  Form of expected instruction(s): `vmov d0, r0, r0`
- int64x2_t vsetq_lane_s64 (int64_t, int64x2_t, const int)
  Form of expected instruction(s): `vmov d0, r0, r0`

5.50.3.41 Create vector from literal bit pattern

- uint32x2_t vcreate_u32 (uint64_t)
- uint16x4_t vcreate_u16 (uint64_t)
- uint8x8_t vcreate_u8 (uint64_t)
- int32x2_t vcreate_s32 (uint64_t)
- int16x4_t vcreate_s16 (uint64_t)
- int8x8_t vcreate_s8 (uint64_t)
- uint64x1_t vcreate_u64 (uint64_t)
- int64x1_t vcreate_s64 (uint64_t)

- float32x2_t vcreate_f32 (uint64_t)
- poly16x4_t vcreate_p16 (uint64_t)
- poly8x8_t vcreate_p8 (uint64_t)

5.50.3.42 Set all lanes to the same value

- uint32x2_t vdup_n_u32 (uint32_t)
  Form of expected instruction(s): **vdup.32 d0, r0**
- uint16x4_t vdup_n_u16 (uint16_t)
  Form of expected instruction(s): **vdup.16 d0, r0**
- uint8x8_t vdup_n_u8 (uint8_t)
  Form of expected instruction(s): **vdup.8 d0, r0**
- int32x2_t vdup_n_s32 (int32_t)
  Form of expected instruction(s): **vdup.32 d0, r0**
- int16x4_t vdup_n_s16 (int16_t)
  Form of expected instruction(s): **vdup.16 d0, r0**
- int8x8_t vdup_n_s8 (int8_t)
  Form of expected instruction(s): **vdup.8 d0, r0**
- float32x2_t vdup_n_f32 (float32_t)
  Form of expected instruction(s): **vdup.32 d0, r0**
- poly16x4_t vdup_n_p16 (poly16_t)
  Form of expected instruction(s): **vdup.16 d0, r0**
- poly8x8_t vdup_n_p8 (poly8_t)
  Form of expected instruction(s): **vdup.8 d0, r0**
- uint64x1_t vdup_n_u64 (uint64_t)
  Form of expected instruction(s): **vmov d0, r0, r0**
- int64x1_t vdup_n_s64 (int64_t)
  Form of expected instruction(s): **vmov d0, r0, r0**
- uint32x4_t vdupq_n_u32 (uint32_t)
  Form of expected instruction(s): **vdup.32 q0, r0**
- uint16x8_t vdupq_n_u16 (uint16_t)
  Form of expected instruction(s): **vdup.16 q0, r0**
- uint8x16_t vdupq_n_u8 (uint8_t)
  Form of expected instruction(s): **vdup.8 q0, r0**
- int32x4_t vdupq_n_s32 (int32_t)
  Form of expected instruction(s): **vdup.32 q0, r0**
- int16x8_t vdupq_n_s16 (int16_t)
  Form of expected instruction(s): **vdup.16 q0, r0**
- int8x16_t vdupq_n_s8 (int8_t)
  Form of expected instruction(s): **vdup.8 q0, r0**
- float32x4_t vdupq_n_f32 (float32_t)
  Form of expected instruction(s): **vdup.32 q0, r0**
- poly16x8_t vdupq_n_p16 (poly16_t)
  Form of expected instruction(s): **vdup.16 q0, r0**

Chapter 5: Extensions to the C Language Family   389

- poly8x16_t vdupq_n_p8 (poly8_t)
  Form of expected instruction(s): vdup.8 q0, r0
- uint64x2_t vdupq_n_u64 (uint64_t)
  Form of expected instruction(s): vmov d0, r0, r0
- int64x2_t vdupq_n_s64 (int64_t)
  Form of expected instruction(s): vmov d0, r0, r0
- uint32x2_t vmov_n_u32 (uint32_t)
  Form of expected instruction(s): vdup.32 d0, r0
- uint16x4_t vmov_n_u16 (uint16_t)
  Form of expected instruction(s): vdup.16 d0, r0
- uint8x8_t vmov_n_u8 (uint8_t)
  Form of expected instruction(s): vdup.8 d0, r0
- int32x2_t vmov_n_s32 (int32_t)
  Form of expected instruction(s): vdup.32 d0, r0
- int16x4_t vmov_n_s16 (int16_t)
  Form of expected instruction(s): vdup.16 d0, r0
- int8x8_t vmov_n_s8 (int8_t)
  Form of expected instruction(s): vdup.8 d0, r0
- float32x2_t vmov_n_f32 (float32_t)
  Form of expected instruction(s): vdup.32 d0, r0
- poly16x4_t vmov_n_p16 (poly16_t)
  Form of expected instruction(s): vdup.16 d0, r0
- poly8x8_t vmov_n_p8 (poly8_t)
  Form of expected instruction(s): vdup.8 d0, r0
- uint64x1_t vmov_n_u64 (uint64_t)
  Form of expected instruction(s): vmov d0, r0, r0
- int64x1_t vmov_n_s64 (int64_t)
  Form of expected instruction(s): vmov d0, r0, r0
- uint32x4_t vmovq_n_u32 (uint32_t)
  Form of expected instruction(s): vdup.32 q0, r0
- uint16x8_t vmovq_n_u16 (uint16_t)
  Form of expected instruction(s): vdup.16 q0, r0
- uint8x16_t vmovq_n_u8 (uint8_t)
  Form of expected instruction(s): vdup.8 q0, r0
- int32x4_t vmovq_n_s32 (int32_t)
  Form of expected instruction(s): vdup.32 q0, r0
- int16x8_t vmovq_n_s16 (int16_t)
  Form of expected instruction(s): vdup.16 q0, r0
- int8x16_t vmovq_n_s8 (int8_t)
  Form of expected instruction(s): vdup.8 q0, r0
- float32x4_t vmovq_n_f32 (float32_t)
  Form of expected instruction(s): vdup.32 q0, r0

- poly16x8_t vmovq_n_p16 (poly16_t)
  Form of expected instruction(s): `vdup.16 q0, r0`
- poly8x16_t vmovq_n_p8 (poly8_t)
  Form of expected instruction(s): `vdup.8 q0, r0`
- uint64x2_t vmovq_n_u64 (uint64_t)
  Form of expected instruction(s): `vmov d0, r0, r0`
- int64x2_t vmovq_n_s64 (int64_t)
  Form of expected instruction(s): `vmov d0, r0, r0`
- uint32x2_t vdup_lane_u32 (uint32x2_t, const int)
  Form of expected instruction(s): `vdup.32 d0, d0[0]`
- uint16x4_t vdup_lane_u16 (uint16x4_t, const int)
  Form of expected instruction(s): `vdup.16 d0, d0[0]`
- uint8x8_t vdup_lane_u8 (uint8x8_t, const int)
  Form of expected instruction(s): `vdup.8 d0, d0[0]`
- int32x2_t vdup_lane_s32 (int32x2_t, const int)
  Form of expected instruction(s): `vdup.32 d0, d0[0]`
- int16x4_t vdup_lane_s16 (int16x4_t, const int)
  Form of expected instruction(s): `vdup.16 d0, d0[0]`
- int8x8_t vdup_lane_s8 (int8x8_t, const int)
  Form of expected instruction(s): `vdup.8 d0, d0[0]`
- float32x2_t vdup_lane_f32 (float32x2_t, const int)
  Form of expected instruction(s): `vdup.32 d0, d0[0]`
- poly16x4_t vdup_lane_p16 (poly16x4_t, const int)
  Form of expected instruction(s): `vdup.16 d0, d0[0]`
- poly8x8_t vdup_lane_p8 (poly8x8_t, const int)
  Form of expected instruction(s): `vdup.8 d0, d0[0]`
- uint64x1_t vdup_lane_u64 (uint64x1_t, const int)
- int64x1_t vdup_lane_s64 (int64x1_t, const int)
- uint32x4_t vdupq_lane_u32 (uint32x2_t, const int)
  Form of expected instruction(s): `vdup.32 q0, d0[0]`
- uint16x8_t vdupq_lane_u16 (uint16x4_t, const int)
  Form of expected instruction(s): `vdup.16 q0, d0[0]`
- uint8x16_t vdupq_lane_u8 (uint8x8_t, const int)
  Form of expected instruction(s): `vdup.8 q0, d0[0]`
- int32x4_t vdupq_lane_s32 (int32x2_t, const int)
  Form of expected instruction(s): `vdup.32 q0, d0[0]`
- int16x8_t vdupq_lane_s16 (int16x4_t, const int)
  Form of expected instruction(s): `vdup.16 q0, d0[0]`
- int8x16_t vdupq_lane_s8 (int8x8_t, const int)
  Form of expected instruction(s): `vdup.8 q0, d0[0]`
- float32x4_t vdupq_lane_f32 (float32x2_t, const int)
  Form of expected instruction(s): `vdup.32 q0, d0[0]`

Chapter 5: Extensions to the C Language Family   391

- poly16x8_t vdupq_lane_p16 (poly16x4_t, const int)
  Form of expected instruction(s): `vdup.16 q0, d0[0]`
- poly8x16_t vdupq_lane_p8 (poly8x8_t, const int)
  Form of expected instruction(s): `vdup.8 q0, d0[0]`
- uint64x2_t vdupq_lane_u64 (uint64x1_t, const int)
- int64x2_t vdupq_lane_s64 (int64x1_t, const int)

5.50.3.43 Combining vectors

- uint32x4_t vcombine_u32 (uint32x2_t, uint32x2_t)
- uint16x8_t vcombine_u16 (uint16x4_t, uint16x4_t)
- uint8x16_t vcombine_u8 (uint8x8_t, uint8x8_t)
- int32x4_t vcombine_s32 (int32x2_t, int32x2_t)
- int16x8_t vcombine_s16 (int16x4_t, int16x4_t)
- int8x16_t vcombine_s8 (int8x8_t, int8x8_t)
- uint64x2_t vcombine_u64 (uint64x1_t, uint64x1_t)
- int64x2_t vcombine_s64 (int64x1_t, int64x1_t)
- float32x4_t vcombine_f32 (float32x2_t, float32x2_t)
- poly16x8_t vcombine_p16 (poly16x4_t, poly16x4_t)
- poly8x16_t vcombine_p8 (poly8x8_t, poly8x8_t)

5.50.3.44 Splitting vectors

- uint32x2_t vget_high_u32 (uint32x4_t)
- uint16x4_t vget_high_u16 (uint16x8_t)
- uint8x8_t vget_high_u8 (uint8x16_t)
- int32x2_t vget_high_s32 (int32x4_t)
- int16x4_t vget_high_s16 (int16x8_t)
- int8x8_t vget_high_s8 (int8x16_t)
- uint64x1_t vget_high_u64 (uint64x2_t)
- int64x1_t vget_high_s64 (int64x2_t)
- float32x2_t vget_high_f32 (float32x4_t)
- poly16x4_t vget_high_p16 (poly16x8_t)
- poly8x8_t vget_high_p8 (poly8x16_t)
- uint32x2_t vget_low_u32 (uint32x4_t)
  Form of expected instruction(s): `vmov d0, d0`
- uint16x4_t vget_low_u16 (uint16x8_t)
  Form of expected instruction(s): `vmov d0, d0`
- uint8x8_t vget_low_u8 (uint8x16_t)
  Form of expected instruction(s): `vmov d0, d0`
- int32x2_t vget_low_s32 (int32x4_t)
  Form of expected instruction(s): `vmov d0, d0`

- int16x4_t vget_low_s16 (int16x8_t)
  Form of expected instruction(s): vmov d0, d0
- int8x8_t vget_low_s8 (int8x16_t)
  Form of expected instruction(s): vmov d0, d0
- uint64x1_t vget_low_u64 (uint64x2_t)
  Form of expected instruction(s): vmov d0, d0
- int64x1_t vget_low_s64 (int64x2_t)
  Form of expected instruction(s): vmov d0, d0
- float32x2_t vget_low_f32 (float32x4_t)
  Form of expected instruction(s): vmov d0, d0
- poly16x4_t vget_low_p16 (poly16x8_t)
  Form of expected instruction(s): vmov d0, d0
- poly8x8_t vget_low_p8 (poly8x16_t)
  Form of expected instruction(s): vmov d0, d0

5.50.3.45 Conversions

- float32x2_t vcvt_f32_u32 (uint32x2_t)
  Form of expected instruction(s): vcvt.f32.u32 d0, d0
- float32x2_t vcvt_f32_s32 (int32x2_t)
  Form of expected instruction(s): vcvt.f32.s32 d0, d0
- uint32x2_t vcvt_u32_f32 (float32x2_t)
  Form of expected instruction(s): vcvt.u32.f32 d0, d0
- int32x2_t vcvt_s32_f32 (float32x2_t)
  Form of expected instruction(s): vcvt.s32.f32 d0, d0
- float32x4_t vcvtq_f32_u32 (uint32x4_t)
  Form of expected instruction(s): vcvt.f32.u32 q0, q0
- float32x4_t vcvtq_f32_s32 (int32x4_t)
  Form of expected instruction(s): vcvt.f32.s32 q0, q0
- uint32x4_t vcvtq_u32_f32 (float32x4_t)
  Form of expected instruction(s): vcvt.u32.f32 q0, q0
- int32x4_t vcvtq_s32_f32 (float32x4_t)
  Form of expected instruction(s): vcvt.s32.f32 q0, q0
- float32x2_t vcvt_n_f32_u32 (uint32x2_t, const int)
  Form of expected instruction(s): vcvt.f32.u32 d0, d0, #0
- float32x2_t vcvt_n_f32_s32 (int32x2_t, const int)
  Form of expected instruction(s): vcvt.f32.s32 d0, d0, #0
- uint32x2_t vcvt_n_u32_f32 (float32x2_t, const int)
  Form of expected instruction(s): vcvt.u32.f32 d0, d0, #0
- int32x2_t vcvt_n_s32_f32 (float32x2_t, const int)
  Form of expected instruction(s): vcvt.s32.f32 d0, d0, #0
- float32x4_t vcvtq_n_f32_u32 (uint32x4_t, const int)
  Form of expected instruction(s): vcvt.f32.u32 q0, q0, #0

- float32x4_t vcvtq_n_f32_s32 (int32x4_t, const int)
  Form of expected instruction(s): `vcvt.f32.s32 q0, q0, #0`
- uint32x4_t vcvtq_n_u32_f32 (float32x4_t, const int)
  Form of expected instruction(s): `vcvt.u32.f32 q0, q0, #0`
- int32x4_t vcvtq_n_s32_f32 (float32x4_t, const int)
  Form of expected instruction(s): `vcvt.s32.f32 q0, q0, #0`

5.50.3.46 Move, single_opcode narrowing

- uint32x2_t vmovn_u64 (uint64x2_t)
  Form of expected instruction(s): `vmovn.i64 d0, q0`
- uint16x4_t vmovn_u32 (uint32x4_t)
  Form of expected instruction(s): `vmovn.i32 d0, q0`
- uint8x8_t vmovn_u16 (uint16x8_t)
  Form of expected instruction(s): `vmovn.i16 d0, q0`
- int32x2_t vmovn_s64 (int64x2_t)
  Form of expected instruction(s): `vmovn.i64 d0, q0`
- int16x4_t vmovn_s32 (int32x4_t)
  Form of expected instruction(s): `vmovn.i32 d0, q0`
- int8x8_t vmovn_s16 (int16x8_t)
  Form of expected instruction(s): `vmovn.i16 d0, q0`
- uint32x2_t vqmovn_u64 (uint64x2_t)
  Form of expected instruction(s): `vqmovn.u64 d0, q0`
- uint16x4_t vqmovn_u32 (uint32x4_t)
  Form of expected instruction(s): `vqmovn.u32 d0, q0`
- uint8x8_t vqmovn_u16 (uint16x8_t)
  Form of expected instruction(s): `vqmovn.u16 d0, q0`
- int32x2_t vqmovn_s64 (int64x2_t)
  Form of expected instruction(s): `vqmovn.s64 d0, q0`
- int16x4_t vqmovn_s32 (int32x4_t)
  Form of expected instruction(s): `vqmovn.s32 d0, q0`
- int8x8_t vqmovn_s16 (int16x8_t)
  Form of expected instruction(s): `vqmovn.s16 d0, q0`
- uint32x2_t vqmovun_s64 (int64x2_t)
  Form of expected instruction(s): `vqmovun.s64 d0, q0`
- uint16x4_t vqmovun_s32 (int32x4_t)
  Form of expected instruction(s): `vqmovun.s32 d0, q0`
- uint8x8_t vqmovun_s16 (int16x8_t)
  Form of expected instruction(s): `vqmovun.s16 d0, q0`

5.50.3.47 Move, single_opcode long

- uint64x2_t vmovl_u32 (uint32x2_t)
  Form of expected instruction(s): `vmovl.u32 q0, d0`

- uint32x4_t vmovl_u16 (uint16x4_t)
  Form of expected instruction(s): `vmovl.u16 q0, d0`
- uint16x8_t vmovl_u8 (uint8x8_t)
  Form of expected instruction(s): `vmovl.u8 q0, d0`
- int64x2_t vmovl_s32 (int32x2_t)
  Form of expected instruction(s): `vmovl.s32 q0, d0`
- int32x4_t vmovl_s16 (int16x4_t)
  Form of expected instruction(s): `vmovl.s16 q0, d0`
- int16x8_t vmovl_s8 (int8x8_t)
  Form of expected instruction(s): `vmovl.s8 q0, d0`

5.50.3.48 Table lookup

- poly8x8_t vtbl1_p8 (poly8x8_t, uint8x8_t)
  Form of expected instruction(s): `vtbl.8 d0, {d0}, d0`
- int8x8_t vtbl1_s8 (int8x8_t, int8x8_t)
  Form of expected instruction(s): `vtbl.8 d0, {d0}, d0`
- uint8x8_t vtbl1_u8 (uint8x8_t, uint8x8_t)
  Form of expected instruction(s): `vtbl.8 d0, {d0}, d0`
- poly8x8_t vtbl2_p8 (poly8x8x2_t, uint8x8_t)
  Form of expected instruction(s): `vtbl.8 d0, {d0, d1}, d0`
- int8x8_t vtbl2_s8 (int8x8x2_t, int8x8_t)
  Form of expected instruction(s): `vtbl.8 d0, {d0, d1}, d0`
- uint8x8_t vtbl2_u8 (uint8x8x2_t, uint8x8_t)
  Form of expected instruction(s): `vtbl.8 d0, {d0, d1}, d0`
- poly8x8_t vtbl3_p8 (poly8x8x3_t, uint8x8_t)
  Form of expected instruction(s): `vtbl.8 d0, {d0, d1, d2}, d0`
- int8x8_t vtbl3_s8 (int8x8x3_t, int8x8_t)
  Form of expected instruction(s): `vtbl.8 d0, {d0, d1, d2}, d0`
- uint8x8_t vtbl3_u8 (uint8x8x3_t, uint8x8_t)
  Form of expected instruction(s): `vtbl.8 d0, {d0, d1, d2}, d0`
- poly8x8_t vtbl4_p8 (poly8x8x4_t, uint8x8_t)
  Form of expected instruction(s): `vtbl.8 d0, {d0, d1, d2, d3}, d0`
- int8x8_t vtbl4_s8 (int8x8x4_t, int8x8_t)
  Form of expected instruction(s): `vtbl.8 d0, {d0, d1, d2, d3}, d0`
- uint8x8_t vtbl4_u8 (uint8x8x4_t, uint8x8_t)
  Form of expected instruction(s): `vtbl.8 d0, {d0, d1, d2, d3}, d0`

5.50.3.49 Extended table lookup

- poly8x8_t vtbx1_p8 (poly8x8_t, poly8x8_t, uint8x8_t)
  Form of expected instruction(s): `vtbx.8 d0, {d0}, d0`
- int8x8_t vtbx1_s8 (int8x8_t, int8x8_t, int8x8_t)
  Form of expected instruction(s): `vtbx.8 d0, {d0}, d0`

Chapter 5: Extensions to the C Language Family   395

- uint8x8_t vtbx1_u8 (uint8x8_t, uint8x8_t, uint8x8_t)
  Form of expected instruction(s): `vtbx.8 d0, {d0}, d0`
- poly8x8_t vtbx2_p8 (poly8x8_t, poly8x8x2_t, uint8x8_t)
  Form of expected instruction(s): `vtbx.8 d0, {d0, d1}, d0`
- int8x8_t vtbx2_s8 (int8x8_t, int8x8x2_t, int8x8_t)
  Form of expected instruction(s): `vtbx.8 d0, {d0, d1}, d0`
- uint8x8_t vtbx2_u8 (uint8x8_t, uint8x8x2_t, uint8x8_t)
  Form of expected instruction(s): `vtbx.8 d0, {d0, d1}, d0`
- poly8x8_t vtbx3_p8 (poly8x8_t, poly8x8x3_t, uint8x8_t)
  Form of expected instruction(s): `vtbx.8 d0, {d0, d1, d2}, d0`
- int8x8_t vtbx3_s8 (int8x8_t, int8x8x3_t, int8x8_t)
  Form of expected instruction(s): `vtbx.8 d0, {d0, d1, d2}, d0`
- uint8x8_t vtbx3_u8 (uint8x8_t, uint8x8x3_t, uint8x8_t)
  Form of expected instruction(s): `vtbx.8 d0, {d0, d1, d2}, d0`
- poly8x8_t vtbx4_p8 (poly8x8_t, poly8x8x4_t, uint8x8_t)
  Form of expected instruction(s): `vtbx.8 d0, {d0, d1, d2, d3}, d0`
- int8x8_t vtbx4_s8 (int8x8_t, int8x8x4_t, int8x8_t)
  Form of expected instruction(s): `vtbx.8 d0, {d0, d1, d2, d3}, d0`
- uint8x8_t vtbx4_u8 (uint8x8_t, uint8x8x4_t, uint8x8_t)
  Form of expected instruction(s): `vtbx.8 d0, {d0, d1, d2, d3}, d0`

5.50.3.50 Multiply, lane

- float32x2_t vmul_lane_f32 (float32x2_t, float32x2_t, const int)
  Form of expected instruction(s): `vmul.f32 d0, d0, d0[0]`
- uint32x2_t vmul_lane_u32 (uint32x2_t, uint32x2_t, const int)
  Form of expected instruction(s): `vmul.i32 d0, d0, d0[0]`
- uint16x4_t vmul_lane_u16 (uint16x4_t, uint16x4_t, const int)
  Form of expected instruction(s): `vmul.i16 d0, d0, d0[0]`
- int32x2_t vmul_lane_s32 (int32x2_t, int32x2_t, const int)
  Form of expected instruction(s): `vmul.i32 d0, d0, d0[0]`
- int16x4_t vmul_lane_s16 (int16x4_t, int16x4_t, const int)
  Form of expected instruction(s): `vmul.i16 d0, d0, d0[0]`
- float32x4_t vmulq_lane_f32 (float32x4_t, float32x2_t, const int)
  Form of expected instruction(s): `vmul.f32 q0, q0, d0[0]`
- uint32x4_t vmulq_lane_u32 (uint32x4_t, uint32x2_t, const int)
  Form of expected instruction(s): `vmul.i32 q0, q0, d0[0]`
- uint16x8_t vmulq_lane_u16 (uint16x8_t, uint16x4_t, const int)
  Form of expected instruction(s): `vmul.i16 q0, q0, d0[0]`
- int32x4_t vmulq_lane_s32 (int32x4_t, int32x2_t, const int)
  Form of expected instruction(s): `vmul.i32 q0, q0, d0[0]`
- int16x8_t vmulq_lane_s16 (int16x8_t, int16x4_t, const int)
  Form of expected instruction(s): `vmul.i16 q0, q0, d0[0]`

5.50.3.51 Long multiply, lane

- uint64x2_t vmull_lane_u32 (uint32x2_t, uint32x2_t, const int)
  Form of expected instruction(s): vmull.u32 q0, d0, d0[0]
- uint32x4_t vmull_lane_u16 (uint16x4_t, uint16x4_t, const int)
  Form of expected instruction(s): vmull.u16 q0, d0, d0[0]
- int64x2_t vmull_lane_s32 (int32x2_t, int32x2_t, const int)
  Form of expected instruction(s): vmull.s32 q0, d0, d0[0]
- int32x4_t vmull_lane_s16 (int16x4_t, int16x4_t, const int)
  Form of expected instruction(s): vmull.s16 q0, d0, d0[0]

5.50.3.52 Saturating doubling long multiply, lane

- int64x2_t vqdmull_lane_s32 (int32x2_t, int32x2_t, const int)
  Form of expected instruction(s): vqdmull.s32 q0, d0, d0[0]
- int32x4_t vqdmull_lane_s16 (int16x4_t, int16x4_t, const int)
  Form of expected instruction(s): vqdmull.s16 q0, d0, d0[0]

5.50.3.53 Saturating doubling multiply high, lane

- int32x4_t vqdmulhq_lane_s32 (int32x4_t, int32x2_t, const int)
  Form of expected instruction(s): vqdmulh.s32 q0, q0, d0[0]
- int16x8_t vqdmulhq_lane_s16 (int16x8_t, int16x4_t, const int)
  Form of expected instruction(s): vqdmulh.s16 q0, q0, d0[0]
- int32x2_t vqdmulh_lane_s32 (int32x2_t, int32x2_t, const int)
  Form of expected instruction(s): vqdmulh.s32 d0, d0, d0[0]
- int16x4_t vqdmulh_lane_s16 (int16x4_t, int16x4_t, const int)
  Form of expected instruction(s): vqdmulh.s16 d0, d0, d0[0]
- int32x4_t vqrdmulhq_lane_s32 (int32x4_t, int32x2_t, const int)
  Form of expected instruction(s): vqrdmulh.s32 q0, q0, d0[0]
- int16x8_t vqrdmulhq_lane_s16 (int16x8_t, int16x4_t, const int)
  Form of expected instruction(s): vqrdmulh.s16 q0, q0, d0[0]
- int32x2_t vqrdmulh_lane_s32 (int32x2_t, int32x2_t, const int)
  Form of expected instruction(s): vqrdmulh.s32 d0, d0, d0[0]
- int16x4_t vqrdmulh_lane_s16 (int16x4_t, int16x4_t, const int)
  Form of expected instruction(s): vqrdmulh.s16 d0, d0, d0[0]

5.50.3.54 Multiply-accumulate, lane

- float32x2_t vmla_lane_f32 (float32x2_t, float32x2_t, float32x2_t, const int)
  Form of expected instruction(s): vmla.f32 d0, d0, d0[0]
- uint32x2_t vmla_lane_u32 (uint32x2_t, uint32x2_t, uint32x2_t, const int)
  Form of expected instruction(s): vmla.i32 d0, d0, d0[0]
- uint16x4_t vmla_lane_u16 (uint16x4_t, uint16x4_t, uint16x4_t, const int)
  Form of expected instruction(s): vmla.i16 d0, d0, d0[0]
- int32x2_t vmla_lane_s32 (int32x2_t, int32x2_t, int32x2_t, const int)
  Form of expected instruction(s): vmla.i32 d0, d0, d0[0]

Chapter 5: Extensions to the C Language Family   397

- int16x4_t vmla_lane_s16 (int16x4_t, int16x4_t, int16x4_t, const int)
  Form of expected instruction(s): `vmla.i16 d0, d0, d0[0]`
- float32x4_t vmlaq_lane_f32 (float32x4_t, float32x4_t, float32x2_t, const int)
  Form of expected instruction(s): `vmla.f32 q0, q0, d0[0]`
- uint32x4_t vmlaq_lane_u32 (uint32x4_t, uint32x4_t, uint32x2_t, const int)
  Form of expected instruction(s): `vmla.i32 q0, q0, d0[0]`
- uint16x8_t vmlaq_lane_u16 (uint16x8_t, uint16x8_t, uint16x4_t, const int)
  Form of expected instruction(s): `vmla.i16 q0, q0, d0[0]`
- int32x4_t vmlaq_lane_s32 (int32x4_t, int32x4_t, int32x2_t, const int)
  Form of expected instruction(s): `vmla.i32 q0, q0, d0[0]`
- int16x8_t vmlaq_lane_s16 (int16x8_t, int16x8_t, int16x4_t, const int)
  Form of expected instruction(s): `vmla.i16 q0, q0, d0[0]`
- uint64x2_t vmlal_lane_u32 (uint64x2_t, uint32x2_t, uint32x2_t, const int)
  Form of expected instruction(s): `vmlal.u32 q0, d0, d0[0]`
- uint32x4_t vmlal_lane_u16 (uint32x4_t, uint16x4_t, uint16x4_t, const int)
  Form of expected instruction(s): `vmlal.u16 q0, d0, d0[0]`
- int64x2_t vmlal_lane_s32 (int64x2_t, int32x2_t, int32x2_t, const int)
  Form of expected instruction(s): `vmlal.s32 q0, d0, d0[0]`
- int32x4_t vmlal_lane_s16 (int32x4_t, int16x4_t, int16x4_t, const int)
  Form of expected instruction(s): `vmlal.s16 q0, d0, d0[0]`
- int64x2_t vqdmlal_lane_s32 (int64x2_t, int32x2_t, int32x2_t, const int)
  Form of expected instruction(s): `vqdmlal.s32 q0, d0, d0[0]`
- int32x4_t vqdmlal_lane_s16 (int32x4_t, int16x4_t, int16x4_t, const int)
  Form of expected instruction(s): `vqdmlal.s16 q0, d0, d0[0]`

5.50.3.55 Multiply-subtract, lane

- float32x2_t vmls_lane_f32 (float32x2_t, float32x2_t, float32x2_t, const int)
  Form of expected instruction(s): `vmls.f32 d0, d0, d0[0]`
- uint32x2_t vmls_lane_u32 (uint32x2_t, uint32x2_t, uint32x2_t, const int)
  Form of expected instruction(s): `vmls.i32 d0, d0, d0[0]`
- uint16x4_t vmls_lane_u16 (uint16x4_t, uint16x4_t, uint16x4_t, const int)
  Form of expected instruction(s): `vmls.i16 d0, d0, d0[0]`
- int32x2_t vmls_lane_s32 (int32x2_t, int32x2_t, int32x2_t, const int)
  Form of expected instruction(s): `vmls.i32 d0, d0, d0[0]`
- int16x4_t vmls_lane_s16 (int16x4_t, int16x4_t, int16x4_t, const int)
  Form of expected instruction(s): `vmls.i16 d0, d0, d0[0]`
- float32x4_t vmlsq_lane_f32 (float32x4_t, float32x4_t, float32x2_t, const int)
  Form of expected instruction(s): `vmls.f32 q0, q0, d0[0]`
- uint32x4_t vmlsq_lane_u32 (uint32x4_t, uint32x4_t, uint32x2_t, const int)
  Form of expected instruction(s): `vmls.i32 q0, q0, d0[0]`
- uint16x8_t vmlsq_lane_u16 (uint16x8_t, uint16x8_t, uint16x4_t, const int)
  Form of expected instruction(s): `vmls.i16 q0, q0, d0[0]`

- int32x4_t vmlsq_lane_s32 (int32x4_t, int32x4_t, int32x2_t, const int)
  Form of expected instruction(s): `vmls.i32 q0, q0, d0[0]`
- int16x8_t vmlsq_lane_s16 (int16x8_t, int16x8_t, int16x4_t, const int)
  Form of expected instruction(s): `vmls.i16 q0, q0, d0[0]`
- uint64x2_t vmlsl_lane_u32 (uint64x2_t, uint32x2_t, uint32x2_t, const int)
  Form of expected instruction(s): `vmlsl.u32 q0, d0, d0[0]`
- uint32x4_t vmlsl_lane_u16 (uint32x4_t, uint16x4_t, uint16x4_t, const int)
  Form of expected instruction(s): `vmlsl.u16 q0, d0, d0[0]`
- int64x2_t vmlsl_lane_s32 (int64x2_t, int32x2_t, int32x2_t, const int)
  Form of expected instruction(s): `vmlsl.s32 q0, d0, d0[0]`
- int32x4_t vmlsl_lane_s16 (int32x4_t, int16x4_t, int16x4_t, const int)
  Form of expected instruction(s): `vmlsl.s16 q0, d0, d0[0]`
- int64x2_t vqdmlsl_lane_s32 (int64x2_t, int32x2_t, int32x2_t, const int)
  Form of expected instruction(s): `vqdmlsl.s32 q0, d0, d0[0]`
- int32x4_t vqdmlsl_lane_s16 (int32x4_t, int16x4_t, int16x4_t, const int)
  Form of expected instruction(s): `vqdmlsl.s16 q0, d0, d0[0]`

5.50.3.56 Vector multiply by scalar

- float32x2_t vmul_n_f32 (float32x2_t, float32_t)
  Form of expected instruction(s): `vmul.f32 d0, d0, d0[0]`
- uint32x2_t vmul_n_u32 (uint32x2_t, uint32_t)
  Form of expected instruction(s): `vmul.i32 d0, d0, d0[0]`
- uint16x4_t vmul_n_u16 (uint16x4_t, uint16_t)
  Form of expected instruction(s): `vmul.i16 d0, d0, d0[0]`
- int32x2_t vmul_n_s32 (int32x2_t, int32_t)
  Form of expected instruction(s): `vmul.i32 d0, d0, d0[0]`
- int16x4_t vmul_n_s16 (int16x4_t, int16_t)
  Form of expected instruction(s): `vmul.i16 d0, d0, d0[0]`
- float32x4_t vmulq_n_f32 (float32x4_t, float32_t)
  Form of expected instruction(s): `vmul.f32 q0, q0, d0[0]`
- uint32x4_t vmulq_n_u32 (uint32x4_t, uint32_t)
  Form of expected instruction(s): `vmul.i32 q0, q0, d0[0]`
- uint16x8_t vmulq_n_u16 (uint16x8_t, uint16_t)
  Form of expected instruction(s): `vmul.i16 q0, q0, d0[0]`
- int32x4_t vmulq_n_s32 (int32x4_t, int32_t)
  Form of expected instruction(s): `vmul.i32 q0, q0, d0[0]`
- int16x8_t vmulq_n_s16 (int16x8_t, int16_t)
  Form of expected instruction(s): `vmul.i16 q0, q0, d0[0]`

5.50.3.57 Vector long multiply by scalar

- uint64x2_t vmull_n_u32 (uint32x2_t, uint32_t)
  Form of expected instruction(s): `vmull.u32 q0, d0, d0[0]`

- uint32x4_t vmull_n_u16 (uint16x4_t, uint16_t)
  Form of expected instruction(s): `vmull.u16 q0, d0, d0[0]`
- int64x2_t vmull_n_s32 (int32x2_t, int32_t)
  Form of expected instruction(s): `vmull.s32 q0, d0, d0[0]`
- int32x4_t vmull_n_s16 (int16x4_t, int16_t)
  Form of expected instruction(s): `vmull.s16 q0, d0, d0[0]`

5.50.3.58 Vector saturating doubling long multiply by scalar

- int64x2_t vqdmull_n_s32 (int32x2_t, int32_t)
  Form of expected instruction(s): `vqdmull.s32 q0, d0, d0[0]`
- int32x4_t vqdmull_n_s16 (int16x4_t, int16_t)
  Form of expected instruction(s): `vqdmull.s16 q0, d0, d0[0]`

5.50.3.59 Vector saturating doubling multiply high by scalar

- int32x4_t vqdmulhq_n_s32 (int32x4_t, int32_t)
  Form of expected instruction(s): `vqdmulh.s32 q0, q0, d0[0]`
- int16x8_t vqdmulhq_n_s16 (int16x8_t, int16_t)
  Form of expected instruction(s): `vqdmulh.s16 q0, q0, d0[0]`
- int32x2_t vqdmulh_n_s32 (int32x2_t, int32_t)
  Form of expected instruction(s): `vqdmulh.s32 d0, d0, d0[0]`
- int16x4_t vqdmulh_n_s16 (int16x4_t, int16_t)
  Form of expected instruction(s): `vqdmulh.s16 d0, d0, d0[0]`
- int32x4_t vqrdmulhq_n_s32 (int32x4_t, int32_t)
  Form of expected instruction(s): `vqrdmulh.s32 q0, q0, d0[0]`
- int16x8_t vqrdmulhq_n_s16 (int16x8_t, int16_t)
  Form of expected instruction(s): `vqrdmulh.s16 q0, q0, d0[0]`
- int32x2_t vqrdmulh_n_s32 (int32x2_t, int32_t)
  Form of expected instruction(s): `vqrdmulh.s32 d0, d0, d0[0]`
- int16x4_t vqrdmulh_n_s16 (int16x4_t, int16_t)
  Form of expected instruction(s): `vqrdmulh.s16 d0, d0, d0[0]`

5.50.3.60 Vector multiply-accumulate by scalar

- float32x2_t vmla_n_f32 (float32x2_t, float32x2_t, float32_t)
  Form of expected instruction(s): `vmla.f32 d0, d0, d0[0]`
- uint32x2_t vmla_n_u32 (uint32x2_t, uint32x2_t, uint32_t)
  Form of expected instruction(s): `vmla.i32 d0, d0, d0[0]`
- uint16x4_t vmla_n_u16 (uint16x4_t, uint16x4_t, uint16_t)
  Form of expected instruction(s): `vmla.i16 d0, d0, d0[0]`
- int32x2_t vmla_n_s32 (int32x2_t, int32x2_t, int32_t)
  Form of expected instruction(s): `vmla.i32 d0, d0, d0[0]`
- int16x4_t vmla_n_s16 (int16x4_t, int16x4_t, int16_t)
  Form of expected instruction(s): `vmla.i16 d0, d0, d0[0]`
- float32x4_t vmlaq_n_f32 (float32x4_t, float32x4_t, float32_t)
  Form of expected instruction(s): `vmla.f32 q0, q0, d0[0]`

- uint32x4_t vmlaq_n_u32 (uint32x4_t, uint32x4_t, uint32_t)
  Form of expected instruction(s): `vmla.i32 q0, q0, d0[0]`
- uint16x8_t vmlaq_n_u16 (uint16x8_t, uint16x8_t, uint16_t)
  Form of expected instruction(s): `vmla.i16 q0, q0, d0[0]`
- int32x4_t vmlaq_n_s32 (int32x4_t, int32x4_t, int32_t)
  Form of expected instruction(s): `vmla.i32 q0, q0, d0[0]`
- int16x8_t vmlaq_n_s16 (int16x8_t, int16x8_t, int16_t)
  Form of expected instruction(s): `vmla.i16 q0, q0, d0[0]`
- uint64x2_t vmlal_n_u32 (uint64x2_t, uint32x2_t, uint32_t)
  Form of expected instruction(s): `vmlal.u32 q0, d0, d0[0]`
- uint32x4_t vmlal_n_u16 (uint32x4_t, uint16x4_t, uint16_t)
  Form of expected instruction(s): `vmlal.u16 q0, d0, d0[0]`
- int64x2_t vmlal_n_s32 (int64x2_t, int32x2_t, int32_t)
  Form of expected instruction(s): `vmlal.s32 q0, d0, d0[0]`
- int32x4_t vmlal_n_s16 (int32x4_t, int16x4_t, int16_t)
  Form of expected instruction(s): `vmlal.s16 q0, d0, d0[0]`
- int64x2_t vqdmlal_n_s32 (int64x2_t, int32x2_t, int32_t)
  Form of expected instruction(s): `vqdmlal.s32 q0, d0, d0[0]`
- int32x4_t vqdmlal_n_s16 (int32x4_t, int16x4_t, int16_t)
  Form of expected instruction(s): `vqdmlal.s16 q0, d0, d0[0]`

5.50.3.61 Vector multiply-subtract by scalar

- float32x2_t vmls_n_f32 (float32x2_t, float32x2_t, float32_t)
  Form of expected instruction(s): `vmls.f32 d0, d0, d0[0]`
- uint32x2_t vmls_n_u32 (uint32x2_t, uint32x2_t, uint32_t)
  Form of expected instruction(s): `vmls.i32 d0, d0, d0[0]`
- uint16x4_t vmls_n_u16 (uint16x4_t, uint16x4_t, uint16_t)
  Form of expected instruction(s): `vmls.i16 d0, d0, d0[0]`
- int32x2_t vmls_n_s32 (int32x2_t, int32x2_t, int32_t)
  Form of expected instruction(s): `vmls.i32 d0, d0, d0[0]`
- int16x4_t vmls_n_s16 (int16x4_t, int16x4_t, int16_t)
  Form of expected instruction(s): `vmls.i16 d0, d0, d0[0]`
- float32x4_t vmlsq_n_f32 (float32x4_t, float32x4_t, float32_t)
  Form of expected instruction(s): `vmls.f32 q0, q0, d0[0]`
- uint32x4_t vmlsq_n_u32 (uint32x4_t, uint32x4_t, uint32_t)
  Form of expected instruction(s): `vmls.i32 q0, q0, d0[0]`
- uint16x8_t vmlsq_n_u16 (uint16x8_t, uint16x8_t, uint16_t)
  Form of expected instruction(s): `vmls.i16 q0, q0, d0[0]`
- int32x4_t vmlsq_n_s32 (int32x4_t, int32x4_t, int32_t)
  Form of expected instruction(s): `vmls.i32 q0, q0, d0[0]`
- int16x8_t vmlsq_n_s16 (int16x8_t, int16x8_t, int16_t)
  Form of expected instruction(s): `vmls.i16 q0, q0, d0[0]`

Chapter 5: Extensions to the C Language Family   401

- uint64x2_t vmlsl_n_u32 (uint64x2_t, uint32x2_t, uint32_t)
  Form of expected instruction(s): `vmlsl.u32 q0, d0, d0[0]`
- uint32x4_t vmlsl_n_u16 (uint32x4_t, uint16x4_t, uint16_t)
  Form of expected instruction(s): `vmlsl.u16 q0, d0, d0[0]`
- int64x2_t vmlsl_n_s32 (int64x2_t, int32x2_t, int32_t)
  Form of expected instruction(s): `vmlsl.s32 q0, d0, d0[0]`
- int32x4_t vmlsl_n_s16 (int32x4_t, int16x4_t, int16_t)
  Form of expected instruction(s): `vmlsl.s16 q0, d0, d0[0]`
- int64x2_t vqdmlsl_n_s32 (int64x2_t, int32x2_t, int32_t)
  Form of expected instruction(s): `vqdmlsl.s32 q0, d0, d0[0]`
- int32x4_t vqdmlsl_n_s16 (int32x4_t, int16x4_t, int16_t)
  Form of expected instruction(s): `vqdmlsl.s16 q0, d0, d0[0]`

5.50.3.62 Vector extract

- uint32x2_t vext_u32 (uint32x2_t, uint32x2_t, const int)
  Form of expected instruction(s): `vext.32 d0, d0, d0, #0`
- uint16x4_t vext_u16 (uint16x4_t, uint16x4_t, const int)
  Form of expected instruction(s): `vext.16 d0, d0, d0, #0`
- uint8x8_t vext_u8 (uint8x8_t, uint8x8_t, const int)
  Form of expected instruction(s): `vext.8 d0, d0, d0, #0`
- int32x2_t vext_s32 (int32x2_t, int32x2_t, const int)
  Form of expected instruction(s): `vext.32 d0, d0, d0, #0`
- int16x4_t vext_s16 (int16x4_t, int16x4_t, const int)
  Form of expected instruction(s): `vext.16 d0, d0, d0, #0`
- int8x8_t vext_s8 (int8x8_t, int8x8_t, const int)
  Form of expected instruction(s): `vext.8 d0, d0, d0, #0`
- uint64x1_t vext_u64 (uint64x1_t, uint64x1_t, const int)
  Form of expected instruction(s): `vext.64 d0, d0, d0, #0`
- int64x1_t vext_s64 (int64x1_t, int64x1_t, const int)
  Form of expected instruction(s): `vext.64 d0, d0, d0, #0`
- float32x2_t vext_f32 (float32x2_t, float32x2_t, const int)
  Form of expected instruction(s): `vext.32 d0, d0, d0, #0`
- poly16x4_t vext_p16 (poly16x4_t, poly16x4_t, const int)
  Form of expected instruction(s): `vext.16 d0, d0, d0, #0`
- poly8x8_t vext_p8 (poly8x8_t, poly8x8_t, const int)
  Form of expected instruction(s): `vext.8 d0, d0, d0, #0`
- uint32x4_t vextq_u32 (uint32x4_t, uint32x4_t, const int)
  Form of expected instruction(s): `vext.32 q0, q0, q0, #0`
- uint16x8_t vextq_u16 (uint16x8_t, uint16x8_t, const int)
  Form of expected instruction(s): `vext.16 q0, q0, q0, #0`
- uint8x16_t vextq_u8 (uint8x16_t, uint8x16_t, const int)
  Form of expected instruction(s): `vext.8 q0, q0, q0, #0`

- int32x4_t vextq_s32 (int32x4_t, int32x4_t, const int)
  Form of expected instruction(s): `vext.32 q0, q0, q0, #0`
- int16x8_t vextq_s16 (int16x8_t, int16x8_t, const int)
  Form of expected instruction(s): `vext.16 q0, q0, q0, #0`
- int8x16_t vextq_s8 (int8x16_t, int8x16_t, const int)
  Form of expected instruction(s): `vext.8 q0, q0, q0, #0`
- uint64x2_t vextq_u64 (uint64x2_t, uint64x2_t, const int)
  Form of expected instruction(s): `vext.64 q0, q0, q0, #0`
- int64x2_t vextq_s64 (int64x2_t, int64x2_t, const int)
  Form of expected instruction(s): `vext.64 q0, q0, q0, #0`
- float32x4_t vextq_f32 (float32x4_t, float32x4_t, const int)
  Form of expected instruction(s): `vext.32 q0, q0, q0, #0`
- poly16x8_t vextq_p16 (poly16x8_t, poly16x8_t, const int)
  Form of expected instruction(s): `vext.16 q0, q0, q0, #0`
- poly8x16_t vextq_p8 (poly8x16_t, poly8x16_t, const int)
  Form of expected instruction(s): `vext.8 q0, q0, q0, #0`

5.50.3.63 Reverse elements

- uint32x2_t vrev64_u32 (uint32x2_t)
  Form of expected instruction(s): `vrev64.32 d0, d0`
- uint16x4_t vrev64_u16 (uint16x4_t)
  Form of expected instruction(s): `vrev64.16 d0, d0`
- uint8x8_t vrev64_u8 (uint8x8_t)
  Form of expected instruction(s): `vrev64.8 d0, d0`
- int32x2_t vrev64_s32 (int32x2_t)
  Form of expected instruction(s): `vrev64.32 d0, d0`
- int16x4_t vrev64_s16 (int16x4_t)
  Form of expected instruction(s): `vrev64.16 d0, d0`
- int8x8_t vrev64_s8 (int8x8_t)
  Form of expected instruction(s): `vrev64.8 d0, d0`
- float32x2_t vrev64_f32 (float32x2_t)
  Form of expected instruction(s): `vrev64.32 d0, d0`
- poly16x4_t vrev64_p16 (poly16x4_t)
  Form of expected instruction(s): `vrev64.16 d0, d0`
- poly8x8_t vrev64_p8 (poly8x8_t)
  Form of expected instruction(s): `vrev64.8 d0, d0`
- uint32x4_t vrev64q_u32 (uint32x4_t)
  Form of expected instruction(s): `vrev64.32 q0, q0`
- uint16x8_t vrev64q_u16 (uint16x8_t)
  Form of expected instruction(s): `vrev64.16 q0, q0`
- uint8x16_t vrev64q_u8 (uint8x16_t)
  Form of expected instruction(s): `vrev64.8 q0, q0`

Chapter 5: Extensions to the C Language Family 403

- int32x4_t vrev64q_s32 (int32x4_t)
  Form of expected instruction(s): `vrev64.32 q0, q0`
- int16x8_t vrev64q_s16 (int16x8_t)
  Form of expected instruction(s): `vrev64.16 q0, q0`
- int8x16_t vrev64q_s8 (int8x16_t)
  Form of expected instruction(s): `vrev64.8 q0, q0`
- float32x4_t vrev64q_f32 (float32x4_t)
  Form of expected instruction(s): `vrev64.32 q0, q0`
- poly16x8_t vrev64q_p16 (poly16x8_t)
  Form of expected instruction(s): `vrev64.16 q0, q0`
- poly8x16_t vrev64q_p8 (poly8x16_t)
  Form of expected instruction(s): `vrev64.8 q0, q0`
- uint16x4_t vrev32_u16 (uint16x4_t)
  Form of expected instruction(s): `vrev32.16 d0, d0`
- int16x4_t vrev32_s16 (int16x4_t)
  Form of expected instruction(s): `vrev32.16 d0, d0`
- uint8x8_t vrev32_u8 (uint8x8_t)
  Form of expected instruction(s): `vrev32.8 d0, d0`
- int8x8_t vrev32_s8 (int8x8_t)
  Form of expected instruction(s): `vrev32.8 d0, d0`
- poly16x4_t vrev32_p16 (poly16x4_t)
  Form of expected instruction(s): `vrev32.16 d0, d0`
- poly8x8_t vrev32_p8 (poly8x8_t)
  Form of expected instruction(s): `vrev32.8 d0, d0`
- uint16x8_t vrev32q_u16 (uint16x8_t)
  Form of expected instruction(s): `vrev32.16 q0, q0`
- int16x8_t vrev32q_s16 (int16x8_t)
  Form of expected instruction(s): `vrev32.16 q0, q0`
- uint8x16_t vrev32q_u8 (uint8x16_t)
  Form of expected instruction(s): `vrev32.8 q0, q0`
- int8x16_t vrev32q_s8 (int8x16_t)
  Form of expected instruction(s): `vrev32.8 q0, q0`
- poly16x8_t vrev32q_p16 (poly16x8_t)
  Form of expected instruction(s): `vrev32.16 q0, q0`
- poly8x16_t vrev32q_p8 (poly8x16_t)
  Form of expected instruction(s): `vrev32.8 q0, q0`
- uint8x8_t vrev16_u8 (uint8x8_t)
  Form of expected instruction(s): `vrev16.8 d0, d0`
- int8x8_t vrev16_s8 (int8x8_t)
  Form of expected instruction(s): `vrev16.8 d0, d0`
- poly8x8_t vrev16_p8 (poly8x8_t)
  Form of expected instruction(s): `vrev16.8 d0, d0`

- uint8x16_t vrev16q_u8 (uint8x16_t)
  Form of expected instruction(s): `vrev16.8 q0, q0`
- int8x16_t vrev16q_s8 (int8x16_t)
  Form of expected instruction(s): `vrev16.8 q0, q0`
- poly8x16_t vrev16q_p8 (poly8x16_t)
  Form of expected instruction(s): `vrev16.8 q0, q0`

5.50.3.64 Bit selection

- uint32x2_t vbsl_u32 (uint32x2_t, uint32x2_t, uint32x2_t)
  Form of expected instruction(s): `vbsl d0, d0, d0` *or* `vbit d0, d0, d0` *or* `vbif d0, d0, d0`
- uint16x4_t vbsl_u16 (uint16x4_t, uint16x4_t, uint16x4_t)
  Form of expected instruction(s): `vbsl d0, d0, d0` *or* `vbit d0, d0, d0` *or* `vbif d0, d0, d0`
- uint8x8_t vbsl_u8 (uint8x8_t, uint8x8_t, uint8x8_t)
  Form of expected instruction(s): `vbsl d0, d0, d0` *or* `vbit d0, d0, d0` *or* `vbif d0, d0, d0`
- int32x2_t vbsl_s32 (uint32x2_t, int32x2_t, int32x2_t)
  Form of expected instruction(s): `vbsl d0, d0, d0` *or* `vbit d0, d0, d0` *or* `vbif d0, d0, d0`
- int16x4_t vbsl_s16 (uint16x4_t, int16x4_t, int16x4_t)
  Form of expected instruction(s): `vbsl d0, d0, d0` *or* `vbit d0, d0, d0` *or* `vbif d0, d0, d0`
- int8x8_t vbsl_s8 (uint8x8_t, int8x8_t, int8x8_t)
  Form of expected instruction(s): `vbsl d0, d0, d0` *or* `vbit d0, d0, d0` *or* `vbif d0, d0, d0`
- uint64x1_t vbsl_u64 (uint64x1_t, uint64x1_t, uint64x1_t)
  Form of expected instruction(s): `vbsl d0, d0, d0` *or* `vbit d0, d0, d0` *or* `vbif d0, d0, d0`
- int64x1_t vbsl_s64 (uint64x1_t, int64x1_t, int64x1_t)
  Form of expected instruction(s): `vbsl d0, d0, d0` *or* `vbit d0, d0, d0` *or* `vbif d0, d0, d0`
- float32x2_t vbsl_f32 (uint32x2_t, float32x2_t, float32x2_t)
  Form of expected instruction(s): `vbsl d0, d0, d0` *or* `vbit d0, d0, d0` *or* `vbif d0, d0, d0`
- poly16x4_t vbsl_p16 (uint16x4_t, poly16x4_t, poly16x4_t)
  Form of expected instruction(s): `vbsl d0, d0, d0` *or* `vbit d0, d0, d0` *or* `vbif d0, d0, d0`
- poly8x8_t vbsl_p8 (uint8x8_t, poly8x8_t, poly8x8_t)
  Form of expected instruction(s): `vbsl d0, d0, d0` *or* `vbit d0, d0, d0` *or* `vbif d0, d0, d0`
- uint32x4_t vbslq_u32 (uint32x4_t, uint32x4_t, uint32x4_t)
  Form of expected instruction(s): `vbsl q0, q0, q0` *or* `vbit q0, q0, q0` *or* `vbif q0, q0, q0`

Chapter 5: Extensions to the C Language Family   405

- uint16x8_t vbslq_u16 (uint16x8_t, uint16x8_t, uint16x8_t)
  Form of expected instruction(s): `vbsl q0, q0, q0` *or* `vbit q0, q0, q0` *or* `vbif q0, q0, q0`
- uint8x16_t vbslq_u8 (uint8x16_t, uint8x16_t, uint8x16_t)
  Form of expected instruction(s): `vbsl q0, q0, q0` *or* `vbit q0, q0, q0` *or* `vbif q0, q0, q0`
- int32x4_t vbslq_s32 (uint32x4_t, int32x4_t, int32x4_t)
  Form of expected instruction(s): `vbsl q0, q0, q0` *or* `vbit q0, q0, q0` *or* `vbif q0, q0, q0`
- int16x8_t vbslq_s16 (uint16x8_t, int16x8_t, int16x8_t)
  Form of expected instruction(s): `vbsl q0, q0, q0` *or* `vbit q0, q0, q0` *or* `vbif q0, q0, q0`
- int8x16_t vbslq_s8 (uint8x16_t, int8x16_t, int8x16_t)
  Form of expected instruction(s): `vbsl q0, q0, q0` *or* `vbit q0, q0, q0` *or* `vbif q0, q0, q0`
- uint64x2_t vbslq_u64 (uint64x2_t, uint64x2_t, uint64x2_t)
  Form of expected instruction(s): `vbsl q0, q0, q0` *or* `vbit q0, q0, q0` *or* `vbif q0, q0, q0`
- int64x2_t vbslq_s64 (uint64x2_t, int64x2_t, int64x2_t)
  Form of expected instruction(s): `vbsl q0, q0, q0` *or* `vbit q0, q0, q0` *or* `vbif q0, q0, q0`
- float32x4_t vbslq_f32 (uint32x4_t, float32x4_t, float32x4_t)
  Form of expected instruction(s): `vbsl q0, q0, q0` *or* `vbit q0, q0, q0` *or* `vbif q0, q0, q0`
- poly16x8_t vbslq_p16 (uint16x8_t, poly16x8_t, poly16x8_t)
  Form of expected instruction(s): `vbsl q0, q0, q0` *or* `vbit q0, q0, q0` *or* `vbif q0, q0, q0`
- poly8x16_t vbslq_p8 (uint8x16_t, poly8x16_t, poly8x16_t)
  Form of expected instruction(s): `vbsl q0, q0, q0` *or* `vbit q0, q0, q0` *or* `vbif q0, q0, q0`

5.50.3.65 Transpose elements

- uint32x2x2_t vtrn_u32 (uint32x2_t, uint32x2_t)
  Form of expected instruction(s): `vtrn.32 d0, d1`
- uint16x4x2_t vtrn_u16 (uint16x4_t, uint16x4_t)
  Form of expected instruction(s): `vtrn.16 d0, d1`
- uint8x8x2_t vtrn_u8 (uint8x8_t, uint8x8_t)
  Form of expected instruction(s): `vtrn.8 d0, d1`
- int32x2x2_t vtrn_s32 (int32x2_t, int32x2_t)
  Form of expected instruction(s): `vtrn.32 d0, d1`
- int16x4x2_t vtrn_s16 (int16x4_t, int16x4_t)
  Form of expected instruction(s): `vtrn.16 d0, d1`
- int8x8x2_t vtrn_s8 (int8x8_t, int8x8_t)
  Form of expected instruction(s): `vtrn.8 d0, d1`

- float32x2x2_t vtrn_f32 (float32x2_t, float32x2_t)
  Form of expected instruction(s): `vtrn.32 d0, d1`
- poly16x4x2_t vtrn_p16 (poly16x4_t, poly16x4_t)
  Form of expected instruction(s): `vtrn.16 d0, d1`
- poly8x8x2_t vtrn_p8 (poly8x8_t, poly8x8_t)
  Form of expected instruction(s): `vtrn.8 d0, d1`
- uint32x4x2_t vtrnq_u32 (uint32x4_t, uint32x4_t)
  Form of expected instruction(s): `vtrn.32 q0, q1`
- uint16x8x2_t vtrnq_u16 (uint16x8_t, uint16x8_t)
  Form of expected instruction(s): `vtrn.16 q0, q1`
- uint8x16x2_t vtrnq_u8 (uint8x16_t, uint8x16_t)
  Form of expected instruction(s): `vtrn.8 q0, q1`
- int32x4x2_t vtrnq_s32 (int32x4_t, int32x4_t)
  Form of expected instruction(s): `vtrn.32 q0, q1`
- int16x8x2_t vtrnq_s16 (int16x8_t, int16x8_t)
  Form of expected instruction(s): `vtrn.16 q0, q1`
- int8x16x2_t vtrnq_s8 (int8x16_t, int8x16_t)
  Form of expected instruction(s): `vtrn.8 q0, q1`
- float32x4x2_t vtrnq_f32 (float32x4_t, float32x4_t)
  Form of expected instruction(s): `vtrn.32 q0, q1`
- poly16x8x2_t vtrnq_p16 (poly16x8_t, poly16x8_t)
  Form of expected instruction(s): `vtrn.16 q0, q1`
- poly8x16x2_t vtrnq_p8 (poly8x16_t, poly8x16_t)
  Form of expected instruction(s): `vtrn.8 q0, q1`

5.50.3.66 Zip elements

- uint32x2x2_t vzip_u32 (uint32x2_t, uint32x2_t)
  Form of expected instruction(s): `vzip.32 d0, d1`
- uint16x4x2_t vzip_u16 (uint16x4_t, uint16x4_t)
  Form of expected instruction(s): `vzip.16 d0, d1`
- uint8x8x2_t vzip_u8 (uint8x8_t, uint8x8_t)
  Form of expected instruction(s): `vzip.8 d0, d1`
- int32x2x2_t vzip_s32 (int32x2_t, int32x2_t)
  Form of expected instruction(s): `vzip.32 d0, d1`
- int16x4x2_t vzip_s16 (int16x4_t, int16x4_t)
  Form of expected instruction(s): `vzip.16 d0, d1`
- int8x8x2_t vzip_s8 (int8x8_t, int8x8_t)
  Form of expected instruction(s): `vzip.8 d0, d1`
- float32x2x2_t vzip_f32 (float32x2_t, float32x2_t)
  Form of expected instruction(s): `vzip.32 d0, d1`
- poly16x4x2_t vzip_p16 (poly16x4_t, poly16x4_t)
  Form of expected instruction(s): `vzip.16 d0, d1`

Chapter 5: Extensions to the C Language Family 407

- poly8x8x2_t vzip_p8 (poly8x8_t, poly8x8_t)
  Form of expected instruction(s): `vzip.8 d0, d1`
- uint32x4x2_t vzipq_u32 (uint32x4_t, uint32x4_t)
  Form of expected instruction(s): `vzip.32 q0, q1`
- uint16x8x2_t vzipq_u16 (uint16x8_t, uint16x8_t)
  Form of expected instruction(s): `vzip.16 q0, q1`
- uint8x16x2_t vzipq_u8 (uint8x16_t, uint8x16_t)
  Form of expected instruction(s): `vzip.8 q0, q1`
- int32x4x2_t vzipq_s32 (int32x4_t, int32x4_t)
  Form of expected instruction(s): `vzip.32 q0, q1`
- int16x8x2_t vzipq_s16 (int16x8_t, int16x8_t)
  Form of expected instruction(s): `vzip.16 q0, q1`
- int8x16x2_t vzipq_s8 (int8x16_t, int8x16_t)
  Form of expected instruction(s): `vzip.8 q0, q1`
- float32x4x2_t vzipq_f32 (float32x4_t, float32x4_t)
  Form of expected instruction(s): `vzip.32 q0, q1`
- poly16x8x2_t vzipq_p16 (poly16x8_t, poly16x8_t)
  Form of expected instruction(s): `vzip.16 q0, q1`
- poly8x16x2_t vzipq_p8 (poly8x16_t, poly8x16_t)
  Form of expected instruction(s): `vzip.8 q0, q1`

5.50.3.67 Unzip elements

- uint32x2x2_t vuzp_u32 (uint32x2_t, uint32x2_t)
  Form of expected instruction(s): `vuzp.32 d0, d1`
- uint16x4x2_t vuzp_u16 (uint16x4_t, uint16x4_t)
  Form of expected instruction(s): `vuzp.16 d0, d1`
- uint8x8x2_t vuzp_u8 (uint8x8_t, uint8x8_t)
  Form of expected instruction(s): `vuzp.8 d0, d1`
- int32x2x2_t vuzp_s32 (int32x2_t, int32x2_t)
  Form of expected instruction(s): `vuzp.32 d0, d1`
- int16x4x2_t vuzp_s16 (int16x4_t, int16x4_t)
  Form of expected instruction(s): `vuzp.16 d0, d1`
- int8x8x2_t vuzp_s8 (int8x8_t, int8x8_t)
  Form of expected instruction(s): `vuzp.8 d0, d1`
- float32x2x2_t vuzp_f32 (float32x2_t, float32x2_t)
  Form of expected instruction(s): `vuzp.32 d0, d1`
- poly16x4x2_t vuzp_p16 (poly16x4_t, poly16x4_t)
  Form of expected instruction(s): `vuzp.16 d0, d1`
- poly8x8x2_t vuzp_p8 (poly8x8_t, poly8x8_t)
  Form of expected instruction(s): `vuzp.8 d0, d1`
- uint32x4x2_t vuzpq_u32 (uint32x4_t, uint32x4_t)
  Form of expected instruction(s): `vuzp.32 q0, q1`

- uint16x8x2_t vuzpq_u16 (uint16x8_t, uint16x8_t)
  Form of expected instruction(s): `vuzp.16 q0, q1`
- uint8x16x2_t vuzpq_u8 (uint8x16_t, uint8x16_t)
  Form of expected instruction(s): `vuzp.8 q0, q1`
- int32x4x2_t vuzpq_s32 (int32x4_t, int32x4_t)
  Form of expected instruction(s): `vuzp.32 q0, q1`
- int16x8x2_t vuzpq_s16 (int16x8_t, int16x8_t)
  Form of expected instruction(s): `vuzp.16 q0, q1`
- int8x16x2_t vuzpq_s8 (int8x16_t, int8x16_t)
  Form of expected instruction(s): `vuzp.8 q0, q1`
- float32x4x2_t vuzpq_f32 (float32x4_t, float32x4_t)
  Form of expected instruction(s): `vuzp.32 q0, q1`
- poly16x8x2_t vuzpq_p16 (poly16x8_t, poly16x8_t)
  Form of expected instruction(s): `vuzp.16 q0, q1`
- poly8x16x2_t vuzpq_p8 (poly8x16_t, poly8x16_t)
  Form of expected instruction(s): `vuzp.8 q0, q1`

5.50.3.68 Element/structure loads, VLD1 variants

- uint32x2_t vld1_u32 (const uint32_t *)
  Form of expected instruction(s): `vld1.32 {d0}, [r0]`
- uint16x4_t vld1_u16 (const uint16_t *)
  Form of expected instruction(s): `vld1.16 {d0}, [r0]`
- uint8x8_t vld1_u8 (const uint8_t *)
  Form of expected instruction(s): `vld1.8 {d0}, [r0]`
- int32x2_t vld1_s32 (const int32_t *)
  Form of expected instruction(s): `vld1.32 {d0}, [r0]`
- int16x4_t vld1_s16 (const int16_t *)
  Form of expected instruction(s): `vld1.16 {d0}, [r0]`
- int8x8_t vld1_s8 (const int8_t *)
  Form of expected instruction(s): `vld1.8 {d0}, [r0]`
- uint64x1_t vld1_u64 (const uint64_t *)
  Form of expected instruction(s): `vld1.64 {d0}, [r0]`
- int64x1_t vld1_s64 (const int64_t *)
  Form of expected instruction(s): `vld1.64 {d0}, [r0]`
- float32x2_t vld1_f32 (const float32_t *)
  Form of expected instruction(s): `vld1.32 {d0}, [r0]`
- poly16x4_t vld1_p16 (const poly16_t *)
  Form of expected instruction(s): `vld1.16 {d0}, [r0]`
- poly8x8_t vld1_p8 (const poly8_t *)
  Form of expected instruction(s): `vld1.8 {d0}, [r0]`
- uint32x4_t vld1q_u32 (const uint32_t *)
  Form of expected instruction(s): `vld1.32 {d0, d1}, [r0]`

Chapter 5: Extensions to the C Language Family   409

- uint16x8_t vld1q_u16 (const uint16_t *)
  Form of expected instruction(s): vld1.16 {d0, d1}, [r0]
- uint8x16_t vld1q_u8 (const uint8_t *)
  Form of expected instruction(s): vld1.8 {d0, d1}, [r0]
- int32x4_t vld1q_s32 (const int32_t *)
  Form of expected instruction(s): vld1.32 {d0, d1}, [r0]
- int16x8_t vld1q_s16 (const int16_t *)
  Form of expected instruction(s): vld1.16 {d0, d1}, [r0]
- int8x16_t vld1q_s8 (const int8_t *)
  Form of expected instruction(s): vld1.8 {d0, d1}, [r0]
- uint64x2_t vld1q_u64 (const uint64_t *)
  Form of expected instruction(s): vld1.64 {d0, d1}, [r0]
- int64x2_t vld1q_s64 (const int64_t *)
  Form of expected instruction(s): vld1.64 {d0, d1}, [r0]
- float32x4_t vld1q_f32 (const float32_t *)
  Form of expected instruction(s): vld1.32 {d0, d1}, [r0]
- poly16x8_t vld1q_p16 (const poly16_t *)
  Form of expected instruction(s): vld1.16 {d0, d1}, [r0]
- poly8x16_t vld1q_p8 (const poly8_t *)
  Form of expected instruction(s): vld1.8 {d0, d1}, [r0]
- uint32x2_t vld1_lane_u32 (const uint32_t *, uint32x2_t, const int)
  Form of expected instruction(s): vld1.32 {d0[0]}, [r0]
- uint16x4_t vld1_lane_u16 (const uint16_t *, uint16x4_t, const int)
  Form of expected instruction(s): vld1.16 {d0[0]}, [r0]
- uint8x8_t vld1_lane_u8 (const uint8_t *, uint8x8_t, const int)
  Form of expected instruction(s): vld1.8 {d0[0]}, [r0]
- int32x2_t vld1_lane_s32 (const int32_t *, int32x2_t, const int)
  Form of expected instruction(s): vld1.32 {d0[0]}, [r0]
- int16x4_t vld1_lane_s16 (const int16_t *, int16x4_t, const int)
  Form of expected instruction(s): vld1.16 {d0[0]}, [r0]
- int8x8_t vld1_lane_s8 (const int8_t *, int8x8_t, const int)
  Form of expected instruction(s): vld1.8 {d0[0]}, [r0]
- float32x2_t vld1_lane_f32 (const float32_t *, float32x2_t, const int)
  Form of expected instruction(s): vld1.32 {d0[0]}, [r0]
- poly16x4_t vld1_lane_p16 (const poly16_t *, poly16x4_t, const int)
  Form of expected instruction(s): vld1.16 {d0[0]}, [r0]
- poly8x8_t vld1_lane_p8 (const poly8_t *, poly8x8_t, const int)
  Form of expected instruction(s): vld1.8 {d0[0]}, [r0]
- uint64x1_t vld1_lane_u64 (const uint64_t *, uint64x1_t, const int)
  Form of expected instruction(s): vld1.64 {d0}, [r0]
- int64x1_t vld1_lane_s64 (const int64_t *, int64x1_t, const int)
  Form of expected instruction(s): vld1.64 {d0}, [r0]

- uint32x4_t vld1q_lane_u32 (const uint32_t *, uint32x4_t, const int)
  Form of expected instruction(s): vld1.32 {d0[0]}, [r0]
- uint16x8_t vld1q_lane_u16 (const uint16_t *, uint16x8_t, const int)
  Form of expected instruction(s): vld1.16 {d0[0]}, [r0]
- uint8x16_t vld1q_lane_u8 (const uint8_t *, uint8x16_t, const int)
  Form of expected instruction(s): vld1.8 {d0[0]}, [r0]
- int32x4_t vld1q_lane_s32 (const int32_t *, int32x4_t, const int)
  Form of expected instruction(s): vld1.32 {d0[0]}, [r0]
- int16x8_t vld1q_lane_s16 (const int16_t *, int16x8_t, const int)
  Form of expected instruction(s): vld1.16 {d0[0]}, [r0]
- int8x16_t vld1q_lane_s8 (const int8_t *, int8x16_t, const int)
  Form of expected instruction(s): vld1.8 {d0[0]}, [r0]
- float32x4_t vld1q_lane_f32 (const float32_t *, float32x4_t, const int)
  Form of expected instruction(s): vld1.32 {d0[0]}, [r0]
- poly16x8_t vld1q_lane_p16 (const poly16_t *, poly16x8_t, const int)
  Form of expected instruction(s): vld1.16 {d0[0]}, [r0]
- poly8x16_t vld1q_lane_p8 (const poly8_t *, poly8x16_t, const int)
  Form of expected instruction(s): vld1.8 {d0[0]}, [r0]
- uint64x2_t vld1q_lane_u64 (const uint64_t *, uint64x2_t, const int)
  Form of expected instruction(s): vld1.64 {d0}, [r0]
- int64x2_t vld1q_lane_s64 (const int64_t *, int64x2_t, const int)
  Form of expected instruction(s): vld1.64 {d0}, [r0]
- uint32x2_t vld1_dup_u32 (const uint32_t *)
  Form of expected instruction(s): vld1.32 {d0[]}, [r0]
- uint16x4_t vld1_dup_u16 (const uint16_t *)
  Form of expected instruction(s): vld1.16 {d0[]}, [r0]
- uint8x8_t vld1_dup_u8 (const uint8_t *)
  Form of expected instruction(s): vld1.8 {d0[]}, [r0]
- int32x2_t vld1_dup_s32 (const int32_t *)
  Form of expected instruction(s): vld1.32 {d0[]}, [r0]
- int16x4_t vld1_dup_s16 (const int16_t *)
  Form of expected instruction(s): vld1.16 {d0[]}, [r0]
- int8x8_t vld1_dup_s8 (const int8_t *)
  Form of expected instruction(s): vld1.8 {d0[]}, [r0]
- float32x2_t vld1_dup_f32 (const float32_t *)
  Form of expected instruction(s): vld1.32 {d0[]}, [r0]
- poly16x4_t vld1_dup_p16 (const poly16_t *)
  Form of expected instruction(s): vld1.16 {d0[]}, [r0]
- poly8x8_t vld1_dup_p8 (const poly8_t *)
  Form of expected instruction(s): vld1.8 {d0[]}, [r0]
- uint64x1_t vld1_dup_u64 (const uint64_t *)
  Form of expected instruction(s): vld1.64 {d0}, [r0]

Chapter 5: Extensions to the C Language Family   411

- int64x1_t vld1_dup_s64 (const int64_t *)
  Form of expected instruction(s): vld1.64 {d0}, [r0]
- uint32x4_t vld1q_dup_u32 (const uint32_t *)
  Form of expected instruction(s): vld1.32 {d0[], d1[]}, [r0]
- uint16x8_t vld1q_dup_u16 (const uint16_t *)
  Form of expected instruction(s): vld1.16 {d0[], d1[]}, [r0]
- uint8x16_t vld1q_dup_u8 (const uint8_t *)
  Form of expected instruction(s): vld1.8 {d0[], d1[]}, [r0]
- int32x4_t vld1q_dup_s32 (const int32_t *)
  Form of expected instruction(s): vld1.32 {d0[], d1[]}, [r0]
- int16x8_t vld1q_dup_s16 (const int16_t *)
  Form of expected instruction(s): vld1.16 {d0[], d1[]}, [r0]
- int8x16_t vld1q_dup_s8 (const int8_t *)
  Form of expected instruction(s): vld1.8 {d0[], d1[]}, [r0]
- float32x4_t vld1q_dup_f32 (const float32_t *)
  Form of expected instruction(s): vld1.32 {d0[], d1[]}, [r0]
- poly16x8_t vld1q_dup_p16 (const poly16_t *)
  Form of expected instruction(s): vld1.16 {d0[], d1[]}, [r0]
- poly8x16_t vld1q_dup_p8 (const poly8_t *)
  Form of expected instruction(s): vld1.8 {d0[], d1[]}, [r0]
- uint64x2_t vld1q_dup_u64 (const uint64_t *)
  Form of expected instruction(s): vld1.64 {d0, d1}, [r0]
- int64x2_t vld1q_dup_s64 (const int64_t *)
  Form of expected instruction(s): vld1.64 {d0, d1}, [r0]

5.50.3.69 Element/structure stores, VST1 variants

- void vst1_u32 (uint32_t *, uint32x2_t)
  Form of expected instruction(s): vst1.32 {d0}, [r0]
- void vst1_u16 (uint16_t *, uint16x4_t)
  Form of expected instruction(s): vst1.16 {d0}, [r0]
- void vst1_u8 (uint8_t *, uint8x8_t)
  Form of expected instruction(s): vst1.8 {d0}, [r0]
- void vst1_s32 (int32_t *, int32x2_t)
  Form of expected instruction(s): vst1.32 {d0}, [r0]
- void vst1_s16 (int16_t *, int16x4_t)
  Form of expected instruction(s): vst1.16 {d0}, [r0]
- void vst1_s8 (int8_t *, int8x8_t)
  Form of expected instruction(s): vst1.8 {d0}, [r0]
- void vst1_u64 (uint64_t *, uint64x1_t)
  Form of expected instruction(s): vst1.64 {d0}, [r0]
- void vst1_s64 (int64_t *, int64x1_t)
  Form of expected instruction(s): vst1.64 {d0}, [r0]

- void vst1_f32 (float32_t *, float32x2_t)
  Form of expected instruction(s): `vst1.32 {d0}, [r0]`
- void vst1_p16 (poly16_t *, poly16x4_t)
  Form of expected instruction(s): `vst1.16 {d0}, [r0]`
- void vst1_p8 (poly8_t *, poly8x8_t)
  Form of expected instruction(s): `vst1.8 {d0}, [r0]`
- void vst1q_u32 (uint32_t *, uint32x4_t)
  Form of expected instruction(s): `vst1.32 {d0, d1}, [r0]`
- void vst1q_u16 (uint16_t *, uint16x8_t)
  Form of expected instruction(s): `vst1.16 {d0, d1}, [r0]`
- void vst1q_u8 (uint8_t *, uint8x16_t)
  Form of expected instruction(s): `vst1.8 {d0, d1}, [r0]`
- void vst1q_s32 (int32_t *, int32x4_t)
  Form of expected instruction(s): `vst1.32 {d0, d1}, [r0]`
- void vst1q_s16 (int16_t *, int16x8_t)
  Form of expected instruction(s): `vst1.16 {d0, d1}, [r0]`
- void vst1q_s8 (int8_t *, int8x16_t)
  Form of expected instruction(s): `vst1.8 {d0, d1}, [r0]`
- void vst1q_u64 (uint64_t *, uint64x2_t)
  Form of expected instruction(s): `vst1.64 {d0, d1}, [r0]`
- void vst1q_s64 (int64_t *, int64x2_t)
  Form of expected instruction(s): `vst1.64 {d0, d1}, [r0]`
- void vst1q_f32 (float32_t *, float32x4_t)
  Form of expected instruction(s): `vst1.32 {d0, d1}, [r0]`
- void vst1q_p16 (poly16_t *, poly16x8_t)
  Form of expected instruction(s): `vst1.16 {d0, d1}, [r0]`
- void vst1q_p8 (poly8_t *, poly8x16_t)
  Form of expected instruction(s): `vst1.8 {d0, d1}, [r0]`
- void vst1_lane_u32 (uint32_t *, uint32x2_t, const int)
  Form of expected instruction(s): `vst1.32 {d0[0]}, [r0]`
- void vst1_lane_u16 (uint16_t *, uint16x4_t, const int)
  Form of expected instruction(s): `vst1.16 {d0[0]}, [r0]`
- void vst1_lane_u8 (uint8_t *, uint8x8_t, const int)
  Form of expected instruction(s): `vst1.8 {d0[0]}, [r0]`
- void vst1_lane_s32 (int32_t *, int32x2_t, const int)
  Form of expected instruction(s): `vst1.32 {d0[0]}, [r0]`
- void vst1_lane_s16 (int16_t *, int16x4_t, const int)
  Form of expected instruction(s): `vst1.16 {d0[0]}, [r0]`
- void vst1_lane_s8 (int8_t *, int8x8_t, const int)
  Form of expected instruction(s): `vst1.8 {d0[0]}, [r0]`
- void vst1_lane_f32 (float32_t *, float32x2_t, const int)
  Form of expected instruction(s): `vst1.32 {d0[0]}, [r0]`

Chapter 5: Extensions to the C Language Family   413

- void vst1_lane_p16 (poly16_t *, poly16x4_t, const int)
  Form of expected instruction(s): `vst1.16 {d0[0]}, [r0]`
- void vst1_lane_p8 (poly8_t *, poly8x8_t, const int)
  Form of expected instruction(s): `vst1.8 {d0[0]}, [r0]`
- void vst1_lane_s64 (int64_t *, int64x1_t, const int)
  Form of expected instruction(s): `vst1.64 {d0}, [r0]`
- void vst1_lane_u64 (uint64_t *, uint64x1_t, const int)
  Form of expected instruction(s): `vst1.64 {d0}, [r0]`
- void vst1q_lane_u32 (uint32_t *, uint32x4_t, const int)
  Form of expected instruction(s): `vst1.32 {d0[0]}, [r0]`
- void vst1q_lane_u16 (uint16_t *, uint16x8_t, const int)
  Form of expected instruction(s): `vst1.16 {d0[0]}, [r0]`
- void vst1q_lane_u8 (uint8_t *, uint8x16_t, const int)
  Form of expected instruction(s): `vst1.8 {d0[0]}, [r0]`
- void vst1q_lane_s32 (int32_t *, int32x4_t, const int)
  Form of expected instruction(s): `vst1.32 {d0[0]}, [r0]`
- void vst1q_lane_s16 (int16_t *, int16x8_t, const int)
  Form of expected instruction(s): `vst1.16 {d0[0]}, [r0]`
- void vst1q_lane_s8 (int8_t *, int8x16_t, const int)
  Form of expected instruction(s): `vst1.8 {d0[0]}, [r0]`
- void vst1q_lane_f32 (float32_t *, float32x4_t, const int)
  Form of expected instruction(s): `vst1.32 {d0[0]}, [r0]`
- void vst1q_lane_p16 (poly16_t *, poly16x8_t, const int)
  Form of expected instruction(s): `vst1.16 {d0[0]}, [r0]`
- void vst1q_lane_p8 (poly8_t *, poly8x16_t, const int)
  Form of expected instruction(s): `vst1.8 {d0[0]}, [r0]`
- void vst1q_lane_s64 (int64_t *, int64x2_t, const int)
  Form of expected instruction(s): `vst1.64 {d0}, [r0]`
- void vst1q_lane_u64 (uint64_t *, uint64x2_t, const int)
  Form of expected instruction(s): `vst1.64 {d0}, [r0]`

5.50.3.70 Element/structure loads, VLD2 variants

- uint32x2x2_t vld2_u32 (const uint32_t *)
  Form of expected instruction(s): `vld2.32 {d0, d1}, [r0]`
- uint16x4x2_t vld2_u16 (const uint16_t *)
  Form of expected instruction(s): `vld2.16 {d0, d1}, [r0]`
- uint8x8x2_t vld2_u8 (const uint8_t *)
  Form of expected instruction(s): `vld2.8 {d0, d1}, [r0]`
- int32x2x2_t vld2_s32 (const int32_t *)
  Form of expected instruction(s): `vld2.32 {d0, d1}, [r0]`
- int16x4x2_t vld2_s16 (const int16_t *)
  Form of expected instruction(s): `vld2.16 {d0, d1}, [r0]`

- int8x8x2_t vld2_s8 (const int8_t *)
  Form of expected instruction(s): `vld2.8 {d0, d1}, [r0]`
- float32x2x2_t vld2_f32 (const float32_t *)
  Form of expected instruction(s): `vld2.32 {d0, d1}, [r0]`
- poly16x4x2_t vld2_p16 (const poly16_t *)
  Form of expected instruction(s): `vld2.16 {d0, d1}, [r0]`
- poly8x8x2_t vld2_p8 (const poly8_t *)
  Form of expected instruction(s): `vld2.8 {d0, d1}, [r0]`
- uint64x1x2_t vld2_u64 (const uint64_t *)
  Form of expected instruction(s): `vld1.64 {d0, d1}, [r0]`
- int64x1x2_t vld2_s64 (const int64_t *)
  Form of expected instruction(s): `vld1.64 {d0, d1}, [r0]`
- uint32x4x2_t vld2q_u32 (const uint32_t *)
  Form of expected instruction(s): `vld2.32 {d0, d1}, [r0]`
- uint16x8x2_t vld2q_u16 (const uint16_t *)
  Form of expected instruction(s): `vld2.16 {d0, d1}, [r0]`
- uint8x16x2_t vld2q_u8 (const uint8_t *)
  Form of expected instruction(s): `vld2.8 {d0, d1}, [r0]`
- int32x4x2_t vld2q_s32 (const int32_t *)
  Form of expected instruction(s): `vld2.32 {d0, d1}, [r0]`
- int16x8x2_t vld2q_s16 (const int16_t *)
  Form of expected instruction(s): `vld2.16 {d0, d1}, [r0]`
- int8x16x2_t vld2q_s8 (const int8_t *)
  Form of expected instruction(s): `vld2.8 {d0, d1}, [r0]`
- float32x4x2_t vld2q_f32 (const float32_t *)
  Form of expected instruction(s): `vld2.32 {d0, d1}, [r0]`
- poly16x8x2_t vld2q_p16 (const poly16_t *)
  Form of expected instruction(s): `vld2.16 {d0, d1}, [r0]`
- poly8x16x2_t vld2q_p8 (const poly8_t *)
  Form of expected instruction(s): `vld2.8 {d0, d1}, [r0]`
- uint32x2x2_t vld2_lane_u32 (const uint32_t *, uint32x2x2_t, const int)
  Form of expected instruction(s): `vld2.32 {d0[0], d1[0]}, [r0]`
- uint16x4x2_t vld2_lane_u16 (const uint16_t *, uint16x4x2_t, const int)
  Form of expected instruction(s): `vld2.16 {d0[0], d1[0]}, [r0]`
- uint8x8x2_t vld2_lane_u8 (const uint8_t *, uint8x8x2_t, const int)
  Form of expected instruction(s): `vld2.8 {d0[0], d1[0]}, [r0]`
- int32x2x2_t vld2_lane_s32 (const int32_t *, int32x2x2_t, const int)
  Form of expected instruction(s): `vld2.32 {d0[0], d1[0]}, [r0]`
- int16x4x2_t vld2_lane_s16 (const int16_t *, int16x4x2_t, const int)
  Form of expected instruction(s): `vld2.16 {d0[0], d1[0]}, [r0]`
- int8x8x2_t vld2_lane_s8 (const int8_t *, int8x8x2_t, const int)
  Form of expected instruction(s): `vld2.8 {d0[0], d1[0]}, [r0]`

Chapter 5: Extensions to the C Language Family 415

- float32x2x2_t vld2_lane_f32 (const float32_t *, float32x2x2_t, const int)
  Form of expected instruction(s): `vld2.32 {d0[0], d1[0]}, [r0]`
- poly16x4x2_t vld2_lane_p16 (const poly16_t *, poly16x4x2_t, const int)
  Form of expected instruction(s): `vld2.16 {d0[0], d1[0]}, [r0]`
- poly8x8x2_t vld2_lane_p8 (const poly8_t *, poly8x8x2_t, const int)
  Form of expected instruction(s): `vld2.8 {d0[0], d1[0]}, [r0]`
- int32x4x2_t vld2q_lane_s32 (const int32_t *, int32x4x2_t, const int)
  Form of expected instruction(s): `vld2.32 {d0[0], d1[0]}, [r0]`
- int16x8x2_t vld2q_lane_s16 (const int16_t *, int16x8x2_t, const int)
  Form of expected instruction(s): `vld2.16 {d0[0], d1[0]}, [r0]`
- uint32x4x2_t vld2q_lane_u32 (const uint32_t *, uint32x4x2_t, const int)
  Form of expected instruction(s): `vld2.32 {d0[0], d1[0]}, [r0]`
- uint16x8x2_t vld2q_lane_u16 (const uint16_t *, uint16x8x2_t, const int)
  Form of expected instruction(s): `vld2.16 {d0[0], d1[0]}, [r0]`
- float32x4x2_t vld2q_lane_f32 (const float32_t *, float32x4x2_t, const int)
  Form of expected instruction(s): `vld2.32 {d0[0], d1[0]}, [r0]`
- poly16x8x2_t vld2q_lane_p16 (const poly16_t *, poly16x8x2_t, const int)
  Form of expected instruction(s): `vld2.16 {d0[0], d1[0]}, [r0]`
- uint32x2x2_t vld2_dup_u32 (const uint32_t *)
  Form of expected instruction(s): `vld2.32 {d0[], d1[]}, [r0]`
- uint16x4x2_t vld2_dup_u16 (const uint16_t *)
  Form of expected instruction(s): `vld2.16 {d0[], d1[]}, [r0]`
- uint8x8x2_t vld2_dup_u8 (const uint8_t *)
  Form of expected instruction(s): `vld2.8 {d0[], d1[]}, [r0]`
- int32x2x2_t vld2_dup_s32 (const int32_t *)
  Form of expected instruction(s): `vld2.32 {d0[], d1[]}, [r0]`
- int16x4x2_t vld2_dup_s16 (const int16_t *)
  Form of expected instruction(s): `vld2.16 {d0[], d1[]}, [r0]`
- int8x8x2_t vld2_dup_s8 (const int8_t *)
  Form of expected instruction(s): `vld2.8 {d0[], d1[]}, [r0]`
- float32x2x2_t vld2_dup_f32 (const float32_t *)
  Form of expected instruction(s): `vld2.32 {d0[], d1[]}, [r0]`
- poly16x4x2_t vld2_dup_p16 (const poly16_t *)
  Form of expected instruction(s): `vld2.16 {d0[], d1[]}, [r0]`
- poly8x8x2_t vld2_dup_p8 (const poly8_t *)
  Form of expected instruction(s): `vld2.8 {d0[], d1[]}, [r0]`
- uint64x1x2_t vld2_dup_u64 (const uint64_t *)
  Form of expected instruction(s): `vld1.64 {d0, d1}, [r0]`
- int64x1x2_t vld2_dup_s64 (const int64_t *)
  Form of expected instruction(s): `vld1.64 {d0, d1}, [r0]`

5.50.3.71 Element/structure stores, VST2 variants

- void vst2_u32 (uint32_t *, uint32x2x2_t)
  Form of expected instruction(s): `vst2.32 {d0, d1}, [r0]`
- void vst2_u16 (uint16_t *, uint16x4x2_t)
  Form of expected instruction(s): `vst2.16 {d0, d1}, [r0]`
- void vst2_u8 (uint8_t *, uint8x8x2_t)
  Form of expected instruction(s): `vst2.8 {d0, d1}, [r0]`
- void vst2_s32 (int32_t *, int32x2x2_t)
  Form of expected instruction(s): `vst2.32 {d0, d1}, [r0]`
- void vst2_s16 (int16_t *, int16x4x2_t)
  Form of expected instruction(s): `vst2.16 {d0, d1}, [r0]`
- void vst2_s8 (int8_t *, int8x8x2_t)
  Form of expected instruction(s): `vst2.8 {d0, d1}, [r0]`
- void vst2_f32 (float32_t *, float32x2x2_t)
  Form of expected instruction(s): `vst2.32 {d0, d1}, [r0]`
- void vst2_p16 (poly16_t *, poly16x4x2_t)
  Form of expected instruction(s): `vst2.16 {d0, d1}, [r0]`
- void vst2_p8 (poly8_t *, poly8x8x2_t)
  Form of expected instruction(s): `vst2.8 {d0, d1}, [r0]`
- void vst2_u64 (uint64_t *, uint64x1x2_t)
  Form of expected instruction(s): `vst1.64 {d0, d1}, [r0]`
- void vst2_s64 (int64_t *, int64x1x2_t)
  Form of expected instruction(s): `vst1.64 {d0, d1}, [r0]`
- void vst2q_u32 (uint32_t *, uint32x4x2_t)
  Form of expected instruction(s): `vst2.32 {d0, d1}, [r0]`
- void vst2q_u16 (uint16_t *, uint16x8x2_t)
  Form of expected instruction(s): `vst2.16 {d0, d1}, [r0]`
- void vst2q_u8 (uint8_t *, uint8x16x2_t)
  Form of expected instruction(s): `vst2.8 {d0, d1}, [r0]`
- void vst2q_s32 (int32_t *, int32x4x2_t)
  Form of expected instruction(s): `vst2.32 {d0, d1}, [r0]`
- void vst2q_s16 (int16_t *, int16x8x2_t)
  Form of expected instruction(s): `vst2.16 {d0, d1}, [r0]`
- void vst2q_s8 (int8_t *, int8x16x2_t)
  Form of expected instruction(s): `vst2.8 {d0, d1}, [r0]`
- void vst2q_f32 (float32_t *, float32x4x2_t)
  Form of expected instruction(s): `vst2.32 {d0, d1}, [r0]`
- void vst2q_p16 (poly16_t *, poly16x8x2_t)
  Form of expected instruction(s): `vst2.16 {d0, d1}, [r0]`
- void vst2q_p8 (poly8_t *, poly8x16x2_t)
  Form of expected instruction(s): `vst2.8 {d0, d1}, [r0]`
- void vst2_lane_u32 (uint32_t *, uint32x2x2_t, const int)
  Form of expected instruction(s): `vst2.32 {d0[0], d1[0]}, [r0]`

Chapter 5: Extensions to the C Language Family   417

- void vst2_lane_u16 (uint16_t *, uint16x4x2_t, const int)
  Form of expected instruction(s): `vst2.16 {d0[0], d1[0]}, [r0]`
- void vst2_lane_u8 (uint8_t *, uint8x8x2_t, const int)
  Form of expected instruction(s): `vst2.8 {d0[0], d1[0]}, [r0]`
- void vst2_lane_s32 (int32_t *, int32x2x2_t, const int)
  Form of expected instruction(s): `vst2.32 {d0[0], d1[0]}, [r0]`
- void vst2_lane_s16 (int16_t *, int16x4x2_t, const int)
  Form of expected instruction(s): `vst2.16 {d0[0], d1[0]}, [r0]`
- void vst2_lane_s8 (int8_t *, int8x8x2_t, const int)
  Form of expected instruction(s): `vst2.8 {d0[0], d1[0]}, [r0]`
- void vst2_lane_f32 (float32_t *, float32x2x2_t, const int)
  Form of expected instruction(s): `vst2.32 {d0[0], d1[0]}, [r0]`
- void vst2_lane_p16 (poly16_t *, poly16x4x2_t, const int)
  Form of expected instruction(s): `vst2.16 {d0[0], d1[0]}, [r0]`
- void vst2_lane_p8 (poly8_t *, poly8x8x2_t, const int)
  Form of expected instruction(s): `vst2.8 {d0[0], d1[0]}, [r0]`
- void vst2q_lane_s32 (int32_t *, int32x4x2_t, const int)
  Form of expected instruction(s): `vst2.32 {d0[0], d1[0]}, [r0]`
- void vst2q_lane_s16 (int16_t *, int16x8x2_t, const int)
  Form of expected instruction(s): `vst2.16 {d0[0], d1[0]}, [r0]`
- void vst2q_lane_u32 (uint32_t *, uint32x4x2_t, const int)
  Form of expected instruction(s): `vst2.32 {d0[0], d1[0]}, [r0]`
- void vst2q_lane_u16 (uint16_t *, uint16x8x2_t, const int)
  Form of expected instruction(s): `vst2.16 {d0[0], d1[0]}, [r0]`
- void vst2q_lane_f32 (float32_t *, float32x4x2_t, const int)
  Form of expected instruction(s): `vst2.32 {d0[0], d1[0]}, [r0]`
- void vst2q_lane_p16 (poly16_t *, poly16x8x2_t, const int)
  Form of expected instruction(s): `vst2.16 {d0[0], d1[0]}, [r0]`

5.50.3.72 Element/structure loads, VLD3 variants

- uint32x2x3_t vld3_u32 (const uint32_t *)
  Form of expected instruction(s): `vld3.32 {d0, d1, d2}, [r0]`
- uint16x4x3_t vld3_u16 (const uint16_t *)
  Form of expected instruction(s): `vld3.16 {d0, d1, d2}, [r0]`
- uint8x8x3_t vld3_u8 (const uint8_t *)
  Form of expected instruction(s): `vld3.8 {d0, d1, d2}, [r0]`
- int32x2x3_t vld3_s32 (const int32_t *)
  Form of expected instruction(s): `vld3.32 {d0, d1, d2}, [r0]`
- int16x4x3_t vld3_s16 (const int16_t *)
  Form of expected instruction(s): `vld3.16 {d0, d1, d2}, [r0]`
- int8x8x3_t vld3_s8 (const int8_t *)
  Form of expected instruction(s): `vld3.8 {d0, d1, d2}, [r0]`

- float32x2x3_t vld3_f32 (const float32_t *)
  Form of expected instruction(s): `vld3.32 {d0, d1, d2}, [r0]`
- poly16x4x3_t vld3_p16 (const poly16_t *)
  Form of expected instruction(s): `vld3.16 {d0, d1, d2}, [r0]`
- poly8x8x3_t vld3_p8 (const poly8_t *)
  Form of expected instruction(s): `vld3.8 {d0, d1, d2}, [r0]`
- uint64x1x3_t vld3_u64 (const uint64_t *)
  Form of expected instruction(s): `vld1.64 {d0, d1, d2}, [r0]`
- int64x1x3_t vld3_s64 (const int64_t *)
  Form of expected instruction(s): `vld1.64 {d0, d1, d2}, [r0]`
- uint32x4x3_t vld3q_u32 (const uint32_t *)
  Form of expected instruction(s): `vld3.32 {d0, d1, d2}, [r0]`
- uint16x8x3_t vld3q_u16 (const uint16_t *)
  Form of expected instruction(s): `vld3.16 {d0, d1, d2}, [r0]`
- uint8x16x3_t vld3q_u8 (const uint8_t *)
  Form of expected instruction(s): `vld3.8 {d0, d1, d2}, [r0]`
- int32x4x3_t vld3q_s32 (const int32_t *)
  Form of expected instruction(s): `vld3.32 {d0, d1, d2}, [r0]`
- int16x8x3_t vld3q_s16 (const int16_t *)
  Form of expected instruction(s): `vld3.16 {d0, d1, d2}, [r0]`
- int8x16x3_t vld3q_s8 (const int8_t *)
  Form of expected instruction(s): `vld3.8 {d0, d1, d2}, [r0]`
- float32x4x3_t vld3q_f32 (const float32_t *)
  Form of expected instruction(s): `vld3.32 {d0, d1, d2}, [r0]`
- poly16x8x3_t vld3q_p16 (const poly16_t *)
  Form of expected instruction(s): `vld3.16 {d0, d1, d2}, [r0]`
- poly8x16x3_t vld3q_p8 (const poly8_t *)
  Form of expected instruction(s): `vld3.8 {d0, d1, d2}, [r0]`
- uint32x2x3_t vld3_lane_u32 (const uint32_t *, uint32x2x3_t, const int)
  Form of expected instruction(s): `vld3.32 {d0[0], d1[0], d2[0]}, [r0]`
- uint16x4x3_t vld3_lane_u16 (const uint16_t *, uint16x4x3_t, const int)
  Form of expected instruction(s): `vld3.16 {d0[0], d1[0], d2[0]}, [r0]`
- uint8x8x3_t vld3_lane_u8 (const uint8_t *, uint8x8x3_t, const int)
  Form of expected instruction(s): `vld3.8 {d0[0], d1[0], d2[0]}, [r0]`
- int32x2x3_t vld3_lane_s32 (const int32_t *, int32x2x3_t, const int)
  Form of expected instruction(s): `vld3.32 {d0[0], d1[0], d2[0]}, [r0]`
- int16x4x3_t vld3_lane_s16 (const int16_t *, int16x4x3_t, const int)
  Form of expected instruction(s): `vld3.16 {d0[0], d1[0], d2[0]}, [r0]`
- int8x8x3_t vld3_lane_s8 (const int8_t *, int8x8x3_t, const int)
  Form of expected instruction(s): `vld3.8 {d0[0], d1[0], d2[0]}, [r0]`
- float32x2x3_t vld3_lane_f32 (const float32_t *, float32x2x3_t, const int)
  Form of expected instruction(s): `vld3.32 {d0[0], d1[0], d2[0]}, [r0]`

Chapter 5: Extensions to the C Language Family   419

- poly16x4x3_t vld3_lane_p16 (const poly16_t *, poly16x4x3_t, const int)
  Form of expected instruction(s): vld3.16 {d0[0], d1[0], d2[0]}, [r0]
- poly8x8x3_t vld3_lane_p8 (const poly8_t *, poly8x8x3_t, const int)
  Form of expected instruction(s): vld3.8 {d0[0], d1[0], d2[0]}, [r0]
- int32x4x3_t vld3q_lane_s32 (const int32_t *, int32x4x3_t, const int)
  Form of expected instruction(s): vld3.32 {d0[0], d1[0], d2[0]}, [r0]
- int16x8x3_t vld3q_lane_s16 (const int16_t *, int16x8x3_t, const int)
  Form of expected instruction(s): vld3.16 {d0[0], d1[0], d2[0]}, [r0]
- uint32x4x3_t vld3q_lane_u32 (const uint32_t *, uint32x4x3_t, const int)
  Form of expected instruction(s): vld3.32 {d0[0], d1[0], d2[0]}, [r0]
- uint16x8x3_t vld3q_lane_u16 (const uint16_t *, uint16x8x3_t, const int)
  Form of expected instruction(s): vld3.16 {d0[0], d1[0], d2[0]}, [r0]
- float32x4x3_t vld3q_lane_f32 (const float32_t *, float32x4x3_t, const int)
  Form of expected instruction(s): vld3.32 {d0[0], d1[0], d2[0]}, [r0]
- poly16x8x3_t vld3q_lane_p16 (const poly16_t *, poly16x8x3_t, const int)
  Form of expected instruction(s): vld3.16 {d0[0], d1[0], d2[0]}, [r0]
- uint32x2x3_t vld3_dup_u32 (const uint32_t *)
  Form of expected instruction(s): vld3.32 {d0[], d1[], d2[]}, [r0]
- uint16x4x3_t vld3_dup_u16 (const uint16_t *)
  Form of expected instruction(s): vld3.16 {d0[], d1[], d2[]}, [r0]
- uint8x8x3_t vld3_dup_u8 (const uint8_t *)
  Form of expected instruction(s): vld3.8 {d0[], d1[], d2[]}, [r0]
- int32x2x3_t vld3_dup_s32 (const int32_t *)
  Form of expected instruction(s): vld3.32 {d0[], d1[], d2[]}, [r0]
- int16x4x3_t vld3_dup_s16 (const int16_t *)
  Form of expected instruction(s): vld3.16 {d0[], d1[], d2[]}, [r0]
- int8x8x3_t vld3_dup_s8 (const int8_t *)
  Form of expected instruction(s): vld3.8 {d0[], d1[], d2[]}, [r0]
- float32x2x3_t vld3_dup_f32 (const float32_t *)
  Form of expected instruction(s): vld3.32 {d0[], d1[], d2[]}, [r0]
- poly16x4x3_t vld3_dup_p16 (const poly16_t *)
  Form of expected instruction(s): vld3.16 {d0[], d1[], d2[]}, [r0]
- poly8x8x3_t vld3_dup_p8 (const poly8_t *)
  Form of expected instruction(s): vld3.8 {d0[], d1[], d2[]}, [r0]
- uint64x1x3_t vld3_dup_u64 (const uint64_t *)
  Form of expected instruction(s): vld1.64 {d0, d1, d2}, [r0]
- int64x1x3_t vld3_dup_s64 (const int64_t *)
  Form of expected instruction(s): vld1.64 {d0, d1, d2}, [r0]

5.50.3.73 Element/structure stores, VST3 variants

- void vst3_u32 (uint32_t *, uint32x2x3_t)
  Form of expected instruction(s): vst3.32 {d0, d1, d2, d3}, [r0]

- void vst3_u16 (uint16_t *, uint16x4x3_t)
  Form of expected instruction(s): **vst3.16** {*d0, d1, d2, d3*}, [*r0*]
- void vst3_u8 (uint8_t *, uint8x8x3_t)
  Form of expected instruction(s): **vst3.8** {*d0, d1, d2, d3*}, [*r0*]
- void vst3_s32 (int32_t *, int32x2x3_t)
  Form of expected instruction(s): **vst3.32** {*d0, d1, d2, d3*}, [*r0*]
- void vst3_s16 (int16_t *, int16x4x3_t)
  Form of expected instruction(s): **vst3.16** {*d0, d1, d2, d3*}, [*r0*]
- void vst3_s8 (int8_t *, int8x8x3_t)
  Form of expected instruction(s): **vst3.8** {*d0, d1, d2, d3*}, [*r0*]
- void vst3_f32 (float32_t *, float32x2x3_t)
  Form of expected instruction(s): **vst3.32** {*d0, d1, d2, d3*}, [*r0*]
- void vst3_p16 (poly16_t *, poly16x4x3_t)
  Form of expected instruction(s): **vst3.16** {*d0, d1, d2, d3*}, [*r0*]
- void vst3_p8 (poly8_t *, poly8x8x3_t)
  Form of expected instruction(s): **vst3.8** {*d0, d1, d2, d3*}, [*r0*]
- void vst3_u64 (uint64_t *, uint64x1x3_t)
  Form of expected instruction(s): **vst1.64** {*d0, d1, d2, d3*}, [*r0*]
- void vst3_s64 (int64_t *, int64x1x3_t)
  Form of expected instruction(s): **vst1.64** {*d0, d1, d2, d3*}, [*r0*]
- void vst3q_u32 (uint32_t *, uint32x4x3_t)
  Form of expected instruction(s): **vst3.32** {*d0, d1, d2*}, [*r0*]
- void vst3q_u16 (uint16_t *, uint16x8x3_t)
  Form of expected instruction(s): **vst3.16** {*d0, d1, d2*}, [*r0*]
- void vst3q_u8 (uint8_t *, uint8x16x3_t)
  Form of expected instruction(s): **vst3.8** {*d0, d1, d2*}, [*r0*]
- void vst3q_s32 (int32_t *, int32x4x3_t)
  Form of expected instruction(s): **vst3.32** {*d0, d1, d2*}, [*r0*]
- void vst3q_s16 (int16_t *, int16x8x3_t)
  Form of expected instruction(s): **vst3.16** {*d0, d1, d2*}, [*r0*]
- void vst3q_s8 (int8_t *, int8x16x3_t)
  Form of expected instruction(s): **vst3.8** {*d0, d1, d2*}, [*r0*]
- void vst3q_f32 (float32_t *, float32x4x3_t)
  Form of expected instruction(s): **vst3.32** {*d0, d1, d2*}, [*r0*]
- void vst3q_p16 (poly16_t *, poly16x8x3_t)
  Form of expected instruction(s): **vst3.16** {*d0, d1, d2*}, [*r0*]
- void vst3q_p8 (poly8_t *, poly8x16x3_t)
  Form of expected instruction(s): **vst3.8** {*d0, d1, d2*}, [*r0*]
- void vst3_lane_u32 (uint32_t *, uint32x2x3_t, const int)
  Form of expected instruction(s): **vst3.32** {*d0[0], d1[0], d2[0]*}, [*r0*]
- void vst3_lane_u16 (uint16_t *, uint16x4x3_t, const int)
  Form of expected instruction(s): **vst3.16** {*d0[0], d1[0], d2[0]*}, [*r0*]

- void vst3_lane_u8 (uint8_t *, uint8x8x3_t, const int)
  Form of expected instruction(s): vst3.8 {d0[0], d1[0], d2[0]}, [r0]
- void vst3_lane_s32 (int32_t *, int32x2x3_t, const int)
  Form of expected instruction(s): vst3.32 {d0[0], d1[0], d2[0]}, [r0]
- void vst3_lane_s16 (int16_t *, int16x4x3_t, const int)
  Form of expected instruction(s): vst3.16 {d0[0], d1[0], d2[0]}, [r0]
- void vst3_lane_s8 (int8_t *, int8x8x3_t, const int)
  Form of expected instruction(s): vst3.8 {d0[0], d1[0], d2[0]}, [r0]
- void vst3_lane_f32 (float32_t *, float32x2x3_t, const int)
  Form of expected instruction(s): vst3.32 {d0[0], d1[0], d2[0]}, [r0]
- void vst3_lane_p16 (poly16_t *, poly16x4x3_t, const int)
  Form of expected instruction(s): vst3.16 {d0[0], d1[0], d2[0]}, [r0]
- void vst3_lane_p8 (poly8_t *, poly8x8x3_t, const int)
  Form of expected instruction(s): vst3.8 {d0[0], d1[0], d2[0]}, [r0]
- void vst3q_lane_s32 (int32_t *, int32x4x3_t, const int)
  Form of expected instruction(s): vst3.32 {d0[0], d1[0], d2[0]}, [r0]
- void vst3q_lane_s16 (int16_t *, int16x8x3_t, const int)
  Form of expected instruction(s): vst3.16 {d0[0], d1[0], d2[0]}, [r0]
- void vst3q_lane_u32 (uint32_t *, uint32x4x3_t, const int)
  Form of expected instruction(s): vst3.32 {d0[0], d1[0], d2[0]}, [r0]
- void vst3q_lane_u16 (uint16_t *, uint16x8x3_t, const int)
  Form of expected instruction(s): vst3.16 {d0[0], d1[0], d2[0]}, [r0]
- void vst3q_lane_f32 (float32_t *, float32x4x3_t, const int)
  Form of expected instruction(s): vst3.32 {d0[0], d1[0], d2[0]}, [r0]
- void vst3q_lane_p16 (poly16_t *, poly16x8x3_t, const int)
  Form of expected instruction(s): vst3.16 {d0[0], d1[0], d2[0]}, [r0]

5.50.3.74 Element/structure loads, VLD4 variants

- uint32x2x4_t vld4_u32 (const uint32_t *)
  Form of expected instruction(s): vld4.32 {d0, d1, d2, d3}, [r0]
- uint16x4x4_t vld4_u16 (const uint16_t *)
  Form of expected instruction(s): vld4.16 {d0, d1, d2, d3}, [r0]
- uint8x8x4_t vld4_u8 (const uint8_t *)
  Form of expected instruction(s): vld4.8 {d0, d1, d2, d3}, [r0]
- int32x2x4_t vld4_s32 (const int32_t *)
  Form of expected instruction(s): vld4.32 {d0, d1, d2, d3}, [r0]
- int16x4x4_t vld4_s16 (const int16_t *)
  Form of expected instruction(s): vld4.16 {d0, d1, d2, d3}, [r0]
- int8x8x4_t vld4_s8 (const int8_t *)
  Form of expected instruction(s): vld4.8 {d0, d1, d2, d3}, [r0]
- float32x2x4_t vld4_f32 (const float32_t *)
  Form of expected instruction(s): vld4.32 {d0, d1, d2, d3}, [r0]

- poly16x4x4_t vld4_p16 (const poly16_t *)
  Form of expected instruction(s): vld4.16 {d0, d1, d2, d3}, [r0]
- poly8x8x4_t vld4_p8 (const poly8_t *)
  Form of expected instruction(s): vld4.8 {d0, d1, d2, d3}, [r0]
- uint64x1x4_t vld4_u64 (const uint64_t *)
  Form of expected instruction(s): vld1.64 {d0, d1, d2, d3}, [r0]
- int64x1x4_t vld4_s64 (const int64_t *)
  Form of expected instruction(s): vld1.64 {d0, d1, d2, d3}, [r0]
- uint32x4x4_t vld4q_u32 (const uint32_t *)
  Form of expected instruction(s): vld4.32 {d0, d1, d2, d3}, [r0]
- uint16x8x4_t vld4q_u16 (const uint16_t *)
  Form of expected instruction(s): vld4.16 {d0, d1, d2, d3}, [r0]
- uint8x16x4_t vld4q_u8 (const uint8_t *)
  Form of expected instruction(s): vld4.8 {d0, d1, d2, d3}, [r0]
- int32x4x4_t vld4q_s32 (const int32_t *)
  Form of expected instruction(s): vld4.32 {d0, d1, d2, d3}, [r0]
- int16x8x4_t vld4q_s16 (const int16_t *)
  Form of expected instruction(s): vld4.16 {d0, d1, d2, d3}, [r0]
- int8x16x4_t vld4q_s8 (const int8_t *)
  Form of expected instruction(s): vld4.8 {d0, d1, d2, d3}, [r0]
- float32x4x4_t vld4q_f32 (const float32_t *)
  Form of expected instruction(s): vld4.32 {d0, d1, d2, d3}, [r0]
- poly16x8x4_t vld4q_p16 (const poly16_t *)
  Form of expected instruction(s): vld4.16 {d0, d1, d2, d3}, [r0]
- poly8x16x4_t vld4q_p8 (const poly8_t *)
  Form of expected instruction(s): vld4.8 {d0, d1, d2, d3}, [r0]
- uint32x2x4_t vld4_lane_u32 (const uint32_t *, uint32x2x4_t, const int)
  Form of expected instruction(s): vld4.32 {d0[0], d1[0], d2[0], d3[0]}, [r0]
- uint16x4x4_t vld4_lane_u16 (const uint16_t *, uint16x4x4_t, const int)
  Form of expected instruction(s): vld4.16 {d0[0], d1[0], d2[0], d3[0]}, [r0]
- uint8x8x4_t vld4_lane_u8 (const uint8_t *, uint8x8x4_t, const int)
  Form of expected instruction(s): vld4.8 {d0[0], d1[0], d2[0], d3[0]}, [r0]
- int32x2x4_t vld4_lane_s32 (const int32_t *, int32x2x4_t, const int)
  Form of expected instruction(s): vld4.32 {d0[0], d1[0], d2[0], d3[0]}, [r0]
- int16x4x4_t vld4_lane_s16 (const int16_t *, int16x4x4_t, const int)
  Form of expected instruction(s): vld4.16 {d0[0], d1[0], d2[0], d3[0]}, [r0]
- int8x8x4_t vld4_lane_s8 (const int8_t *, int8x8x4_t, const int)
  Form of expected instruction(s): vld4.8 {d0[0], d1[0], d2[0], d3[0]}, [r0]
- float32x2x4_t vld4_lane_f32 (const float32_t *, float32x2x4_t, const int)
  Form of expected instruction(s): vld4.32 {d0[0], d1[0], d2[0], d3[0]}, [r0]
- poly16x4x4_t vld4_lane_p16 (const poly16_t *, poly16x4x4_t, const int)
  Form of expected instruction(s): vld4.16 {d0[0], d1[0], d2[0], d3[0]}, [r0]

Chapter 5: Extensions to the C Language Family   423

- poly8x8x4_t vld4_lane_p8 (const poly8_t *, poly8x8x4_t, const int)
  Form of expected instruction(s): `vld4.8 {d0[0], d1[0], d2[0], d3[0]}, [r0]`
- int32x4x4_t vld4q_lane_s32 (const int32_t *, int32x4x4_t, const int)
  Form of expected instruction(s): `vld4.32 {d0[0], d1[0], d2[0], d3[0]}, [r0]`
- int16x8x4_t vld4q_lane_s16 (const int16_t *, int16x8x4_t, const int)
  Form of expected instruction(s): `vld4.16 {d0[0], d1[0], d2[0], d3[0]}, [r0]`
- uint32x4x4_t vld4q_lane_u32 (const uint32_t *, uint32x4x4_t, const int)
  Form of expected instruction(s): `vld4.32 {d0[0], d1[0], d2[0], d3[0]}, [r0]`
- uint16x8x4_t vld4q_lane_u16 (const uint16_t *, uint16x8x4_t, const int)
  Form of expected instruction(s): `vld4.16 {d0[0], d1[0], d2[0], d3[0]}, [r0]`
- float32x4x4_t vld4q_lane_f32 (const float32_t *, float32x4x4_t, const int)
  Form of expected instruction(s): `vld4.32 {d0[0], d1[0], d2[0], d3[0]}, [r0]`
- poly16x8x4_t vld4q_lane_p16 (const poly16_t *, poly16x8x4_t, const int)
  Form of expected instruction(s): `vld4.16 {d0[0], d1[0], d2[0], d3[0]}, [r0]`
- uint32x2x4_t vld4_dup_u32 (const uint32_t *)
  Form of expected instruction(s): `vld4.32 {d0[], d1[], d2[], d3[]}, [r0]`
- uint16x4x4_t vld4_dup_u16 (const uint16_t *)
  Form of expected instruction(s): `vld4.16 {d0[], d1[], d2[], d3[]}, [r0]`
- uint8x8x4_t vld4_dup_u8 (const uint8_t *)
  Form of expected instruction(s): `vld4.8 {d0[], d1[], d2[], d3[]}, [r0]`
- int32x2x4_t vld4_dup_s32 (const int32_t *)
  Form of expected instruction(s): `vld4.32 {d0[], d1[], d2[], d3[]}, [r0]`
- int16x4x4_t vld4_dup_s16 (const int16_t *)
  Form of expected instruction(s): `vld4.16 {d0[], d1[], d2[], d3[]}, [r0]`
- int8x8x4_t vld4_dup_s8 (const int8_t *)
  Form of expected instruction(s): `vld4.8 {d0[], d1[], d2[], d3[]}, [r0]`
- float32x2x4_t vld4_dup_f32 (const float32_t *)
  Form of expected instruction(s): `vld4.32 {d0[], d1[], d2[], d3[]}, [r0]`
- poly16x4x4_t vld4_dup_p16 (const poly16_t *)
  Form of expected instruction(s): `vld4.16 {d0[], d1[], d2[], d3[]}, [r0]`
- poly8x8x4_t vld4_dup_p8 (const poly8_t *)
  Form of expected instruction(s): `vld4.8 {d0[], d1[], d2[], d3[]}, [r0]`
- uint64x1x4_t vld4_dup_u64 (const uint64_t *)
  Form of expected instruction(s): `vld1.64 {d0, d1, d2, d3}, [r0]`
- int64x1x4_t vld4_dup_s64 (const int64_t *)
  Form of expected instruction(s): `vld1.64 {d0, d1, d2, d3}, [r0]`

5.50.3.75 Element/structure stores, VST4 variants

- void vst4_u32 (uint32_t *, uint32x2x4_t)
  Form of expected instruction(s): `vst4.32 {d0, d1, d2, d3}, [r0]`
- void vst4_u16 (uint16_t *, uint16x4x4_t)
  Form of expected instruction(s): `vst4.16 {d0, d1, d2, d3}, [r0]`

- void vst4_u8 (uint8_t *, uint8x8x4_t)
  Form of expected instruction(s): `vst4.8 {d0, d1, d2, d3}, [r0]`
- void vst4_s32 (int32_t *, int32x2x4_t)
  Form of expected instruction(s): `vst4.32 {d0, d1, d2, d3}, [r0]`
- void vst4_s16 (int16_t *, int16x4x4_t)
  Form of expected instruction(s): `vst4.16 {d0, d1, d2, d3}, [r0]`
- void vst4_s8 (int8_t *, int8x8x4_t)
  Form of expected instruction(s): `vst4.8 {d0, d1, d2, d3}, [r0]`
- void vst4_f32 (float32_t *, float32x2x4_t)
  Form of expected instruction(s): `vst4.32 {d0, d1, d2, d3}, [r0]`
- void vst4_p16 (poly16_t *, poly16x4x4_t)
  Form of expected instruction(s): `vst4.16 {d0, d1, d2, d3}, [r0]`
- void vst4_p8 (poly8_t *, poly8x8x4_t)
  Form of expected instruction(s): `vst4.8 {d0, d1, d2, d3}, [r0]`
- void vst4_u64 (uint64_t *, uint64x1x4_t)
  Form of expected instruction(s): `vst1.64 {d0, d1, d2, d3}, [r0]`
- void vst4_s64 (int64_t *, int64x1x4_t)
  Form of expected instruction(s): `vst1.64 {d0, d1, d2, d3}, [r0]`
- void vst4q_u32 (uint32_t *, uint32x4x4_t)
  Form of expected instruction(s): `vst4.32 {d0, d1, d2, d3}, [r0]`
- void vst4q_u16 (uint16_t *, uint16x8x4_t)
  Form of expected instruction(s): `vst4.16 {d0, d1, d2, d3}, [r0]`
- void vst4q_u8 (uint8_t *, uint8x16x4_t)
  Form of expected instruction(s): `vst4.8 {d0, d1, d2, d3}, [r0]`
- void vst4q_s32 (int32_t *, int32x4x4_t)
  Form of expected instruction(s): `vst4.32 {d0, d1, d2, d3}, [r0]`
- void vst4q_s16 (int16_t *, int16x8x4_t)
  Form of expected instruction(s): `vst4.16 {d0, d1, d2, d3}, [r0]`
- void vst4q_s8 (int8_t *, int8x16x4_t)
  Form of expected instruction(s): `vst4.8 {d0, d1, d2, d3}, [r0]`
- void vst4q_f32 (float32_t *, float32x4x4_t)
  Form of expected instruction(s): `vst4.32 {d0, d1, d2, d3}, [r0]`
- void vst4q_p16 (poly16_t *, poly16x8x4_t)
  Form of expected instruction(s): `vst4.16 {d0, d1, d2, d3}, [r0]`
- void vst4q_p8 (poly8_t *, poly8x16x4_t)
  Form of expected instruction(s): `vst4.8 {d0, d1, d2, d3}, [r0]`
- void vst4_lane_u32 (uint32_t *, uint32x2x4_t, const int)
  Form of expected instruction(s): `vst4.32 {d0[0], d1[0], d2[0], d3[0]}, [r0]`
- void vst4_lane_u16 (uint16_t *, uint16x4x4_t, const int)
  Form of expected instruction(s): `vst4.16 {d0[0], d1[0], d2[0], d3[0]}, [r0]`
- void vst4_lane_u8 (uint8_t *, uint8x8x4_t, const int)
  Form of expected instruction(s): `vst4.8 {d0[0], d1[0], d2[0], d3[0]}, [r0]`

Chapter 5: Extensions to the C Language Family   425

- void vst4_lane_s32 (int32_t *, int32x2x4_t, const int)
  Form of expected instruction(s): vst4.32 {d0[0], d1[0], d2[0], d3[0]}, [r0]
- void vst4_lane_s16 (int16_t *, int16x4x4_t, const int)
  Form of expected instruction(s): vst4.16 {d0[0], d1[0], d2[0], d3[0]}, [r0]
- void vst4_lane_s8 (int8_t *, int8x8x4_t, const int)
  Form of expected instruction(s): vst4.8 {d0[0], d1[0], d2[0], d3[0]}, [r0]
- void vst4_lane_f32 (float32_t *, float32x2x4_t, const int)
  Form of expected instruction(s): vst4.32 {d0[0], d1[0], d2[0], d3[0]}, [r0]
- void vst4_lane_p16 (poly16_t *, poly16x4x4_t, const int)
  Form of expected instruction(s): vst4.16 {d0[0], d1[0], d2[0], d3[0]}, [r0]
- void vst4_lane_p8 (poly8_t *, poly8x8x4_t, const int)
  Form of expected instruction(s): vst4.8 {d0[0], d1[0], d2[0], d3[0]}, [r0]
- void vst4q_lane_s32 (int32_t *, int32x4x4_t, const int)
  Form of expected instruction(s): vst4.32 {d0[0], d1[0], d2[0], d3[0]}, [r0]
- void vst4q_lane_s16 (int16_t *, int16x8x4_t, const int)
  Form of expected instruction(s): vst4.16 {d0[0], d1[0], d2[0], d3[0]}, [r0]
- void vst4q_lane_u32 (uint32_t *, uint32x4x4_t, const int)
  Form of expected instruction(s): vst4.32 {d0[0], d1[0], d2[0], d3[0]}, [r0]
- void vst4q_lane_u16 (uint16_t *, uint16x8x4_t, const int)
  Form of expected instruction(s): vst4.16 {d0[0], d1[0], d2[0], d3[0]}, [r0]
- void vst4q_lane_f32 (float32_t *, float32x4x4_t, const int)
  Form of expected instruction(s): vst4.32 {d0[0], d1[0], d2[0], d3[0]}, [r0]
- void vst4q_lane_p16 (poly16_t *, poly16x8x4_t, const int)
  Form of expected instruction(s): vst4.16 {d0[0], d1[0], d2[0], d3[0]}, [r0]

5.50.3.76 Logical operations (AND)

- uint32x2_t vand_u32 (uint32x2_t, uint32x2_t)
  Form of expected instruction(s): vand d0, d0, d0
- uint16x4_t vand_u16 (uint16x4_t, uint16x4_t)
  Form of expected instruction(s): vand d0, d0, d0
- uint8x8_t vand_u8 (uint8x8_t, uint8x8_t)
  Form of expected instruction(s): vand d0, d0, d0
- int32x2_t vand_s32 (int32x2_t, int32x2_t)
  Form of expected instruction(s): vand d0, d0, d0
- int16x4_t vand_s16 (int16x4_t, int16x4_t)
  Form of expected instruction(s): vand d0, d0, d0
- int8x8_t vand_s8 (int8x8_t, int8x8_t)
  Form of expected instruction(s): vand d0, d0, d0
- uint64x1_t vand_u64 (uint64x1_t, uint64x1_t)
  Form of expected instruction(s): vand d0, d0, d0
- int64x1_t vand_s64 (int64x1_t, int64x1_t)
  Form of expected instruction(s): vand d0, d0, d0

- uint32x4_t vandq_u32 (uint32x4_t, uint32x4_t)
  Form of expected instruction(s): **vand** *q0, q0, q0*
- uint16x8_t vandq_u16 (uint16x8_t, uint16x8_t)
  Form of expected instruction(s): **vand** *q0, q0, q0*
- uint8x16_t vandq_u8 (uint8x16_t, uint8x16_t)
  Form of expected instruction(s): **vand** *q0, q0, q0*
- int32x4_t vandq_s32 (int32x4_t, int32x4_t)
  Form of expected instruction(s): **vand** *q0, q0, q0*
- int16x8_t vandq_s16 (int16x8_t, int16x8_t)
  Form of expected instruction(s): **vand** *q0, q0, q0*
- int8x16_t vandq_s8 (int8x16_t, int8x16_t)
  Form of expected instruction(s): **vand** *q0, q0, q0*
- uint64x2_t vandq_u64 (uint64x2_t, uint64x2_t)
  Form of expected instruction(s): **vand** *q0, q0, q0*
- int64x2_t vandq_s64 (int64x2_t, int64x2_t)
  Form of expected instruction(s): **vand** *q0, q0, q0*

5.50.3.77 Logical operations (OR)

- uint32x2_t vorr_u32 (uint32x2_t, uint32x2_t)
  Form of expected instruction(s): **vorr** *d0, d0, d0*
- uint16x4_t vorr_u16 (uint16x4_t, uint16x4_t)
  Form of expected instruction(s): **vorr** *d0, d0, d0*
- uint8x8_t vorr_u8 (uint8x8_t, uint8x8_t)
  Form of expected instruction(s): **vorr** *d0, d0, d0*
- int32x2_t vorr_s32 (int32x2_t, int32x2_t)
  Form of expected instruction(s): **vorr** *d0, d0, d0*
- int16x4_t vorr_s16 (int16x4_t, int16x4_t)
  Form of expected instruction(s): **vorr** *d0, d0, d0*
- int8x8_t vorr_s8 (int8x8_t, int8x8_t)
  Form of expected instruction(s): **vorr** *d0, d0, d0*
- uint64x1_t vorr_u64 (uint64x1_t, uint64x1_t)
  Form of expected instruction(s): **vorr** *d0, d0, d0*
- int64x1_t vorr_s64 (int64x1_t, int64x1_t)
  Form of expected instruction(s): **vorr** *d0, d0, d0*
- uint32x4_t vorrq_u32 (uint32x4_t, uint32x4_t)
  Form of expected instruction(s): **vorr** *q0, q0, q0*
- uint16x8_t vorrq_u16 (uint16x8_t, uint16x8_t)
  Form of expected instruction(s): **vorr** *q0, q0, q0*
- uint8x16_t vorrq_u8 (uint8x16_t, uint8x16_t)
  Form of expected instruction(s): **vorr** *q0, q0, q0*
- int32x4_t vorrq_s32 (int32x4_t, int32x4_t)
  Form of expected instruction(s): **vorr** *q0, q0, q0*

Chapter 5: Extensions to the C Language Family   427

- int16x8_t vorrq_s16 (int16x8_t, int16x8_t)
  Form of expected instruction(s): vorr q0, q0, q0
- int8x16_t vorrq_s8 (int8x16_t, int8x16_t)
  Form of expected instruction(s): vorr q0, q0, q0
- uint64x2_t vorrq_u64 (uint64x2_t, uint64x2_t)
  Form of expected instruction(s): vorr q0, q0, q0
- int64x2_t vorrq_s64 (int64x2_t, int64x2_t)
  Form of expected instruction(s): vorr q0, q0, q0

5.50.3.78 Logical operations (exclusive OR)

- uint32x2_t veor_u32 (uint32x2_t, uint32x2_t)
  Form of expected instruction(s): veor d0, d0, d0
- uint16x4_t veor_u16 (uint16x4_t, uint16x4_t)
  Form of expected instruction(s): veor d0, d0, d0
- uint8x8_t veor_u8 (uint8x8_t, uint8x8_t)
  Form of expected instruction(s): veor d0, d0, d0
- int32x2_t veor_s32 (int32x2_t, int32x2_t)
  Form of expected instruction(s): veor d0, d0, d0
- int16x4_t veor_s16 (int16x4_t, int16x4_t)
  Form of expected instruction(s): veor d0, d0, d0
- int8x8_t veor_s8 (int8x8_t, int8x8_t)
  Form of expected instruction(s): veor d0, d0, d0
- uint64x1_t veor_u64 (uint64x1_t, uint64x1_t)
  Form of expected instruction(s): veor d0, d0, d0
- int64x1_t veor_s64 (int64x1_t, int64x1_t)
  Form of expected instruction(s): veor d0, d0, d0
- uint32x4_t veorq_u32 (uint32x4_t, uint32x4_t)
  Form of expected instruction(s): veor q0, q0, q0
- uint16x8_t veorq_u16 (uint16x8_t, uint16x8_t)
  Form of expected instruction(s): veor q0, q0, q0
- uint8x16_t veorq_u8 (uint8x16_t, uint8x16_t)
  Form of expected instruction(s): veor q0, q0, q0
- int32x4_t veorq_s32 (int32x4_t, int32x4_t)
  Form of expected instruction(s): veor q0, q0, q0
- int16x8_t veorq_s16 (int16x8_t, int16x8_t)
  Form of expected instruction(s): veor q0, q0, q0
- int8x16_t veorq_s8 (int8x16_t, int8x16_t)
  Form of expected instruction(s): veor q0, q0, q0
- uint64x2_t veorq_u64 (uint64x2_t, uint64x2_t)
  Form of expected instruction(s): veor q0, q0, q0
- int64x2_t veorq_s64 (int64x2_t, int64x2_t)
  Form of expected instruction(s): veor q0, q0, q0

5.50.3.79 Logical operations (AND-NOT)

- uint32x2_t vbic_u32 (uint32x2_t, uint32x2_t)
  Form of expected instruction(s): vbic d0, d0, d0
- uint16x4_t vbic_u16 (uint16x4_t, uint16x4_t)
  Form of expected instruction(s): vbic d0, d0, d0
- uint8x8_t vbic_u8 (uint8x8_t, uint8x8_t)
  Form of expected instruction(s): vbic d0, d0, d0
- int32x2_t vbic_s32 (int32x2_t, int32x2_t)
  Form of expected instruction(s): vbic d0, d0, d0
- int16x4_t vbic_s16 (int16x4_t, int16x4_t)
  Form of expected instruction(s): vbic d0, d0, d0
- int8x8_t vbic_s8 (int8x8_t, int8x8_t)
  Form of expected instruction(s): vbic d0, d0, d0
- uint64x1_t vbic_u64 (uint64x1_t, uint64x1_t)
  Form of expected instruction(s): vbic d0, d0, d0
- int64x1_t vbic_s64 (int64x1_t, int64x1_t)
  Form of expected instruction(s): vbic d0, d0, d0
- uint32x4_t vbicq_u32 (uint32x4_t, uint32x4_t)
  Form of expected instruction(s): vbic q0, q0, q0
- uint16x8_t vbicq_u16 (uint16x8_t, uint16x8_t)
  Form of expected instruction(s): vbic q0, q0, q0
- uint8x16_t vbicq_u8 (uint8x16_t, uint8x16_t)
  Form of expected instruction(s): vbic q0, q0, q0
- int32x4_t vbicq_s32 (int32x4_t, int32x4_t)
  Form of expected instruction(s): vbic q0, q0, q0
- int16x8_t vbicq_s16 (int16x8_t, int16x8_t)
  Form of expected instruction(s): vbic q0, q0, q0
- int8x16_t vbicq_s8 (int8x16_t, int8x16_t)
  Form of expected instruction(s): vbic q0, q0, q0
- uint64x2_t vbicq_u64 (uint64x2_t, uint64x2_t)
  Form of expected instruction(s): vbic q0, q0, q0
- int64x2_t vbicq_s64 (int64x2_t, int64x2_t)
  Form of expected instruction(s): vbic q0, q0, q0

5.50.3.80 Logical operations (OR-NOT)

- uint32x2_t vorn_u32 (uint32x2_t, uint32x2_t)
  Form of expected instruction(s): vorn d0, d0, d0
- uint16x4_t vorn_u16 (uint16x4_t, uint16x4_t)
  Form of expected instruction(s): vorn d0, d0, d0
- uint8x8_t vorn_u8 (uint8x8_t, uint8x8_t)
  Form of expected instruction(s): vorn d0, d0, d0
- int32x2_t vorn_s32 (int32x2_t, int32x2_t)
  Form of expected instruction(s): vorn d0, d0, d0

Chapter 5: Extensions to the C Language Family   429

- int16x4_t vorn_s16 (int16x4_t, int16x4_t)
  Form of expected instruction(s): **vorn d0, d0, d0**
- int8x8_t vorn_s8 (int8x8_t, int8x8_t)
  Form of expected instruction(s): **vorn d0, d0, d0**
- uint64x1_t vorn_u64 (uint64x1_t, uint64x1_t)
  Form of expected instruction(s): **vorn d0, d0, d0**
- int64x1_t vorn_s64 (int64x1_t, int64x1_t)
  Form of expected instruction(s): **vorn d0, d0, d0**
- uint32x4_t vornq_u32 (uint32x4_t, uint32x4_t)
  Form of expected instruction(s): **vorn q0, q0, q0**
- uint16x8_t vornq_u16 (uint16x8_t, uint16x8_t)
  Form of expected instruction(s): **vorn q0, q0, q0**
- uint8x16_t vornq_u8 (uint8x16_t, uint8x16_t)
  Form of expected instruction(s): **vorn q0, q0, q0**
- int32x4_t vornq_s32 (int32x4_t, int32x4_t)
  Form of expected instruction(s): **vorn q0, q0, q0**
- int16x8_t vornq_s16 (int16x8_t, int16x8_t)
  Form of expected instruction(s): **vorn q0, q0, q0**
- int8x16_t vornq_s8 (int8x16_t, int8x16_t)
  Form of expected instruction(s): **vorn q0, q0, q0**
- uint64x2_t vornq_u64 (uint64x2_t, uint64x2_t)
  Form of expected instruction(s): **vorn q0, q0, q0**
- int64x2_t vornq_s64 (int64x2_t, int64x2_t)
  Form of expected instruction(s): **vorn q0, q0, q0**

5.50.3.81 Reinterpret casts

- poly8x8_t vreinterpret_p8_u32 (uint32x2_t)
- poly8x8_t vreinterpret_p8_u16 (uint16x4_t)
- poly8x8_t vreinterpret_p8_u8 (uint8x8_t)
- poly8x8_t vreinterpret_p8_s32 (int32x2_t)
- poly8x8_t vreinterpret_p8_s16 (int16x4_t)
- poly8x8_t vreinterpret_p8_s8 (int8x8_t)
- poly8x8_t vreinterpret_p8_u64 (uint64x1_t)
- poly8x8_t vreinterpret_p8_s64 (int64x1_t)
- poly8x8_t vreinterpret_p8_f32 (float32x2_t)
- poly8x8_t vreinterpret_p8_p16 (poly16x4_t)
- poly8x16_t vreinterpretq_p8_u32 (uint32x4_t)
- poly8x16_t vreinterpretq_p8_u16 (uint16x8_t)
- poly8x16_t vreinterpretq_p8_u8 (uint8x16_t)
- poly8x16_t vreinterpretq_p8_s32 (int32x4_t)
- poly8x16_t vreinterpretq_p8_s16 (int16x8_t)

- poly8x16_t vreinterpretq_p8_s8 (int8x16_t)
- poly8x16_t vreinterpretq_p8_u64 (uint64x2_t)
- poly8x16_t vreinterpretq_p8_s64 (int64x2_t)
- poly8x16_t vreinterpretq_p8_f32 (float32x4_t)
- poly8x16_t vreinterpretq_p8_p16 (poly16x8_t)
- poly16x4_t vreinterpret_p16_u32 (uint32x2_t)
- poly16x4_t vreinterpret_p16_u16 (uint16x4_t)
- poly16x4_t vreinterpret_p16_u8 (uint8x8_t)
- poly16x4_t vreinterpret_p16_s32 (int32x2_t)
- poly16x4_t vreinterpret_p16_s16 (int16x4_t)
- poly16x4_t vreinterpret_p16_s8 (int8x8_t)
- poly16x4_t vreinterpret_p16_u64 (uint64x1_t)
- poly16x4_t vreinterpret_p16_s64 (int64x1_t)
- poly16x4_t vreinterpret_p16_f32 (float32x2_t)
- poly16x4_t vreinterpret_p16_p8 (poly8x8_t)
- poly16x8_t vreinterpretq_p16_u32 (uint32x4_t)
- poly16x8_t vreinterpretq_p16_u16 (uint16x8_t)
- poly16x8_t vreinterpretq_p16_u8 (uint8x16_t)
- poly16x8_t vreinterpretq_p16_s32 (int32x4_t)
- poly16x8_t vreinterpretq_p16_s16 (int16x8_t)
- poly16x8_t vreinterpretq_p16_s8 (int8x16_t)
- poly16x8_t vreinterpretq_p16_u64 (uint64x2_t)
- poly16x8_t vreinterpretq_p16_s64 (int64x2_t)
- poly16x8_t vreinterpretq_p16_f32 (float32x4_t)
- poly16x8_t vreinterpretq_p16_p8 (poly8x16_t)
- float32x2_t vreinterpret_f32_u32 (uint32x2_t)
- float32x2_t vreinterpret_f32_u16 (uint16x4_t)
- float32x2_t vreinterpret_f32_u8 (uint8x8_t)
- float32x2_t vreinterpret_f32_s32 (int32x2_t)
- float32x2_t vreinterpret_f32_s16 (int16x4_t)
- float32x2_t vreinterpret_f32_s8 (int8x8_t)
- float32x2_t vreinterpret_f32_u64 (uint64x1_t)
- float32x2_t vreinterpret_f32_s64 (int64x1_t)
- float32x2_t vreinterpret_f32_p16 (poly16x4_t)
- float32x2_t vreinterpret_f32_p8 (poly8x8_t)
- float32x4_t vreinterpretq_f32_u32 (uint32x4_t)
- float32x4_t vreinterpretq_f32_u16 (uint16x8_t)
- float32x4_t vreinterpretq_f32_u8 (uint8x16_t)
- float32x4_t vreinterpretq_f32_s32 (int32x4_t)

Chapter 5: Extensions to the C Language Family   431

- float32x4_t vreinterpretq_f32_s16 (int16x8_t)
- float32x4_t vreinterpretq_f32_s8 (int8x16_t)
- float32x4_t vreinterpretq_f32_u64 (uint64x2_t)
- float32x4_t vreinterpretq_f32_s64 (int64x2_t)
- float32x4_t vreinterpretq_f32_p16 (poly16x8_t)
- float32x4_t vreinterpretq_f32_p8 (poly8x16_t)
- int64x1_t vreinterpret_s64_u32 (uint32x2_t)
- int64x1_t vreinterpret_s64_u16 (uint16x4_t)
- int64x1_t vreinterpret_s64_u8 (uint8x8_t)
- int64x1_t vreinterpret_s64_s32 (int32x2_t)
- int64x1_t vreinterpret_s64_s16 (int16x4_t)
- int64x1_t vreinterpret_s64_s8 (int8x8_t)
- int64x1_t vreinterpret_s64_u64 (uint64x1_t)
- int64x1_t vreinterpret_s64_f32 (float32x2_t)
- int64x1_t vreinterpret_s64_p16 (poly16x4_t)
- int64x1_t vreinterpret_s64_p8 (poly8x8_t)
- int64x2_t vreinterpretq_s64_u32 (uint32x4_t)
- int64x2_t vreinterpretq_s64_u16 (uint16x8_t)
- int64x2_t vreinterpretq_s64_u8 (uint8x16_t)
- int64x2_t vreinterpretq_s64_s32 (int32x4_t)
- int64x2_t vreinterpretq_s64_s16 (int16x8_t)
- int64x2_t vreinterpretq_s64_s8 (int8x16_t)
- int64x2_t vreinterpretq_s64_u64 (uint64x2_t)
- int64x2_t vreinterpretq_s64_f32 (float32x4_t)
- int64x2_t vreinterpretq_s64_p16 (poly16x8_t)
- int64x2_t vreinterpretq_s64_p8 (poly8x16_t)
- uint64x1_t vreinterpret_u64_u32 (uint32x2_t)
- uint64x1_t vreinterpret_u64_u16 (uint16x4_t)
- uint64x1_t vreinterpret_u64_u8 (uint8x8_t)
- uint64x1_t vreinterpret_u64_s32 (int32x2_t)
- uint64x1_t vreinterpret_u64_s16 (int16x4_t)
- uint64x1_t vreinterpret_u64_s8 (int8x8_t)
- uint64x1_t vreinterpret_u64_s64 (int64x1_t)
- uint64x1_t vreinterpret_u64_f32 (float32x2_t)
- uint64x1_t vreinterpret_u64_p16 (poly16x4_t)
- uint64x1_t vreinterpret_u64_p8 (poly8x8_t)
- uint64x2_t vreinterpretq_u64_u32 (uint32x4_t)
- uint64x2_t vreinterpretq_u64_u16 (uint16x8_t)
- uint64x2_t vreinterpretq_u64_u8 (uint8x16_t)

- uint64x2_t vreinterpretq_u64_s32 (int32x4_t)
- uint64x2_t vreinterpretq_u64_s16 (int16x8_t)
- uint64x2_t vreinterpretq_u64_s8 (int8x16_t)
- uint64x2_t vreinterpretq_u64_s64 (int64x2_t)
- uint64x2_t vreinterpretq_u64_f32 (float32x4_t)
- uint64x2_t vreinterpretq_u64_p16 (poly16x8_t)
- uint64x2_t vreinterpretq_u64_p8 (poly8x16_t)
- int8x8_t vreinterpret_s8_u32 (uint32x2_t)
- int8x8_t vreinterpret_s8_u16 (uint16x4_t)
- int8x8_t vreinterpret_s8_u8 (uint8x8_t)
- int8x8_t vreinterpret_s8_s32 (int32x2_t)
- int8x8_t vreinterpret_s8_s16 (int16x4_t)
- int8x8_t vreinterpret_s8_u64 (uint64x1_t)
- int8x8_t vreinterpret_s8_s64 (int64x1_t)
- int8x8_t vreinterpret_s8_f32 (float32x2_t)
- int8x8_t vreinterpret_s8_p16 (poly16x4_t)
- int8x8_t vreinterpret_s8_p8 (poly8x8_t)
- int8x16_t vreinterpretq_s8_u32 (uint32x4_t)
- int8x16_t vreinterpretq_s8_u16 (uint16x8_t)
- int8x16_t vreinterpretq_s8_u8 (uint8x16_t)
- int8x16_t vreinterpretq_s8_s32 (int32x4_t)
- int8x16_t vreinterpretq_s8_s16 (int16x8_t)
- int8x16_t vreinterpretq_s8_u64 (uint64x2_t)
- int8x16_t vreinterpretq_s8_s64 (int64x2_t)
- int8x16_t vreinterpretq_s8_f32 (float32x4_t)
- int8x16_t vreinterpretq_s8_p16 (poly16x8_t)
- int8x16_t vreinterpretq_s8_p8 (poly8x16_t)
- int16x4_t vreinterpret_s16_u32 (uint32x2_t)
- int16x4_t vreinterpret_s16_u16 (uint16x4_t)
- int16x4_t vreinterpret_s16_u8 (uint8x8_t)
- int16x4_t vreinterpret_s16_s32 (int32x2_t)
- int16x4_t vreinterpret_s16_s8 (int8x8_t)
- int16x4_t vreinterpret_s16_u64 (uint64x1_t)
- int16x4_t vreinterpret_s16_s64 (int64x1_t)
- int16x4_t vreinterpret_s16_f32 (float32x2_t)
- int16x4_t vreinterpret_s16_p16 (poly16x4_t)
- int16x4_t vreinterpret_s16_p8 (poly8x8_t)
- int16x8_t vreinterpretq_s16_u32 (uint32x4_t)
- int16x8_t vreinterpretq_s16_u16 (uint16x8_t)

Chapter 5: Extensions to the C Language Family   433

- int16x8_t vreinterpretq_s16_u8 (uint8x16_t)
- int16x8_t vreinterpretq_s16_s32 (int32x4_t)
- int16x8_t vreinterpretq_s16_s8 (int8x16_t)
- int16x8_t vreinterpretq_s16_u64 (uint64x2_t)
- int16x8_t vreinterpretq_s16_s64 (int64x2_t)
- int16x8_t vreinterpretq_s16_f32 (float32x4_t)
- int16x8_t vreinterpretq_s16_p16 (poly16x8_t)
- int16x8_t vreinterpretq_s16_p8 (poly8x16_t)
- int32x2_t vreinterpret_s32_u32 (uint32x2_t)
- int32x2_t vreinterpret_s32_u16 (uint16x4_t)
- int32x2_t vreinterpret_s32_u8 (uint8x8_t)
- int32x2_t vreinterpret_s32_s16 (int16x4_t)
- int32x2_t vreinterpret_s32_s8 (int8x8_t)
- int32x2_t vreinterpret_s32_u64 (uint64x1_t)
- int32x2_t vreinterpret_s32_s64 (int64x1_t)
- int32x2_t vreinterpret_s32_f32 (float32x2_t)
- int32x2_t vreinterpret_s32_p16 (poly16x4_t)
- int32x2_t vreinterpret_s32_p8 (poly8x8_t)
- int32x4_t vreinterpretq_s32_u32 (uint32x4_t)
- int32x4_t vreinterpretq_s32_u16 (uint16x8_t)
- int32x4_t vreinterpretq_s32_u8 (uint8x16_t)
- int32x4_t vreinterpretq_s32_s16 (int16x8_t)
- int32x4_t vreinterpretq_s32_s8 (int8x16_t)
- int32x4_t vreinterpretq_s32_u64 (uint64x2_t)
- int32x4_t vreinterpretq_s32_s64 (int64x2_t)
- int32x4_t vreinterpretq_s32_f32 (float32x4_t)
- int32x4_t vreinterpretq_s32_p16 (poly16x8_t)
- int32x4_t vreinterpretq_s32_p8 (poly8x16_t)
- uint8x8_t vreinterpret_u8_u32 (uint32x2_t)
- uint8x8_t vreinterpret_u8_u16 (uint16x4_t)
- uint8x8_t vreinterpret_u8_s32 (int32x2_t)
- uint8x8_t vreinterpret_u8_s16 (int16x4_t)
- uint8x8_t vreinterpret_u8_s8 (int8x8_t)
- uint8x8_t vreinterpret_u8_u64 (uint64x1_t)
- uint8x8_t vreinterpret_u8_s64 (int64x1_t)
- uint8x8_t vreinterpret_u8_f32 (float32x2_t)
- uint8x8_t vreinterpret_u8_p16 (poly16x4_t)
- uint8x8_t vreinterpret_u8_p8 (poly8x8_t)
- uint8x16_t vreinterpretq_u8_u32 (uint32x4_t)

- uint8x16_t vreinterpretq_u8_u16 (uint16x8_t)
- uint8x16_t vreinterpretq_u8_s32 (int32x4_t)
- uint8x16_t vreinterpretq_u8_s16 (int16x8_t)
- uint8x16_t vreinterpretq_u8_s8 (int8x16_t)
- uint8x16_t vreinterpretq_u8_u64 (uint64x2_t)
- uint8x16_t vreinterpretq_u8_s64 (int64x2_t)
- uint8x16_t vreinterpretq_u8_f32 (float32x4_t)
- uint8x16_t vreinterpretq_u8_p16 (poly16x8_t)
- uint8x16_t vreinterpretq_u8_p8 (poly8x16_t)
- uint16x4_t vreinterpret_u16_u32 (uint32x2_t)
- uint16x4_t vreinterpret_u16_u8 (uint8x8_t)
- uint16x4_t vreinterpret_u16_s32 (int32x2_t)
- uint16x4_t vreinterpret_u16_s16 (int16x4_t)
- uint16x4_t vreinterpret_u16_s8 (int8x8_t)
- uint16x4_t vreinterpret_u16_u64 (uint64x1_t)
- uint16x4_t vreinterpret_u16_s64 (int64x1_t)
- uint16x4_t vreinterpret_u16_f32 (float32x2_t)
- uint16x4_t vreinterpret_u16_p16 (poly16x4_t)
- uint16x4_t vreinterpret_u16_p8 (poly8x8_t)
- uint16x8_t vreinterpretq_u16_u32 (uint32x4_t)
- uint16x8_t vreinterpretq_u16_u8 (uint8x16_t)
- uint16x8_t vreinterpretq_u16_s32 (int32x4_t)
- uint16x8_t vreinterpretq_u16_s16 (int16x8_t)
- uint16x8_t vreinterpretq_u16_s8 (int8x16_t)
- uint16x8_t vreinterpretq_u16_u64 (uint64x2_t)
- uint16x8_t vreinterpretq_u16_s64 (int64x2_t)
- uint16x8_t vreinterpretq_u16_f32 (float32x4_t)
- uint16x8_t vreinterpretq_u16_p16 (poly16x8_t)
- uint16x8_t vreinterpretq_u16_p8 (poly8x16_t)
- uint32x2_t vreinterpret_u32_u16 (uint16x4_t)
- uint32x2_t vreinterpret_u32_u8 (uint8x8_t)
- uint32x2_t vreinterpret_u32_s32 (int32x2_t)
- uint32x2_t vreinterpret_u32_s16 (int16x4_t)
- uint32x2_t vreinterpret_u32_s8 (int8x8_t)
- uint32x2_t vreinterpret_u32_u64 (uint64x1_t)
- uint32x2_t vreinterpret_u32_s64 (int64x1_t)
- uint32x2_t vreinterpret_u32_f32 (float32x2_t)
- uint32x2_t vreinterpret_u32_p16 (poly16x4_t)
- uint32x2_t vreinterpret_u32_p8 (poly8x8_t)

Chapter 5: Extensions to the C Language Family   435

- uint32x4_t vreinterpretq_u32_u16 (uint16x8_t)
- uint32x4_t vreinterpretq_u32_u8 (uint8x16_t)
- uint32x4_t vreinterpretq_u32_s32 (int32x4_t)
- uint32x4_t vreinterpretq_u32_s16 (int16x8_t)
- uint32x4_t vreinterpretq_u32_s8 (int8x16_t)
- uint32x4_t vreinterpretq_u32_u64 (uint64x2_t)
- uint32x4_t vreinterpretq_u32_s64 (int64x2_t)
- uint32x4_t vreinterpretq_u32_f32 (float32x4_t)
- uint32x4_t vreinterpretq_u32_p16 (poly16x8_t)
- uint32x4_t vreinterpretq_u32_p8 (poly8x16_t)

5.50.4 Blackfin Built-in Functions

Currently, there are two Blackfin-specific built-in functions. These are used for generating `CSYNC` and `SSYNC` machine insns without using inline assembly; by using these built-in functions the compiler can automatically add workarounds for hardware errata involving these instructions. These functions are named as follows:

```
void __builtin_bfin_csync (void)
void __builtin_bfin_ssync (void)
```

5.50.5 FR-V Built-in Functions

GCC provides many FR-V-specific built-in functions. In general, these functions are intended to be compatible with those described by *FR-V Family, Softune C/C++ Compiler Manual (V6), Fujitsu Semiconductor*. The two exceptions are `__MDUNPACKH` and `__MBTOHE`, the gcc forms of which pass 128-bit values by pointer rather than by value.

Most of the functions are named after specific FR-V instructions. Such functions are said to be "directly mapped" and are summarized here in tabular form.

5.50.5.1 Argument Types

The arguments to the built-in functions can be divided into three groups: register numbers, compile-time constants and run-time values. In order to make this classification clear at a glance, the arguments and return values are given the following pseudo types:

Pseudo type	Real C type	Constant?	Description
uh	unsigned short	No	an unsigned halfword
uw1	unsigned int	No	an unsigned word
sw1	int	No	a signed word
uw2	unsigned long long	No	an unsigned doubleword
sw2	long long	No	a signed doubleword
const	int	Yes	an integer constant
acc	int	Yes	an ACC register number
iacc	int	Yes	an IACC register number

These pseudo types are not defined by GCC, they are simply a notational convenience used in this manual.

Arguments of type `uh`, `uw1`, `sw1`, `uw2` and `sw2` are evaluated at run time. They correspond to register operands in the underlying FR-V instructions.

`const` arguments represent immediate operands in the underlying FR-V instructions. They must be compile-time constants.

`acc` arguments are evaluated at compile time and specify the number of an accumulator register. For example, an `acc` argument of 2 will select the ACC2 register.

`iacc` arguments are similar to `acc` arguments but specify the number of an IACC register. See see Section 5.50.5.5 [Other Built-in Functions], page 438 for more details.

5.50.5.2 Directly-mapped Integer Functions

The functions listed below map directly to FR-V I-type instructions.

Function prototype	Example usage	Assembly output
sw1 __ADDSS (sw1, sw1)	c = __ADDSS (a, b)	ADDSS a,b,c
sw1 __SCAN (sw1, sw1)	c = __SCAN (a, b)	SCAN a,b,c
sw1 __SCUTSS (sw1)	b = __SCUTSS (a)	SCUTSS a,b
sw1 __SLASS (sw1, sw1)	c = __SLASS (a, b)	SLASS a,b,c
void __SMASS (sw1, sw1)	__SMASS (a, b)	SMASS a,b
void __SMSSS (sw1, sw1)	__SMSSS (a, b)	SMSSS a,b
void __SMU (sw1, sw1)	__SMU (a, b)	SMU a,b
sw2 __SMUL (sw1, sw1)	c = __SMUL (a, b)	SMUL a,b,c
sw1 __SUBSS (sw1, sw1)	c = __SUBSS (a, b)	SUBSS a,b,c
uw2 __UMUL (uw1, uw1)	c = __UMUL (a, b)	UMUL a,b,c

5.50.5.3 Directly-mapped Media Functions

The functions listed below map directly to FR-V M-type instructions.

Function prototype	Example usage	Assembly output
uw1 __MABSHS (sw1)	b = __MABSHS (a)	MABSHS a,b
void __MADDACCS (acc, acc)	__MADDACCS (b, a)	MADDACCS a,b
sw1 __MADDHSS (sw1, sw1)	c = __MADDHSS (a, b)	MADDHSS a,b,c
uw1 __MADDHUS (uw1, uw1)	c = __MADDHUS (a, b)	MADDHUS a,b,c
uw1 __MAND (uw1, uw1)	c = __MAND (a, b)	MAND a,b,c
void __MASACCS (acc, acc)	__MASACCS (b, a)	MASACCS a,b
uw1 __MAVEH (uw1, uw1)	c = __MAVEH (a, b)	MAVEH a,b,c
uw2 __MBTOH (uw1)	b = __MBTOH (a)	MBTOH a,b
void __MBTOHE (uw1 *, uw1)	__MBTOHE (&b, a)	MBTOHE a,b
void __MCLRACC (acc)	__MCLRACC (a)	MCLRACC a
void __MCLRACCA (void)	__MCLRACCA ()	MCLRACCA
uw1 __Mcop1 (uw1, uw1)	c = __Mcop1 (a, b)	Mcop1 a,b,c
uw1 __Mcop2 (uw1, uw1)	c = __Mcop2 (a, b)	Mcop2 a,b,c
uw1 __MCPLHI (uw2, const)	c = __MCPLHI (a, b)	MCPLHI a,#b,c
uw1 __MCPLI (uw2, const)	c = __MCPLI (a, b)	MCPLI a,#b,c
void __MCPXIS (acc, sw1, sw1)	__MCPXIS (c, a, b)	MCPXIS a,b,c
void __MCPXIU (acc, uw1, uw1)	__MCPXIU (c, a, b)	MCPXIU a,b,c
void __MCPXRS (acc, sw1, sw1)	__MCPXRS (c, a, b)	MCPXRS a,b,c
void __MCPXRU (acc, uw1, uw1)	__MCPXRU (c, a, b)	MCPXRU a,b,c
uw1 __MCUT (acc, uw1)	c = __MCUT (a, b)	MCUT a,b,c
uw1 __MCUTSS (acc, sw1)	c = __MCUTSS (a, b)	MCUTSS a,b,c
void __MDADDACCS (acc, acc)	__MDADDACCS (b, a)	MDADDACCS a,b

Chapter 5: Extensions to the C Language Family   437

void __MDASACCS (acc, acc)	__MDASACCS (b, a)	MDASACCS a,b
uw2 __MDCUTSSI (acc, const)	c = __MDCUTSSI (a, b)	MDCUTSSI a,#b,c
uw2 __MDPACKH (uw2, uw2)	c = __MDPACKH (a, b)	MDPACKH a,b,c
uw2 __MDROTLI (uw2, const)	c = __MDROTLI (a, b)	MDROTLI a,#b,c
void __MDSUBACCS (acc, acc)	__MDSUBACCS (b, a)	MDSUBACCS a,b
void __MDUNPACKH (uw1 *, uw2)	__MDUNPACKH (&b, a)	MDUNPACKH a,b
uw2 __MEXPDHD (uw1, const)	c = __MEXPDHD (a, b)	MEXPDHD a,#b,c
uw1 __MEXPDHW (uw1, const)	c = __MEXPDHW (a, b)	MEXPDHW a,#b,c
uw1 __MHDSETH (uw1, const)	c = __MHDSETH (a, b)	MHDSETH a,#b,c
sw1 __MHDSETS (const)	b = __MHDSETS (a)	MHDSETS #a,b
uw1 __MHSETHIH (uw1, const)	b = __MHSETHIH (b, a)	MHSETHIH #a,b
sw1 __MHSETHIS (sw1, const)	b = __MHSETHIS (b, a)	MHSETHIS #a,b
uw1 __MHSETLOH (uw1, const)	b = __MHSETLOH (b, a)	MHSETLOH #a,b
sw1 __MHSETLOS (sw1, const)	b = __MHSETLOS (b, a)	MHSETLOS #a,b
uw1 __MHTOB (uw2)	b = __MHTOB (a)	MHTOB a,b
void __MMACHS (acc, sw1, sw1)	__MMACHS (c, a, b)	MMACHS a,b,c
void __MMACHU (acc, uw1, uw1)	__MMACHU (c, a, b)	MMACHU a,b,c
void __MMRDHS (acc, sw1, sw1)	__MMRDHS (c, a, b)	MMRDHS a,b,c
void __MMRDHU (acc, uw1, uw1)	__MMRDHU (c, a, b)	MMRDHU a,b,c
void __MMULHS (acc, sw1, sw1)	__MMULHS (c, a, b)	MMULHS a,b,c
void __MMULHU (acc, uw1, uw1)	__MMULHU (c, a, b)	MMULHU a,b,c
void __MMULXHS (acc, sw1, sw1)	__MMULXHS (c, a, b)	MMULXHS a,b,c
void __MMULXHU (acc, uw1, uw1)	__MMULXHU (c, a, b)	MMULXHU a,b,c
uw1 __MNOT (uw1)	b = __MNOT (a)	MNOT a,b
uw1 __MOR (uw1, uw1)	c = __MOR (a, b)	MOR a,b,c
uw1 __MPACKH (uh, uh)	c = __MPACKH (a, b)	MPACKH a,b,c
sw2 __MQADDHSS (sw2, sw2)	c = __MQADDHSS (a, b)	MQADDHSS a,b,c
uw2 __MQADDHUS (uw2, uw2)	c = __MQADDHUS (a, b)	MQADDHUS a,b,c
void __MQCPXIS (acc, sw2, sw2)	__MQCPXIS (c, a, b)	MQCPXIS a,b,c
void __MQCPXIU (acc, uw2, uw2)	__MQCPXIU (c, a, b)	MQCPXIU a,b,c
void __MQCPXRS (acc, sw2, sw2)	__MQCPXRS (c, a, b)	MQCPXRS a,b,c
void __MQCPXRU (acc, uw2, uw2)	__MQCPXRU (c, a, b)	MQCPXRU a,b,c
sw2 __MQLCLRHS (sw2, sw2)	c = __MQLCLRHS (a, b)	MQLCLRHS a,b,c
sw2 __MQLMTHS (sw2, sw2)	c = __MQLMTHS (a, b)	MQLMTHS a,b,c
void __MQMACHS (acc, sw2, sw2)	__MQMACHS (c, a, b)	MQMACHS a,b,c
void __MQMACHU (acc, uw2, uw2)	__MQMACHU (c, a, b)	MQMACHU a,b,c
void __MQMACXHS (acc, sw2, sw2)	__MQMACXHS (c, a, b)	MQMACXHS a,b,c
void __MQMULHS (acc, sw2, sw2)	__MQMULHS (c, a, b)	MQMULHS a,b,c
void __MQMULHU (acc, uw2, uw2)	__MQMULHU (c, a, b)	MQMULHU a,b,c
void __MQMULXHS (acc, sw2, sw2)	__MQMULXHS (c, a, b)	MQMULXHS a,b,c
void __MQMULXHU (acc, uw2, uw2)	__MQMULXHU (c, a, b)	MQMULXHU a,b,c
sw2 __MQSATHS (sw2, sw2)	c = __MQSATHS (a, b)	MQSATHS a,b,c
uw2 __MQSLLHI (uw2, int)	c = __MQSLLHI (a, b)	MQSLLHI a,b,c
sw2 __MQSRAHI (sw2, int)	c = __MQSRAHI (a, b)	MQSRAHI a,b,c
sw2 __MQSUBHSS (sw2, sw2)	c = __MQSUBHSS (a, b)	MQSUBHSS a,b,c
uw2 __MQSUBHUS (uw2, uw2)	c = __MQSUBHUS (a, b)	MQSUBHUS a,b,c
void __MQXMACHS (acc, sw2, sw2)	__MQXMACHS (c, a, b)	MQXMACHS a,b,c

void __MQXMACXHS (acc, sw2, sw2)	__MQXMACXHS (c, a, b)	MQXMACXHS a,b,c
uw1 __MRDACC (acc)	b = __MRDACC (a)	MRDACC a,b
uw1 __MRDACCG (acc)	b = __MRDACCG (a)	MRDACCG a,b
uw1 __MROTLI (uw1, const)	c = __MROTLI (a, b)	MROTLI a,#b,c
uw1 __MROTRI (uw1, const)	c = __MROTRI (a, b)	MROTRI a,#b,c
sw1 __MSATHS (sw1, sw1)	c = __MSATHS (a, b)	MSATHS a,b,c
uw1 __MSATHU (uw1, uw1)	c = __MSATHU (a, b)	MSATHU a,b,c
uw1 __MSLLHI (uw1, const)	c = __MSLLHI (a, b)	MSLLHI a,#b,c
sw1 __MSRAHI (sw1, const)	c = __MSRAHI (a, b)	MSRAHI a,#b,c
uw1 __MSRLHI (uw1, const)	c = __MSRLHI (a, b)	MSRLHI a,#b,c
void __MSUBACCS (acc, acc)	__MSUBACCS (b, a)	MSUBACCS a,b
sw1 __MSUBHSS (sw1, sw1)	c = __MSUBHSS (a, b)	MSUBHSS a,b,c
uw1 __MSUBHUS (uw1, uw1)	c = __MSUBHUS (a, b)	MSUBHUS a,b,c
void __MTRAP (void)	__MTRAP ()	MTRAP
uw2 __MUNPACKH (uw1)	b = __MUNPACKH (a)	MUNPACKH a,b
uw1 __MWCUT (uw2, uw1)	c = __MWCUT (a, b)	MWCUT a,b,c
void __MWTACC (acc, uw1)	__MWTACC (b, a)	MWTACC a,b
void __MWTACCG (acc, uw1)	__MWTACCG (b, a)	MWTACCG a,b
uw1 __MXOR (uw1, uw1)	c = __MXOR (a, b)	MXOR a,b,c

5.50.5.4 Raw read/write Functions

This sections describes built-in functions related to read and write instructions to access memory. These functions generate `membar` instructions to flush the I/O load and stores where appropriate, as described in Fujitsu's manual described above.

```
unsigned char __builtin_read8 (void *data)
unsigned short __builtin_read16 (void *data)
unsigned long __builtin_read32 (void *data)
unsigned long long __builtin_read64 (void *data)
void __builtin_write8 (void *data, unsigned char datum)
void __builtin_write16 (void *data, unsigned short datum)
void __builtin_write32 (void *data, unsigned long datum)
void __builtin_write64 (void *data, unsigned long long datum)
```

5.50.5.5 Other Built-in Functions

This section describes built-in functions that are not named after a specific FR-V instruction.

`sw2 __IACCreadll (iacc reg)`
: Return the full 64-bit value of IACC0. The reg argument is reserved for future expansion and must be 0.

`sw1 __IACCreadl (iacc reg)`
: Return the value of IACC0H if reg is 0 and IACC0L if reg is 1. Other values of reg are rejected as invalid.

`void __IACCsetll (iacc reg, sw2 x)`
: Set the full 64-bit value of IACC0 to x. The reg argument is reserved for future expansion and must be 0.

Chapter 5: Extensions to the C Language Family   439

`void __IACCsetl (iacc reg, sw1 x)`
> Set IACC0H to *x* if *reg* is 0 and IACC0L to *x* if *reg* is 1. Other values of *reg* are rejected as invalid.

`void __data_prefetch0 (const void *x)`
> Use the `dcpl` instruction to load the contents of address *x* into the data cache.

`void __data_prefetch (const void *x)`
> Use the `nldub` instruction to load the contents of address *x* into the data cache. The instruction will be issued in slot I1.

5.50.6 X86 Built-in Functions

These built-in functions are available for the i386 and x86-64 family of computers, depending on the command-line switches used.

Note that, if you specify command-line switches such as '`-msse`', the compiler could use the extended instruction sets even if the built-ins are not used explicitly in the program. For this reason, applications which perform runtime CPU detection must compile separate files for each supported architecture, using the appropriate flags. In particular, the file containing the CPU detection code should be compiled without these options.

The following machine modes are available for use with MMX built-in functions (see Section 5.45 [Vector Extensions], page 332): `V2SI` for a vector of two 32-bit integers, `V4HI` for a vector of four 16-bit integers, and `V8QI` for a vector of eight 8-bit integers. Some of the built-in functions operate on MMX registers as a whole 64-bit entity, these use `DI` as their mode.

If 3Dnow extensions are enabled, `V2SF` is used as a mode for a vector of two 32-bit floating point values.

If SSE extensions are enabled, `V4SF` is used for a vector of four 32-bit floating point values. Some instructions use a vector of four 32-bit integers, these use `V4SI`. Finally, some instructions operate on an entire vector register, interpreting it as a 128-bit integer, these use mode `TI`.

In 64-bit mode, the x86-64 family of processors uses additional built-in functions for efficient use of `TF` (`__float128`) 128-bit floating point and `TC` 128-bit complex floating point values.

The following floating point built-in functions are available in 64-bit mode. All of them implement the function that is part of the name.

```
__float128 __builtin_fabsq (__float128)
__float128 __builtin_copysignq (__float128, __float128)
```

The following floating point built-in functions are made available in the 64-bit mode.

`__float128 __builtin_infq (void)`
> Similar to `__builtin_inf`, except the return type is `__float128`.

The following built-in functions are made available by '`-mmmx`'. All of them generate the machine instruction that is part of the name.

```
v8qi __builtin_ia32_paddb (v8qi, v8qi)
v4hi __builtin_ia32_paddw (v4hi, v4hi)
v2si __builtin_ia32_paddd (v2si, v2si)
v8qi __builtin_ia32_psubb (v8qi, v8qi)
```

```
v4hi __builtin_ia32_psubw (v4hi, v4hi)
v2si __builtin_ia32_psubd (v2si, v2si)
v8qi __builtin_ia32_paddsb (v8qi, v8qi)
v4hi __builtin_ia32_paddsw (v4hi, v4hi)
v8qi __builtin_ia32_psubsb (v8qi, v8qi)
v4hi __builtin_ia32_psubsw (v4hi, v4hi)
v8qi __builtin_ia32_paddusb (v8qi, v8qi)
v4hi __builtin_ia32_paddusw (v4hi, v4hi)
v8qi __builtin_ia32_psubusb (v8qi, v8qi)
v4hi __builtin_ia32_psubusw (v4hi, v4hi)
v4hi __builtin_ia32_pmullw (v4hi, v4hi)
v4hi __builtin_ia32_pmulhw (v4hi, v4hi)
di __builtin_ia32_pand (di, di)
di __builtin_ia32_pandn (di,di)
di __builtin_ia32_por (di, di)
di __builtin_ia32_pxor (di, di)
v8qi __builtin_ia32_pcmpeqb (v8qi, v8qi)
v4hi __builtin_ia32_pcmpeqw (v4hi, v4hi)
v2si __builtin_ia32_pcmpeqd (v2si, v2si)
v8qi __builtin_ia32_pcmpgtb (v8qi, v8qi)
v4hi __builtin_ia32_pcmpgtw (v4hi, v4hi)
v2si __builtin_ia32_pcmpgtd (v2si, v2si)
v8qi __builtin_ia32_punpckhbw (v8qi, v8qi)
v4hi __builtin_ia32_punpckhwd (v4hi, v4hi)
v2si __builtin_ia32_punpckhdq (v2si, v2si)
v8qi __builtin_ia32_punpcklbw (v8qi, v8qi)
v4hi __builtin_ia32_punpcklwd (v4hi, v4hi)
v2si __builtin_ia32_punpckldq (v2si, v2si)
v8qi __builtin_ia32_packsswb (v4hi, v4hi)
v4hi __builtin_ia32_packssdw (v2si, v2si)
v8qi __builtin_ia32_packuswb (v4hi, v4hi)
```

The following built-in functions are made available either with '-msse', or with a combination of '-m3dnow' and '-march=athlon'. All of them generate the machine instruction that is part of the name.

```
v4hi __builtin_ia32_pmulhuw (v4hi, v4hi)
v8qi __builtin_ia32_pavgb (v8qi, v8qi)
v4hi __builtin_ia32_pavgw (v4hi, v4hi)
v4hi __builtin_ia32_psadbw (v8qi, v8qi)
v8qi __builtin_ia32_pmaxub (v8qi, v8qi)
v4hi __builtin_ia32_pmaxsw (v4hi, v4hi)
v8qi __builtin_ia32_pminub (v8qi, v8qi)
v4hi __builtin_ia32_pminsw (v4hi, v4hi)
int __builtin_ia32_pextrw (v4hi, int)
v4hi __builtin_ia32_pinsrw (v4hi, int, int)
int __builtin_ia32_pmovmskb (v8qi)
void __builtin_ia32_maskmovq (v8qi, v8qi, char *)
void __builtin_ia32_movntq (di *, di)
void __builtin_ia32_sfence (void)
```

The following built-in functions are available when '-msse' is used. All of them generate the machine instruction that is part of the name.

```
int __builtin_ia32_comieq (v4sf, v4sf)
int __builtin_ia32_comineq (v4sf, v4sf)
int __builtin_ia32_comilt (v4sf, v4sf)
int __builtin_ia32_comile (v4sf, v4sf)
int __builtin_ia32_comigt (v4sf, v4sf)
int __builtin_ia32_comige (v4sf, v4sf)
```

Chapter 5: Extensions to the C Language Family

```
int __builtin_ia32_ucomieq (v4sf, v4sf)
int __builtin_ia32_ucomineq (v4sf, v4sf)
int __builtin_ia32_ucomilt (v4sf, v4sf)
int __builtin_ia32_ucomile (v4sf, v4sf)
int __builtin_ia32_ucomigt (v4sf, v4sf)
int __builtin_ia32_ucomige (v4sf, v4sf)
v4sf __builtin_ia32_addps (v4sf, v4sf)
v4sf __builtin_ia32_subps (v4sf, v4sf)
v4sf __builtin_ia32_mulps (v4sf, v4sf)
v4sf __builtin_ia32_divps (v4sf, v4sf)
v4sf __builtin_ia32_addss (v4sf, v4sf)
v4sf __builtin_ia32_subss (v4sf, v4sf)
v4sf __builtin_ia32_mulss (v4sf, v4sf)
v4sf __builtin_ia32_divss (v4sf, v4sf)
v4si __builtin_ia32_cmpeqps (v4sf, v4sf)
v4si __builtin_ia32_cmpltps (v4sf, v4sf)
v4si __builtin_ia32_cmpleps (v4sf, v4sf)
v4si __builtin_ia32_cmpgtps (v4sf, v4sf)
v4si __builtin_ia32_cmpgeps (v4sf, v4sf)
v4si __builtin_ia32_cmpunordps (v4sf, v4sf)
v4si __builtin_ia32_cmpneqps (v4sf, v4sf)
v4si __builtin_ia32_cmpnltps (v4sf, v4sf)
v4si __builtin_ia32_cmpnleps (v4sf, v4sf)
v4si __builtin_ia32_cmpngtps (v4sf, v4sf)
v4si __builtin_ia32_cmpngeps (v4sf, v4sf)
v4si __builtin_ia32_cmpordps (v4sf, v4sf)
v4si __builtin_ia32_cmpeqss (v4sf, v4sf)
v4si __builtin_ia32_cmpltss (v4sf, v4sf)
v4si __builtin_ia32_cmpless (v4sf, v4sf)
v4si __builtin_ia32_cmpunordss (v4sf, v4sf)
v4si __builtin_ia32_cmpneqss (v4sf, v4sf)
v4si __builtin_ia32_cmpnlts (v4sf, v4sf)
v4si __builtin_ia32_cmpnless (v4sf, v4sf)
v4si __builtin_ia32_cmpordss (v4sf, v4sf)
v4sf __builtin_ia32_maxps (v4sf, v4sf)
v4sf __builtin_ia32_maxss (v4sf, v4sf)
v4sf __builtin_ia32_minps (v4sf, v4sf)
v4sf __builtin_ia32_minss (v4sf, v4sf)
v4sf __builtin_ia32_andps (v4sf, v4sf)
v4sf __builtin_ia32_andnps (v4sf, v4sf)
v4sf __builtin_ia32_orps (v4sf, v4sf)
v4sf __builtin_ia32_xorps (v4sf, v4sf)
v4sf __builtin_ia32_movss (v4sf, v4sf)
v4sf __builtin_ia32_movhlps (v4sf, v4sf)
v4sf __builtin_ia32_movlhps (v4sf, v4sf)
v4sf __builtin_ia32_unpckhps (v4sf, v4sf)
v4sf __builtin_ia32_unpcklps (v4sf, v4sf)
v4sf __builtin_ia32_cvtpi2ps (v4sf, v2si)
v4sf __builtin_ia32_cvtsi2ss (v4sf, int)
v2si __builtin_ia32_cvtps2pi (v4sf)
int __builtin_ia32_cvtss2si (v4sf)
v2si __builtin_ia32_cvttps2pi (v4sf)
int __builtin_ia32_cvttss2si (v4sf)
v4sf __builtin_ia32_rcpps (v4sf)
v4sf __builtin_ia32_rsqrtps (v4sf)
v4sf __builtin_ia32_sqrtps (v4sf)
v4sf __builtin_ia32_rcpss (v4sf)
v4sf __builtin_ia32_rsqrtss (v4sf)
```

```
v4sf __builtin_ia32_sqrtss (v4sf)
v4sf __builtin_ia32_shufps (v4sf, v4sf, int)
void __builtin_ia32_movntps (float *, v4sf)
int __builtin_ia32_movmskps (v4sf)
```

The following built-in functions are available when '-msse' is used.

`v4sf __builtin_ia32_loadaps (float *)`
: Generates the movaps machine instruction as a load from memory.

`void __builtin_ia32_storeaps (float *, v4sf)`
: Generates the movaps machine instruction as a store to memory.

`v4sf __builtin_ia32_loadups (float *)`
: Generates the movups machine instruction as a load from memory.

`void __builtin_ia32_storeups (float *, v4sf)`
: Generates the movups machine instruction as a store to memory.

`v4sf __builtin_ia32_loadsss (float *)`
: Generates the movss machine instruction as a load from memory.

`void __builtin_ia32_storess (float *, v4sf)`
: Generates the movss machine instruction as a store to memory.

`v4sf __builtin_ia32_loadhps (v4sf, v2si *)`
: Generates the movhps machine instruction as a load from memory.

`v4sf __builtin_ia32_loadlps (v4sf, v2si *)`
: Generates the movlps machine instruction as a load from memory

`void __builtin_ia32_storehps (v4sf, v2si *)`
: Generates the movhps machine instruction as a store to memory.

`void __builtin_ia32_storelps (v4sf, v2si *)`
: Generates the movlps machine instruction as a store to memory.

The following built-in functions are available when '-msse2' is used. All of them generate the machine instruction that is part of the name.

```
int __builtin_ia32_comisdeq (v2df, v2df)
int __builtin_ia32_comisdlt (v2df, v2df)
int __builtin_ia32_comisdle (v2df, v2df)
int __builtin_ia32_comisdgt (v2df, v2df)
int __builtin_ia32_comisdge (v2df, v2df)
int __builtin_ia32_comisdneq (v2df, v2df)
int __builtin_ia32_ucomisdeq (v2df, v2df)
int __builtin_ia32_ucomisdlt (v2df, v2df)
int __builtin_ia32_ucomisdle (v2df, v2df)
int __builtin_ia32_ucomisdgt (v2df, v2df)
int __builtin_ia32_ucomisdge (v2df, v2df)
int __builtin_ia32_ucomisdneq (v2df, v2df)
v2df __builtin_ia32_cmpeqpd (v2df, v2df)
v2df __builtin_ia32_cmpltpd (v2df, v2df)
v2df __builtin_ia32_cmplepd (v2df, v2df)
v2df __builtin_ia32_cmpgtpd (v2df, v2df)
v2df __builtin_ia32_cmpgepd (v2df, v2df)
v2df __builtin_ia32_cmpunordpd (v2df, v2df)
v2df __builtin_ia32_cmpneqpd (v2df, v2df)
```

Chapter 5: Extensions to the C Language Family   443

```
v2df __builtin_ia32_cmpnltpd (v2df, v2df)
v2df __builtin_ia32_cmpnlepd (v2df, v2df)
v2df __builtin_ia32_cmpngtpd (v2df, v2df)
v2df __builtin_ia32_cmpngepd (v2df, v2df)
v2df __builtin_ia32_cmpordpd (v2df, v2df)
v2df __builtin_ia32_cmpeqsd (v2df, v2df)
v2df __builtin_ia32_cmpltsd (v2df, v2df)
v2df __builtin_ia32_cmplesd (v2df, v2df)
v2df __builtin_ia32_cmpunordsd (v2df, v2df)
v2df __builtin_ia32_cmpneqsd (v2df, v2df)
v2df __builtin_ia32_cmpnltsd (v2df, v2df)
v2df __builtin_ia32_cmpnlesd (v2df, v2df)
v2df __builtin_ia32_cmpordsd (v2df, v2df)
v2di __builtin_ia32_paddq (v2di, v2di)
v2di __builtin_ia32_psubq (v2di, v2di)
v2df __builtin_ia32_addpd (v2df, v2df)
v2df __builtin_ia32_subpd (v2df, v2df)
v2df __builtin_ia32_mulpd (v2df, v2df)
v2df __builtin_ia32_divpd (v2df, v2df)
v2df __builtin_ia32_addsd (v2df, v2df)
v2df __builtin_ia32_subsd (v2df, v2df)
v2df __builtin_ia32_mulsd (v2df, v2df)
v2df __builtin_ia32_divsd (v2df, v2df)
v2df __builtin_ia32_minpd (v2df, v2df)
v2df __builtin_ia32_maxpd (v2df, v2df)
v2df __builtin_ia32_minsd (v2df, v2df)
v2df __builtin_ia32_maxsd (v2df, v2df)
v2df __builtin_ia32_andpd (v2df, v2df)
v2df __builtin_ia32_andnpd (v2df, v2df)
v2df __builtin_ia32_orpd (v2df, v2df)
v2df __builtin_ia32_xorpd (v2df, v2df)
v2df __builtin_ia32_movsd (v2df, v2df)
v2df __builtin_ia32_unpckhpd (v2df, v2df)
v2df __builtin_ia32_unpcklpd (v2df, v2df)
v16qi __builtin_ia32_paddb128 (v16qi, v16qi)
v8hi __builtin_ia32_paddw128 (v8hi, v8hi)
v4si __builtin_ia32_paddd128 (v4si, v4si)
v2di __builtin_ia32_paddq128 (v2di, v2di)
v16qi __builtin_ia32_psubb128 (v16qi, v16qi)
v8hi __builtin_ia32_psubw128 (v8hi, v8hi)
v4si __builtin_ia32_psubd128 (v4si, v4si)
v2di __builtin_ia32_psubq128 (v2di, v2di)
v8hi __builtin_ia32_pmullw128 (v8hi, v8hi)
v8hi __builtin_ia32_pmulhw128 (v8hi, v8hi)
v2di __builtin_ia32_pand128 (v2di, v2di)
v2di __builtin_ia32_pandn128 (v2di, v2di)
v2di __builtin_ia32_por128 (v2di, v2di)
v2di __builtin_ia32_pxor128 (v2di, v2di)
v16qi __builtin_ia32_pavgb128 (v16qi, v16qi)
v8hi __builtin_ia32_pavgw128 (v8hi, v8hi)
v16qi __builtin_ia32_pcmpeqb128 (v16qi, v16qi)
v8hi __builtin_ia32_pcmpeqw128 (v8hi, v8hi)
v4si __builtin_ia32_pcmpeqd128 (v4si, v4si)
v16qi __builtin_ia32_pcmpgtb128 (v16qi, v16qi)
v8hi __builtin_ia32_pcmpgtw128 (v8hi, v8hi)
v4si __builtin_ia32_pcmpgtd128 (v4si, v4si)
v16qi __builtin_ia32_pmaxub128 (v16qi, v16qi)
v8hi __builtin_ia32_pmaxsw128 (v8hi, v8hi)
```

```
v16qi __builtin_ia32_pminub128 (v16qi, v16qi)
v8hi  __builtin_ia32_pminsw128 (v8hi, v8hi)
v16qi __builtin_ia32_punpckhbw128 (v16qi, v16qi)
v8hi  __builtin_ia32_punpckhwd128 (v8hi, v8hi)
v4si  __builtin_ia32_punpckhdq128 (v4si, v4si)
v2di  __builtin_ia32_punpckhqdq128 (v2di, v2di)
v16qi __builtin_ia32_punpcklbw128 (v16qi, v16qi)
v8hi  __builtin_ia32_punpcklwd128 (v8hi, v8hi)
v4si  __builtin_ia32_punpckldq128 (v4si, v4si)
v2di  __builtin_ia32_punpcklqdq128 (v2di, v2di)
v16qi __builtin_ia32_packsswb128 (v16qi, v16qi)
v8hi  __builtin_ia32_packssdw128 (v8hi, v8hi)
v16qi __builtin_ia32_packuswb128 (v16qi, v16qi)
v8hi  __builtin_ia32_pmulhuw128 (v8hi, v8hi)
void  __builtin_ia32_maskmovdqu (v16qi, v16qi)
v2df  __builtin_ia32_loadupd (double *)
void  __builtin_ia32_storeupd (double *, v2df)
v2df  __builtin_ia32_loadhpd (v2df, double *)
v2df  __builtin_ia32_loadlpd (v2df, double *)
int   __builtin_ia32_movmskpd (v2df)
int   __builtin_ia32_pmovmskb128 (v16qi)
void  __builtin_ia32_movnti (int *, int)
void  __builtin_ia32_movntpd (double *, v2df)
void  __builtin_ia32_movntdq (v2df *, v2df)
v4si  __builtin_ia32_pshufd (v4si, int)
v8hi  __builtin_ia32_pshuflw (v8hi, int)
v8hi  __builtin_ia32_pshufhw (v8hi, int)
v2di  __builtin_ia32_psadbw128 (v16qi, v16qi)
v2df  __builtin_ia32_sqrtpd (v2df)
v2df  __builtin_ia32_sqrtsd (v2df)
v2df  __builtin_ia32_shufpd (v2df, v2df, int)
v2df  __builtin_ia32_cvtdq2pd (v4si)
v4sf  __builtin_ia32_cvtdq2ps (v4si)
v4si  __builtin_ia32_cvtpd2dq (v2df)
v2si  __builtin_ia32_cvtpd2pi (v2df)
v4sf  __builtin_ia32_cvtpd2ps (v2df)
v4si  __builtin_ia32_cvttpd2dq (v2df)
v2si  __builtin_ia32_cvttpd2pi (v2df)
v2df  __builtin_ia32_cvtpi2pd (v2si)
int   __builtin_ia32_cvtsd2si (v2df)
int   __builtin_ia32_cvttsd2si (v2df)
long long __builtin_ia32_cvtsd2si64 (v2df)
long long __builtin_ia32_cvttsd2si64 (v2df)
v4si  __builtin_ia32_cvtps2dq (v4sf)
v2df  __builtin_ia32_cvtps2pd (v4sf)
v4si  __builtin_ia32_cvttps2dq (v4sf)
v2df  __builtin_ia32_cvtsi2sd (v2df, int)
v2df  __builtin_ia32_cvtsi642sd (v2df, long long)
v4sf  __builtin_ia32_cvtsd2ss (v4sf, v2df)
v2df  __builtin_ia32_cvtss2sd (v2df, v4sf)
void  __builtin_ia32_clflush (const void *)
void  __builtin_ia32_lfence (void)
void  __builtin_ia32_mfence (void)
v16qi __builtin_ia32_loaddqu (const char *)
void  __builtin_ia32_storedqu (char *, v16qi)
unsigned long long __builtin_ia32_pmuludq (v2si, v2si)
v2di  __builtin_ia32_pmuludq128 (v4si, v4si)
v8hi  __builtin_ia32_psllw128 (v8hi, v2di)
```

Chapter 5: Extensions to the C Language Family   445

```
v4si __builtin_ia32_pslld128 (v4si, v2di)
v2di __builtin_ia32_psllq128 (v4si, v2di)
v8hi __builtin_ia32_psrlw128 (v8hi, v2di)
v4si __builtin_ia32_psrld128 (v4si, v2di)
v2di __builtin_ia32_psrlq128 (v2di, v2di)
v8hi __builtin_ia32_psraw128 (v8hi, v2di)
v4si __builtin_ia32_psrad128 (v4si, v2di)
v2di __builtin_ia32_pslldqi128 (v2di, int)
v8hi __builtin_ia32_psllwi128 (v8hi, int)
v4si __builtin_ia32_pslldi128 (v4si, int)
v2di __builtin_ia32_psllqi128 (v2di, int)
v2di __builtin_ia32_psrldqi128 (v2di, int)
v8hi __builtin_ia32_psrlwi128 (v8hi, int)
v4si __builtin_ia32_psrldi128 (v4si, int)
v2di __builtin_ia32_psrlqi128 (v2di, int)
v8hi __builtin_ia32_psrawi128 (v8hi, int)
v4si __builtin_ia32_psradi128 (v4si, int)
v4si __builtin_ia32_pmaddwd128 (v8hi, v8hi)
```

The following built-in functions are available when '-msse3' is used. All of them generate the machine instruction that is part of the name.

```
v2df __builtin_ia32_addsubpd (v2df, v2df)
v4sf __builtin_ia32_addsubps (v4sf, v4sf)
v2df __builtin_ia32_haddpd (v2df, v2df)
v4sf __builtin_ia32_haddps (v4sf, v4sf)
v2df __builtin_ia32_hsubpd (v2df, v2df)
v4sf __builtin_ia32_hsubps (v4sf, v4sf)
v16qi __builtin_ia32_lddqu (char const *)
void __builtin_ia32_monitor (void *, unsigned int, unsigned int)
v2df __builtin_ia32_movddup (v2df)
v4sf __builtin_ia32_movshdup (v4sf)
v4sf __builtin_ia32_movsldup (v4sf)
void __builtin_ia32_mwait (unsigned int, unsigned int)
```

The following built-in functions are available when '-msse3' is used.

`v2df __builtin_ia32_loadddup (double const *)`
    Generates the `movddup` machine instruction as a load from memory.

The following built-in functions are available when '-mssse3' is used. All of them generate the machine instruction that is part of the name with MMX registers.

```
v2si __builtin_ia32_phaddd (v2si, v2si)
v4hi __builtin_ia32_phaddw (v4hi, v4hi)
v4hi __builtin_ia32_phaddsw (v4hi, v4hi)
v2si __builtin_ia32_phsubd (v2si, v2si)
v4hi __builtin_ia32_phsubw (v4hi, v4hi)
v4hi __builtin_ia32_phsubsw (v4hi, v4hi)
v8qi __builtin_ia32_pmaddubsw (v8qi, v8qi)
v4hi __builtin_ia32_pmulhrsw (v4hi, v4hi)
v8qi __builtin_ia32_pshufb (v8qi, v8qi)
v8qi __builtin_ia32_psignb (v8qi, v8qi)
v2si __builtin_ia32_psignd (v2si, v2si)
v4hi __builtin_ia32_psignw (v4hi, v4hi)
long long __builtin_ia32_palignr (long long, long long, int)
v8qi __builtin_ia32_pabsb (v8qi)
v2si __builtin_ia32_pabsd (v2si)
v4hi __builtin_ia32_pabsw (v4hi)
```

The following built-in functions are available when '-mssse3' is used. All of them generate the machine instruction that is part of the name with SSE registers.

```
v4si __builtin_ia32_phaddd128 (v4si, v4si)
v8hi __builtin_ia32_phaddw128 (v8hi, v8hi)
v8hi __builtin_ia32_phaddsw128 (v8hi, v8hi)
v4si __builtin_ia32_phsubd128 (v4si, v4si)
v8hi __builtin_ia32_phsubw128 (v8hi, v8hi)
v8hi __builtin_ia32_phsubsw128 (v8hi, v8hi)
v16qi __builtin_ia32_pmaddubsw128 (v16qi, v16qi)
v8hi __builtin_ia32_pmulhrsw128 (v8hi, v8hi)
v16qi __builtin_ia32_pshufb128 (v16qi, v16qi)
v16qi __builtin_ia32_psignb128 (v16qi, v16qi)
v4si __builtin_ia32_psignd128 (v4si, v4si)
v8hi __builtin_ia32_psignw128 (v8hi, v8hi)
v2di __builtin_ia32_palignr (v2di, v2di, int)
v16qi __builtin_ia32_pabsb128 (v16qi)
v4si __builtin_ia32_pabsd128 (v4si)
v8hi __builtin_ia32_pabsw128 (v8hi)
```

The following built-in functions are available when '-msse4.1' is used. All of them generate the machine instruction that is part of the name.

```
v2df __builtin_ia32_blendpd (v2df, v2df, const int)
v4sf __builtin_ia32_blendps (v4sf, v4sf, const int)
v2df __builtin_ia32_blendvpd (v2df, v2df, v2df)
v4sf __builtin_ia32_blendvps (v4sf, v4sf, v4sf)
v2df __builtin_ia32_dppd (v2df, v2df, const int)
v4sf __builtin_ia32_dpps (v4sf, v4sf, const int)
v4sf __builtin_ia32_insertps128 (v4sf, v4sf, const int)
v2di __builtin_ia32_movntdqa (v2di *);
v16qi __builtin_ia32_mpsadbw128 (v16qi, v16qi, const int)
v8hi __builtin_ia32_packusdw128 (v4si, v4si)
v16qi __builtin_ia32_pblendvb128 (v16qi, v16qi, v16qi)
v8hi __builtin_ia32_pblendw128 (v8hi, v8hi, const int)
v2di __builtin_ia32_pcmpeqq (v2di, v2di)
v8hi __builtin_ia32_phminposuw128 (v8hi)
v16qi __builtin_ia32_pmaxsb128 (v16qi, v16qi)
v4si __builtin_ia32_pmaxsd128 (v4si, v4si)
v4si __builtin_ia32_pmaxud128 (v4si, v4si)
v8hi __builtin_ia32_pmaxuw128 (v8hi, v8hi)
v16qi __builtin_ia32_pminsb128 (v16qi, v16qi)
v4si __builtin_ia32_pminsd128 (v4si, v4si)
v4si __builtin_ia32_pminud128 (v4si, v4si)
v8hi __builtin_ia32_pminuw128 (v8hi, v8hi)
v4si __builtin_ia32_pmovsxbd128 (v16qi)
v2di __builtin_ia32_pmovsxbq128 (v16qi)
v8hi __builtin_ia32_pmovsxbw128 (v16qi)
v2di __builtin_ia32_pmovsxdq128 (v4si)
v4si __builtin_ia32_pmovsxwd128 (v8hi)
v2di __builtin_ia32_pmovsxwq128 (v8hi)
v4si __builtin_ia32_pmovzxbd128 (v16qi)
v2di __builtin_ia32_pmovzxbq128 (v16qi)
v8hi __builtin_ia32_pmovzxbw128 (v16qi)
v2di __builtin_ia32_pmovzxdq128 (v4si)
v4si __builtin_ia32_pmovzxwd128 (v8hi)
v2di __builtin_ia32_pmovzxwq128 (v8hi)
v2di __builtin_ia32_pmuldq128 (v4si, v4si)
v4si __builtin_ia32_pmulld128 (v4si, v4si)
int __builtin_ia32_ptestc128 (v2di, v2di)
```

Chapter 5: Extensions to the C Language Family   447

```
int __builtin_ia32_ptestnzc128 (v2di, v2di)
int __builtin_ia32_ptestz128 (v2di, v2di)
v2df __builtin_ia32_roundpd (v2df, const int)
v4sf __builtin_ia32_roundps (v4sf, const int)
v2df __builtin_ia32_roundsd (v2df, v2df, const int)
v4sf __builtin_ia32_roundss (v4sf, v4sf, const int)
```

The following built-in functions are available when '-msse4.1' is used.

`v4sf __builtin_ia32_vec_set_v4sf (v4sf, float, const int)`
    Generates the `insertps` machine instruction.

`int __builtin_ia32_vec_ext_v16qi (v16qi, const int)`
    Generates the `pextrb` machine instruction.

`v16qi __builtin_ia32_vec_set_v16qi (v16qi, int, const int)`
    Generates the `pinsrb` machine instruction.

`v4si __builtin_ia32_vec_set_v4si (v4si, int, const int)`
    Generates the `pinsrd` machine instruction.

`v2di __builtin_ia32_vec_set_v2di (v2di, long long, const int)`
    Generates the `pinsrq` machine instruction in 64bit mode.

The following built-in functions are changed to generate new SSE4.1 instructions when '-msse4.1' is used.

`float __builtin_ia32_vec_ext_v4sf (v4sf, const int)`
    Generates the `extractps` machine instruction.

`int __builtin_ia32_vec_ext_v4si (v4si, const int)`
    Generates the `pextrd` machine instruction.

`long long __builtin_ia32_vec_ext_v2di (v2di, const int)`
    Generates the `pextrq` machine instruction in 64bit mode.

The following built-in functions are available when '-msse4.2' is used. All of them generate the machine instruction that is part of the name.

```
v16qi __builtin_ia32_pcmpestrm128 (v16qi, int, v16qi, int, const int)
int __builtin_ia32_pcmpestri128 (v16qi, int, v16qi, int, const int)
int __builtin_ia32_pcmpestria128 (v16qi, int, v16qi, int, const int)
int __builtin_ia32_pcmpestric128 (v16qi, int, v16qi, int, const int)
int __builtin_ia32_pcmpestrio128 (v16qi, int, v16qi, int, const int)
int __builtin_ia32_pcmpestris128 (v16qi, int, v16qi, int, const int)
int __builtin_ia32_pcmpestriz128 (v16qi, int, v16qi, int, const int)
v16qi __builtin_ia32_pcmpistrm128 (v16qi, v16qi, const int)
int __builtin_ia32_pcmpistri128 (v16qi, v16qi, const int)
int __builtin_ia32_pcmpistria128 (v16qi, v16qi, const int)
int __builtin_ia32_pcmpistric128 (v16qi, v16qi, const int)
int __builtin_ia32_pcmpistrio128 (v16qi, v16qi, const int)
int __builtin_ia32_pcmpistris128 (v16qi, v16qi, const int)
int __builtin_ia32_pcmpistriz128 (v16qi, v16qi, const int)
v2di __builtin_ia32_pcmpgtq (v2di, v2di)
```

The following built-in functions are available when '-msse4.2' is used.

`unsigned int __builtin_ia32_crc32qi (unsigned int, unsigned char)`
    Generates the `crc32b` machine instruction.

unsigned int __builtin_ia32_crc32hi (unsigned int, unsigned short)
: Generates the crc32w machine instruction.

unsigned int __builtin_ia32_crc32si (unsigned int, unsigned int)
: Generates the crc32l machine instruction.

unsigned long long __builtin_ia32_crc32di (unsigned long long, unsigned long long)

The following built-in functions are changed to generate new SSE4.2 instructions when '-msse4.2' is used.

int __builtin_popcount (unsigned int)
: Generates the popcntl machine instruction.

int __builtin_popcountl (unsigned long)
: Generates the popcntl or popcntq machine instruction, depending on the size of unsigned long.

int __builtin_popcountll (unsigned long long)
: Generates the popcntq machine instruction.

The following built-in functions are available when '-msse4a' is used. All of them generate the machine instruction that is part of the name.

```
void __builtin_ia32_movntsd (double *, v2df)
void __builtin_ia32_movntss (float *, v4sf)
v2di __builtin_ia32_extrq  (v2di, v16qi)
v2di __builtin_ia32_extrqi (v2di, const unsigned int, const unsigned int)
v2di __builtin_ia32_insertq (v2di, v2di)
v2di __builtin_ia32_insertqi (v2di, v2di, const unsigned int, const unsigned int)
```

The following built-in functions are available when '-msse5' is used. All of them generate the machine instruction that is part of the name with MMX registers.

```
v2df __builtin_ia32_comeqpd (v2df, v2df)
v2df __builtin_ia32_comeqps (v2df, v2df)
v4sf __builtin_ia32_comeqsd (v4sf, v4sf)
v4sf __builtin_ia32_comeqss (v4sf, v4sf)
v2df __builtin_ia32_comfalsepd (v2df, v2df)
v2df __builtin_ia32_comfalseps (v2df, v2df)
v4sf __builtin_ia32_comfalsesd (v4sf, v4sf)
v4sf __builtin_ia32_comfalsess (v4sf, v4sf)
v2df __builtin_ia32_comgepd (v2df, v2df)
v2df __builtin_ia32_comgeps (v2df, v2df)
v4sf __builtin_ia32_comgesd (v4sf, v4sf)
v4sf __builtin_ia32_comgess (v4sf, v4sf)
v2df __builtin_ia32_comgtpd (v2df, v2df)
v2df __builtin_ia32_comgtps (v2df, v2df)
v4sf __builtin_ia32_comgtsd (v4sf, v4sf)
v4sf __builtin_ia32_comgtss (v4sf, v4sf)
v2df __builtin_ia32_comlepd (v2df, v2df)
v2df __builtin_ia32_comleps (v2df, v2df)
v4sf __builtin_ia32_comlesd (v4sf, v4sf)
v4sf __builtin_ia32_comless (v4sf, v4sf)
v2df __builtin_ia32_comltpd (v2df, v2df)
v2df __builtin_ia32_comltps (v2df, v2df)
v4sf __builtin_ia32_comltsd (v4sf, v4sf)
v4sf __builtin_ia32_comltss (v4sf, v4sf)
v2df __builtin_ia32_comnepd (v2df, v2df)
```

Chapter 5: Extensions to the C Language Family   449

```
v2df __builtin_ia32_comneps (v2df, v2df)
v4sf __builtin_ia32_comnesd (v4sf, v4sf)
v4sf __builtin_ia32_comness (v4sf, v4sf)
v2df __builtin_ia32_comordpd (v2df, v2df)
v2df __builtin_ia32_comordps (v2df, v2df)
v4sf __builtin_ia32_comordsd (v4sf, v4sf)
v4sf __builtin_ia32_comordss (v4sf, v4sf)
v2df __builtin_ia32_comtruepd (v2df, v2df)
v2df __builtin_ia32_comtrueps (v2df, v2df)
v4sf __builtin_ia32_comtruesd (v4sf, v4sf)
v4sf __builtin_ia32_comtruess (v4sf, v4sf)
v2df __builtin_ia32_comueqpd (v2df, v2df)
v2df __builtin_ia32_comueqps (v2df, v2df)
v4sf __builtin_ia32_comueqsd (v4sf, v4sf)
v4sf __builtin_ia32_comueqss (v4sf, v4sf)
v2df __builtin_ia32_comugepd (v2df, v2df)
v2df __builtin_ia32_comugeps (v2df, v2df)
v4sf __builtin_ia32_comugesd (v4sf, v4sf)
v4sf __builtin_ia32_comugess (v4sf, v4sf)
v2df __builtin_ia32_comugtpd (v2df, v2df)
v2df __builtin_ia32_comugtps (v2df, v2df)
v4sf __builtin_ia32_comugtsd (v4sf, v4sf)
v4sf __builtin_ia32_comugtss (v4sf, v4sf)
v2df __builtin_ia32_comulepd (v2df, v2df)
v2df __builtin_ia32_comuleps (v2df, v2df)
v4sf __builtin_ia32_comulesd (v4sf, v4sf)
v4sf __builtin_ia32_comuless (v4sf, v4sf)
v2df __builtin_ia32_comultpd (v2df, v2df)
v2df __builtin_ia32_comultps (v2df, v2df)
v4sf __builtin_ia32_comultsd (v4sf, v4sf)
v4sf __builtin_ia32_comultss (v4sf, v4sf)
v2df __builtin_ia32_comunepd (v2df, v2df)
v2df __builtin_ia32_comuneps (v2df, v2df)
v4sf __builtin_ia32_comunesd (v4sf, v4sf)
v4sf __builtin_ia32_comuness (v4sf, v4sf)
v2df __builtin_ia32_comunordpd (v2df, v2df)
v2df __builtin_ia32_comunordps (v2df, v2df)
v4sf __builtin_ia32_comunordsd (v4sf, v4sf)
v4sf __builtin_ia32_comunordss (v4sf, v4sf)
v2df __builtin_ia32_fmaddpd (v2df, v2df, v2df)
v4sf __builtin_ia32_fmaddps (v4sf, v4sf, v4sf)
v2df __builtin_ia32_fmaddsd (v2df, v2df, v2df)
v4sf __builtin_ia32_fmaddss (v4sf, v4sf, v4sf)
v2df __builtin_ia32_fmsubpd (v2df, v2df, v2df)
v4sf __builtin_ia32_fmsubps (v4sf, v4sf, v4sf)
v2df __builtin_ia32_fmsubsd (v2df, v2df, v2df)
v4sf __builtin_ia32_fmsubss (v4sf, v4sf, v4sf)
v2df __builtin_ia32_fnmaddpd (v2df, v2df, v2df)
v4sf __builtin_ia32_fnmaddps (v4sf, v4sf, v4sf)
v2df __builtin_ia32_fnmaddsd (v2df, v2df, v2df)
v4sf __builtin_ia32_fnmaddss (v4sf, v4sf, v4sf)
v2df __builtin_ia32_fnmsubpd (v2df, v2df, v2df)
v4sf __builtin_ia32_fnmsubps (v4sf, v4sf, v4sf)
v2df __builtin_ia32_fnmsubsd (v2df, v2df, v2df)
v4sf __builtin_ia32_fnmsubss (v4sf, v4sf, v4sf)
v2df __builtin_ia32_frczpd (v2df)
v4sf __builtin_ia32_frczps (v4sf)
v2df __builtin_ia32_frczsd (v2df, v2df)
```

```
v4sf __builtin_ia32_frczss (v4sf, v4sf)
v2di __builtin_ia32_pcmov (v2di, v2di, v2di)
v2di __builtin_ia32_pcmov_v2di (v2di, v2di, v2di)
v4si __builtin_ia32_pcmov_v4si (v4si, v4si, v4si)
v8hi __builtin_ia32_pcmov_v8hi (v8hi, v8hi, v8hi)
v16qi __builtin_ia32_pcmov_v16qi (v16qi, v16qi, v16qi)
v2df __builtin_ia32_pcmov_v2df (v2df, v2df, v2df)
v4sf __builtin_ia32_pcmov_v4sf (v4sf, v4sf, v4sf)
v16qi __builtin_ia32_pcomeqb (v16qi, v16qi)
v8hi __builtin_ia32_pcomeqw (v8hi, v8hi)
v4si __builtin_ia32_pcomeqd (v4si, v4si)
v2di __builtin_ia32_pcomeqq (v2di, v2di)
v16qi __builtin_ia32_pcomequb (v16qi, v16qi)
v4si __builtin_ia32_pcomequd (v4si, v4si)
v2di __builtin_ia32_pcomequq (v2di, v2di)
v8hi __builtin_ia32_pcomequw (v8hi, v8hi)
v8hi __builtin_ia32_pcomeqw (v8hi, v8hi)
v16qi __builtin_ia32_pcomfalseb (v16qi, v16qi)
v4si __builtin_ia32_pcomfalsed (v4si, v4si)
v2di __builtin_ia32_pcomfalseq (v2di, v2di)
v16qi __builtin_ia32_pcomfalseub (v16qi, v16qi)
v4si __builtin_ia32_pcomfalseud (v4si, v4si)
v2di __builtin_ia32_pcomfalseuq (v2di, v2di)
v8hi __builtin_ia32_pcomfalseuw (v8hi, v8hi)
v8hi __builtin_ia32_pcomfalsew (v8hi, v8hi)
v16qi __builtin_ia32_pcomgeb (v16qi, v16qi)
v4si __builtin_ia32_pcomged (v4si, v4si)
v2di __builtin_ia32_pcomgeq (v2di, v2di)
v16qi __builtin_ia32_pcomgeub (v16qi, v16qi)
v4si __builtin_ia32_pcomgeud (v4si, v4si)
v2di __builtin_ia32_pcomgeuq (v2di, v2di)
v8hi __builtin_ia32_pcomgeuw (v8hi, v8hi)
v8hi __builtin_ia32_pcomgew (v8hi, v8hi)
v16qi __builtin_ia32_pcomgtb (v16qi, v16qi)
v4si __builtin_ia32_pcomgtd (v4si, v4si)
v2di __builtin_ia32_pcomgtq (v2di, v2di)
v16qi __builtin_ia32_pcomgtub (v16qi, v16qi)
v4si __builtin_ia32_pcomgtud (v4si, v4si)
v2di __builtin_ia32_pcomgtuq (v2di, v2di)
v8hi __builtin_ia32_pcomgtuw (v8hi, v8hi)
v8hi __builtin_ia32_pcomgtw (v8hi, v8hi)
v16qi __builtin_ia32_pcomleb (v16qi, v16qi)
v4si __builtin_ia32_pcomled (v4si, v4si)
v2di __builtin_ia32_pcomleq (v2di, v2di)
v16qi __builtin_ia32_pcomleub (v16qi, v16qi)
v4si __builtin_ia32_pcomleud (v4si, v4si)
v2di __builtin_ia32_pcomleuq (v2di, v2di)
v8hi __builtin_ia32_pcomleuw (v8hi, v8hi)
v8hi __builtin_ia32_pcomlew (v8hi, v8hi)
v16qi __builtin_ia32_pcomltb (v16qi, v16qi)
v4si __builtin_ia32_pcomltd (v4si, v4si)
v2di __builtin_ia32_pcomltq (v2di, v2di)
v16qi __builtin_ia32_pcomltub (v16qi, v16qi)
v4si __builtin_ia32_pcomltud (v4si, v4si)
v2di __builtin_ia32_pcomltuq (v2di, v2di)
v8hi __builtin_ia32_pcomltuw (v8hi, v8hi)
v8hi __builtin_ia32_pcomltw (v8hi, v8hi)
v16qi __builtin_ia32_pcomneb (v16qi, v16qi)
```

Chapter 5: Extensions to the C Language Family

```
v4si __builtin_ia32_pcomned (v4si, v4si)
v2di __builtin_ia32_pcomneq (v2di, v2di)
v16qi __builtin_ia32_pcomneub (v16qi, v16qi)
v4si __builtin_ia32_pcomneud (v4si, v4si)
v2di __builtin_ia32_pcomneuq (v2di, v2di)
v8hi __builtin_ia32_pcomneuw (v8hi, v8hi)
v8hi __builtin_ia32_pcomnew (v8hi, v8hi)
v16qi __builtin_ia32_pcomtrueb (v16qi, v16qi)
v4si __builtin_ia32_pcomtrued (v4si, v4si)
v2di __builtin_ia32_pcomtrueq (v2di, v2di)
v16qi __builtin_ia32_pcomtrueub (v16qi, v16qi)
v4si __builtin_ia32_pcomtrueud (v4si, v4si)
v2di __builtin_ia32_pcomtrueuq (v2di, v2di)
v8hi __builtin_ia32_pcomtrueuw (v8hi, v8hi)
v8hi __builtin_ia32_pcomtruew (v8hi, v8hi)
v4df __builtin_ia32_permpd (v2df, v2df, v16qi)
v4sf __builtin_ia32_permps (v4sf, v4sf, v16qi)
v4si __builtin_ia32_phaddbd (v16qi)
v2di __builtin_ia32_phaddbq (v16qi)
v8hi __builtin_ia32_phaddbw (v16qi)
v2di __builtin_ia32_phadddq (v4si)
v4si __builtin_ia32_phaddubd (v16qi)
v2di __builtin_ia32_phaddubq (v16qi)
v8hi __builtin_ia32_phaddubw (v16qi)
v2di __builtin_ia32_phaddudq (v4si)
v4si __builtin_ia32_phadduwd (v8hi)
v2di __builtin_ia32_phadduwq (v8hi)
v4si __builtin_ia32_phaddwd (v8hi)
v2di __builtin_ia32_phaddwq (v8hi)
v8hi __builtin_ia32_phsubbw (v16qi)
v2di __builtin_ia32_phsubdq (v4si)
v4si __builtin_ia32_phsubwd (v8hi)
v4si __builtin_ia32_pmacsdd (v4si, v4si, v4si)
v2di __builtin_ia32_pmacsdqh (v4si, v4si, v2di)
v2di __builtin_ia32_pmacsdql (v4si, v4si, v2di)
v4si __builtin_ia32_pmacssdd (v4si, v4si, v4si)
v2di __builtin_ia32_pmacssdqh (v4si, v4si, v2di)
v2di __builtin_ia32_pmacssdql (v4si, v4si, v2di)
v4si __builtin_ia32_pmacsswd (v8hi, v8hi, v4si)
v8hi __builtin_ia32_pmacssww (v8hi, v8hi, v8hi)
v4si __builtin_ia32_pmacswd (v8hi, v8hi, v4si)
v8hi __builtin_ia32_pmacsww (v8hi, v8hi, v8hi)
v4si __builtin_ia32_pmadcsswd (v8hi, v8hi, v4si)
v4si __builtin_ia32_pmadcswd (v8hi, v8hi, v4si)
v16qi __builtin_ia32_pperm (v16qi, v16qi, v16qi)
v16qi __builtin_ia32_protb (v16qi, v16qi)
v4si __builtin_ia32_protd (v4si, v4si)
v2di __builtin_ia32_protq (v2di, v2di)
v8hi __builtin_ia32_protw (v8hi, v8hi)
v16qi __builtin_ia32_pshab (v16qi, v16qi)
v4si __builtin_ia32_pshad (v4si, v4si)
v2di __builtin_ia32_pshaq (v2di, v2di)
v8hi __builtin_ia32_pshaw (v8hi, v8hi)
v16qi __builtin_ia32_pshlb (v16qi, v16qi)
v4si __builtin_ia32_pshld (v4si, v4si)
v2di __builtin_ia32_pshlq (v2di, v2di)
v8hi __builtin_ia32_pshlw (v8hi, v8hi)
```

The following builtin-in functions are available when '`-msse5`' is used. The second argument must be an integer constant and generate the machine instruction that is part of the name with the '`_imm`' suffix removed.

```
v16qi __builtin_ia32_protb_imm (v16qi, int)
v4si  __builtin_ia32_protd_imm (v4si, int)
v2di  __builtin_ia32_protq_imm (v2di, int)
v8hi  __builtin_ia32_protw_imm (v8hi, int)
```

The following built-in functions are available when '`-m3dnow`' is used. All of them generate the machine instruction that is part of the name.

```
void __builtin_ia32_femms (void)
v8qi __builtin_ia32_pavgusb (v8qi, v8qi)
v2si __builtin_ia32_pf2id (v2sf)
v2sf __builtin_ia32_pfacc (v2sf, v2sf)
v2sf __builtin_ia32_pfadd (v2sf, v2sf)
v2si __builtin_ia32_pfcmpeq (v2sf, v2sf)
v2si __builtin_ia32_pfcmpge (v2sf, v2sf)
v2si __builtin_ia32_pfcmpgt (v2sf, v2sf)
v2sf __builtin_ia32_pfmax (v2sf, v2sf)
v2sf __builtin_ia32_pfmin (v2sf, v2sf)
v2sf __builtin_ia32_pfmul (v2sf, v2sf)
v2sf __builtin_ia32_pfrcp (v2sf)
v2sf __builtin_ia32_pfrcpit1 (v2sf, v2sf)
v2sf __builtin_ia32_pfrcpit2 (v2sf, v2sf)
v2sf __builtin_ia32_pfrsqrt (v2sf)
v2sf __builtin_ia32_pfrsqrtit1 (v2sf, v2sf)
v2sf __builtin_ia32_pfsub (v2sf, v2sf)
v2sf __builtin_ia32_pfsubr (v2sf, v2sf)
v2sf __builtin_ia32_pi2fd (v2si)
v4hi __builtin_ia32_pmulhrw (v4hi, v4hi)
```

The following built-in functions are available when both '`-m3dnow`' and '`-march=athlon`' are used. All of them generate the machine instruction that is part of the name.

```
v2si __builtin_ia32_pf2iw (v2sf)
v2sf __builtin_ia32_pfnacc (v2sf, v2sf)
v2sf __builtin_ia32_pfpnacc (v2sf, v2sf)
v2sf __builtin_ia32_pi2fw (v2si)
v2sf __builtin_ia32_pswapdsf (v2sf)
v2si __builtin_ia32_pswapdsi (v2si)
```

5.50.7 MIPS DSP Built-in Functions

The MIPS DSP Application-Specific Extension (ASE) includes new instructions that are designed to improve the performance of DSP and media applications. It provides instructions that operate on packed 8-bit/16-bit integer data, Q7, Q15 and Q31 fractional data.

GCC supports MIPS DSP operations using both the generic vector extensions (see Section 5.45 [Vector Extensions], page 332) and a collection of MIPS-specific built-in functions. Both kinds of support are enabled by the '`-mdsp`' command-line option.

Revision 2 of the ASE was introduced in the second half of 2006. This revision adds extra instructions to the original ASE, but is otherwise backwards-compatible with it. You can select revision 2 using the command-line option '`-mdspr2`'; this option implies '`-mdsp`'.

At present, GCC only provides support for operations on 32-bit vectors. The vector type associated with 8-bit integer data is usually called `v4i8`, the vector type associated with Q7 is usually called `v4q7`, the vector type associated with 16-bit integer data is usually

Chapter 5: Extensions to the C Language Family   453

called v2i16, and the vector type associated with Q15 is usually called v2q15. They can be defined in C as follows:

```
typedef signed char v4i8 __attribute__ ((vector_size(4)));
typedef signed char v4q7 __attribute__ ((vector_size(4)));
typedef short v2i16 __attribute__ ((vector_size(4)));
typedef short v2q15 __attribute__ ((vector_size(4)));
```

v4i8, v4q7, v2i16 and v2q15 values are initialized in the same way as aggregates. For example:

```
v4i8 a = {1, 2, 3, 4};
v4i8 b;
b = (v4i8) {5, 6, 7, 8};

v2q15 c = {0x0fcb, 0x3a75};
v2q15 d;
d = (v2q15) {0.1234 * 0x1.0p15, 0.4567 * 0x1.0p15};
```

Note: The CPU's endianness determines the order in which values are packed. On little-endian targets, the first value is the least significant and the last value is the most significant. The opposite order applies to big-endian targets. For example, the code above will set the lowest byte of a to 1 on little-endian targets and 4 on big-endian targets.

Note: Q7, Q15 and Q31 values must be initialized with their integer representation. As shown in this example, the integer representation of a Q7 value can be obtained by multiplying the fractional value by 0x1.0p7. The equivalent for Q15 values is to multiply by 0x1.0p15. The equivalent for Q31 values is to multiply by 0x1.0p31.

The table below lists the v4i8 and v2q15 operations for which hardware support exists. a and b are v4i8 values, and c and d are v2q15 values.

C code	MIPS instruction
a + b	addu.qb
c + d	addq.ph
a - b	subu.qb
c - d	subq.ph

The table below lists the v2i16 operation for which hardware support exists for the DSP ASE REV 2. e and f are v2i16 values.

C code	MIPS instruction
e * f	mul.ph

It is easier to describe the DSP built-in functions if we first define the following types:

```
typedef int q31;
typedef int i32;
typedef unsigned int ui32;
typedef long long a64;
```

q31 and i32 are actually the same as int, but we use q31 to indicate a Q31 fractional value and i32 to indicate a 32-bit integer value. Similarly, a64 is the same as long long, but we use a64 to indicate values that will be placed in one of the four DSP accumulators ($ac0, $ac1, $ac2 or $ac3).

Also, some built-in functions prefer or require immediate numbers as parameters, because the corresponding DSP instructions accept both immediate numbers and register operands, or accept immediate numbers only. The immediate parameters are listed as follows.

```
imm0_3: 0 to 3.
imm0_7: 0 to 7.
imm0_15: 0 to 15.
imm0_31: 0 to 31.
imm0_63: 0 to 63.
imm0_255: 0 to 255.
imm_n32_31: -32 to 31.
imm_n512_511: -512 to 511.
```

The following built-in functions map directly to a particular MIPS DSP instruction. Please refer to the architecture specification for details on what each instruction does.

```
v2q15 __builtin_mips_addq_ph (v2q15, v2q15)
v2q15 __builtin_mips_addq_s_ph (v2q15, v2q15)
q31 __builtin_mips_addq_s_w (q31, q31)
v4i8 __builtin_mips_addu_qb (v4i8, v4i8)
v4i8 __builtin_mips_addu_s_qb (v4i8, v4i8)
v2q15 __builtin_mips_subq_ph (v2q15, v2q15)
v2q15 __builtin_mips_subq_s_ph (v2q15, v2q15)
q31 __builtin_mips_subq_s_w (q31, q31)
v4i8 __builtin_mips_subu_qb (v4i8, v4i8)
v4i8 __builtin_mips_subu_s_qb (v4i8, v4i8)
i32 __builtin_mips_addsc (i32, i32)
i32 __builtin_mips_addwc (i32, i32)
i32 __builtin_mips_modsub (i32, i32)
i32 __builtin_mips_raddu_w_qb (v4i8)
v2q15 __builtin_mips_absq_s_ph (v2q15)
q31 __builtin_mips_absq_s_w (q31)
v4i8 __builtin_mips_precrq_qb_ph (v2q15, v2q15)
v2q15 __builtin_mips_precrq_ph_w (q31, q31)
v2q15 __builtin_mips_precrq_rs_ph_w (q31, q31)
v4i8 __builtin_mips_precrqu_s_qb_ph (v2q15, v2q15)
q31 __builtin_mips_preceq_w_phl (v2q15)
q31 __builtin_mips_preceq_w_phr (v2q15)
v2q15 __builtin_mips_precequ_ph_qbl (v4i8)
v2q15 __builtin_mips_precequ_ph_qbr (v4i8)
v2q15 __builtin_mips_precequ_ph_qbla (v4i8)
v2q15 __builtin_mips_precequ_ph_qbra (v4i8)
v2q15 __builtin_mips_preceu_ph_qbl (v4i8)
v2q15 __builtin_mips_preceu_ph_qbr (v4i8)
v2q15 __builtin_mips_preceu_ph_qbla (v4i8)
v2q15 __builtin_mips_preceu_ph_qbra (v4i8)
v4i8 __builtin_mips_shll_qb (v4i8, imm0_7)
v4i8 __builtin_mips_shll_qb (v4i8, i32)
v2q15 __builtin_mips_shll_ph (v2q15, imm0_15)
v2q15 __builtin_mips_shll_ph (v2q15, i32)
v2q15 __builtin_mips_shll_s_ph (v2q15, imm0_15)
v2q15 __builtin_mips_shll_s_ph (v2q15, i32)
q31 __builtin_mips_shll_s_w (q31, imm0_31)
q31 __builtin_mips_shll_s_w (q31, i32)
v4i8 __builtin_mips_shrl_qb (v4i8, imm0_7)
v4i8 __builtin_mips_shrl_qb (v4i8, i32)
v2q15 __builtin_mips_shra_ph (v2q15, imm0_15)
v2q15 __builtin_mips_shra_ph (v2q15, i32)
v2q15 __builtin_mips_shra_r_ph (v2q15, imm0_15)
v2q15 __builtin_mips_shra_r_ph (v2q15, i32)
q31 __builtin_mips_shra_r_w (q31, imm0_31)
q31 __builtin_mips_shra_r_w (q31, i32)
v2q15 __builtin_mips_muleu_s_ph_qbl (v4i8, v2q15)
```

Chapter 5: Extensions to the C Language Family   455

```
v2q15 __builtin_mips_muleu_s_ph_qbr (v4i8, v2q15)
v2q15 __builtin_mips_mulq_rs_ph (v2q15, v2q15)
q31 __builtin_mips_muleq_s_w_phl (v2q15, v2q15)
q31 __builtin_mips_muleq_s_w_phr (v2q15, v2q15)
a64 __builtin_mips_dpau_h_qbl (a64, v4i8, v4i8)
a64 __builtin_mips_dpau_h_qbr (a64, v4i8, v4i8)
a64 __builtin_mips_dpsu_h_qbl (a64, v4i8, v4i8)
a64 __builtin_mips_dpsu_h_qbr (a64, v4i8, v4i8)
a64 __builtin_mips_dpaq_s_w_ph (a64, v2q15, v2q15)
a64 __builtin_mips_dpaq_sa_l_w (a64, q31, q31)
a64 __builtin_mips_dpsq_s_w_ph (a64, v2q15, v2q15)
a64 __builtin_mips_dpsq_sa_l_w (a64, q31, q31)
a64 __builtin_mips_mulsaq_s_w_ph (a64, v2q15, v2q15)
a64 __builtin_mips_maq_s_w_phl (a64, v2q15, v2q15)
a64 __builtin_mips_maq_s_w_phr (a64, v2q15, v2q15)
a64 __builtin_mips_maq_sa_w_phl (a64, v2q15, v2q15)
a64 __builtin_mips_maq_sa_w_phr (a64, v2q15, v2q15)
i32 __builtin_mips_bitrev (i32)
i32 __builtin_mips_insv (i32, i32)
v4i8 __builtin_mips_repl_qb (imm0_255)
v4i8 __builtin_mips_repl_qb (i32)
v2q15 __builtin_mips_repl_ph (imm_n512_511)
v2q15 __builtin_mips_repl_ph (i32)
void __builtin_mips_cmpu_eq_qb (v4i8, v4i8)
void __builtin_mips_cmpu_lt_qb (v4i8, v4i8)
void __builtin_mips_cmpu_le_qb (v4i8, v4i8)
i32 __builtin_mips_cmpgu_eq_qb (v4i8, v4i8)
i32 __builtin_mips_cmpgu_lt_qb (v4i8, v4i8)
i32 __builtin_mips_cmpgu_le_qb (v4i8, v4i8)
void __builtin_mips_cmp_eq_ph (v2q15, v2q15)
void __builtin_mips_cmp_lt_ph (v2q15, v2q15)
void __builtin_mips_cmp_le_ph (v2q15, v2q15)
v4i8 __builtin_mips_pick_qb (v4i8, v4i8)
v2q15 __builtin_mips_pick_ph (v2q15, v2q15)
v2q15 __builtin_mips_packrl_ph (v2q15, v2q15)
i32 __builtin_mips_extr_w (a64, imm0_31)
i32 __builtin_mips_extr_w (a64, i32)
i32 __builtin_mips_extr_r_w (a64, imm0_31)
i32 __builtin_mips_extr_s_h (a64, i32)
i32 __builtin_mips_extr_rs_w (a64, imm0_31)
i32 __builtin_mips_extr_rs_w (a64, i32)
i32 __builtin_mips_extr_s_h (a64, imm0_31)
i32 __builtin_mips_extr_r_w (a64, i32)
i32 __builtin_mips_extp (a64, imm0_31)
i32 __builtin_mips_extp (a64, i32)
i32 __builtin_mips_extpdp (a64, imm0_31)
i32 __builtin_mips_extpdp (a64, i32)
a64 __builtin_mips_shilo (a64, imm_n32_31)
a64 __builtin_mips_shilo (a64, i32)
a64 __builtin_mips_mthlip (a64, i32)
void __builtin_mips_wrdsp (i32, imm0_63)
i32 __builtin_mips_rddsp (imm0_63)
i32 __builtin_mips_lbux (void *, i32)
i32 __builtin_mips_lhx (void *, i32)
i32 __builtin_mips_lwx (void *, i32)
i32 __builtin_mips_bposge32 (void)
```

The following built-in functions map directly to a particular MIPS DSP REV 2 instruction. Please refer to the architecture specification for details on what each instruction does.

```
v4q7   __builtin_mips_absq_s_qb (v4q7);
v2i16  __builtin_mips_addu_ph (v2i16, v2i16);
v2i16  __builtin_mips_addu_s_ph (v2i16, v2i16);
v4i8   __builtin_mips_adduh_qb (v4i8, v4i8);
v4i8   __builtin_mips_adduh_r_qb (v4i8, v4i8);
i32    __builtin_mips_append (i32, i32, imm0_31);
i32    __builtin_mips_balign (i32, i32, imm0_3);
i32    __builtin_mips_cmpgdu_eq_qb (v4i8, v4i8);
i32    __builtin_mips_cmpgdu_lt_qb (v4i8, v4i8);
i32    __builtin_mips_cmpgdu_le_qb (v4i8, v4i8);
a64    __builtin_mips_dpa_w_ph (a64, v2i16, v2i16);
a64    __builtin_mips_dps_w_ph (a64, v2i16, v2i16);
a64    __builtin_mips_madd (a64, i32, i32);
a64    __builtin_mips_maddu (a64, ui32, ui32);
a64    __builtin_mips_msub (a64, i32, i32);
a64    __builtin_mips_msubu (a64, ui32, ui32);
v2i16  __builtin_mips_mul_ph (v2i16, v2i16);
v2i16  __builtin_mips_mul_s_ph (v2i16, v2i16);
q31    __builtin_mips_mulq_rs_w (q31, q31);
v2q15  __builtin_mips_mulq_s_ph (v2q15, v2q15);
q31    __builtin_mips_mulq_s_w (q31, q31);
a64    __builtin_mips_mulsa_w_ph (a64, v2i16, v2i16);
a64    __builtin_mips_mult (i32, i32);
a64    __builtin_mips_multu (ui32, ui32);
v4i8   __builtin_mips_precr_qb_ph (v2i16, v2i16);
v2i16  __builtin_mips_precr_sra_ph_w (i32, i32, imm0_31);
v2i16  __builtin_mips_precr_sra_r_ph_w (i32, i32, imm0_31);
i32    __builtin_mips_prepend (i32, i32, imm0_31);
v4i8   __builtin_mips_shra_qb (v4i8, imm0_7);
v4i8   __builtin_mips_shra_r_qb (v4i8, imm0_7);
v4i8   __builtin_mips_shra_qb (v4i8, i32);
v4i8   __builtin_mips_shra_r_qb (v4i8, i32);
v2i16  __builtin_mips_shrl_ph (v2i16, imm0_15);
v2i16  __builtin_mips_shrl_ph (v2i16, i32);
v2i16  __builtin_mips_subu_ph (v2i16, v2i16);
v2i16  __builtin_mips_subu_s_ph (v2i16, v2i16);
v4i8   __builtin_mips_subuh_qb (v4i8, v4i8);
v4i8   __builtin_mips_subuh_r_qb (v4i8, v4i8);
v2q15  __builtin_mips_addqh_ph (v2q15, v2q15);
v2q15  __builtin_mips_addqh_r_ph (v2q15, v2q15);
q31    __builtin_mips_addqh_w (q31, q31);
q31    __builtin_mips_addqh_r_w (q31, q31);
v2q15  __builtin_mips_subqh_ph (v2q15, v2q15);
v2q15  __builtin_mips_subqh_r_ph (v2q15, v2q15);
q31    __builtin_mips_subqh_w (q31, q31);
q31    __builtin_mips_subqh_r_w (q31, q31);
a64    __builtin_mips_dpax_w_ph (a64, v2i16, v2i16);
a64    __builtin_mips_dpsx_w_ph (a64, v2i16, v2i16);
a64    __builtin_mips_dpaqx_s_w_ph (a64, v2q15, v2q15);
a64    __builtin_mips_dpaqx_sa_w_ph (a64, v2q15, v2q15);
a64    __builtin_mips_dpsqx_s_w_ph (a64, v2q15, v2q15);
a64    __builtin_mips_dpsqx_sa_w_ph (a64, v2q15, v2q15);
```

5.50.8 MIPS Paired-Single Support

The MIPS64 architecture includes a number of instructions that operate on pairs of single-precision floating-point values. Each pair is packed into a 64-bit floating-point register, with

Chapter 5: Extensions to the C Language Family   457

one element being designated the "upper half" and the other being designated the "lower half".

GCC supports paired-single operations using both the generic vector extensions (see Section 5.45 [Vector Extensions], page 332) and a collection of MIPS-specific built-in functions. Both kinds of support are enabled by the '-mpaired-single' command-line option.

The vector type associated with paired-single values is usually called **v2sf**. It can be defined in C as follows:

```
typedef float v2sf __attribute__ ((vector_size (8)));
```

v2sf values are initialized in the same way as aggregates. For example:

```
v2sf a = {1.5, 9.1};
v2sf b;
float e, f;
b = (v2sf) {e, f};
```

Note: The CPU's endianness determines which value is stored in the upper half of a register and which value is stored in the lower half. On little-endian targets, the first value is the lower one and the second value is the upper one. The opposite order applies to big-endian targets. For example, the code above will set the lower half of **a** to **1.5** on little-endian targets and **9.1** on big-endian targets.

5.50.8.1 Paired-Single Arithmetic

The table below lists the **v2sf** operations for which hardware support exists. **a**, **b** and **c** are **v2sf** values and **x** is an integral value.

C code	MIPS instruction
a + b	add.ps
a - b	sub.ps
-a	neg.ps
a * b	mul.ps
a * b + c	madd.ps
a * b - c	msub.ps
-(a * b + c)	nmadd.ps
-(a * b - c)	nmsub.ps
x ? a : b	movn.ps/movz.ps

Note that the multiply-accumulate instructions can be disabled using the command-line option -mno-fused-madd.

5.50.8.2 Paired-Single Built-in Functions

The following paired-single functions map directly to a particular MIPS instruction. Please refer to the architecture specification for details on what each instruction does.

v2sf __builtin_mips_pll_ps (v2sf, v2sf)
        Pair lower lower (pll.ps).

v2sf __builtin_mips_pul_ps (v2sf, v2sf)
        Pair upper lower (pul.ps).

v2sf __builtin_mips_plu_ps (v2sf, v2sf)
        Pair lower upper (plu.ps).

`v2sf __builtin_mips_puu_ps (v2sf, v2sf)`
> Pair upper upper (`puu.ps`).

`v2sf __builtin_mips_cvt_ps_s (float, float)`
> Convert pair to paired single (`cvt.ps.s`).

`float __builtin_mips_cvt_s_pl (v2sf)`
> Convert pair lower to single (`cvt.s.pl`).

`float __builtin_mips_cvt_s_pu (v2sf)`
> Convert pair upper to single (`cvt.s.pu`).

`v2sf __builtin_mips_abs_ps (v2sf)`
> Absolute value (`abs.ps`).

`v2sf __builtin_mips_alnv_ps (v2sf, v2sf, int)`
> Align variable (`alnv.ps`).
>
> *Note:* The value of the third parameter must be 0 or 4 modulo 8, otherwise the result will be unpredictable. Please read the instruction description for details.

The following multi-instruction functions are also available. In each case, *cond* can be any of the 16 floating-point conditions: `f`, `un`, `eq`, `ueq`, `olt`, `ult`, `ole`, `ule`, `sf`, `ngle`, `seq`, `ngl`, `lt`, `nge`, `le` or `ngt`.

`v2sf __builtin_mips_movt_c_`*cond*`_ps (v2sf a, v2sf b, v2sf c, v2sf d)`
`v2sf __builtin_mips_movf_c_`*cond*`_ps (v2sf a, v2sf b, v2sf c, v2sf d)`
> Conditional move based on floating point comparison (`c.`*cond*`.ps`, `movt.ps`/`movf.ps`).
>
> The `movt` functions return the value *x* computed by:
>> `c.`*cond*`.ps cc,a,b`
>> `mov.ps x,c`
>> `movt.ps x,d,cc`
>
> The `movf` functions are similar but use `movf.ps` instead of `movt.ps`.

`int __builtin_mips_upper_c_`*cond*`_ps (v2sf a, v2sf b)`
`int __builtin_mips_lower_c_`*cond*`_ps (v2sf a, v2sf b)`
> Comparison of two paired-single values (`c.`*cond*`.ps`, `bc1t`/`bc1f`).
>
> These functions compare *a* and *b* using `c.`*cond*`.ps` and return either the upper or lower half of the result. For example:
>> ```
>> v2sf a, b;
>> if (__builtin_mips_upper_c_eq_ps (a, b))
>>   upper_halves_are_equal ();
>> else
>>   upper_halves_are_unequal ();
>>
>> if (__builtin_mips_lower_c_eq_ps (a, b))
>>   lower_halves_are_equal ();
>> else
>>   lower_halves_are_unequal ();
>> ```

5.50.8.3 MIPS-3D Built-in Functions

The MIPS-3D Application-Specific Extension (ASE) includes additional paired-single instructions that are designed to improve the performance of 3D graphics operations. Support for these instructions is controlled by the '`-mips3d`' command-line option.

Chapter 5: Extensions to the C Language Family 459

The functions listed below map directly to a particular MIPS-3D instruction. Please refer to the architecture specification for more details on what each instruction does.

v2sf __builtin_mips_addr_ps (v2sf, v2sf)
: Reduction add (addr.ps).

v2sf __builtin_mips_mulr_ps (v2sf, v2sf)
: Reduction multiply (mulr.ps).

v2sf __builtin_mips_cvt_pw_ps (v2sf)
: Convert paired single to paired word (cvt.pw.ps).

v2sf __builtin_mips_cvt_ps_pw (v2sf)
: Convert paired word to paired single (cvt.ps.pw).

float __builtin_mips_recip1_s (float)
double __builtin_mips_recip1_d (double)
v2sf __builtin_mips_recip1_ps (v2sf)
: Reduced precision reciprocal (sequence step 1) (recip1.*fmt*).

float __builtin_mips_recip2_s (float, float)
double __builtin_mips_recip2_d (double, double)
v2sf __builtin_mips_recip2_ps (v2sf, v2sf)
: Reduced precision reciprocal (sequence step 2) (recip2.*fmt*).

float __builtin_mips_rsqrt1_s (float)
double __builtin_mips_rsqrt1_d (double)
v2sf __builtin_mips_rsqrt1_ps (v2sf)
: Reduced precision reciprocal square root (sequence step 1) (rsqrt1.*fmt*).

float __builtin_mips_rsqrt2_s (float, float)
double __builtin_mips_rsqrt2_d (double, double)
v2sf __builtin_mips_rsqrt2_ps (v2sf, v2sf)
: Reduced precision reciprocal square root (sequence step 2) (rsqrt2.*fmt*).

The following multi-instruction functions are also available. In each case, *cond* can be any of the 16 floating-point conditions: f, un, eq, ueq, olt, ult, ole, ule, sf, ngle, seq, ngl, lt, nge, le or ngt.

int __builtin_mips_cabs_*cond*_s (float a, float b)
int __builtin_mips_cabs_*cond*_d (double a, double b)
: Absolute comparison of two scalar values (cabs.*cond*.fmt, bc1t/bc1f).

    These functions compare a and b using cabs.*cond*.s or cabs.*cond*.d and return the result as a boolean value. For example:

        float a, b;
        if (__builtin_mips_cabs_eq_s (a, b))
          true ();
        else
          false ();

int __builtin_mips_upper_cabs_*cond*_ps (v2sf a, v2sf b)
int __builtin_mips_lower_cabs_*cond*_ps (v2sf a, v2sf b)
: Absolute comparison of two paired-single values (cabs.*cond*.ps, bc1t/bc1f).

These functions compare a and b using cabs.*cond*.ps and return either the upper or lower half of the result. For example:
```
v2sf a, b;
if (__builtin_mips_upper_cabs_eq_ps (a, b))
  upper_halves_are_equal ();
else
  upper_halves_are_unequal ();

if (__builtin_mips_lower_cabs_eq_ps (a, b))
  lower_halves_are_equal ();
else
  lower_halves_are_unequal ();
```

`v2sf __builtin_mips_movt_cabs_`*cond*`_ps (v2sf a, v2sf b, v2sf c, v2sf d)`
`v2sf __builtin_mips_movf_cabs_`*cond*`_ps (v2sf a, v2sf b, v2sf c, v2sf d)`

Conditional move based on absolute comparison (cabs.*cond*.ps, movt.ps/movf.ps).

The movt functions return the value x computed by:
```
cabs.cond.ps cc,a,b
mov.ps x,c
movt.ps x,d,cc
```

The movf functions are similar but use movf.ps instead of movt.ps.

`int __builtin_mips_any_c_`*cond*`_ps (v2sf a, v2sf b)`
`int __builtin_mips_all_c_`*cond*`_ps (v2sf a, v2sf b)`
`int __builtin_mips_any_cabs_`*cond*`_ps (v2sf a, v2sf b)`
`int __builtin_mips_all_cabs_`*cond*`_ps (v2sf a, v2sf b)`

Comparison of two paired-single values (c.*cond*.ps/cabs.*cond*.ps, bc1any2t/bc1any2f).

These functions compare a and b using c.*cond*.ps or cabs.*cond*.ps. The **any** forms return true if either result is true and the **all** forms return true if both results are true. For example:
```
v2sf a, b;
if (__builtin_mips_any_c_eq_ps (a, b))
  one_is_true ();
else
  both_are_false ();

if (__builtin_mips_all_c_eq_ps (a, b))
  both_are_true ();
else
  one_is_false ();
```

`int __builtin_mips_any_c_`*cond*`_4s (v2sf a, v2sf b, v2sf c, v2sf d)`
`int __builtin_mips_all_c_`*cond*`_4s (v2sf a, v2sf b, v2sf c, v2sf d)`
`int __builtin_mips_any_cabs_`*cond*`_4s (v2sf a, v2sf b, v2sf c, v2sf d)`
`int __builtin_mips_all_cabs_`*cond*`_4s (v2sf a, v2sf b, v2sf c, v2sf d)`

Comparison of four paired-single values (c.*cond*.ps/cabs.*cond*.ps, bc1any4t/bc1any4f).

These functions use c.*cond*.ps or cabs.*cond*.ps to compare a with b and to compare c with d. The **any** forms return true if any of the four results are true and the **all** forms return true if all four results are true. For example:

Chapter 5: Extensions to the C Language Family   461

```
v2sf a, b, c, d;
if (__builtin_mips_any_c_eq_4s (a, b, c, d))
  some_are_true ();
else
  all_are_false ();

if (__builtin_mips_all_c_eq_4s (a, b, c, d))
  all_are_true ();
else
  some_are_false ();
```

5.50.9 PowerPC AltiVec Built-in Functions

GCC provides an interface for the PowerPC family of processors to access the AltiVec operations described in Motorola's AltiVec Programming Interface Manual. The interface is made available by including `<altivec.h>` and using '-maltivec' and '-mabi=altivec'. The interface supports the following vector types.

```
vector unsigned char
vector signed char
vector bool char

vector unsigned short
vector signed short
vector bool short
vector pixel

vector unsigned int
vector signed int
vector bool int
vector float
```

GCC's implementation of the high-level language interface available from C and C++ code differs from Motorola's documentation in several ways.

- A vector constant is a list of constant expressions within curly braces.
- A vector initializer requires no cast if the vector constant is of the same type as the variable it is initializing.
- If `signed` or `unsigned` is omitted, the signedness of the vector type is the default signedness of the base type. The default varies depending on the operating system, so a portable program should always specify the signedness.
- Compiling with '-maltivec' adds keywords `__vector`, `__pixel`, and `__bool`. Macros 'vector', `pixel`, and `bool` are defined in `<altivec.h>` and can be undefined.
- GCC allows using a `typedef` name as the type specifier for a vector type.
- For C, overloaded functions are implemented with macros so the following does not work:

    ```
    vec_add ((vector signed int){1, 2, 3, 4}, foo);
    ```

    Since `vec_add` is a macro, the vector constant in the example is treated as four separate arguments. Wrap the entire argument in parentheses for this to work.

Note: Only the `<altivec.h>` interface is supported. Internally, GCC uses built-in functions to achieve the functionality in the aforementioned header file, but they are not supported and are subject to change without notice.

The following interfaces are supported for the generic and specific AltiVec operations and the AltiVec predicates. In cases where there is a direct mapping between generic and specific operations, only the generic names are shown here, although the specific operations can also be used.

Arguments that are documented as `const int` require literal integral values within the range required for that operation.

```
vector signed char vec_abs (vector signed char);
vector signed short vec_abs (vector signed short);
vector signed int vec_abs (vector signed int);
vector float vec_abs (vector float);

vector signed char vec_abss (vector signed char);
vector signed short vec_abss (vector signed short);
vector signed int vec_abss (vector signed int);

vector signed char vec_add (vector bool char, vector signed char);
vector signed char vec_add (vector signed char, vector bool char);
vector signed char vec_add (vector signed char, vector signed char);
vector unsigned char vec_add (vector bool char, vector unsigned char);
vector unsigned char vec_add (vector unsigned char, vector bool char);
vector unsigned char vec_add (vector unsigned char,
                              vector unsigned char);
vector signed short vec_add (vector bool short, vector signed short);
vector signed short vec_add (vector signed short, vector bool short);
vector signed short vec_add (vector signed short, vector signed short);
vector unsigned short vec_add (vector bool short,
                               vector unsigned short);
vector unsigned short vec_add (vector unsigned short,
                               vector bool short);
vector unsigned short vec_add (vector unsigned short,
                               vector unsigned short);
vector signed int vec_add (vector bool int, vector signed int);
vector signed int vec_add (vector signed int, vector bool int);
vector signed int vec_add (vector signed int, vector signed int);
vector unsigned int vec_add (vector bool int, vector unsigned int);
vector unsigned int vec_add (vector unsigned int, vector bool int);
vector unsigned int vec_add (vector unsigned int, vector unsigned int);
vector float vec_add (vector float, vector float);

vector float vec_vaddfp (vector float, vector float);

vector signed int vec_vadduwm (vector bool int, vector signed int);
vector signed int vec_vadduwm (vector signed int, vector bool int);
vector signed int vec_vadduwm (vector signed int, vector signed int);
vector unsigned int vec_vadduwm (vector bool int, vector unsigned int);
vector unsigned int vec_vadduwm (vector unsigned int, vector bool int);
vector unsigned int vec_vadduwm (vector unsigned int,
                                 vector unsigned int);

vector signed short vec_vadduhm (vector bool short,
                                 vector signed short);
vector signed short vec_vadduhm (vector signed short,
                                 vector bool short);
vector signed short vec_vadduhm (vector signed short,
                                 vector signed short);
vector unsigned short vec_vadduhm (vector bool short,
                                   vector unsigned short);
```

Chapter 5: Extensions to the C Language Family

```
vector unsigned short vec_vadduhm (vector unsigned short,
                                   vector bool short);
vector unsigned short vec_vadduhm (vector unsigned short,
                                   vector unsigned short);

vector signed char vec_vaddubm (vector bool char, vector signed char);
vector signed char vec_vaddubm (vector signed char, vector bool char);
vector signed char vec_vaddubm (vector signed char, vector signed char);
vector unsigned char vec_vaddubm (vector bool char,
                                  vector unsigned char);
vector unsigned char vec_vaddubm (vector unsigned char,
                                  vector bool char);
vector unsigned char vec_vaddubm (vector unsigned char,
                                  vector unsigned char);

vector unsigned int vec_addc (vector unsigned int, vector unsigned int);

vector unsigned char vec_adds (vector bool char, vector unsigned char);
vector unsigned char vec_adds (vector unsigned char, vector bool char);
vector unsigned char vec_adds (vector unsigned char,
                               vector unsigned char);
vector signed char vec_adds (vector bool char, vector signed char);
vector signed char vec_adds (vector signed char, vector bool char);
vector signed char vec_adds (vector signed char, vector signed char);
vector unsigned short vec_adds (vector bool short,
                                vector unsigned short);
vector unsigned short vec_adds (vector unsigned short,
                                vector bool short);
vector unsigned short vec_adds (vector unsigned short,
                                vector unsigned short);
vector signed short vec_adds (vector bool short, vector signed short);
vector signed short vec_adds (vector signed short, vector bool short);
vector signed short vec_adds (vector signed short, vector signed short);
vector unsigned int vec_adds (vector bool int, vector unsigned int);
vector unsigned int vec_adds (vector unsigned int, vector bool int);
vector unsigned int vec_adds (vector unsigned int, vector unsigned int);
vector signed int vec_adds (vector bool int, vector signed int);
vector signed int vec_adds (vector signed int, vector bool int);
vector signed int vec_adds (vector signed int, vector signed int);

vector signed int vec_vaddsws (vector bool int, vector signed int);
vector signed int vec_vaddsws (vector signed int, vector bool int);
vector signed int vec_vaddsws (vector signed int, vector signed int);

vector unsigned int vec_vadduws (vector bool int, vector unsigned int);
vector unsigned int vec_vadduws (vector unsigned int, vector bool int);
vector unsigned int vec_vadduws (vector unsigned int,
                                 vector unsigned int);

vector signed short vec_vaddshs (vector bool short,
                                 vector signed short);
vector signed short vec_vaddshs (vector signed short,
                                 vector bool short);
vector signed short vec_vaddshs (vector signed short,
                                 vector signed short);

vector unsigned short vec_vadduhs (vector bool short,
                                   vector unsigned short);
```

```
vector unsigned short vec_vadduhs (vector unsigned short,
                                   vector bool short);
vector unsigned short vec_vadduhs (vector unsigned short,
                                   vector unsigned short);

vector signed char vec_vaddsbs (vector bool char, vector signed char);
vector signed char vec_vaddsbs (vector signed char, vector bool char);
vector signed char vec_vaddsbs (vector signed char, vector signed char);

vector unsigned char vec_vaddubs (vector bool char,
                                  vector unsigned char);
vector unsigned char vec_vaddubs (vector unsigned char,
                                  vector bool char);
vector unsigned char vec_vaddubs (vector unsigned char,
                                  vector unsigned char);

vector float vec_and (vector float, vector float);
vector float vec_and (vector float, vector bool int);
vector float vec_and (vector bool int, vector float);
vector bool int vec_and (vector bool int, vector bool int);
vector signed int vec_and (vector bool int, vector signed int);
vector signed int vec_and (vector signed int, vector bool int);
vector signed int vec_and (vector signed int, vector signed int);
vector unsigned int vec_and (vector bool int, vector unsigned int);
vector unsigned int vec_and (vector unsigned int, vector bool int);
vector unsigned int vec_and (vector unsigned int, vector unsigned int);
vector bool short vec_and (vector bool short, vector bool short);
vector signed short vec_and (vector bool short, vector signed short);
vector signed short vec_and (vector signed short, vector bool short);
vector signed short vec_and (vector signed short, vector signed short);
vector unsigned short vec_and (vector bool short,
                               vector unsigned short);
vector unsigned short vec_and (vector unsigned short,
                               vector bool short);
vector unsigned short vec_and (vector unsigned short,
                               vector unsigned short);
vector signed char vec_and (vector bool char, vector signed char);
vector bool char vec_and (vector bool char, vector bool char);
vector signed char vec_and (vector signed char, vector bool char);
vector signed char vec_and (vector signed char, vector signed char);
vector unsigned char vec_and (vector bool char, vector unsigned char);
vector unsigned char vec_and (vector unsigned char, vector bool char);
vector unsigned char vec_and (vector unsigned char,
                              vector unsigned char);

vector float vec_andc (vector float, vector float);
vector float vec_andc (vector float, vector bool int);
vector float vec_andc (vector bool int, vector float);
vector bool int vec_andc (vector bool int, vector bool int);
vector signed int vec_andc (vector bool int, vector signed int);
vector signed int vec_andc (vector signed int, vector bool int);
vector signed int vec_andc (vector signed int, vector signed int);
vector unsigned int vec_andc (vector bool int, vector unsigned int);
vector unsigned int vec_andc (vector unsigned int, vector bool int);
vector unsigned int vec_andc (vector unsigned int, vector unsigned int);
vector bool short vec_andc (vector bool short, vector bool short);
vector signed short vec_andc (vector bool short, vector signed short);
vector signed short vec_andc (vector signed short, vector bool short);
```

Chapter 5: Extensions to the C Language Family

```
vector signed short vec_andc (vector signed short, vector signed short);
vector unsigned short vec_andc (vector bool short,
                                vector unsigned short);
vector unsigned short vec_andc (vector unsigned short,
                                vector bool short);
vector unsigned short vec_andc (vector unsigned short,
                                vector unsigned short);
vector signed char vec_andc (vector bool char, vector signed char);
vector bool char vec_andc (vector bool char, vector bool char);
vector signed char vec_andc (vector signed char, vector bool char);
vector signed char vec_andc (vector signed char, vector signed char);
vector unsigned char vec_andc (vector bool char, vector unsigned char);
vector unsigned char vec_andc (vector unsigned char, vector bool char);
vector unsigned char vec_andc (vector unsigned char,
                               vector unsigned char);

vector unsigned char vec_avg (vector unsigned char,
                              vector unsigned char);
vector signed char vec_avg (vector signed char, vector signed char);
vector unsigned short vec_avg (vector unsigned short,
                               vector unsigned short);
vector signed short vec_avg (vector signed short, vector signed short);
vector unsigned int vec_avg (vector unsigned int, vector unsigned int);
vector signed int vec_avg (vector signed int, vector signed int);

vector signed int vec_vavgsw (vector signed int, vector signed int);

vector unsigned int vec_vavguw (vector unsigned int,
                                vector unsigned int);

vector signed short vec_vavgsh (vector signed short,
                                vector signed short);

vector unsigned short vec_vavguh (vector unsigned short,
                                  vector unsigned short);

vector signed char vec_vavgsb (vector signed char, vector signed char);

vector unsigned char vec_vavgub (vector unsigned char,
                                 vector unsigned char);

vector float vec_ceil (vector float);

vector signed int vec_cmpb (vector float, vector float);

vector bool char vec_cmpeq (vector signed char, vector signed char);
vector bool char vec_cmpeq (vector unsigned char, vector unsigned char);
vector bool short vec_cmpeq (vector signed short, vector signed short);
vector bool short vec_cmpeq (vector unsigned short,
                             vector unsigned short);
vector bool int vec_cmpeq (vector signed int, vector signed int);
vector bool int vec_cmpeq (vector unsigned int, vector unsigned int);
vector bool int vec_cmpeq (vector float, vector float);

vector bool int vec_vcmpeqfp (vector float, vector float);

vector bool int vec_vcmpequw (vector signed int, vector signed int);
vector bool int vec_vcmpequw (vector unsigned int, vector unsigned int);
```

```
vector bool short vec_vcmpequh (vector signed short,
                                vector signed short);
vector bool short vec_vcmpequh (vector unsigned short,
                                vector unsigned short);

vector bool char vec_vcmpequb (vector signed char, vector signed char);
vector bool char vec_vcmpequb (vector unsigned char,
                               vector unsigned char);

vector bool int vec_cmpge (vector float, vector float);

vector bool char vec_cmpgt (vector unsigned char, vector unsigned char);
vector bool char vec_cmpgt (vector signed char, vector signed char);
vector bool short vec_cmpgt (vector unsigned short,
                             vector unsigned short);
vector bool short vec_cmpgt (vector signed short, vector signed short);
vector bool int vec_cmpgt (vector unsigned int, vector unsigned int);
vector bool int vec_cmpgt (vector signed int, vector signed int);
vector bool int vec_cmpgt (vector float, vector float);

vector bool int vec_vcmpgtfp (vector float, vector float);

vector bool int vec_vcmpgtsw (vector signed int, vector signed int);

vector bool int vec_vcmpgtuw (vector unsigned int, vector unsigned int);

vector bool short vec_vcmpgtsh (vector signed short,
                                vector signed short);

vector bool short vec_vcmpgtuh (vector unsigned short,
                                vector unsigned short);

vector bool char vec_vcmpgtsb (vector signed char, vector signed char);

vector bool char vec_vcmpgtub (vector unsigned char,
                               vector unsigned char);

vector bool int vec_cmple (vector float, vector float);

vector bool char vec_cmplt (vector unsigned char, vector unsigned char);
vector bool char vec_cmplt (vector signed char, vector signed char);
vector bool short vec_cmplt (vector unsigned short,
                             vector unsigned short);
vector bool short vec_cmplt (vector signed short, vector signed short);
vector bool int vec_cmplt (vector unsigned int, vector unsigned int);
vector bool int vec_cmplt (vector signed int, vector signed int);
vector bool int vec_cmplt (vector float, vector float);

vector float vec_ctf (vector unsigned int, const int);
vector float vec_ctf (vector signed int, const int);

vector float vec_vcfsx (vector signed int, const int);

vector float vec_vcfux (vector unsigned int, const int);

vector signed int vec_cts (vector float, const int);
```

Chapter 5: Extensions to the C Language Family 467

```
vector unsigned int vec_ctu (vector float, const int);

void vec_dss (const int);

void vec_dssall (void);

void vec_dst (const vector unsigned char *, int, const int);
void vec_dst (const vector signed char *, int, const int);
void vec_dst (const vector bool char *, int, const int);
void vec_dst (const vector unsigned short *, int, const int);
void vec_dst (const vector signed short *, int, const int);
void vec_dst (const vector bool short *, int, const int);
void vec_dst (const vector pixel *, int, const int);
void vec_dst (const vector unsigned int *, int, const int);
void vec_dst (const vector signed int *, int, const int);
void vec_dst (const vector bool int *, int, const int);
void vec_dst (const vector float *, int, const int);
void vec_dst (const unsigned char *, int, const int);
void vec_dst (const signed char *, int, const int);
void vec_dst (const unsigned short *, int, const int);
void vec_dst (const short *, int, const int);
void vec_dst (const unsigned int *, int, const int);
void vec_dst (const int *, int, const int);
void vec_dst (const unsigned long *, int, const int);
void vec_dst (const long *, int, const int);
void vec_dst (const float *, int, const int);

void vec_dstst (const vector unsigned char *, int, const int);
void vec_dstst (const vector signed char *, int, const int);
void vec_dstst (const vector bool char *, int, const int);
void vec_dstst (const vector unsigned short *, int, const int);
void vec_dstst (const vector signed short *, int, const int);
void vec_dstst (const vector bool short *, int, const int);
void vec_dstst (const vector pixel *, int, const int);
void vec_dstst (const vector unsigned int *, int, const int);
void vec_dstst (const vector signed int *, int, const int);
void vec_dstst (const vector bool int *, int, const int);
void vec_dstst (const vector float *, int, const int);
void vec_dstst (const unsigned char *, int, const int);
void vec_dstst (const signed char *, int, const int);
void vec_dstst (const unsigned short *, int, const int);
void vec_dstst (const short *, int, const int);
void vec_dstst (const unsigned int *, int, const int);
void vec_dstst (const int *, int, const int);
void vec_dstst (const unsigned long *, int, const int);
void vec_dstst (const long *, int, const int);
void vec_dstst (const float *, int, const int);

void vec_dststt (const vector unsigned char *, int, const int);
void vec_dststt (const vector signed char *, int, const int);
void vec_dststt (const vector bool char *, int, const int);
void vec_dststt (const vector unsigned short *, int, const int);
void vec_dststt (const vector signed short *, int, const int);
void vec_dststt (const vector bool short *, int, const int);
void vec_dststt (const vector pixel *, int, const int);
void vec_dststt (const vector unsigned int *, int, const int);
void vec_dststt (const vector signed int *, int, const int);
void vec_dststt (const vector bool int *, int, const int);
```

```
void vec_dststt (const vector float *, int, const int);
void vec_dststt (const unsigned char *, int, const int);
void vec_dststt (const signed char *, int, const int);
void vec_dststt (const unsigned short *, int, const int);
void vec_dststt (const short *, int, const int);
void vec_dststt (const unsigned int *, int, const int);
void vec_dststt (const int *, int, const int);
void vec_dststt (const unsigned long *, int, const int);
void vec_dststt (const long *, int, const int);
void vec_dststt (const float *, int, const int);

void vec_dstt (const vector unsigned char *, int, const int);
void vec_dstt (const vector signed char *, int, const int);
void vec_dstt (const vector bool char *, int, const int);
void vec_dstt (const vector unsigned short *, int, const int);
void vec_dstt (const vector signed short *, int, const int);
void vec_dstt (const vector bool short *, int, const int);
void vec_dstt (const vector pixel *, int, const int);
void vec_dstt (const vector unsigned int *, int, const int);
void vec_dstt (const vector signed int *, int, const int);
void vec_dstt (const vector bool int *, int, const int);
void vec_dstt (const vector float *, int, const int);
void vec_dstt (const unsigned char *, int, const int);
void vec_dstt (const signed char *, int, const int);
void vec_dstt (const unsigned short *, int, const int);
void vec_dstt (const short *, int, const int);
void vec_dstt (const unsigned int *, int, const int);
void vec_dstt (const int *, int, const int);
void vec_dstt (const unsigned long *, int, const int);
void vec_dstt (const long *, int, const int);
void vec_dstt (const float *, int, const int);

vector float vec_expte (vector float);

vector float vec_floor (vector float);

vector float vec_ld (int, const vector float *);
vector float vec_ld (int, const float *);
vector bool int vec_ld (int, const vector bool int *);
vector signed int vec_ld (int, const vector signed int *);
vector signed int vec_ld (int, const int *);
vector signed int vec_ld (int, const long *);
vector unsigned int vec_ld (int, const vector unsigned int *);
vector unsigned int vec_ld (int, const unsigned int *);
vector unsigned int vec_ld (int, const unsigned long *);
vector bool short vec_ld (int, const vector bool short *);
vector pixel vec_ld (int, const vector pixel *);
vector signed short vec_ld (int, const vector signed short *);
vector signed short vec_ld (int, const short *);
vector unsigned short vec_ld (int, const vector unsigned short *);
vector unsigned short vec_ld (int, const unsigned short *);
vector bool char vec_ld (int, const vector bool char *);
vector signed char vec_ld (int, const vector signed char *);
vector signed char vec_ld (int, const signed char *);
vector unsigned char vec_ld (int, const vector unsigned char *);
vector unsigned char vec_ld (int, const unsigned char *);

vector signed char vec_lde (int, const signed char *);
```

Chapter 5: Extensions to the C Language Family

```
vector unsigned char vec_lde (int, const unsigned char *);
vector signed short vec_lde (int, const short *);
vector unsigned short vec_lde (int, const unsigned short *);
vector float vec_lde (int, const float *);
vector signed int vec_lde (int, const int *);
vector unsigned int vec_lde (int, const unsigned int *);
vector signed int vec_lde (int, const long *);
vector unsigned int vec_lde (int, const unsigned long *);

vector float vec_lvewx (int, float *);
vector signed int vec_lvewx (int, int *);
vector unsigned int vec_lvewx (int, unsigned int *);
vector signed int vec_lvewx (int, long *);
vector unsigned int vec_lvewx (int, unsigned long *);

vector signed short vec_lvehx (int, short *);
vector unsigned short vec_lvehx (int, unsigned short *);

vector signed char vec_lvebx (int, char *);
vector unsigned char vec_lvebx (int, unsigned char *);

vector float vec_ldl (int, const vector float *);
vector float vec_ldl (int, const float *);
vector bool int vec_ldl (int, const vector bool int *);
vector signed int vec_ldl (int, const vector signed int *);
vector signed int vec_ldl (int, const int *);
vector signed int vec_ldl (int, const long *);
vector unsigned int vec_ldl (int, const vector unsigned int *);
vector unsigned int vec_ldl (int, const unsigned int *);
vector unsigned int vec_ldl (int, const unsigned long *);
vector bool short vec_ldl (int, const vector bool short *);
vector pixel vec_ldl (int, const vector pixel *);
vector signed short vec_ldl (int, const vector signed short *);
vector signed short vec_ldl (int, const short *);
vector unsigned short vec_ldl (int, const vector unsigned short *);
vector unsigned short vec_ldl (int, const unsigned short *);
vector bool char vec_ldl (int, const vector bool char *);
vector signed char vec_ldl (int, const vector signed char *);
vector signed char vec_ldl (int, const signed char *);
vector unsigned char vec_ldl (int, const vector unsigned char *);
vector unsigned char vec_ldl (int, const unsigned char *);

vector float vec_loge (vector float);

vector unsigned char vec_lvsl (int, const volatile unsigned char *);
vector unsigned char vec_lvsl (int, const volatile signed char *);
vector unsigned char vec_lvsl (int, const volatile unsigned short *);
vector unsigned char vec_lvsl (int, const volatile short *);
vector unsigned char vec_lvsl (int, const volatile unsigned int *);
vector unsigned char vec_lvsl (int, const volatile int *);
vector unsigned char vec_lvsl (int, const volatile unsigned long *);
vector unsigned char vec_lvsl (int, const volatile long *);
vector unsigned char vec_lvsl (int, const volatile float *);

vector unsigned char vec_lvsr (int, const volatile unsigned char *);
vector unsigned char vec_lvsr (int, const volatile signed char *);
vector unsigned char vec_lvsr (int, const volatile unsigned short *);
vector unsigned char vec_lvsr (int, const volatile short *);
```

```
vector unsigned char vec_lvsr (int, const volatile unsigned int *);
vector unsigned char vec_lvsr (int, const volatile int *);
vector unsigned char vec_lvsr (int, const volatile unsigned long *);
vector unsigned char vec_lvsr (int, const volatile long *);
vector unsigned char vec_lvsr (int, const volatile float *);

vector float vec_madd (vector float, vector float, vector float);

vector signed short vec_madds (vector signed short,
                               vector signed short,
                               vector signed short);

vector unsigned char vec_max (vector bool char, vector unsigned char);
vector unsigned char vec_max (vector unsigned char, vector bool char);
vector unsigned char vec_max (vector unsigned char,
                              vector unsigned char);
vector signed char vec_max (vector bool char, vector signed char);
vector signed char vec_max (vector signed char, vector bool char);
vector signed char vec_max (vector signed char, vector signed char);
vector unsigned short vec_max (vector bool short,
                               vector unsigned short);
vector unsigned short vec_max (vector unsigned short,
                               vector bool short);
vector unsigned short vec_max (vector unsigned short,
                               vector unsigned short);
vector signed short vec_max (vector bool short, vector signed short);
vector signed short vec_max (vector signed short, vector bool short);
vector signed short vec_max (vector signed short, vector signed short);
vector unsigned int vec_max (vector bool int, vector unsigned int);
vector unsigned int vec_max (vector unsigned int, vector bool int);
vector unsigned int vec_max (vector unsigned int, vector unsigned int);
vector signed int vec_max (vector bool int, vector signed int);
vector signed int vec_max (vector signed int, vector bool int);
vector signed int vec_max (vector signed int, vector signed int);
vector float vec_max (vector float, vector float);

vector float vec_vmaxfp (vector float, vector float);

vector signed int vec_vmaxsw (vector bool int, vector signed int);
vector signed int vec_vmaxsw (vector signed int, vector bool int);
vector signed int vec_vmaxsw (vector signed int, vector signed int);

vector unsigned int vec_vmaxuw (vector bool int, vector unsigned int);
vector unsigned int vec_vmaxuw (vector unsigned int, vector bool int);
vector unsigned int vec_vmaxuw (vector unsigned int,
                                vector unsigned int);

vector signed short vec_vmaxsh (vector bool short, vector signed short);
vector signed short vec_vmaxsh (vector signed short, vector bool short);
vector signed short vec_vmaxsh (vector signed short,
                                vector signed short);

vector unsigned short vec_vmaxuh (vector bool short,
                                  vector unsigned short);
vector unsigned short vec_vmaxuh (vector unsigned short,
                                  vector bool short);
vector unsigned short vec_vmaxuh (vector unsigned short,
                                  vector unsigned short);
```

Chapter 5: Extensions to the C Language Family   471

```
vector signed char vec_vmaxsb (vector bool char, vector signed char);
vector signed char vec_vmaxsb (vector signed char, vector bool char);
vector signed char vec_vmaxsb (vector signed char, vector signed char);

vector unsigned char vec_vmaxub (vector bool char,
                                 vector unsigned char);
vector unsigned char vec_vmaxub (vector unsigned char,
                                 vector bool char);
vector unsigned char vec_vmaxub (vector unsigned char,
                                 vector unsigned char);

vector bool char vec_mergeh (vector bool char, vector bool char);
vector signed char vec_mergeh (vector signed char, vector signed char);
vector unsigned char vec_mergeh (vector unsigned char,
                                 vector unsigned char);
vector bool short vec_mergeh (vector bool short, vector bool short);
vector pixel vec_mergeh (vector pixel, vector pixel);
vector signed short vec_mergeh (vector signed short,
                                vector signed short);
vector unsigned short vec_mergeh (vector unsigned short,
                                  vector unsigned short);
vector float vec_mergeh (vector float, vector float);
vector bool int vec_mergeh (vector bool int, vector bool int);
vector signed int vec_mergeh (vector signed int, vector signed int);
vector unsigned int vec_mergeh (vector unsigned int,
                                vector unsigned int);

vector float vec_vmrghw (vector float, vector float);
vector bool int vec_vmrghw (vector bool int, vector bool int);
vector signed int vec_vmrghw (vector signed int, vector signed int);
vector unsigned int vec_vmrghw (vector unsigned int,
                                vector unsigned int);

vector bool short vec_vmrghh (vector bool short, vector bool short);
vector signed short vec_vmrghh (vector signed short,
                                vector signed short);
vector unsigned short vec_vmrghh (vector unsigned short,
                                  vector unsigned short);
vector pixel vec_vmrghh (vector pixel, vector pixel);

vector bool char vec_vmrghb (vector bool char, vector bool char);
vector signed char vec_vmrghb (vector signed char, vector signed char);
vector unsigned char vec_vmrghb (vector unsigned char,
                                 vector unsigned char);

vector bool char vec_mergel (vector bool char, vector bool char);
vector signed char vec_mergel (vector signed char, vector signed char);
vector unsigned char vec_mergel (vector unsigned char,
                                 vector unsigned char);
vector bool short vec_mergel (vector bool short, vector bool short);
vector pixel vec_mergel (vector pixel, vector pixel);
vector signed short vec_mergel (vector signed short,
                                vector signed short);
vector unsigned short vec_mergel (vector unsigned short,
                                  vector unsigned short);
vector float vec_mergel (vector float, vector float);
vector bool int vec_mergel (vector bool int, vector bool int);
```

```c
vector signed int vec_mergel (vector signed int, vector signed int);
vector unsigned int vec_mergel (vector unsigned int,
                                vector unsigned int);

vector float vec_vmrglw (vector float, vector float);
vector signed int vec_vmrglw (vector signed int, vector signed int);
vector unsigned int vec_vmrglw (vector unsigned int,
                                vector unsigned int);
vector bool int vec_vmrglw (vector bool int, vector bool int);

vector bool short vec_vmrglh (vector bool short, vector bool short);
vector signed short vec_vmrglh (vector signed short,
                                vector signed short);
vector unsigned short vec_vmrglh (vector unsigned short,
                                  vector unsigned short);
vector pixel vec_vmrglh (vector pixel, vector pixel);

vector bool char vec_vmrglb (vector bool char, vector bool char);
vector signed char vec_vmrglb (vector signed char, vector signed char);
vector unsigned char vec_vmrglb (vector unsigned char,
                                 vector unsigned char);

vector unsigned short vec_mfvscr (void);

vector unsigned char vec_min (vector bool char, vector unsigned char);
vector unsigned char vec_min (vector unsigned char, vector bool char);
vector unsigned char vec_min (vector unsigned char,
                              vector unsigned char);
vector signed char vec_min (vector bool char, vector signed char);
vector signed char vec_min (vector signed char, vector bool char);
vector signed char vec_min (vector signed char, vector signed char);
vector unsigned short vec_min (vector bool short,
                               vector unsigned short);
vector unsigned short vec_min (vector unsigned short,
                               vector bool short);
vector unsigned short vec_min (vector unsigned short,
                               vector unsigned short);
vector signed short vec_min (vector bool short, vector signed short);
vector signed short vec_min (vector signed short, vector bool short);
vector signed short vec_min (vector signed short, vector signed short);
vector unsigned int vec_min (vector bool int, vector unsigned int);
vector unsigned int vec_min (vector unsigned int, vector bool int);
vector unsigned int vec_min (vector unsigned int, vector unsigned int);
vector signed int vec_min (vector bool int, vector signed int);
vector signed int vec_min (vector signed int, vector bool int);
vector signed int vec_min (vector signed int, vector signed int);
vector float vec_min (vector float, vector float);

vector float vec_vminfp (vector float, vector float);

vector signed int vec_vminsw (vector bool int, vector signed int);
vector signed int vec_vminsw (vector signed int, vector bool int);
vector signed int vec_vminsw (vector signed int, vector signed int);

vector unsigned int vec_vminuw (vector bool int, vector unsigned int);
vector unsigned int vec_vminuw (vector unsigned int, vector bool int);
vector unsigned int vec_vminuw (vector unsigned int,
                                vector unsigned int);
```

Chapter 5: Extensions to the C Language Family

```
vector signed short vec_vminsh (vector bool short, vector signed short);
vector signed short vec_vminsh (vector signed short, vector bool short);
vector signed short vec_vminsh (vector signed short,
                                vector signed short);

vector unsigned short vec_vminuh (vector bool short,
                                  vector unsigned short);
vector unsigned short vec_vminuh (vector unsigned short,
                                  vector bool short);
vector unsigned short vec_vminuh (vector unsigned short,
                                  vector unsigned short);

vector signed char vec_vminsb (vector bool char, vector signed char);
vector signed char vec_vminsb (vector signed char, vector bool char);
vector signed char vec_vminsb (vector signed char, vector signed char);

vector unsigned char vec_vminub (vector bool char,
                                 vector unsigned char);
vector unsigned char vec_vminub (vector unsigned char,
                                 vector bool char);
vector unsigned char vec_vminub (vector unsigned char,
                                 vector unsigned char);

vector signed short vec_mladd (vector signed short,
                               vector signed short,
                               vector signed short);
vector signed short vec_mladd (vector signed short,
                               vector unsigned short,
                               vector unsigned short);
vector signed short vec_mladd (vector unsigned short,
                               vector signed short,
                               vector signed short);
vector unsigned short vec_mladd (vector unsigned short,
                                 vector unsigned short,
                                 vector unsigned short);

vector signed short vec_mradds (vector signed short,
                                vector signed short,
                                vector signed short);

vector unsigned int vec_msum (vector unsigned char,
                              vector unsigned char,
                              vector unsigned int);
vector signed int vec_msum (vector signed char,
                            vector unsigned char,
                            vector signed int);
vector unsigned int vec_msum (vector unsigned short,
                              vector unsigned short,
                              vector unsigned int);
vector signed int vec_msum (vector signed short,
                            vector signed short,
                            vector signed int);

vector signed int vec_vmsumshm (vector signed short,
                                vector signed short,
                                vector signed int);
```

```
vector unsigned int vec_vmsumuhm (vector unsigned short,
                                  vector unsigned short,
                                  vector unsigned int);

vector signed int vec_vmsummbm (vector signed char,
                                vector unsigned char,
                                vector signed int);

vector unsigned int vec_vmsumubm (vector unsigned char,
                                  vector unsigned char,
                                  vector unsigned int);

vector unsigned int vec_msums (vector unsigned short,
                               vector unsigned short,
                               vector unsigned int);
vector signed int vec_msums (vector signed short,
                             vector signed short,
                             vector signed int);

vector signed int vec_vmsumshs (vector signed short,
                                vector signed short,
                                vector signed int);

vector unsigned int vec_vmsumuhs (vector unsigned short,
                                  vector unsigned short,
                                  vector unsigned int);

void vec_mtvscr (vector signed int);
void vec_mtvscr (vector unsigned int);
void vec_mtvscr (vector bool int);
void vec_mtvscr (vector signed short);
void vec_mtvscr (vector unsigned short);
void vec_mtvscr (vector bool short);
void vec_mtvscr (vector pixel);
void vec_mtvscr (vector signed char);
void vec_mtvscr (vector unsigned char);
void vec_mtvscr (vector bool char);

vector unsigned short vec_mule (vector unsigned char,
                                vector unsigned char);
vector signed short vec_mule (vector signed char,
                              vector signed char);
vector unsigned int vec_mule (vector unsigned short,
                              vector unsigned short);
vector signed int vec_mule (vector signed short, vector signed short);

vector signed int vec_vmulesh (vector signed short,
                               vector signed short);

vector unsigned int vec_vmuleuh (vector unsigned short,
                                 vector unsigned short);

vector signed short vec_vmulesb (vector signed char,
                                 vector signed char);

vector unsigned short vec_vmuleub (vector unsigned char,
                                   vector unsigned char);
```

Chapter 5: Extensions to the C Language Family 475

```
vector unsigned short vec_mulo (vector unsigned char,
                                vector unsigned char);
vector signed short vec_mulo (vector signed char, vector signed char);
vector unsigned int vec_mulo (vector unsigned short,
                              vector unsigned short);
vector signed int vec_mulo (vector signed short, vector signed short);

vector signed int vec_vmulosh (vector signed short,
                               vector signed short);

vector unsigned int vec_vmulouh (vector unsigned short,
                                 vector unsigned short);

vector signed short vec_vmulosb (vector signed char,
                                 vector signed char);

vector unsigned short vec_vmuloub (vector unsigned char,
                                   vector unsigned char);

vector float vec_nmsub (vector float, vector float, vector float);

vector float vec_nor (vector float, vector float);
vector signed int vec_nor (vector signed int, vector signed int);
vector unsigned int vec_nor (vector unsigned int, vector unsigned int);
vector bool int vec_nor (vector bool int, vector bool int);
vector signed short vec_nor (vector signed short, vector signed short);
vector unsigned short vec_nor (vector unsigned short,
                               vector unsigned short);
vector bool short vec_nor (vector bool short, vector bool short);
vector signed char vec_nor (vector signed char, vector signed char);
vector unsigned char vec_nor (vector unsigned char,
                              vector unsigned char);
vector bool char vec_nor (vector bool char, vector bool char);

vector float vec_or (vector float, vector float);
vector float vec_or (vector float, vector bool int);
vector float vec_or (vector bool int, vector float);
vector bool int vec_or (vector bool int, vector bool int);
vector signed int vec_or (vector bool int, vector signed int);
vector signed int vec_or (vector signed int, vector bool int);
vector signed int vec_or (vector signed int, vector signed int);
vector unsigned int vec_or (vector bool int, vector unsigned int);
vector unsigned int vec_or (vector unsigned int, vector bool int);
vector unsigned int vec_or (vector unsigned int, vector unsigned int);
vector bool short vec_or (vector bool short, vector bool short);
vector signed short vec_or (vector bool short, vector signed short);
vector signed short vec_or (vector signed short, vector bool short);
vector signed short vec_or (vector signed short, vector signed short);
vector unsigned short vec_or (vector bool short, vector unsigned short);
vector unsigned short vec_or (vector unsigned short, vector bool short);
vector unsigned short vec_or (vector unsigned short,
                              vector unsigned short);
vector signed char vec_or (vector bool char, vector signed char);
vector bool char vec_or (vector bool char, vector bool char);
vector signed char vec_or (vector signed char, vector bool char);
vector signed char vec_or (vector signed char, vector signed char);
vector unsigned char vec_or (vector bool char, vector unsigned char);
vector unsigned char vec_or (vector unsigned char, vector bool char);
```

```
vector unsigned char vec_or (vector unsigned char,
                             vector unsigned char);

vector signed char vec_pack (vector signed short, vector signed short);
vector unsigned char vec_pack (vector unsigned short,
                               vector unsigned short);
vector bool char vec_pack (vector bool short, vector bool short);
vector signed short vec_pack (vector signed int, vector signed int);
vector unsigned short vec_pack (vector unsigned int,
                                vector unsigned int);
vector bool short vec_pack (vector bool int, vector bool int);

vector bool short vec_vpkuwum (vector bool int, vector bool int);
vector signed short vec_vpkuwum (vector signed int, vector signed int);
vector unsigned short vec_vpkuwum (vector unsigned int,
                                   vector unsigned int);

vector bool char vec_vpkuhum (vector bool short, vector bool short);
vector signed char vec_vpkuhum (vector signed short,
                                vector signed short);
vector unsigned char vec_vpkuhum (vector unsigned short,
                                  vector unsigned short);

vector pixel vec_packpx (vector unsigned int, vector unsigned int);

vector unsigned char vec_packs (vector unsigned short,
                                vector unsigned short);
vector signed char vec_packs (vector signed short, vector signed short);
vector unsigned short vec_packs (vector unsigned int,
                                 vector unsigned int);
vector signed short vec_packs (vector signed int, vector signed int);

vector signed short vec_vpkswss (vector signed int, vector signed int);

vector unsigned short vec_vpkuwus (vector unsigned int,
                                   vector unsigned int);

vector signed char vec_vpkshss (vector signed short,
                                vector signed short);

vector unsigned char vec_vpkuhus (vector unsigned short,
                                  vector unsigned short);

vector unsigned char vec_packsu (vector unsigned short,
                                 vector unsigned short);
vector unsigned char vec_packsu (vector signed short,
                                 vector signed short);
vector unsigned short vec_packsu (vector unsigned int,
                                  vector unsigned int);
vector unsigned short vec_packsu (vector signed int, vector signed int);

vector unsigned short vec_vpkswus (vector signed int,
                                   vector signed int);

vector unsigned char vec_vpkshus (vector signed short,
                                  vector signed short);

vector float vec_perm (vector float,
```

Chapter 5: Extensions to the C Language Family 477

```
                        vector float,
                        vector unsigned char);
vector signed int vec_perm (vector signed int,
                        vector signed int,
                        vector unsigned char);
vector unsigned int vec_perm (vector unsigned int,
                        vector unsigned int,
                        vector unsigned char);
vector bool int vec_perm (vector bool int,
                        vector bool int,
                        vector unsigned char);
vector signed short vec_perm (vector signed short,
                        vector signed short,
                        vector unsigned char);
vector unsigned short vec_perm (vector unsigned short,
                        vector unsigned short,
                        vector unsigned char);
vector bool short vec_perm (vector bool short,
                        vector bool short,
                        vector unsigned char);
vector pixel vec_perm (vector pixel,
                        vector pixel,
                        vector unsigned char);
vector signed char vec_perm (vector signed char,
                        vector signed char,
                        vector unsigned char);
vector unsigned char vec_perm (vector unsigned char,
                        vector unsigned char,
                        vector unsigned char);
vector bool char vec_perm (vector bool char,
                        vector bool char,
                        vector unsigned char);

vector float vec_re (vector float);

vector signed char vec_rl (vector signed char,
                        vector unsigned char);
vector unsigned char vec_rl (vector unsigned char,
                        vector unsigned char);
vector signed short vec_rl (vector signed short, vector unsigned short);
vector unsigned short vec_rl (vector unsigned short,
                        vector unsigned short);
vector signed int vec_rl (vector signed int, vector unsigned int);
vector unsigned int vec_rl (vector unsigned int, vector unsigned int);

vector signed int vec_vrlw (vector signed int, vector unsigned int);
vector unsigned int vec_vrlw (vector unsigned int, vector unsigned int);

vector signed short vec_vrlh (vector signed short,
                        vector unsigned short);
vector unsigned short vec_vrlh (vector unsigned short,
                        vector unsigned short);

vector signed char vec_vrlb (vector signed char, vector unsigned char);
vector unsigned char vec_vrlb (vector unsigned char,
                        vector unsigned char);

vector float vec_round (vector float);
```

```
vector float vec_rsqrte (vector float);

vector float vec_sel (vector float, vector float, vector bool int);
vector float vec_sel (vector float, vector float, vector unsigned int);
vector signed int vec_sel (vector signed int,
                           vector signed int,
                           vector bool int);
vector signed int vec_sel (vector signed int,
                           vector signed int,
                           vector unsigned int);
vector unsigned int vec_sel (vector unsigned int,
                             vector unsigned int,
                             vector bool int);
vector unsigned int vec_sel (vector unsigned int,
                             vector unsigned int,
                             vector unsigned int);
vector bool int vec_sel (vector bool int,
                         vector bool int,
                         vector bool int);
vector bool int vec_sel (vector bool int,
                         vector bool int,
                         vector unsigned int);
vector signed short vec_sel (vector signed short,
                             vector signed short,
                             vector bool short);
vector signed short vec_sel (vector signed short,
                             vector signed short,
                             vector unsigned short);
vector unsigned short vec_sel (vector unsigned short,
                               vector unsigned short,
                               vector bool short);
vector unsigned short vec_sel (vector unsigned short,
                               vector unsigned short,
                               vector unsigned short);
vector bool short vec_sel (vector bool short,
                           vector bool short,
                           vector bool short);
vector bool short vec_sel (vector bool short,
                           vector bool short,
                           vector unsigned short);
vector signed char vec_sel (vector signed char,
                            vector signed char,
                            vector bool char);
vector signed char vec_sel (vector signed char,
                            vector signed char,
                            vector unsigned char);
vector unsigned char vec_sel (vector unsigned char,
                              vector unsigned char,
                              vector bool char);
vector unsigned char vec_sel (vector unsigned char,
                              vector unsigned char,
                              vector unsigned char);
vector bool char vec_sel (vector bool char,
                          vector bool char,
                          vector bool char);
vector bool char vec_sel (vector bool char,
                          vector bool char,
```

Chapter 5: Extensions to the C Language Family   479

```
                        vector unsigned char);

vector signed char vec_sl (vector signed char,
                          vector unsigned char);
vector unsigned char vec_sl (vector unsigned char,
                             vector unsigned char);
vector signed short vec_sl (vector signed short, vector unsigned short);
vector unsigned short vec_sl (vector unsigned short,
                              vector unsigned short);
vector signed int vec_sl (vector signed int, vector unsigned int);
vector unsigned int vec_sl (vector unsigned int, vector unsigned int);

vector signed int vec_vslw (vector signed int, vector unsigned int);
vector unsigned int vec_vslw (vector unsigned int, vector unsigned int);

vector signed short vec_vslh (vector signed short,
                              vector unsigned short);
vector unsigned short vec_vslh (vector unsigned short,
                                vector unsigned short);

vector signed char vec_vslb (vector signed char, vector unsigned char);
vector unsigned char vec_vslb (vector unsigned char,
                               vector unsigned char);

vector float vec_sld (vector float, vector float, const int);
vector signed int vec_sld (vector signed int,
                           vector signed int,
                           const int);
vector unsigned int vec_sld (vector unsigned int,
                             vector unsigned int,
                             const int);
vector bool int vec_sld (vector bool int,
                         vector bool int,
                         const int);
vector signed short vec_sld (vector signed short,
                             vector signed short,
                             const int);
vector unsigned short vec_sld (vector unsigned short,
                               vector unsigned short,
                               const int);
vector bool short vec_sld (vector bool short,
                           vector bool short,
                           const int);
vector pixel vec_sld (vector pixel,
                      vector pixel,
                      const int);
vector signed char vec_sld (vector signed char,
                            vector signed char,
                            const int);
vector unsigned char vec_sld (vector unsigned char,
                              vector unsigned char,
                              const int);
vector bool char vec_sld (vector bool char,
                          vector bool char,
                          const int);

vector signed int vec_sll (vector signed int,
                           vector unsigned int);
```

```
vector signed int vec_sll (vector signed int,
                          vector unsigned short);
vector signed int vec_sll (vector signed int,
                          vector unsigned char);
vector unsigned int vec_sll (vector unsigned int,
                             vector unsigned int);
vector unsigned int vec_sll (vector unsigned int,
                             vector unsigned short);
vector unsigned int vec_sll (vector unsigned int,
                             vector unsigned char);
vector bool int vec_sll (vector bool int,
                         vector unsigned int);
vector bool int vec_sll (vector bool int,
                         vector unsigned short);
vector bool int vec_sll (vector bool int,
                         vector unsigned char);
vector signed short vec_sll (vector signed short,
                             vector unsigned int);
vector signed short vec_sll (vector signed short,
                             vector unsigned short);
vector signed short vec_sll (vector signed short,
                             vector unsigned char);
vector unsigned short vec_sll (vector unsigned short,
                               vector unsigned int);
vector unsigned short vec_sll (vector unsigned short,
                               vector unsigned short);
vector unsigned short vec_sll (vector unsigned short,
                               vector unsigned char);
vector bool short vec_sll (vector bool short, vector unsigned int);
vector bool short vec_sll (vector bool short, vector unsigned short);
vector bool short vec_sll (vector bool short, vector unsigned char);
vector pixel vec_sll (vector pixel, vector unsigned int);
vector pixel vec_sll (vector pixel, vector unsigned short);
vector pixel vec_sll (vector pixel, vector unsigned char);
vector signed char vec_sll (vector signed char, vector unsigned int);
vector signed char vec_sll (vector signed char, vector unsigned short);
vector signed char vec_sll (vector signed char, vector unsigned char);
vector unsigned char vec_sll (vector unsigned char,
                              vector unsigned int);
vector unsigned char vec_sll (vector unsigned char,
                              vector unsigned short);
vector unsigned char vec_sll (vector unsigned char,
                              vector unsigned char);
vector bool char vec_sll (vector bool char, vector unsigned int);
vector bool char vec_sll (vector bool char, vector unsigned short);
vector bool char vec_sll (vector bool char, vector unsigned char);

vector float vec_slo (vector float, vector signed char);
vector float vec_slo (vector float, vector unsigned char);
vector signed int vec_slo (vector signed int, vector signed char);
vector signed int vec_slo (vector signed int, vector unsigned char);
vector unsigned int vec_slo (vector unsigned int, vector signed char);
vector unsigned int vec_slo (vector unsigned int, vector unsigned char);
vector signed short vec_slo (vector signed short, vector signed char);
vector signed short vec_slo (vector signed short, vector unsigned char);
vector unsigned short vec_slo (vector unsigned short,
                               vector signed char);
vector unsigned short vec_slo (vector unsigned short,
```

Chapter 5: Extensions to the C Language Family   481

```
                              vector unsigned char);
vector pixel vec_slo (vector pixel, vector signed char);
vector pixel vec_slo (vector pixel, vector unsigned char);
vector signed char vec_slo (vector signed char, vector signed char);
vector signed char vec_slo (vector signed char, vector unsigned char);
vector unsigned char vec_slo (vector unsigned char, vector signed char);
vector unsigned char vec_slo (vector unsigned char,
                              vector unsigned char);

vector signed char vec_splat (vector signed char, const int);
vector unsigned char vec_splat (vector unsigned char, const int);
vector bool char vec_splat (vector bool char, const int);
vector signed short vec_splat (vector signed short, const int);
vector unsigned short vec_splat (vector unsigned short, const int);
vector bool short vec_splat (vector bool short, const int);
vector pixel vec_splat (vector pixel, const int);
vector float vec_splat (vector float, const int);
vector signed int vec_splat (vector signed int, const int);
vector unsigned int vec_splat (vector unsigned int, const int);
vector bool int vec_splat (vector bool int, const int);

vector float vec_vspltw (vector float, const int);
vector signed int vec_vspltw (vector signed int, const int);
vector unsigned int vec_vspltw (vector unsigned int, const int);
vector bool int vec_vspltw (vector bool int, const int);

vector bool short vec_vsplth (vector bool short, const int);
vector signed short vec_vsplth (vector signed short, const int);
vector unsigned short vec_vsplth (vector unsigned short, const int);
vector pixel vec_vsplth (vector pixel, const int);

vector signed char vec_vspltb (vector signed char, const int);
vector unsigned char vec_vspltb (vector unsigned char, const int);
vector bool char vec_vspltb (vector bool char, const int);

vector signed char vec_splat_s8 (const int);

vector signed short vec_splat_s16 (const int);

vector signed int vec_splat_s32 (const int);

vector unsigned char vec_splat_u8 (const int);

vector unsigned short vec_splat_u16 (const int);

vector unsigned int vec_splat_u32 (const int);

vector signed char vec_sr (vector signed char, vector unsigned char);
vector unsigned char vec_sr (vector unsigned char,
                             vector unsigned char);
vector signed short vec_sr (vector signed short,
                            vector unsigned short);
vector unsigned short vec_sr (vector unsigned short,
                              vector unsigned short);
vector signed int vec_sr (vector signed int, vector unsigned int);
vector unsigned int vec_sr (vector unsigned int, vector unsigned int);

vector signed int vec_vsrw (vector signed int, vector unsigned int);
```

```
vector unsigned int vec_vsrw (vector unsigned int, vector unsigned int);

vector signed short vec_vsrh (vector signed short,
                              vector unsigned short);
vector unsigned short vec_vsrh (vector unsigned short,
                                vector unsigned short);

vector signed char vec_vsrb (vector signed char, vector unsigned char);
vector unsigned char vec_vsrb (vector unsigned char,
                               vector unsigned char);

vector signed char vec_sra (vector signed char, vector unsigned char);
vector unsigned char vec_sra (vector unsigned char,
                              vector unsigned char);
vector signed short vec_sra (vector signed short,
                             vector unsigned short);
vector unsigned short vec_sra (vector unsigned short,
                               vector unsigned short);
vector signed int vec_sra (vector signed int, vector unsigned int);
vector unsigned int vec_sra (vector unsigned int, vector unsigned int);

vector signed int vec_vsraw (vector signed int, vector unsigned int);
vector unsigned int vec_vsraw (vector unsigned int,
                               vector unsigned int);

vector signed short vec_vsrah (vector signed short,
                               vector unsigned short);
vector unsigned short vec_vsrah (vector unsigned short,
                                 vector unsigned short);

vector signed char vec_vsrab (vector signed char, vector unsigned char);
vector unsigned char vec_vsrab (vector unsigned char,
                                vector unsigned char);

vector signed int vec_srl (vector signed int, vector unsigned int);
vector signed int vec_srl (vector signed int, vector unsigned short);
vector signed int vec_srl (vector signed int, vector unsigned char);
vector unsigned int vec_srl (vector unsigned int, vector unsigned int);
vector unsigned int vec_srl (vector unsigned int,
                             vector unsigned short);
vector unsigned int vec_srl (vector unsigned int, vector unsigned char);
vector bool int vec_srl (vector bool int, vector unsigned int);
vector bool int vec_srl (vector bool int, vector unsigned short);
vector bool int vec_srl (vector bool int, vector unsigned char);
vector signed short vec_srl (vector signed short, vector unsigned int);
vector signed short vec_srl (vector signed short,
                             vector unsigned short);
vector signed short vec_srl (vector signed short, vector unsigned char);
vector unsigned short vec_srl (vector unsigned short,
                               vector unsigned int);
vector unsigned short vec_srl (vector unsigned short,
                               vector unsigned short);
vector unsigned short vec_srl (vector unsigned short,
                               vector unsigned char);
vector bool short vec_srl (vector bool short, vector unsigned int);
vector bool short vec_srl (vector bool short, vector unsigned short);
vector bool short vec_srl (vector bool short, vector unsigned char);
vector pixel vec_srl (vector pixel, vector unsigned int);
```

Chapter 5: Extensions to the C Language Family 483

```
vector pixel vec_srl (vector pixel, vector unsigned short);
vector pixel vec_srl (vector pixel, vector unsigned char);
vector signed char vec_srl (vector signed char, vector unsigned int);
vector signed char vec_srl (vector signed char, vector unsigned short);
vector signed char vec_srl (vector signed char, vector unsigned char);
vector unsigned char vec_srl (vector unsigned char,
                              vector unsigned int);
vector unsigned char vec_srl (vector unsigned char,
                              vector unsigned short);
vector unsigned char vec_srl (vector unsigned char,
                              vector unsigned char);
vector bool char vec_srl (vector bool char, vector unsigned int);
vector bool char vec_srl (vector bool char, vector unsigned short);
vector bool char vec_srl (vector bool char, vector unsigned char);

vector float vec_sro (vector float, vector signed char);
vector float vec_sro (vector float, vector unsigned char);
vector signed int vec_sro (vector signed int, vector signed char);
vector signed int vec_sro (vector signed int, vector unsigned char);
vector unsigned int vec_sro (vector unsigned int, vector signed char);
vector unsigned int vec_sro (vector unsigned int, vector unsigned char);
vector signed short vec_sro (vector signed short, vector signed char);
vector signed short vec_sro (vector signed short, vector unsigned char);
vector unsigned short vec_sro (vector unsigned short,
                               vector signed char);
vector unsigned short vec_sro (vector unsigned short,
                               vector unsigned char);
vector pixel vec_sro (vector pixel, vector signed char);
vector pixel vec_sro (vector pixel, vector unsigned char);
vector signed char vec_sro (vector signed char, vector signed char);
vector signed char vec_sro (vector signed char, vector unsigned char);
vector unsigned char vec_sro (vector unsigned char, vector signed char);
vector unsigned char vec_sro (vector unsigned char,
                              vector unsigned char);

void vec_st (vector float, int, vector float *);
void vec_st (vector float, int, float *);
void vec_st (vector signed int, int, vector signed int *);
void vec_st (vector signed int, int, int *);
void vec_st (vector unsigned int, int, vector unsigned int *);
void vec_st (vector unsigned int, int, unsigned int *);
void vec_st (vector bool int, int, vector bool int *);
void vec_st (vector bool int, int, unsigned int *);
void vec_st (vector bool int, int, int *);
void vec_st (vector signed short, int, vector signed short *);
void vec_st (vector signed short, int, short *);
void vec_st (vector unsigned short, int, vector unsigned short *);
void vec_st (vector unsigned short, int, unsigned short *);
void vec_st (vector bool short, int, vector bool short *);
void vec_st (vector bool short, int, unsigned short *);
void vec_st (vector pixel, int, vector pixel *);
void vec_st (vector pixel, int, unsigned short *);
void vec_st (vector pixel, int, short *);
void vec_st (vector bool short, int, short *);
void vec_st (vector signed char, int, vector signed char *);
void vec_st (vector signed char, int, signed char *);
void vec_st (vector unsigned char, int, vector unsigned char *);
void vec_st (vector unsigned char, int, unsigned char *);
```

```
void vec_st (vector bool char, int, vector bool char *);
void vec_st (vector bool char, int, unsigned char *);
void vec_st (vector bool char, int, signed char *);

void vec_ste (vector signed char, int, signed char *);
void vec_ste (vector unsigned char, int, unsigned char *);
void vec_ste (vector bool char, int, signed char *);
void vec_ste (vector bool char, int, unsigned char *);
void vec_ste (vector signed short, int, short *);
void vec_ste (vector unsigned short, int, unsigned short *);
void vec_ste (vector bool short, int, short *);
void vec_ste (vector bool short, int, unsigned short *);
void vec_ste (vector pixel, int, short *);
void vec_ste (vector pixel, int, unsigned short *);
void vec_ste (vector float, int, float *);
void vec_ste (vector signed int, int, int *);
void vec_ste (vector unsigned int, int, unsigned int *);
void vec_ste (vector bool int, int, int *);
void vec_ste (vector bool int, int, unsigned int *);

void vec_stvewx (vector float, int, float *);
void vec_stvewx (vector signed int, int, int *);
void vec_stvewx (vector unsigned int, int, unsigned int *);
void vec_stvewx (vector bool int, int, int *);
void vec_stvewx (vector bool int, int, unsigned int *);

void vec_stvehx (vector signed short, int, short *);
void vec_stvehx (vector unsigned short, int, unsigned short *);
void vec_stvehx (vector bool short, int, short *);
void vec_stvehx (vector bool short, int, unsigned short *);
void vec_stvehx (vector pixel, int, short *);
void vec_stvehx (vector pixel, int, unsigned short *);

void vec_stvebx (vector signed char, int, signed char *);
void vec_stvebx (vector unsigned char, int, unsigned char *);
void vec_stvebx (vector bool char, int, signed char *);
void vec_stvebx (vector bool char, int, unsigned char *);

void vec_stl (vector float, int, vector float *);
void vec_stl (vector float, int, float *);
void vec_stl (vector signed int, int, vector signed int *);
void vec_stl (vector signed int, int, int *);
void vec_stl (vector unsigned int, int, vector unsigned int *);
void vec_stl (vector unsigned int, int, unsigned int *);
void vec_stl (vector bool int, int, vector bool int *);
void vec_stl (vector bool int, int, unsigned int *);
void vec_stl (vector bool int, int, int *);
void vec_stl (vector signed short, int, vector signed short *);
void vec_stl (vector signed short, int, short *);
void vec_stl (vector unsigned short, int, vector unsigned short *);
void vec_stl (vector unsigned short, int, unsigned short *);
void vec_stl (vector bool short, int, vector bool short *);
void vec_stl (vector bool short, int, unsigned short *);
void vec_stl (vector bool short, int, short *);
void vec_stl (vector pixel, int, vector pixel *);
void vec_stl (vector pixel, int, unsigned short *);
void vec_stl (vector pixel, int, short *);
void vec_stl (vector signed char, int, vector signed char *);
```

Chapter 5: Extensions to the C Language Family

```
void vec_stl (vector signed char, int, signed char *);
void vec_stl (vector unsigned char, int, vector unsigned char *);
void vec_stl (vector unsigned char, int, unsigned char *);
void vec_stl (vector bool char, int, vector bool char *);
void vec_stl (vector bool char, int, unsigned char *);
void vec_stl (vector bool char, int, signed char *);

vector signed char vec_sub (vector bool char, vector signed char);
vector signed char vec_sub (vector signed char, vector bool char);
vector signed char vec_sub (vector signed char, vector signed char);
vector unsigned char vec_sub (vector bool char, vector unsigned char);
vector unsigned char vec_sub (vector unsigned char, vector bool char);
vector unsigned char vec_sub (vector unsigned char,
                              vector unsigned char);
vector signed short vec_sub (vector bool short, vector signed short);
vector signed short vec_sub (vector signed short, vector bool short);
vector signed short vec_sub (vector signed short, vector signed short);
vector unsigned short vec_sub (vector bool short,
                               vector unsigned short);
vector unsigned short vec_sub (vector unsigned short,
                               vector bool short);
vector unsigned short vec_sub (vector unsigned short,
                               vector unsigned short);
vector signed int vec_sub (vector bool int, vector signed int);
vector signed int vec_sub (vector signed int, vector bool int);
vector signed int vec_sub (vector signed int, vector signed int);
vector unsigned int vec_sub (vector bool int, vector unsigned int);
vector unsigned int vec_sub (vector unsigned int, vector bool int);
vector unsigned int vec_sub (vector unsigned int, vector unsigned int);
vector float vec_sub (vector float, vector float);

vector float vec_vsubfp (vector float, vector float);

vector signed int vec_vsubuwm (vector bool int, vector signed int);
vector signed int vec_vsubuwm (vector signed int, vector bool int);
vector signed int vec_vsubuwm (vector signed int, vector signed int);
vector unsigned int vec_vsubuwm (vector bool int, vector unsigned int);
vector unsigned int vec_vsubuwm (vector unsigned int, vector bool int);
vector unsigned int vec_vsubuwm (vector unsigned int,
                                 vector unsigned int);

vector signed short vec_vsubuhm (vector bool short,
                                 vector signed short);
vector signed short vec_vsubuhm (vector signed short,
                                 vector bool short);
vector signed short vec_vsubuhm (vector signed short,
                                 vector signed short);
vector unsigned short vec_vsubuhm (vector bool short,
                                   vector unsigned short);
vector unsigned short vec_vsubuhm (vector unsigned short,
                                   vector bool short);
vector unsigned short vec_vsubuhm (vector unsigned short,
                                   vector unsigned short);

vector signed char vec_vsububm (vector bool char, vector signed char);
vector signed char vec_vsububm (vector signed char, vector bool char);
vector signed char vec_vsububm (vector signed char, vector signed char);
vector unsigned char vec_vsububm (vector bool char,
```

```
                                       vector unsigned char);
vector unsigned char vec_vsububm (vector unsigned char,
                                  vector bool char);
vector unsigned char vec_vsububm (vector unsigned char,
                                  vector unsigned char);

vector unsigned int vec_subc (vector unsigned int, vector unsigned int);

vector unsigned char vec_subs (vector bool char, vector unsigned char);
vector unsigned char vec_subs (vector unsigned char, vector bool char);
vector unsigned char vec_subs (vector unsigned char,
                               vector unsigned char);
vector signed char vec_subs (vector bool char, vector signed char);
vector signed char vec_subs (vector signed char, vector bool char);
vector signed char vec_subs (vector signed char, vector signed char);
vector unsigned short vec_subs (vector bool short,
                                vector unsigned short);
vector unsigned short vec_subs (vector unsigned short,
                                vector bool short);
vector unsigned short vec_subs (vector unsigned short,
                                vector unsigned short);
vector signed short vec_subs (vector bool short, vector signed short);
vector signed short vec_subs (vector signed short, vector bool short);
vector signed short vec_subs (vector signed short, vector signed short);
vector unsigned int vec_subs (vector bool int, vector unsigned int);
vector unsigned int vec_subs (vector unsigned int, vector bool int);
vector unsigned int vec_subs (vector unsigned int, vector unsigned int);
vector signed int vec_subs (vector bool int, vector signed int);
vector signed int vec_subs (vector signed int, vector bool int);
vector signed int vec_subs (vector signed int, vector signed int);

vector signed int vec_vsubsws (vector bool int, vector signed int);
vector signed int vec_vsubsws (vector signed int, vector bool int);
vector signed int vec_vsubsws (vector signed int, vector signed int);

vector unsigned int vec_vsubuws (vector bool int, vector unsigned int);
vector unsigned int vec_vsubuws (vector unsigned int, vector bool int);
vector unsigned int vec_vsubuws (vector unsigned int,
                                 vector unsigned int);

vector signed short vec_vsubshs (vector bool short,
                                 vector signed short);
vector signed short vec_vsubshs (vector signed short,
                                 vector bool short);
vector signed short vec_vsubshs (vector signed short,
                                 vector signed short);

vector unsigned short vec_vsubuhs (vector bool short,
                                   vector unsigned short);
vector unsigned short vec_vsubuhs (vector unsigned short,
                                   vector bool short);
vector unsigned short vec_vsubuhs (vector unsigned short,
                                   vector unsigned short);

vector signed char vec_vsubsbs (vector bool char, vector signed char);
vector signed char vec_vsubsbs (vector signed char, vector bool char);
vector signed char vec_vsubsbs (vector signed char, vector signed char);
```

Chapter 5: Extensions to the C Language Family

```
vector unsigned char vec_vsububs (vector bool char,
                                  vector unsigned char);
vector unsigned char vec_vsububs (vector unsigned char,
                                  vector bool char);
vector unsigned char vec_vsububs (vector unsigned char,
                                  vector unsigned char);

vector unsigned int vec_sum4s (vector unsigned char,
                               vector unsigned int);
vector signed int vec_sum4s (vector signed char, vector signed int);
vector signed int vec_sum4s (vector signed short, vector signed int);

vector signed int vec_vsum4shs (vector signed short, vector signed int);

vector signed int vec_vsum4sbs (vector signed char, vector signed int);

vector unsigned int vec_vsum4ubs (vector unsigned char,
                                  vector unsigned int);

vector signed int vec_sum2s (vector signed int, vector signed int);

vector signed int vec_sums (vector signed int, vector signed int);

vector float vec_trunc (vector float);

vector signed short vec_unpackh (vector signed char);
vector bool short vec_unpackh (vector bool char);
vector signed int vec_unpackh (vector signed short);
vector bool int vec_unpackh (vector bool short);
vector unsigned int vec_unpackh (vector pixel);

vector bool int vec_vupkhsh (vector bool short);
vector signed int vec_vupkhsh (vector signed short);

vector unsigned int vec_vupkhpx (vector pixel);

vector bool short vec_vupkhsb (vector bool char);
vector signed short vec_vupkhsb (vector signed char);

vector signed short vec_unpackl (vector signed char);
vector bool short vec_unpackl (vector bool char);
vector unsigned int vec_unpackl (vector pixel);
vector signed int vec_unpackl (vector signed short);
vector bool int vec_unpackl (vector bool short);

vector unsigned int vec_vupklpx (vector pixel);

vector bool int vec_vupklsh (vector bool short);
vector signed int vec_vupklsh (vector signed short);

vector bool short vec_vupklsb (vector bool char);
vector signed short vec_vupklsb (vector signed char);

vector float vec_xor (vector float, vector float);
vector float vec_xor (vector float, vector bool int);
vector float vec_xor (vector bool int, vector float);
vector bool int vec_xor (vector bool int, vector bool int);
vector signed int vec_xor (vector bool int, vector signed int);
```

```
vector signed int vec_xor (vector signed int, vector bool int);
vector signed int vec_xor (vector signed int, vector signed int);
vector unsigned int vec_xor (vector bool int, vector unsigned int);
vector unsigned int vec_xor (vector unsigned int, vector bool int);
vector unsigned int vec_xor (vector unsigned int, vector unsigned int);
vector bool short vec_xor (vector bool short, vector bool short);
vector signed short vec_xor (vector bool short, vector signed short);
vector signed short vec_xor (vector signed short, vector bool short);
vector signed short vec_xor (vector signed short, vector signed short);
vector unsigned short vec_xor (vector bool short,
                               vector unsigned short);
vector unsigned short vec_xor (vector unsigned short,
                               vector bool short);
vector unsigned short vec_xor (vector unsigned short,
                               vector unsigned short);
vector signed char vec_xor (vector bool char, vector signed char);
vector bool char vec_xor (vector bool char, vector bool char);
vector signed char vec_xor (vector signed char, vector bool char);
vector signed char vec_xor (vector signed char, vector signed char);
vector unsigned char vec_xor (vector bool char, vector unsigned char);
vector unsigned char vec_xor (vector unsigned char, vector bool char);
vector unsigned char vec_xor (vector unsigned char,
                              vector unsigned char);

int vec_all_eq (vector signed char, vector bool char);
int vec_all_eq (vector signed char, vector signed char);
int vec_all_eq (vector unsigned char, vector bool char);
int vec_all_eq (vector unsigned char, vector unsigned char);
int vec_all_eq (vector bool char, vector bool char);
int vec_all_eq (vector bool char, vector unsigned char);
int vec_all_eq (vector bool char, vector signed char);
int vec_all_eq (vector signed short, vector bool short);
int vec_all_eq (vector signed short, vector signed short);
int vec_all_eq (vector unsigned short, vector bool short);
int vec_all_eq (vector unsigned short, vector unsigned short);
int vec_all_eq (vector bool short, vector bool short);
int vec_all_eq (vector bool short, vector unsigned short);
int vec_all_eq (vector bool short, vector signed short);
int vec_all_eq (vector pixel, vector pixel);
int vec_all_eq (vector signed int, vector bool int);
int vec_all_eq (vector signed int, vector signed int);
int vec_all_eq (vector unsigned int, vector bool int);
int vec_all_eq (vector unsigned int, vector unsigned int);
int vec_all_eq (vector bool int, vector bool int);
int vec_all_eq (vector bool int, vector unsigned int);
int vec_all_eq (vector bool int, vector signed int);
int vec_all_eq (vector float, vector float);

int vec_all_ge (vector bool char, vector unsigned char);
int vec_all_ge (vector unsigned char, vector bool char);
int vec_all_ge (vector unsigned char, vector unsigned char);
int vec_all_ge (vector bool char, vector signed char);
int vec_all_ge (vector signed char, vector bool char);
int vec_all_ge (vector signed char, vector signed char);
int vec_all_ge (vector bool short, vector unsigned short);
int vec_all_ge (vector unsigned short, vector bool short);
int vec_all_ge (vector unsigned short, vector unsigned short);
int vec_all_ge (vector signed short, vector signed short);
```

```
int vec_all_ge (vector bool short, vector signed short);
int vec_all_ge (vector signed short, vector bool short);
int vec_all_ge (vector bool int, vector unsigned int);
int vec_all_ge (vector unsigned int, vector bool int);
int vec_all_ge (vector unsigned int, vector unsigned int);
int vec_all_ge (vector bool int, vector signed int);
int vec_all_ge (vector signed int, vector bool int);
int vec_all_ge (vector signed int, vector signed int);
int vec_all_ge (vector float, vector float);

int vec_all_gt (vector bool char, vector unsigned char);
int vec_all_gt (vector unsigned char, vector bool char);
int vec_all_gt (vector unsigned char, vector unsigned char);
int vec_all_gt (vector bool char, vector signed char);
int vec_all_gt (vector signed char, vector bool char);
int vec_all_gt (vector signed char, vector signed char);
int vec_all_gt (vector bool short, vector unsigned short);
int vec_all_gt (vector unsigned short, vector bool short);
int vec_all_gt (vector unsigned short, vector unsigned short);
int vec_all_gt (vector bool short, vector signed short);
int vec_all_gt (vector signed short, vector bool short);
int vec_all_gt (vector signed short, vector signed short);
int vec_all_gt (vector bool int, vector unsigned int);
int vec_all_gt (vector unsigned int, vector bool int);
int vec_all_gt (vector unsigned int, vector unsigned int);
int vec_all_gt (vector bool int, vector signed int);
int vec_all_gt (vector signed int, vector bool int);
int vec_all_gt (vector signed int, vector signed int);
int vec_all_gt (vector float, vector float);

int vec_all_in (vector float, vector float);

int vec_all_le (vector bool char, vector unsigned char);
int vec_all_le (vector unsigned char, vector bool char);
int vec_all_le (vector unsigned char, vector unsigned char);
int vec_all_le (vector bool char, vector signed char);
int vec_all_le (vector signed char, vector bool char);
int vec_all_le (vector signed char, vector signed char);
int vec_all_le (vector bool short, vector unsigned short);
int vec_all_le (vector unsigned short, vector bool short);
int vec_all_le (vector unsigned short, vector unsigned short);
int vec_all_le (vector bool short, vector signed short);
int vec_all_le (vector signed short, vector bool short);
int vec_all_le (vector signed short, vector signed short);
int vec_all_le (vector bool int, vector unsigned int);
int vec_all_le (vector unsigned int, vector bool int);
int vec_all_le (vector unsigned int, vector unsigned int);
int vec_all_le (vector bool int, vector signed int);
int vec_all_le (vector signed int, vector bool int);
int vec_all_le (vector signed int, vector signed int);
int vec_all_le (vector float, vector float);

int vec_all_lt (vector bool char, vector unsigned char);
int vec_all_lt (vector unsigned char, vector bool char);
int vec_all_lt (vector unsigned char, vector unsigned char);
int vec_all_lt (vector bool char, vector signed char);
int vec_all_lt (vector signed char, vector bool char);
int vec_all_lt (vector signed char, vector signed char);
```

```
int vec_all_lt (vector bool short, vector unsigned short);
int vec_all_lt (vector unsigned short, vector bool short);
int vec_all_lt (vector unsigned short, vector unsigned short);
int vec_all_lt (vector bool short, vector signed short);
int vec_all_lt (vector signed short, vector bool short);
int vec_all_lt (vector signed short, vector signed short);
int vec_all_lt (vector bool int, vector unsigned int);
int vec_all_lt (vector unsigned int, vector bool int);
int vec_all_lt (vector unsigned int, vector unsigned int);
int vec_all_lt (vector bool int, vector signed int);
int vec_all_lt (vector signed int, vector bool int);
int vec_all_lt (vector signed int, vector signed int);
int vec_all_lt (vector float, vector float);

int vec_all_nan (vector float);

int vec_all_ne (vector signed char, vector bool char);
int vec_all_ne (vector signed char, vector signed char);
int vec_all_ne (vector unsigned char, vector bool char);
int vec_all_ne (vector unsigned char, vector unsigned char);
int vec_all_ne (vector bool char, vector bool char);
int vec_all_ne (vector bool char, vector unsigned char);
int vec_all_ne (vector bool char, vector signed char);
int vec_all_ne (vector signed short, vector bool short);
int vec_all_ne (vector signed short, vector signed short);
int vec_all_ne (vector unsigned short, vector bool short);
int vec_all_ne (vector unsigned short, vector unsigned short);
int vec_all_ne (vector bool short, vector bool short);
int vec_all_ne (vector bool short, vector unsigned short);
int vec_all_ne (vector bool short, vector signed short);
int vec_all_ne (vector pixel, vector pixel);
int vec_all_ne (vector signed int, vector bool int);
int vec_all_ne (vector signed int, vector signed int);
int vec_all_ne (vector unsigned int, vector bool int);
int vec_all_ne (vector unsigned int, vector unsigned int);
int vec_all_ne (vector bool int, vector bool int);
int vec_all_ne (vector bool int, vector unsigned int);
int vec_all_ne (vector bool int, vector signed int);
int vec_all_ne (vector float, vector float);

int vec_all_nge (vector float, vector float);

int vec_all_ngt (vector float, vector float);

int vec_all_nle (vector float, vector float);

int vec_all_nlt (vector float, vector float);

int vec_all_numeric (vector float);

int vec_any_eq (vector signed char, vector bool char);
int vec_any_eq (vector signed char, vector signed char);
int vec_any_eq (vector unsigned char, vector bool char);
int vec_any_eq (vector unsigned char, vector unsigned char);
int vec_any_eq (vector bool char, vector bool char);
int vec_any_eq (vector bool char, vector unsigned char);
int vec_any_eq (vector bool char, vector signed char);
int vec_any_eq (vector signed short, vector bool short);
```

Chapter 5: Extensions to the C Language Family

```
int vec_any_eq (vector signed short, vector signed short);
int vec_any_eq (vector unsigned short, vector bool short);
int vec_any_eq (vector unsigned short, vector unsigned short);
int vec_any_eq (vector bool short, vector bool short);
int vec_any_eq (vector bool short, vector unsigned short);
int vec_any_eq (vector bool short, vector signed short);
int vec_any_eq (vector pixel, vector pixel);
int vec_any_eq (vector signed int, vector bool int);
int vec_any_eq (vector signed int, vector signed int);
int vec_any_eq (vector unsigned int, vector bool int);
int vec_any_eq (vector unsigned int, vector unsigned int);
int vec_any_eq (vector bool int, vector bool int);
int vec_any_eq (vector bool int, vector unsigned int);
int vec_any_eq (vector bool int, vector signed int);
int vec_any_eq (vector float, vector float);

int vec_any_ge (vector signed char, vector bool char);
int vec_any_ge (vector unsigned char, vector bool char);
int vec_any_ge (vector unsigned char, vector unsigned char);
int vec_any_ge (vector signed char, vector signed char);
int vec_any_ge (vector bool char, vector unsigned char);
int vec_any_ge (vector bool char, vector signed char);
int vec_any_ge (vector unsigned short, vector bool short);
int vec_any_ge (vector unsigned short, vector unsigned short);
int vec_any_ge (vector signed short, vector signed short);
int vec_any_ge (vector signed short, vector bool short);
int vec_any_ge (vector bool short, vector unsigned short);
int vec_any_ge (vector bool short, vector signed short);
int vec_any_ge (vector signed int, vector bool int);
int vec_any_ge (vector unsigned int, vector bool int);
int vec_any_ge (vector unsigned int, vector unsigned int);
int vec_any_ge (vector signed int, vector signed int);
int vec_any_ge (vector bool int, vector unsigned int);
int vec_any_ge (vector bool int, vector signed int);
int vec_any_ge (vector float, vector float);

int vec_any_gt (vector bool char, vector unsigned char);
int vec_any_gt (vector unsigned char, vector bool char);
int vec_any_gt (vector unsigned char, vector unsigned char);
int vec_any_gt (vector bool char, vector signed char);
int vec_any_gt (vector signed char, vector bool char);
int vec_any_gt (vector signed char, vector signed char);
int vec_any_gt (vector bool short, vector unsigned short);
int vec_any_gt (vector unsigned short, vector bool short);
int vec_any_gt (vector unsigned short, vector unsigned short);
int vec_any_gt (vector bool short, vector signed short);
int vec_any_gt (vector signed short, vector bool short);
int vec_any_gt (vector signed short, vector signed short);
int vec_any_gt (vector bool int, vector unsigned int);
int vec_any_gt (vector unsigned int, vector bool int);
int vec_any_gt (vector unsigned int, vector unsigned int);
int vec_any_gt (vector bool int, vector signed int);
int vec_any_gt (vector signed int, vector bool int);
int vec_any_gt (vector signed int, vector signed int);
int vec_any_gt (vector float, vector float);

int vec_any_le (vector bool char, vector unsigned char);
int vec_any_le (vector unsigned char, vector bool char);
```

```
int vec_any_le (vector unsigned char, vector unsigned char);
int vec_any_le (vector bool char, vector signed char);
int vec_any_le (vector signed char, vector bool char);
int vec_any_le (vector signed char, vector signed char);
int vec_any_le (vector bool short, vector unsigned short);
int vec_any_le (vector unsigned short, vector bool short);
int vec_any_le (vector unsigned short, vector unsigned short);
int vec_any_le (vector bool short, vector signed short);
int vec_any_le (vector signed short, vector bool short);
int vec_any_le (vector signed short, vector signed short);
int vec_any_le (vector bool int, vector unsigned int);
int vec_any_le (vector unsigned int, vector bool int);
int vec_any_le (vector unsigned int, vector unsigned int);
int vec_any_le (vector bool int, vector signed int);
int vec_any_le (vector signed int, vector bool int);
int vec_any_le (vector signed int, vector signed int);
int vec_any_le (vector float, vector float);

int vec_any_lt (vector bool char, vector unsigned char);
int vec_any_lt (vector unsigned char, vector bool char);
int vec_any_lt (vector unsigned char, vector unsigned char);
int vec_any_lt (vector bool char, vector signed char);
int vec_any_lt (vector signed char, vector bool char);
int vec_any_lt (vector signed char, vector signed char);
int vec_any_lt (vector bool short, vector unsigned short);
int vec_any_lt (vector unsigned short, vector bool short);
int vec_any_lt (vector unsigned short, vector unsigned short);
int vec_any_lt (vector bool short, vector signed short);
int vec_any_lt (vector signed short, vector bool short);
int vec_any_lt (vector signed short, vector signed short);
int vec_any_lt (vector bool int, vector unsigned int);
int vec_any_lt (vector unsigned int, vector bool int);
int vec_any_lt (vector unsigned int, vector unsigned int);
int vec_any_lt (vector bool int, vector signed int);
int vec_any_lt (vector signed int, vector bool int);
int vec_any_lt (vector signed int, vector signed int);
int vec_any_lt (vector float, vector float);

int vec_any_nan (vector float);

int vec_any_ne (vector signed char, vector bool char);
int vec_any_ne (vector signed char, vector signed char);
int vec_any_ne (vector unsigned char, vector bool char);
int vec_any_ne (vector unsigned char, vector unsigned char);
int vec_any_ne (vector bool char, vector bool char);
int vec_any_ne (vector bool char, vector unsigned char);
int vec_any_ne (vector bool char, vector signed char);
int vec_any_ne (vector signed short, vector bool short);
int vec_any_ne (vector signed short, vector signed short);
int vec_any_ne (vector unsigned short, vector bool short);
int vec_any_ne (vector unsigned short, vector unsigned short);
int vec_any_ne (vector bool short, vector bool short);
int vec_any_ne (vector bool short, vector unsigned short);
int vec_any_ne (vector bool short, vector signed short);
int vec_any_ne (vector pixel, vector pixel);
int vec_any_ne (vector signed int, vector bool int);
int vec_any_ne (vector signed int, vector signed int);
int vec_any_ne (vector unsigned int, vector bool int);
```

Chapter 5: Extensions to the C Language Family   493

```
int vec_any_ne (vector unsigned int, vector unsigned int);
int vec_any_ne (vector bool int, vector bool int);
int vec_any_ne (vector bool int, vector unsigned int);
int vec_any_ne (vector bool int, vector signed int);
int vec_any_ne (vector float, vector float);

int vec_any_nge (vector float, vector float);

int vec_any_ngt (vector float, vector float);

int vec_any_nle (vector float, vector float);

int vec_any_nlt (vector float, vector float);

int vec_any_numeric (vector float);

int vec_any_out (vector float, vector float);
```

5.50.10 SPARC VIS Built-in Functions

GCC supports SIMD operations on the SPARC using both the generic vector extensions (see Section 5.45 [Vector Extensions], page 332) as well as built-in functions for the SPARC Visual Instruction Set (VIS). When you use the '-mvis' switch, the VIS extension is exposed as the following built-in functions:

```
typedef int v2si __attribute__ ((vector_size (8)));
typedef short v4hi __attribute__ ((vector_size (8)));
typedef short v2hi __attribute__ ((vector_size (4)));
typedef char v8qi __attribute__ ((vector_size (8)));
typedef char v4qi __attribute__ ((vector_size (4)));

void * __builtin_vis_alignaddr (void *, long);
int64_t __builtin_vis_faligndatadi (int64_t, int64_t);
v2si __builtin_vis_faligndatav2si (v2si, v2si);
v4hi __builtin_vis_faligndatav4hi (v4si, v4si);
v8qi __builtin_vis_faligndatav8qi (v8qi, v8qi);

v4hi __builtin_vis_fexpand (v4qi);

v4hi __builtin_vis_fmul8x16 (v4qi, v4hi);
v4hi __builtin_vis_fmul8x16au (v4qi, v4hi);
v4hi __builtin_vis_fmul8x16al (v4qi, v4hi);
v4hi __builtin_vis_fmul8sux16 (v8qi, v4hi);
v4hi __builtin_vis_fmul8ulx16 (v8qi, v4hi);
v2si __builtin_vis_fmuld8sux16 (v4qi, v2hi);
v2si __builtin_vis_fmuld8ulx16 (v4qi, v2hi);

v4qi __builtin_vis_fpack16 (v4hi);
v8qi __builtin_vis_fpack32 (v2si, v2si);
v2hi __builtin_vis_fpackfix (v2si);
v8qi __builtin_vis_fpmerge (v4qi, v4qi);

int64_t __builtin_vis_pdist (v8qi, v8qi, int64_t);
```

5.50.11 SPU Built-in Functions

GCC provides extensions for the SPU processor as described in the Sony/Toshiba/IBM SPU Language Extensions Specification, which can be found at http://cell.scei.co.jp/

or http://www.ibm.com/developerworks/power/cell/. GCC's implementation differs in several ways.

- The optional extension of specifying vector constants in parentheses is not supported.
- A vector initializer requires no cast if the vector constant is of the same type as the variable it is initializing.
- If `signed` or `unsigned` is omitted, the signedness of the vector type is the default signedness of the base type. The default varies depending on the operating system, so a portable program should always specify the signedness.
- By default, the keyword `__vector` is added. The macro `vector` is defined in `<spu_intrinsics.h>` and can be undefined.
- GCC allows using a `typedef` name as the type specifier for a vector type.
- For C, overloaded functions are implemented with macros so the following does not work:

    ```
    spu_add ((vector signed int){1, 2, 3, 4}, foo);
    ```

    Since `spu_add` is a macro, the vector constant in the example is treated as four separate arguments. Wrap the entire argument in parentheses for this to work.
- The extended version of `__builtin_expect` is not supported.

Note: Only the interface described in the aforementioned specification is supported. Internally, GCC uses built-in functions to implement the required functionality, but these are not supported and are subject to change without notice.

5.51 Format Checks Specific to Particular Target Machines

For some target machines, GCC supports additional options to the format attribute (see Section 5.27 [Declaring Attributes of Functions], page 264).

5.51.1 Solaris Format Checks

Solaris targets support the `cmn_err` (or `__cmn_err__`) format check. `cmn_err` accepts a subset of the standard `printf` conversions, and the two-argument %b conversion for displaying bit-fields. See the Solaris man page for `cmn_err` for more information.

5.52 Pragmas Accepted by GCC

GCC supports several types of pragmas, primarily in order to compile code originally written for other compilers. Note that in general we do not recommend the use of pragmas; See Section 5.27 [Function Attributes], page 264, for further explanation.

5.52.1 ARM Pragmas

The ARM target defines pragmas for controlling the default addition of `long_call` and `short_call` attributes to functions. See Section 5.27 [Function Attributes], page 264, for information about the effects of these attributes.

`long_calls`
    Set all subsequent functions to have the `long_call` attribute.

`no_long_calls`
    Set all subsequent functions to have the `short_call` attribute.

Chapter 5: Extensions to the C Language Family   495

`long_calls_off`
> Do not affect the `long_call` or `short_call` attributes of subsequent functions.

5.52.2 M32C Pragmas

`memregs number`
> Overrides the command line option `-memregs=` for the current file. Use with care! This pragma must be before any function in the file, and mixing different memregs values in different objects may make them incompatible. This pragma is useful when a performance-critical function uses a memreg for temporary values, as it may allow you to reduce the number of memregs used.

5.52.3 RS/6000 and PowerPC Pragmas

The RS/6000 and PowerPC targets define one pragma for controlling whether or not the `longcall` attribute is added to function declarations by default. This pragma overrides the '`-mlongcall`' option, but not the `longcall` and `shortcall` attributes. See Section 3.17.27 [RS/6000 and PowerPC Options], page 194, for more information about when long calls are and are not necessary.

`longcall (1)`
> Apply the `longcall` attribute to all subsequent function declarations.

`longcall (0)`
> Do not apply the `longcall` attribute to subsequent function declarations.

5.52.4 Darwin Pragmas

The following pragmas are available for all architectures running the Darwin operating system. These are useful for compatibility with other Mac OS compilers.

`mark tokens...`
> This pragma is accepted, but has no effect.

`options align=alignment`
> This pragma sets the alignment of fields in structures. The values of *alignment* may be `mac68k`, to emulate m68k alignment, or `power`, to emulate PowerPC alignment. Uses of this pragma nest properly; to restore the previous setting, use `reset` for the *alignment*.

`segment tokens...`
> This pragma is accepted, but has no effect.

`unused (var [, var]...)`
> This pragma declares variables to be possibly unused. GCC will not produce warnings for the listed variables. The effect is similar to that of the `unused` attribute, except that this pragma may appear anywhere within the variables' scopes.

5.52.5 Solaris Pragmas

The Solaris target supports `#pragma redefine_extname` (see Section 5.52.6 [Symbol-Renaming Pragmas], page 496). It also supports additional `#pragma` directives for compatibility with the system compiler.

align *alignment* (*variable* [, *variable*]...)
> Increase the minimum alignment of each *variable* to *alignment*. This is the same as GCC's **aligned** attribute see Section 5.34 [Variable Attributes], page 286). Macro expansion occurs on the arguments to this pragma when compiling C and Objective-C. It does not currently occur when compiling C++, but this is a bug which may be fixed in a future release.

fini (*function* [, *function*]...)
> This pragma causes each listed *function* to be called after main, or during shared module unloading, by adding a call to the .fini section.

init (*function* [, *function*]...)
> This pragma causes each listed *function* to be called during initialization (before main) or during shared module loading, by adding a call to the .init section.

5.52.6 Symbol-Renaming Pragmas

For compatibility with the Solaris and Tru64 UNIX system headers, GCC supports two **#pragma** directives which change the name used in assembly for a given declaration. These pragmas are only available on platforms whose system headers need them. To get this effect on all platforms supported by GCC, use the asm labels extension (see Section 5.39 [Asm Labels], page 326).

redefine_extname *oldname newname*
> This pragma gives the C function *oldname* the assembly symbol *newname*. The preprocessor macro __PRAGMA_REDEFINE_EXTNAME will be defined if this pragma is available (currently only on Solaris).

extern_prefix *string*
> This pragma causes all subsequent external function and variable declarations to have *string* prepended to their assembly symbols. This effect may be terminated with another **extern_prefix** pragma whose argument is an empty string. The preprocessor macro __PRAGMA_EXTERN_PREFIX will be defined if this pragma is available (currently only on Tru64 UNIX).

These pragmas and the asm labels extension interact in a complicated manner. Here are some corner cases you may want to be aware of.

1. Both pragmas silently apply only to declarations with external linkage. Asm labels do not have this restriction.
2. In C++, both pragmas silently apply only to declarations with "C" linkage. Again, asm labels do not have this restriction.
3. If any of the three ways of changing the assembly name of a declaration is applied to a declaration whose assembly name has already been determined (either by a previous use of one of these features, or because the compiler needed the assembly name in order to generate code), and the new name is different, a warning issues and the name does not change.
4. The *oldname* used by **#pragma redefine_extname** is always the C-language name.
5. If **#pragma extern_prefix** is in effect, and a declaration occurs with an asm label attached, the prefix is silently ignored for that declaration.

Chapter 5: Extensions to the C Language Family   497

6. If #pragma extern_prefix and #pragma redefine_extname apply to the same declaration, whichever triggered first wins, and a warning issues if they contradict each other. (We would like to have #pragma redefine_extname always win, for consistency with asm labels, but if #pragma extern_prefix triggers first we have no way of knowing that that happened.)

5.52.7 Structure-Packing Pragmas

For compatibility with Win32, GCC supports a set of #pragma directives which change the maximum alignment of members of structures (other than zero-width bitfields), unions, and classes subsequently defined. The *n* value below always is required to be a small power of two and specifies the new alignment in bytes.

1. #pragma pack(*n*) simply sets the new alignment.
2. #pragma pack() sets the alignment to the one that was in effect when compilation started (see also command line option '-fpack-struct[=<n>]' see Section 3.18 [Code Gen Options], page 222).
3. #pragma pack(push[,*n*]) pushes the current alignment setting on an internal stack and then optionally sets the new alignment.
4. #pragma pack(pop) restores the alignment setting to the one saved at the top of the internal stack (and removes that stack entry). Note that #pragma pack([*n*]) does not influence this internal stack; thus it is possible to have #pragma pack(push) followed by multiple #pragma pack(*n*) instances and finalized by a single #pragma pack(pop).

Some targets, e.g. i386 and powerpc, support the ms_struct #pragma which lays out a structure as the documented __attribute__ ((ms_struct)).

1. #pragma ms_struct on turns on the layout for structures declared.
2. #pragma ms_struct off turns off the layout for structures declared.
3. #pragma ms_struct reset goes back to the default layout.

5.52.8 Weak Pragmas

For compatibility with SVR4, GCC supports a set of #pragma directives for declaring symbols to be weak, and defining weak aliases.

#pragma weak *symbol*

> This pragma declares *symbol* to be weak, as if the declaration had the attribute of the same name. The pragma may appear before or after the declaration of *symbol*, but must appear before either its first use or its definition. It is not an error for *symbol* to never be defined at all.

#pragma weak *symbol1* = *symbol2*

> This pragma declares *symbol1* to be a weak alias of *symbol2*. It is an error if *symbol2* is not defined in the current translation unit.

5.52.9 Diagnostic Pragmas

GCC allows the user to selectively enable or disable certain types of diagnostics, and change the kind of the diagnostic. For example, a project's policy might require that all sources compile with '-Werror' but certain files might have exceptions allowing specific types of warnings. Or, a project might selectively enable diagnostics and treat them as errors depending on which preprocessor macros are defined.

#pragma GCC diagnostic *kind option*

> Modifies the disposition of a diagnostic. Note that not all diagnostics are modifiable; at the moment only warnings (normally controlled by '-W...') can be controlled, and not all of them. Use '-fdiagnostics-show-option' to determine which diagnostics are controllable and which option controls them.
>
> *kind* is 'error' to treat this diagnostic as an error, 'warning' to treat it like a warning (even if '-Werror' is in effect), or 'ignored' if the diagnostic is to be ignored. *option* is a double quoted string which matches the command line option.
>
> ```
> #pragma GCC diagnostic warning "-Wformat"
> #pragma GCC diagnostic error "-Wformat"
> #pragma GCC diagnostic ignored "-Wformat"
> ```
>
> Note that these pragmas override any command line options. Also, while it is syntactically valid to put these pragmas anywhere in your sources, the only supported location for them is before any data or functions are defined. Doing otherwise may result in unpredictable results depending on how the optimizer manages your sources. If the same option is listed multiple times, the last one specified is the one that is in effect. This pragma is not intended to be a general purpose replacement for command line options, but for implementing strict control over project policies.

5.52.10 Visibility Pragmas

#pragma GCC visibility push(*visibility*)
#pragma GCC visibility pop

> This pragma allows the user to set the visibility for multiple declarations without having to give each a visibility attribute See Section 5.27 [Function Attributes], page 264, for more information about visibility and the attribute syntax.
>
> In C++, '#pragma GCC visibility' affects only namespace-scope declarations. Class members and template specializations are not affected; if you want to override the visibility for a particular member or instantiation, you must use an attribute.

5.53 Unnamed struct/union fields within structs/unions

For compatibility with other compilers, GCC allows you to define a structure or union that contains, as fields, structures and unions without names. For example:

```
struct {
  int a;
  union {
    int b;
    float c;
  };
  int d;
} foo;
```

Chapter 5: Extensions to the C Language Family   499

In this example, the user would be able to access members of the unnamed union with code like 'foo.b'. Note that only unnamed structs and unions are allowed, you may not have, for example, an unnamed int.

You must never create such structures that cause ambiguous field definitions. For example, this structure:

```
struct {
  int a;
  struct {
    int a;
  };
} foo;
```

It is ambiguous which `a` is being referred to with 'foo.a'. Such constructs are not supported and must be avoided. In the future, such constructs may be detected and treated as compilation errors.

Unless '-fms-extensions' is used, the unnamed field must be a structure or union definition without a tag (for example, 'struct { int a; };'). If '-fms-extensions' is used, the field may also be a definition with a tag such as 'struct foo { int a; };', a reference to a previously defined structure or union such as 'struct foo;', or a reference to a typedef name for a previously defined structure or union type.

5.54 Thread-Local Storage

Thread-local storage (TLS) is a mechanism by which variables are allocated such that there is one instance of the variable per extant thread. The run-time model GCC uses to implement this originates in the IA-64 processor-specific ABI, but has since been migrated to other processors as well. It requires significant support from the linker (ld), dynamic linker (ld.so), and system libraries ('libc.so' and 'libpthread.so'), so it is not available everywhere.

At the user level, the extension is visible with a new storage class keyword: __thread. For example:

```
__thread int i;
extern __thread struct state s;
static __thread char *p;
```

The __thread specifier may be used alone, with the extern or static specifiers, but with no other storage class specifier. When used with extern or static, __thread must appear immediately after the other storage class specifier.

The __thread specifier may be applied to any global, file-scoped static, function-scoped static, or static data member of a class. It may not be applied to block-scoped automatic or non-static data member.

When the address-of operator is applied to a thread-local variable, it is evaluated at run-time and returns the address of the current thread's instance of that variable. An address so obtained may be used by any thread. When a thread terminates, any pointers to thread-local variables in that thread become invalid.

No static initialization may refer to the address of a thread-local variable.

In C++, if an initializer is present for a thread-local variable, it must be a *constant-expression*, as defined in 5.19.2 of the ANSI/ISO C++ standard.

See ELF Handling For Thread-Local Storage for a detailed explanation of the four thread-local storage addressing models, and how the run-time is expected to function.

5.54.1 ISO/IEC 9899:1999 Edits for Thread-Local Storage

The following are a set of changes to ISO/IEC 9899:1999 (aka C99) that document the exact semantics of the language extension.

- *5.1.2 Execution environments*

    Add new text after paragraph 1

    > Within either execution environment, a *thread* is a flow of control within a program. It is implementation defined whether or not there may be more than one thread associated with a program. It is implementation defined how threads beyond the first are created, the name and type of the function called at thread startup, and how threads may be terminated. However, objects with thread storage duration shall be initialized before thread startup.

- *6.2.4 Storage durations of objects*

    Add new text before paragraph 3

    > An object whose identifier is declared with the storage-class specifier `__thread` has *thread storage duration*. Its lifetime is the entire execution of the thread, and its stored value is initialized only once, prior to thread startup.

- *6.4.1 Keywords*

    Add `__thread`.

- *6.7.1 Storage-class specifiers*

    Add `__thread` to the list of storage class specifiers in paragraph 1.

    Change paragraph 2 to

    > With the exception of `__thread`, at most one storage-class specifier may be given [...]. The `__thread` specifier may be used alone, or immediately following `extern` or `static`.

    Add new text after paragraph 6

    > The declaration of an identifier for a variable that has block scope that specifies `__thread` shall also specify either `extern` or `static`.
    >
    > The `__thread` specifier shall be used only with variables.

5.54.2 ISO/IEC 14882:1998 Edits for Thread-Local Storage

The following are a set of changes to ISO/IEC 14882:1998 (aka C++98) that document the exact semantics of the language extension.

- [intro.execution]

    New text after paragraph 4

    > A *thread* is a flow of control within the abstract machine. It is implementation defined whether or not there may be more than one thread.

    New text after paragraph 7

Chapter 5: Extensions to the C Language Family   501

It is unspecified whether additional action must be taken to ensure when and whether side effects are visible to other threads.

- [lex.key]

  Add `__thread`.

- [basic.start.main]

  Add after paragraph 5

  The thread that begins execution at the `main` function is called the *main thread*. It is implementation defined how functions beginning threads other than the main thread are designated or typed. A function so designated, as well as the `main` function, is called a *thread startup function*. It is implementation defined what happens if a thread startup function returns. It is implementation defined what happens to other threads when any thread calls `exit`.

- [basic.start.init]

  Add after paragraph 4

  The storage for an object of thread storage duration shall be statically initialized before the first statement of the thread startup function. An object of thread storage duration shall not require dynamic initialization.

- [basic.start.term]

  Add after paragraph 3

  The type of an object with thread storage duration shall not have a non-trivial destructor, nor shall it be an array type whose elements (directly or indirectly) have non-trivial destructors.

- [basic.stc]

  Add "thread storage duration" to the list in paragraph 1.

  Change paragraph 2

  Thread, static, and automatic storage durations are associated with objects introduced by declarations [...].

  Add `__thread` to the list of specifiers in paragraph 3.

- [basic.stc.thread]

  New section before [basic.stc.static]

  The keyword `__thread` applied to a non-local object gives the object thread storage duration.

  A local variable or class data member declared both `static` and `__thread` gives the variable or member thread storage duration.

- [basic.stc.static]

  Change paragraph 1

  All objects which have neither thread storage duration, dynamic storage duration nor are local [...].

- [dcl.stc]

  Add `__thread` to the list in paragraph 1.

Change paragraph 1

With the exception of __thread, at most one *storage-class-specifier* shall appear in a given *decl-specifier-seq*. The __thread specifier may be used alone, or immediately following the extern or static specifiers. [...]

Add after paragraph 5

The __thread specifier can be applied only to the names of objects and to anonymous unions.

- [class.mem]

Add after paragraph 6

Non-static members shall not be __thread.

5.55 Binary constants using the '0b' prefix

Integer constants can be written as binary constants, consisting of a sequence of '0' and '1' digits, prefixed by '0b' or '0B'. This is particularly useful in environments that operate a lot on the bit-level (like microcontrollers).

The following statements are identical:
```
i =         42;
i =       0x2a;
i =        052;
i = 0b101010;
```

The type of these constants follows the same rules as for octal or hexadecimal integer constants, so suffixes like 'L' or 'UL' can be applied.

6 Extensions to the C++ Language

The GNU compiler provides these extensions to the C++ language (and you can also use most of the C language extensions in your C++ programs). If you want to write code that checks whether these features are available, you can test for the GNU compiler the same way as for C programs: check for a predefined macro __GNUC__. You can also use __GNUG__ to test specifically for GNU C++ (see Section "Predefined Macros" in *The GNU C Preprocessor*).

6.1 When is a Volatile Object Accessed?

Both the C and C++ standard have the concept of volatile objects. These are normally accessed by pointers and used for accessing hardware. The standards encourage compilers to refrain from optimizations concerning accesses to volatile objects. The C standard leaves it implementation defined as to what constitutes a volatile access. The C++ standard omits to specify this, except to say that C++ should behave in a similar manner to C with respect to volatiles, where possible. The minimum either standard specifies is that at a sequence point all previous accesses to volatile objects have stabilized and no subsequent accesses have occurred. Thus an implementation is free to reorder and combine volatile accesses which occur between sequence points, but cannot do so for accesses across a sequence point. The use of volatiles does not allow you to violate the restriction on updating objects multiple times within a sequence point.

See Section 4.10 [Volatile qualifier and the C compiler], page 242.

The behavior differs slightly between C and C++ in the non-obvious cases:

```
volatile int *src = somevalue;
*src;
```

With C, such expressions are rvalues, and GCC interprets this either as a read of the volatile object being pointed to or only as request to evaluate the side-effects. The C++ standard specifies that such expressions do not undergo lvalue to rvalue conversion, and that the type of the dereferenced object may be incomplete. The C++ standard does not specify explicitly that it is this lvalue to rvalue conversion which may be responsible for causing an access. However, there is reason to believe that it is, because otherwise certain simple expressions become undefined. However, because it would surprise most programmers, G++ treats dereferencing a pointer to volatile object of complete type when the value is unused as GCC would do for an equivalent type in C. When the object has incomplete type, G++ issues a warning; if you wish to force an error, you must force a conversion to rvalue with, for instance, a static cast.

When using a reference to volatile, G++ does not treat equivalent expressions as accesses to volatiles, but instead issues a warning that no volatile is accessed. The rationale for this is that otherwise it becomes difficult to determine where volatile access occur, and not possible to ignore the return value from functions returning volatile references. Again, if you wish to force a read, cast the reference to an rvalue.

6.2 Restricting Pointer Aliasing

As with the C front end, G++ understands the C99 feature of restricted pointers, specified with the __restrict__, or __restrict type qualifier. Because you cannot compile C++ by specifying the '-std=c99' language flag, restrict is not a keyword in C++.

In addition to allowing restricted pointers, you can specify restricted references, which
indicate that the reference is not aliased in the local context.

```
void fn (int *__restrict__ rptr, int &__restrict__ rref)
{
  /* ... */
}
```

In the body of **fn**, *rptr* points to an unaliased integer and *rref* refers to a (different) unaliased
integer.

You may also specify whether a member function's *this* pointer is unaliased by using
`__restrict__` as a member function qualifier.

```
void T::fn () __restrict__
{
  /* ... */
}
```

Within the body of T::fn, *this* will have the effective definition T *__restrict__ const
this. Notice that the interpretation of a `__restrict__` member function qualifier is different to that of `const` or `volatile` qualifier, in that it is applied to the pointer rather than
the object. This is consistent with other compilers which implement restricted pointers.

As with all outermost parameter qualifiers, `__restrict__` is ignored in function definition
matching. This means you only need to specify `__restrict__` in a function definition,
rather than in a function prototype as well.

6.3 Vague Linkage

There are several constructs in C++ which require space in the object file but are not
clearly tied to a single translation unit. We say that these constructs have "vague linkage".
Typically such constructs are emitted wherever they are needed, though sometimes we can
be more clever.

Inline Functions

> Inline functions are typically defined in a header file which can be included
> in many different compilations. Hopefully they can usually be inlined, but
> sometimes an out-of-line copy is necessary, if the address of the function is taken
> or if inlining fails. In general, we emit an out-of-line copy in all translation units
> where one is needed. As an exception, we only emit inline virtual functions with
> the vtable, since it will always require a copy.
>
> Local static variables and string constants used in an inline function are also
> considered to have vague linkage, since they must be shared between all inlined
> and out-of-line instances of the function.

VTables
> C++ virtual functions are implemented in most compilers using a lookup table,
> known as a vtable. The vtable contains pointers to the virtual functions provided by a class, and each object of the class contains a pointer to its vtable (or
> vtables, in some multiple-inheritance situations). If the class declares any non-inline, non-pure virtual functions, the first one is chosen as the "key method"
> for the class, and the vtable is only emitted in the translation unit where the
> key method is defined.

Chapter 6: Extensions to the C++ Language   505

> *Note:* If the chosen key method is later defined as inline, the vtable will still
> be emitted in every translation unit which defines it. Make sure that any inline
> virtuals are declared inline in the class body, even if they are not defined there.

type_info objects
> C++ requires information about types to be written out in order to implement
> 'dynamic_cast', 'typeid' and exception handling. For polymorphic classes
> (classes with virtual functions), the type_info object is written out along with
> the vtable so that 'dynamic_cast' can determine the dynamic type of a class
> object at runtime. For all other types, we write out the type_info object when
> it is used: when applying 'typeid' to an expression, throwing an object, or
> referring to a type in a catch clause or exception specification.

Template Instantiations
> Most everything in this section also applies to template instantiations, but there
> are other options as well. See Section 6.5 [Where's the Template?], page 507.

When used with GNU ld version 2.8 or later on an ELF system such as GNU/Linux or Solaris 2, or on Microsoft Windows, duplicate copies of these constructs will be discarded at link time. This is known as COMDAT support.

On targets that don't support COMDAT, but do support weak symbols, GCC will use them. This way one copy will override all the others, but the unused copies will still take up space in the executable.

For targets which do not support either COMDAT or weak symbols, most entities with vague linkage will be emitted as local symbols to avoid duplicate definition errors from the linker. This will not happen for local statics in inlines, however, as having multiple copies will almost certainly break things.

See Section 6.4 [Declarations and Definitions in One Header], page 505, for another way to control placement of these constructs.

6.4 #pragma interface and implementation

`#pragma interface` and `#pragma implementation` provide the user with a way of explicitly directing the compiler to emit entities with vague linkage (and debugging information) in a particular translation unit.

Note: As of GCC 2.7.2, these `#pragma`s are not useful in most cases, because of COMDAT support and the "key method" heuristic mentioned in Section 6.3 [Vague Linkage], page 504. Using them can actually cause your program to grow due to unnecessary out-of-line copies of inline functions. Currently (3.4) the only benefit of these `#pragma`s is reduced duplication of debugging information, and that should be addressed soon on DWARF 2 targets with the use of COMDAT groups.

`#pragma interface`
`#pragma interface "subdir/objects.h"`
> Use this directive in *header files* that define object classes, to save space in
> most of the object files that use those classes. Normally, local copies of certain
> information (backup copies of inline member functions, debugging information,
> and the internal tables that implement virtual functions) must be kept in each
> object file that includes class definitions. You can use this pragma to avoid such

duplication. When a header file containing '`#pragma interface`' is included in a compilation, this auxiliary information will not be generated (unless the main input source file itself uses '`#pragma implementation`'). Instead, the object files will contain references to be resolved at link time.

The second form of this directive is useful for the case where you have multiple headers with the same name in different directories. If you use this form, you must specify the same string to '`#pragma implementation`'.

`#pragma implementation`
`#pragma implementation "objects.h"`

    Use this pragma in a *main input file*, when you want full output from included header files to be generated (and made globally visible). The included header file, in turn, should use '`#pragma interface`'. Backup copies of inline member functions, debugging information, and the internal tables used to implement virtual functions are all generated in implementation files.

    If you use '`#pragma implementation`' with no argument, it applies to an include file with the same basename[1] as your source file. For example, in '`allclass.cc`', giving just '`#pragma implementation`' by itself is equivalent to '`#pragma implementation "allclass.h"`'.

    In versions of GNU C++ prior to 2.6.0 '`allclass.h`' was treated as an implementation file whenever you would include it from '`allclass.cc`' even if you never specified '`#pragma implementation`'. This was deemed to be more trouble than it was worth, however, and disabled.

    Use the string argument if you want a single implementation file to include code from multiple header files. (You must also use '`#include`' to include the header file; '`#pragma implementation`' only specifies how to use the file—it doesn't actually include it.)

    There is no way to split up the contents of a single header file into multiple implementation files.

'`#pragma implementation`' and '`#pragma interface`' also have an effect on function inlining.

If you define a class in a header file marked with '`#pragma interface`', the effect on an inline function defined in that class is similar to an explicit **extern** declaration—the compiler emits no code at all to define an independent version of the function. Its definition is used only for inlining with its callers.

Conversely, when you include the same header file in a main source file that declares it as '`#pragma implementation`', the compiler emits code for the function itself; this defines a version of the function that can be found via pointers (or by callers compiled without inlining). If all calls to the function can be inlined, you can avoid emitting the function by compiling with '`-fno-implement-inlines`'. If any calls were not inlined, you will get linker errors.

---

[1] A file's *basename* was the name stripped of all leading path information and of trailing suffixes, such as '.h' or '.C' or '.cc'.

Chapter 6: Extensions to the C++ Language   507

6.5 Where's the Template?

C++ templates are the first language feature to require more intelligence from the environment than one usually finds on a UNIX system. Somehow the compiler and linker have to make sure that each template instance occurs exactly once in the executable if it is needed, and not at all otherwise. There are two basic approaches to this problem, which are referred to as the Borland model and the Cfront model.

Borland model
: Borland C++ solved the template instantiation problem by adding the code equivalent of common blocks to their linker; the compiler emits template instances in each translation unit that uses them, and the linker collapses them together. The advantage of this model is that the linker only has to consider the object files themselves; there is no external complexity to worry about. This disadvantage is that compilation time is increased because the template code is being compiled repeatedly. Code written for this model tends to include definitions of all templates in the header file, since they must be seen to be instantiated.

Cfront model
: The AT&T C++ translator, Cfront, solved the template instantiation problem by creating the notion of a template repository, an automatically maintained place where template instances are stored. A more modern version of the repository works as follows: As individual object files are built, the compiler places any template definitions and instantiations encountered in the repository. At link time, the link wrapper adds in the objects in the repository and compiles any needed instances that were not previously emitted. The advantages of this model are more optimal compilation speed and the ability to use the system linker; to implement the Borland model a compiler vendor also needs to replace the linker. The disadvantages are vastly increased complexity, and thus potential for error; for some code this can be just as transparent, but in practice it can been very difficult to build multiple programs in one directory and one program in multiple directories. Code written for this model tends to separate definitions of non-inline member templates into a separate file, which should be compiled separately.

When used with GNU ld version 2.8 or later on an ELF system such as GNU/Linux or Solaris 2, or on Microsoft Windows, G++ supports the Borland model. On other systems, G++ implements neither automatic model.

A future version of G++ will support a hybrid model whereby the compiler will emit any instantiations for which the template definition is included in the compile, and store template definitions and instantiation context information into the object file for the rest. The link wrapper will extract that information as necessary and invoke the compiler to produce the remaining instantiations. The linker will then combine duplicate instantiations.

In the mean time, you have the following options for dealing with template instantiations:

1. Compile your template-using code with '-frepo'. The compiler will generate files with the extension '.rpo' listing all of the template instantiations used in the corresponding object files which could be instantiated there; the link wrapper, 'collect2', will then

update the '.rpo' files to tell the compiler where to place those instantiations and rebuild any affected object files. The link-time overhead is negligible after the first pass, as the compiler will continue to place the instantiations in the same files.

This is your best option for application code written for the Borland model, as it will just work. Code written for the Cfront model will need to be modified so that the template definitions are available at one or more points of instantiation; usually this is as simple as adding #include <tmethods.cc> to the end of each template header.

For library code, if you want the library to provide all of the template instantiations it needs, just try to link all of its object files together; the link will fail, but cause the instantiations to be generated as a side effect. Be warned, however, that this may cause conflicts if multiple libraries try to provide the same instantiations. For greater control, use explicit instantiation as described in the next option.

2. Compile your code with '-fno-implicit-templates' to disable the implicit generation of template instances, and explicitly instantiate all the ones you use. This approach requires more knowledge of exactly which instances you need than do the others, but it's less mysterious and allows greater control. You can scatter the explicit instantiations throughout your program, perhaps putting them in the translation units where the instances are used or the translation units that define the templates themselves; you can put all of the explicit instantiations you need into one big file; or you can create small files like

   ```
   #include "Foo.h"
   #include "Foo.cc"

   template class Foo<int>;
   template ostream& operator <<
                   (ostream&, const Foo<int>&);
   ```

   for each of the instances you need, and create a template instantiation library from those.

   If you are using Cfront-model code, you can probably get away with not using '-fno-implicit-templates' when compiling files that don't '#include' the member template definitions.

   If you use one big file to do the instantiations, you may want to compile it without '-fno-implicit-templates' so you get all of the instances required by your explicit instantiations (but not by any other files) without having to specify them as well.

   G++ has extended the template instantiation syntax given in the ISO standard to allow forward declaration of explicit instantiations (with **extern**), instantiation of the compiler support data for a template class (i.e. the vtable) without instantiating any of its members (with **inline**), and instantiation of only the static data members of a template class, without the support data or member functions (with (**static**):

   ```
   extern template int max (int, int);
   inline template class Foo<int>;
   static template class Foo<int>;
   ```

3. Do nothing. Pretend G++ does implement automatic instantiation management. Code written for the Borland model will work fine, but each translation unit will contain instances of each of the templates it uses. In a large program, this can lead to an unacceptable amount of code duplication.

Chapter 6: Extensions to the C++ Language   509

6.6 Extracting the function pointer from a bound pointer to member function

In C++, pointer to member functions (PMFs) are implemented using a wide pointer of sorts to handle all the possible call mechanisms; the PMF needs to store information about how to adjust the 'this' pointer, and if the function pointed to is virtual, where to find the vtable, and where in the vtable to look for the member function. If you are using PMFs in an inner loop, you should really reconsider that decision. If that is not an option, you can extract the pointer to the function that would be called for a given object/PMF pair and call it directly inside the inner loop, to save a bit of time.

Note that you will still be paying the penalty for the call through a function pointer; on most modern architectures, such a call defeats the branch prediction features of the CPU. This is also true of normal virtual function calls.

The syntax for this extension is

```
extern A a;
extern int (A::*fp)();
typedef int (*fptr)(A *);

fptr p = (fptr)(a.*fp);
```

For PMF constants (i.e. expressions of the form '&Klasse::Member'), no object is needed to obtain the address of the function. They can be converted to function pointers directly:

```
fptr p1 = (fptr)(&A::foo);
```

You must specify '-Wno-pmf-conversions' to use this extension.

6.7 C++-Specific Variable, Function, and Type Attributes

Some attributes only make sense for C++ programs.

`init_priority (priority)`
> In Standard C++, objects defined at namespace scope are guaranteed to be initialized in an order in strict accordance with that of their definitions *in a given translation unit*. No guarantee is made for initializations across translation units. However, GNU C++ allows users to control the order of initialization of objects defined at namespace scope with the `init_priority` attribute by specifying a relative *priority*, a constant integral expression currently bounded between 101 and 65535 inclusive. Lower numbers indicate a higher priority.
>
> In the following example, A would normally be created before B, but the `init_priority` attribute has reversed that order:
>
> ```
> Some_Class  A  __attribute__ ((init_priority (2000)));
> Some_Class  B  __attribute__ ((init_priority (543)));
> ```
>
> Note that the particular values of *priority* do not matter; only their relative ordering.

`java_interface`
> This type attribute informs C++ that the class is a Java interface. It may only be applied to classes declared within an `extern "Java"` block. Calls to methods declared in this interface will be dispatched using GCJ's interface table mechanism, instead of regular virtual table dispatch.

See also See Section 6.8 [Namespace Association], page 510.

6.8 Namespace Association

Caution: The semantics of this extension are not fully defined. Users should refrain from using this extension as its semantics may change subtly over time. It is possible that this extension will be removed in future versions of G++.

A using-directive with `__attribute ((strong))` is stronger than a normal using-directive in two ways:

- Templates from the used namespace can be specialized and explicitly instantiated as though they were members of the using namespace.
- The using namespace is considered an associated namespace of all templates in the used namespace for purposes of argument-dependent name lookup.

The used namespace must be nested within the using namespace so that normal unqualified lookup works properly.

This is useful for composing a namespace transparently from implementation namespaces. For example:

```
namespace std {
  namespace debug {
    template <class T> struct A { };
  }
  using namespace debug __attribute ((__strong__));
  template <> struct A<int> { };    // ok to specialize

  template <class T> void f (A<T>);
}

int main()
{
  f (std::A<float>());              // lookup finds std::f
  f (std::A<int>());
}
```

6.9 Type Traits

The C++ front-end implements syntactic extensions that allow to determine at compile time various characteristics of a type (or of a pair of types).

`__has_nothrow_assign (type)`
    If `type` is const qualified or is a reference type then the trait is false. Otherwise if `__has_trivial_assign (type)` is true then the trait is true, else if `type` is a cv class or union type with copy assignment operators that are known not to throw an exception then the trait is true, else it is false. Requires: `type` shall be a complete type, an array type of unknown bound, or is a `void` type.

`__has_nothrow_copy (type)`
    If `__has_trivial_copy (type)` is true then the trait is true, else if `type` is a cv class or union type with copy constructors that are known not to throw an exception then the trait is true, else it is false. Requires: `type` shall be a complete type, an array type of unknown bound, or is a `void` type.

`__has_nothrow_constructor (type)`
    If `__has_trivial_constructor (type)` is true then the trait is true, else if `type` is a cv class or union type (or array thereof) with a default constructor

Chapter 6: Extensions to the C++ Language   511

that is known not to throw an exception then the trait is true, else it is false. Requires: type shall be a complete type, an array type of unknown bound, or is a void type.

__has_trivial_assign (type)
: If type is const qualified or is a reference type then the trait is false. Otherwise if __is_pod (type) is true then the trait is true, else if type is a cv class or union type with a trivial copy assignment ([class.copy]) then the trait is true, else it is false. Requires: type shall be a complete type, an array type of unknown bound, or is a void type.

__has_trivial_copy (type)
: If __is_pod (type) is true or type is a reference type then the trait is true, else if type is a cv class or union type with a trivial copy constructor ([class.copy]) then the trait is true, else it is false. Requires: type shall be a complete type, an array type of unknown bound, or is a void type.

__has_trivial_constructor (type)
: If __is_pod (type) is true then the trait is true, else if type is a cv class or union type (or array thereof) with a trivial default constructor ([class.ctor]) then the trait is true, else it is false. Requires: type shall be a complete type, an array type of unknown bound, or is a void type.

__has_trivial_destructor (type)
: If __is_pod (type) is true or type is a reference type then the trait is true, else if type is a cv class or union type (or array thereof) with a trivial destructor ([class.dtor]) then the trait is true, else it is false. Requires: type shall be a complete type, an array type of unknown bound, or is a void type.

__has_virtual_destructor (type)
: If type is a class type with a virtual destructor ([class.dtor]) then the trait is true, else it is false. Requires: type shall be a complete type, an array type of unknown bound, or is a void type.

__is_abstract (type)
: If type is an abstract class ([class.abstract]) then the trait is true, else it is false. Requires: type shall be a complete type, an array type of unknown bound, or is a void type.

__is_base_of (base_type, derived_type)
: If base_type is a base class of derived_type ([class.derived]) then the trait is true, otherwise it is false. Top-level cv qualifications of base_type and derived_type are ignored. For the purposes of this trait, a class type is considered is own base. Requires: if __is_class (base_type) and __is_class (derived_type) are true and base_type and derived_type are not the same type (disregarding cv-qualifiers), derived_type shall be a complete type. Diagnostic is produced if this requirement is not met.

__is_class (type)
: If type is a cv class type, and not a union type ([basic.compound]) the the trait is true, else it is false.

`__is_empty (type)`
> If `__is_class (type)` is false then the trait is false. Otherwise `type` is considered empty if and only if: `type` has no non-static data members, or all non-static data members, if any, are bit-fields of lenght 0, and `type` has no virtual members, and `type` has no virtual base classes, and `type` has no base classes `base_type` for which `__is_empty (base_type)` is false. Requires: `type` shall be a complete type, an array type of unknown bound, or is a `void` type.

`__is_enum (type)`
> If `type` is a cv enumeration type ([basic.compound]) the the trait is true, else it is false.

`__is_pod (type)`
> If `type` is a cv POD type ([basic.types]) then the trait is true, else it is false. Requires: `type` shall be a complete type, an array type of unknown bound, or is a `void` type.

`__is_polymorphic (type)`
> If `type` is a polymorphic class ([class.virtual]) then the trait is true, else it is false. Requires: `type` shall be a complete type, an array type of unknown bound, or is a `void` type.

`__is_union (type)`
> If `type` is a cv union type ([basic.compound]) the the trait is true, else it is false.

6.10 Java Exceptions

The Java language uses a slightly different exception handling model from C++. Normally, GNU C++ will automatically detect when you are writing C++ code that uses Java exceptions, and handle them appropriately. However, if C++ code only needs to execute destructors when Java exceptions are thrown through it, GCC will guess incorrectly. Sample problematic code is:

```
struct S { ~S(); };
extern void bar();    // is written in Java, and may throw exceptions
void foo()
{
  S s;
  bar();
}
```

The usual effect of an incorrect guess is a link failure, complaining of a missing routine called '`__gxx_personality_v0`'.

You can inform the compiler that Java exceptions are to be used in a translation unit, irrespective of what it might think, by writing '`#pragma GCC java_exceptions`' at the head of the file. This '`#pragma`' must appear before any functions that throw or catch exceptions, or run destructors when exceptions are thrown through them.

You cannot mix Java and C++ exceptions in the same translation unit. It is believed to be safe to throw a C++ exception from one file through another file compiled for the Java exception model, or vice versa, but there may be bugs in this area.

Chapter 6: Extensions to the C++ Language 513

6.11 Deprecated Features

In the past, the GNU C++ compiler was extended to experiment with new features, at a time when the C++ language was still evolving. Now that the C++ standard is complete, some of those features are superseded by superior alternatives. Using the old features might cause a warning in some cases that the feature will be dropped in the future. In other cases, the feature might be gone already.

While the list below is not exhaustive, it documents some of the options that are now deprecated:

`-fexternal-templates`
`-falt-external-templates`
>These are two of the many ways for G++ to implement template instantiation. See Section 6.5 [Template Instantiation], page 507. The C++ standard clearly defines how template definitions have to be organized across implementation units. G++ has an implicit instantiation mechanism that should work just fine for standard-conforming code.

`-fstrict-prototype`
`-fno-strict-prototype`
>Previously it was possible to use an empty prototype parameter list to indicate an unspecified number of parameters (like C), rather than no parameters, as C++ demands. This feature has been removed, except where it is required for backwards compatibility See Section 6.12 [Backwards Compatibility], page 514.

G++ allows a virtual function returning 'void *' to be overridden by one returning a different pointer type. This extension to the covariant return type rules is now deprecated and will be removed from a future version.

The G++ minimum and maximum operators ('<?' and '>?') and their compound forms ('<?=') and '>?=') have been deprecated and are now removed from G++. Code using these operators should be modified to use `std::min` and `std::max` instead.

The named return value extension has been deprecated, and is now removed from G++.

The use of initializer lists with new expressions has been deprecated, and is now removed from G++.

Floating and complex non-type template parameters have been deprecated, and are now removed from G++.

The implicit typename extension has been deprecated and is now removed from G++.

The use of default arguments in function pointers, function typedefs and other places where they are not permitted by the standard is deprecated and will be removed from a future version of G++.

G++ allows floating-point literals to appear in integral constant expressions, e.g. ' `enum E { e = int(2.2 * 3.7) }` ' This extension is deprecated and will be removed from a future version.

G++ allows static data members of const floating-point type to be declared with an initializer in a class definition. The standard only allows initializers for static members of const integral types and const enumeration types so this extension has been deprecated and will be removed from a future version.

6.12 Backwards Compatibility

Now that there is a definitive ISO standard C++, G++ has a specification to adhere to. The C++ language evolved over time, and features that used to be acceptable in previous drafts of the standard, such as the ARM [Annotated C++ Reference Manual], are no longer accepted. In order to allow compilation of C++ written to such drafts, G++ contains some backwards compatibilities. *All such backwards compatibility features are liable to disappear in future versions of G++.* They should be considered deprecated See Section 6.11 [Deprecated Features], page 513.

For scope
: If a variable is declared at for scope, it used to remain in scope until the end of the scope which contained the for statement (rather than just within the for scope). G++ retains this, but issues a warning, if such a variable is accessed outside the for scope.

Implicit C language
: Old C system header files did not contain an `extern "C" {...}` scope to set the language. On such systems, all header files are implicitly scoped inside a C language scope. Also, an empty prototype () will be treated as an unspecified number of arguments, rather than no arguments, as C++ demands.

Chapter 7: GNU Objective-C runtime features   515

7 GNU Objective-C runtime features

This document is meant to describe some of the GNU Objective-C runtime features. It is not intended to teach you Objective-C, there are several resources on the Internet that present the language. Questions and comments about this document to Ovidiu Predescu ovidiu@cup.hp.com.

7.1 +load: Executing code before main

The GNU Objective-C runtime provides a way that allows you to execute code before the execution of the program enters the **main** function. The code is executed on a per-class and a per-category basis, through a special class method **+load**.

This facility is very useful if you want to initialize global variables which can be accessed by the program directly, without sending a message to the class first. The usual way to initialize global variables, in the **+initialize** method, might not be useful because **+initialize** is only called when the first message is sent to a class object, which in some cases could be too late.

Suppose for example you have a `FileStream` class that declares `Stdin`, `Stdout` and `Stderr` as global variables, like below:

```
FileStream *Stdin = nil;
FileStream *Stdout = nil;
FileStream *Stderr = nil;

@implementation FileStream

+ (void)initialize
{
    Stdin = [[FileStream new] initWithFd:0];
    Stdout = [[FileStream new] initWithFd:1];
    Stderr = [[FileStream new] initWithFd:2];
}

/* Other methods here */
@end
```

In this example, the initialization of `Stdin`, `Stdout` and `Stderr` in **+initialize** occurs too late. The programmer can send a message to one of these objects before the variables are actually initialized, thus sending messages to the `nil` object. The **+initialize** method which actually initializes the global variables is not invoked until the first message is sent to the class object. The solution would require these variables to be initialized just before entering **main**.

The correct solution of the above problem is to use the **+load** method instead of **+initialize**:

```
@implementation FileStream

+ (void)load
{
    Stdin = [[FileStream new] initWithFd:0];
    Stdout = [[FileStream new] initWithFd:1];
```

```
        Stderr = [[FileStream new] initWithFd:2];
}

/* Other methods here */
@end
```

The +load is a method that is not overridden by categories. If a class and a category of it both implement +load, both methods are invoked. This allows some additional initializations to be performed in a category.

This mechanism is not intended to be a replacement for +initialize. You should be aware of its limitations when you decide to use it instead of +initialize.

7.1.1 What you can and what you cannot do in +load

The +load implementation in the GNU runtime guarantees you the following things:

- you can write whatever C code you like;
- you can send messages to Objective-C constant strings (@"this is a constant string");
- you can allocate and send messages to objects whose class is implemented in the same file;
- the +load implementation of all super classes of a class are executed before the +load of that class is executed;
- the +load implementation of a class is executed before the +load implementation of any category.

In particular, the following things, even if they can work in a particular case, are not guaranteed:

- allocation of or sending messages to arbitrary objects;
- allocation of or sending messages to objects whose classes have a category implemented in the same file;

You should make no assumptions about receiving +load in sibling classes when you write +load of a class. The order in which sibling classes receive +load is not guaranteed.

The order in which +load and +initialize are called could be problematic if this matters. If you don't allocate objects inside +load, it is guaranteed that +load is called before +initialize. If you create an object inside +load the +initialize method of object's class is invoked even if +load was not invoked. Note if you explicitly call +load on a class, +initialize will be called first. To avoid possible problems try to implement only one of these methods.

The +load method is also invoked when a bundle is dynamically loaded into your running program. This happens automatically without any intervening operation from you. When you write bundles and you need to write +load you can safely create and send messages to objects whose classes already exist in the running program. The same restrictions as above apply to classes defined in bundle.

7.2 Type encoding

The Objective-C compiler generates type encodings for all the types. These type encodings are used at runtime to find out information about selectors and methods and about objects and classes.

The types are encoded in the following way:

`_Bool`	B
`char`	c
`unsigned char`	C
`short`	s
`unsigned short`	S
`int`	i
`unsigned int`	I
`long`	l
`unsigned long`	L
`long long`	q
`unsigned long long`	Q
`float`	f
`double`	d
`void`	v
`id`	@
`Class`	#
`SEL`	:
`char*`	*
unknown type	?
Complex types	j followed by the inner type. For example `_Complex double` is encoded as "jd".
bit-fields	b followed by the starting position of the bit-field, the type of the bit-field and the size of the bit-field (the bit-fields encoding was changed from the NeXT's compiler encoding, see below)

The encoding of bit-fields has changed to allow bit-fields to be properly handled by the runtime functions that compute sizes and alignments of types that contain bit-fields. The previous encoding contained only the size of the bit-field. Using only this information it is not possible to reliably compute the size occupied by the bit-field. This is very important in the presence of the Boehm's garbage collector because the objects are allocated using the typed memory facility available in this collector. The typed memory allocation requires information about where the pointers are located inside the object.

The position in the bit-field is the position, counting in bits, of the bit closest to the beginning of the structure.

The non-atomic types are encoded as follows:

pointers	'^' followed by the pointed type.
arrays	'[' followed by the number of elements in the array followed by the type of the elements followed by ']'
structures	'{' followed by the name of the structure (or '?' if the structure is unnamed), the '=' sign, the type of the members and by '}'

unions '(' followed by the name of the structure (or '?' if the union is unnamed), the '=' sign, the type of the members followed by ')'

Here are some types and their encodings, as they are generated by the compiler on an i386 machine:

Objective-C type	Compiler encoding
`int a[10];`	`[10i]`

`struct {`
`  int i;`
`  float f[3];`
`  int a:3;`
`  int b:2;`
`  char c;`
`}`
	`{?=i[3f]b128i3b131i2c}`

In addition to the types the compiler also encodes the type specifiers. The table below describes the encoding of the current Objective-C type specifiers:

Specifier	Encoding
`const`	r
`in`	n
`inout`	N
`out`	o
`bycopy`	O
`oneway`	V

The type specifiers are encoded just before the type. Unlike types however, the type specifiers are only encoded when they appear in method argument types.

7.3 Garbage Collection

Support for a new memory management policy has been added by using a powerful conservative garbage collector, known as the Boehm-Demers-Weiser conservative garbage collector. It is available from http://www.hpl.hp.com/personal/Hans_Boehm/gc/.

To enable the support for it you have to configure the compiler using an additional argument, '--enable-objc-gc'. You need to have garbage collector installed before building the compiler. This will build an additional runtime library which has several enhancements to support the garbage collector. The new library has a new name, 'libobjc_gc.a' to not conflict with the non-garbage-collected library.

When the garbage collector is used, the objects are allocated using the so-called typed memory allocation mechanism available in the Boehm-Demers-Weiser collector. This mode requires precise information on where pointers are located inside objects. This information is computed once per class, immediately after the class has been initialized.

There is a new runtime function `class_ivar_set_gcinvisible()` which can be used to declare a so-called *weak pointer* reference. Such a pointer is basically hidden for the garbage

Chapter 7: GNU Objective-C runtime features   519

collector; this can be useful in certain situations, especially when you want to keep track of the allocated objects, yet allow them to be collected. This kind of pointers can only be members of objects, you cannot declare a global pointer as a weak reference. Every type which is a pointer type can be declared a weak pointer, including id, `Class` and `SEL`.

Here is an example of how to use this feature. Suppose you want to implement a class whose instances hold a weak pointer reference; the following class does this:

```
@interface WeakPointer : Object
{
    const void* weakPointer;
}

- initWithPointer:(const void*)p;
- (const void*)weakPointer;
@end


@implementation WeakPointer

+ (void)initialize
{
  class_ivar_set_gcinvisible (self, "weakPointer", YES);
}

- initWithPointer:(const void*)p
{
  weakPointer = p;
  return self;
}

- (const void*)weakPointer
{
  return weakPointer;
}

@end
```

Weak pointers are supported through a new type character specifier represented by the '!' character. The `class_ivar_set_gcinvisible()` function adds or removes this specifier to the string type description of the instance variable named as argument.

7.4 Constant string objects

GNU Objective-C provides constant string objects that are generated directly by the compiler. You declare a constant string object by prefixing a C constant string with the character '@':

```
id myString = @"this is a constant string object";
```

The constant string objects are by default instances of the `NXConstantString` class which is provided by the GNU Objective-C runtime. To get the definition of this class you must include the 'objc/NXConstStr.h' header file.

User defined libraries may want to implement their own constant string class. To be able to support them, the GNU Objective-C compiler provides a new command line options

'-fconstant-string-class=*class-name*'. The provided class should adhere to a strict structure, the same as `NXConstantString`'s structure:

```
@interface MyConstantStringClass
{
  Class isa;
  char *c_string;
  unsigned int len;
}
@end
```

`NXConstantString` inherits from `Object`; user class libraries may choose to inherit the customized constant string class from a different class than `Object`. There is no requirement in the methods the constant string class has to implement, but the final ivar layout of the class must be the compatible with the given structure.

When the compiler creates the statically allocated constant string object, the `c_string` field will be filled by the compiler with the string; the `length` field will be filled by the compiler with the string length; the `isa` pointer will be filled with `NULL` by the compiler, and it will later be fixed up automatically at runtime by the GNU Objective-C runtime library to point to the class which was set by the '-fconstant-string-class' option when the object file is loaded (if you wonder how it works behind the scenes, the name of the class to use, and the list of static objects to fixup, are stored by the compiler in the object file in a place where the GNU runtime library will find them at runtime).

As a result, when a file is compiled with the '-fconstant-string-class' option, all the constant string objects will be instances of the class specified as argument to this option. It is possible to have multiple compilation units referring to different constant string classes, neither the compiler nor the linker impose any restrictions in doing this.

7.5 compatibility_alias

This is a feature of the Objective-C compiler rather than of the runtime, anyway since it is documented nowhere and its existence was forgotten, we are documenting it here.

The keyword `@compatibility_alias` allows you to define a class name as equivalent to another class name. For example:

    @compatibility_alias WOApplication GSWApplication;

tells the compiler that each time it encounters `WOApplication` as a class name, it should replace it with `GSWApplication` (that is, `WOApplication` is just an alias for `GSWApplication`).

There are some constraints on how this can be used—

- `WOApplication` (the alias) must not be an existing class;
- `GSWApplication` (the real class) must be an existing class.

8 Binary Compatibility

Binary compatibility encompasses several related concepts:

application binary interface (ABI)
: The set of runtime conventions followed by all of the tools that deal with binary representations of a program, including compilers, assemblers, linkers, and language runtime support. Some ABIs are formal with a written specification, possibly designed by multiple interested parties. Others are simply the way things are actually done by a particular set of tools.

ABI conformance
: A compiler conforms to an ABI if it generates code that follows all of the specifications enumerated by that ABI. A library conforms to an ABI if it is implemented according to that ABI. An application conforms to an ABI if it is built using tools that conform to that ABI and does not contain source code that specifically changes behavior specified by the ABI.

calling conventions
: Calling conventions are a subset of an ABI that specify of how arguments are passed and function results are returned.

interoperability
: Different sets of tools are interoperable if they generate files that can be used in the same program. The set of tools includes compilers, assemblers, linkers, libraries, header files, startup files, and debuggers. Binaries produced by different sets of tools are not interoperable unless they implement the same ABI. This applies to different versions of the same tools as well as tools from different vendors.

intercallability
: Whether a function in a binary built by one set of tools can call a function in a binary built by a different set of tools is a subset of interoperability.

implementation-defined features
: Language standards include lists of implementation-defined features whose behavior can vary from one implementation to another. Some of these features are normally covered by a platform's ABI and others are not. The features that are not covered by an ABI generally affect how a program behaves, but not intercallability.

compatibility
: Conformance to the same ABI and the same behavior of implementation-defined features are both relevant for compatibility.

The application binary interface implemented by a C or C++ compiler affects code generation and runtime support for:

- size and alignment of data types
- layout of structured types
- calling conventions

- register usage conventions
- interfaces for runtime arithmetic support
- object file formats

In addition, the application binary interface implemented by a C++ compiler affects code generation and runtime support for:

- name mangling
- exception handling
- invoking constructors and destructors
- layout, alignment, and padding of classes
- layout and alignment of virtual tables

Some GCC compilation options cause the compiler to generate code that does not conform to the platform's default ABI. Other options cause different program behavior for implementation-defined features that are not covered by an ABI. These options are provided for consistency with other compilers that do not follow the platform's default ABI or the usual behavior of implementation-defined features for the platform. Be very careful about using such options.

Most platforms have a well-defined ABI that covers C code, but ABIs that cover C++ functionality are not yet common.

Starting with GCC 3.2, GCC binary conventions for C++ are based on a written, vendor-neutral C++ ABI that was designed to be specific to 64-bit Itanium but also includes generic specifications that apply to any platform. This C++ ABI is also implemented by other compiler vendors on some platforms, notably GNU/Linux and BSD systems. We have tried hard to provide a stable ABI that will be compatible with future GCC releases, but it is possible that we will encounter problems that make this difficult. Such problems could include different interpretations of the C++ ABI by different vendors, bugs in the ABI, or bugs in the implementation of the ABI in different compilers. GCC's '-Wabi' switch warns when G++ generates code that is probably not compatible with the C++ ABI.

The C++ library used with a C++ compiler includes the Standard C++ Library, with functionality defined in the C++ Standard, plus language runtime support. The runtime support is included in a C++ ABI, but there is no formal ABI for the Standard C++ Library. Two implementations of that library are interoperable if one follows the de-facto ABI of the other and if they are both built with the same compiler, or with compilers that conform to the same ABI for C++ compiler and runtime support.

When G++ and another C++ compiler conform to the same C++ ABI, but the implementations of the Standard C++ Library that they normally use do not follow the same ABI for the Standard C++ Library, object files built with those compilers can be used in the same program only if they use the same C++ library. This requires specifying the location of the C++ library header files when invoking the compiler whose usual library is not being used. The location of GCC's C++ header files depends on how the GCC build was configured, but can be seen by using the G++ '-v' option. With default configuration options for G++ 3.3 the compile line for a different C++ compiler needs to include

    -Igcc_install_directory/include/c++/3.3

Similarly, compiling code with G++ that must use a C++ library other than the GNU C++ library requires specifying the location of the header files for that other library.

Chapter 8: Binary Compatibility

The most straightforward way to link a program to use a particular C++ library is to use a C++ driver that specifies that C++ library by default. The g++ driver, for example, tells the linker where to find GCC's C++ library ('`libstdc++`') plus the other libraries and startup files it needs, in the proper order.

If a program must use a different C++ library and it's not possible to do the final link using a C++ driver that uses that library by default, it is necessary to tell g++ the location and name of that library. It might also be necessary to specify different startup files and other runtime support libraries, and to suppress the use of GCC's support libraries with one or more of the options '`-nostdlib`', '`-nostartfiles`', and '`-nodefaultlibs`'.

9 gcov—a Test Coverage Program

gcov is a tool you can use in conjunction with GCC to test code coverage in your programs.

9.1 Introduction to gcov

gcov is a test coverage program. Use it in concert with GCC to analyze your programs to help create more efficient, faster running code and to discover untested parts of your program. You can use gcov as a profiling tool to help discover where your optimization efforts will best affect your code. You can also use gcov along with the other profiling tool, gprof, to assess which parts of your code use the greatest amount of computing time.

Profiling tools help you analyze your code's performance. Using a profiler such as gcov or gprof, you can find out some basic performance statistics, such as:

- how often each line of code executes
- what lines of code are actually executed
- how much computing time each section of code uses

Once you know these things about how your code works when compiled, you can look at each module to see which modules should be optimized. gcov helps you determine where to work on optimization.

Software developers also use coverage testing in concert with testsuites, to make sure software is actually good enough for a release. Testsuites can verify that a program works as expected; a coverage program tests to see how much of the program is exercised by the testsuite. Developers can then determine what kinds of test cases need to be added to the testsuites to create both better testing and a better final product.

You should compile your code without optimization if you plan to use gcov because the optimization, by combining some lines of code into one function, may not give you as much information as you need to look for 'hot spots' where the code is using a great deal of computer time. Likewise, because gcov accumulates statistics by line (at the lowest resolution), it works best with a programming style that places only one statement on each line. If you use complicated macros that expand to loops or to other control structures, the statistics are less helpful—they only report on the line where the macro call appears. If your complex macros behave like functions, you can replace them with inline functions to solve this problem.

gcov creates a logfile called '*sourcefile*.gcov' which indicates how many times each line of a source file '*sourcefile*.c' has executed. You can use these logfiles along with gprof to aid in fine-tuning the performance of your programs. gprof gives timing information you can use along with the information you get from gcov.

gcov works only on code compiled with GCC. It is not compatible with any other profiling or test coverage mechanism.

9.2 Invoking gcov

    gcov [options] sourcefiles

gcov accepts the following options:

`-h`
`--help`
>Display help about using `gcov` (on the standard output), and exit without doing any further processing.

`-v`
`--version`
>Display the `gcov` version number (on the standard output), and exit without doing any further processing.

`-a`
`--all-blocks`
>Write individual execution counts for every basic block. Normally gcov outputs execution counts only for the main blocks of a line. With this option you can determine if blocks within a single line are not being executed.

`-b`
`--branch-probabilities`
>Write branch frequencies to the output file, and write branch summary info to the standard output. This option allows you to see how often each branch in your program was taken. Unconditional branches will not be shown, unless the '-u' option is given.

`-c`
`--branch-counts`
>Write branch frequencies as the number of branches taken, rather than the percentage of branches taken.

`-n`
`--no-output`
>Do not create the gcov output file.

`-l`
`--long-file-names`
>Create long file names for included source files. For example, if the header file 'x.h' contains code, and was included in the file 'a.c', then running gcov on the file 'a.c' will produce an output file called 'a.c##x.h.gcov' instead of 'x.h.gcov'. This can be useful if 'x.h' is included in multiple source files. If you use the '-p' option, both the including and included file names will be complete path names.

`-p`
`--preserve-paths`
>Preserve complete path information in the names of generated '.gcov' files. Without this option, just the filename component is used. With this option, all directories are used, with '/' characters translated to '#' characters, '.' directory components removed and '..' components renamed to '^'. This is useful if sourcefiles are in several different directories. It also affects the '-l' option.

`-f`
`--function-summaries`
>Output summaries for each function in addition to the file level summary.

Chapter 9: gcov—a Test Coverage Program

`-o `*`directory|file`*
`--object-directory `*`directory`*
`--object-file `*`file`*
> Specify either the directory containing the gcov data files, or the object path name. The '.gcno', and '.gcda' data files are searched for using this option. If a directory is specified, the data files are in that directory and named after the source file name, without its extension. If a file is specified here, the data files are named after that file, without its extension. If this option is not supplied, it defaults to the current directory.

`-u`
`--unconditional-branches`
> When branch probabilities are given, include those of unconditional branches. Unconditional branches are normally not interesting.

gcov should be run with the current directory the same as that when you invoked the compiler. Otherwise it will not be able to locate the source files. gcov produces files called '*manglename*.gcov' in the current directory. These contain the coverage information of the source file they correspond to. One '.gcov' file is produced for each source file containing code, which was compiled to produce the data files. The *manglename* part of the output file name is usually simply the source file name, but can be something more complicated if the '-l' or '-p' options are given. Refer to those options for details.

The '.gcov' files contain the ':' separated fields along with program source code. The format is

    `execution_count``:`*`line_number`*`:`*`source line text`*

Additional block information may succeed each line, when requested by command line option. The *execution_count* is '-' for lines containing no code and '#####' for lines which were never executed. Some lines of information at the start have *line_number* of zero.

The preamble lines are of the form

    `-:0:`*`tag`*`:`*`value`*

The ordering and number of these preamble lines will be augmented as gcov development progresses — do not rely on them remaining unchanged. Use *tag* to locate a particular preamble line.

The additional block information is of the form

    `tag information`

The *information* is human readable, but designed to be simple enough for machine parsing too.

When printing percentages, 0% and 100% are only printed when the values are *exactly* 0% and 100% respectively. Other values which would conventionally be rounded to 0% or 100% are instead printed as the nearest non-boundary value.

When using gcov, you must first compile your program with two special GCC options: '-fprofile-arcs -ftest-coverage'. This tells the compiler to generate additional information needed by gcov (basically a flow graph of the program) and also includes additional code in the object files for generating the extra profiling information needed by gcov. These additional files are placed in the directory where the object file is located.

Running the program will cause profile output to be generated. For each source file compiled with '-fprofile-arcs', an accompanying '.gcda' file will be placed in the object file directory.

Running gcov with your program's source file names as arguments will now produce a listing of the code along with frequency of execution for each line. For example, if your program is called 'tmp.c', this is what you see when you use the basic gcov facility:

```
$ gcc -fprofile-arcs -ftest-coverage tmp.c
$ a.out
$ gcov tmp.c
90.00% of 10 source lines executed in file tmp.c
Creating tmp.c.gcov.
```

The file 'tmp.c.gcov' contains output from gcov. Here is a sample:

```
        -:    0:Source:tmp.c
        -:    0:Graph:tmp.gcno
        -:    0:Data:tmp.gcda
        -:    0:Runs:1
        -:    0:Programs:1
        -:    1:#include <stdio.h>
        -:    2:
        -:    3:int main (void)
        1:    4:{
        1:    5:  int i, total;
        -:    6:
        1:    7:  total = 0;
        -:    8:
       11:    9:  for (i = 0; i < 10; i++)
       10:   10:    total += i;
        -:   11:
        1:   12:  if (total != 45)
    #####:   13:    printf ("Failure\n");
        -:   14:  else
        1:   15:    printf ("Success\n");
        1:   16:  return 0;
        -:   17:}
```

When you use the '-a' option, you will get individual block counts, and the output looks like this:

```
        -:    0:Source:tmp.c
        -:    0:Graph:tmp.gcno
        -:    0:Data:tmp.gcda
        -:    0:Runs:1
        -:    0:Programs:1
        -:    1:#include <stdio.h>
        -:    2:
        -:    3:int main (void)
        1:    4:{
        1:    4-block  0
        1:    5:  int i, total;
        -:    6:
        1:    7:  total = 0;
        -:    8:
       11:    9:  for (i = 0; i < 10; i++)
       11:    9-block  0
       10:   10:    total += i;
       10:   10-block  0
        -:   11:
```

Chapter 9: gcov—a Test Coverage Program   529

```
           1:    12:    if (total != 45)
           1:    12-block  0
       #####:    13:        printf ("Failure\n");
       $$$$$:    13-block  0
          -:    14:    else
           1:    15:        printf ("Success\n");
           1:    15-block  0
           1:    16:    return 0;
           1:    16-block  0
          -:    17:}
```

In this mode, each basic block is only shown on one line – the last line of the block. A multi-line block will only contribute to the execution count of that last line, and other lines will not be shown to contain code, unless previous blocks end on those lines. The total execution count of a line is shown and subsequent lines show the execution counts for individual blocks that end on that line. After each block, the branch and call counts of the block will be shown, if the '-b' option is given.

Because of the way GCC instruments calls, a call count can be shown after a line with no individual blocks. As you can see, line 13 contains a basic block that was not executed.

When you use the '-b' option, your output looks like this:

```
$ gcov -b tmp.c
90.00% of 10 source lines executed in file tmp.c
80.00% of 5 branches executed in file tmp.c
80.00% of 5 branches taken at least once in file tmp.c
50.00% of 2 calls executed in file tmp.c
Creating tmp.c.gcov.
```

Here is a sample of a resulting 'tmp.c.gcov' file:

```
          -:    0:Source:tmp.c
          -:    0:Graph:tmp.gcno
          -:    0:Data:tmp.gcda
          -:    0:Runs:1
          -:    0:Programs:1
          -:    1:#include <stdio.h>
          -:    2:
          -:    3:int main (void)
function main called 1 returned 1 blocks executed 75%
           1:    4:{
           1:    5:    int i, total;
          -:    6:
           1:    7:    total = 0;
          -:    8:
          11:    9:    for (i = 0; i < 10; i++)
branch  0 taken 91% (fallthrough)
branch  1 taken 9%
          10:   10:        total += i;
          -:   11:
           1:   12:    if (total != 45)
branch  0 taken 0% (fallthrough)
branch  1 taken 100%
       #####:   13:        printf ("Failure\n");
call    0 never executed
          -:   14:    else
           1:   15:        printf ("Success\n");
call    0 called 1 returned 100%
           1:   16:    return 0;
```

```
        -:   17:}
```

For each function, a line is printed showing how many times the function is called, how many times it returns and what percentage of the function's blocks were executed.

For each basic block, a line is printed after the last line of the basic block describing the branch or call that ends the basic block. There can be multiple branches and calls listed for a single source line if there are multiple basic blocks that end on that line. In this case, the branches and calls are each given a number. There is no simple way to map these branches and calls back to source constructs. In general, though, the lowest numbered branch or call will correspond to the leftmost construct on the source line.

For a branch, if it was executed at least once, then a percentage indicating the number of times the branch was taken divided by the number of times the branch was executed will be printed. Otherwise, the message "never executed" is printed.

For a call, if it was executed at least once, then a percentage indicating the number of times the call returned divided by the number of times the call was executed will be printed. This will usually be 100%, but may be less for functions that call `exit` or `longjmp`, and thus may not return every time they are called.

The execution counts are cumulative. If the example program were executed again without removing the '.gcda' file, the count for the number of times each line in the source was executed would be added to the results of the previous run(s). This is potentially useful in several ways. For example, it could be used to accumulate data over a number of program runs as part of a test verification suite, or to provide more accurate long-term information over a large number of program runs.

The data in the '.gcda' files is saved immediately before the program exits. For each source file compiled with '-fprofile-arcs', the profiling code first attempts to read in an existing '.gcda' file; if the file doesn't match the executable (differing number of basic block counts) it will ignore the contents of the file. It then adds in the new execution counts and finally writes the data to the file.

9.3 Using `gcov` with GCC Optimization

If you plan to use `gcov` to help optimize your code, you must first compile your program with two special GCC options: '-fprofile-arcs -ftest-coverage'. Aside from that, you can use any other GCC options; but if you want to prove that every single line in your program was executed, you should not compile with optimization at the same time. On some machines the optimizer can eliminate some simple code lines by combining them with other lines. For example, code like this:

```
if (a != b)
  c = 1;
else
  c = 0;
```

can be compiled into one instruction on some machines. In this case, there is no way for `gcov` to calculate separate execution counts for each line because there isn't separate code for each line. Hence the gcov output looks like this if you compiled the program with optimization:

```
       100:   12:if (a != b)
       100:   13:  c = 1;
       100:   14:else
```

Chapter 9: gcov—a Test Coverage Program   531

```
        100:   15:   c = 0;
```
The output shows that this block of code, combined by optimization, executed 100 times. In one sense this result is correct, because there was only one instruction representing all four of these lines. However, the output does not indicate how many times the result was 0 and how many times the result was 1.

Inlineable functions can create unexpected line counts. Line counts are shown for the source code of the inlineable function, but what is shown depends on where the function is inlined, or if it is not inlined at all.

If the function is not inlined, the compiler must emit an out of line copy of the function, in any object file that needs it. If 'fileA.o' and 'fileB.o' both contain out of line bodies of a particular inlineable function, they will also both contain coverage counts for that function. When 'fileA.o' and 'fileB.o' are linked together, the linker will, on many systems, select one of those out of line bodies for all calls to that function, and remove or ignore the other. Unfortunately, it will not remove the coverage counters for the unused function body. Hence when instrumented, all but one use of that function will show zero counts.

If the function is inlined in several places, the block structure in each location might not be the same. For instance, a condition might now be calculable at compile time in some instances. Because the coverage of all the uses of the inline function will be shown for the same source lines, the line counts themselves might seem inconsistent.

9.4 Brief description of gcov data files

gcov uses two files for profiling. The names of these files are derived from the original *object* file by substituting the file suffix with either '.gcno', or '.gcda'. All of these files are placed in the same directory as the object file, and contain data stored in a platform-independent format.

The '.gcno' file is generated when the source file is compiled with the GCC '-ftest-coverage' option. It contains information to reconstruct the basic block graphs and assign source line numbers to blocks.

The '.gcda' file is generated when a program containing object files built with the GCC '-fprofile-arcs' option is executed. A separate '.gcda' file is created for each object file compiled with this option. It contains arc transition counts, and some summary information.

The full details of the file format is specified in 'gcov-io.h', and functions provided in that header file should be used to access the coverage files.

9.5 Data file relocation to support cross-profiling

Running the program will cause profile output to be generated. For each source file compiled with '-fprofile-arcs', an accompanying '.gcda' file will be placed in the object file directory. That implicitly requires running the program on the same system as it was built or having the same absolute directory structure on the target system. The program will try to create the needed directory structure, if it is not already present.

To support cross-profiling, a program compiled with '-fprofile-arcs' can relocate the data files based on two environment variables:

- GCOV_PREFIX contains the prefix to add to the absolute paths in the object file. Prefix must be absolute as well, otherwise its value is ignored. The default is no prefix.

- GCOV_PREFIX_STRIP indicates the how many initial directory names to strip off the hardwired absolute paths. Default value is 0.

  Note: GCOV_PREFIX_STRIP has no effect if GCOV_PREFIX is undefined, empty or non-absolute.

For example, if the object file '`/user/build/foo.o`' was built with '`-fprofile-arcs`', the final executable will try to create the data file '`/user/build/foo.gcda`' when running on the target system. This will fail if the corresponding directory does not exist and it is unable to create it. This can be overcome by, for example, setting the environment as '`GCOV_PREFIX=/target/run`' and '`GCOV_PREFIX_STRIP=1`'. Such a setting will name the data file '`/target/run/build/foo.gcda`'.

You must move the data files to the expected directory tree in order to use them for profile directed optimizations ('`--use-profile`'), or to use the gcov tool.

10 Known Causes of Trouble with GCC

This section describes known problems that affect users of GCC. Most of these are not GCC bugs per se—if they were, we would fix them. But the result for a user may be like the result of a bug.

Some of these problems are due to bugs in other software, some are missing features that are too much work to add, and some are places where people's opinions differ as to what is best.

10.1 Actual Bugs We Haven't Fixed Yet

- The `fixincludes` script interacts badly with automounters; if the directory of system header files is automounted, it tends to be unmounted while `fixincludes` is running. This would seem to be a bug in the automounter. We don't know any good way to work around it.

- The `fixproto` script will sometimes add prototypes for the `sigsetjmp` and `siglongjmp` functions that reference the `jmp_buf` type before that type is defined. To work around this, edit the offending file and place the typedef in front of the prototypes.

10.2 Cross-Compiler Problems

You may run into problems with cross compilation on certain machines, for several reasons.

- At present, the program '`mips-tfile`' which adds debug support to object files on MIPS systems does not work in a cross compile environment.

10.3 Interoperation

This section lists various difficulties encountered in using GCC together with other compilers or with the assemblers, linkers, libraries and debuggers on certain systems.

- On many platforms, GCC supports a different ABI for C++ than do other compilers, so the object files compiled by GCC cannot be used with object files generated by another C++ compiler.

  An area where the difference is most apparent is name mangling. The use of different name mangling is intentional, to protect you from more subtle problems. Compilers differ as to many internal details of C++ implementation, including: how class instances are laid out, how multiple inheritance is implemented, and how virtual function calls are handled. If the name encoding were made the same, your programs would link against libraries provided from other compilers—but the programs would then crash when run. Incompatible libraries are then detected at link time, rather than at run time.

- On some BSD systems, including some versions of Ultrix, use of profiling causes static variable destructors (currently used only in C++) not to be run.

- On some SGI systems, when you use '`-lgl_s`' as an option, it gets translated magically to '`-lgl_s -lX11_s -lc_s`'. Naturally, this does not happen when you use GCC. You must specify all three options explicitly.

- On a SPARC, GCC aligns all values of type `double` on an 8-byte boundary, and it expects every `double` to be so aligned. The Sun compiler usually gives `double` values 8-byte alignment, with one exception: function arguments of type `double` may not be aligned.

  As a result, if a function compiled with Sun CC takes the address of an argument of type `double` and passes this pointer of type `double *` to a function compiled with GCC, dereferencing the pointer may cause a fatal signal.

  One way to solve this problem is to compile your entire program with GCC. Another solution is to modify the function that is compiled with Sun CC to copy the argument into a local variable; local variables are always properly aligned. A third solution is to modify the function that uses the pointer to dereference it via the following function `access_double` instead of directly with '*':

  ```
  inline double
  access_double (double *unaligned_ptr)
  {
    union d2i { double d; int i[2]; };

    union d2i *p = (union d2i *) unaligned_ptr;
    union d2i u;

    u.i[0] = p->i[0];
    u.i[1] = p->i[1];

    return u.d;
  }
  ```

  Storing into the pointer can be done likewise with the same union.

- On Solaris, the `malloc` function in the 'libmalloc.a' library may allocate memory that is only 4 byte aligned. Since GCC on the SPARC assumes that doubles are 8 byte aligned, this may result in a fatal signal if doubles are stored in memory allocated by the 'libmalloc.a' library.

  The solution is to not use the 'libmalloc.a' library. Use instead `malloc` and related functions from 'libc.a'; they do not have this problem.

- On the HP PA machine, ADB sometimes fails to work on functions compiled with GCC. Specifically, it fails to work on functions that use `alloca` or variable-size arrays. This is because GCC doesn't generate HP-UX unwind descriptors for such functions. It may even be impossible to generate them.

- Debugging ('-g') is not supported on the HP PA machine, unless you use the preliminary GNU tools.

- Taking the address of a label may generate errors from the HP-UX PA assembler. GAS for the PA does not have this problem.

- Using floating point parameters for indirect calls to static functions will not work when using the HP assembler. There simply is no way for GCC to specify what registers hold arguments for static functions when using the HP assembler. GAS for the PA does not have this problem.

- In extremely rare cases involving some very large functions you may receive errors from the HP linker complaining about an out of bounds unconditional branch offset. This

Chapter 10: Known Causes of Trouble with GCC   535

- used to occur more often in previous versions of GCC, but is now exceptionally rare. If you should run into it, you can work around by making your function smaller.
- GCC compiled code sometimes emits warnings from the HP-UX assembler of the form:

    ```
    (warning) Use of GR3 when
         frame >= 8192 may cause conflict.
    ```

    These warnings are harmless and can be safely ignored.
- In extremely rare cases involving some very large functions you may receive errors from the AIX Assembler complaining about a displacement that is too large. If you should run into it, you can work around by making your function smaller.
- The 'libstdc++.a' library in GCC relies on the SVR4 dynamic linker semantics which merges global symbols between libraries and applications, especially necessary for C++ streams functionality. This is not the default behavior of AIX shared libraries and dynamic linking. 'libstdc++.a' is built on AIX with "runtime-linking" enabled so that symbol merging can occur. To utilize this feature, the application linked with 'libstdc++.a' must include the '-Wl,-brtl' flag on the link line. G++ cannot impose this because this option may interfere with the semantics of the user program and users may not always use 'g++' to link his or her application. Applications are not required to use the '-Wl,-brtl' flag on the link line—the rest of the 'libstdc++.a' library which is not dependent on the symbol merging semantics will continue to function correctly.
- An application can interpose its own definition of functions for functions invoked by 'libstdc++.a' with "runtime-linking" enabled on AIX. To accomplish this the application must be linked with "runtime-linking" option and the functions explicitly must be exported by the application ('-Wl,-brtl,-bE:exportfile').
- AIX on the RS/6000 provides support (NLS) for environments outside of the United States. Compilers and assemblers use NLS to support locale-specific representations of various objects including floating-point numbers ('.' vs ',' for separating decimal fractions). There have been problems reported where the library linked with GCC does not produce the same floating-point formats that the assembler accepts. If you have this problem, set the LANG environment variable to 'C' or 'En_US'.
- Even if you specify '-fdollars-in-identifiers', you cannot successfully use '$' in identifiers on the RS/6000 due to a restriction in the IBM assembler. GAS supports these identifiers.

10.4 Incompatibilities of GCC

There are several noteworthy incompatibilities between GNU C and K&R (non-ISO) versions of C.

- GCC normally makes string constants read-only. If several identical-looking string constants are used, GCC stores only one copy of the string.

    One consequence is that you cannot call mktemp with a string constant argument. The function mktemp always alters the string its argument points to.

    Another consequence is that sscanf does not work on some very old systems when passed a string constant as its format control string or input. This is because sscanf incorrectly tries to write into the string constant. Likewise fscanf and scanf.

    The solution to these problems is to change the program to use char-array variables with initialization strings for these purposes instead of string constants.

- -2147483648 is positive.

  This is because 2147483648 cannot fit in the type int, so (following the ISO C rules) its data type is **unsigned long int**. Negating this value yields 2147483648 again.

- GCC does not substitute macro arguments when they appear inside of string constants. For example, the following macro in GCC

    ```
    #define foo(a) "a"
    ```

  will produce output "a" regardless of what the argument a is.

- When you use setjmp and longjmp, the only automatic variables guaranteed to remain valid are those declared **volatile**. This is a consequence of automatic register allocation. Consider this function:

    ```
    jmp_buf j;

    foo ()
    {
      int a, b;

      a = fun1 ();
      if (setjmp (j))
        return a;

      a = fun2 ();
      /* longjmp (j) may occur in fun3. */
      return a + fun3 ();
    }
    ```

  Here a may or may not be restored to its first value when the longjmp occurs. If a is allocated in a register, then its first value is restored; otherwise, it keeps the last value stored in it.

  If you use the '-W' option with the '-O' option, you will get a warning when GCC thinks such a problem might be possible.

- Programs that use preprocessing directives in the middle of macro arguments do not work with GCC. For example, a program like this will not work:

    ```
    foobar (
    #define luser
            hack)
    ```

  ISO C does not permit such a construct.

- K&R compilers allow comments to cross over an inclusion boundary (i.e. started in an include file and ended in the including file).

- Declarations of external variables and functions within a block apply only to the block containing the declaration. In other words, they have the same scope as any other declaration in the same place.

  In some other C compilers, a **extern** declaration affects all the rest of the file even if it happens within a block.

- In traditional C, you can combine long, etc., with a typedef name, as shown here:

    ```
    typedef int foo;
    typedef long foo bar;
    ```

  In ISO C, this is not allowed: long and other type modifiers require an explicit int.

- PCC allows typedef names to be used as function parameters.

Chapter 10: Known Causes of Trouble with GCC   537

- Traditional C allows the following erroneous pair of declarations to appear together in a given scope:
  ```
  typedef int foo;
  typedef foo foo;
  ```
- GCC treats all characters of identifiers as significant. According to K&R-1 (2.2), "No more than the first eight characters are significant, although more may be used.". Also according to K&R-1 (2.2), "An identifier is a sequence of letters and digits; the first character must be a letter. The underscore _ counts as a letter.", but GCC also allows dollar signs in identifiers.
- PCC allows whitespace in the middle of compound assignment operators such as '+='. GCC, following the ISO standard, does not allow this.
- GCC complains about unterminated character constants inside of preprocessing conditionals that fail. Some programs have English comments enclosed in conditionals that are guaranteed to fail; if these comments contain apostrophes, GCC will probably report an error. For example, this code would produce an error:
  ```
  #if 0
  You can't expect this to work.
  #endif
  ```
  The best solution to such a problem is to put the text into an actual C comment delimited by '/*...*/'.
- Many user programs contain the declaration 'long time ();'. In the past, the system header files on many systems did not actually declare time, so it did not matter what type your program declared it to return. But in systems with ISO C headers, time is declared to return time_t, and if that is not the same as long, then 'long time ();' is erroneous.

  The solution is to change your program to use appropriate system headers (<time.h> on systems with ISO C headers) and not to declare time if the system header files declare it, or failing that to use time_t as the return type of time.
- When compiling functions that return float, PCC converts it to a double. GCC actually returns a float. If you are concerned with PCC compatibility, you should declare your functions to return double; you might as well say what you mean.
- When compiling functions that return structures or unions, GCC output code normally uses a method different from that used on most versions of Unix. As a result, code compiled with GCC cannot call a structure-returning function compiled with PCC, and vice versa.

  The method used by GCC is as follows: a structure or union which is 1, 2, 4 or 8 bytes long is returned like a scalar. A structure or union with any other size is stored into an address supplied by the caller (usually in a special, fixed register, but on some machines it is passed on the stack). The target hook TARGET_STRUCT_VALUE_RTX tells GCC where to pass this address.

  By contrast, PCC on most target machines returns structures and unions of any size by copying the data into an area of static storage, and then returning the address of that storage as if it were a pointer value. The caller must copy the data from that memory area to the place where the value is wanted. GCC does not use this method because it is slower and nonreentrant.

On some newer machines, PCC uses a reentrant convention for all structure and union returning. GCC on most of these machines uses a compatible convention when returning structures and unions in memory, but still returns small structures and unions in registers.

You can tell GCC to use a compatible convention for all structure and union returning with the option '`-fpcc-struct-return`'.

- GCC complains about program fragments such as '`0x74ae-0x4000`' which appear to be two hexadecimal constants separated by the minus operator. Actually, this string is a single *preprocessing token*. Each such token must correspond to one token in C. Since this does not, GCC prints an error message. Although it may appear obvious that what is meant is an operator and two values, the ISO C standard specifically requires that this be treated as erroneous.

  A *preprocessing token* is a *preprocessing number* if it begins with a digit and is followed by letters, underscores, digits, periods and 'e+', 'e-', 'E+', 'E-', 'p+', 'p-', 'P+', or 'P-' character sequences. (In strict C89 mode, the sequences 'p+', 'p-', 'P+' and 'P-' cannot appear in preprocessing numbers.)

  To make the above program fragment valid, place whitespace in front of the minus sign. This whitespace will end the preprocessing number.

10.5 Fixed Header Files

GCC needs to install corrected versions of some system header files. This is because most target systems have some header files that won't work with GCC unless they are changed. Some have bugs, some are incompatible with ISO C, and some depend on special features of other compilers.

Installing GCC automatically creates and installs the fixed header files, by running a program called `fixincludes`. Normally, you don't need to pay attention to this. But there are cases where it doesn't do the right thing automatically.

- If you update the system's header files, such as by installing a new system version, the fixed header files of GCC are not automatically updated. They can be updated using the `mkheaders` script installed in '*libexecdir*/gcc/*target*/*version*/`install-tools`/'.
- On some systems, header file directories contain machine-specific symbolic links in certain places. This makes it possible to share most of the header files among hosts running the same version of the system on different machine models.

  The programs that fix the header files do not understand this special way of using symbolic links; therefore, the directory of fixed header files is good only for the machine model used to build it.

  It is possible to make separate sets of fixed header files for the different machine models, and arrange a structure of symbolic links so as to use the proper set, but you'll have to do this by hand.

10.6 Standard Libraries

GCC by itself attempts to be a conforming freestanding implementation. See Chapter 2 [Language Standards Supported by GCC], page 5, for details of what this means. Beyond

Chapter 10: Known Causes of Trouble with GCC   539

the library facilities required of such an implementation, the rest of the C library is supplied by the vendor of the operating system. If that C library doesn't conform to the C standards, then your programs might get warnings (especially when using '-Wall') that you don't expect.

For example, the `sprintf` function on SunOS 4.1.3 returns `char *` while the C standard says that `sprintf` returns an `int`. The `fixincludes` program could make the prototype for this function match the Standard, but that would be wrong, since the function will still return `char *`.

If you need a Standard compliant library, then you need to find one, as GCC does not provide one. The GNU C library (called `glibc`) provides ISO C, POSIX, BSD, SystemV and X/Open compatibility for GNU/Linux and HURD-based GNU systems; no recent version of it supports other systems, though some very old versions did. Version 2.2 of the GNU C library includes nearly complete C99 support. You could also ask your operating system vendor if newer libraries are available.

10.7 Disappointments and Misunderstandings

These problems are perhaps regrettable, but we don't know any practical way around them.

- Certain local variables aren't recognized by debuggers when you compile with optimization.

    This occurs because sometimes GCC optimizes the variable out of existence. There is no way to tell the debugger how to compute the value such a variable "would have had", and it is not clear that would be desirable anyway. So GCC simply does not mention the eliminated variable when it writes debugging information.

    You have to expect a certain amount of disagreement between the executable and your source code, when you use optimization.

- Users often think it is a bug when GCC reports an error for code like this:

    ```
    int foo (struct mumble *);

    struct mumble { ... };

    int foo (struct mumble *x)
    { ... }
    ```

    This code really is erroneous, because the scope of `struct mumble` in the prototype is limited to the argument list containing it. It does not refer to the `struct mumble` defined with file scope immediately below—they are two unrelated types with similar names in different scopes.

    But in the definition of `foo`, the file-scope type is used because that is available to be inherited. Thus, the definition and the prototype do not match, and you get an error.

    This behavior may seem silly, but it's what the ISO standard specifies. It is easy enough for you to make your code work by moving the definition of `struct mumble` above the prototype. It's not worth being incompatible with ISO C just to avoid an error for the example shown above.

- Accesses to bit-fields even in volatile objects works by accessing larger objects, such as a byte or a word. You cannot rely on what size of object is accessed in order to read or write the bit-field; it may even vary for a given bit-field according to the precise usage.

If you care about controlling the amount of memory that is accessed, use volatile but
  do not use bit-fields.

- GCC comes with shell scripts to fix certain known problems in system header files.
  They install corrected copies of various header files in a special directory where only
  GCC will normally look for them. The scripts adapt to various systems by searching
  all the system header files for the problem cases that we know about.

  If new system header files are installed, nothing automatically arranges to update the
  corrected header files. They can be updated using the `mkheaders` script installed in
  '`libexecdir/gcc/target/version/install-tools/`'.

- On 68000 and x86 systems, for instance, you can get paradoxical results if you test
  the precise values of floating point numbers. For example, you can find that a floating
  point value which is not a NaN is not equal to itself. This results from the fact that
  the floating point registers hold a few more bits of precision than fit in a `double` in
  memory. Compiled code moves values between memory and floating point registers at
  its convenience, and moving them into memory truncates them.

  You can partially avoid this problem by using the '`-ffloat-store`' option (see
  Section 3.10 [Optimize Options], page 77).

- On AIX and other platforms without weak symbol support, templates need to be instantiated explicitly and symbols for static members of templates will not be generated.

- On AIX, GCC scans object files and library archives for static constructors and destructors when linking an application before the linker prunes unreferenced symbols. This is necessary to prevent the AIX linker from mistakenly assuming that static constructor or destructor are unused and removing them before the scanning can occur. All static constructors and destructors found will be referenced even though the modules in which they occur may not be used by the program. This may lead to both increased executable size and unexpected symbol references.

10.8 Common Misunderstandings with GNU C++

C++ is a complex language and an evolving one, and its standard definition (the ISO C++ standard) was only recently completed. As a result, your C++ compiler may occasionally surprise you, even when its behavior is correct. This section discusses some areas that frequently give rise to questions of this sort.

10.8.1 Declare *and* Define Static Members

When a class has static data members, it is not enough to *declare* the static member; you must also *define* it. For example:

```
class Foo
{
  ...
  void method();
  static int bar;
};
```

This declaration only establishes that the class `Foo` has an `int` named `Foo::bar`, and a member function named `Foo::method`. But you still need to define *both* `method` and `bar` elsewhere. According to the ISO standard, you must supply an initializer in one (and only one) source file, such as:

Chapter 10: Known Causes of Trouble with GCC   541

```
int Foo::bar = 0;
```

Other C++ compilers may not correctly implement the standard behavior. As a result, when you switch to g++ from one of these compilers, you may discover that a program that appeared to work correctly in fact does not conform to the standard: g++ reports as undefined symbols any static data members that lack definitions.

10.8.2 Name lookup, templates, and accessing members of base classes

The C++ standard prescribes that all names that are not dependent on template parameters are bound to their present definitions when parsing a template function or class.[1] Only names that are dependent are looked up at the point of instantiation. For example, consider

```
void foo(double);

struct A {
  template <typename T>
  void f () {
    foo (1);        // 1
    int i = N;      // 2
    T t;
    t.bar();        // 3
    foo (t);        // 4
  }

  static const int N;
};
```

Here, the names foo and N appear in a context that does not depend on the type of T. The compiler will thus require that they are defined in the context of use in the template, not only before the point of instantiation, and will here use ::foo(double) and A::N, respectively. In particular, it will convert the integer value to a double when passing it to ::foo(double).

Conversely, bar and the call to foo in the fourth marked line are used in contexts that do depend on the type of T, so they are only looked up at the point of instantiation, and you can provide declarations for them after declaring the template, but before instantiating it. In particular, if you instantiate A::f<int>, the last line will call an overloaded ::foo(int) if one was provided, even if after the declaration of struct A.

This distinction between lookup of dependent and non-dependent names is called two-stage (or dependent) name lookup. G++ implements it since version 3.4.

Two-stage name lookup sometimes leads to situations with behavior different from non-template codes. The most common is probably this:

```
template <typename T> struct Base {
  int i;
};

template <typename T> struct Derived : public Base<T> {
  int get_i() { return i; }
};
```

---

[1] The C++ standard just uses the term "dependent" for names that depend on the type or value of template parameters. This shorter term will also be used in the rest of this section.

In `get_i()`, `i` is not used in a dependent context, so the compiler will look for a name declared at the enclosing namespace scope (which is the global scope here). It will not look into the base class, since that is dependent and you may declare specializations of `Base` even after declaring `Derived`, so the compiler can't really know what `i` would refer to. If there is no global variable `i`, then you will get an error message.

In order to make it clear that you want the member of the base class, you need to defer lookup until instantiation time, at which the base class is known. For this, you need to access `i` in a dependent context, by either using `this->i` (remember that `this` is of type `Derived<T>*`, so is obviously dependent), or using `Base<T>::i`. Alternatively, `Base<T>::i` might be brought into scope by a `using`-declaration.

Another, similar example involves calling member functions of a base class:

```
template <typename T> struct Base {
    int f();
};

template <typename T> struct Derived : Base<T> {
    int g() { return f(); };
};
```

Again, the call to `f()` is not dependent on template arguments (there are no arguments that depend on the type `T`, and it is also not otherwise specified that the call should be in a dependent context). Thus a global declaration of such a function must be available, since the one in the base class is not visible until instantiation time. The compiler will consequently produce the following error message:

```
x.cc: In member function 'int Derived<T>::g()':
x.cc:6: error: there are no arguments to 'f' that depend on a template
    parameter, so a declaration of 'f' must be available
x.cc:6: error: (if you use '-fpermissive', G++ will accept your code, but
    allowing the use of an undeclared name is deprecated)
```

To make the code valid either use `this->f()`, or `Base<T>::f()`. Using the '-fpermissive' flag will also let the compiler accept the code, by marking all function calls for which no declaration is visible at the time of definition of the template for later lookup at instantiation time, as if it were a dependent call. We do not recommend using '-fpermissive' to work around invalid code, and it will also only catch cases where functions in base classes are called, not where variables in base classes are used (as in the example above).

Note that some compilers (including G++ versions prior to 3.4) get these examples wrong and accept above code without an error. Those compilers do not implement two-stage name lookup correctly.

10.8.3 Temporaries May Vanish Before You Expect

It is dangerous to use pointers or references to *portions* of a temporary object. The compiler may very well delete the object before you expect it to, leaving a pointer to garbage. The most common place where this problem crops up is in classes like string classes, especially ones that define a conversion function to type `char *` or `const char *`—which is one reason why the standard `string` class requires you to call the `c_str` member function. However, any class that returns a pointer to some internal structure is potentially subject to this problem.

Chapter 10: Known Causes of Trouble with GCC   543

For example, a program may use a function `strfunc` that returns `string` objects, and another function `charfunc` that operates on pointers to `char`:

```
string strfunc ();
void charfunc (const char *);

void
f ()
{
  const char *p = strfunc().c_str();
  ...
  charfunc (p);
  ...
  charfunc (p);
}
```

In this situation, it may seem reasonable to save a pointer to the C string returned by the `c_str` member function and use that rather than call `c_str` repeatedly. However, the temporary string created by the call to `strfunc` is destroyed after `p` is initialized, at which point `p` is left pointing to freed memory.

Code like this may run successfully under some other compilers, particularly obsolete cfront-based compilers that delete temporaries along with normal local variables. However, the GNU C++ behavior is standard-conforming, so if your program depends on late destruction of temporaries it is not portable.

The safe way to write such code is to give the temporary a name, which forces it to remain until the end of the scope of the name. For example:

```
const string& tmp = strfunc ();
charfunc (tmp.c_str ());
```

10.8.4 Implicit Copy-Assignment for Virtual Bases

When a base class is virtual, only one subobject of the base class belongs to each full object. Also, the constructors and destructors are invoked only once, and called from the most-derived class. However, such objects behave unspecified when being assigned. For example:

```
struct Base{
  char *name;
  Base(char *n) : name(strdup(n)){}
  Base& operator= (const Base& other){
   free (name);
   name = strdup (other.name);
  }
};

struct A:virtual Base{
  int val;
  A():Base("A"){}
};

struct B:virtual Base{
  int bval;
  B():Base("B"){}
};

struct Derived:public A, public B{
```

```
      Derived():Base("Derived"){}
    };

    void func(Derived &d1, Derived &d2)
    {
      d1 = d2;
    }
```

The C++ standard specifies that 'Base::Base' is only called once when constructing or copy-constructing a Derived object. It is unspecified whether 'Base::operator=' is called more than once when the implicit copy-assignment for Derived objects is invoked (as it is inside 'func' in the example).

G++ implements the "intuitive" algorithm for copy-assignment: assign all direct bases, then assign all members. In that algorithm, the virtual base subobject can be encountered more than once. In the example, copying proceeds in the following order: 'val', 'name' (via strdup), 'bval', and 'name' again.

If application code relies on copy-assignment, a user-defined copy-assignment operator removes any uncertainties. With such an operator, the application can define whether and how the virtual base subobject is assigned.

10.9 Caveats of using protoize

The conversion programs **protoize** and **unprotoize** can sometimes change a source file in a way that won't work unless you rearrange it.

- **protoize** can insert references to a type name or type tag before the definition, or in a file where they are not defined.

  If this happens, compiler error messages should show you where the new references are, so fixing the file by hand is straightforward.

- There are some C constructs which **protoize** cannot figure out. For example, it can't determine argument types for declaring a pointer-to-function variable; this you must do by hand. **protoize** inserts a comment containing '???' each time it finds such a variable; so you can find all such variables by searching for this string. ISO C does not require declaring the argument types of pointer-to-function types.

- Using **unprotoize** can easily introduce bugs. If the program relied on prototypes to bring about conversion of arguments, these conversions will not take place in the program without prototypes. One case in which you can be sure **unprotoize** is safe is when you are removing prototypes that were made with **protoize**; if the program worked before without any prototypes, it will work again without them.

  You can find all the places where this problem might occur by compiling the program with the '-Wtraditional-conversion' option. It prints a warning whenever an argument is converted.

- Both conversion programs can be confused if there are macro calls in and around the text to be converted. In other words, the standard syntax for a declaration or definition must not result from expanding a macro. This problem is inherent in the design of C and cannot be fixed. If only a few functions have confusing macro calls, you can easily convert them manually.

- **protoize** cannot get the argument types for a function whose definition was not actually compiled due to preprocessing conditionals. When this happens, **protoize** changes

Chapter 10: Known Causes of Trouble with GCC   545

nothing in regard to such a function. `protoize` tries to detect such instances and warn about them.

You can generally work around this problem by using `protoize` step by step, each time specifying a different set of '`-D`' options for compilation, until all of the functions have been converted. There is no automatic way to verify that you have got them all, however.

- Confusion may result if there is an occasion to convert a function declaration or definition in a region of source code where there is more than one formal parameter list present. Thus, attempts to convert code containing multiple (conditionally compiled) versions of a single function header (in the same vicinity) may not produce the desired (or expected) results.

  If you plan on converting source files which contain such code, it is recommended that you first make sure that each conditionally compiled region of source code which contains an alternative function header also contains at least one additional follower token (past the final right parenthesis of the function header). This should circumvent the problem.

- `unprotoize` can become confused when trying to convert a function definition or declaration which contains a declaration for a pointer-to-function formal argument which has the same name as the function being defined or declared. We recommend you avoid such choices of formal parameter names.

- You might also want to correct some of the indentation by hand and break long lines. (The conversion programs don't write lines longer than eighty characters in any case.)

10.10 Certain Changes We Don't Want to Make

This section lists changes that people frequently request, but which we do not make because we think GCC is better without them.

- Checking the number and type of arguments to a function which has an old-fashioned definition and no prototype.

  Such a feature would work only occasionally—only for calls that appear in the same file as the called function, following the definition. The only way to check all calls reliably is to add a prototype for the function. But adding a prototype eliminates the motivation for this feature. So the feature is not worthwhile.

- Warning about using an expression whose type is signed as a shift count.

  Shift count operands are probably signed more often than unsigned. Warning about this would cause far more annoyance than good.

- Warning about assigning a signed value to an unsigned variable.

  Such assignments must be very common; warning about them would cause more annoyance than good.

- Warning when a non-void function value is ignored.

  C contains many standard functions that return a value that most programs choose to ignore. One obvious example is `printf`. Warning about this practice only leads the defensive programmer to clutter programs with dozens of casts to `void`. Such casts are required so frequently that they become visual noise. Writing those casts becomes so automatic that they no longer convey useful information about the intentions of the programmer. For functions where the return value should never be ignored, use the `warn_unused_result` function attribute (see Section 5.27 [Function Attributes], page 264).

- Making '-fshort-enums' the default.

  This would cause storage layout to be incompatible with most other C compilers. And it doesn't seem very important, given that you can get the same result in other ways. The case where it matters most is when the enumeration-valued object is inside a structure, and in that case you can specify a field width explicitly.

- Making bit-fields unsigned by default on particular machines where "the ABI standard" says to do so.

  The ISO C standard leaves it up to the implementation whether a bit-field declared plain int is signed or not. This in effect creates two alternative dialects of C.

  The GNU C compiler supports both dialects; you can specify the signed dialect with '-fsigned-bitfields' and the unsigned dialect with '-funsigned-bitfields'. However, this leaves open the question of which dialect to use by default.

  Currently, the preferred dialect makes plain bit-fields signed, because this is simplest. Since int is the same as signed int in every other context, it is cleanest for them to be the same in bit-fields as well.

  Some computer manufacturers have published Application Binary Interface standards which specify that plain bit-fields should be unsigned. It is a mistake, however, to say anything about this issue in an ABI. This is because the handling of plain bit-fields distinguishes two dialects of C. Both dialects are meaningful on every type of machine. Whether a particular object file was compiled using signed bit-fields or unsigned is of no concern to other object files, even if they access the same bit-fields in the same data structures.

  A given program is written in one or the other of these two dialects. The program stands a chance to work on most any machine if it is compiled with the proper dialect. It is unlikely to work at all if compiled with the wrong dialect.

  Many users appreciate the GNU C compiler because it provides an environment that is uniform across machines. These users would be inconvenienced if the compiler treated plain bit-fields differently on certain machines.

  Occasionally users write programs intended only for a particular machine type. On these occasions, the users would benefit if the GNU C compiler were to support by default the same dialect as the other compilers on that machine. But such applications are rare. And users writing a program to run on more than one type of machine cannot possibly benefit from this kind of compatibility.

  This is why GCC does and will treat plain bit-fields in the same fashion on all types of machines (by default).

  There are some arguments for making bit-fields unsigned by default on all machines. If, for example, this becomes a universal de facto standard, it would make sense for GCC to go along with it. This is something to be considered in the future.

  (Of course, users strongly concerned about portability should indicate explicitly in each bit-field whether it is signed or not. In this way, they write programs which have the same meaning in both C dialects.)

Chapter 10: Known Causes of Trouble with GCC   547

- Undefining `__STDC__` when '-ansi' is not used.

  Currently, GCC defines `__STDC__` unconditionally. This provides good results in practice.

  Programmers normally use conditionals on `__STDC__` to ask whether it is safe to use certain features of ISO C, such as function prototypes or ISO token concatenation. Since plain gcc supports all the features of ISO C, the correct answer to these questions is "yes".

  Some users try to use `__STDC__` to check for the availability of certain library facilities. This is actually incorrect usage in an ISO C program, because the ISO C standard says that a conforming freestanding implementation should define `__STDC__` even though it does not have the library facilities. 'gcc -ansi -pedantic' is a conforming freestanding implementation, and it is therefore required to define `__STDC__`, even though it does not come with an ISO C library.

  Sometimes people say that defining `__STDC__` in a compiler that does not completely conform to the ISO C standard somehow violates the standard. This is illogical. The standard is a standard for compilers that claim to support ISO C, such as 'gcc -ansi'— not for other compilers such as plain gcc. Whatever the ISO C standard says is relevant to the design of plain gcc without '-ansi' only for pragmatic reasons, not as a requirement.

  GCC normally defines `__STDC__` to be 1, and in addition defines `__STRICT_ANSI__` if you specify the '-ansi' option, or a '-std' option for strict conformance to some version of ISO C. On some hosts, system include files use a different convention, where `__STDC__` is normally 0, but is 1 if the user specifies strict conformance to the C Standard. GCC follows the host convention when processing system include files, but when processing user files it follows the usual GNU C convention.

- Undefining `__STDC__` in C++.

  Programs written to compile with C++-to-C translators get the value of `__STDC__` that goes with the C compiler that is subsequently used. These programs must test `__STDC__` to determine what kind of C preprocessor that compiler uses: whether they should concatenate tokens in the ISO C fashion or in the traditional fashion.

  These programs work properly with GNU C++ if `__STDC__` is defined. They would not work otherwise.

  In addition, many header files are written to provide prototypes in ISO C but not in traditional C. Many of these header files can work without change in C++ provided `__STDC__` is defined. If `__STDC__` is not defined, they will all fail, and will all need to be changed to test explicitly for C++ as well.

- Deleting "empty" loops.

  Historically, GCC has not deleted "empty" loops under the assumption that the most likely reason you would put one in a program is to have a delay, so deleting them will not make real programs run any faster.

  However, the rationale here is that optimization of a nonempty loop cannot produce an empty one. This held for carefully written C compiled with less powerful optimizers but is not always the case for carefully written C++ or with more powerful optimizers. Thus GCC will remove operations from loops whenever it can determine those operations are not externally visible (apart from the time taken to execute them, of course). In case the loop can be proved to be finite, GCC will also remove the loop itself.

Be aware of this when performing timing tests, for instance the following loop can be completely removed, provided `some_expression` can provably not change any global state.

```
{
    int sum = 0;
    int ix;

    for (ix = 0; ix != 10000; ix++)
        sum += some_expression;
}
```

Even though `sum` is accumulated in the loop, no use is made of that summation, so the accumulation can be removed.

- Making side effects happen in the same order as in some other compiler.

  It is never safe to depend on the order of evaluation of side effects. For example, a function call like this may very well behave differently from one compiler to another:

  ```
  void func (int, int);

  int i = 2;
  func (i++, i++);
  ```

  There is no guarantee (in either the C or the C++ standard language definitions) that the increments will be evaluated in any particular order. Either increment might happen first. `func` might get the arguments '2, 3', or it might get '3, 2', or even '2, 2'.

- Making certain warnings into errors by default.

  Some ISO C testsuites report failure when the compiler does not produce an error message for a certain program.

  ISO C requires a "diagnostic" message for certain kinds of invalid programs, but a warning is defined by GCC to count as a diagnostic. If GCC produces a warning but not an error, that is correct ISO C support. If testsuites call this "failure", they should be run with the GCC option '-pedantic-errors', which will turn these warnings into errors.

10.11 Warning Messages and Error Messages

The GNU compiler can produce two kinds of diagnostics: errors and warnings. Each kind has a different purpose:

Errors report problems that make it impossible to compile your program. GCC reports errors with the source file name and line number where the problem is apparent.

Warnings report other unusual conditions in your code that *may* indicate a problem, although compilation can (and does) proceed. Warning messages also report the source file name and line number, but include the text '`warning:`' to distinguish them from error messages.

Warnings may indicate danger points where you should check to make sure that your program really does what you intend; or the use of obsolete features; or the use of nonstandard features of GNU C or C++. Many warnings are issued only if you ask for them, with one of the '-W' options (for instance, '-Wall' requests a variety of useful warnings).

Chapter 10: Known Causes of Trouble with GCC

GCC always tries to compile your program if possible; it never gratuitously rejects a program whose meaning is clear merely because (for instance) it fails to conform to a standard. In some cases, however, the C and C++ standards specify that certain extensions are forbidden, and a diagnostic *must* be issued by a conforming compiler. The '`-pedantic`' option tells GCC to issue warnings in such cases; '`-pedantic-errors`' says to make them errors instead. This does not mean that *all* non-ISO constructs get warnings or errors.

See Section 3.8 [Options to Request or Suppress Warnings], page 43, for more detail on these and related command-line options.

11 Reporting Bugs

Your bug reports play an essential role in making GCC reliable.

When you encounter a problem, the first thing to do is to see if it is already known. See Chapter 10 [Trouble], page 533. If it isn't known, then you should report the problem.

11.1 Have You Found a Bug?

If you are not sure whether you have found a bug, here are some guidelines:

- If the compiler gets a fatal signal, for any input whatever, that is a compiler bug. Reliable compilers never crash.

- If the compiler produces invalid assembly code, for any input whatever (except an `asm` statement), that is a compiler bug, unless the compiler reports errors (not just warnings) which would ordinarily prevent the assembler from being run.

- If the compiler produces valid assembly code that does not correctly execute the input source code, that is a compiler bug.

  However, you must double-check to make sure, because you may have a program whose behavior is undefined, which happened by chance to give the desired results with another C or C++ compiler.

  For example, in many nonoptimizing compilers, you can write 'x;' at the end of a function instead of 'return x;', with the same results. But the value of the function is undefined if return is omitted; it is not a bug when GCC produces different results.

  Problems often result from expressions with two increment operators, as in f (*p++, *p++). Your previous compiler might have interpreted that expression the way you intended; GCC might interpret it another way. Neither compiler is wrong. The bug is in your code.

  After you have localized the error to a single source line, it should be easy to check for these things. If your program is correct and well defined, you have found a compiler bug.

- If the compiler produces an error message for valid input, that is a compiler bug.

- If the compiler does not produce an error message for invalid input, that is a compiler bug. However, you should note that your idea of "invalid input" might be someone else's idea of "an extension" or "support for traditional practice".

- If you are an experienced user of one of the languages GCC supports, your suggestions for improvement of GCC are welcome in any case.

11.2 How and where to Report Bugs

Bugs should be reported to the bug database at http://gcc.gnu.org/bugs.html.

12 How To Get Help with GCC

If you need help installing, using or changing GCC, there are two ways to find it:

- Send a message to a suitable network mailing list. First try gcc-help@gcc.gnu.org (for help installing or using GCC), and if that brings no response, try gcc@gcc.gnu.org. For help changing GCC, ask gcc@gcc.gnu.org. If you think you have found a bug in GCC, please report it following the instructions at see Section 11.2 [Bug Reporting], page 551.

- Look in the service directory for someone who might help you for a fee. The service directory is found at http://www.gnu.org/prep/service.html.

For further information, see http://gcc.gnu.org/faq.html#support.

13 Contributing to GCC Development

If you would like to help pretest GCC releases to assure they work well, current development sources are available by SVN (see http://gcc.gnu.org/svn.html). Source and binary snapshots are also available for FTP; see http://gcc.gnu.org/snapshots.html.

If you would like to work on improvements to GCC, please read the advice at these URLs:

    http://gcc.gnu.org/contribute.html
    http://gcc.gnu.org/contributewhy.html

for information on how to make useful contributions and avoid duplication of effort. Suggested projects are listed at http://gcc.gnu.org/projects/.

Funding Free Software

If you want to have more free software a few years from now, it makes sense for you to help encourage people to contribute funds for its development. The most effective approach known is to encourage commercial redistributors to donate.

Users of free software systems can boost the pace of development by encouraging for-a-fee distributors to donate part of their selling price to free software developers—the Free Software Foundation, and others.

The way to convince distributors to do this is to demand it and expect it from them. So when you compare distributors, judge them partly by how much they give to free software development. Show distributors they must compete to be the one who gives the most.

To make this approach work, you must insist on numbers that you can compare, such as, "We will donate ten dollars to the Frobnitz project for each disk sold." Don't be satisfied with a vague promise, such as "A portion of the profits are donated," since it doesn't give a basis for comparison.

Even a precise fraction "of the profits from this disk" is not very meaningful, since creative accounting and unrelated business decisions can greatly alter what fraction of the sales price counts as profit. If the price you pay is $50, ten percent of the profit is probably less than a dollar; it might be a few cents, or nothing at all.

Some redistributors do development work themselves. This is useful too; but to keep everyone honest, you need to inquire how much they do, and what kind. Some kinds of development make much more long-term difference than others. For example, maintaining a separate version of a program contributes very little; maintaining the standard version of a program for the whole community contributes much. Easy new ports contribute little, since someone else would surely do them; difficult ports such as adding a new CPU to the GNU Compiler Collection contribute more; major new features or packages contribute the most.

By establishing the idea that supporting further development is "the proper thing to do" when distributing free software for a fee, we can assure a steady flow of resources into making more free software.

> Copyright © 1994 Free Software Foundation, Inc.
> Verbatim copying and redistribution of this section is permitted
> without royalty; alteration is not permitted.

The GNU Project and GNU/Linux

The GNU Project was launched in 1984 to develop a complete Unix-like operating system which is free software: the GNU system. (GNU is a recursive acronym for "GNU's Not Unix"; it is pronounced "guh-NEW".) Variants of the GNU operating system, which use the kernel Linux, are now widely used; though these systems are often referred to as "Linux", they are more accurately called GNU/Linux systems.

For more information, see:
```
http://www.gnu.org/
http://www.gnu.org/gnu/linux-and-gnu.html
```

GNU General Public License

Version 3, 29 June 2007

Copyright © 2007 Free Software Foundation, Inc. http://fsf.org/

Everyone is permitted to copy and distribute verbatim copies of this license document, but changing it is not allowed.

Preamble

The GNU General Public License is a free, copyleft license for software and other kinds of works.

The licenses for most software and other practical works are designed to take away your freedom to share and change the works. By contrast, the GNU General Public License is intended to guarantee your freedom to share and change all versions of a program—to make sure it remains free software for all its users. We, the Free Software Foundation, use the GNU General Public License for most of our software; it applies also to any other work released this way by its authors. You can apply it to your programs, too.

When we speak of free software, we are referring to freedom, not price. Our General Public Licenses are designed to make sure that you have the freedom to distribute copies of free software (and charge for them if you wish), that you receive source code or can get it if you want it, that you can change the software or use pieces of it in new free programs, and that you know you can do these things.

To protect your rights, we need to prevent others from denying you these rights or asking you to surrender the rights. Therefore, you have certain responsibilities if you distribute copies of the software, or if you modify it: responsibilities to respect the freedom of others.

For example, if you distribute copies of such a program, whether gratis or for a fee, you must pass on to the recipients the same freedoms that you received. You must make sure that they, too, receive or can get the source code. And you must show them these terms so they know their rights.

Developers that use the GNU GPL protect your rights with two steps: (1) assert copyright on the software, and (2) offer you this License giving you legal permission to copy, distribute and/or modify it.

For the developers' and authors' protection, the GPL clearly explains that there is no warranty for this free software. For both users' and authors' sake, the GPL requires that modified versions be marked as changed, so that their problems will not be attributed erroneously to authors of previous versions.

Some devices are designed to deny users access to install or run modified versions of the software inside them, although the manufacturer can do so. This is fundamentally incompatible with the aim of protecting users' freedom to change the software. The systematic pattern of such abuse occurs in the area of products for individuals to use, which is precisely where it is most unacceptable. Therefore, we have designed this version of the GPL to prohibit the practice for those products. If such problems arise substantially in other domains, we stand ready to extend this provision to those domains in future versions of the GPL, as needed to protect the freedom of users.

Finally, every program is threatened constantly by software patents. States should not allow patents to restrict development and use of software on general-purpose computers, but in those that do, we wish to avoid the special danger that patents applied to a free program could make it effectively proprietary. To prevent this, the GPL assures that patents cannot be used to render the program non-free.

The precise terms and conditions for copying, distribution and modification follow.

TERMS AND CONDITIONS

0. Definitions.

    "This License" refers to version 3 of the GNU General Public License.

    "Copyright" also means copyright-like laws that apply to other kinds of works, such as semiconductor masks.

    "The Program" refers to any copyrightable work licensed under this License. Each licensee is addressed as "you". "Licensees" and "recipients" may be individuals or organizations.

    To "modify" a work means to copy from or adapt all or part of the work in a fashion requiring copyright permission, other than the making of an exact copy. The resulting work is called a "modified version" of the earlier work or a work "based on" the earlier work.

    A "covered work" means either the unmodified Program or a work based on the Program.

    To "propagate" a work means to do anything with it that, without permission, would make you directly or secondarily liable for infringement under applicable copyright law, except executing it on a computer or modifying a private copy. Propagation includes copying, distribution (with or without modification), making available to the public, and in some countries other activities as well.

    To "convey" a work means any kind of propagation that enables other parties to make or receive copies. Mere interaction with a user through a computer network, with no transfer of a copy, is not conveying.

    An interactive user interface displays "Appropriate Legal Notices" to the extent that it includes a convenient and prominently visible feature that (1) displays an appropriate copyright notice, and (2) tells the user that there is no warranty for the work (except to the extent that warranties are provided), that licensees may convey the work under this License, and how to view a copy of this License. If the interface presents a list of user commands or options, such as a menu, a prominent item in the list meets this criterion.

1. Source Code.

    The "source code" for a work means the preferred form of the work for making modifications to it. "Object code" means any non-source form of a work.

    A "Standard Interface" means an interface that either is an official standard defined by a recognized standards body, or, in the case of interfaces specified for a particular programming language, one that is widely used among developers working in that language.

GNU General Public License

The "System Libraries" of an executable work include anything, other than the work as a whole, that (a) is included in the normal form of packaging a Major Component, but which is not part of that Major Component, and (b) serves only to enable use of the work with that Major Component, or to implement a Standard Interface for which an implementation is available to the public in source code form. A "Major Component", in this context, means a major essential component (kernel, window system, and so on) of the specific operating system (if any) on which the executable work runs, or a compiler used to produce the work, or an object code interpreter used to run it.

The "Corresponding Source" for a work in object code form means all the source code needed to generate, install, and (for an executable work) run the object code and to modify the work, including scripts to control those activities. However, it does not include the work's System Libraries, or general-purpose tools or generally available free programs which are used unmodified in performing those activities but which are not part of the work. For example, Corresponding Source includes interface definition files associated with source files for the work, and the source code for shared libraries and dynamically linked subprograms that the work is specifically designed to require, such as by intimate data communication or control flow between those subprograms and other parts of the work.

The Corresponding Source need not include anything that users can regenerate automatically from other parts of the Corresponding Source.

The Corresponding Source for a work in source code form is that same work.

2. Basic Permissions.

   All rights granted under this License are granted for the term of copyright on the Program, and are irrevocable provided the stated conditions are met. This License explicitly affirms your unlimited permission to run the unmodified Program. The output from running a covered work is covered by this License only if the output, given its content, constitutes a covered work. This License acknowledges your rights of fair use or other equivalent, as provided by copyright law.

   You may make, run and propagate covered works that you do not convey, without conditions so long as your license otherwise remains in force. You may convey covered works to others for the sole purpose of having them make modifications exclusively for you, or provide you with facilities for running those works, provided that you comply with the terms of this License in conveying all material for which you do not control copyright. Those thus making or running the covered works for you must do so exclusively on your behalf, under your direction and control, on terms that prohibit them from making any copies of your copyrighted material outside their relationship with you.

   Conveying under any other circumstances is permitted solely under the conditions stated below. Sublicensing is not allowed; section 10 makes it unnecessary.

3. Protecting Users' Legal Rights From Anti-Circumvention Law.

   No covered work shall be deemed part of an effective technological measure under any applicable law fulfilling obligations under article 11 of the WIPO copyright treaty adopted on 20 December 1996, or similar laws prohibiting or restricting circumvention of such measures.

When you convey a covered work, you waive any legal power to forbid circumvention of technological measures to the extent such circumvention is effected by exercising rights under this License with respect to the covered work, and you disclaim any intention to limit operation or modification of the work as a means of enforcing, against the work's users, your or third parties' legal rights to forbid circumvention of technological measures.

4. Conveying Verbatim Copies.

   You may convey verbatim copies of the Program's source code as you receive it, in any medium, provided that you conspicuously and appropriately publish on each copy an appropriate copyright notice; keep intact all notices stating that this License and any non-permissive terms added in accord with section 7 apply to the code; keep intact all notices of the absence of any warranty; and give all recipients a copy of this License along with the Program.

   You may charge any price or no price for each copy that you convey, and you may offer support or warranty protection for a fee.

5. Conveying Modified Source Versions.

   You may convey a work based on the Program, or the modifications to produce it from the Program, in the form of source code under the terms of section 4, provided that you also meet all of these conditions:

   a. The work must carry prominent notices stating that you modified it, and giving a relevant date.

   b. The work must carry prominent notices stating that it is released under this License and any conditions added under section 7. This requirement modifies the requirement in section 4 to "keep intact all notices".

   c. You must license the entire work, as a whole, under this License to anyone who comes into possession of a copy. This License will therefore apply, along with any applicable section 7 additional terms, to the whole of the work, and all its parts, regardless of how they are packaged. This License gives no permission to license the work in any other way, but it does not invalidate such permission if you have separately received it.

   d. If the work has interactive user interfaces, each must display Appropriate Legal Notices; however, if the Program has interactive interfaces that do not display Appropriate Legal Notices, your work need not make them do so.

   A compilation of a covered work with other separate and independent works, which are not by their nature extensions of the covered work, and which are not combined with it such as to form a larger program, in or on a volume of a storage or distribution medium, is called an "aggregate" if the compilation and its resulting copyright are not used to limit the access or legal rights of the compilation's users beyond what the individual works permit. Inclusion of a covered work in an aggregate does not cause this License to apply to the other parts of the aggregate.

6. Conveying Non-Source Forms.

   You may convey a covered work in object code form under the terms of sections 4 and 5, provided that you also convey the machine-readable Corresponding Source under the terms of this License, in one of these ways:

a. Convey the object code in, or embodied in, a physical product (including a physical distribution medium), accompanied by the Corresponding Source fixed on a durable physical medium customarily used for software interchange.
b. Convey the object code in, or embodied in, a physical product (including a physical distribution medium), accompanied by a written offer, valid for at least three years and valid for as long as you offer spare parts or customer support for that product model, to give anyone who possesses the object code either (1) a copy of the Corresponding Source for all the software in the product that is covered by this License, on a durable physical medium customarily used for software interchange, for a price no more than your reasonable cost of physically performing this conveying of source, or (2) access to copy the Corresponding Source from a network server at no charge.
c. Convey individual copies of the object code with a copy of the written offer to provide the Corresponding Source. This alternative is allowed only occasionally and noncommercially, and only if you received the object code with such an offer, in accord with subsection 6b.
d. Convey the object code by offering access from a designated place (gratis or for a charge), and offer equivalent access to the Corresponding Source in the same way through the same place at no further charge. You need not require recipients to copy the Corresponding Source along with the object code. If the place to copy the object code is a network server, the Corresponding Source may be on a different server (operated by you or a third party) that supports equivalent copying facilities, provided you maintain clear directions next to the object code saying where to find the Corresponding Source. Regardless of what server hosts the Corresponding Source, you remain obligated to ensure that it is available for as long as needed to satisfy these requirements.
e. Convey the object code using peer-to-peer transmission, provided you inform other peers where the object code and Corresponding Source of the work are being offered to the general public at no charge under subsection 6d.

A separable portion of the object code, whose source code is excluded from the Corresponding Source as a System Library, need not be included in conveying the object code work.

A "User Product" is either (1) a "consumer product", which means any tangible personal property which is normally used for personal, family, or household purposes, or (2) anything designed or sold for incorporation into a dwelling. In determining whether a product is a consumer product, doubtful cases shall be resolved in favor of coverage. For a particular product received by a particular user, "normally used" refers to a typical or common use of that class of product, regardless of the status of the particular user or of the way in which the particular user actually uses, or expects or is expected to use, the product. A product is a consumer product regardless of whether the product has substantial commercial, industrial or non-consumer uses, unless such uses represent the only significant mode of use of the product.

"Installation Information" for a User Product means any methods, procedures, authorization keys, or other information required to install and execute modified versions of a covered work in that User Product from a modified version of its Corresponding Source.

The information must suffice to ensure that the continued functioning of the modified object code is in no case prevented or interfered with solely because modification has been made.

If you convey an object code work under this section in, or with, or specifically for use in, a User Product, and the conveying occurs as part of a transaction in which the right of possession and use of the User Product is transferred to the recipient in perpetuity or for a fixed term (regardless of how the transaction is characterized), the Corresponding Source conveyed under this section must be accompanied by the Installation Information. But this requirement does not apply if neither you nor any third party retains the ability to install modified object code on the User Product (for example, the work has been installed in ROM).

The requirement to provide Installation Information does not include a requirement to continue to provide support service, warranty, or updates for a work that has been modified or installed by the recipient, or for the User Product in which it has been modified or installed. Access to a network may be denied when the modification itself materially and adversely affects the operation of the network or violates the rules and protocols for communication across the network.

Corresponding Source conveyed, and Installation Information provided, in accord with this section must be in a format that is publicly documented (and with an implementation available to the public in source code form), and must require no special password or key for unpacking, reading or copying.

7. Additional Terms.

"Additional permissions" are terms that supplement the terms of this License by making exceptions from one or more of its conditions. Additional permissions that are applicable to the entire Program shall be treated as though they were included in this License, to the extent that they are valid under applicable law. If additional permissions apply only to part of the Program, that part may be used separately under those permissions, but the entire Program remains governed by this License without regard to the additional permissions.

When you convey a copy of a covered work, you may at your option remove any additional permissions from that copy, or from any part of it. (Additional permissions may be written to require their own removal in certain cases when you modify the work.) You may place additional permissions on material, added by you to a covered work, for which you have or can give appropriate copyright permission.

Notwithstanding any other provision of this License, for material you add to a covered work, you may (if authorized by the copyright holders of that material) supplement the terms of this License with terms:

   a. Disclaiming warranty or limiting liability differently from the terms of sections 15 and 16 of this License; or

   b. Requiring preservation of specified reasonable legal notices or author attributions in that material or in the Appropriate Legal Notices displayed by works containing it; or

   c. Prohibiting misrepresentation of the origin of that material, or requiring that modified versions of such material be marked in reasonable ways as different from the original version; or

GNU General Public License

d. Limiting the use for publicity purposes of names of licensors or authors of the material; or

e. Declining to grant rights under trademark law for use of some trade names, trademarks, or service marks; or

f. Requiring indemnification of licensors and authors of that material by anyone who conveys the material (or modified versions of it) with contractual assumptions of liability to the recipient, for any liability that these contractual assumptions directly impose on those licensors and authors.

All other non-permissive additional terms are considered "further restrictions" within the meaning of section 10. If the Program as you received it, or any part of it, contains a notice stating that it is governed by this License along with a term that is a further restriction, you may remove that term. If a license document contains a further restriction but permits relicensing or conveying under this License, you may add to a covered work material governed by the terms of that license document, provided that the further restriction does not survive such relicensing or conveying.

If you add terms to a covered work in accord with this section, you must place, in the relevant source files, a statement of the additional terms that apply to those files, or a notice indicating where to find the applicable terms.

Additional terms, permissive or non-permissive, may be stated in the form of a separately written license, or stated as exceptions; the above requirements apply either way.

8. Termination.

You may not propagate or modify a covered work except as expressly provided under this License. Any attempt otherwise to propagate or modify it is void, and will automatically terminate your rights under this License (including any patent licenses granted under the third paragraph of section 11).

However, if you cease all violation of this License, then your license from a particular copyright holder is reinstated (a) provisionally, unless and until the copyright holder explicitly and finally terminates your license, and (b) permanently, if the copyright holder fails to notify you of the violation by some reasonable means prior to 60 days after the cessation.

Moreover, your license from a particular copyright holder is reinstated permanently if the copyright holder notifies you of the violation by some reasonable means, this is the first time you have received notice of violation of this License (for any work) from that copyright holder, and you cure the violation prior to 30 days after your receipt of the notice.

Termination of your rights under this section does not terminate the licenses of parties who have received copies or rights from you under this License. If your rights have been terminated and not permanently reinstated, you do not qualify to receive new licenses for the same material under section 10.

9. Acceptance Not Required for Having Copies.

You are not required to accept this License in order to receive or run a copy of the Program. Ancillary propagation of a covered work occurring solely as a consequence of using peer-to-peer transmission to receive a copy likewise does not require acceptance.

However, nothing other than this License grants you permission to propagate or modify any covered work. These actions infringe copyright if you do not accept this License. Therefore, by modifying or propagating a covered work, you indicate your acceptance of this License to do so.

10. Automatic Licensing of Downstream Recipients.

Each time you convey a covered work, the recipient automatically receives a license from the original licensors, to run, modify and propagate that work, subject to this License. You are not responsible for enforcing compliance by third parties with this License.

An "entity transaction" is a transaction transferring control of an organization, or substantially all assets of one, or subdividing an organization, or merging organizations. If propagation of a covered work results from an entity transaction, each party to that transaction who receives a copy of the work also receives whatever licenses to the work the party's predecessor in interest had or could give under the previous paragraph, plus a right to possession of the Corresponding Source of the work from the predecessor in interest, if the predecessor has it or can get it with reasonable efforts.

You may not impose any further restrictions on the exercise of the rights granted or affirmed under this License. For example, you may not impose a license fee, royalty, or other charge for exercise of rights granted under this License, and you may not initiate litigation (including a cross-claim or counterclaim in a lawsuit) alleging that any patent claim is infringed by making, using, selling, offering for sale, or importing the Program or any portion of it.

11. Patents.

A "contributor" is a copyright holder who authorizes use under this License of the Program or a work on which the Program is based. The work thus licensed is called the contributor's "contributor version".

A contributor's "essential patent claims" are all patent claims owned or controlled by the contributor, whether already acquired or hereafter acquired, that would be infringed by some manner, permitted by this License, of making, using, or selling its contributor version, but do not include claims that would be infringed only as a consequence of further modification of the contributor version. For purposes of this definition, "control" includes the right to grant patent sublicenses in a manner consistent with the requirements of this License.

Each contributor grants you a non-exclusive, worldwide, royalty-free patent license under the contributor's essential patent claims, to make, use, sell, offer for sale, import and otherwise run, modify and propagate the contents of its contributor version.

In the following three paragraphs, a "patent license" is any express agreement or commitment, however denominated, not to enforce a patent (such as an express permission to practice a patent or covenant not to sue for patent infringement). To "grant" such a patent license to a party means to make such an agreement or commitment not to enforce a patent against the party.

If you convey a covered work, knowingly relying on a patent license, and the Corresponding Source of the work is not available for anyone to copy, free of charge and under the terms of this License, through a publicly available network server or other readily accessible means, then you must either (1) cause the Corresponding Source to be so available, or (2) arrange to deprive yourself of the benefit of the patent license for this particular work, or (3) arrange, in a manner consistent with the requirements of this License, to extend the patent license to downstream recipients. "Knowingly relying" means you have actual knowledge that, but for the patent license, your conveying the covered work in a country, or your recipient's use of the covered work in a country, would infringe one or more identifiable patents in that country that you have reason to believe are valid.

If, pursuant to or in connection with a single transaction or arrangement, you convey, or propagate by procuring conveyance of, a covered work, and grant a patent license to some of the parties receiving the covered work authorizing them to use, propagate, modify or convey a specific copy of the covered work, then the patent license you grant is automatically extended to all recipients of the covered work and works based on it.

A patent license is "discriminatory" if it does not include within the scope of its coverage, prohibits the exercise of, or is conditioned on the non-exercise of one or more of the rights that are specifically granted under this License. You may not convey a covered work if you are a party to an arrangement with a third party that is in the business of distributing software, under which you make payment to the third party based on the extent of your activity of conveying the work, and under which the third party grants, to any of the parties who would receive the covered work from you, a discriminatory patent license (a) in connection with copies of the covered work conveyed by you (or copies made from those copies), or (b) primarily for and in connection with specific products or compilations that contain the covered work, unless you entered into that arrangement, or that patent license was granted, prior to 28 March 2007.

Nothing in this License shall be construed as excluding or limiting any implied license or other defenses to infringement that may otherwise be available to you under applicable patent law.

12. No Surrender of Others' Freedom.

   If conditions are imposed on you (whether by court order, agreement or otherwise) that contradict the conditions of this License, they do not excuse you from the conditions of this License. If you cannot convey a covered work so as to satisfy simultaneously your obligations under this License and any other pertinent obligations, then as a consequence you may not convey it at all. For example, if you agree to terms that obligate you to collect a royalty for further conveying from those to whom you convey the Program, the only way you could satisfy both those terms and this License would be to refrain entirely from conveying the Program.

13. Use with the GNU Affero General Public License.

   Notwithstanding any other provision of this License, you have permission to link or combine any covered work with a work licensed under version 3 of the GNU Affero General Public License into a single combined work, and to convey the resulting work. The terms of this License will continue to apply to the part which is the covered work, but the special requirements of the GNU Affero General Public License, section 13, concerning interaction through a network will apply to the combination as such.

14. Revised Versions of this License.

The Free Software Foundation may publish revised and/or new versions of the GNU General Public License from time to time. Such new versions will be similar in spirit to the present version, but may differ in detail to address new problems or concerns.

Each version is given a distinguishing version number. If the Program specifies that a certain numbered version of the GNU General Public License "or any later version" applies to it, you have the option of following the terms and conditions either of that numbered version or of any later version published by the Free Software Foundation. If the Program does not specify a version number of the GNU General Public License, you may choose any version ever published by the Free Software Foundation.

If the Program specifies that a proxy can decide which future versions of the GNU General Public License can be used, that proxy's public statement of acceptance of a version permanently authorizes you to choose that version for the Program.

Later license versions may give you additional or different permissions. However, no additional obligations are imposed on any author or copyright holder as a result of your choosing to follow a later version.

15. Disclaimer of Warranty.

THERE IS NO WARRANTY FOR THE PROGRAM, TO THE EXTENT PERMITTED BY APPLICABLE LAW. EXCEPT WHEN OTHERWISE STATED IN WRITING THE COPYRIGHT HOLDERS AND/OR OTHER PARTIES PROVIDE THE PROGRAM "AS IS" WITHOUT WARRANTY OF ANY KIND, EITHER EXPRESSED OR IMPLIED, INCLUDING, BUT NOT LIMITED TO, THE IMPLIED WARRANTIES OF MERCHANTABILITY AND FITNESS FOR A PARTICULAR PURPOSE. THE ENTIRE RISK AS TO THE QUALITY AND PERFORMANCE OF THE PROGRAM IS WITH YOU. SHOULD THE PROGRAM PROVE DEFECTIVE, YOU ASSUME THE COST OF ALL NECESSARY SERVICING, REPAIR OR CORRECTION.

16. Limitation of Liability.

IN NO EVENT UNLESS REQUIRED BY APPLICABLE LAW OR AGREED TO IN WRITING WILL ANY COPYRIGHT HOLDER, OR ANY OTHER PARTY WHO MODIFIES AND/OR CONVEYS THE PROGRAM AS PERMITTED ABOVE, BE LIABLE TO YOU FOR DAMAGES, INCLUDING ANY GENERAL, SPECIAL, INCIDENTAL OR CONSEQUENTIAL DAMAGES ARISING OUT OF THE USE OR INABILITY TO USE THE PROGRAM (INCLUDING BUT NOT LIMITED TO LOSS OF DATA OR DATA BEING RENDERED INACCURATE OR LOSSES SUSTAINED BY YOU OR THIRD PARTIES OR A FAILURE OF THE PROGRAM TO OPERATE WITH ANY OTHER PROGRAMS), EVEN IF SUCH HOLDER OR OTHER PARTY HAS BEEN ADVISED OF THE POSSIBILITY OF SUCH DAMAGES.

17. Interpretation of Sections 15 and 16.

If the disclaimer of warranty and limitation of liability provided above cannot be given local legal effect according to their terms, reviewing courts shall apply local law that most closely approximates an absolute waiver of all civil liability in connection with the Program, unless a warranty or assumption of liability accompanies a copy of the Program in return for a fee.

GNU General Public License

END OF TERMS AND CONDITIONS

How to Apply These Terms to Your New Programs

If you develop a new program, and you want it to be of the greatest possible use to the public, the best way to achieve this is to make it free software which everyone can redistribute and change under these terms.

To do so, attach the following notices to the program. It is safest to attach them to the start of each source file to most effectively state the exclusion of warranty; and each file should have at least the "copyright" line and a pointer to where the full notice is found.

```
one line to give the program's name and a brief idea of what it does.
Copyright (C) year name of author

This program is free software: you can redistribute it and/or modify
it under the terms of the GNU General Public License as published by
the Free Software Foundation, either version 3 of the License, or (at
your option) any later version.

This program is distributed in the hope that it will be useful, but
WITHOUT ANY WARRANTY; without even the implied warranty of
MERCHANTABILITY or FITNESS FOR A PARTICULAR PURPOSE.  See the GNU
General Public License for more details.

You should have received a copy of the GNU General Public License
along with this program.  If not, see http://www.gnu.org/licenses/.
```

Also add information on how to contact you by electronic and paper mail.

If the program does terminal interaction, make it output a short notice like this when it starts in an interactive mode:

```
program Copyright (C) year name of author
This program comes with ABSOLUTELY NO WARRANTY; for details type 'show w'.
This is free software, and you are welcome to redistribute it
under certain conditions; type 'show c' for details.
```

The hypothetical commands 'show w' and 'show c' should show the appropriate parts of the General Public License. Of course, your program's commands might be different; for a GUI interface, you would use an "about box".

You should also get your employer (if you work as a programmer) or school, if any, to sign a "copyright disclaimer" for the program, if necessary. For more information on this, and how to apply and follow the GNU GPL, see http://www.gnu.org/licenses/.

The GNU General Public License does not permit incorporating your program into proprietary programs. If your program is a subroutine library, you may consider it more useful to permit linking proprietary applications with the library. If this is what you want to do, use the GNU Lesser General Public License instead of this License. But first, please read http://www.gnu.org/philosophy/why-not-lgpl.html.

GNU Free Documentation License

Version 1.2, November 2002

Copyright © 2000,2001,2002 Free Software Foundation, Inc.
51 Franklin Street, Fifth Floor, Boston, MA 02110-1301, USA

Everyone is permitted to copy and distribute verbatim copies
of this license document, but changing it is not allowed.

0. PREAMBLE

   The purpose of this License is to make a manual, textbook, or other functional and useful document free in the sense of freedom: to assure everyone the effective freedom to copy and redistribute it, with or without modifying it, either commercially or noncommercially. Secondarily, this License preserves for the author and publisher a way to get credit for their work, while not being considered responsible for modifications made by others.

   This License is a kind of "copyleft", which means that derivative works of the document must themselves be free in the same sense. It complements the GNU General Public License, which is a copyleft license designed for free software.

   We have designed this License in order to use it for manuals for free software, because free software needs free documentation: a free program should come with manuals providing the same freedoms that the software does. But this License is not limited to software manuals; it can be used for any textual work, regardless of subject matter or whether it is published as a printed book. We recommend this License principally for works whose purpose is instruction or reference.

1. APPLICABILITY AND DEFINITIONS

   This License applies to any manual or other work, in any medium, that contains a notice placed by the copyright holder saying it can be distributed under the terms of this License. Such a notice grants a world-wide, royalty-free license, unlimited in duration, to use that work under the conditions stated herein. The "Document", below, refers to any such manual or work. Any member of the public is a licensee, and is addressed as "you". You accept the license if you copy, modify or distribute the work in a way requiring permission under copyright law.

   A "Modified Version" of the Document means any work containing the Document or a portion of it, either copied verbatim, or with modifications and/or translated into another language.

   A "Secondary Section" is a named appendix or a front-matter section of the Document that deals exclusively with the relationship of the publishers or authors of the Document to the Document's overall subject (or to related matters) and contains nothing that could fall directly within that overall subject. (Thus, if the Document is in part a textbook of mathematics, a Secondary Section may not explain any mathematics.) The relationship could be a matter of historical connection with the subject or with related matters, or of legal, commercial, philosophical, ethical or political position regarding them.

   The "Invariant Sections" are certain Secondary Sections whose titles are designated, as being those of Invariant Sections, in the notice that says that the Document is released under this License. If a section does not fit the above definition of Secondary then it is not allowed to be designated as Invariant. The Document may contain zero Invariant Sections. If the Document does not identify any Invariant Sections then there are none.

The "Cover Texts" are certain short passages of text that are listed, as Front-Cover Texts or Back-Cover Texts, in the notice that says that the Document is released under this License. A Front-Cover Text may be at most 5 words, and a Back-Cover Text may be at most 25 words.

A "Transparent" copy of the Document means a machine-readable copy, represented in a format whose specification is available to the general public, that is suitable for revising the document straightforwardly with generic text editors or (for images composed of pixels) generic paint programs or (for drawings) some widely available drawing editor, and that is suitable for input to text formatters or for automatic translation to a variety of formats suitable for input to text formatters. A copy made in an otherwise Transparent file format whose markup, or absence of markup, has been arranged to thwart or discourage subsequent modification by readers is not Transparent. An image format is not Transparent if used for any substantial amount of text. A copy that is not "Transparent" is called "Opaque".

Examples of suitable formats for Transparent copies include plain ASCII without markup, Texinfo input format, LaTeX input format, SGML or XML using a publicly available DTD, and standard-conforming simple HTML, PostScript or PDF designed for human modification. Examples of transparent image formats include PNG, XCF and JPG. Opaque formats include proprietary formats that can be read and edited only by proprietary word processors, SGML or XML for which the DTD and/or processing tools are not generally available, and the machine-generated HTML, PostScript or PDF produced by some word processors for output purposes only.

The "Title Page" means, for a printed book, the title page itself, plus such following pages as are needed to hold, legibly, the material this License requires to appear in the title page. For works in formats which do not have any title page as such, "Title Page" means the text near the most prominent appearance of the work's title, preceding the beginning of the body of the text.

A section "Entitled XYZ" means a named subunit of the Document whose title either is precisely XYZ or contains XYZ in parentheses following text that translates XYZ in another language. (Here XYZ stands for a specific section name mentioned below, such as "Acknowledgements", "Dedications", "Endorsements", or "History".) To "Preserve the Title" of such a section when you modify the Document means that it remains a section "Entitled XYZ" according to this definition.

The Document may include Warranty Disclaimers next to the notice which states that this License applies to the Document. These Warranty Disclaimers are considered to be included by reference in this License, but only as regards disclaiming warranties: any other implication that these Warranty Disclaimers may have is void and has no effect on the meaning of this License.

2. VERBATIM COPYING

You may copy and distribute the Document in any medium, either commercially or noncommercially, provided that this License, the copyright notices, and the license notice saying this License applies to the Document are reproduced in all copies, and that you add no other conditions whatsoever to those of this License. You may not use technical measures to obstruct or control the reading or further copying of the copies you make or distribute. However, you may accept compensation in exchange for copies. If you distribute a large enough number of copies you must also follow the conditions in section 3.

You may also lend copies, under the same conditions stated above, and you may publicly display copies.

3. COPYING IN QUANTITY

If you publish printed copies (or copies in media that commonly have printed covers) of the Document, numbering more than 100, and the Document's license notice requires Cover Texts, you must enclose the copies in covers that carry, clearly and legibly, all these Cover Texts: Front-Cover Texts on the front cover, and Back-Cover Texts on the back cover. Both covers must also clearly and legibly identify you as the publisher of these copies. The front cover must present the full title with all words of the title equally prominent and visible. You may add other material on the covers in addition. Copying with changes limited to the covers, as long as they preserve the title of the Document and satisfy these conditions, can be treated as verbatim copying in other respects.

If the required texts for either cover are too voluminous to fit legibly, you should put the first ones listed (as many as fit reasonably) on the actual cover, and continue the rest onto adjacent pages.

If you publish or distribute Opaque copies of the Document numbering more than 100, you must either include a machine-readable Transparent copy along with each Opaque copy, or state in or with each Opaque copy a computer-network location from which the general network-using public has access to download using public-standard network protocols a complete Transparent copy of the Document, free of added material. If you use the latter option, you must take reasonably prudent steps, when you begin distribution of Opaque copies in quantity, to ensure that this Transparent copy will remain thus accessible at the stated location until at least one year after the last time you distribute an Opaque copy (directly or through your agents or retailers) of that edition to the public.

It is requested, but not required, that you contact the authors of the Document well before redistributing any large number of copies, to give them a chance to provide you with an updated version of the Document.

4. MODIFICATIONS

You may copy and distribute a Modified Version of the Document under the conditions of sections 2 and 3 above, provided that you release the Modified Version under precisely this License, with the Modified Version filling the role of the Document, thus licensing distribution and modification of the Modified Version to whoever possesses a copy of it. In addition, you must do these things in the Modified Version:

   A. Use in the Title Page (and on the covers, if any) a title distinct from that of the Document, and from those of previous versions (which should, if there were any, be listed in the History section of the Document). You may use the same title as a previous version if the original publisher of that version gives permission.

B. List on the Title Page, as authors, one or more persons or entities responsible for authorship of the modifications in the Modified Version, together with at least five of the principal authors of the Document (all of its principal authors, if it has fewer than five), unless they release you from this requirement.

C. State on the Title page the name of the publisher of the Modified Version, as the publisher.

D. Preserve all the copyright notices of the Document.

E. Add an appropriate copyright notice for your modifications adjacent to the other copyright notices.

F. Include, immediately after the copyright notices, a license notice giving the public permission to use the Modified Version under the terms of this License, in the form shown in the Addendum below.

G. Preserve in that license notice the full lists of Invariant Sections and required Cover Texts given in the Document's license notice.

H. Include an unaltered copy of this License.

I. Preserve the section Entitled "History", Preserve its Title, and add to it an item stating at least the title, year, new authors, and publisher of the Modified Version as given on the Title Page. If there is no section Entitled "History" in the Document, create one stating the title, year, authors, and publisher of the Document as given on its Title Page, then add an item describing the Modified Version as stated in the previous sentence.

J. Preserve the network location, if any, given in the Document for public access to a Transparent copy of the Document, and likewise the network locations given in the Document for previous versions it was based on. These may be placed in the "History" section. You may omit a network location for a work that was published at least four years before the Document itself, or if the original publisher of the version it refers to gives permission.

K. For any section Entitled "Acknowledgements" or "Dedications", Preserve the Title of the section, and preserve in the section all the substance and tone of each of the contributor acknowledgements and/or dedications given therein.

L. Preserve all the Invariant Sections of the Document, unaltered in their text and in their titles. Section numbers or the equivalent are not considered part of the section titles.

M. Delete any section Entitled "Endorsements". Such a section may not be included in the Modified Version.

N. Do not retitle any existing section to be Entitled "Endorsements" or to conflict in title with any Invariant Section.

O. Preserve any Warranty Disclaimers.

If the Modified Version includes new front-matter sections or appendices that qualify as Secondary Sections and contain no material copied from the Document, you may at your option designate some or all of these sections as invariant. To do this, add their titles to the list of Invariant Sections in the Modified Version's license notice. These titles must be distinct from any other section titles.

You may add a section Entitled "Endorsements", provided it contains nothing but endorsements of your Modified Version by various parties—for example, statements of peer review or that the text has been approved by an organization as the authoritative definition of a standard.

You may add a passage of up to five words as a Front-Cover Text, and a passage of up to 25 words as a Back-Cover Text, to the end of the list of Cover Texts in the Modified Version. Only one passage of Front-Cover Text and one of Back-Cover Text may be added by (or through arrangements made by) any one entity. If the Document already includes a cover text for the same cover, previously added by you or by arrangement made by the same entity you are acting on behalf of, you may not add another; but you may replace the old one, on explicit permission from the previous publisher that added the old one.

The author(s) and publisher(s) of the Document do not by this License give permission to use their names for publicity for or to assert or imply endorsement of any Modified Version.

5. COMBINING DOCUMENTS

    You may combine the Document with other documents released under this License, under the terms defined in section 4 above for modified versions, provided that you include in the combination all of the Invariant Sections of all of the original documents, unmodified, and list them all as Invariant Sections of your combined work in its license notice, and that you preserve all their Warranty Disclaimers.

    The combined work need only contain one copy of this License, and multiple identical Invariant Sections may be replaced with a single copy. If there are multiple Invariant Sections with the same name but different contents, make the title of each such section unique by adding at the end of it, in parentheses, the name of the original author or publisher of that section if known, or else a unique number. Make the same adjustment to the section titles in the list of Invariant Sections in the license notice of the combined work.

    In the combination, you must combine any sections Entitled "History" in the various original documents, forming one section Entitled "History"; likewise combine any sections Entitled "Acknowledgements", and any sections Entitled "Dedications". You must delete all sections Entitled "Endorsements."

6. COLLECTIONS OF DOCUMENTS

    You may make a collection consisting of the Document and other documents released under this License, and replace the individual copies of this License in the various documents with a single copy that is included in the collection, provided that you follow the rules of this License for verbatim copying of each of the documents in all other respects.

    You may extract a single document from such a collection, and distribute it individually under this License, provided you insert a copy of this License into the extracted document, and follow this License in all other respects regarding verbatim copying of that document.

7. AGGREGATION WITH INDEPENDENT WORKS

    A compilation of the Document or its derivatives with other separate and independent documents or works, in or on a volume of a storage or distribution medium, is called an "aggregate" if the copyright resulting from the compilation is not used to limit the legal rights of the compilation's users beyond what the individual works permit. When the Document is included in an aggregate, this License does not apply to the other works in the aggregate which are not themselves derivative works of the Document.

If the Cover Text requirement of section 3 is applicable to these copies of the Document, then if the Document is less than one half of the entire aggregate, the Document's Cover Texts may be placed on covers that bracket the Document within the aggregate, or the electronic equivalent of covers if the Document is in electronic form. Otherwise they must appear on printed covers that bracket the whole aggregate.

8. TRANSLATION

Translation is considered a kind of modification, so you may distribute translations of the Document under the terms of section 4. Replacing Invariant Sections with translations requires special permission from their copyright holders, but you may include translations of some or all Invariant Sections in addition to the original versions of these Invariant Sections. You may include a translation of this License, and all the license notices in the Document, and any Warranty Disclaimers, provided that you also include the original English version of this License and the original versions of those notices and disclaimers. In case of a disagreement between the translation and the original version of this License or a notice or disclaimer, the original version will prevail.

If a section in the Document is Entitled "Acknowledgements", "Dedications", or "History", the requirement (section 4) to Preserve its Title (section 1) will typically require changing the actual title.

9. TERMINATION

You may not copy, modify, sublicense, or distribute the Document except as expressly provided for under this License. Any other attempt to copy, modify, sublicense or distribute the Document is void, and will automatically terminate your rights under this License. However, parties who have received copies, or rights, from you under this License will not have their licenses terminated so long as such parties remain in full compliance.

10. FUTURE REVISIONS OF THIS LICENSE

The Free Software Foundation may publish new, revised versions of the GNU Free Documentation License from time to time. Such new versions will be similar in spirit to the present version, but may differ in detail to address new problems or concerns. See http://www.gnu.org/copyleft/.

Each version of the License is given a distinguishing version number. If the Document specifies that a particular numbered version of this License "or any later version" applies to it, you have the option of following the terms and conditions either of that specified version or of any later version that has been published (not as a draft) by the Free Software Foundation. If the Document does not specify a version number of this License, you may choose any version ever published (not as a draft) by the Free Software Foundation.

ADDENDUM: How to use this License for your documents

To use this License in a document you have written, include a copy of the License in the document and put the following copyright and license notices just after the title page:

```
Copyright (C)  year  your name.
Permission is granted to copy, distribute and/or modify this document
under the terms of the GNU Free Documentation License, Version 1.2
or any later version published by the Free Software Foundation;
with no Invariant Sections, no Front-Cover Texts, and no Back-Cover
Texts.  A copy of the license is included in the section entitled ``GNU
Free Documentation License''.
```

If you have Invariant Sections, Front-Cover Texts and Back-Cover Texts, replace the "with...Texts." line with this:

```
with the Invariant Sections being list their titles, with
the Front-Cover Texts being list, and with the Back-Cover Texts
being list.
```

If you have Invariant Sections without Cover Texts, or some other combination of the three, merge those two alternatives to suit the situation.

If your document contains nontrivial examples of program code, we recommend releasing these examples in parallel under your choice of free software license, such as the GNU General Public License, to permit their use in free software.

Contributors to GCC

The GCC project would like to thank its many contributors. Without them the project would not have been nearly as successful as it has been. Any omissions in this list are accidental. Feel free to contact law@redhat.com or gerald@pfeifer.com if you have been left out or some of your contributions are not listed. Please keep this list in alphabetical order.

- Analog Devices helped implement the support for complex data types and iterators.
- John David Anglin for threading-related fixes and improvements to libstdc++-v3, and the HP-UX port.
- James van Artsdalen wrote the code that makes efficient use of the Intel 80387 register stack.
- Abramo and Roberto Bagnara for the SysV68 Motorola 3300 Delta Series port.
- Alasdair Baird for various bug fixes.
- Giovanni Bajo for analyzing lots of complicated C++ problem reports.
- Peter Barada for his work to improve code generation for new ColdFire cores.
- Gerald Baumgartner added the signature extension to the C++ front end.
- Godmar Back for his Java improvements and encouragement.
- Scott Bambrough for help porting the Java compiler.
- Wolfgang Bangerth for processing tons of bug reports.
- Jon Beniston for his Microsoft Windows port of Java.
- Daniel Berlin for better DWARF2 support, faster/better optimizations, improved alias analysis, plus migrating GCC to Bugzilla.
- Geoff Berry for his Java object serialization work and various patches.
- Uros Bizjak for the implementation of x87 math built-in functions and for various middle end and i386 back end improvements and bug fixes.
- Eric Blake for helping to make GCJ and libgcj conform to the specifications.
- Janne Blomqvist for contributions to GNU Fortran.
- Segher Boessenkool for various fixes.
- Hans-J. Boehm for his garbage collector, IA-64 libffi port, and other Java work.
- Neil Booth for work on cpplib, lang hooks, debug hooks and other miscellaneous clean-ups.
- Steven Bosscher for integrating the GNU Fortran front end into GCC and for contributing to the tree-ssa branch.
- Eric Botcazou for fixing middle- and backend bugs left and right.
- Per Bothner for his direction via the steering committee and various improvements to the infrastructure for supporting new languages. Chill front end implementation. Initial implementations of cpplib, fix-header, config.guess, libio, and past C++ library (libg++) maintainer. Dreaming up, designing and implementing much of GCJ.
- Devon Bowen helped port GCC to the Tahoe.
- Don Bowman for mips-vxworks contributions.

- Dave Brolley for work on cpplib and Chill.
- Paul Brook for work on the ARM architecture and maintaining GNU Fortran.
- Robert Brown implemented the support for Encore 32000 systems.
- Christian Bruel for improvements to local store elimination.
- Herman A.J. ten Brugge for various fixes.
- Joerg Brunsmann for Java compiler hacking and help with the GCJ FAQ.
- Joe Buck for his direction via the steering committee.
- Craig Burley for leadership of the G77 Fortran effort.
- Stephan Buys for contributing Doxygen notes for libstdc++.
- Paolo Carlini for libstdc++ work: lots of efficiency improvements to the C++ strings, streambufs and formatted I/O, hard detective work on the frustrating localization issues, and keeping up with the problem reports.
- John Carr for his alias work, SPARC hacking, infrastructure improvements, previous contributions to the steering committee, loop optimizations, etc.
- Stephane Carrez for 68HC11 and 68HC12 ports.
- Steve Chamberlain for support for the Renesas SH and H8 processors and the PicoJava processor, and for GCJ config fixes.
- Glenn Chambers for help with the GCJ FAQ.
- John-Marc Chandonia for various libgcj patches.
- Scott Christley for his Objective-C contributions.
- Eric Christopher for his Java porting help and clean-ups.
- Branko Cibej for more warning contributions.
- The GNU Classpath project for all of their merged runtime code.
- Nick Clifton for arm, mcore, fr30, v850, m32r work, '--help', and other random hacking.
- Michael Cook for libstdc++ cleanup patches to reduce warnings.
- R. Kelley Cook for making GCC buildable from a read-only directory as well as other miscellaneous build process and documentation clean-ups.
- Ralf Corsepius for SH testing and minor bug fixing.
- Stan Cox for care and feeding of the x86 port and lots of behind the scenes hacking.
- Alex Crain provided changes for the 3b1.
- Ian Dall for major improvements to the NS32k port.
- Paul Dale for his work to add uClinux platform support to the m68k backend.
- Dario Dariol contributed the four varieties of sample programs that print a copy of their source.
- Russell Davidson for fstream and stringstream fixes in libstdc++.
- Bud Davis for work on the G77 and GNU Fortran compilers.
- Mo DeJong for GCJ and libgcj bug fixes.
- DJ Delorie for the DJGPP port, build and libiberty maintenance, various bug fixes, and the M32C port.

- Arnaud Desitter for helping to debug GNU Fortran.
- Gabriel Dos Reis for contributions to G++, contributions and maintenance of GCC diagnostics infrastructure, libstdc++-v3, including `valarray<>`, `complex<>`, maintaining the numerics library (including that pesky `<limits>` :-) and keeping up-to-date anything to do with numbers.
- Ulrich Drepper for his work on glibc, testing of GCC using glibc, ISO C99 support, CFG dumping support, etc., plus support of the C++ runtime libraries including for all kinds of C interface issues, contributing and maintaining `complex<>`, sanity checking and disbursement, configuration architecture, libio maintenance, and early math work.
- Zdenek Dvorak for a new loop unroller and various fixes.
- Richard Earnshaw for his ongoing work with the ARM.
- David Edelsohn for his direction via the steering committee, ongoing work with the RS6000/PowerPC port, help cleaning up Haifa loop changes, doing the entire AIX port of libstdc++ with his bare hands, and for ensuring GCC properly keeps working on AIX.
- Kevin Ediger for the floating point formatting of num_put::do_put in libstdc++.
- Phil Edwards for libstdc++ work including configuration hackery, documentation maintainer, chief breaker of the web pages, the occasional iostream bug fix, and work on shared library symbol versioning.
- Paul Eggert for random hacking all over GCC.
- Mark Elbrecht for various DJGPP improvements, and for libstdc++ configuration support for locales and fstream-related fixes.
- Vadim Egorov for libstdc++ fixes in strings, streambufs, and iostreams.
- Christian Ehrhardt for dealing with bug reports.
- Ben Elliston for his work to move the Objective-C runtime into its own subdirectory and for his work on autoconf.
- Revital Eres for work on the PowerPC 750CL port.
- Marc Espie for OpenBSD support.
- Doug Evans for much of the global optimization framework, arc, m32r, and SPARC work.
- Christopher Faylor for his work on the Cygwin port and for caring and feeding the gcc.gnu.org box and saving its users tons of spam.
- Fred Fish for BeOS support and Ada fixes.
- Ivan Fontes Garcia for the Portuguese translation of the GCJ FAQ.
- Peter Gerwinski for various bug fixes and the Pascal front end.
- Kaveh R. Ghazi for his direction via the steering committee, amazing work to make '`-W -Wall -W* -Werror`' useful, and continuously testing GCC on a plethora of platforms. Kaveh extends his gratitude to the CAIP Center at Rutgers University for providing him with computing resources to work on Free Software since the late 1980s.
- John Gilmore for a donation to the FSF earmarked improving GNU Java.
- Judy Goldberg for c++ contributions.

- Torbjorn Granlund for various fixes and the c-torture testsuite, multiply- and divide-by-constant optimization, improved long long support, improved leaf function register allocation, and his direction via the steering committee.
- Anthony Green for his '-Os' contributions and Java front end work.
- Stu Grossman for gdb hacking, allowing GCJ developers to debug Java code.
- Michael K. Gschwind contributed the port to the PDP-11.
- Ron Guilmette implemented the protoize and unprotoize tools, the support for Dwarf symbolic debugging information, and much of the support for System V Release 4. He has also worked heavily on the Intel 386 and 860 support.
- Mostafa Hagog for Swing Modulo Scheduling (SMS) and post reload GCSE.
- Bruno Haible for improvements in the runtime overhead for EH, new warnings and assorted bug fixes.
- Andrew Haley for his amazing Java compiler and library efforts.
- Chris Hanson assisted in making GCC work on HP-UX for the 9000 series 300.
- Michael Hayes for various thankless work he's done trying to get the c30/c40 ports functional. Lots of loop and unroll improvements and fixes.
- Dara Hazeghi for wading through myriads of target-specific bug reports.
- Kate Hedstrom for staking the G77 folks with an initial testsuite.
- Richard Henderson for his ongoing SPARC, alpha, ia32, and ia64 work, loop opts, and generally fixing lots of old problems we've ignored for years, flow rewrite and lots of further stuff, including reviewing tons of patches.
- Aldy Hernandez for working on the PowerPC port, SIMD support, and various fixes.
- Nobuyuki Hikichi of Software Research Associates, Tokyo, contributed the support for the Sony NEWS machine.
- Kazu Hirata for caring and feeding the Renesas H8/300 port and various fixes.
- Katherine Holcomb for work on GNU Fortran.
- Manfred Hollstein for his ongoing work to keep the m88k alive, lots of testing and bug fixing, particularly of GCC configury code.
- Steve Holmgren for MachTen patches.
- Jan Hubicka for his x86 port improvements.
- Falk Hueffner for working on C and optimization bug reports.
- Bernardo Innocenti for his m68k work, including merging of ColdFire improvements and uClinux support.
- Christian Iseli for various bug fixes.
- Kamil Iskra for general m68k hacking.
- Lee Iverson for random fixes and MIPS testing.
- Andreas Jaeger for testing and benchmarking of GCC and various bug fixes.
- Jakub Jelinek for his SPARC work and sibling call optimizations as well as lots of bug fixes and test cases, and for improving the Java build system.
- Janis Johnson for ia64 testing and fixes, her quality improvement sidetracks, and web page maintenance.

Contributors to GCC 585

- Kean Johnston for SCO OpenServer support and various fixes.
- Tim Josling for the sample language treelang based originally on Richard Kenner's "toy" language.
- Nicolai Josuttis for additional libstdc++ documentation.
- Klaus Kaempf for his ongoing work to make alpha-vms a viable target.
- Steven G. Kargl for work on GNU Fortran.
- David Kashtan of SRI adapted GCC to VMS.
- Ryszard Kabatek for many, many libstdc++ bug fixes and optimizations of strings, especially member functions, and for auto_ptr fixes.
- Geoffrey Keating for his ongoing work to make the PPC work for GNU/Linux and his automatic regression tester.
- Brendan Kehoe for his ongoing work with G++ and for a lot of early work in just about every part of libstdc++.
- Oliver M. Kellogg of Deutsche Aerospace contributed the port to the MIL-STD-1750A.
- Richard Kenner of the New York University Ultracomputer Research Laboratory wrote the machine descriptions for the AMD 29000, the DEC Alpha, the IBM RT PC, and the IBM RS/6000 as well as the support for instruction attributes. He also made changes to better support RISC processors including changes to common subexpression elimination, strength reduction, function calling sequence handling, and condition code support, in addition to generalizing the code for frame pointer elimination and delay slot scheduling. Richard Kenner was also the head maintainer of GCC for several years.
- Mumit Khan for various contributions to the Cygwin and Mingw32 ports and maintaining binary releases for Microsoft Windows hosts, and for massive libstdc++ porting work to Cygwin/Mingw32.
- Robin Kirkham for cpu32 support.
- Mark Klein for PA improvements.
- Thomas Koenig for various bug fixes.
- Bruce Korb for the new and improved fixincludes code.
- Benjamin Kosnik for his G++ work and for leading the libstdc++-v3 effort.
- Charles LaBrec contributed the support for the Integrated Solutions 68020 system.
- Asher Langton and Mike Kumbera for contributing Cray pointer support to GNU Fortran, and for other GNU Fortran improvements.
- Jeff Law for his direction via the steering committee, coordinating the entire egcs project and GCC 2.95, rolling out snapshots and releases, handling merges from GCC2, reviewing tons of patches that might have fallen through the cracks else, and random but extensive hacking.
- Marc Lehmann for his direction via the steering committee and helping with analysis and improvements of x86 performance.
- Victor Leikehman for work on GNU Fortran.
- Ted Lemon wrote parts of the RTL reader and printer.
- Kriang Lerdsuwanakij for C++ improvements including template as template parameter support, and many C++ fixes.

- Warren Levy for tremendous work on libgcj (Java Runtime Library) and random work on the Java front end.
- Alain Lichnewsky ported GCC to the MIPS CPU.
- Oskar Liljeblad for hacking on AWT and his many Java bug reports and patches.
- Robert Lipe for OpenServer support, new testsuites, testing, etc.
- Chen Liqin for various S+core related fixes/improvement, and for maintaining the S+core port.
- Weiwen Liu for testing and various bug fixes.
- Manuel López-Ibáñez for improving '-Wconversion' and many other diagnostics fixes and improvements.
- Dave Love for his ongoing work with the Fortran front end and runtime libraries.
- Martin von Löwis for internal consistency checking infrastructure, various C++ improvements including namespace support, and tons of assistance with libstdc++/compiler merges.
- H.J. Lu for his previous contributions to the steering committee, many x86 bug reports, prototype patches, and keeping the GNU/Linux ports working.
- Greg McGary for random fixes and (someday) bounded pointers.
- Andrew MacLeod for his ongoing work in building a real EH system, various code generation improvements, work on the global optimizer, etc.
- Vladimir Makarov for hacking some ugly i960 problems, PowerPC hacking improvements to compile-time performance, overall knowledge and direction in the area of instruction scheduling, and design and implementation of the automaton based instruction scheduler.
- Bob Manson for his behind the scenes work on dejagnu.
- Philip Martin for lots of libstdc++ string and vector iterator fixes and improvements, and string clean up and testsuites.
- All of the Mauve project contributors, for Java test code.
- Bryce McKinlay for numerous GCJ and libgcj fixes and improvements.
- Adam Megacz for his work on the Microsoft Windows port of GCJ.
- Michael Meissner for LRS framework, ia32, m32r, v850, m88k, MIPS, powerpc, haifa, ECOFF debug support, and other assorted hacking.
- Jason Merrill for his direction via the steering committee and leading the G++ effort.
- Martin Michlmayr for testing GCC on several architectures using the entire Debian archive.
- David Miller for his direction via the steering committee, lots of SPARC work, improvements in jump.c and interfacing with the Linux kernel developers.
- Gary Miller ported GCC to Charles River Data Systems machines.
- Alfred Minarik for libstdc++ string and ios bug fixes, and turning the entire libstdc++ testsuite namespace-compatible.
- Mark Mitchell for his direction via the steering committee, mountains of C++ work, load/store hoisting out of loops, alias analysis improvements, ISO C `restrict` support, and serving as release manager for GCC 3.x.

Contributors to GCC

- Alan Modra for various GNU/Linux bits and testing.
- Toon Moene for his direction via the steering committee, Fortran maintenance, and his ongoing work to make us make Fortran run fast.
- Jason Molenda for major help in the care and feeding of all the services on the gcc.gnu.org (formerly egcs.cygnus.com) machine—mail, web services, ftp services, etc etc. Doing all this work on scrap paper and the backs of envelopes would have been... difficult.
- Catherine Moore for fixing various ugly problems we have sent her way, including the haifa bug which was killing the Alpha & PowerPC Linux kernels.
- Mike Moreton for his various Java patches.
- David Mosberger-Tang for various Alpha improvements, and for the initial IA-64 port.
- Stephen Moshier contributed the floating point emulator that assists in cross-compilation and permits support for floating point numbers wider than 64 bits and for ISO C99 support.
- Bill Moyer for his behind the scenes work on various issues.
- Philippe De Muyter for his work on the m68k port.
- Joseph S. Myers for his work on the PDP-11 port, format checking and ISO C99 support, and continuous emphasis on (and contributions to) documentation.
- Nathan Myers for his work on libstdc++-v3: architecture and authorship through the first three snapshots, including implementation of locale infrastructure, string, shadow C headers, and the initial project documentation (DESIGN, CHECKLIST, and so forth). Later, more work on MT-safe string and shadow headers.
- Felix Natter for documentation on porting libstdc++.
- Nathanael Nerode for cleaning up the configuration/build process.
- NeXT, Inc. donated the front end that supports the Objective-C language.
- Hans-Peter Nilsson for the CRIS and MMIX ports, improvements to the search engine setup, various documentation fixes and other small fixes.
- Geoff Noer for his work on getting cygwin native builds working.
- Diego Novillo for his work on Tree SSA, OpenMP, SPEC performance tracking web pages and assorted fixes.
- David O'Brien for the FreeBSD/alpha, FreeBSD/AMD x86-64, FreeBSD/ARM, FreeBSD/PowerPC, and FreeBSD/SPARC64 ports and related infrastructure improvements.
- Alexandre Oliva for various build infrastructure improvements, scripts and amazing testing work, including keeping libtool issues sane and happy.
- Stefan Olsson for work on mt_alloc.
- Melissa O'Neill for various NeXT fixes.
- Rainer Orth for random MIPS work, including improvements to GCC's o32 ABI support, improvements to dejagnu's MIPS support, Java configuration clean-ups and porting work, etc.
- Hartmut Penner for work on the s390 port.
- Paul Petersen wrote the machine description for the Alliant FX/8.

- Alexandre Petit-Bianco for implementing much of the Java compiler and continued Java maintainership.
- Matthias Pfaller for major improvements to the NS32k port.
- Gerald Pfeifer for his direction via the steering committee, pointing out lots of problems we need to solve, maintenance of the web pages, and taking care of documentation maintenance in general.
- Andrew Pinski for processing bug reports by the dozen.
- Ovidiu Predescu for his work on the Objective-C front end and runtime libraries.
- Jerry Quinn for major performance improvements in C++ formatted I/O.
- Ken Raeburn for various improvements to checker, MIPS ports and various cleanups in the compiler.
- Rolf W. Rasmussen for hacking on AWT.
- David Reese of Sun Microsystems contributed to the Solaris on PowerPC port.
- Volker Reichelt for keeping up with the problem reports.
- Joern Rennecke for maintaining the sh port, loop, regmove & reload hacking.
- Loren J. Rittle for improvements to libstdc++-v3 including the FreeBSD port, threading fixes, thread-related configury changes, critical threading documentation, and solutions to really tricky I/O problems, as well as keeping GCC properly working on FreeBSD and continuous testing.
- Craig Rodrigues for processing tons of bug reports.
- Ola Rönnerup for work on mt_alloc.
- Gavin Romig-Koch for lots of behind the scenes MIPS work.
- David Ronis inspired and encouraged Craig to rewrite the G77 documentation in texinfo format by contributing a first pass at a translation of the old 'g77-0.5.16/f/DOC' file.
- Ken Rose for fixes to GCC's delay slot filling code.
- Paul Rubin wrote most of the preprocessor.
- Pétur Runólfsson for major performance improvements in C++ formatted I/O and large file support in C++ filebuf.
- Chip Salzenberg for libstdc++ patches and improvements to locales, traits, Makefiles, libio, libtool hackery, and "long long" support.
- Juha Sarlin for improvements to the H8 code generator.
- Greg Satz assisted in making GCC work on HP-UX for the 9000 series 300.
- Roger Sayle for improvements to constant folding and GCC's RTL optimizers as well as for fixing numerous bugs.
- Bradley Schatz for his work on the GCJ FAQ.
- Peter Schauer wrote the code to allow debugging to work on the Alpha.
- William Schelter did most of the work on the Intel 80386 support.
- Tobias Schlüter for work on GNU Fortran.
- Bernd Schmidt for various code generation improvements and major work in the reload pass as well a serving as release manager for GCC 2.95.3.

Contributors to GCC

- Peter Schmid for constant testing of libstdc++—especially application testing, going above and beyond what was requested for the release criteria—and libstdc++ header file tweaks.
- Jason Schroeder for jcf-dump patches.
- Andreas Schwab for his work on the m68k port.
- Lars Segerlund for work on GNU Fortran.
- Joel Sherrill for his direction via the steering committee, RTEMS contributions and RTEMS testing.
- Nathan Sidwell for many C++ fixes/improvements.
- Jeffrey Siegal for helping RMS with the original design of GCC, some code which handles the parse tree and RTL data structures, constant folding and help with the original VAX & m68k ports.
- Kenny Simpson for prompting libstdc++ fixes due to defect reports from the LWG (thereby keeping GCC in line with updates from the ISO).
- Franz Sirl for his ongoing work with making the PPC port stable for GNU/Linux.
- Andrey Slepuhin for assorted AIX hacking.
- Trevor Smigiel for contributing the SPU port.
- Christopher Smith did the port for Convex machines.
- Danny Smith for his major efforts on the Mingw (and Cygwin) ports.
- Randy Smith finished the Sun FPA support.
- Scott Snyder for queue, iterator, istream, and string fixes and libstdc++ testsuite entries. Also for providing the patch to G77 to add rudimentary support for `INTEGER*1`, `INTEGER*2`, and `LOGICAL*1`.
- Brad Spencer for contributions to the GLIBCPP_FORCE_NEW technique.
- Richard Stallman, for writing the original GCC and launching the GNU project.
- Jan Stein of the Chalmers Computer Society provided support for Genix, as well as part of the 32000 machine description.
- Nigel Stephens for various mips16 related fixes/improvements.
- Jonathan Stone wrote the machine description for the Pyramid computer.
- Graham Stott for various infrastructure improvements.
- John Stracke for his Java HTTP protocol fixes.
- Mike Stump for his Elxsi port, G++ contributions over the years and more recently his vxworks contributions
- Jeff Sturm for Java porting help, bug fixes, and encouragement.
- Shigeya Suzuki for this fixes for the bsdi platforms.
- Ian Lance Taylor for his mips16 work, general configury hacking, fixincludes, etc.
- Holger Teutsch provided the support for the Clipper CPU.
- Gary Thomas for his ongoing work to make the PPC work for GNU/Linux.
- Philipp Thomas for random bug fixes throughout the compiler
- Jason Thorpe for thread support in libstdc++ on NetBSD.

- Kresten Krab Thorup wrote the run time support for the Objective-C language and the fantastic Java bytecode interpreter.
- Michael Tiemann for random bug fixes, the first instruction scheduler, initial C++ support, function integration, NS32k, SPARC and M88k machine description work, delay slot scheduling.
- Andreas Tobler for his work porting libgcj to Darwin.
- Teemu Torma for thread safe exception handling support.
- Leonard Tower wrote parts of the parser, RTL generator, and RTL definitions, and of the VAX machine description.
- Tom Tromey for internationalization support and for his many Java contributions and libgcj maintainership.
- Lassi Tuura for improvements to config.guess to determine HP processor types.
- Petter Urkedal for libstdc++ CXXFLAGS, math, and algorithms fixes.
- Andy Vaught for the design and initial implementation of the GNU Fortran front end.
- Brent Verner for work with the libstdc++ cshadow files and their associated configure steps.
- Todd Vierling for contributions for NetBSD ports.
- Jonathan Wakely for contributing libstdc++ Doxygen notes and XHTML guidance.
- Dean Wakerley for converting the install documentation from HTML to texinfo in time for GCC 3.0.
- Krister Walfridsson for random bug fixes.
- Feng Wang for contributions to GNU Fortran.
- Stephen M. Webb for time and effort on making libstdc++ shadow files work with the tricky Solaris 8+ headers, and for pushing the build-time header tree.
- John Wehle for various improvements for the x86 code generator, related infrastructure improvements to help x86 code generation, value range propagation and other work, WE32k port.
- Ulrich Weigand for work on the s390 port.
- Zack Weinberg for major work on cpplib and various other bug fixes.
- Matt Welsh for help with Linux Threads support in GCJ.
- Urban Widmark for help fixing java.io.
- Mark Wielaard for new Java library code and his work integrating with Classpath.
- Dale Wiles helped port GCC to the Tahoe.
- Bob Wilson from Tensilica, Inc. for the Xtensa port.
- Jim Wilson for his direction via the steering committee, tackling hard problems in various places that nobody else wanted to work on, strength reduction and other loop optimizations.
- Paul Woegerer and Tal Agmon for the CRX port.
- Carlo Wood for various fixes.
- Tom Wood for work on the m88k port.
- Canqun Yang for work on GNU Fortran.

Contributors to GCC

- Masanobu Yuhara of Fujitsu Laboratories implemented the machine description for the Tron architecture (specifically, the Gmicro).
- Kevin Zachmann helped port GCC to the Tahoe.
- Ayal Zaks for Swing Modulo Scheduling (SMS).
- Xiaoqiang Zhang for work on GNU Fortran.
- Gilles Zunino for help porting Java to Irix.

The following people are recognized for their contributions to GNAT, the Ada front end of GCC:

- Bernard Banner
- Romain Berrendonner
- Geert Bosch
- Emmanuel Briot
- Joel Brobecker
- Ben Brosgol
- Vincent Celier
- Arnaud Charlet
- Chien Chieng
- Cyrille Comar
- Cyrille Crozes
- Robert Dewar
- Gary Dismukes
- Robert Duff
- Ed Falis
- Ramon Fernandez
- Sam Figueroa
- Vasiliy Fofanov
- Michael Friess
- Franco Gasperoni
- Ted Giering
- Matthew Gingell
- Laurent Guerby
- Jerome Guitton
- Olivier Hainque
- Jerome Hugues
- Hristian Kirtchev
- Jerome Lambourg
- Bruno Leclerc
- Albert Lee
- Sean McNeil

- Javier Miranda
- Laurent Nana
- Pascal Obry
- Dong-Ik Oh
- Laurent Pautet
- Brett Porter
- Thomas Quinot
- Nicolas Roche
- Pat Rogers
- Jose Ruiz
- Douglas Rupp
- Sergey Rybin
- Gail Schenker
- Ed Schonberg
- Nicolas Setton
- Samuel Tardieu

The following people are recognized for their contributions of new features, bug reports, testing and integration of classpath/libgcj for GCC version 4.1:

- Lillian Angel for `JTree` implementation and lots Free Swing additions and bug fixes.
- Wolfgang Baer for `GapContent` bug fixes.
- Anthony Balkissoon for `JList`, Free Swing 1.5 updates and mouse event fixes, lots of Free Swing work including `JTable` editing.
- Stuart Ballard for RMI constant fixes.
- Goffredo Baroncelli for `HTTPURLConnection` fixes.
- Gary Benson for `MessageFormat` fixes.
- Daniel Bonniot for `Serialization` fixes.
- Chris Burdess for lots of gnu.xml and http protocol fixes, `StAX` and `DOM` `xml:id` support.
- Ka-Hing Cheung for `TreePath` and `TreeSelection` fixes.
- Archie Cobbs for build fixes, VM interface updates, `URLClassLoader` updates.
- Kelley Cook for build fixes.
- Martin Cordova for Suggestions for better `SocketTimeoutException`.
- David Daney for `BitSet` bug fixes, `HttpURLConnection` rewrite and improvements.
- Thomas Fitzsimmons for lots of upgrades to the gtk+ AWT and Cairo 2D support. Lots of imageio framework additions, lots of AWT and Free Swing bug fixes.
- Jeroen Frijters for `ClassLoader` and nio cleanups, serialization fixes, better `Proxy` support, bug fixes and IKVM integration.
- Santiago Gala for `AccessControlContext` fixes.
- Nicolas Geoffray for `VMClassLoader` and `AccessController` improvements.
- David Gilbert for `basic` and `metal` icon and plaf support and lots of documenting, Lots of Free Swing and metal theme additions. `MetalIconFactory` implementation.

Contributors to GCC 593

- Anthony Green for `MIDI` framework, `ALSA` and `DSSI` providers.
- Andrew Haley for `Serialization` and `URLClassLoader` fixes, gcj build speedups.
- Kim Ho for `JFileChooser` implementation.
- Andrew John Hughes for `Locale` and net fixes, URI RFC2986 updates, `Serialization` fixes, `Properties` XML support and generic branch work, VMIntegration guide update.
- Bastiaan Huisman for `TimeZone` bug fixing.
- Andreas Jaeger for mprec updates.
- Paul Jenner for better '-`Werror`' support.
- Ito Kazumitsu for `NetworkInterface` implementation and updates.
- Roman Kennke for `BoxLayout`, `GrayFilter` and `SplitPane`, plus bug fixes all over. Lots of Free Swing work including styled text.
- Simon Kitching for `String` cleanups and optimization suggestions.
- Michael Koch for configuration fixes, `Locale` updates, bug and build fixes.
- Guilhem Lavaux for configuration, thread and channel fixes and Kaffe integration. JCL native `Pointer` updates. Logger bug fixes.
- David Lichteblau for JCL support library global/local reference cleanups.
- Aaron Luchko for JDWP updates and documentation fixes.
- Ziga Mahkovec for `Graphics2D` upgraded to Cairo 0.5 and new regex features.
- Sven de Marothy for BMP imageio support, CSS and `TextLayout` fixes. `GtkImage` rewrite, 2D, awt, free swing and date/time fixes and implementing the Qt4 peers.
- Casey Marshall for crypto algorithm fixes, `FileChannel` lock, `SystemLogger` and `FileHandler` rotate implementations, NIO `FileChannel.map` support, security and policy updates.
- Bryce McKinlay for RMI work.
- Audrius Meskauskas for lots of Free Corba, RMI and HTML work plus testing and documenting.
- Kalle Olavi Niemitalo for build fixes.
- Rainer Orth for build fixes.
- Andrew Overholt for `File` locking fixes.
- Ingo Proetel for `Image`, `Logger` and `URLClassLoader` updates.
- Olga Rodimina for `MenuSelectionManager` implementation.
- Jan Roehrich for `BasicTreeUI` and `JTree` fixes.
- Julian Scheid for documentation updates and gjdoc support.
- Christian Schlichtherle for zip fixes and cleanups.
- Robert Schuster for documentation updates and beans fixes, `TreeNode` enumerations and `ActionCommand` and various fixes, XML and URL, AWT and Free Swing bug fixes.
- Keith Seitz for lots of JDWP work.
- Christian Thalinger for 64-bit cleanups, Configuration and VM interface fixes and `CACAO` integration, `fdlibm` updates.
- Gael Thomas for `VMClassLoader` boot packages support suggestions.

- Andreas Tobler for Darwin and Solaris testing and fixing, `Qt4` support for Darwin/OS X, `Graphics2D` support, `gtk+` updates.
- Dalibor Topic for better `DEBUG` support, build cleanups and Kaffe integration. `Qt4` build infrastructure, `SHA1PRNG` and `GdkPixbugDecoder` updates.
- Tom Tromey for Eclipse integration, generics work, lots of bug fixes and gcj integration including coordinating The Big Merge.
- Mark Wielaard for bug fixes, packaging and release management, `Clipboard` implementation, system call interrupts and network timeouts and `GdkPixpufDecoder` fixes.

In addition to the above, all of which also contributed time and energy in testing GCC, we would like to thank the following for their contributions to testing:

- Michael Abd-El-Malek
- Thomas Arend
- Bonzo Armstrong
- Steven Ashe
- Chris Baldwin
- David Billinghurst
- Jim Blandy
- Stephane Bortzmeyer
- Horst von Brand
- Frank Braun
- Rodney Brown
- Sidney Cadot
- Bradford Castalia
- Jonathan Corbet
- Ralph Doncaster
- Richard Emberson
- Levente Farkas
- Graham Fawcett
- Mark Fernyhough
- Robert A. French
- Jörgen Freyh
- Mark K. Gardner
- Charles-Antoine Gauthier
- Yung Shing Gene
- David Gilbert
- Simon Gornall
- Fred Gray
- John Griffin
- Patrik Hagglund

Contributors to GCC

- Phil Hargett
- Amancio Hasty
- Takafumi Hayashi
- Bryan W. Headley
- Kevin B. Hendricks
- Joep Jansen
- Christian Joensson
- Michel Kern
- David Kidd
- Tobias Kuipers
- Anand Krishnaswamy
- A. O. V. Le Blanc
- llewelly
- Damon Love
- Brad Lucier
- Matthias Klose
- Martin Knoblauch
- Rick Lutowski
- Jesse Macnish
- Stefan Morrell
- Anon A. Mous
- Matthias Mueller
- Pekka Nikander
- Rick Niles
- Jon Olson
- Magnus Persson
- Chris Pollard
- Richard Polton
- Derk Reefman
- David Rees
- Paul Reilly
- Tom Reilly
- Torsten Rueger
- Danny Sadinoff
- Marc Schifer
- Erik Schnetter
- Wayne K. Schroll
- David Schuler
- Vin Shelton

- Tim Souder
- Adam Sulmicki
- Bill Thorson
- George Talbot
- Pedro A. M. Vazquez
- Gregory Warnes
- Ian Watson
- David E. Young
- And many others

And finally we'd like to thank everyone who uses the compiler, submits bug reports and generally reminds us why we're doing this work in the first place.

Option Index

GCC's command line options are indexed here without any initial '-' or '--'. Where an option has both positive and negative forms (such as '-f*option*' and '-fno-*option*'), relevant entries in the manual are indexed under the most appropriate form; it may sometimes be useful to look up both forms.

#
.... 23

A
A 121
all_load 147
allowable_client 148
ansi 5, 26, 117, 337, 547
arch_errors_fatal 147
aux-info 28

B
b 135
B 126
bcopy-builtin 193
Bdynamic 220
bind_at_load 147
Bstatic 220
bundle 147
bundle_loader 147

C
c 22, 123
C 122
client_name 148
combine 23
compatibility_version 148
coverage 67
current_version 148

D
d 68
D 113
da 71
dA 68
dB 69
dc 69
dC 69
dd 69
dD 69, 121
dE 69
dead_strip 148
dependency-file 148
df 69
dg 69
dG 69
dh 70
dH 71
di 70
dI 121
dj 70
dk 70
dl 70
dL 70
dm 70, 71
dM 70, 121
dn 70
dN 70, 121
do 70
dp 71
dP 71
dr 70
dR 70
ds 71
dS 71
dt 71
dT 71
dumpmachine 77
dumpspecs 77
dumpversion 77
dv 72
dV 71
dw 71
dx 72
dy 72
dylib_file 148
dylinker_install_name 148
dynamic 148
dynamiclib 147
dz 71
dZ 71

E
E 23, 123
EB 135, 182
EL 135, 182
exported_symbols_list 148

F
F 145
fabi-version 31
falign-functions 94

falign-jumps	95	fdump-rtl-flow2	71
falign-labels	94	fdump-rtl-gcse	69
falign-loops	94	fdump-rtl-greg	69
fargument-alias	227	fdump-rtl-jump	70
fargument-noalias	227	fdump-rtl-life	69
fargument-noalias-anything	227	fdump-rtl-loop2	70
fargument-noalias-global	227	fdump-rtl-lreg	70
fassociative-math	97	fdump-rtl-mach	70
fasynchronous-unwind-tables	222	fdump-rtl-peephole2	71
fauto-inc-dec	85	fdump-rtl-postreload	70
fbounds-check	222	fdump-rtl-regmove	70
fbranch-probabilities	99	fdump-rtl-rnreg	70
fbranch-target-load-optimize	101	fdump-rtl-sched1	71
fbranch-target-load-optimize2	101	fdump-rtl-sched2	70
fbtr-bb-exclusive	101	fdump-rtl-sibling	70
fcall-saved	225	fdump-rtl-sms	70
fcall-used	225	fdump-rtl-stack	70
fcaller-saves	87	fdump-rtl-tracer	71
fcheck-data-deps	89	fdump-rtl-vartrack	71
fcheck-new	31	fdump-rtl-vpt	71
fcommon	287	fdump-rtl-web	71
fcond-mismatch	30	fdump-translation-unit	72
fconserve-space	31	fdump-tree	72
fconstant-string-class	39	fdump-tree-alias	74
fcprop-registers	96	fdump-tree-all	75
fcrossjumping	84	fdump-tree-ccp	74
fcse-follow-jumps	83	fdump-tree-cfg	73
fcse-skip-blocks	83	fdump-tree-ch	73
fcx-limited-range	99	fdump-tree-copyprop	74
fdata-sections	101	fdump-tree-copyrename	75
fdbg-cnt	68	fdump-tree-dce	74
fdbg-cnt-list	68	fdump-tree-dom	74
fdce	85	fdump-tree-dse	74
fdebug-prefix-map	66	fdump-tree-forwprop	74
fdelayed-branch	85	fdump-tree-fre	74
fdelete-null-pointer-checks	85	fdump-tree-gimple	73
fdiagnostics-show-location	42	fdump-tree-mudflap	74
fdiagnostics-show-option	43	fdump-tree-nrv	75
fdirectives-only	119	fdump-tree-phiopt	74
fdollars-in-identifiers	120, 535	fdump-tree-pre	74
fdse	85	fdump-tree-salias	74
fdump-class-hierarchy	72	fdump-tree-sink	74
fdump-ipa	72	fdump-tree-sra	74
fdump-noaddr	72	fdump-tree-ssa	73
fdump-rtl-all	71	fdump-tree-store_copyprop	74
fdump-rtl-bbro	69	fdump-tree-storeccp	74
fdump-rtl-btl	69	fdump-tree-vcg	73
fdump-rtl-bypass	69	fdump-tree-vect	75
fdump-rtl-ce1	69	fdump-tree-vrp	75
fdump-rtl-ce2	69	fdump-unnumbered	72
fdump-rtl-ce3	69	fearly-inlining	81
fdump-rtl-cfg	69	feliminate-dwarf2-dups	65
fdump-rtl-combine	69	feliminate-unused-debug-symbols	64
fdump-rtl-cse	71	feliminate-unused-debug-types	77
fdump-rtl-cse2	71	fexceptions	222
fdump-rtl-dbr	69	fexec-charset	120
fdump-rtl-eh	70	fexpensive-optimizations	85
fdump-rtl-expand	70	fextended-identifiers	120

Option Index

ffast-math	97	fno-access-control	31
ffinite-math-only	98	fno-asm	28
ffix-and-continue	147	fno-branch-count-reg	82
ffixed	225	fno-builtin	28, 46, 270, 337
ffloat-store	96, 540	fno-common	224, 287
ffor-scope	32	fno-default-inline	35, 80, 300
fforward-propagate	80	fno-defer-pop	80
ffreestanding	6, 29, 46, 270	fno-elide-constructors	32
ffriend-injection	31	fno-enforce-eh-specs	32
ffunction-sections	101	fno-for-scope	32
fgcse	84	fno-function-cse	82
fgcse-after-reload	84	fno-gnu-keywords	32
fgcse-las	84	fno-guess-branch-probability	92
fgcse-lm	84	fno-ident	224
fgcse-sm	84	fno-implement-inlines	32, 506
fgnu-runtime	39	fno-implicit-inline-templates	32
fgnu89-inline	28	fno-implicit-templates	32, 508
fhosted	29	fno-inline	80
fif-conversion	85	fno-jump-tables	225
fif-conversion2	85	fno-math-errno	97
filelist	148	fno-merge-debug-strings	66
findirect-data	147	fno-nil-receivers	39
finhibit-size-directive	224	fno-nonansi-builtins	33
finline-functions	80	fno-operator-names	33
finline-functions-called-once	81	fno-optional-diags	33
finline-limit	81	fno-peephole	92
finline-small-functions	80	fno-peephole2	92
finput-charset	120	fno-rtti	33
finstrument-functions	226, 274	fno-sched-interblock	86
finstrument-functions-exclude-file-list		fno-sched-spec	86
	226	fno-show-column	121
finstrument-functions-exclude-function-list		fno-signed-bitfields	30
	227	fno-signed-zeros	98
fipa-cp	88	fno-stack-limit	227
fipa-matrix-reorg	88	fno-threadsafe-statics	33
fipa-pta	88	fno-toplevel-reorder	95
fipa-pure-const	88	fno-trapping-math	98
fipa-reference	88	fno-unsigned-bitfields	30
fipa-struct-reorg	88	fno-use-cxa-get-exception-ptr	34
fivopts	90	fno-weak	35
fkeep-inline-functions	81, 299	fno-working-directory	121
fkeep-static-consts	81	fno-zero-initialized-in-bss	82
flat_namespace	148	fnon-call-exceptions	222
flax-vector-conversions	30	fobjc-call-cxx-cdtors	39
fleading-underscore	228	fobjc-direct-dispatch	39
fmem-report	67	fobjc-exceptions	40
fmerge-all-constants	82	fobjc-gc	41
fmerge-constants	82	fomit-frame-pointer	80
fmerge-debug-strings	66	fopenmp	29
fmessage-length	42	foptimize-register-move	85
fmodulo-sched	82	foptimize-sibling-calls	80
fmodulo-sched-allow-regmoves	82	force_cpusubtype_ALL	147
fmove-loop-invariants	101	force_flat_namespace	148
fms-extensions	29, 32, 499	fpack-struct	226
fmudflap	83	fpcc-struct-return	223, 538
fmudflapir	83	fpch-deps	117
fmudflapth	83	fpch-preprocess	117
fnext-runtime	39	fpeel-loops	100

fpermissive	33	ftabstop	120
fpic	224	ftemplate-depth	33
fPIC	225	ftest-coverage	68
fpie	225	fthread-jumps	83
fPIE	225	ftime-report	67
fpost-ipa-mem-report	67	ftls-model	228
fpre-ipa-mem-report	67	ftracer	91, 100
fpredictive-commoning	91	ftrapv	222
fprefetch-loop-arrays	91	ftree-ccp	89
fpreprocessed	120	ftree-ch	89
fprofile-arcs	67, 340	ftree-copy-prop	88
fprofile-generate	96	ftree-copyrename	90
fprofile-use	96	ftree-dce	89
fprofile-values	100	ftree-dominator-opts	89
frandom-string	75	ftree-dse	89
freciprocal-math	98	ftree-fre	87
frecord-gcc-switches	224	ftree-loop-im	89
freg-struct-return	223	ftree-loop-ivcanon	90
fregmove	85	ftree-loop-linear	89
frename-registers	100	ftree-loop-optimize	89
freorder-blocks	92	ftree-parallelize-loops	90
freorder-blocks-and-partition	92	ftree-pre	87
freorder-functions	92	ftree-reassoc	87
freplace-objc-classes	41	ftree-salias	88
frepo	33, 507	ftree-sink	89
frerun-cse-after-loop	84	ftree-sra	90
freschedule-modulo-scheduled-loops	87	ftree-store-ccp	89
frounding-math	98	ftree-ter	90
frtl-abstract-sequences	99	ftree-vect-loop-version	90
fsched-spec-load	86	ftree-vectorize	90
fsched-spec-load-dangerous	86	ftree-vectorizer-verbose	75
fsched-stalled-insns	86	ftree-vrp	91
fsched-stalled-insns-dep	86	funit-at-a-time	95
fsched-verbose	75	funroll-all-loops	91, 100
fsched2-use-superblocks	87	funroll-loops	91, 100
fsched2-use-traces	87	funsafe-loop-optimizations	84
fschedule-insns	86	funsafe-math-optimizations	97
fschedule-insns2	86	funsigned-bitfields	30, 241, 546
fsection-anchors	101	funsigned-char	30, 238
fsee	87	funswitch-loops	101
fshort-double	223	funwind-tables	222
fshort-enums	223, 241, 295, 546	fuse-cxa-atexit	33
fshort-wchar	223	fvar-tracking	76
fsignaling-nans	99	fvariable-expansion-in-unroller	91
fsigned-bitfields	30, 546	fvect-cost-model	90
fsigned-char	30, 238	fverbose-asm	224
fsingle-precision-constant	99	fvisibility	228
fsplit-ivs-in-unroller	91	fvisibility-inlines-hidden	34
fsplit-wide-types	83	fvisibility-ms-compat	34
fstack-check	227	fvpt	100
fstack-limit-register	227	fweb	95
fstack-limit-symbol	227	fwhole-program	96
fstack-protector	101	fwide-exec-charset	120
fstack-protector-all	101	fworking-directory	121
fstats	33	fwrapv	222
fstrict-aliasing	92	fzero-link	41
fstrict-overflow	93		
fsyntax-only	43		

G

g	63
G	175, 186, 205, 218
gcoff	64
gdwarf-2	64
gen-decls	41
gfull	146
ggdb	64
gnu-ld	159
gstabs	64
gstabs+	64
gused	146
gvms	65
gxcoff	64
gxcoff+	64

H

H	122
headerpad_max_install_names	148
help	23, 122
hp-ld	159

I

I	113, 126
I-	118, 127
idirafter	119
iframework	146
imacros	119
image_base	148
imultilib	119
include	118
init	148
install_name	148
iprefix	119
iquote	119, 126
isysroot	119
isystem	119
iwithprefix	119
iwithprefixbefore	119

K

keep_private_externs	148

L

l	123
L	126
lobjc	124

M

M	115
m1	209
m10	193
m128bit-long-double	165
m16-bit	144
m2	209
m210	182
m3	209
m31	207
m32	170, 198, 216
m32-bit	144
m32r	175
m32r2	174
m32rx	175
m340	182
m3dnow	168
m3e	209
m4	209
m4-nofpu	209
m4-single	209
m4-single-only	209
m40	193
m45	193
m4a	210
m4a-nofpu	209
m4a-single	210
m4a-single-only	209
m4al	210
m4byte-functions	182
m5200	178
m5206e	178
m528x	178
m5307	178
m5407	178
m64	170, 198, 207, 216
m68000	177
m68010	177
m68020	178
m68020-40	178
m68020-60	179
m68030	178
m68040	178
m68060	178
m6811	181
m6812	181
m68881	179
m68hc11	181
m68hc12	181
m68hcs12	181
m68S12	181
m8-bit	144
m96bit-long-double	165
mabi	136, 203
mabi-mmixware	191
mabi=32	184
mabi=64	184
mabi=eabi	184
mabi=gnu	191
mabi=ibmlongdouble	203
mabi=ieeelongdouble	203
mabi=n32	184

mabi=no-spe	203	mcall-linux	203
mabi=o64	184	mcall-netbsd	203
mabi=spe	203	mcall-prologues	141
mabicalls	184	mcall-solaris	203
mabort-on-noreturn	138	mcall-sysv	202
mabshi	194	mcall-sysv-eabi	202
mac0	193	mcall-sysv-noeabi	203
macc-4	155	mcallee-super-interworking	140
macc-8	155	mcaller-super-interworking	140
maccumulate-outgoing-args	169	mcallgraph-data	182
madjust-unroll	212	mcc-init	144
mads	204	mcfv4e	178
maix-struct-return	203	mcheck-zero-division	188
maix32	199	mcirrus-fix-invalid-insns	139
maix64	199	mcix	151
malign-300	157	mcld	168
malign-double	165	mcmodel=embmedany	216
malign-int	180	mcmodel=kernel	170
malign-labels	155	mcmodel=large	171
malign-loops	175	mcmodel=medany	216
malign-natural	200	mcmodel=medium	171
malign-power	200	mcmodel=medlow	216
malloc-cc	154	mcmodel=medmid	216
malpha-as	151	mcmodel=small	170
maltivec	197	mcmpb	195
mam33	192	mcode-readable	188
maout	145	mcond-exec	156
mapcs	136	mcond-move	155
mapcs-frame	136	mconst-align	144
mapp-regs	213, 219	mconst16	220
march .. 138, 143, 158, 160, 163, 176, 182, 193, 208		mconstant-gp	171
masm=*dialect*	164	mcpu ... 136, 137, 143, 152, 157, 163, 176, 196, 214	
mauto-incdec	181	mcpu=	141, 174
mauto-pic	171	mcpu32	178
mb	210	mcsync-anomaly	142
mbacc	193	mcx16	168
mbackchain	206	MD	116
mbase-addresses	192	mdalign	210
mbcopy	193	mdata	136
mbig	202	mdata-align	144
mbig-endian	137, 171, 182, 202	mdebug	175, 207
mbig-switch	158, 219	mdec-asm	194
mbigtable	210	mdisable-callt	219
mbit-align	201	mdisable-fpregs	158
mbitfield	179	mdisable-indexing	158
mbranch-cheap	194	mdiv	179, 181
mbranch-cost	190	mdiv=*strategy*	211
mbranch-cost=*number*	176	mdivide-breaks	188
mbranch-expensive	194	mdivide-traps	188
mbranch-hints	217	mdivsi3_libfunc=*name*	212
mbranch-likely	190	mdlmzb	201
mbranch-predict	192	mdmx	186
mbss-plt	198	mdouble	154
mbuild-constants	151	mdouble-float	185
mbwx	151	mdsp	185
mc68000	177	mdspr2	186
mc68020	178	mdual-nops	217
mcall-gnu	203	mdwarf2-asm	172

Option Index

mdword	154
mdynamic-no-pic	202
meabi	204
mearly-stop-bits	172
meb	209
mel	209
melf	145, 192
melinux	145
melinux-stacksize	143
memb	204
membedded-data	187
memregs=	174
mep	218
mepsilon	191
merror-reloc	217
mesa	207
metrax100	144
metrax4	144
mexplicit-relocs	151, 188
mextern-sdata	187
MF	116
mfast-fp	143
mfast-indirect-calls	158
mfaster-structs	214
mfdpic	154
mfix	151
mfix-and-continue	147
mfix-r4000	189
mfix-r4400	189
mfix-sb1	190
mfix-vr4120	190
mfix-vr4130	190
mfixed-cc	154
mfixed-range	158, 172, 217
mflip-mips16	183
mfloat-abi	137
mfloat-gprs	198
mfloat-ieee	151
mfloat-vax	151
mfloat32	194
mfloat64	194
mflush-func	190
mflush-func=name	176
mflush-trap=number	176
mfmovd	210
mfp	138
mfp-exceptions	191
mfp-reg	149
mfp-rounding-mode	150
mfp-trap-mode	150
mfp32	185
mfp64	185
mfpe	138
mfpr-32	153
mfpr-64	153
mfprnd	195
mfpu	138, 193, 213
mfull-toc	199
mfused-madd	170, 189, 201, 208, 220
mg	219
MG	116
mgas	151, 159
mgettrcost=number	212
mglibc	157
mgnu	219
mgnu-as	171
mgnu-ld	171
mgotplt	145
mgp32	185
mgp64	185
mgpopt	187
mgpr-32	153
mgpr-64	153
mgprel-ro	155
mh	157
mhard-dfp	195, 206
mhard-float	136, 153, 179, 185, 200, 206, 213
mhard-quad-float	213
mhardlit	181
mhint-max-distance	218
mhint-max-nops	218
mhitachi	210
mid-shared-library	142
mieee	149, 210
mieee-conformant	151
mieee-fp	164
mieee-with-inexact	149
milp32	173
mimpure-text	214
mindexed-addressing	212
minit-stack	140
minline-all-stringops	169
minline-float-divide-max-throughput	172
minline-float-divide-min-latency	172
minline-ic_invalidate	210
minline-int-divide-max-throughput	172
minline-int-divide-min-latency	172
minline-plt	143, 154
minline-sqrt-max-throughput	172
minline-sqrt-min-latency	172
minline-stringops-dynamically	169
minmax	181
minsert-sched-nops	202
mint16	193
mint32	157, 194
mint8	141
minterlink-mips16	183
minvalid-symbols	212
mips1	183
mips16	183
mips2	183
mips3	183
mips32	183
mips32r2	183
mips3d	186
mips4	183

mips64	183	mmvme	204
misel	198	mn	157
misize	211	mnested-cond-exec	156
missue-rate=number	176	mnew-mnemonics	196
mjump-in-delay	158	mnhwloop	209
mkernel	146	mno-3dnow	168
mknuthdiv	191	mno-4byte-functions	182
ml	210	mno-abicalls	184
mlarge-data	152	mno-abshi	194
mlarge-data-threshold=number	165	mno-ac0	193
mlarge-mem	217	mno-align-double	165
mlarge-text	152	mno-align-int	180
mleaf-id-shared-library	142	mno-align-loops	175
mlibfuncs	191	mno-align-stringops	169
mlibrary-pic	155	mno-altivec	197
mlinked-fp	155	mno-am33	192
mlinker-opt	159	mno-app-regs	213, 219
mlinux	145	mno-bacc	193
mlittle	202	mno-backchain	206
mlittle-endian	137, 171, 182, 202, 216	mno-base-addresses	192
mllsc	185	mno-bit-align	201
mlocal-sdata	187	mno-bitfield	179
mlong-calls	138, 143, 155, 181, 189, 218	mno-branch-likely	190
mlong-double-128	206	mno-branch-predict	192
mlong-double-64	206	mno-bwx	151
mlong-load-store	159	mno-callgraph-data	182
mlong32	186	mno-check-zero-division	188
mlong64	186	mno-cirrus-fix-invalid-insns	139
mlongcall	205	mno-cix	151
mlongcalls	221	mno-cmpb	195
mlow-64k	142	mno-cond-exec	156
mlp64	173	mno-cond-move	155
MM	116	mno-const-align	144
mmac	145, 209	mno-const16	220
mmad	189	mno-crt0	192, 193
mmangle-cpu	135	mno-csync-anomaly	142
mmax	151	mno-data-align	144
mmax-stack-frame	143	mno-debug	207
mmcu	140	mno-div	179, 181
MMD	117	mno-dlmzb	201
mmedia	154	mno-double	154
mmemcpy	189	mno-dsp	185
mmemory-latency	153	mno-dspr2	186
mmfcrf	195	mno-dwarf2-asm	172
mmfpgpr	195	mno-dword	154
mminimal-toc	199	mno-eabi	204
mmmx	168	mno-early-stop-bits	172
mmodel=large	175	mno-eflags	155
mmodel=medium	175	mno-embedded-data	187
mmodel=small	175	mno-ep	218
mmt	186	mno-epsilon	191
mmul-bug-workaround	144	mno-explicit-relocs	151, 188
mmuladd	154	mno-extern-sdata	187
mmulhw	201	mno-fancy-math-387	164
mmult-bug	192	mno-faster-structs	214
mmulti-cond-exec	156	mno-fix	151
mmultiple	200	mno-fix-r4000	189
mmvcle	207	mno-fix-r4400	189

Option Index

mno-float32	194
mno-float64	194
mno-flush-func	176
mno-flush-trap	176
mno-fp-in-toc	199
mno-fp-regs	149
mno-fp-ret-in-387	164
mno-fprnd	195
mno-fpu	213
mno-fused-madd	189, 201, 208, 220
mno-gnu-as	171
mno-gnu-ld	171
mno-gotplt	145
mno-gpopt	187
mno-hard-dfp	195, 206
mno-hardlit	181
mno-id-shared-library	142
mno-ieee-fp	164
mno-int16	194
mno-int32	193
mno-interlink-mips16	183
mno-interrupts	140
mno-isel	198
mno-knuthdiv	191
mno-leaf-id-shared-library	142
mno-libfuncs	191
mno-llsc	185
mno-local-sdata	187
mno-long-calls	138, 143, 160, 181, 189, 218
mno-longcall	205
mno-longcalls	221
mno-low-64k	142
mno-mad	189
mno-max	151
mno-mdmx	186
mno-media	154
mno-memcpy	189
mno-mfcrf	195
mno-mfpgpr	195
mno-mips16	183
mno-mips3d	186
mno-mmx	168
mno-mt	186
mno-mul-bug-workaround	144
mno-muladd	154
mno-mulhw	201
mno-mult-bug	192
mno-multi-cond-exec	156
mno-multiple	200
mno-mvcle	207
mno-nested-cond-exec	156
mno-optimize-membar	157
mno-pack	155
mno-packed-stack	206
mno-paired	198
mno-paired-single	186
mno-pic	171
mno-popcntb	195
mno-power	195
mno-power2	195
mno-powerpc	195
mno-powerpc-gfxopt	195
mno-powerpc-gpopt	195
mno-powerpc64	195
mno-prolog-function	218
mno-prologue-epilogue	144
mno-prototype	203
mno-push-args	169
mno-register-names	171
mno-regnames	205
mno-relax-immediate	181
mno-relocatable	201
mno-relocatable-lib	201
mno-rtd	180
mno-scc	156
mno-sched-ar-data-spec	173
mno-sched-ar-in-data-spec	173
mno-sched-br-data-spec	173
mno-sched-br-in-data-spec	173
mno-sched-control-ldc	173
mno-sched-control-spec	173
mno-sched-count-spec-in-critical-path	174
mno-sched-in-control-spec	173
mno-sched-ldc	173
mno-sched-prefer-non-control-spec-insns	174
mno-sched-prefer-non-data-spec-insns	174
mno-sched-prolog	136
mno-sched-spec-verbose	174
mno-sdata	171, 205
mno-sep-data	143
mno-short	179
mno-side-effects	144
mno-single-exit	192
mno-slow-bytes	182
mno-small-exec	207
mno-smartmips	186
mno-soft-float	149
mno-space-regs	158
mno-spe	198
mno-specld-anomaly	142
mno-split	194
mno-split-addresses	188
mno-sse	168
mno-stack-align	144
mno-stack-bias	216
mno-strict-align	180, 201
mno-string	200
mno-sum-in-toc	199
mno-swdiv	197
mno-sym32	186
mno-tablejump	141
mno-target-align	221
mno-text-section-literals	221
mno-toc	202
mno-toplevel-symbols	192

mno-tpf-trace	208	mregparm	166
mno-unaligned-doubles	213	mrelax	157, 193, 210
mno-uninit-const-in-rodata	188	mrelax-immediate	181
mno-update	200	mrelocatable	201
mno-v8plus	215	mrelocatable-lib	201
mno-vis	215	mreturn-pointer-on-d0	192
mno-vliw-branch	156	mrodata	136
mno-volatile-asm-stop	171	mrtd	165, 179, 266
mno-vrsave	198	mrtp	220
mno-wide-bitfields	182	ms	157
mno-xgot	184	ms2600	157
mno-xl-compat	199	msafe-dma	217
mno-zero-extend	191	msafe-hints	218
mnobitfield	179	msahf	168
mnomacsave	210	mscc	156
mnominmax	181	msched-ar-data-spec	173
mnop-fun-dllimport	139	msched-ar-in-data-spec	173
mold-mnemonics	196	msched-br-data-spec	173
momit-leaf-frame-pointer	141, 170	msched-br-in-data-spec	173
mone-byte-bool	146	msched-control-ldc	173
moptimize-membar	157	msched-control-spec	173
MP	116	msched-costly-dep	202
mpa-risc-1-0	158	msched-count-spec-in-critical-path	174
mpa-risc-1-1	158	msched-in-control-spec	173
mpa-risc-2-0	158	msched-ldc	173
mpack	155	msched-prefer-non-control-spec-insns	174
mpacked-stack	206	msched-prefer-non-data-spec-insns	174
mpadstruct	211	msched-spec-verbose	174
mpaired	198	mschedule	159
mpaired-single	186	mscore5	209
mpc32	166	mscore5u	209
mpc64	166	mscore7	209
mpc80	166	mscore7d	209
mpcrel	180	msda	219
mpdebug	144	msdata	171, 205
mpe	200	msdata-data	205
mpic-register	139	msdata=default	205
mpoke-function-name	139	msdata=eabi	204
mpopcntb	195	msdata=none	175, 205
mportable-runtime	159	msdata=sdata	175
mpower	195	msdata=sysv	204
mpower2	195	msdata=use	175
mpowerpc	195	msecure-plt	198
mpowerpc-gfxopt	195	msep-data	143
mpowerpc-gpopt	195	mshared-library-id	142
mpowerpc64	195	mshort	179, 181
mprefergot	211	msim	141, 174, 193, 204, 220
mpreferred-stack-boundary	167	msingle-exit	192
mprioritize-restricted-insns	202	msingle-float	185
mprolog-function	218	msingle-pic-base	139
mprologue-epilogue	144	msio	159
mprototype	203	msize	140
mpt-fixed	212	mslow-bytes	182
mpush-args	145, 169	msmall-data	152
MQ	116	msmall-exec	207
mrecip	168	msmall-mem	217
mregister-names	171	msmall-text	152
mregnames	205	msmartmips	186

```
msoft-float ....  136, 149, 154, 159, 164, 179, 185,
        193, 200, 206, 213
msoft-quad-float ............................ 213
msoft-reg-count ............................. 181
mspace ................................ 211, 219
mspe ........................................ 198
mspecld-anomaly ............................. 142
msplit ...................................... 194
msplit-addresses ............................ 188
msse ........................................ 168
msseregparm ................................. 166
mstack-align ................................ 144
mstack-bias ................................. 216
mstack-check-l1 ............................. 142
mstack-guard ................................ 208
mstack-size ................................. 208
mstackrealign ............................... 166
mstdmain .................................... 217
mstrict-align ......................... 180, 201
mstring ..................................... 200
mstringop-strategy=alg ...................... 170
mstructure-size-boundary .................... 138
msvr4-struct-return ......................... 203
mswdiv ...................................... 197
msym32 ...................................... 186
mt .......................................... 172
MT .......................................... 116
mtarget-align ............................... 221
mtda ........................................ 219
mtext ....................................... 136
mtext-section-literals ...................... 221
mthreads .................................... 169
mthumb ...................................... 139
mthumb-interwork ............................ 136
mtiny-stack ................................. 141
mtls-direct-seg-refs ........................ 170
mtls-size ................................... 172
mtoc ........................................ 202
mtomcat-stats ............................... 157
mtoplevel-symbols ........................... 192
mtp ......................................... 140
mtpcs-frame ................................. 139
mtpcs-leaf-frame ............................ 140
mtpf-trace .................................. 208
mtrap-precision ............................. 150
mtune .. 137, 143, 153, 161, 172, 177, 183, 197, 208,
        215
muclibc ..................................... 157
muls ........................................ 209
multcost=number ............................. 211
multi_module ................................ 148
multilib-library-pic ........................ 155
multiply_defined ............................ 148
multiply_defined_unused ..................... 148
munaligned-doubles .......................... 213
muninit-const-in-rodata ..................... 188
munix ....................................... 219
munix-asm ................................... 194
munsafe-dma ................................. 217
mupdate ..................................... 200
musermode ................................... 211
mv850 ....................................... 219
mv850e ...................................... 219
mv850e1 ..................................... 219
mv8plus ..................................... 215
mveclibabi .................................. 169
mvis ........................................ 215
mvliw-branch ................................ 156
mvms-return-codes ........................... 153
mvolatile-asm-stop .......................... 171
mvr4130-align ............................... 191
mvrsave ..................................... 198
mvxworks .................................... 204
mwarn-dynamicstack .......................... 208
mwarn-framesize ............................. 208
mwarn-reloc ................................. 217
mwide-bitfields ............................. 182
mwindiss .................................... 204
mwords-little-endian ........................ 137
mxgot ....................................... 184
mxl-compat .................................. 199
myellowknife ................................ 204
mzarch ...................................... 207
mzda ........................................ 219
mzero-extend ................................ 191
```

N

```
no-integrated-cpp ............................ 29
no-red-zone ................................. 170
no_dead_strip_inits_and_terms ............... 148
noall_load .................................. 148
nocpp ....................................... 189
nodefaultlibs ............................... 124
nofixprebinding ............................. 148
nolibdld .................................... 160
nomultidefs ................................. 148
non-static .................................. 220
noprebind ................................... 148
noseglinkedit ............................... 148
nostartfiles ................................ 124
nostdinc .................................... 118
nostdinc++ ............................. 35, 118
nostdlib .................................... 124
```

O

```
o ...................................... 23, 114
0 ........................................... 78
00 .......................................... 79
01 .......................................... 78
02 .......................................... 78
03 .......................................... 79
0s .......................................... 79
```

P

p	66
P	122
pagezero_size	148
param	102
pass-exit-codes	22
pedantic	5, 44, 115, 245, 330, 548
pedantic-errors	5, 44, 115, 548
pg	67
pie	124
pipe	23
prebind	148
prebind_all_twolevel_modules	148
preprocessor	113
print-file-name	76
print-libgcc-file-name	77
print-multi-directory	76
print-multi-lib	76
print-objc-runtime-info	42
print-prog-name	77
print-search-dirs	77
print-sysroot-headers-suffix	77
private_bundle	148
pthread	172, 206, 217
pthreads	216

Q

Q	67
Qn	218
Qy	218

R

rdynamic	124
read_only_relocs	148
remap	122

S

s	125
S	23, 123
save-temps	76
sectalign	148
sectcreate	148
sectobjectsymbols	148
sectorder	148
seg_addr_table	148
seg_addr_table_filename	148
seg1addr	148
segaddr	148
seglinkedit	148
segprot	148
segs_read_only_addr	148
segs_read_write_addr	148
shared	125
shared-libgcc	125

sim	145
sim2	145
single_module	148
specs	127
static	125, 148, 161
static-libgcc	125
std	5, 26, 337, 547
std=	117
sub_library	148
sub_umbrella	148
symbolic	125
sysroot	127

T

target-help	24, 122
threads	161, 216
time	76
tls	154
TLS	154
traditional	30, 535
traditional-cpp	30, 122
trigraphs	29, 122
twolevel_namespace	148

U

u	126
U	113
umbrella	148
undef	113
undefined	148
unexported_symbols_list	148

V

v	23, 122
V	135
version	25, 123

W

w	43, 115
W	45, 59, 61, 536
Wa	123
Wabi	35
Waddress	58
Waggregate-return	58
Wall	44, 114, 538
Warray-bounds	54
Wassign-intercept	41
Wattributes	58
Wbad-function-cast	57
Wcast-align	57
Wcast-qual	57
Wchar-subscripts	46
Wclobbered	57

Option Index

Wcomment	46, 114
Wcomments	114
Wconversion	57
Wcoverage-mismatch	43
Wctor-dtor-privacy	36
Wdeclaration-after-statement	56
Wdeprecated	37
Wdeprecated-declarations	60
Wdisabled-optimization	63
Wdiv-by-zero	54
weak_reference_mismatches	148
Weffc++	37
Wempty-body	58
Wendif-labels	56, 115
Werror	43, 115
Werror=	43
Wextra	45, 59, 61
Wfatal-errors	44
Wfloat-equal	54
Wformat	46, 59, 269
Wformat-extra-args	47
Wformat-nonliteral	47, 270
Wformat-security	47
Wformat-y2k	47
Wformat-zero-length	47
Wformat=2	47
whatsloaded	148
whyload	148
Wignored-qualifiers	48
Wimplicit	48
Wimplicit-function-declaration	48
Wimplicit-int	48
Wimport	46, 114
Winit-self	47
Winline	62, 299
Wint-to-pointer-cast	62
Winvalid-offsetof	62
Winvalid-pch	62
Wl	126
Wlarger-than-*len*	56
Wlogical-op	58
Wlong-long	62
Wmain	48
Wmissing-braces	48
Wmissing-declarations	59
Wmissing-field-initializers	59
Wmissing-format-attribute	59
Wmissing-include-dirs	48
Wmissing-noreturn	59
Wmissing-parameter-type	59
Wmissing-prototypes	59
Wmultichar	60
Wnested-externs	61
Wno-abi	35
Wno-address	58
Wno-aggregate-return	58
Wno-all	44
Wno-array-bounds	54

Wno-assign-intercept	41
Wno-attributes	58
Wno-bad-function-cast	57
Wno-cast-align	57
Wno-cast-qual	57
Wno-char-subscripts	46
Wno-clobbered	57
Wno-comment	46
Wno-conversion	57
Wno-ctor-dtor-privacy	36
Wno-declaration-after-statement	56
Wno-deprecated	37
Wno-deprecated-declarations	60
Wno-disabled-optimization	63
Wno-div-by-zero	54
Wno-effc++	37
Wno-empty-body	58
Wno-endif-labels	56
Wno-error	43
Wno-error=	43
Wno-extra	45, 59, 61
Wno-fatal-errors	44
Wno-float-equal	54
Wno-format	46, 59
Wno-format-extra-args	47
Wno-format-nonliteral	47
Wno-format-security	47
Wno-format-y2k	47
Wno-format-zero-length	47
Wno-format=2	47
Wno-ignored-qualifiers	48
Wno-implicit	48
Wno-implicit-function-declaration	48
Wno-implicit-int	48
Wno-import	46
Wno-init-self	47
Wno-inline	62
Wno-int-to-pointer-cast	62
Wno-invalid-offsetof	62
Wno-invalid-pch	62
Wno-logical-op	58
Wno-long-long	62
Wno-main	48
Wno-missing-braces	48
Wno-missing-declarations	59
Wno-missing-field-initializers	59
Wno-missing-format-attribute	59
Wno-missing-include-dirs	48
Wno-missing-noreturn	59
Wno-missing-parameter-type	59
Wno-missing-prototypes	59
Wno-multichar	60
Wno-nested-externs	61
Wno-non-template-friend	37
Wno-non-virtual-dtor	36
Wno-nonnull	47
Wno-old-style-cast	37
Wno-old-style-declaration	58

Wno-old-style-definition	59	Wold-style-cast	37
Wno-overflow	61	Wold-style-declaration	58
Wno-overlength-strings	63	Wold-style-definition	59
Wno-overloaded-virtual	38	Woverflow	61
Wno-override-init	61	Woverlength-strings	63
Wno-packed	61	Woverloaded-virtual	38
Wno-padded	61	Woverride-init	61
Wno-parentheses	48	Wp	113
Wno-pmf-conversions	38, 509	Wpacked	61
Wno-pointer-arith	56	Wpadded	61
Wno-pointer-sign	63	Wparentheses	48
Wno-pointer-to-int-cast	62	Wpmf-conversions	38
Wno-pragmas	52	Wpointer-arith	56, 260
Wno-protocol	41	Wpointer-sign	63
Wno-redundant-decls	61	Wpointer-to-int-cast	62
Wno-reorder	36	Wpragmas	52
Wno-return-type	50	Wprotocol	41
Wno-selector	42	Wredundant-decls	61
Wno-sequence-point	49	Wreorder	36
Wno-shadow	56	Wreturn-type	50
Wno-sign-compare	58	Wselector	42
Wno-sign-conversion	58	Wsequence-point	49
Wno-sign-promo	38	Wshadow	56
Wno-stack-protector	63	Wsign-compare	58
Wno-strict-aliasing	52	Wsign-conversion	58
Wno-strict-aliasing=n	53	Wsign-promo	38
Wno-strict-null-sentinel	37	Wstack-protector	63
Wno-strict-overflow	53	Wstrict-aliasing	52
Wno-strict-prototypes	58	Wstrict-aliasing=n	53
Wno-strict-selector-match	42	Wstrict-null-sentinel	37
Wno-switch	50	Wstrict-overflow	53
Wno-switch-default	50	Wstrict-prototypes	58
Wno-switch-enum	50	Wstrict-selector-match	42
Wno-system-headers	54	Wswitch	50
Wno-traditional	55	Wswitch-default	50
Wno-traditional-conversion	56	Wswitch-enum	50
Wno-trigraphs	50	Wsystem-headers	54, 115
Wno-type-limits	56	Wtraditional	55, 114
Wno-undeclared-selector	42	Wtraditional-conversion	56, 544
Wno-undef	56	Wtrigraphs	50, 114
Wno-uninitialized	51	Wtype-limits	56
Wno-unknown-pragmas	52	Wundeclared-selector	42
Wno-unreachable-code	61	Wundef	56, 114
Wno-unsafe-loop-optimizations	56	Wuninitialized	51
Wno-unused	51	Wunknown-pragmas	52
Wno-unused-function	50	Wunreachable-code	61
Wno-unused-label	50	Wunsafe-loop-optimizations	56
Wno-unused-parameter	51	Wunused	51
Wno-unused-value	51	Wunused-function	50
Wno-unused-variable	51	Wunused-label	50
Wno-variadic-macros	62	Wunused-macros	114
Wno-vla	62	Wunused-parameter	51
Wno-volatile-register-var	63	Wunused-value	51
Wno-write-strings	57	Wunused-variable	51
Wnon-template-friend	37	Wvariadic-macros	62
Wnon-virtual-dtor	36	Wvla	62
Wnonnull	47	Wvolatile-register-var	63
Wnormalized=	60	Wwrite-strings	57

X

x 22, 117
Xassembler 123
Xbind-lazy 220
Xbind-now 220

Xlinker 126

Y

Ym 218
YP 218

Keyword Index

!
'!' in constraint 309

#
'#' in constraint 310
#pragma 494
`#pragma implementation` 506
`#pragma implementation`, implied 506
`#pragma interface` 505
`#pragma`, reason for not using 281

$
$ 285

%
'%' in constraint 310
%include 128
%include_noerr 128
%rename 128

&
'&' in constraint 309

ʼ
ʼ 537

(
() 251

*
'*' in constraint 310

+
'+' in constraint 309

-
'-lgcc', use with '-nodefaultlibs' 124
'-lgcc', use with '-nostdlib' 124
'-nodefaultlibs' and unresolved references 124
'-nostdlib' and unresolved references 124

.
.sdata/.sdata2 references (PowerPC) 205

/
// 285

<
'<' in constraint 307

=
'=' in constraint 309

>
'>' in constraint 307

?
'?' in constraint 309
?: extensions 253
?: side effect 253

_
'_' in variables in macros 252
`__builtin___clear_cache` 340
`__builtin___fprintf_chk` 335
`__builtin___memcpy_chk` 335
`__builtin___memmove_chk` 335
`__builtin___mempcpy_chk` 335
`__builtin___memset_chk` 335
`__builtin___printf_chk` 335
`__builtin___snprintf_chk` 335
`__builtin___sprintf_chk` 335
`__builtin___stpcpy_chk` 335
`__builtin___strcat_chk` 335
`__builtin___strcpy_chk` 335
`__builtin___strncat_chk` 335
`__builtin___strncpy_chk` 335
`__builtin___vfprintf_chk` 335
`__builtin___vprintf_chk` 335
`__builtin___vsnprintf_chk` 335
`__builtin___vsprintf_chk` 335
`__builtin_apply` 251
`__builtin_apply_args` 250
`__builtin_bswap32` 344
`__builtin_bswap64` 344
`__builtin_choose_expr` 339
`__builtin_clz` 343
`__builtin_clzl` 343
`__builtin_clzll` 343
`__builtin_constant_p` 339
`__builtin_ctz` 343
`__builtin_ctzl` 343
`__builtin_ctzll` 343

`__builtin_expect`	340	`__STDC_HOSTED__`	5
`__builtin_ffs`	342	`__sync_add_and_fetch`	334
`__builtin_ffsl`	343	`__sync_and_and_fetch`	334
`__builtin_ffsll`	343	`__sync_bool_compare_and_swap`	334
`__builtin_frame_address`	331	`__sync_fetch_and_add`	334
`__builtin_huge_val`	341	`__sync_fetch_and_and`	334
`__builtin_huge_valf`	341	`__sync_fetch_and_nand`	334
`__builtin_huge_vall`	341	`__sync_fetch_and_or`	334
`__builtin_inf`	341	`__sync_fetch_and_sub`	334
`__builtin_infd128`	342	`__sync_fetch_and_xor`	334
`__builtin_infd32`	341	`__sync_lock_release`	335
`__builtin_infd64`	342	`__sync_lock_test_and_set`	334
`__builtin_inff`	342	`__sync_nand_and_fetch`	334
`__builtin_infl`	342	`__sync_or_and_fetch`	334
`__builtin_isfinite`	337	`__sync_sub_and_fetch`	334
`__builtin_isgreater`	337	`__sync_synchronize`	334
`__builtin_isgreaterequal`	337	`__sync_val_compare_and_swap`	334
`__builtin_isless`	337	`__sync_xor_and_fetch`	334
`__builtin_islessequal`	337	`__thread`	499
`__builtin_islessgreater`	337	`_Accum` data type	256
`__builtin_isnormal`	337	`_Complex` keyword	254
`__builtin_isunordered`	337	`_Decimal128` data type	255
`__builtin_nan`	342	`_Decimal32` data type	255
`__builtin_nand128`	342	`_Decimal64` data type	255
`__builtin_nand32`	342	`_exit`	337
`__builtin_nand64`	342	`_Exit`	337
`__builtin_nanf`	342	`_Fract` data type	256
`__builtin_nanl`	342	`_Sat` data type	256
`__builtin_nans`	342		
`__builtin_nansf`	342		
`__builtin_nansl`	342	**0**	
`__builtin_object_size`	335	'0' in constraint	308
`__builtin_offsetof`	333		
`__builtin_parity`	343	**A**	
`__builtin_parityl`	343		
`__builtin_parityll`	343	ABI	521
`__builtin_popcount`	343	abort	337
`__builtin_popcountl`	343	abs	337
`__builtin_popcountll`	343	accessing volatiles	503
`__builtin_powi`	337, 343	acos	337
`__builtin_powif`	337, 343	acosf	337
`__builtin_powil`	337, 343	acosh	337
`__builtin_prefetch`	341	acoshf	337
`__builtin_return`	251	acoshl	337
`__builtin_return_address`	331	acosl	337
`__builtin_trap`	340	Ada	3
`__builtin_types_compatible_p`	338	additional floating types	255
`__complex__` keyword	254	address constraints	308
`__declspec(dllexport)`	267	address of a label	247
`__declspec(dllimport)`	268	address_operand	308
`__extension__`	330	alias attribute	264
`__float128` data type	255	aliasing of parameters	227
`__float80` data type	255	aligned attribute	264, 286, 294
`__func__` identifier	330	alignment	285
`__FUNCTION__` identifier	330	alloc_size attribute	265
`__imag__` keyword	254	alloca	337
`__PRETTY_FUNCTION__` identifier	330	alloca vs variable-length arrays	258
`__real__` keyword	254		

Keyword Index

Allow nesting in an interrupt handler on the
    Blackfin processor........................ 274
alternate keywords 329
`always_inline` function attribute............. 265
AMD x86-64 Options......................... 161
AMD1... 5
ANSI C....................................... 5
ANSI C standard.............................. 5
ANSI C89..................................... 5
ANSI support 26
ANSI X3.159-1989............................. 5
apostrophes................................. 537
application binary interface.................. 521
ARC Options................................ 135
ARM [Annotated C++ Reference Manual]..... 514
ARM Options............................... 136
arrays of length zero........................ 257
arrays of variable length 258
arrays, non-lvalue 260
`artificial` function attribute................ 266
`asin` 337
`asinf` 337
`asinh` 337
`asinhf` 337
`asinhl` 337
`asinl` 337
asm constraints 306
asm expressions 300
assembler instructions 300
assembler names for identifiers............... 326
assembly code, invalid 551
`atan` 337
`atan2` 337
`atan2f` 337
`atan2l` 337
`atanf` 337
`atanh` 337
`atanhf` 337
`atanhl` 337
`atanl` 337
attribute of types........................... 293
attribute of variables 286
attribute syntax 281
autoincrement/decrement addressing.......... 307
automatic `inline` for C++ member fns 300
AVR Options............................... 140

B

Backwards Compatibility 514
base class members.......................... 541
`bcmp` 337
`below100` attribute 293
binary compatibility......................... 521
Binary constants using the '0b' prefix 502
Blackfin Options 141
bound pointer to member function............ 509
bounds checking............................. 83

bug criteria................................. 551
bugs 551
bugs, known................................ 533
built-in functions 28, 337
`bzero` 337

C

C compilation options 9
C intermediate output, nonexistent 3
C language extensions 245
C language, traditional 30
C standard................................... 5
C standards.................................. 5
c++.. 25
C++ 3
C++ comments 285
C++ compilation options 9
C++ interface and implementation headers 505
C++ language extensions..................... 503
C++ member fns, automatically `inline` 300
C++ misunderstandings 540
C++ options, command line 31
C++ pragmas, effect on inlining 506
C++ source file suffixes...................... 25
C++ static data, declaring and defining........ 540
`C_INCLUDE_PATH`........................... 231
C89 5
C90 5
C94 5
C95 5
C99 5
C9X 5
`cabs` 337
`cabsf` 337
`cabsl` 337
`cacos` 337
`cacosf` 337
`cacosh` 337
`cacoshf` 337
`cacoshl` 337
`cacosl` 337
calling functions through the function vector on
    H8/300, M16C, and M32C processors 271
`calloc` 337
`carg` 337
`cargf` 337
`cargl` 337
case labels in initializers..................... 261
case ranges 263
`casin` 337
`casinf` 337
`casinh` 337
`casinhf` 337
`casinhl` 337
`casinl` 337
cast to a union 263
`catan` 337

catanf	337
catanh	337
catanhf	337
catanhl	337
catanl	337
cbrt	337
cbrtf	337
cbrtl	337
ccos	337
ccosf	337
ccosh	337
ccoshf	337
ccoshl	337
ccosl	337
ceil	337
ceilf	337
ceill	337
cexp	337
cexpf	337
cexpl	337
character set, execution	120
character set, input	120
character set, input normalization	60
character set, wide execution	120
cimag	337
cimagf	337
cimagl	337
cleanup attribute	287
clog	337
clogf	337
clogl	337
COBOL	3
code generation conventions	222
code, mixed with declarations	264
cold function attribute	276
command options	9
comments, C++ style	285
common attribute	287
comparison of signed and unsigned values, warning	58
compiler bugs, reporting	551
compiler compared to C++ preprocessor	3
compiler options, C++	31
compiler options, Objective-C and Objective-C++	38
compiler version, specifying	135
COMPILER_PATH	230
complex conjugation	254
complex numbers	254
compound literals	261
computed gotos	247
conditional expressions, extensions	253
conflicting types	539
conj	337
conjf	337
conjl	337
const applied to function	264
const function attribute	266

constants in constraints	307
constraint modifier characters	309
constraint, matching	308
constraints, asm	306
constraints, machine specific	310
constructing calls	250
constructor expressions	261
constructor function attribute	267
contributors	581
copysign	337
copysignf	337
copysignl	337
core dump	551
cos	337
cosf	337
cosh	337
coshf	337
coshl	337
cosl	337
CPATH	231
CPLUS_INCLUDE_PATH	231
cpow	337
cpowf	337
cpowl	337
cproj	337
cprojf	337
cprojl	337
creal	337
crealf	337
creall	337
CRIS Options	143
cross compiling	135
CRX Options	145
csin	337
csinf	337
csinh	337
csinhf	337
csinhl	337
csinl	337
csqrt	337
csqrtf	337
csqrtl	337
ctan	337
ctanf	337
ctanh	337
ctanhf	337
ctanhl	337
ctanl	337

D

Darwin options	145
dcgettext	337
dd integer suffix	255
DD integer suffix	255
deallocating variable length arrays	258
debugging information options	63
decimal floating types	255

Keyword Index

declaration scope 536
declarations inside expressions 245
declarations, mixed with code 264
declaring attributes of functions 264
declaring static data in C++ 540
defining static data in C++ 540
dependencies for make as output 231, 232
dependencies, make 115
DEPENDENCIES_OUTPUT 231
dependent name lookup 541
deprecated attribute 287
deprecated attribute 267
designated initializers 261
designator lists 262
designators 262
destructor function attribute 267
df integer suffix 255
DF integer suffix 255
dgettext 337
diagnostic messages 42
dialect options 26
digits in constraint 308
directory options 126
dl integer suffix 255
DL integer suffix 255
dollar signs in identifier names 285
double-word arithmetic 254
downward funargs 248
drem 337
dremf 337
dreml 337

E

'E' in constraint 307
earlyclobber operand 309
eight bit data on the H8/300, H8/300H, and H8S
.... 269
empty structures 258
environment variables 229
erf 337
erfc 337
erfcf 337
erfcl 337
erff 337
erfl 337
error function attribute 266
error messages 548
escaped newlines 260
exception handler functions on the Blackfin
    processor 269
exclamation point 309
exit 337
exp 337
exp10 337
exp10f 337
exp10l 337
exp2 337

exp2f 337
exp2l 337
expf 337
expl 337
explicit register variables 327
expm1 337
expm1f 337
expm1l 337
expressions containing statements 245
expressions, constructor 261
extended asm 300
extensible constraints 309
extensions, ?: 253
extensions, C language 245
extensions, C++ language 503
external declaration scope 536
externally_visible attribute 281

F

'F' in constraint 308
fabs 337
fabsf 337
fabsl 337
fatal signal 551
fdim 337
fdimf 337
fdiml 337
FDL, GNU Free Documentation License 573
ffs 337
file name suffix 20
file names 123
fixed-point types 256
flatten function attribute 266
flexible array members 257
float as function value type 537
floating point precision 96, 540
floor 337
floorf 337
floorl 337
fma 337
fmaf 337
fmal 337
fmax 337
fmaxf 337
fmaxl 337
fmin 337
fminf 337
fminl 337
fmod 337
fmodf 337
fmodl 337
force_align_arg_pointer attribute 276
format function attribute 269
format_arg function attribute 270
Fortran 3
forwarding calls 250
fprintf 337

fprintf_unlocked............................ 337
fputs....................................... 337
fputs_unlocked.............................. 337
freestanding environment...................... 5
freestanding implementation................... 5
frexp...................................... 337
frexpf..................................... 337
frexpl..................................... 337
FRV Options............................... 153
fscanf..................................... 337
fscanf, and constant strings................. 535
function addressability on the M32R/D....... 273
function attributes......................... 264
function pointers, arithmetic................ 260
function prototype declarations.............. 284
function without a prologue/epilogue code.... 274
function, size of pointer to................. 260
functions called via pointer on the RS/6000 and
    PowerPC............................... 272
functions in arbitrary sections.............. 264
functions that are passed arguments in registers on
    the 386........................... 264, 276
functions that behave like malloc............ 264
functions that do not pop the argument stack on
    the 386.............................. 264
functions that do pop the argument stack on the
    386................................. 266
functions that have no side effects.......... 264
functions that never return.................. 264
functions that pop the argument stack on the 386
    .... 264, 269, 278
functions that return more than once......... 264
functions which do not handle memory bank
    switching on 68HC11/68HC12............ 274
functions which handle memory bank switching
    269
functions with non-null pointer arguments.... 264
functions with printf, scanf, strftime or
    strfmon style arguments.................. 264

G

'g' in constraint............................ 308
'G' in constraint............................ 308
g++.. 25
G++.. 3
gamma...................................... 337
gamma_r.................................... 337
gammaf..................................... 337
gammaf_r................................... 337
gammal..................................... 337
gammal_r................................... 337
GCC.. 3
GCC command options.......................... 9
GCC_EXEC_PREFIX............................ 230
gcc_struct................................. 298
gcc_struct attribute....................... 291
gcov.. 67

gettext.................................... 337
global offset table........................ 224
global register after longjmp.............. 328
global register variables.................. 327
GNAT... 3
GNU C Compiler............................... 3
GNU Compiler Collection...................... 3
gnu_inline function attribute.............. 265
goto with computed label................... 247
gprof....................................... 66
grouping options............................. 9

H

'H' in constraint.......................... 308
hardware models and configurations, specifying
    135
hex floats................................. 255
hk fixed-suffix............................ 256
HK fixed-suffix............................ 256
hosted environment........................ 5, 29
hosted implementation........................ 5
hot function attribute..................... 276
HPPA Options............................... 158
hr fixed-suffix............................ 256
HR fixed-suffix............................ 256
hypot...................................... 337
hypotf..................................... 337
hypotl..................................... 337

I

'i' in constraint.......................... 307
'I' in constraint.......................... 307
i386 Options............................... 161
IA-64 Options.............................. 171
IBM RS/6000 and PowerPC Options............ 194
identifier names, dollar signs in........... 285
identifiers, names in assembler code........ 326
ilogb...................................... 337
ilogbf..................................... 337
ilogbl..................................... 337
imaxabs.................................... 337
implementation-defined behavior, C language
    237
implied #pragma implementation.............. 506
incompatibilities of GCC................... 535
increment operators........................ 551
index...................................... 337
indirect calls on ARM...................... 272
indirect calls on MIPS..................... 273
init_priority attribute.................... 509
initializations in expressions............. 261
initializers with labeled elements......... 261
initializers, non-constant................. 260
inline automatic for C++ member fns........ 300
inline functions........................... 299
inline functions, omission of.............. 299

Keyword Index

inlining and C++ pragmas 506
installation trouble 533
integrating function code 299
Intel 386 Options 161
interface and implementation headers, C++.... 505
intermediate C version, nonexistent 3
interrupt handler functions 271
interrupt handler functions on the Blackfin, m68k, H8/300 and SH processors 272
interrupt thread functions on fido 272
introduction 1
invalid assembly code 551
invalid input 551
invoking g++ 26
isalnum 337
isalpha 337
isascii 337
isblank 337
iscntrl 337
isdigit 337
isgraph 337
islower 337
ISO 9899 5
ISO C 5
ISO C standard 5
ISO C90 5
ISO C94 5
ISO C95 5
ISO C99 5
ISO C9X 5
ISO support 26
ISO/IEC 9899 5
isprint 337
ispunct 337
isspace 337
isupper 337
iswalnum 337
iswalpha 337
iswblank 337
iswcntrl 337
iswdigit 337
iswgraph 337
iswlower 337
iswprint 337
iswpunct 337
iswspace 337
iswupper 337
iswxdigit 337
isxdigit 337

J

j0 337
j0f 337
j0l 337
j1 337
j1f 337
j1l 337

Java 3
java_interface attribute 509
jn 337
jnf 337
jnl 337

K

k fixed-suffix 256
K fixed-suffix 256
keywords, alternate 329
known causes of trouble 533

L

l1_data variable attribute 290
l1_data_A variable attribute 290
l1_data_B variable attribute 290
l1_text function attribute 272
labeled elements in initializers 261
labels as values 247
labs 337
LANG 229, 231
language dialect options 26
LC_ALL 229
LC_CTYPE 229
LC_MESSAGES 229
ldexp 337
ldexpf 337
ldexpl 337
length-zero arrays 257
lgamma 337
lgamma_r 337
lgammaf 337
lgammaf_r 337
lgammal 337
lgammal_r 337
Libraries 123
LIBRARY_PATH 230
link options 123
lk fixed-suffix 256
LK fixed-suffix 256
LL integer suffix 254
llabs 337
llk fixed-suffix 256
LLK fixed-suffix 256
llr fixed-suffix 256
LLR fixed-suffix 256
llrint 337
llrintf 337
llrintl 337
llround 337
llroundf 337
llroundl 337
load address instruction 308
local labels 246
local variables in macros 252
local variables, specifying registers 328

locale	229	Mercury	3
locale definition	231	message formatting	42
`log`	337	messages, warning	43
`log10`	337	messages, warning and error	548
`log10f`	337	middle-operands, omitted	253
`log10l`	337	MIPS options	182
`log1p`	337	`mips16` attribute	273
`log1pf`	337	misunderstandings in C++	540
`log1pl`	337	mixed declarations and code	264
`log2`	337	`mktemp`, and constant strings	535
`log2f`	337	MMIX Options	191
`log2l`	337	MN10300 options	192
`logb`	337	`mode` attribute	288
`logbf`	337	`modf`	337
`logbl`	337	`modff`	337
`logf`	337	`modfl`	337
`logl`	337	modifiers in constraints	309
long long data types	254	`ms_struct`	298
longjmp	328	`ms_struct` attribute	291
longjmp incompatibilities	536	MT options	193
longjmp warnings	52	mudflap	83
`lr` fixed-suffix	256	multiple alternative constraints	309
`LR` fixed-suffix	256	multiprecision arithmetic	254
`lrint`	337		
`lrintf`	337	**N**	
`lrintl`	337	'n' in constraint	307
`lround`	337	names used in assembler code	326
`lroundf`	337	naming convention, implementation headers	506
`lroundl`	337	`nearbyint`	337
		`nearbyintf`	337
M		`nearbyintl`	337
'm' in constraint	307	nested functions	248
M32C options	174	newlines (escaped)	260
M32R/D options	174	`nextafter`	337
M680x0 options	176	`nextafterf`	337
M68hc1x options	181	`nextafterl`	337
machine dependent options	135	`nexttoward`	337
machine specific constraints	310	`nexttowardf`	337
macro with variable arguments	259	`nexttowardl`	337
macros containing `asm`	304	NFC	60
macros, inline alternative	299	NFKC	60
macros, local labels	246	NMI handler functions on the Blackfin processor	274
macros, local variables in	252	`no_instrument_function` function attribute	274
macros, statements in expressions	245	`nocommon` attribute	287
macros, types of arguments	252	`noinline` function attribute	274
make	115	`nomips16` attribute	273
`malloc`	337	non-constant initializers	260
`malloc` attribute	273	non-static inline function	300
matching constraint	308	`nonnull` function attribute	274
MCore options	181	`noreturn` function attribute	275
member fns, automatically `inline`	300	`nothrow` function attribute	275
`memchr`	337		
`memcmp`	337	**O**	
`memcpy`	337	'o' in constraint	307
memory references in constraints	307	`OBJC_INCLUDE_PATH`	231
`mempcpy`	337		
`memset`	337		

Keyword Index

Objective-C 3, 7
Objective-C and Objective-C++ options, command
 line 38
Objective-C++ 3, 7
offsettable address 307
old-style function definitions 284
omitted middle-operands 253
open coding 299
openmp parallel 29
operand constraints, `asm` 306
optimize options 77
options to control diagnostics formatting 42
options to control warnings 43
options, C++ 31
options, code generation 222
options, debugging 63
options, dialect 26
options, directory search 126
options, GCC command 9
options, grouping 9
options, linking 123
options, Objective-C and Objective-C++ 38
options, optimization 77
options, order 9
options, preprocessor 113
order of evaluation, side effects 548
order of options 9
other register constraints 309
output file option 23
overloaded virtual fn, warning 38

P

'p' in constraint 308
`packed` attribute 288
parameter forward declaration 259
parameters, aliased 227
Pascal 3
PDP-11 Options 193
PIC 224
pmf 509
pointer arguments 266
pointer to member function 509
portions of temporary objects, pointers to ... 542
pow 337
pow10 337
pow10f 337
pow10l 337
PowerPC options 194
powf 337
powl 337
pragma, align 496
pragma, diagnostic 498
pragma, extern_prefix 496
pragma, fini 496
pragma, init 496
pragma, long_calls 494
pragma, long_calls_off 495

pragma, longcall 495
pragma, mark 495
pragma, memregs 495
pragma, no_long_calls 494
pragma, options align 495
pragma, reason for not using 281
pragma, redefine_extname 496
pragma, segment 495
pragma, unused 495
pragma, visibility 498
pragma, weak 497
pragmas 494
pragmas in C++, effect on inlining 506
pragmas, interface and implementation 505
pragmas, warning of unknown 52
precompiled headers 232
preprocessing numbers 538
preprocessing tokens 538
preprocessor options 113
`printf` 337
`printf_unlocked` 337
prof 66
`progmem` variable attribute 293
promotion of formal parameters 284
pure function attribute 275
push address instruction 308
`putchar` 337
`puts` 337

Q

q floating point suffix 255
Q floating point suffix 255
`qsort`, and global register variables 328
question mark 309

R

r fixed-suffix 256
R fixed-suffix 256
'r' in constraint 307
ranges in case statements 263
read-only strings 535
register variable after `longjmp` 328
registers 300
registers for local variables 328
registers in constraints 307
registers, global allocation 327
registers, global variables in 327
`regparm` attribute 276
relocation truncated to fit (MIPS) 185
`remainder` 337
`remainderf` 337
`remainderl` 337
`remquo` 337
`remquof` 337
`remquol` 337
reordering, warning 36

reporting bugs 551
rest argument (in macro) 259
restricted pointers 503
restricted references 503
restricted this pointer 503
`returns_twice` attribute 277
`rindex` 337
`rint` 337
`rintf` 337
`rintl` 337
`round` 337
`roundf` 337
`roundl` 337
RS/6000 and PowerPC Options 194
RTTI 505
run-time options 222

S

's' in constraint 308
S/390 and zSeries Options 206
save all registers on the Blackfin, H8/300,
   H8/300H, and H8S 277
`scalb` 337
`scalbf` 337
`scalbl` 337
`scalbln` 337
`scalblnf` 337
`scalbn` 337
`scalbnf` 337
`scanf`, and constant strings 535
`scanfnl` 337
scope of a variable length array 258
scope of declaration 539
scope of external declarations 536
Score Options 209
search path 126
`section` function attribute 277
`section` variable attribute 288
`sentinel` function attribute 277
`setjmp` 328
`setjmp` incompatibilities 536
shared strings 535
`shared` variable attribute 289
side effect in ?: 253
side effects, macro argument 245
side effects, order of evaluation 548
signal handler functions on the AVR processors
   278
`signbit` 337
`signbitd128` 337
`signbitd32` 337
`signbitd64` 337
`signbitf` 337
`signbitl` 337
signed and unsigned values, comparison warning
   58
`significand` 337

`significandf` 337
`significandl` 337
simple constraints 307
`sin` 337
`sincos` 337
`sincosf` 337
`sincosl` 337
`sinf` 337
`sinh` 337
`sinhf` 337
`sinhl` 337
`sinl` 337
`sizeof` 252
smaller data references 175
smaller data references (PowerPC) 205
`snprintf` 337
SPARC options 213
Spec Files 128
specified registers 327
specifying compiler version and target machine
   135
specifying hardware config 135
specifying machine version 135
specifying registers for local variables 328
speed of compilation 232
`sprintf` 337
SPU options 217
`sqrt` 337
`sqrtf` 337
`sqrtl` 337
`sscanf` 337
`sscanf`, and constant strings 535
`sseregparm` attribute 276
statements inside expressions 245
static data in C++, declaring and defining 540
`stpcpy` 337
`stpncpy` 337
`strcasecmp` 337
`strcat` 337
`strchr` 337
`strcmp` 337
`strcpy` 337
`strcspn` 337
`strdup` 337
`strfmon` 337
`strftime` 337
string constants 535
`strlen` 337
`strncasecmp` 337
`strncat` 337
`strncmp` 337
`strncpy` 337
`strndup` 337
`strpbrk` 337
`strrchr` 337
`strspn` 337
`strstr` 337
struct 498

Keyword Index

structures 537
structures, constructor expression 261
submodel options 135
subscripting 260
subscripting and function values 260
suffixes for C++ source 25
SUNPRO_DEPENDENCIES 232
suppressing warnings 43
surprises in C++ 540
syntax checking 43
system headers, warnings from 54

T

tan 337
tanf 337
tanh 337
tanhf 337
tanhl 337
tanl 337
target machine, specifying 135
target options 135
TC1 5
TC2 5
TC3 5
Technical Corrigenda 5
Technical Corrigendum 1 5
Technical Corrigendum 2 5
Technical Corrigendum 3 5
template instantiation 507
temporaries, lifetime of 542
tgamma 337
tgammaf 337
tgammal 337
Thread-Local Storage 499
thunks 248
tiny data section on the H8/300H and H8S ... 278
TLS 499
tls_model attribute 289
TMPDIR 230
toascii 337
tolower 337
toupper 337
towlower 337
towupper 337
traditional C language 30
treelang 3, 7
trunc 337
truncf 337
truncl 337
two-stage name lookup 541
type alignment 285
type attributes 293
type_info 505
typedef names as function parameters 536
typeof 252

U

uhk fixed-suffix 256
UHK fixed-suffix 256
uhr fixed-suffix 256
UHR fixed-suffix 256
uk fixed-suffix 256
UK fixed-suffix 256
ulk fixed-suffix 256
ULK fixed-suffix 256
ULL integer suffix 254
ullk fixed-suffix 256
ULLK fixed-suffix 256
ullr fixed-suffix 256
ULLR fixed-suffix 256
ulr fixed-suffix 256
ULR fixed-suffix 256
undefined behavior 551
undefined function value 551
underscores in variables in macros 252
union 498
union, casting to a 263
unions 537
unknown pragmas, warning 52
unresolved references and '-nodefaultlibs'... 124
unresolved references and '-nostdlib' 124
unused attribute 278
ur fixed-suffix 256
UR fixed-suffix 256
used attribute 278
User stack pointer in interrupts on the Blackfin
  272

V

'V' in constraint 307
V850 Options 218
vague linkage 504
value after longjmp 328
variable addressability on the IA-64 273
variable addressability on the M32R/D 291
variable alignment 285
variable attributes 286
variable number of arguments 259
variable-length array scope 258
variable-length arrays 258
variables in specified registers 327
variables, local, in macros 252
variadic macros 259
VAX options 219
version_id attribute on IA64 HP-UX 278
vfprintf 337
vfscanf 337
visibility attribute 278
VLAs 258
void pointers, arithmetic 260
void, size of pointer to 260
volatile access 503
volatile applied to function 264

volatile read	503
volatile write	503
`vprintf`	337
`vscanf`	337
`vsnprintf`	337
`vsprintf`	337
`vsscanf`	337
vtable	504
VxWorks Options	220

W

`w` floating point suffix	255
`W` floating point suffix	255
`warn_unused_result` attribute	280
warning for comparison of signed and unsigned values	58
warning for overloaded virtual fn	38
warning for reordering of member initializers	36
warning for unknown pragmas	52
`warning` function attribute	266
warning messages	43
warnings from system headers	54
warnings vs errors	548
`weak` attribute	280
`weakref` attribute	280
whitespace	537

X

'X' in constraint	308
X3.159-1989	5
x86-64 options	220
x86-64 Options	161
Xstormy16 Options	220
Xtensa Options	220

Y

y0	337
y0f	337
y0l	337
y1	337
y1f	337
y1l	337
yn	337
ynf	337
ynl	337

Z

zero-length arrays	257
zero-size structures	258
zSeries options	221